PHILOSOPHISCHE UNTERSUCHUNGEN

PHILOSOPHICAL INVESTIGATIONS

PHILOSOPHISCHE UNTERSUCHUNGEN

PHILOSOPHICAL INVESTIGATIONS

LUDWIG WITTGENSTEIN

Translated by

G. E. M. Anscombe, P. M. S. Hacker and
Joachim Schulte

Revised fourth edition by

P. M. S. Hacker and Joachim Schulte

WILEY-
BLACKWELL

This fourth edition first published 2009
© 2009 Blackwell Publishing Ltd

Edition history: Basil Blackwell Ltd (1e, 1953; 2e, 1958);
Blackwell Publishing Ltd (3e, 2001)

Blackwell Publishing was acquired by John Wiley & Sons in February 2007.
Blackwell's publishing program has been merged with Wiley's global Scientific,
Technical, and Medical business to form Wiley-Blackwell.

Registered Office
John Wiley & Sons Ltd, The Atrium, Southern Gate, Chichester, West Sussex,
PO19 8SQ, United Kingdom

Editorial Offices
350 Main Street, Malden, MA 02148-5020, USA
9600 Garsington Road, Oxford, OX4 2DQ, UK
The Atrium, Southern Gate, Chichester, West Sussex, PO19 8SQ, UK

For details of our global editorial offices, for customer services, and for
information about how to apply for permission to reuse the copyright
material in this book please see our website at www.wiley.com/wiley-blackwell.

The right of Peter Hacker and Joachim Schulte to be identified as the authors of
the editorial material in this work has been asserted in accordance with the
Copyright, Designs and Patents Act 1988.

Library of Congress Cataloging-in-Publication Data
Wittgenstein, Ludwig, 1889–1951.
    [Philosophische Untersuchungen. English]
    Philosophical investigations / Ludwig Wittgenstein ; translated by G.E.M. Anscombe,
P.M.S. Hacker, and Joachim Schulte. — Rev. 4th ed. / by P.M.S. Hacker and Joachim
Schulte.
        p. cm.
    English and German.
    Includes bibliographical references and index.
    ISBN 978-1-4051-5928-9 (hardcover : alk. paper) — ISBN 978-1-4051-5929-6
(pbk. : alk. paper)   1. Philosophy.   2. Language and languages—Philosophy.   3. Semantics
(Philosophy)   I. Anscombe, G. E. M. (Gertrude Elizabeth Margaret)   II. Hacker, P. M. S.
(Peter Michael Stephan)   III. Schulte, Joachim.   IV. Title.
    B3376.W563P53 2009
    192—dc22

                                                                            2009023572

A catalogue record for this book is available from the British Library.

Set in 10.5/13pt Sabon by Graphicraft Limited, Hong Kong
Printed in United States of America.

SKYD886CDE2-5708-4985-A6B1-42DDB857895D_120321

Editors' and Translators' Acknowledgements for the Fourth Edition

The idea that we should produce a revised translation of Wittgenstein's *Philosophische Untersuchungen* was brought up at what turned out to be one of the last meetings of the Wittgenstein trustees. We and our colleagues — Nicholas Denyer, Anthony Kenny and Anselm Müller — came to the conclusion that it would be best to build on the foundations laid by G. E. M. Anscombe in her translation of Wittgenstein's second great work. The trustees, with the exception of Anthony Kenny, became members of what is now the Wittgenstein editorial advisory committee. This group was joined by David McKitterick, the Librarian of Trinity College, Cambridge, who has been an enthusiastic supporter of our project. We are greatly indebted to him for his help.

We thought that a few months' individual work and three or four weeks together would suffice to complete the task. With that in mind, we applied to the Rockefeller Center at Bellagio on Lake Como for a period of residence to work together, and were granted a stay of four weeks in these beautiful surroundings. But although each of us had spent several months preparing for our meeting, we found that the amount of work still necessary was far greater than anticipated. The shock of discovering that we would be lucky to reach §189 by the end of our stay was mitigated by the generous hospitality offered by the Rockefeller Center in September–October 2006.

It was evident that far more time than originally anticipated was necessary, and we had to ensure that we could meet periodically to discuss the work each of us did independently. In this we were greatly helped by St John's College, Oxford, and the Philosophy Department of the University of Zürich, whose assistance enabled us to have a further four extended meetings. Moreover, in the summer of 2007 the Kalischer family gave us the use of their magnificent home in Berlin, which made it possible for us to spend a fortnight's intense discussions in this *locus amoenus*.

When we had a complete draft, we thought to benefit from responses of Wittgenstein scholars to our revised translation. We applied to the European Translation Centre in Athens for a week's stay in their residence at Lefkes on the island of Paros. Generous financial support was forthcoming from Trinity College, Cambridge, and when it was found that we had failed to allow for the fact that the value of currencies tends to fluctuate, the Faculty of Philosophy of Oxford University and the University of Athens stepped in to help. So, we met for a week at Lefkes to discuss the fruit of our labours with Hanjo Glock, Anthony Kenny, Vassiliki Kindi, Brian McGuinness, Eike von Savigny, Severin Schroeder, Edna Ullmann-Margalit and Stelios Virvidakis. Anthony Kenny's chairmanship of the meetings was exemplary, and we are grateful to him for steering us through the shoals and rapids. We are especially indebted to Vassiliki Kindi, who surpassed herself as organizer, helpmate, contributor to our discussions and friend. These intense and lengthy discussions led to a great number of changes in our revised translation.

In addition, we received long and invaluable lists of specific comments and questions from Brian McGuinness and Eike von Savigny, both before and after the meetings on Paros. Questions on or relevant to our revised translation were raised in correspondence with Hanoch Ben-Yami, Stewart Candlish, Lars Hertzberg, Wolfgang Kienzler, Grant Luckhardt and Josef Rothhaupt. We also profited from examining specific points discussed in writings by Stewart Candlish, Roland Hall and David Stern.

Patience is a publisher's crowning virtue. We thank Nick Bellorini of Wiley-Blackwell for unstintingly exercising this virtue in our regard. And we are most grateful to Jean van Altena for her copy-editing and invaluable suggestions for improvement.

P. M. S. Hacker
Joachim Schulte

Contents

Editorial Preface to the Fourth Edition and Modified
Translation   viii

The Text of the *Philosophische Untersuchungen*   xviii

Philosophische Untersuchungen
Philosophical Investigations   1

Philosophie der Psychologie – Ein Fragment
Philosophy of Psychology – A Fragment   182

Endnotes   244

Register   267
Index   288

Editorial Preface to the Fourth Edition and Modified Translation

1. *The previous editions and translation*

The *Philosophical Investigations* was published in 1953, edited by G. E. M. Anscombe and Rush Rhees, and translated by Anscombe. A second edition was published in 1958, in which minor corrections (misspellings and punctuation) to the German text were made, and a large number of small changes and 28 significant alterations were made to the English text. In 2003, after Anscombe's death, a third, 50-year anniversary edition was published by Nicholas Denyer with a small number of further alterations to the translation that Anscombe had made over the years in her copy of the previously published text. The third edition unfortunately did not follow the pagination of the first two editions.

Anscombe's translation was an impressive achievement. She invented an English equivalent for Wittgenstein's distinctive, often colloquial, style. This was no mean feat. For she had to find not only English analogues of Wittgenstein's stylistic idiosyncrasies, but also an English rhythm that would convey the character of Wittgenstein's carefully crafted prose. Her success is indisputable.

Nevertheless, there are errors of different kinds in the first three editions and in the translation. It was because of these that the Wittgenstein editorial advisory committee agreed to the production of a new edition. But, given the excellence of the Anscombe translation, it was resolved that rather than making a completely new one, we should build on Anscombe's achievement and produce a modified translation, rectifying any errors or misjudgements we discerned in hers. It should be emphasized that many of the errors in the Anscombe–Rhees editions could not have been identified in the 1950s, prior to the availability and extensive study of the Wittgenstein *Nachlass*, some crucial items of which did not come to light until decades later.

2. *The fourth edition*

The most important editorial change we have made is to drop the division of the book into two parts. What was Part I is now the *Philosophical Investigations*, and what was Part II is now named *Philosophy of Psychology — A Fragment* (which we abbreviate 'PPF'). We explain our reasons for this alteration in the essay on the history of the text of the *Investigations* below.

A further important change we have introduced is to print the slips that were added by Wittgenstein to the typed text of the *Philosophical Investigations* in boxes in their designated places wherever that is now known, rather than at the foot of the relevant page as *Randbemerkungen*. The rationales for their relocations are given severally in endnotes.

In a couple of places, we have introduced Wittgenstein's original squiggles or drawings. In §169 a meaningless sequence of typographical symbols was typed into the text as a *substitute* for the 'arbitrary pothooks and squiggles' (mentioned in §168) that are evident in *Eine Philosophische Betrachtung*, p. 182. So we have reproduced the latter. Again, PPF §108 benefits from the insertion of the little drawing, printed in *Last Writings on the Philosophy of Psychology* I, §88, which illustrates the remark that different concepts touch and run side by side for a stretch, but one shouldn't think that all such lines are circles.

Because the new edition is also a modified translation, with some translated sentences longer than hitherto and others shorter, it has not been possible to preserve the identical pagination of the first and second editions. Since the vast majority of English writings on Wittgenstein have made copious references to those editions, we have inserted the pagination of the first two editions in the text between small verticals (e.g. |123|) at the points of page-breaks.

There are some editorial changes in the new edition of what was previously referred to as 'Part II'. The lost TS 234 was based on MS 144, which consists of loose sheets clipped into a folder.[1] It is not known to what extent the present order of sheets was Wittgenstein's (the foliation is not in his hand). Most of the remarks collected in this folder come from MSS 137 and 138, that is, from manuscripts that were written between October 1948 and spring 1949 and hence *not* used for the dictation of TSS 229 and 232 (published as *Remarks on the*

---

[1] All references to Wittgenstein's Nachlass are to von Wright number, followed by page number or section number (§) or both, as in the Bergen electronic edition. References to Wittgenstein's published works are by title and either section or page number.

Philosophy of Psychology I and II). A few remarks are taken from these earlier typescripts; some originate in MS 169 (which is contemporary with the later part of MS 137); another few have not been traced to earlier manuscript sources. It is not known whether the typescript used for printing the first edition of 'Part II' of the *Investigations* (TS 234) was copied by a typist from MS 144 or dictated to the typist by Wittgenstein. There is evidence that some mistakes were made in the composition of the typescript. It can safely be said that there are at least two points where the order of remarks intended by Wittgenstein and clearly indicated in MS 144 was not respected in TS 234. These errors were pointed out by G. H. von Wright;[2] they have been rectified here (see PPF §§220–1 and §§235–6).

It is clear that the remarks that were collected together in TS 234, as well as their arrangement, are very uneven. There is every reason to think that Wittgenstein would have made many changes had he continued to work on this material. Some of these changes would have consisted in shifting individual remarks to different positions, in joining separate paragraphs to other ones, and in severing sentences or paragraphs from certain remarks. Other changes would have involved redrafting and correcting sentences that were badly drafted or poorly adjusted to their context (some of these requirements will be pointed out in the endnotes). Readers of *Philosophy of Psychology — A Fragment* will be well advised to bear in mind that what we have there, unlike the *Investigations*, is work in progress.

A prominent feature of the Anscombe–Rhees edition of what they called 'Part II' is the subdivision of the text into 'sections' numbered i to xiv. The editors' reasons for inserting these headings were in part external. As von Wright pointed out, in the manuscript 'each section begins and ends on a sheet of its own'.[3] However, as no copy of TS 234 is extant, we know nothing about the external characteristics of this typescript, and accordingly we cannot judge to what extent the criterion mentioned by von Wright may have been relevant to the editors' decisions. In the case of the earlier sections it is often clear on the basis of the content of the remarks why they were grouped as they are. However, when one turns to section xi, it becomes equally clear that

---

[2]   G. H. von Wright, 'The Troubled History of Part II of the *Investigations*', *Grazer philosophische Studien* 42 (1992), p. 184. Cf. J. Schulte's Kritisch-genetische Edition of *Philosophische Untersuchungen* (Suhrkamp, Frankfurt am Main, 2001).
[3]   von Wright, 'Troubled History', p. 183.

Wittgenstein or his editors simply abandoned the project of arranging these remarks in an order analogous to that of sections i to x and xii to xiv. In the present edition, we have retained the old section headings, but our principal means of organizing the text and facilitating reference to passages from it is a simple numbering of individual remarks along the lines of Wittgenstein's own system in the *Investigations*. This method has the additional advantage of forestalling doubts about whether a paragraph beginning on a new page belongs to the same remark as the last paragraph on the previous page — a difficulty encountered on several pages of former editions.

3. *The German text*

The most important source for the German text of *Philosophische Untersuchungen* printed here is the first edition of the book (1953). This was based on one of three copies of the typescript of the *Investigations* and on what was apparently the sole copy (the missing TS 234) of what became 'Part II' of the book.[4] As far as we know, the text of the 1953 edition is on the whole very reliable.

Work on Wittgenstein's *Nachlass* led to the critical edition (2001) of the currently extant typescripts of the earlier drafts of the *Philosophical Investigations*, as well as of the manuscript (MS 144) on which Part II was based. In this critical-genetic edition, many passages were elucidated by quotations from earlier manuscript versions of relevant remarks. In the light of this edition and additional work on the *Nachlass*, we have prepared a German text which differs from that of the first three editions in various respects. We have corrected a few obvious misprints like 'Wage' (§§142, 182, 259) in place of 'Waage' (often but by no means always misspelled by Wittgenstein); 'wir' in place of 'wie' (§282), and 'Sinneneindrücke' in place of 'Sinneseindrücke' (§486). A few oddities could be clarified by consulting the manuscripts. For example, in §433 the correct version reads, not 'in welchem Zeichen', but 'in welchen Zeichen'; and in §441 the unintelligible 'daß wir . . . Wunschäußerungen von uns machen' should read 'daß wir . . . Wunschäußerungen machen'

---

[4]   The typescripts from which the book was printed were lost sometime after publication. The third copy of the *Untersuchungen* proper came to light only in 1993. The few points where it deviates from the published text and/or the other extant copy of the typescript are described in J. Schulte's critical-genetic edition.

(Wittgenstein forgot to cross out part of the variant formulation 'Wunschäußerungen von uns geben'). In TS 227(a), one of the two surviving typescripts, Wittgenstein crossed out the 'k' in 'keinen' in §85(b), thus changing the sentence from 'der Wegweiser lässt doch keinen Zweifel offen' ('the signpost does after all leave no room for doubt') to 'der Wegweiser lässt doch einen Zweifel offen' ('the signpost does after all leave room for doubt'). This, in the context, makes much better sense. Similarly, 'Gesichtseindruck' ('visual impression') in PPF §231 is a misprint for 'Gesichtsausdruck' ('facial expression'), as is evident from MS 138, 6b. So too in PPF §306 'beim innerlichen Rechnen' ('when we made internal calculations', according to Anscombe's translation) is almost certainly meant to be 'beim innerlichen Reden' ('when we speak to ourselves silently') on the model of MS 144, 92.

We have made no attempt to normalize Wittgenstein's characteristic use of commas; the only exceptions are two or three passages where we omitted a particularly distracting comma after the last item of a long list. An example is PPF §93: 'daß die Verben "glauben", "wünschen", "wollen", alle die grammatischen Formen aufweisen'; the comma before 'alle' has been dropped in our edition. We have, however, standardized his dots signifying 'and so on', reducing them to three, without any closing full stop when they occur at the end of a sentence.

In the typescripts as well as in the previous editions of the *Untersuchungen* there are many occurrences of forms like 'etc.' where a closing full stop follows an abbreviation. We have decided to print only one full stop in such cases. There are a number of sentences where a closing full stop or question mark is missing. In such cases we have supplied the missing sign. In the case of complete quoted sentences we print the last quotation mark after the closing punctuation mark. This is in conformity with Wittgenstein's normal practice.

A few common expressions have been standardized in the light of Wittgenstein's usual practice in his manuscripts. These are: 'gar nicht', 'gar nichts' in place of 'garnicht', 'garnichts'; 'inwiefern' in place of 'in wiefern'; 'derselbe' in place of 'der selbe'; 'so daß' in place of 'sodaß'; 'statt dessen' in place of 'stattdessen'. In accordance with German typographical practice, we have spaced 'z. B.', 'd. h.', 'u. s. w.', etc.

We have capitalized nominalized forms where Wittgenstein forgot to do so. In such cases, however, we have exercised our judgement and proceeded with discretion, restricting modifications of the text to particularly clear and distracting cases where, for example, only one out of several nominalized words in the same sentence is spelled without a capital letter.

4. *The modified translation*

Anscombe's translation is now more than 50 years old, and English has moved on apace. Some of her orthographic conventions have become definitely archaic, such as her spelling of 'connexion' and 'shew'. These we have replaced by contemporary orthographic conventions. We have also favoured colloquial compression, as in 'I'm', 'I'll', 'he'd', 'we'd', 'isn't', 'aren't', 'won't' and 'wouldn't', rather more than Anscombe, in order to bring out the conversational tone of the writing. She was meticulous in her use of 'shall' and 'will', and 'should' and 'would', but time has eroded these distinctions, and we have tried to conform to current usage.

In the changes we have introduced to the first 107 remarks of the *Investigations*, we have paid careful attention to Wittgenstein's responses to Rush Rhees's translation of 1938–9 (TS 226). Wittgenstein went over Rhees's often imperfect draft carefully, together with Yorick Smythies, and he made numerous changes and corrections on the typescript by hand. To be sure, he was not a native English speaker, and not all of his corrections are improvements. But where he changed a translation that was subsequently used also by Anscombe, his proposal always merits close attention. Moreover, many of the changes he introduced make his intentions at that time (1939) clear, and the fact that he did *not* change some of Rhees's translation where it differs importantly in meaning from Anscombe's is always noteworthy.

Some of the substantive changes we have introduced into the translation are systematic. Anscombe had a marked preference for minimizing the use of the third-person impersonal pronoun 'one', often translating Wittgenstein's use of the German word *man* by the second-person pronoun 'you'. This made the text appear to be more of a conversation with the reader than it actually is. We have throughout respected Wittgenstein's choice of pronominal form. Anscombe translated *seltsam* and *merkwürdig* by 'queer'. We have translated *seltsam* by 'odd', 'strange' or 'curious', and *merkwürdig* by 'remarkable', 'strange', 'curious' or 'extraordinary'. Wittgenstein's use of *Erklärung* ('explanation') and *Definition* ('definition') was not always respected in Anscombe's translation, but we have kept to Wittgenstein's choice of words. So too, his choice of *Sinn* in some contexts and *Bedeutung* in others was not observed in the translation, but we have abided by Wittgenstein's preferences. Hence, where he speaks of ' "primäre" und "sekundäre" Bedeutung' (PPF §276; p. 216(d) in the first two editions), we have translated ' "primary" and "secondary" meaning' rather than Anscombe's ' "primary" and

"secondary" sense'. Anscombe was not consistent in her translation of *Gebrauch*, *Verwendung* and *Anwendung*. We have translated *Gebrauch* by 'use', *Verwendung* by 'use' or 'employment', and *Anwendung* by 'application'. 'Use' also does service for *benützen*. In general, however, we have not allowed ourselves to be hidebound by the multiple occurrence of the same German word or phrase in different contexts. It by no means requires always translating by the same English expression, but rather depends on the exigencies of the context and the author's intention. So, for example, we have translated *Praxis der Sprache* in *Investigations* §21 by 'linguistic practice' rather than by the more ponderous 'practice of the language', and *Praxis des Spiels* in §54(b) as 'the way the game is played', because this is how Wittgenstein wanted it translated.

Some German words that Wittgenstein employs are problematic for any translator. So, for example, his use of *Satz* has no obvious English equivalent, and choices have to be made between 'sentence', 'proposition', and even 'remark'. So, for example, in *Investigations* §§134–5 the German has *Satz* throughout, but it would be infelicitous to translate the word by 'sentence' in all its occurrences here. In many cases, we have gone along with Anscombe's choice between 'sentence' and 'proposition', but not in all. For example, in §105(a) Wittgenstein wrote 'Wenn wir glauben, jene Ordnung, das Ideal, in der wirklichen Sprache finden zu müssen, werden wir nun mit dem unzufrieden, was man im gewöhnlichen Leben "Satz", "Wort", "Zeichen" nennt.' Anscombe translated the latter clause by 'We become dissatisfied with what are ordinarily called "propositions", "words", "signs".' But Wittgenstein here is focusing on linguistic *signs* (as is evident from the subsequent paragraph ('And we rack our brains over the nature of the *real* sign') — so we have opted for 'sentence' here. Again, in §§395–6, it is clearly the *sentence*, not the proposition, that is supposedly guaranteed its sense by the imagination. And in §554, Wittgenstein is talking about applying the operation of negation to *sentences*.

Similar recurrent difficulties arise with the translation of *Seele*, since it cannot always be correctly rendered by 'soul'. Anscombe was clearly aware of the problem, and in many remarks rightly opted for 'mind' as a correct translation of *Seele* (e.g. §§6, 37, 188, 196, 357, 358, 648, 651, 652), and usually translated *Zustand der Seele* correctly as 'state of mind'. However, in some remarks she questionably opted for 'soul'. For example, in §283(d): 'And can one say of the stone that it has a *Seele* and *that* is what has the pain? What has a *Seele*, or pain, to do with a stone?' — what is at issue is *mind*, not *soul*, and the problems of mind and body, not of the soul and the body. Similarly, in the final

paragraph of this remark: 'For one has to say it of a body, or, if you like of a *Seele* which some body *has*. And how can a body *have* a *Seele*', it is clear that the discussion concerns *mind* and body. So too, in §§357, 391, 424, 454, and PPF §76. By contrast, in PPF §§23–6 it is primarily the soul that is under discussion, because §23 opens with the observation that 'religion teaches that the soul can exist when the body has disintegrated'. However, §24 requires some indication that 'mind' or 'soul' are equally apt.

In the case of *Empfindung* the German noun has a much wider application than the English 'sensation'. In many contexts, the translation 'sensation' is unproblematic. But in some cases the use of the German *Empfindung* is perfectly natural, while 'sensation' would be quite mistaken. So, for example, in §151 'Vielleicht hatte er eine Empfindung, die man "das ist leicht" nennen kann' is to be rendered '. . . what may be called the feeling [not "the sensation"] "that's easy!" '. So too, in §160, one can speak of reading something with the *feeling* of saying something one has learnt by heart, but not with the *sensation* of saying something one has learnt by heart. §§272–5 are very problematic in this respect, for 'Empfindung von Rot' is neither 'sensation of red' (where is this sensation? — in the eye?) nor 'feeling of red'. Since Wittgenstein switched from 'Rotempfindung' in §272 and §273 to 'Farbeindruck' and 'visueller Eindruck' in §§275–7, we have translated 'Empfindung von Rot' as 'visual impression of red' in §§272–3 and 'colour impression' in §274. Similarly, in §312, where Wittgenstein speaks of *Gesichtsempfindung*, we have changed Anscombe's 'visual sensation' (visual sensations are, for example, sensations of glare when blinded by strong light) to 'visual impression'. In §400 *Empfindung* presents yet another difficulty: what the idealist has discovered in speaking of the *visual room* 'was a new way of speaking, a new comparison, and one could even say, a new *Empfindung*' — here neither 'sensation' or 'feeling' nor 'impression' will do. We have opted for 'experience' as the closest approximation, but perhaps what Wittgenstein had in mind was 'a new sensibility'. Similar systematic difficulties attend the German use of '*wollen*' and its relation to '*Wille*' (especially in §§611–19). Anscombe chose to translate the verb in these contexts uniformly by 'to will' and its cognates, which is highly artificial as well as misleading. There is no easy solution to the problem, but we have used 'to want' and its derivatives where possible, and sometimes (as in §611) both. So too, *Vorstellung* and its cognates present formidable difficulties for the translator, which we have sometimes resolved differently from Anscombe, e.g. §§300–1, 389, 402.

Occasional Anglicisms crept into Wittgenstein's German. At one point, Anscombe failed to notice his (mis)use of *Meinung* to signify 'meaning (something)', translating §639 as 'One would like to say that *an opinion* develops' (which is perfectly accurate) instead of '. . . that meaning something develops' (which is surely what Wittgenstein meant (see MS 129, 166f.)).

Three recurrent errors run through Anscombe's translation. First, she commonly mistranslated *manch(er, -e, -es)*: for example, as 'much of the use of (§7)' rather than 'certain uses', 'much else besides' (§21) rather than 'some other things', 'many ways' (§73) rather than 'various ways', 'a good deal that you will not say' (§79(d)) rather than 'some things you won't say', 'many mathematical proofs' (§517) instead of 'some mathematical proofs', and so on. Second, she apparently misunderstood the usage of *wohl*, taking it to be more categorical than it is. So, for example, she translated 'Aber es wird wohl auch der Ton . . .' (§21) as 'No doubt the tone . . .' where we prefer 'But probably the tone . . .'; she translated 'Ähnlich dachte sich wohl Frege die "Annahme" ' (boxed note after §22) as 'This will be how Frege thought of the "assumption" ' instead of 'It may well be that this is how . . .', 'der wohl nur beim Philosophieren vorkommt' (§38) as 'which doubtless only occurs when doing philosophy', instead of 'which may well occur only when . . .'; and so on. Finally, there are occasions where the use of the German definite article *der* (*die, das*) should not be translated by a definite, but by an *indefinite* article. For example, it is mistaken to translate 'so nenne ich sie deswegen nicht den Befehl, mich anzustarren etc. . . .' as 'I don't on that account call it *the* order to stare . . .' rather than '. . . an order to stare' (§498). Again, the slogan quoted in §560 should not run 'The meaning of a word is what is explained by *the* explanation of its meaning' but rather: 'The meaning of a word is what *an* explanation of its meaning explains'. And so on. Since in German the indefinite article and the number word 'one' are homonyms (*ein*) Wittgenstein tended to italicize *ein* when he meant 'one' as opposed to 'a'. Anscombe preserved these italics in translation, but in English such italicization is unnecessary.

Wittgenstein's punctuation was often idiosyncratic. It is, of course, impossible to transfer into English the elaborate punctuation conventions of German, let alone all of Wittgenstein's idiosyncratic additions to it. Anscombe was sparing with her use of punctuation. But Wittgenstein explicitly noted his own preference for heavy punctuation, in order to slow the reader down (MS 136, 128)[5], so we have been a

---

[5]   See Wittgenstein, *Culture and Value*, 2nd edn (Blackwell Oxford, 1980), p. 68.

little more liberal in our use of commas than Anscombe. On the other hand, we have reduced his frequent use of colons before quoted sentences and replaced his colons by commas. We have respected Wittgenstein's use of short and long dashes, but wherever possible, have avoided following a comma or semi-colon by a dash — which looks uncommonly ugly, preferring to delete one or the other. In some cases, however, we have replaced a pair of short dashes by commas. As in the German text, we have standardized his 'dots of laziness', but in conformity with English convention have added one as a full stop when they occur at the end of a sentence. We have accepted his practice of using double quotation marks to begin a quotation, with single quotation marks for quotes within quotes. He also used single quotation marks as scare-quotes, and this too we have accepted. Wittgenstein wrote before the days of systematic and methodical differentiation of the use from the mention of a word or phrase by quotation marks (which became uniform in the second half of the twentieth century). His use, and lack of use, of quotation marks is not always systematic. We have for the most part abided by it, since it is usually perfectly clear. But in a couple of places it renders a passage almost unintelligible, and there we have changed it (e.g. §458, see endnote). We have by and large not followed his practice of employing both question mark and exclamation mark at the end of an interrogative sentence that is surprising or especially emphatic. For reasons that should be obvious from case to case, we have sometimes added italics and sometimes removed italics from Anscombe's translation.

There are various quotations, references and allusions in Wittgenstein's text. These we have attempted to identify. But, not wanting to clutter up his text with footnotes, we have relegated these identifications to the endnotes. It is there too that we have explained, where we could, the import of Wittgenstein's occasional double-bracketed notes to himself. Our primary use of endnotes, however, is to explain our differences with Anscombe's translation, where they do not speak for themselves. All endnotes are indicated by a marginal asterisk adjacent to the relevant remark or paragraph within a remark.

The Text of the *Philosophische Untersuchungen*

In his Preface, dated January 1945 (prior to the composition of the final draft of the *Investigations* in 1945–6), Wittgenstein wrote that the book consists of the precipitate of his work over the previous sixteen years. He had returned to Cambridge, and to philosophy, in January 1929. His first attempt to compose a book which would present his new thoughts was *The Big Typescript* (TS 213), a 768-page untitled typescript, with an eight-page annotated table of contents, dictated in 1933. This was based on his MSS Volumes I–X (MSS 105–114) written between 1929 and 1932. No sooner was the dictation completed than Wittgenstein started to amend it extensively, first by manuscript additions written on the typescript, and then by attempts at rewriting the material in fresh manuscripts. The first revision ('Umarbeitung') is in MSS Volumes X and XI (MSS 114 and 115) written in late 1933 and early 1934. This too was unsatisfactory, and Wittgenstein immediately embarked on a second revision (the 'Zweite Umarbeitung') in MS 140 (known as the 'Grosses Format'). However, after writing 39 pages of this, he abandoned it too. Thereafter, *The Big Typescript* was used primarily as a store from which remarks could be selected for use elsewhere.

The second attempt at composing a book took place in Norway in the autumn of 1936. In the academic year of 1934–5 in Cambridge, Wittgenstein had dictated the *Brown Book* to Alice Ambrose and Francis Skinner. In August 1936, he travelled to Norway with the intention of continuing his philosophical work in solitude in his small house in Skjolden. At the end of August, he began translating the English text of the *Brown Book* into German in MS 115 (Volume XI), pp. 118–292, under the title 'Philosophische Untersuchungen, Versuch einer Umarbeitung' ('Philosophical Investigations, Attempted Revision'), revising it as he was going along. But in early November he gave up,

writing on page 292 of the MS volume 'This whole "attempted revision" from page 118 to here is WORTHLESS.'

He immediately began a new endeavour in MS 142 — the first, prewar, version of the *Philosophical Investigations*, which corresponds roughly to §§1–189(a) of the published book. This is a 167-page manuscript, written as consecutive paragraphed prose, with the title *Philosophische Untersuchungen* (*Philosophical Investigations*). It was compiled during two separate periods. Pages 1–76 were probably written between early November and early December 1936, after which Wittgenstein left Norway to spend Christmas with his family in Vienna. Pages 77–167 were presumably composed after his return to Skjolden between February and May 1937, when he left Skjolden for Britain. This manuscript material was typed in two instalments later in 1937, producing the 137-page typescript TS 220.

Wittgenstein returned to Skjolden in mid-August 1937 and began working on the continuation of TS 220. At this stage, the continuation of his reflections beyond §189 was intended to pursue questions in the philosophy of mathematics pertaining to inference, proof and calculation, and logical compulsion. So the initial discussion of following rules, which is common both to this Early Draft and to the final version of the *Investigations*, was designed to support an investigation into logical and mathematical necessity. The upshot of his work on the sequel to TS 220 was the dictation in 1938 of TS 221, a typescript that corresponds, in a different arrangement (see below), to Part I of the *Remarks on the Foundations of Mathematics*. It was with the conjunction of TS 220 and 221[1] that Wittgenstein approached the Syndics of Cambridge University Press in the late summer of 1938 with the intention of publishing it in a bilingual edition under the title 'Philosophical Remarks'. However, by October 1938, Wittgenstein was already having qualms about publication and expressing hesitation about it to the Syndics.

Sometime between late 1939 and 1943, Wittgenstein revised the Early Draft. One of the typescripts of TS 220 was extensively revised by hand (TS 239).[2] TS 221 was reworked, cut up and re-arranged. The subsequently dictated typescript, TS 222, has been printed as Part I of the *Remarks on the Foundations of Mathematics*. It was with these revised

[1]   The conjunction of the two typescripts has been published as the 'Frühfassung' ('Early Draft') in *Philosophische Untersuchungen, Kritisch-genetische Edition*, ed. Joachim Schulte (Suhrkamp, Frankfurt am Main, 2001).

[2]   It has been published in the critical-genetic edition as the 'Bearbeitete Frühfassung' ('Reworked Early Draft').

typescripts that Wittgenstein again approached the Syndics of the Press in September 1943, proposing publication of a book with the title *Philosophical Investigations*, to be printed together with a new impression of the *Tractatus*. The idea of juxtaposing these two texts, as he explained later in the Preface to the *Investigations*, had occurred to him in the course of re-reading the *Tractatus* together with a friend (probably Nicholas Bachtin). For it seemed to him that his new philosophical ideas could be seen in the right light only by contrast with his old ones. The Syndics agreed to the proposal in January 1944, but by then Wittgenstein had already moved on to something else.

His next attempt was embodied in a 195-page typescript (which no longer exists as a separate typescript, but which has been reconstructed by G. H. von Wright) consisting of 300 (mis)numbered remarks (303 being the correct number) corresponding roughly to *Investigations* §§1–421. It was for this typescript that Wittgenstein wrote the Preface to the *Investigations* dated January 1945. This so called Intermediate Draft[3] consists of the reworked draft of TS 220 (i.e. TS 239), corresponding to *Investigations* §§1–189(a), together with eight pages from TS 221, corresponding to §§189(b)–197, followed by new material, written in 1944, that corresponds roughly to half the remarks in *Investigations* §§198–421. It was at this stage that Wittgenstein apparently abandoned the idea of a logico-mathematical sequel to the early draft of §§1–189, resolving instead to continue the remarks on following rules with the discussion of a private language, thought, imagination, and so forth — in short, the material we are now familiar with from the final version. The mathematical project was, it seems, deferred for a second book, with the subsequently proposed tentative title of 'Beginning Mathematics' (see MS 169, 36v).

Still not satisfied with what he had done, Wittgenstein turned in mid-1945 to selecting further materials for this first volume,[4] i.e. the *Investigations*, from his manuscript volumes MSS 115–119 and MSS 129–30, some from pre-war sources (MSS 115–17 and 119) and the rest from 1944–5 (the final part of MS 116 and MSS 129–30). From these he dictated a typescript he entitled 'Bemerkungen I' (MS 228), which consists of 698 numbered remarks, some 400 of which he then incorporated

---

[3] Published in the critical-genetic edition as the 'Zwischenfassung' ('Intermediate Draft').

[4] See letter to Rhees 13 June 1945 (letter no. 328 in B. F. McGuinness (ed.), *Wittgenstein in Cambridge — Letters and Documents 1911–51* (Blackwell, Oxford, 2008), p. 377).

into the final draft of the *Investigations*. The latter (TS 227) was probably dictated in the course of the academic year 1945–6. The Intermediate Draft had been 195 pages long; the final typescript is 324 pages long.

The final typescript contains no remarks the manuscript sources of which post-date June 1945. But Wittgenstein made minor handwritten alterations to the typescript over the next few years. He also added the slips that were cut from typescripts or scribbled on notes, which were probably meant to be taken into account in further revisions of the text. On some he indicated their intended location. These notes, mostly printed in previous editions at the bottom of a given page[5] and referred to as *Randbemerkungen*, are printed in this edition in boxes placed, wherever possible, in their designated location.

The task of publishing the *Philosophical Investigations* fell to two of Wittgenstein's three literary executors, Elizabeth Anscombe and Rush Rhees. Three typescripts of the *Investigations* were found among Wittgenstein's papers after his death in April 1951. His manuscript modifications to one of the carbon copies were transcribed by various hands into the other two copies, and the original corrected copy was sent to the publisher Basil Blackwell, who produced the first edition from it in 1953. Unfortunately, sometime after publication, the original corrected copy was lost.

Among Wittgenstein's papers, the editors found a typescript based on manuscript MS 144. This was a collection of 372 unnumbered remarks selected mostly from manuscripts written between May 1946 and May 1949. Anscombe and Rhees decided that this typescript was part of the same book as the 693 numbered remarks which they called 'Part I'. Indeed, in the editorial note to their edition, they remarked that 'If Wittgenstein had published his work himself, he would have suppressed a good deal of what is in the last 30 pages or so of Part I and worked what is in Part II, with further material, into its place.' Accordingly, they published the typescript of MS 144 (TS 234) as Part II of the *Philosophical Investigations*. Unfortunately, that typescript, from which the text was printed, has been lost.

---

[5]   There are two exceptions. One is the boxed remark after §108, consisting of three paragraphs. In the Anscombe–Rhees editions these were incorporated in §108 as paragraphs (b)–(d). The other is the boxed remark after §133, previously printed as §133(d) without indicating that it is an added slip cut from TS 228, §140.

There is no written evidence in Wittgenstein's *Nachlass* or correspondence to suggest that MS 144 was intended to collect together materials that would be incorporated into the *Philosophical Investigations*. Nor is there any indication that he intended to suppress 'a good deal of what is in the last thirty pages or so of Part I'. One question that arises in this connection is the date when he might have made this remark to Anscombe and Rhees. G. H. von Wright, the third of Wittgenstein's literary executors, conjectured that it was probably when they visited Wittgenstein in Dublin in December 1948.[6] At that time a major part of what was collected in MS 144 had been written in much more extensive manuscript volumes (MS 137 and MS 138). But neither MS 144 nor, of course, the subsequent typescript TS 234, had been compiled. It may well have been that at this stage Wittgenstein contemplated revising the last 30 pages of his book, and intended to use some of the large amount of material that he had written since 1946 in the process. But he never carried out any such intentions, and we do not know whether he continued to intend to change the book in this radical way. What we do know is that he compiled MS 144 and dictated it to, or had it typed by, a typist in late June and early July 1949. It may well be that this was done at least in part in order to show his friend Norman Malcolm his current work in philosophy of psychology when he visited Malcolm at Cornell in late July 1949. We also know that when he visited Malcolm he said that

> if he had the money he thought he would have his book (TS 227, the typescript of the *Investigations*) mimeographed and distributed among his friends. He said that it was not in a completely finished state, but that he did not think that he could give the final polish to it in his lifetime. The plan would have the merit that he could put in parentheses after a remark, expressions of dissatisfaction, like 'This is not quite right' or 'This is fishy'. He would like to put his book into the hands of his friends, but to take it to a publisher right then was out of the question.[7]

This remark, made in the late summer of 1949, certainly does not suggest plans for the radical rewriting and extension of the last 30 pages (approximately 170 remarks) of the book.

---

[6] See G. H. von Wright, 'The Troubled History of Part II of the *Investigations*', *Grazer Philosophische Studien* 42 (1992), p. 186. He added: 'For all I have been able to ascertain, Wittgenstein did not talk about his plans to the future editors of the *Investigations* after he had left Dublin in 1949' (p. 187).

[7] N. Malcolm, *Ludwig Wittgenstein — A Memoir*, 2nd edn (Oxford University Press, Oxford, 1984), p. 75.

Whatever Wittgenstein's final intentions were, the fact is that the closest he ever came to completing the *Philosophical Investigations* is the current text consisting of §§1–693. It is, we believe, this text that should be known as Wittgenstein's *Philosophical Investigations*. What has hitherto been called '*Philosophical Investigations*, Part II' was a re-arranged set of remarks written between 1946 and 1949 dealing chiefly with questions in what Wittgenstein called 'philosophy of psychology'. We have named it *Philosophy of Psychology — A Fragment*. This is, in effect, a reconstruction of the lost typescript 234, based on MS 144 and the printed version in the previous editions of the *Investigations*.

Philosophische Untersuchungen

Philosophical Investigations

Überhaupt hat der Fortschritt das an sich, daß er viel größer ausschaut als er wirklich ist.

The trouble about progress is that it always looks much greater than it really is.

Nestroy

Vorwort

In dem Folgenden veröffentliche ich Gedanken, den Niederschlag philosophischer Untersuchungen, die mich in den letzten 16 Jahren beschäftigt haben. Sie betreffen viele Gegenstände: Den Begriff der Bedeutung, des Verstehens, des Satzes, der Logik, die Grundlagen der Mathematik, die Bewußtseinszustände und Anderes. Ich habe diese Gedanken alle als *Bemerkungen*, kurze Absätze, niedergeschrieben. Manchmal in längeren Ketten, über den gleichen Gegenstand, manchmal in raschem Wechsel von einem Gebiet zum andern überspringend. — Meine Absicht war es von Anfang, alles dies einmal in einem Buche zusammenzufassen, von dessen Form ich mir zu verschiedenen Zeiten verschiedene Vorstellungen machte. Wesentlich aber schien es mir, daß darin die Gedanken von einem Gegenstand zum andern in einer natürlichen und lückenlosen Folge fortschreiten sollten.

Nach manchen mißglückten Versuchen, meine Ergebnisse zu einem solchen Ganzen zusammenzuschweißen, sah ich ein, daß mir dies nie gelingen würde. Daß das Beste, was ich schreiben konnte, immer nur philosophische Bemerkungen bleiben würden; daß meine Gedanken bald erlahmten, wenn ich versuchte, sie, gegen ihre natürliche Neigung, in *einer* Richtung weiterzuzwingen. —— Und dies hing freilich mit der Natur der Untersuchung selbst zusammen. Sie nämlich zwingt uns, ein weites Gedankengebiet, kreuz und quer, nach allen Richtungen hin zu durchreisen. —— Die philosophischen Bemerkungen dieses Buches sind gleichsam eine Menge von Landschaftsskizzen, die auf diesen langen und verwickelten Fahrten entstanden sind.

Die gleichen Punkte, oder beinahe die gleichen, wurden stets von neuem von verschiedenen Richtungen her berührt und immer neue Bilder entworfen. Eine Unzahl dieser war verzeichnet, oder uncharakteristisch, mit allen Mängeln eines schwachen Zeichners behaftet. Und wenn man diese ausschied, blieb eine Anzahl halbwegser übrig, die nun so angeordnet,

Preface

The thoughts that I publish in what follows are the precipitate of philosophical investigations which have occupied me for the last sixteen years. They concern many subjects: the concepts of meaning, of understanding, of a proposition and sentence, of logic, the foundations of mathematics, states of consciousness, and other things. I have written down all these thoughts as *remarks*, short paragraphs, sometimes in longer chains about the same subject, sometimes jumping, in a sudden change, from one area to another. — Originally it was my intention to bring all this together in a book whose form I thought of differently at different times. But it seemed to me essential that in the book the thoughts should proceed from one subject to another in a natural, smooth sequence.

After several unsuccessful attempts to weld my results together into such a whole, I realized that I should never succeed. The best that I could write would never be more than philosophical remarks; my thoughts soon grew feeble if I tried to force them along a single track against their natural inclination. —— And this was, of course, connected with the very nature of the investigation. For it compels us to travel criss-cross in every direction over a wide field of thought. —— The philosophical remarks in this book are, as it were, a number of sketches of landscapes which were made in the course of these long and meandering journeys.

The same or almost the same points were always being approached afresh from different directions, and new sketches made. Very many of these were badly drawn or lacking in character, marked by all the defects of a weak draughtsman. And when they were rejected, a number of half-way decent ones were left, which then had to be arranged and often

oftmals beschnitten, werden mußten, daß sie dem Betrachter ein Bild der Landschaft geben konnten. — So ist also dieses Buch eigentlich nur ein Album.

Ich hatte bis vor Kurzem den Gedanken an eine Veröffentlichung meiner Arbeit bei meinen Lebzeiten eigentlich aufgegeben. Er wurde allerdings von Zeit zu Zeit rege gemacht, und zwar hauptsächlich dadurch, daß ich erfahren mußte, daß meine Ergebnisse, die ich in Vorlesungen, Skripten und Diskussionen weitergegeben hatte, vielfach mißverstanden, mehr oder weniger verwässert oder verstümmelt im Umlauf waren. Hierdurch wurde meine Eitelkeit aufgestachelt und ich hatte Mühe, sie zu beruhigen.

Vor vier Jahren aber hatte ich Veranlassung, mein erstes Buch (die "Logisch-Philosophische Abhandlung") wieder zu lesen und seine Gedanken zu erklären. Da schien es mir plötzlich, daß ich jene alten Gedanken und die neuen zusammen veröffentlichen sollte: daß diese nur durch den Gegensatz und auf dem Hintergrund meiner ältern Denkweise ihre rechte Beleuchtung erhalten könnten.

Seit ich nämlich vor 16 Jahren mich wieder mit Philosophie zu beschäftigen anfing, mußte ich schwere Irrtümer in dem erkennen, was ich in jenem ersten Buche niedergelegt hatte. Diese Irrtümer einzusehen, hat mir — in einem Maße, das ich kaum selbst zu beurteilen vermag — die Kritik geholfen, die meine Ideen durch Frank Ramsey erfahren haben, — mit welchem ich sie während der zwei letzten Jahre seines Lebens in zahllosen Gesprächen erörtert habe. — Mehr noch als dieser — stets kraftvollen und sichern — Kritik verdanke ich derjenigen, die ein Lehrer dieser Universität, Herr P. Sraffa durch viele Jahre unablässig an meinen Gedanken geübt hat. *Diesem* Ansporn verdanke ich die folgereichsten der Ideen dieser Schrift.

Aus mehr als *einem* Grunde wird, was ich hier veröffentliche, sich mit dem berühren, was Andre heute schreiben. — Tragen meine Bemerkungen keinen Stempel an sich, der sie als die meinen kennzeichnet, so will ich sie auch weiter nicht als mein Eigentum beanspruchen.

Ich übergebe sie mit zweifelhaften Gefühlen der Öffentlichkeit. Daß es dieser Arbeit in ihrer Dürftigkeit und der Finsternis dieser Zeit beschieden sein sollte, Licht in ein oder das andere Gehirn zu werfen, ist nicht unmöglich; aber freilich nicht wahrscheinlich.

Ich möchte nicht mit meiner Schrift Andern das Denken ersparen. Sondern, wenn es möglich wäre, jemand zu eigenen Gedanken anregen.

Ich hätte gerne ein gutes Buch hervorgebracht. Es ist nicht so ausgefallen; aber die Zeit ist vorbei, in der es von mir verbessert werden könnte.

Cambridge, im Januar 1945.

cut down, in order to give the viewer an idea of the landscape. — So this book is really just an album.

Until recently I had really given up the idea of publishing my work in my lifetime. All the same, it was revived from time to time, mainly because I could not help noticing that the results of my work (which I had conveyed in lectures, typescripts and discussions), were in $|x|$ circulation, frequently misunderstood and more or less watered down or mangled. This stung my vanity, and I had difficulty in quieting it.

Four years ago, however, I had occasion to reread my first book (the *Tractatus Logico-Philosophicus*) and to explain its ideas. Then it suddenly seemed to me that I should publish those old ideas and the new ones together: that the latter could be seen in the right light only by contrast with and against the background of my older way of thinking.

For since I began to occupy myself with philosophy again, sixteen years ago, I could not but recognize grave mistakes in what I set out in that first book. I was helped to realize these mistakes — to a degree which I myself am hardly able to estimate — by the criticism which my ideas encountered from Frank Ramsey, with whom I discussed them in innumerable conversations during the last two years of his life. — Even more than to this — always powerful and assured — criticism, I am indebted to that which a teacher of this university, Mr P. Sraffa, for many years unceasingly applied to my thoughts. It is to this stimulus that I owe the most fruitful ideas of this book.

For more than one reason, what I publish here will have points of contact with what other people are writing today. — If my remarks do not bear a stamp which marks them as mine, then I do not wish to lay any further claim to them as my property.

I make them public with misgivings. It is not impossible that it should fall to the lot of this work, in its poverty and in the darkness of this time, to bring light into one brain or another — but, of course, it is not likely.

I should not like my writing to spare other people the trouble of thinking. But if possible, to stimulate someone to thoughts of his own.

I should have liked to produce a good book. It has not turned out that way, but the time is past in which I could improve it.

Cambridge, January 1945.

1. *Augustinus*, in den Confessionen I/8: cum ipsi (majores homines) appellabant rem aliquam, et cum secundum eam vocem corpus ad aliquid movebant, videbam, et tenebam hoc ab eis vocari rem illam, quod sonabant, cum eam vellent ostendere. Hoc autem eos velle ex motu corporis aperiebatur: tamquam verbis naturalibus omnium gentium, quae fiunt vultu et nutu oculorum, ceterorumque membrorum actu, et sonitu vocis indicante affectionem animi in petendis, habendis, rejiciendis, fugiendisve rebus. Ita verba in variis sententiis locis suis posita, et crebro audita, quarum rerum signa essent, paulatim colligebam, measque jam voluntates, edomito in eis signis ore, per haec enuntiabam.[1]

In diesen Worten erhalten wir, so scheint es mir, ein bestimmtes Bild von dem Wesen der menschlichen Sprache. Nämlich dieses: Die Wörter der Sprache benennen Gegenstände — Sätze sind Verbindungen von solchen Benennungen. —— In diesem Bild von der Sprache finden wir die Wurzeln der Idee: Jedes Wort hat eine Bedeutung. Diese Bedeutung ist dem Wort zugeordnet. Sie ist der Gegenstand, für welchen das Wort steht.

Von einem Unterschied der Wortarten spricht Augustinus nicht. Wer das Lernen der Sprache so beschreibt, denkt, so möchte ich glauben, zunächst an Hauptwörter, wie "Tisch", "Stuhl", "Brot", und die Namen von Personen, erst in zweiter Linie an die Namen gewisser Tätigkeiten und Eigenschaften, und an die übrigen Wortarten als etwas, was sich finden wird.

Denke nun an diese Verwendung der Sprache: Ich schicke jemand einkaufen. Ich gebe ihm einen Zettel, auf diesem stehen die Zeichen: "fünf rote Äpfel". Er trägt den Zettel zum Kaufmann; der öffnet die

---

[1] Nannten die Erwachsenen irgend einen Gegenstand und wandten sie sich dabei ihm zu, so nahm ich das wahr und ich begriff, daß der Gegenstand durch die Laute, die sie aussprachen, bezeichnet wurde, da sie auf *ihn* hinweisen wollten. Dies aber entnahm ich aus ihren Gebärden, der natürlichen Sprache aller Völker, der Sprache, die durch Mienen- und Augenspiel, durch die Bewegungen der Glieder und den Klang der Stimme die Empfindungen der Seele anzeigt, wenn diese irgend etwas begehrt, oder festhält, oder zurückweist, oder flieht. So lernte ich nach und nach verstehen, welche Dinge die Wörter bezeichneten, die ich wieder und wieder, an ihren bestimmten Stellen in verschiedenen Sätzen, aussprechen hörte. Und ich brachte, als nun mein Mund sich an diese Zeichen gewöhnt hatte, durch sie meine Wünsche zum Ausdruck.

1. Cum ipsi (majores homines) appellabant rem aliquam, et cum secundum eam vocem corpus ad aliquid movebant, videbam, et tenebam hoc ab eis vocari rem illam, quod sonabant, cum eam vellent ostendere. Hoc autem eos velle ex motu corporis aperiebatur: tamquam verbis naturalibus omnium gentium, quae fiunt vultu et nutu oculorum, ceterorumque membrorum actu, et sonitu vocis indicante affectionem animi in petendis, habendis, rejiciendis, fugiendisve rebus. Ita verba in variis sententiis locis suis posita, et crebro audita, quarum rerum signa essent, paulatim colligebam, measque jam voluntates, edomito in eis signis ore, per haec enuntiabam. (Augustine, *Confessions*, I. 8.)[1]

These words, it seems to me, give us a particular picture of the essence of human language. It is this: the words in language name objects — sentences are combinations of such names. —— In this picture of language we find the roots of the following idea: Every word has a meaning. This meaning is correlated with the word. It is the object for which the word stands.

Augustine does not mention any difference between kinds of word. Someone who describes the learning of language in this way is, I believe, thinking primarily of nouns like "table", "chair", "bread", and of people's names, and only secondarily of the names of certain actions and properties; and of the remaining kinds of word as something that will take care of itself.

* Now think of the following use of language: I send someone shopping. I give him a slip of paper marked "five red apples". He takes the slip to |3| the shopkeeper, who opens the drawer marked "apples"; then

---

* [1] When grown-ups named some object and at the same time turned towards it, I perceived this, and I grasped that the thing was signified by the sound they uttered, since they meant to point *it* out. This, however, I gathered from their gestures, the natural language of all peoples, the language that by means of facial expression and the play of eyes, of the movements of the limbs and the tone of voice, indicates the affections of the soul when it desires, or clings to, or rejects, or recoils from, something. In this way, little by little, I learnt to understand what things the words, which I heard uttered in their respective places in various sentences, signified. And once I got my tongue around these signs, I used them to express my wishes.

Lade, auf welcher das Zeichen "Äpfel" steht; dann sucht er in einer Tabelle das Wort "rot" auf und findet ihm gegenüber ein Farbmuster; nun sagt er die Reihe der Grundzahlwörter — ich nehme an, er weiß sie auswendig — bis zum Worte "fünf" und bei jedem Zahlwort nimmt er einen Apfel aus der Lade, der die Farbe des Musters hat. —— So, und ähnlich, operiert man mit Worten. —— "Wie weiß er aber, wo und wie er das Wort 'rot' nachschlagen soll und was er mit dem Wort 'fünf' anzufangen hat?" —— Nun, ich nehme an, er *handelt*, wie ich es beschrieben habe. Die Erklärungen haben irgendwo ein Ende. — Was ist aber die Bedeutung des Wortes "fünf"? — Von einer solchen war hier gar nicht die Rede; nur davon, wie das Wort "fünf" gebraucht wird.

2. Jener philosophische Begriff der Bedeutung ist in einer primitiven Vorstellung von der Art und Weise, wie die Sprache funktioniert, zu Hause. Man kann aber auch sagen, es sei die Vorstellung einer primitiveren Sprache, als der unsern.

Denken wir uns eine Sprache, für die die Beschreibung, wie Augustinus sie gegeben hat, stimmt: Die Sprache soll der Verständigung eines Bauenden A mit einem Gehilfen B dienen. A führt einen Bau auf aus Bausteinen; es sind Würfel, Säulen, Platten und Balken vorhanden. B hat ihm die Bausteine zuzureichen, und zwar nach der Reihe, wie A sie braucht. Zu dem Zweck bedienen sie sich einer Sprache, bestehend aus den Wörtern: "Würfel", "Säule", "Platte", "Balken". A ruft sie aus; — B bringt den Stein, den er gelernt hat, auf diesen Ruf zu bringen. —— Fasse dies als vollständige primitive Sprache auf.

3. Augustinus beschreibt, könnten wir sagen, ein System der Verständigung; nur ist nicht alles, was wir Sprache nennen, dieses System. Und das muß man in so manchen Fällen sagen, wo sich die Frage erhebt: "Ist diese Darstellung brauchbar, oder unbrauchbar?" Die Antwort ist dann: "Ja, brauchbar; aber nur für dieses eng umschriebene Gebiet, nicht für das Ganze, das du darzustellen vorgabst."

Es ist, als erklärte jemand: "Spielen besteht darin, daß man Dinge, gewissen Regeln gemäß, auf einer Fläche verschiebt . . ." — und wir ihm antworten: Du scheinst an die Brettspiele zu denken; aber das sind nicht alle Spiele. Du kannst deine Erklärung richtigstellen, indem du sie ausdrücklich auf diese Spiele einschränkst.

4. Denk dir eine Schrift, in welcher Buchstaben zur Bezeichnung von Lauten benützt würden, aber auch zur Bezeichnung der Betonung und als Interpunktionszeichen. (Eine Schrift kann man auffassen als eine Sprache zur Beschreibung von Lautbildern.) Denk dir nun, daß Einer

he looks up the word "red" in a chart and finds a colour sample next to it; then he says the series of elementary number-words — I assume that he knows them by heart — up to the word "five", and for each number-word he takes an apple of the same colour as the sample out of the drawer. —— It is in this and similar ways that one operates with words. —— "But how does he know where and how he is to look up the word 'red' and what he is to do with the word 'five'?" —— Well, I assume that he *acts* as I have described. Explanations come to an end somewhere. — But what is the meaning of the word "five"? — No such thing was in question here, only how the word "five" is used.

2. That philosophical notion of meaning is at home in a primitive idea of the way language functions. But one might instead say that it is the idea of a language more primitive than ours.

Let us imagine a language for which the description given by Augustine is right: the language is meant to serve for communication between a builder A and an assistant B. A is building with building stones: there are blocks, pillars, slabs and beams. B has to pass him the stones and to do so in the order in which A needs them. For this purpose they make use of a language consisting of the words "block", "pillar", "slab", "beam". A calls them out; B brings the stone which he has learnt to bring at such-and-such a call. —— Conceive of this as a complete primitive language.

3. Augustine, we might say, does describe a system of communication; only not everything that we call language is this system. And one has to say this in several cases where the question arises "Will that description do or not?" The answer is: "Yes, it will, but only for this narrowly circumscribed area, not for the whole of what you were purporting to describe."

It is as if someone were to say, "Playing a game consists in moving objects about on a surface according to certain rules . . ." — and we replied: You seem to be thinking of board-games, but they are not all the games there are. You can rectify your explanation by expressly restricting it to those games.

4. Imagine a script in which letters were used for sounds, but also for signs of emphasis and punctuation. (A script can be conceived as a language for describing sound-patterns.) Now imagine someone construing that script as if there were just a |4| correspondence of letters to

jene Schrift so verstünde, als entspräche einfach jedem Buchstaben ein
Laut und als hätten die Buchstaben nicht auch ganz andere Funktionen.
So einer, zu einfachen, Auffassung der Schrift gleicht Augustinus'
Auffassung der Sprache.

5. Wenn man das Beispiel im §1 betrachtet, so ahnt man vielleicht,
inwiefern der allgemeine Begriff der Bedeutung der Worte das Funktionieren der Sprache mit einem Dunst umgibt, der das klare Sehen
unmöglich macht. — Es zerstreut den Nebel, wenn wir die Erscheinungen der Sprache an primitiven Arten ihrer Verwendung studieren, in denen
man den Zweck und das Funktionieren der Wörter klar übersehen kann.

Solche primitive Formen der Sprache verwendet das Kind, wenn es
sprechen lernt. Das Lehren der Sprache ist hier kein Erklären, sondern
ein Abrichten.

6. Wir könnten uns vorstellen, daß die Sprache im §2 die *ganze*
Sprache des A und B ist; ja, die ganze Sprache eines Volksstamms. Die
Kinder werden dazu erzogen, *diese* Tätigkeiten zu verrichten, *diese* Wörter
dabei zu gebrauchen, und *so* auf die Worte des Anderen zu reagieren.

Ein wichtiger Teil der Abrichtung wird darin bestehen, daß der Lehrende
auf die Gegenstände weist, die Aufmerksamkeit des Kindes auf sie lenkt,
und dabei ein Wort ausspricht; z. B. das Wort "Platte" beim Vorzeigen
dieser Form. (Dies will ich nicht "hinweisende Erklärung", oder
"Definition", nennen, weil ja das Kind noch nicht nach der Benennung
fragen kann. Ich will es "hinweisendes Lehren der Wörter" nennen. ——
Ich sage, es wird einen wichtigen Teil der Abrichtung bilden, weil es
bei Menschen so der Fall ist; nicht, weil es sich nicht anders vorstellen
ließe.) Dieses hinweisende Lehren der Wörter, kann man sagen, schlägt
eine assoziative Verbindung zwischen dem Wort und dem Ding. Aber
was heißt das? Nun, es kann Verschiedenes heißen; aber man denkt wohl
zunächst daran, daß dem Kind das Bild des Dings vor die Seele tritt,
wenn es das Wort hört. Aber wenn das nun geschieht, — ist das der
Zweck des Worts? — Ja, es *kann* der Zweck sein. — Ich kann mir eine
solche Verwendung von Wörtern (Lautreihen) denken. (Das Aussprechen
eines Wortes ist gleichsam ein Anschlagen einer Taste auf dem
Vorstellungsklavier.) Aber in der Sprache im §2 ist es *nicht* der Zweck
der Wörter, Vorstellungen zu erwecken. (Es kann freilich auch gefunden werden, daß dies dem eigentlichen Zweck förderlich ist.)

Wenn aber das das hinweisende Lehren bewirkt, — soll ich sagen, es
bewirkt das Verstehen des Worts? Versteht nicht der den Ruf "Platte!",
der so und so nach ihm handelt? — Aber dies half wohl das hinweisende

sounds and as if the letters did not also have completely different functions. Augustine's conception of language is like such an over-simple conception of the script.

5. If one looks at the example in §1, one can perhaps get an idea of how much the general concept of the meaning of a word surrounds the working of language with a haze which makes clear vision impossible. — It disperses the fog if we study the phenomena of language in primitive kinds of use in which one can clearly survey the purpose and functioning of the words.

A child uses such primitive forms of language when he learns to talk. Here the teaching of language is not explaining, but training.

6. We could imagine that the language of §2 was the *whole* language of A and B, even the whole language of a tribe. The children are brought up to perform *these* actions, to use *these* words as they do so, and to react in *this* way to the words of others.

An important part of the training will consist in the teacher's pointing to the objects, directing the child's attention to them, and at the same time uttering a word; for instance, the word "slab" as he displays that shape. (I do not want to call this "ostensive explanation" or "definition", because the child cannot as yet *ask* what the name is. I'll call it "ostensive teaching of words". —— I say that it will form an important part of the training, because it is so with human beings; not because it could not be imagined otherwise.) This ostensive teaching of words can be said to establish an associative connection between word and thing. But what does this mean? Well, it may mean various things; but one very likely thinks first of all that a picture of the object comes before the child's mind when it hears the word. But now, if this does happen — is it the purpose of the word? — Yes, it *may* be the purpose. — I can imagine such a use of words (of sequences of sounds). (Uttering a word is like striking a note on the keyboard of the imagination.) But in the language of §2 it is *not* the purpose of the words to evoke images. (It may, of course, be discovered that it helps to attain the actual purpose.)

But if this is the effect of the ostensive teaching, am I to say that it effects an understanding of the word? Doesn't someone who acts on the call "Slab!" in such-and-such a way understand it? — No doubt it

Lehren herbeiführen; aber doch nur zusammen mit einem bestimmten Unterricht. Mit einem anderen Unterricht hätte dasselbe hinweisende Lehren dieser Wörter ein ganz anderes Verständnis bewirkt.

"Indem ich die Stange mit dem Hebel verbinde, setze ich die Bremse instand." — Ja, gegeben den ganzen übrigen Mechanismus. Nur mit diesem ist er der Bremshebel; und losgelöst von seiner Unterstützung ist er nicht einmal Hebel, sondern kann alles Mögliche sein, oder nichts.

7. In der Praxis des Gebrauchs der Sprache (2) ruft der eine Teil die Wörter, der andere handelt nach ihnen; im Unterricht der Sprache aber wird sich *dieser* Vorgang finden: Der Lernende *benennt* die Gegenstände. D. h. er spricht das Wort, wenn der Lehrer auf den Stein zeigt. — Ja, es wird sich hier die noch einfachere Übung finden: der Schüler spricht die Worte nach, die der Lehrer ihm vorsagt —— beides sprachähnliche Vorgänge.

Wir können uns auch denken, daß der ganze Vorgang des Gebrauchs der Worte in (2) eines jener Spiele ist, mittels welcher Kinder ihre Muttersprache erlernen. Ich will diese Spiele "*Sprachspiele*" nennen, und von einer primitiven Sprache manchmal als einem Sprachspiel reden.

Und man könnte die Vorgänge des Benennens der Steine und des Nachsprechens des vorgesagten Wortes auch Sprachspiele nennen. Denke an manchen Gebrauch, der von Worten in Reigenspielen gemacht wird.

Ich werde auch das Ganze: der Sprache und der Tätigkeiten, mit denen sie verwoben ist, das "Sprachspiel" nennen.

8. Sehen wir eine Erweiterung der Sprache (2) an. Außer den vier Wörtern "Würfel", "Säule", etc. enthalte sie eine Wörterreihe, die verwendet wird, wie der Kaufmann in (1) die Zahlwörter verwendet (es kann die Reihe der Buchstaben des Alphabets sein); ferner, zwei Wörter, sie mögen "dorthin" und "dieses" lauten (weil dies schon ungefähr ihren Zweck andeutet), sie werden in Verbindung mit einer zeigenden Handbewegung gebraucht; und endlich eine Anzahl von Farbmustern. A gibt einen Befehl von der Art: "d-Platte-dorthin". Dabei läßt er den Gehilfen ein Farbmuster sehen, und beim Worte "dorthin" zeigt er an eine Stelle des Bauplatzes. B nimmt von dem Vorrat der Platten je eine von der Farbe des Musters für jeden Buchstaben des Alphabets bis zum "d" und bringt sie an den Ort, den A bezeichnet. — Bei anderen Gelegenheiten gibt A den Befehl: "dieses-dorthin". Bei "dieses" zeigt er auf einen Baustein. U. s. w.

was the ostensive teaching that helped to bring this about; but only together with a particular |5| kind of instruction. With different instruction the same ostensive teaching of these words would have effected a quite different understanding.

"I set the brake up by connecting up rod and lever." — Yes, given the whole of the rest of the mechanism. Only in conjunction with that is it a brake-lever, and separated from its support it is not even a lever; it may be anything, or nothing.

7. In the practice of the use of language (2) one party calls out the words, the other acts on them. However, in instruction in the language the following process will occur: the learner *names* the objects; that is, he utters the word when the teacher points at the stone. — Indeed, there will be an even simpler exercise: the pupil repeats the words after the teacher —— both of these being speech-like processes.

We can also think of the whole process of using words in (2) as one of those games by means of which children learn their native language. I will call these games *"language-games"* and will sometimes speak of a primitive language as a language-game.

And the processes of naming the stones and of repeating words after someone might also be called language-games. Think of certain uses that are made of words in games like ring-a-ring-a-roses.

I shall also call the whole, consisting of language and the activities into which it is woven, a "language-game".

8. Let us now look at an expansion of language (2). Besides the four words "block", "pillar", etc., let it contain a sequence of words used as the shopkeeper in (1) uses number-words (it may be the series of letters of the alphabet); further, let it contain two words which may as well be "there" and "this" (because that roughly indicates their purpose), which are used in connection with a pointing gesture; and finally a number of colour samples. A gives an order like "d–slab–there". At the same time he shows the assistant a colour sample, and when he utters the word "there" he points to a place on the building site. From the stock of slabs, B takes one for each letter of the alphabet up to "d", of the same colour as the sample, and brings them to the place A indicates. — On other occasions A gives the order "this-there". At "this" he points at a building stone. And so on.

9. Wenn das Kind diese Sprache lernt, muß es die Reihe der 'Zahlwörter' a, b, c, . . . auswendiglernen. Und es muß ihren Gebrauch lernen. — Wird in diesem Unterricht auch ein hinweisendes Lehren der Wörter vorkommen? — Nun, es wird z. B. auf Platten gewiesen und gezählt werden: "a, b, c Platten". — Mehr Ähnlichkeit mit dem hinweisenden Lehren der Wörter "Würfel", "Säule", etc. hätte das hinweisende Lehren von Zahlwörtern, die nicht zum Zählen dienen, sondern zur Bezeichnung mit dem Auge erfaßbarer Gruppen von Dingen. So lernen ja Kinder den Gebrauch der ersten fünf oder sechs Grundzahlwörter.

Wird auch "dorthin" und "dieses" hinweisend gelehrt? — Stell dir vor, wie man ihren Gebrauch etwa lehren könnte! Es wird dabei auf Örter und Dinge gezeigt werden, — aber hier geschieht ja dieses Zeigen auch im *Gebrauch* der Wörter und nicht nur beim Lernen des Gebrauchs. —

10. Was *bezeichnen* nun die Wörter dieser Sprache? — Was sie bezeichnen, wie soll sich das zeigen, es sei denn in der Art ihres Gebrauchs? Und den haben wir ja beschrieben. Der Ausdruck "dieses Wort bezeichnet *das*" müßte also ein Teil dieser Beschreibung werden. Oder: die Beschreibung soll auf die Form gebracht werden "Das Wort . . . bezeichnet . . .".

Nun, man kann ja die Beschreibung des Gebrauchs des Wortes "Platte" dahin abkürzen, daß man sagt, dieses Wort bezeichne diesen Gegenstand. Das wird man tun, wenn es sich z. B. nurmehr darum handelt, das Mißverständnis zu beseitigen, das Wort "Platte" beziehe sich auf die Bausteinform, die wir tatsächlich "Würfel" nennen, — die Art und Weise dieses '*Bezugs*' aber, d. h. der Gebrauch dieser Worte im übrigen, bekannt ist.

Und ebenso kann man sagen, die Zeichen "a", "b", etc. bezeichnen Zahlen; wenn dies etwa das Mißverständnis behebt, "a", "b", "c", spielten in der Sprache die Rolle, die in Wirklichkeit "Würfel", "Platte", "Säule", spielen. Und man kann auch sagen, "c" bezeichne diese Zahl und nicht jene; wenn damit etwa erklärt wird, die Buchstaben seien in der Reihenfolge a, b, c, d, etc. zu verwenden und nicht in der: a, b, d, c.

Aber dadurch, daß man so die Beschreibungen des Gebrauchs der Wörter einander anähnelt, kann doch dieser Gebrauch nicht ähnlicher werden! Denn, wie wir sehen, ist er ganz und gar ungleichartig.

11. Denk an die Werkzeuge in einem Werkzeugkasten: es ist da ein Hammer, eine Zange, eine Säge, ein Schraubenzieher, ein Maßstab, ein Leimtopf, Leim, Nägel und Schrauben. — So verschieden die Funktionen dieser Gegenstände, so verschieden sind die Funktionen der Wörter. (Und es gibt Ähnlichkeiten hier und dort.)

9. When a child learns this language, he has to learn the series of number-words a, b, c, . . . by heart. And he has to learn their use. — Will this training include ostensive teaching of the words? — Well, people |6| will, for example, point to slabs and count: "a, b, c slabs". — Something more like the ostensive teaching of the words "block", "pillar", etc. would be the ostensive teaching of number-words that serve not to count but to signify groups of objects that can be taken in at a glance. Children do learn the use of the first five or six elementary number-words in this way.

Are "there" and "this" also taught ostensively? — Imagine how one might perhaps teach their use. One will point at places and things, but in this case the pointing occurs in the *use* of the words too and not merely in learning the use. —

10. Now what do the words of this language *signify*? — How is what they signify supposed to come out other than in the kind of use they have? And we have already described that. So the expression "This word signifies *that*" would have to become a part of our description. In other words, the description ought to take the form: "The word . . . signifies . . ."

Well, one can abbreviate the description of the use of the word "slab" by saying that this word signifies this object. This will be done if, for example, it is merely a matter of removing the misunderstanding that the word "slab" refers to the building stone that we in fact call "block" — but the kind of '*referring*' this is, that is to say, the rest of the use of these words, is already known.

Equally one may say that the signs "a", "b", etc. signify numbers: when, for example, this removes the misunderstanding that "a", "b", "c" play the part actually played in the language by "block", "slab", "pillar". And one may also say that "c" signifies this number and not that one; if, for example, this serves to explain that the letters are to be used in the order a, b, c, d, etc., and not in the order a, b, d, c.

But making the descriptions of the uses of these words similar in this way cannot make the uses themselves any more like one another! For, as we see, they are absolutely unlike.

11. Think of the tools in a toolbox: there is a hammer, pliers, a saw, a screwdriver, a rule, a glue-pot, glue, nails and screws. — The functions of words are as diverse as the functions of these objects. (And in both cases there are similarities.)

Freilich, was uns verwirrt ist die Gleichförmigkeit ihrer Erscheinung, wenn die Wörter uns gesprochen, oder in der Schrift und im Druck entgegentreten. Denn ihre *Verwendung* steht nicht so deutlich vor uns. Besonders nicht, wenn wir philosophieren!

12. Wie wenn wir in den Führerstand einer Lokomotive schauen: da sind Handgriffe, die alle mehr oder weniger gleich aussehen. (Das ist begreiflich, denn sie sollen alle mit der Hand angefaßt werden.) Aber einer ist der Handgriff einer Kurbel, die kontinuierlich verstellt werden kann (sie reguliert die Öffnung eines Ventils); ein andrer ist der Handgriff eines Schalters, der nur zweierlei wirksame Stellungen hat, er ist entweder umgelegt, oder aufgestellt; ein dritter ist der Griff eines Bremshebels, je stärker man zieht, desto stärker wird gebremst; ein vierter, der Handgriff einer Pumpe; er wirkt nur, solange er hin und her bewegt wird.

13. Wenn wir sagen: "jedes Wort der Sprache bezeichnet etwas", so ist damit vorerst noch *gar* nichts gesagt; es sei denn, daß wir genau erklärten, *welche* Unterscheidung wir zu machen wünschen. (Es könnte ja sein, daß wir die Wörter der Sprache (8) von Wörtern 'ohne Bedeutung' unterscheiden wollten, wie sie in Gedichten Lewis Carroll's vorkommen, oder von Worten wie "juwiwallera" in einem Lied.)

14. Denke dir, jemand sagte: "*Alle* Werkzeuge dienen dazu, etwas zu modifizieren. So, der Hammer die Lage des Nagels, die Säge die Form des Bretts, etc." — Und was modifiziert der Maßstab, der Leimtopf, die Nägel? — "Unser Wissen um die Länge eines Dings, die Temperatur des Leims, und die Festigkeit der Kiste." —— Wäre mit dieser Assimilation des Ausdrucks etwas gewonnen? —

15. Am direktesten ist das Wort "bezeichnen" vielleicht da angewandt, wo das Zeichen auf dem Gegenstand steht, den es bezeichnet. Nimm an, die Werkzeuge, die A beim Bauen benützt, tragen gewisse Zeichen. Zeigt A dem Gehilfen ein solches Zeichen, so bringt dieser das Werkzeug, das mit dem Zeichen versehen ist.

So, und auf mehr oder weniger ähnliche Weise, bezeichnet ein Name ein Ding, und wird ein Name einem Ding gegeben. — Es wird sich oft nützlich erweisen, wenn wir uns beim Philosophieren sagen: Etwas benennen, das ist etwas Ähnliches, wie einem Ding ein Namentäfelchen anheften.

16. Wie ist es mit den Farbmustern, die A dem B zeigt, — gehören sie zur *Sprache*? Nun, wie man will. Zur Wortsprache gehören sie nicht;

*   Of course, what confuses us is the uniform appearance of words when we hear them in speech, or see them written or in print. For their *use* is not that obvious. Especially when we are doing philosophy! |7|

12. It is like looking into the cabin of a locomotive. There are handles there, all looking more or less alike. (This stands to reason, since they are all supposed to be handled.) But one is the handle of a crank, which can be moved continuously (it regulates the opening of a valve); another is the handle of a switch, which has only two operative positions: it is either off or on; a third is the handle of a brake-lever, the harder one pulls on it, the harder the braking; a fourth, the handle of a pump: it has an effect only so long as it is moved to and fro.

13. If we say, "Every word in the language signifies something", we have so far said nothing *whatever*; unless we explain exactly *what* distinction we wish to make. (It might be, of course, that we wanted to distinguish the words of language (8) from words 'without meaning' such as occur in Lewis Carroll's poems, or words like "Tra-la-la" in a song.)

14. Suppose someone said, "*All* tools serve to modify something. So, a hammer modifies the position of a nail, a saw the shape of a board, and so on." — And what is modified by a rule, a glue-pot and nails? — "Our knowledge of a thing's length, the temperature of the glue, and the solidity of a box." —— Would anything be gained by this assimilation of expressions? —

15. The word "signify" is perhaps most straightforwardly applied when the name is actually a mark on the object signified. Suppose that the tools A uses in building bear certain marks. When A shows his assistant such a mark, the assistant brings the tool that has that mark on it.

In this way, and in more or less similar ways, a name signifies a thing, and is given to a thing. — When philosophizing, it will often prove useful to say to ourselves: naming something is rather like attaching a name tag to a thing.

16. What about the colour samples that A shows to B: are they part of the *language*? Well, it is as you please. They do not belong to

aber wenn ich jemandem sage: "Sprich das Wort 'das' aus", so wirst du doch dieses zweite " 'das' " auch noch zum Satz rechnen. Und doch spielt es eine ganz ähnliche Rolle, wie ein Farbmuster im Sprachspiel (8); es ist nämlich ein Muster dessen, was der Andre sagen soll.

Es ist das Natürlichste, und richtet am wenigsten Verwirrung an, wenn wir die Muster zu den Werkzeugen der Sprache rechnen.

((Bemerkung über das reflexive Fürwort "*dieser* Satz".))

17. Wir werden sagen können: in der Sprache (8) haben wir verschiedene *Wortarten*. Denn die Funktion des Wortes "Platte" und des Wortes "Würfel" sind einander ähnlicher, als die von "Platte" und von "d". Wie wir aber die Worte nach Arten zusammenfassen, wird vom Zweck der Einteilung abhängen, — und von unserer Neigung.

Denke an die verschiedenen Gesichtspunkte, nach denen man Werkzeuge in Werkzeugarten einteilen kann. Oder Schachfiguren in Figurenarten.

18. Daß die Sprachen (2) und (8) nur aus Befehlen bestehen, laß dich nicht stören. Willst du sagen, sie seien darum nicht vollständig, so frage dich, ob unsere Sprache vollständig ist; — ob sie es war, ehe ihr der chemische Symbolismus und die Infinitesimalnotation einverleibt wurden; denn dies sind, sozusagen, Vorstädte unserer Sprache. (Und mit wieviel Häusern, oder Straßen, fängt eine Stadt an, Stadt zu sein?) Unsere Sprache kann man ansehen als eine alte Stadt: Ein Gewinkel von Gäßchen und Plätzen, alten und neuen Häusern, und Häusern mit Zubauten aus verschiedenen Zeiten; und dies umgeben von einer Menge neuer Vororte mit geraden und regelmäßigen Straßen und mit einförmigen Häusern.

19. Man kann sich leicht eine Sprache vorstellen, die nur aus Befehlen und Meldungen in der Schlacht besteht. — Oder eine Sprache, die nur aus Fragen besteht und einem Ausdruck der Bejahung und der Verneinung. Und unzähliges Andere. —— Und eine Sprache vorstellen heißt, sich eine Lebensform vorstellen.

Wie ist es aber: Ist der Ruf "Platte!" im Beispiel (2) ein Satz oder ein Wort? — Wenn ein Wort, so hat es doch nicht dieselbe Bedeutung, wie das gleichlautende unserer gewöhnlichen Sprache, denn im §2 ist es ja ein Ruf. Wenn aber ein Satz, so ist es doch nicht der elliptische Satz "Platte!" unserer Sprache. —— Was die erste Frage anbelangt, so kannst du "Platte!" ein Wort, und auch einen Satz nennen; vielleicht treffend einen 'degenerierten Satz' (wie man von einer degenerierten Hyperbel

spoken language; yet when I say to someone, "Pronounce the word 'the' ", you will also count the second " 'the' " as part of the sentence. Yet it has a role just like that of a colour sample in language-game (8); that is, it is a sample of what the other is meant to say.

It is most natural, and causes least confusion, if we count the samples as tools of the language.

    ((Remark on the reflexive pronoun "*this* proposition".)) |8|

17. We could say: In language (8) we have different *kinds of word*. For the functions of the word "slab" and the word "block" are more alike than those of "slab" and "d". But how we group words into kinds will depend on the aim of the classification — and on our own inclination.

Think of the different points of view according to which one can classify tools into kinds of tools. Or chess pieces into kinds of chess pieces.

18. Don't let it bother you that languages (2) and (8) consist only of orders. If you want to say that they are therefore incomplete, ask yourself whether our own language is complete — whether it was so before the symbolism of chemistry and the notation of the infinitesimal calculus were incorporated in to it; for these are, so to speak, suburbs of our language. (And how many houses or streets does it take before a town begins to be a town?) Our language can be regarded as an ancient city: a maze of little streets and squares, of old and new houses, of houses with extensions from various periods, and all this surrounded by a multitude of new suburbs with straight and regular streets and uniform houses.

19. It is easy to imagine a language consisting only of orders and reports in battle. — Or a language consisting only of questions and expressions for answering Yes and No — and countless other things. —— And to imagine a language means to imagine a form of life.

But what about this: is the call "Slab!" in example (2) a sentence or a word? — If a word, surely it has not the same meaning as the like-sounding word of our ordinary language, for in §2 it is a call. But if a sentence, it is surely not the elliptical sentence "Slab!" of our language. —— As far as the first question goes, you can call "Slab!" a word and also a sentence; perhaps it could aptly be called a 'degenerate sentence' (as one speaks of a degenerate hyperbola); in fact it is our 'elliptical'

spricht), und zwar ist es eben unser 'elliptischer' Satz. — Aber der ist
doch nur eine verkürzte Form des Satzes "Bring mir eine Platte!" und
diesen Satz gibt es doch in Beispiel (2) nicht. — Aber warum sollte ich
nicht, umgekehrt, den Satz "Bring mir eine Platte!" eine *Verlängerung*
des Satzes "Platte!" nennen? — Weil der, der "Platte!" ruft, eigentlich
meint: "Bring mir eine Platte!" — Aber wie machst du das, *dies meinen*,
während du "Platte" *sagst*? Sprichst du dir inwendig den unverkürzten
Satz vor? Und warum soll ich, um zu sagen, was Einer mit dem Ruf
"Platte!" meint, diesen Ausdruck in einen andern übersetzen? Und
wenn sie das Gleiche bedeuten, — warum soll ich nicht sagen: "wenn er
'Platte!' sagt, meint er 'Platte!' "? Oder: warum sollst du nicht "Platte!"
meinen können, wenn du "Bring mir die Platte" meinen kannst? —— Aber
wenn ich "Platte!" rufe, so will ich doch, *er soll mir eine Platte bringen*! —— Gewiß, aber besteht 'dies wollen' darin, daß du in irgend einer
Form einen andern Satz denkst, als den, den du sagst? —

20. Aber wenn nun Einer sagt "Bring mir eine Platte!", so scheint es
ja jetzt, als könnte er diesen Ausdruck als *ein* langes Wort meinen:
entsprechend nämlich dem einen Worte "Platte!". —— Kann man ihn
also einmal als *ein* Wort, einmal als vier Wörter meinen? Und wie meint
man ihn gewöhnlich? —— Ich glaube, wir werden geneigt sein, zu sagen:
Wir meinen den Satz als einen von *vier* Wörtern, wenn wir ihn im
Gegensatz zu andern Sätzen gebrauchen, wie "*Reich* mir eine Platte zu",
"Bring *ihm* eine Platte", "Bring *zwei* Platten", etc.; also im Gegensatz
zu Sätzen, welche die Wörter unseres Befehls in andern Verbindungen
enthalten. —— Aber worin besteht es, einen Satz im Gegensatz zu
andern Sätzen gebrauchen? Schweben einem dabei etwa diese Sätze vor?
Und *alle*? Und *während* man den einen Satz sagt, oder vor-, oder nachher? — Nein! Wenn auch so eine Erklärung einige Versuchung für uns
hat, so brauchen wir doch nur einen Augenblick zu bedenken, was wirklich geschieht, um zu sehen, daß wir hier auf falschem Weg sind. Wir
sagen, wir gebrauchen den Befehl im Gegensatz zu andern Sätzen, weil
unsere Sprache die Möglichkeit dieser andern Sätze enthält. Wer unsere
Sprache nicht versteht, ein Ausländer, der öfter gehört hätte, wie
jemand den Befehl gibt "Bring mir eine Platte!", könnte der Meinung
sein, diese ganze Lautreihe sei ein Wort und entspräche etwa dem Wort
für "Baustein" in seiner Sprache. Wenn er selbst dann diesen Befehl
gegeben hätte, würde er ihn vielleicht anders aussprechen, und wir würden sagen: Er spricht ihn so sonderbar aus, weil er ihn für *ein* Wort
hält. —— Aber geht also nicht, wenn er ihn ausspricht, eben auch etwas
anderes in ihm vor, — *dem* entsprechend, daß er den Satz als *ein* Wort

sentence. — But that is surely only a shortened form of the sentence "Bring me a slab", and there is no such sentence in example (2). — But why shouldn't I conversely have called the sentence "Bring me a slab" a *lengthening* of the sentence "Slab!"? — Because anyone who calls out "Slab!" really means "Bring me a slab". — But how do you do this: how do you *mean* that while *saying* "Slab!"? Do you say the unshortened sentence to yourself? And why should I translate the call "Slab!" into a different expression in order to say |9| what someone means by it? And if they mean the same thing, why shouldn't I say, "When he says 'Slab!' he means 'Slab!' "? Again, why shouldn't you be able to mean "Slab!", if you can mean "Bring me the slab!"? —— But when I call out "Slab!", then what I want is *that he should bring me a slab*! —— Certainly, but does 'wanting this' consist in thinking in some form or other a different sentence from the one you utter? —

* 20. But now it looks as if when someone says "Bring me a slab", he could mean this expression as one long word corresponding indeed to the single word "Slab!" —— Then can one mean it sometimes as one word, and sometimes as four? And how does one usually mean it? —— I think we'll be inclined to say: we mean the sentence as one consisting of *four* words when we use it in contrast to other sentences such as "*Hand* me a slab", "Bring *him* a slab", "Bring *two* slabs", etc.; that is, in contrast with sentences containing the words of our command in other combinations. —— But what does using one sentence in contrast to others consist in? Does one have the others in mind at the same time? *All* of them? And *while* one is saying the one sentence, or before, or afterwards? — No! Even if such an explanation rather tempts us, we need only think for a moment of what actually happens in order to see that we are on the wrong track here. We say that we use the command in contrast with other sentences because *our language* contains the possibility of those other sentences. Someone who did not understand our language, a foreigner, who had fairly often heard someone giving the order "Bring me a slab!", might believe that this whole sequence of sounds was one word corresponding perhaps to the word for "building stone" in his language. If he himself had then given this order, perhaps he would have pronounced it differently, and we'd say: he pronounces it so oddly because he takes it for a single word. —— But then is there not also something different going on in him when he pronounces it — something corresponding to the fact that he conceives the sentence as a single word? —— The same thing may go on in him, or

auffaßt? —— Es kann das Gleiche in ihm vorgehen, oder auch anderes. Was geht denn in dir vor, wenn du so einen Befehl gibst; bist du dir bewußt, daß er aus vier Wörtern besteht, *während* du ihn aussprichst? Freilich, du *beherrschst* diese Sprache — in der es auch jene andern Sätze gibt — aber ist dieses Beherrschen etwas, was '*geschieht*', während du den Satz aussprichst? — Und ich habe ja zugegeben: der Fremde wird den Satz, den er anders auffaßt, wahrscheinlich anders aussprechen; aber, was wir die falsche Auffassung nennen, *muß* nicht in irgend etwas liegen, was das Aussprechen des Befehls begleitet.

'Elliptisch' ist der Satz nicht, weil er etwas ausläßt, was wir meinen, wenn wir ihn aussprechen, sondern weil er gekürzt ist — im Vergleich mit einem bestimmten Vorbild unserer Grammatik. — Man könnte hier freilich den Einwand machen: "Du gibst zu, daß der verkürzte und der unverkürzte Satz den gleichen Sinn haben. — Welchen Sinn haben sie also? Gibt es denn für diesen Sinn nicht einen Wortausdruck?" —— Aber besteht der gleiche Sinn der Sätze nicht in ihrer gleichen *Verwendung*? — (Im Russischen heißt es "Stein rot" statt "der Stein ist rot"; geht ihnen die Kopula im Sinn ab, oder *denken* sie sich die Kopula dazu?)

21. Denke dir ein Sprachspiel, in welchem B dem A auf dessen Frage die Anzahl der Platten, oder Würfel in einem Stoß meldet, oder die Farben und Formen der Bausteine, die dort und dort liegen. — So eine Meldung könnte also lauten: "Fünf Platten". Was ist nun der Unterschied zwischen der Meldung, oder Behauptung, "Fünf Platten" und dem Befehl "Fünf Platten!"? — Nun, die Rolle, die das Aussprechen dieser Worte im Sprachspiel spielt. Aber es wird wohl auch der Ton, in dem sie ausgesprochen werden, ein anderer sein, und die Miene, und noch manches andere. Aber wir können uns auch denken, daß der Ton der gleiche ist, — denn ein Befehl und eine Meldung können in *mancherlei* Ton ausgesprochen werden und mit mancherlei Miene — und daß der Unterschied allein in der Verwendung liegt. (Freilich könnten wir auch die Worte "Behauptung" und "Befehl" zur Bezeichnung einer grammatischen Satzform und eines Tonfalls gebrauchen; wie wir ja "Ist das Wetter heute nicht herrlich?" eine Frage nennen, obwohl sie als Behauptung verwendet wird.) Wir könnten uns eine Sprache denken, in der *alle* Behauptungen die Form und den Ton rhetorischer Fragen hätten; oder jeder Befehl die Form der Frage: "Möchtest du das tun?". Man wird dann vielleicht sagen: "Was er sagt, hat die Form der Frage, ist aber wirklich ein Befehl" — d. h., hat die Funktion des Befehls in der Praxis der Sprache. (Ähnlich sagt man "Du wirst das tun", nicht als Prophezeiung, sondern als Befehl. Was macht es zu dem einen, was zu dem andern?)

something different. What goes on in you when you give such an order? Are you conscious of its consisting of four words *while* you are uttering it? Of course you *know* this language — which contains those other sentences as well — but is this knowing something that '*happens*' while you are uttering the sentence? — And I have conceded that the foreigner, who conceives the sentence differently, will probably also pro-nounce it differently; but what we call his wrong conception does not *have* to lie in anything that accompanies the utterance of the command. |10|

* The sentence is 'elliptical', not because it leaves out something that we mean when we utter it, but because it is shortened — in compari-son with a particular paradigm of our grammar. — Of course someone might object here: "You grant that the shortened and the unshortened sentence have the same sense. — What is this sense, then? Isn't there a verbal expression for this sense?" —— But doesn't their having the same sense consist in their having the same *use*? — (In Russian one says "Stone red" instead of "The stone is red". Does the sense they grasp lack the copula? Or do they add the copula *in thought*?)

21. Imagine a language-game in which A asks, and B reports, the num-ber of slabs or blocks in a pile, or the colours and shapes of the build-ing stones that are stacked in such-and-such a place. — Such a report might run: "Five slabs." Now what is the difference between the report or assertion "Five slabs" and the order "Five slabs!"? — Well, it is the part which uttering these words plays in the language-game. But the tone of voice in which they are uttered is likely to be different too, as are the facial expression and some other things. But we could also ima-gine the tone's being the same — for an order and a report can be spoken in a *variety* of tones of voice and with various facial expressions — the difference being only in the use that is made of these words. (Of course, we might also use the words "assertion" and "command" to signify a grammatical form of a sentence and a particular intonation; just as we would call the sentence "Isn't the weather glorious to-day?" a question, although it is used as an assertion.) We could imagine a lan-guage in which *all* assertions had the form and tone of rhetorical ques-tions; or every command had the form of the question "Would you like to . . . ?". Perhaps it will then be said: "What he says has the form of a question but is really a command" — that is, has the function of a command in linguistic practice. (Similarly, one says "You will do this" not as a prophecy, but as a command. What makes it the one or the other?)

22. Freges Ansicht, daß in einer Behauptung eine Annahme steckt, die
dasjenige ist, was behauptet wird, basiert eigentlich auf der Möglichkeit,
die es in unserer Sprache gibt, jeden Behauptungssatz in der Form zu
schreiben "Es wird behauptet, daß das und das der Fall ist". — Aber
"daß das und das der Fall ist" ist eben in unsrer Sprache kein Satz —
es ist noch kein *Zug* im Sprachspiel. Und schreibe ich statt "Es wird
behauptet, daß . . ." "Es wird behauptet: das und das ist der Fall", dann
sind hier die Worte "Es wird behauptet" eben überflüssig.

Wir könnten sehr gut auch jede Behauptung in der Form einer Frage
mit nachgesetzter Bejahung schreiben; etwa: "Regnet es? Ja!". Würde
das zeigen, daß in jeder Behauptung eine Frage steckt?

Man hat wohl das Recht, ein Behauptungszeichen zu verwenden im
Gegensatz z. B. zu einem Fragezeichen; oder wenn man eine Behauptung
unterscheiden will von einer Fiktion, oder einer Annahme. Irrig ist es
nur, wenn man meint, daß die Behauptung nun aus zwei Akten besteht,
dem Erwägen und dem Behaupten (Beilegen des Wahrheitswerts, oder
dergl.) und daß wir diese Akte nach den Zeichen des Satzes vollziehen,
ungefähr wie wir nach Noten singen. Mit dem Singen nach Noten ist
allerdings das laute, oder leise Lesen des geschriebenen Satzes zu
vergleichen, aber nicht das '*Meinen*' (Denken) des gelesenen Satzes.

Das Fregesche Behauptungszeichen betont den *Satzanfang*. Es hat also
eine ähnliche Funktion, wie der Schlußpunkt. Es unterscheidet die
ganze Periode vom Satz *in* der Periode. Wenn ich Einen sagen höre "es
regnet", aber nicht weiß, ob ich den Anfang und den Schluß der
Periode gehört habe, so ist dieser Satz für mich noch kein Mittel der
Verständigung.

Denken wir uns ein Bild, einen Boxer in bestimmter Kampfstellung
darstellend. Dieses Bild kann nun dazu gebraucht werden, um
jemand mitzuteilen, wie er stehen, sich halten soll; oder, wie er
sich nicht halten soll; oder, wie ein bestimmter Mann dort und
dort gestanden hat; oder etc. etc. Man könnte dieses Bild
(chemisch gesprochen) ein Satzradikal nennen. Ähnlich dachte sich
wohl Frege die "Annahme".

---

23. Wieviele Arten der Sätze gibt es aber? Etwa Behauptung, Frage
und Befehl? — Es gibt *unzählige* solcher Arten: unzählige verschiedene
Arten der Verwendung alles dessen, was wir "Zeichen", "Worte",
"Sätze" nennen. Und diese Mannigfaltigkeit ist nichts Festes, ein für allemal Gegebenes; sondern neue Typen der Sprache, neue Sprachspiele, wie

*   22. Frege's opinion that every assertion contains an assumption, which is the thing that is asserted, really rests on the possibility, found in our language, of writing every assertoric sentence in the form "It is asserted that such-and-such is the case". — But "that such-and-such is the case" is *not* a sentence in our language — it is not yet a *move* in the language-game. And if I write, not "It is asserted that . . .", but "It is asserted: such-and-such is the case", the words "It is asserted" simply become superfluous.

We might very well also write every assertion in the form of a |11| question followed by an affirmative expression; for instance, "Is it raining? Yes!" Would this show that every assertion contained a question?

Of course, one has the right to use an assertion sign in contrast with a question-mark, for example, or if one wants to distinguish an assertion from a fiction or an assumption. It is a mistake only if one thinks that the assertion consists of two acts, entertaining and asserting (assigning a truth-value, or something of the kind), and that in performing these acts we follow the sentence sign by sign roughly as we sing from sheet music. Reading the written sentence loudly or softly is indeed comparable to singing from sheet music, but *'meaning'* (thinking) the sentence that is read is not.

*   The Fregean assertion sign marks the *beginning of a sentence*. So its function is like that of the full stop. It distinguishes the whole period from a clause *within* the period. If I hear someone say "it's raining", but do not know whether I have heard the beginning and end of the period, then so far this sentence fails to convey anything to me.

*   > Imagine a picture representing a boxer in a particular fighting stance.
> Well, this picture can be used to tell someone how he should stand,
> should hold himself; or how he should not hold himself; or how
> a particular man did stand in such-and-such a place; and so on.
> One might (using the language of chemistry) call this picture a
> sentence-radical. Frege probably conceived of the "assumption"
> along these lines. |p. 11 n.|

23. But how many kinds of sentence are there? Say assertion, question and command? — There are *countless* kinds; countless different kinds of use of all the things we call "signs", "words", "sentences". And this diversity is not something fixed, given once for all; but new types of language, new language-games, as we may say, come into existence, and

wir sagen können, entstehen und andre veralten und werden vergessen. (Ein *ungefähres Bild* davon können uns die Wandlungen der Mathematik geben.)

Das Wort "Sprach*spiel*" soll hier hervorheben, daß das *Sprechen* der Sprache ein Teil ist einer Tätigkeit, oder einer Lebensform.

Führe dir die Mannigfaltigkeit der Sprachspiele an diesen Beispielen, und andern, vor Augen:

Befehlen, und nach Befehlen handeln —
Beschreiben eines Gegenstands nach dem Ansehen, oder nach Messungen —
Herstellen eines Gegenstands nach einer Beschreibung (Zeichnung) —
Berichten eines Hergangs —
Über den Hergang Vermutungen anstellen —
Eine Hypothese aufstellen und prüfen —
Darstellen der Ergebnisse eines Experiments durch Tabellen und Diagramme —
Eine Geschichte erfinden; und lesen —
Theater spielen —
Reigen singen —
Rätsel raten —
Einen Witz machen; erzählen —
Ein angewandtes Rechenexempel lösen —
Aus einer Sprache in die andere übersetzen —
Bitten, Danken, Fluchen, Grüßen, Beten.

— Es ist interessant, die Mannigfaltigkeit der Werkzeuge der Sprache und ihrer Verwendungsweisen, die Mannigfaltigkeit der Wort- und Satzarten, mit dem zu vergleichen, was Logiker über den Bau der Sprache gesagt haben. (Und auch der Verfasser der Logisch-Philosophischen Abhandlung.)

24. Wem die Mannigfaltigkeit der Sprachspiele nicht vor Augen ist, der wird etwa zu Fragen geneigt sein, wie dieser: "Was ist eine Frage?" — Ist es die Feststellung, daß ich das und das nicht weiß, oder die Feststellung, daß ich wünsche, der Andre möchte mir sagen . . . ? Oder ist es die Beschreibung meines seelischen Zustandes der Ungewißheit? — Und ist der Ruf "Hilfe!" so eine Beschreibung?

Denke daran, wieviel Verschiedenartiges "Beschreibung" genannt wird: Beschreibung der Lage eines Körpers durch seine Koordinaten;

others become obsolete and get forgotten. (We can get a *rough picture* of this from the changes in mathematics.)

The word "language-*game*" is used here to emphasize the fact that the *speaking* of language is part of an activity, or of a form of life.

Consider the variety of language-games in the following examples, and in others:

Giving orders, and acting on them —
Describing an object by its appearance, or by its measurements —
Constructing an object from a description (a drawing) —
Reporting an event —
Speculating about the event — |12|
Forming and testing a hypothesis —
Presenting the results of an experiment in tables and diagrams —
Making up a story; and reading one —
Acting in a play —
Singing rounds —
Guessing riddles —
Cracking a joke; telling one —
Solving a problem in applied arithmetic —
Translating from one language into another —
Requesting, thanking, cursing, greeting, praying.

— It is interesting to compare the diversity of the tools of language and of the ways they are used, the diversity of kinds of word and sentence, with what logicians have said about the structure of language. (This includes the author of the *Tractatus Logico-Philosophicus*.)

24. Someone who does not bear in mind the variety of language-games will perhaps be inclined to ask questions like: "What is a question?" — Is it a way of stating that I do not know such-and-such, or that I wish the other person would tell me . . . ? Or is it a description of my mental state of uncertainty? — And is the cry "Help!" such a description?

Remember how many different kinds of thing are called "description": description of a body's position by means of its co-ordinates,

Beschreibung eines Gesichtsausdrucks; Beschreibung einer Tastempfindung; einer Stimmung.

Man kann freilich statt der gewöhnlichen Form der Frage die der Feststellung, oder Beschreibung setzen: "Ich will wissen, ob . . .", oder "Ich bin im Zweifel, ob . . ." — aber damit hat man die verschiedenen Sprachspiele einander nicht näher gebracht.

Die Bedeutsamkeit solcher Umformungsmöglichkeiten, z. B. aller Behauptungssätze in Sätze, die mit der Klausel "Ich denke", oder "Ich glaube" anfangen (also sozusagen in Beschreibungen *meines* Innenlebens) wird sich an anderer Stelle deutlicher zeigen. (Solipsismus.)

25. Man sagt manchmal: die Tiere sprechen nicht, weil ihnen die geistigen Fähigkeiten fehlen. Und das heißt: "Sie denken nicht, darum sprechen sie nicht." Aber: sie sprechen eben nicht. Oder besser: sie verwenden die Sprache nicht — wenn wir von den primitivsten Sprachformen absehen. — Befehlen, fragen, erzählen, plauschen gehören zu unserer Naturgeschichte so, wie gehen, essen, trinken, spielen.

26. Man meint, das Lernen der Sprache bestehe darin, daß man Gegenstände benennt. Und zwar: Menschen, Formen, Farben, Schmerzen, Stimmungen, Zahlen, etc. Wie gesagt — das Benennen ist etwas Ähnliches, wie, einem Ding ein Namentäfelchen anheften. Man kann das eine Vorbereitung zum Gebrauch eines Wortes nennen. Aber *worauf* ist es eine Vorbereitung?

27. "Wir benennen die Dinge und können nun über sie reden. Uns in der Rede auf sie beziehen." — Als ob mit dem Akt des Benennens schon das, was wir weiter tun, gegeben wäre. Als ob es nur Eines gäbe, was heißt: "von Dingen reden". Während wir doch das Verschiedenartigste mit unsern Sätzen tun. Denken wir allein an die Ausrufe. Mit ihren ganz verschiedenen Funktionen.

Wasser!

Fort!

Au!

Hilfe!

Schön!

Nicht!

Bist du nun noch geneigt, diese Wörter "Benennungen von Gegenständen" zu nennen?

description of a facial expression, description of a sensation of touch, of a mood.

Of course, it is possible to substitute for the usual form of a question the form of a statement or description: "I want to know whether . . ." or "I am in doubt whether . . ." — but this does not bring the different language-games any closer together.

The significance of such possibilities of transformation, for example, of turning all assertoric sentences into sentences beginning with the prefix "I think" or "I believe" (and thus, as it were, into descriptions of *my* inner life) will become clearer in another place. (Solipsism.)

* 25. It is sometimes said: animals do not talk because they lack the mental abilities. And this means: "They do not think, and that is why they do not talk." But — they simply do not talk. Or better: they do not use language — if we disregard the most primitive forms of language. — Giving orders, asking questions, telling stories, having a chat, are as much a part of our natural history as walking, eating, drinking, playing.

26. One thinks that learning language consists in giving names to objects. For example, to human beings, to shapes, to colours, to pains, to |13| moods, to numbers, etc. To repeat — naming is something like attaching a name tag to a thing. One can call this a preparation for the use of a word. But *what* is it a preparation *for*?

27. "We name things and then we can talk about them: can refer to them in talk." — As if what we did next were given with the mere act of naming. As if there were only one thing called "talking about things". Whereas in fact we do the most various things with our sentences. Think just of exclamations, with their completely different functions.

Water!
Away!
Ow!
Help!
Splendid!
No!

Are you still inclined to call these words "names of objects"?

In den Sprachen (2) und (8) gab es ein Fragen nach der Benennung nicht. Dies und sein Korrelat, die hinweisende Erklärung, ist, wie wir sagen könnten, ein eigenes Sprachspiel. Das heißt eigentlich: wir werden erzogen, abgerichtet dazu, zu fragen: "Wie heißt das?" — worauf dann das Benennen erfolgt. Und es gibt auch ein Sprachspiel: Für etwas einen Namen erfinden. Also, zu sagen: "Das heißt . . .", und nun den neuen Namen zu verwenden. (So benennen Kinder z. B. ihre Puppen und reden dann von ihnen, und zu ihnen. Dabei bedenke gleich, wie eigenartig der Gebrauch des Personennamens ist, mit welchem wir den Benannten *rufen*!)

28. Man kann nun einen Personennamen, ein Farbwort, einen Stoffnamen, ein Zahlwort, den Namen einer Himmelsrichtung, etc. hinweisend definieren. Die Definition der Zahl Zwei "Das heißt 'zwei' " — wobei man auf zwei Nüsse zeigt — ist vollkommen exakt. — Aber wie kann man denn die Zwei so definieren? Der, dem man die Definition gibt, weiß ja dann nicht, *was* man mit "zwei" benennen will; er wird annehmen, daß du *diese* Gruppe von Nüssen "zwei" nennst! — — Er *kann* dies annehmen; vielleicht nimmt er es aber nicht an. Er könnte ja auch, umgekehrt, wenn ich dieser Gruppe von Nüssen einen Namen beilegen will, ihn als Zahlnamen mißverstehen. Und ebensogut, wenn ich einen Personennamen hinweisend erkläre, diesen als Farbnamen, als Bezeichnung der Rasse, ja als Namen einer Himmelsrichtung auffassen. Das heißt, die hinweisende Definition kann in *jedem* Fall so und anders gedeutet werden.

Könnte man zur Erklärung des Wortes "rot" auf etwas weisen, was *nicht rot* ist? Das wäre ähnlich, wie wenn man Einem, der der deutschen Sprache nicht mächtig ist, das Wort "bescheiden" erklären sollte, und man zeigte zur Erklärung auf einen arroganten Menschen und sagte "Dieser ist *nicht* bescheiden". Es ist kein Argument gegen eine solche Erklärungsweise, daß sie vieldeutig ist. Jede Erklärung kann mißverstanden werden.

Wohl aber könnte man fragen: Sollen wir das noch eine "Erklärung" nennen? — Denn sie spielt im Kalkül natürlich eine andere Rolle, als das was wir gewöhnlich "hinweisende Erklärung" des Wortes "rot" nennen; auch wenn sie dieselben praktischen Folgen, dieselbe *Wirkung* auf den Lernenden hätte.

In languages (2) and (8), there was no such thing as asking something's name. This, with its correlate, ostensive explanation, is, we might say, a language-game in its own right. That is really to say: we are brought up, trained, to ask "What is that called?" — upon which the name is given. And there is also a language-game of inventing a name for something, that is, of saying "This is called . . ." and then using the new name. (So, for example, children give names to their dolls and then talk about them and to them. Consider in this connection how singular is the use of a person's name to *call* him!)

28. Now, one can ostensively define a person's name, the name of a colour, the name of a material, a number-word, the name of a point of the compass, and so on. The definition of the number two, "That is called 'two' " — pointing to two nuts — is perfectly exact. — But how can the number two be defined like that? The person one gives the definition to doesn't know *what* it is that one wants to call "two"; he will suppose that "two" is the name given to *this* group of nuts! —— He *may* suppose this; but perhaps he does not. He might make the opposite mistake: when I want to assign a name to this group of nuts, he might take it to be the name of a number. And he might equally well take a person's name, which I explain ostensively, as that of a colour, of a race, or even of a point |14| of the compass. That is to say, an ostensive definition can be variously interpreted in *any* case.

*

> Could one explain the word "red" by pointing to something that was *not red*? That would be as if one had to explain the word "modest" to someone whose English was poor, and one pointed to an arrogant man and said "That man is *not* modest". That it is ambiguous is no argument against such a form of explanation. Any explanation can be misunderstood.
>
> But one might well ask: are we still to call this an "explanation"? — For, of course, it plays a different role in the calculus from what we ordinarily call an "ostensive explanation" of the word "red", even if it has the same practical consequences, the same *effect* on the learner. |p. 14 n.|

29. Vielleicht sagt man: die Zwei kann nur *so* hinweisend definiert werden: "Diese *Zahl* heißt 'zwei'". Denn das Wort "Zahl" zeigt hier an, an welchen *Platz* der Sprache, der Grammatik, wir das Wort setzen. Das heißt aber, es muß das Wort "Zahl" erklärt sein, ehe jene hinweisende Definition verstanden werden kann. — Das Wort "Zahl" in der Definition zeigt allerdings diesen Platz an; den Posten, an den wir das Wort stellen. Und wir können so Mißverständnissen vorbeugen, indem wir sagen: "Diese *Farbe* heißt so und so", "Diese *Länge* heißt so und so", u. s. w. Das heißt: Mißverständnisse werden manchmal so vermieden. Aber läßt sich denn das Wort "Farbe", oder "Länge" nur *so* auffassen? — Nun, wir müssen sie eben erklären. — Also erklären durch andere Wörter! Und wie ist es mit der letzten Erklärung in dieser Kette? (Sag nicht "Es gibt keine 'letzte' Erklärung". Das ist gerade so, als wolltest du sagen: "Es gibt kein letztes Haus in dieser Straße; man kann immer noch eines dazubauen.")

Ob das Wort "Zahl" in der hinweisenden Definition der Zwei nötig ist, das hängt davon ab, ob er sie ohne dieses Wort anders auffaßt, als ich es wünsche. Und das wird wohl von den Umständen abhängen, unter welchen sie gegeben wird, und von dem Menschen, dem ich sie gebe.

Und wie er die Erklärung 'auffaßt', zeigt sich darin, wie er von dem erklärten Wort Gebrauch macht.

30. Man könnte also sagen: Die hinweisende Definition erklärt den Gebrauch — die Bedeutung — des Wortes, wenn es schon klar ist, welche Rolle das Wort in der Sprache überhaupt spielen soll. Wenn ich also weiß, daß Einer mir ein Farbwort erklären will, so wird mir die hinweisende Erklärung "Das heißt 'Sepia'" zum Verständnis des Wortes verhelfen. — Und dies kann man sagen, wenn man nicht vergißt, daß sich nun allerlei Fragen an das Wort "wissen", oder "klar sein" anknüpfen.

Man muß schon etwas wissen (oder können), um nach der Benennung fragen zu können. Aber was muß man wissen?

31. Wenn man jemandem die Königsfigur im Schachspiel zeigt und sagt "Das ist der Schachkönig", so erklärt man ihm dadurch nicht den Gebrauch dieser Figur, — es sei denn, daß er die Regeln des Spiels schon kennt, bis auf diese letzte Bestimmung: die Form einer Königsfigur. Man kann sich denken, er habe die Regeln des Spiels gelernt, ohne daß ihm je eine wirkliche Spielfigur gezeigt wurde. Die Form der Spielfigur entspricht hier dem Klang, oder der Gestalt eines Wortes.

Man kann sich aber auch denken, Einer habe das Spiel gelernt, ohne je Regeln zu lernen, oder zu formulieren. Er hat etwa zuerst durch

29. Perhaps someone will say, "two" can be ostensively defined only in *this* way: "This *number* is called 'two'." For the word "number" here shows what *place* in language, in grammar, we assign to the word. But this means that the word "number" must be explained before that ostensive definition can be understood. — The word "number" in the definition does indeed indicate this place — the post at which we station the word. And we can prevent misunderstandings by saying "This *colour* is called so-and-so", "This *length* is called so-and-so", and so on. That is to say, misunderstandings are sometimes averted in this way. But does one have to take the words "colour" and "length" in just *this* way? — Well, we'll just have to explain them. Explain, then, by means of other words! And what about the last explanation in this chain? (Don't say: "There isn't a 'last' explanation." That is just as if you were to say: "There isn't a last house in this road; one can always build an additional one.")

Whether the word "number" is necessary in an ostensive definition of "two" depends on whether without this word the other person takes the definition otherwise than I wish. And that will depend on the circumstances under which it is given, and on the person I give it to.

And how he 'takes' the explanation shows itself in how he uses the word explained.

30. So, one could say: an ostensive definition explains the use — the meaning — of a word if the role the word is supposed to play in the language is already clear. So if I know that someone means to explain a colour-word to me, the ostensive explanation "That is called 'sepia' " will enable me to understand the word. — And one can say this, as long as |15| one does not forget that now all sorts of questions are tied up with the words "to know" or "to be clear".

One has already to know (or be able to do) something before one can ask what something is called. But what does one have to know?

31. When one shows someone the king in chess and says "This is the king", one does not thereby explain to him the use of this piece — unless he already knows the rules of the game except for this last point: the shape of the king. One can imagine his having learnt the rules of the game without ever having been shown an actual piece. The shape of the chess piece corresponds here to the sound or shape of a word.

However, one can also imagine someone's having learnt the game without ever learning or formulating rules. He might have learnt quite

Zusehen ganz einfache Brettspiele gelernt und ist zu immer komplizierteren fortgeschritten. Auch diesem könnte man die Erklärung geben: "Das ist der König" — wenn man ihm z. B. Schachfiguren von einer ihm ungewohnten Form zeigt. Auch diese Erklärung lehrt ihn den Gebrauch der Figur nur darum, weil, wie wir sagen könnten, der Platz schon vorbereitet war, an den sie gestellt wurde. Oder auch: Wir werden nur dann sagen, sie lehre ihn den Gebrauch, wenn der Platz schon vorbereitet ist. Und er ist es hier nicht dadurch, daß der, dem wir die Erklärung geben, schon Regeln weiß, sondern dadurch, daß er in anderm Sinne schon ein Spiel beherrscht.

Betrachte noch diesen Fall: Ich erkläre jemandem das Schachspiel; und fange damit an, indem ich auf eine Figur zeige und sage: "Das ist der König. Er kann so und so ziehen, etc. etc." — In diesem Fall werden wir sagen: die Worte "Das ist der König" (oder "Das heißt 'König'") sind nur dann eine Worterklärung, wenn der Lernende schon 'weiß, was eine Spielfigur ist'. Wenn er also etwa schon andere Spiele gespielt hat, oder dem Spielen Anderer 'mit Verständnis' zugesehen hat — *und dergleichen*. Auch nur dann wird er beim Lernen des Spiels relevant fragen können: "Wie heißt das?" — nämlich, diese Spielfigur.

Wir können sagen: Nach der Benennung fragt nur der sinnvoll, der schon etwas mit ihr anzufangen weiß.

Wir können uns ja auch denken, daß der Gefragte antwortet: "Bestimm die Benennung selber" — und nun müßte, der gefragt hat, für alles selber aufkommen.

32. Wer in ein fremdes Land kommt, wird manchmal die Sprache der Einheimischen durch hinweisende Erklärungen lernen, die sie ihm geben; und er wird die Deutung dieser Erklärungen oft *raten* müssen und manchmal richtig, manchmal falsch raten.

Und nun können wir, glaube ich, sagen: Augustinus beschreibe das Lernen der menschlichen Sprache so, als käme das Kind in ein fremdes Land und verstehe die Sprache des Landes nicht; das heißt: so als habe es bereits eine Sprache, nur nicht diese. Oder auch: als könne das Kind schon *denken*, nur noch nicht sprechen. Und "denken" hieße hier etwas, wie: zu sich selber reden.

33. Wie aber, wenn man einwendete: "Es ist nicht wahr, daß Einer schon ein Sprachspiel beherrschen muß, um eine hinweisende Definition zu verstehen, sondern er muß nur — selbstverständlich — wissen (oder erraten) worauf der Erklärende zeigt! Ob also z. B. auf die Form des Gegenstandes, oder auf seine Farbe, oder auf die Anzahl, etc. etc." —— Und worin besteht es denn — 'auf die Form zeigen', 'auf die Farbe zeigen'?

simple board-games first, by watching, and have progressed to more and more complicated ones. He too might be given the explanation "This is the king" — if, for instance, he were being shown chess pieces of a shape unfamiliar to him. This explanation again informs him of the use of the piece only because, as we might say, the place for it was already prepared. In other words, we'll say that it informs him of the use only if the place is already prepared. And in that case it is so, not because the person to whom we give the explanation already knows rules, but because, in another sense, he has already mastered a game.

Consider this further case: I am explaining chess to someone; and I begin by pointing to a chess piece and saying "This is the king; it can move in this-and-this way", and so on. — In this case we shall say: the words "This is the king" (or "This is called 'the king'") are an explanation of a word only if the learner already 'knows what a piece in a game is'. That is, if, for example, he has already played other games, or has watched 'with understanding' how other people play — *and similar things*. Only then will he, while learning the game, be able to ask relevantly, "What is this called?" — that is, this chess piece.

We may say: it only makes sense for someone to ask what something is called if he already knows how to make use of the name.

We can, after all, imagine the person who is asked replying: "Decide what to call it yourself" — and now the one who asked would himself be answerable for everything.

32. Someone coming into a foreign country will sometimes learn the language of the inhabitants from ostensive explanations that they give him; and he will often have to *guess* how to interpret these explanations; and sometimes he will guess right, sometimes wrong.

And now, I think, we can say: Augustine describes the learning |16| of human language as if the child came into a foreign country and did not understand the language of the country; that is, as if he already had a language, only not this one. Or again, as if the child could already *think*, only not yet speak. And "think" would here mean something like "talk to himself".

33. But what if someone objected: "It is not true that one must already be master of a language-game in order to understand an ostensive definition: rather, one need only — obviously — know (or guess) what the person giving the explanation is pointing at. That is, whether, for example, at the shape of the object, or its colour, or the number and so on." —— And what does 'pointing at the shape', 'pointing at the colour',

Zeig auf ein Stück Papier! — Und nun zeig auf seine Form, — nun auf seine Farbe, — nun auf seine Anzahl (das klingt seltsam)! — Nun, wie hast du es gemacht? — Du wirst sagen, du habest jedesmal etwas anderes beim Zeigen 'gemeint'. Und wenn ich frage, wie das vor sich geht, wirst du sagen, du habest deine Aufmerksamkeit auf die Farbe, Form, etc. konzentriert. Nun aber frage ich noch einmal, wie *das* vor sich geht.

Denke, jemand zeigt auf eine Vase und sagt: "Schau das herrliche Blau an! — auf die Form kommt es nicht an. —" Oder: "Schau die herrliche Form an! — die Farbe ist gleichgültig." Es ist zweifellos, du wirst *Verschiedenes* tun, wenn du diesen beiden Aufforderungen nachkommst. Aber tust du immer das *Gleiche*, wenn du deine Aufmerksamkeit auf die Farbe richtest? Stell dir doch verschiedene Fälle vor! Ich will einige andeuten:

> "Ist dieses Blau das gleiche, wie das dort? Siehst du einen Unterschied?"—
> Du mischst Farben und sagst: "Dieses Blau des Himmels ist schwer zu treffen."
> "Es wird schön, man sieht schon wieder blauen Himmel!"
> "Schau, wie verschieden diese beiden Blau wirken!"
> "Siehst du dort das blaue Buch? Bring es her."
> "Dieses blaue Lichtsignal bedeutet . . ."
> "Wie heißt nur dieses Blau? — ist es 'Indigo'?"

Die Aufmerksamkeit auf die Farbe richten, das tut man manchmal, indem man sich die Umrisse der Form mit der Hand weghält; oder den Blick nicht auf die Kontur des Dinges richtet; oder auf den Gegenstand starrt und sich zu erinnern trachtet, wo man diese Farbe schon gesehen hat.

Man richtet seine Aufmerksamkeit auf die Form, manchmal, indem man sie nachzeichnet, manchmal, indem man blinzelt, um die Farbe nicht deutlich zu sehen, etc. etc. Ich will sagen: dies und Ähnliches geschieht, *während* man 'die Aufmerksamkeit auf das und das richtet'. Aber das ist es nicht allein, was uns sagen läßt, Einer richte seine Aufmerksamkeit auf die Form, die Farbe, etc. Wie ein Schachzug nicht allein darin besteht, daß ein Stein so und so auf dem Brett verschoben wird, — aber auch nicht in den Gedanken und Gefühlen des Ziehenden, die den Zug begleiten; sondern in den Umständen, die wir nennen: "eine Schachpartie spielen", "ein Schachproblem lösen", und dergl.

34. Aber nimm an, Einer sagte: "Ich tue immer das Gleiche, wenn ich meine Aufmerksamkeit auf die Form richte: ich folge der Kontur mit

consist in? Point at a piece of paper. — And now point at its shape — now at its colour — now at its number (that sounds odd). — Well, how did you do it? — You'll say that you 'meant' something different each time you pointed. And if I ask how that is done, you'll say you concentrated your attention on the colour, the shape, and so on. But now I ask again: how is *that* done?

Suppose someone points to a vase and says "Look at that marvellous blue — forget about the shape". Or: "Look at the marvellous shape — the colour doesn't matter." No doubt you'll do something *different* in each case, when you do what he asks you. But do you always do the *same* thing when you direct your attention to the colour? Imagine various different cases! To indicate a few:

"Is this blue the same as the blue over there? Do you see any difference?" —
You are mixing paints and you say, "It's hard to get the blue of this sky".
"It's turning fine, you can already see blue sky again."
"Note how different these two blues look."
"Do you see the blue book over there? Bring it here."
"This blue light means . . ."
"What's this blue called? — Is it 'indigo'?"

One attends to the colour sometimes by blocking the contour from view with one's hand, or by not focusing on the contour of the thing, or by staring at the object and trying to remember where one saw that colour before.

One attends to the shape, sometimes by tracing it, sometimes by screwing up one's eyes so as not to see the colour clearly, and so forth. I want to say: this and similar things are what one does *while* one 'directs one's attention to this or that'. But it isn't only these things |17| that make us say that someone is attending to the shape, the colour, etc. Just as making a move in chess doesn't consist only in pushing a piece from here to there on the board — nor yet in the thoughts and feelings that accompany the move: but in the circumstances that we call "playing a game of chess", "solving a chess problem", and the like.

34. But suppose someone said: "I always do the same thing when I attend to a shape: I follow the contour with my eyes and feel . . ." And

den Augen und fühle dabei ..." Und nimm an, dieser gibt einem Andern die hinweisende Erklärung "Das heißt 'Kreis'", indem er, mit all diesen Erlebnissen, auf einen kreisförmigen Gegenstand zeigt —— kann der Andre die Erklärung nicht dennoch anders deuten, auch wenn er sieht, daß der Erklärende der Form mit den Augen folgt, und auch wenn er fühlt, was der Erklärende fühlt? Das heißt: Diese 'Deutung' kann auch darin bestehen, wie er nun von dem erklärten Wort Gebrauch macht, z. B., worauf er zeigt, wenn er den Befehl erhält "Zeige auf einen Kreis!". — Denn weder der Ausdruck "die Erklärung so und so meinen", noch der, "die Erklärung so und so deuten", bezeichnen einen Vorgang, der das Geben und Hören der Erklärung begleitet.

35. Es gibt freilich, was man "charakteristische Erlebnisse", für das Zeigen auf die Form etwa, nennen kann. Zum Beispiel, das Nachfahren der Kontur mit dem Finger, oder mit dem Blick, beim Zeigen. — Aber so wenig, wie *dies* in allen Fällen geschieht, in denen ich 'die Form meine', so wenig geschieht irgend ein anderer charakteristischer Vorgang in allen diesen Fällen. — Aber auch, wenn ein solcher sich in allen wiederholte, so käme es doch auf die Umstände an — d. h., auf das, was vor und nach dem Zeigen geschieht — ob wir sagen würden "Er hat auf die Form und nicht auf die Farbe gezeigt".

Denn es werden die Worte "auf die Form zeigen", "die Form meinen", etc. nicht so gebraucht, wie *die*: "auf dies Buch zeigen" (nicht auf jenes), "auf den Stuhl zeigen, nicht auf den Tisch", etc. — Denn denk nur, wie anders wir den Gebrauch der Worte *lernen*: "auf dieses Ding zeigen", "auf jenes Ding zeigen", und andersteits: "auf die Farbe, nicht auf die Form, zeigen", "die *Farbe* meinen", etc. etc.

Wie gesagt, in gewissen Fällen, besonders beim Zeigen 'auf die Form', oder 'auf die Anzahl' gibt es charakteristische Erlebnisse und Arten des Zeigens — 'charakteristisch', weil sie sich oft (nicht immer) wiederholen, wo Form, oder Anzahl 'gemeint' werden. Aber kennst du auch ein charakteristisches Erlebnis für das Zeigen auf die Spielfigur, als *Spielfigur*? Und doch kann man sagen: "Ich meine, diese *Spielfigur* heißt 'König', nicht dieses bestimmte Stück Holz, worauf ich zeige." (Wiedererkennen, wünschen, sich erinnern, etc.)

suppose this person gives someone else the ostensive explanation "That is called a 'circle'", pointing to a circular object and having all these experiences — can't his hearer still interpret the explanation differently, even though he sees the other's eyes following the contour, and even though he feels what the other feels? That is to say, this 'interpretation' may also consist in how he now makes use of the explained word; in what he points at, for example, when told "Point to a circle!" — For neither the expression "to mean the explanation in such-and-such a way" nor the expression "to interpret the explanation in such-and-such a way" signifies a process which accompanies the giving and hearing of an explanation.

35. There are, indeed, what may be called "characteristic experiences" of pointing, say, to the shape. For example, following the contour with one's finger or with one's eyes as one points. — *This*, however, does not happen in all cases in which I 'mean the shape', and no more does any other one characteristic process occur in all these cases. — But even if something of the sort did recur in all cases, it would still depend on the circumstances — that is, on what happened before and after the pointing — whether we would say "He pointed at the shape and not at the colour".

For the words "to point at the shape", "to mean the shape", and so on, are not used in the same way as *these*: "to point at this book" (not that one), "to point at the chair, not at the table", and so on. — Just think how differently we *learn* the use of the words "to point at this thing", "to point at that thing", and on the other hand, "to point at the colour, not shape", "to mean the *colour*", and so on.

To repeat: in certain cases, especially when one points 'at the shape' or 'at the number', there are characteristic experiences and ways of pointing — 'characteristic' because they recur often (not always) when shape or number are 'meant'. But do you also know of an experience characteristic of pointing at a piece in a game as *a piece in a game*? |18| All the same, one can say: "I mean that this *piece* is called the 'king', not this particular bit of wood I am pointing at." (Recognizing, wishing, remembering, and so on.)

Wie geht es vor sich: die Worte *"Das* ist blau" einmal als Aussage über den Gegenstand, auf den man zeigt — einmal als Erklärung des Wortes "blau" *meinen*? Im zweiten Falle meint man also eigentlich "Das heißt 'blau' ". — Kann man also das Wort "ist" einmal als "heißt" meinen, und das Wort "blau" als " 'blau' "? und ein andermal das "ist" wirklich als "ist"?

Es kann auch geschehen, daß jemand aus dem, was als Mitteilung gemeint war, eine Worterklärung zieht. [Hier liegt ein folgenschwerer Aberglaube verborgen.]

Kann ich mit dem Wort "bububu" meinen "Wenn es nicht regnet, werde ich spazieren gehen"? — Nur in einer Sprache kann ich etwas mit etwas meinen. Das zeigt klar, daß die Grammatik von "meinen" nicht ähnlich der ist des Ausdrucks "sich etwas vorstellen" und dergl.

36. Und wir tun hier, was wir in tausend ähnlichen Fällen tun: Weil wir nicht *eine* körperliche Handlung angeben können, die wir das Zeigen auf die Form (im Gegensatz z. B. zur Farbe) nennen, so sagen wir, es entspreche diesen Worten eine *geistige* Tätigkeit.

Wo unsere Sprache uns einen Körper vermuten läßt, und kein Körper ist, dort, möchten wir sagen, sei ein *Geist*.

37. Was ist die Beziehung zwischen Namen und Benanntem? — Nun, was *ist* sie? Schau auf das Sprachspiel (2), oder ein anderes! dort ist zu sehen, worin diese Beziehung etwa besteht. Diese Beziehung kann, unter vielem andern, auch darin bestehen, daß das Hören des Namens uns das Bild des Benannten vor die Seele ruft, und sie besteht unter anderem auch darin, daß der Name auf das Benannte geschrieben ist, oder daß er beim Zeigen auf das Benannte ausgesprochen wird.

38. Was benennt aber z. B. das Wort "dieses" im Sprachspiel (8), oder das Wort "das" in der hinweisenden Erklärung "Das heißt . . ."? — Wenn man keine Verwirrung anrichten will, so ist es am besten, man sagt gar nicht, daß diese Wörter etwas benennen. — Und merkwürdigerweise wurde von dem Worte "dieses" einmal gesagt, es sei der *eigentliche* Name. Alles, was wir sonst "Name" nennen, sei dies also nur in einem ungenauen, angenäherten Sinn.

Diese seltsame Auffassung rührt von einer Tendenz her, die Logik unserer Sprache zu sublimieren — wie man es nennen könnte. Die

* What is going on when one *means* the words "*That* is blue" at
one time as a statement about the object one is pointing at — at
another as an explanation of the word "blue"? Well, in the second case, one really means "That is called 'blue'". — Then can
one at one time mean the word "is" as "is called" and the word
"blue" as " 'blue' ", and another time mean "is" really as "is"?

It can also happen that from what was meant as a piece of information, someone derives an explanation of a word. [Here lurks
a superstition of great consequence.]

Can I say "bububu" and mean "If it doesn't rain, I shall go for
a walk"? — It is only in a language that I can mean something by
something. This shows clearly that the grammar of "to mean" does
not resemble that of the expression "to imagine" and the like.
|p. 18 n.|

36. And we do here what we do in a host of similar cases: because we
cannot specify any *one* bodily action which we call pointing at the shape
(as opposed to the colour, for example), we say that a *mental, spiritual*
activity corresponds to these words.

Where our language suggests a body and there is none: there, we should
like to say, is a *spirit*.

37. What is the relation between name and thing named? — Well, what
is it? Look at language-game (2) or at some other one: that's where one
can see what this relation may consist in. Among many other things,
this relation may also consist in the fact that hearing a name calls before
our mind the picture of what is named; and sometimes in the name's
being written on the thing named or in its being uttered when the thing
named is pointed at.

* 38. But what, for example, does the word "this" name in language-game
(8) or the word "that" in the ostensive explanation "That is called
...."? — If you don't want to produce confusion, then it is best not to
say that these words name anything. — Yet, strange to say, the word
"this" has been called the *real* name; so that anything else we call a
name was one only in an inexact, approximate sense.

This odd conception springs from a tendency to sublimate the logic
of our language — as one might put it. The proper answer to it is: we

eigentliche Antwort darauf ist: "Name" nennen wir *sehr Verschiedenes*; das Wort "Name" charakterisiert viele verschiedene, mit einander auf viele verschiedene Weisen verwandte, Arten des Gebrauchs eines Worts; — aber unter diesen Arten des Gebrauchs ist nicht die des Wortes "dieses".

Es ist wohl wahr, daß wir oft, z. B. in der hinweisenden Definition, auf das Benannte zeigen und dabei den Namen aussprechen. Und ebenso sprechen wir, z. B. in der hinweisenden Definition, das Wort "dieses" aus, indem wir auf ein Ding zeigen. Und das Wort "dieses" und ein Name stehen auch oft an der gleichen Stelle im Satzzusammenhang. Aber charakteristisch für den Namen ist es gerade, daß er durch das hinweisende "Das ist N" (oder "Das heißt 'N' ") erklärt wird. Erklären wir aber auch: "Das heißt 'dieses' ", oder "Dieses heißt 'dieses' "?

Dies hängt mit der Auffassung des Benennens als eines, sozusagen, okkulten Vorgangs zusammen. Das Benennen erscheint als eine *seltsame* Verbindung eines Wortes mit einem Gegenstand. — Und so eine seltsame Verbindung hat wirklich statt, wenn nämlich der Philosoph, um herauszubringen, was *die* Beziehung zwischen Namen und Benanntem ist, auf einen Gegenstand vor sich starrt und dabei unzählige Male einen Namen wiederholt, oder auch das Wort "dieses". Denn die philosophischen Probleme entstehen, wenn die Sprache *feiert*. Und *da* können wir uns allerdings einbilden, das Benennen sei irgend ein merkwürdiger seelischer Akt, quasi eine Taufe eines Gegenstandes. Und wir können so auch das Wort "dieses" gleichsam *zu* dem Gegenstand sagen, ihn damit *ansprechen* — ein seltsamer Gebrauch dieses Wortes, der wohl nur beim Philosophieren vorkommt.

39. Aber warum kommt man auf die Idee, gerade dieses Wort zum Namen machen zu wollen, wo es offenbar *kein* Name ist? — Gerade darum. Denn man ist versucht, gegen das, was gewöhnlich "Name" heißt, einen Einwand zu machen; und den kann man so ausdrücken: *daß der Name eigentlich Einfaches bezeichnen soll*. Und man könnte dies etwa so begründen: Ein Eigenname im gewöhnlichen Sinn ist etwa das Wort "Nothung". Das Schwert Nothung besteht aus Teilen in einer bestimmten Zusammensetzung. Sind sie anders zusammengesetzt, so existiert Nothung nicht. Nun hat aber offenbar der Satz "Nothung hat eine scharfe Schneide" *Sinn*, ob Nothung noch ganz ist, oder schon zerschlagen. Ist aber "Nothung" der Name eines Gegenstandes, so gibt es diesen Gegenstand nicht mehr, wenn Nothung zerschlagen ist; und da dem Namen dann kein Gegenstand entspräche, so hätte er keine Bedeutung. Dann aber stünde in dem Satz "Nothung hat eine scharfe Schneide" ein Wort, das keine Bedeutung hat, und daher wäre der Satz Unsinn.

call *very different* things "names"; the word "name" serves to |19| characterize many different, variously related, kinds of use of a word — but the kind of use that the word "this" has is not among them.

It is quite true that in giving an ostensive definition, for instance, we often point to the object named and utter the name. And likewise, in giving an ostensive definition, we utter the word "this" while pointing to a thing. And also, the word "this" and a name often occupy the same position in the context of a sentence. But it is precisely characteristic of a name that it is explained by means of the demonstrative expression "That is N" (or "That is called 'N' "). But do we also explain "That is called 'this' ", or "This is called 'this' "?

This is connected with the conception of naming as a process that is, so to speak, occult. Naming seems to be a *strange* connection of a word with an object. — And such a strange connection really obtains, particularly when a philosopher tries to fathom *the* relation between name and what is named by staring at an object in front of him and repeating a name, or even the word "this", innumerable times. For philosophical problems arise when language *goes on holiday*. And *then* we may indeed imagine naming to be some remarkable mental act, as it were the baptism of an object. And we can also say the word "this" *to* the object, as it were *address* the object as "this" — a strange use of this word, which perhaps occurs only when philosophizing.

*   39. But why does it occur to one to want to make precisely this word into a name, when it obviously is *not* a name? — That is just the reason. For one is tempted to make an objection against what is ordinarily called a name. It can be put like this: *a name ought really to signify a simple*. And one might perhaps give the following reasons for this: the word "Nothung", say, is a proper name in the ordinary sense. The sword Nothung consists of parts combined in a particular way. If they are combined differently, Nothung does not exist. But it is clear that the sentence "Nothung has a sharp blade" has a *sense*, whether Nothung is still whole or has already been shattered. But if "Nothung" is the name of an object, this object no longer exists when Nothung is shattered into pieces; and as no object would then correspond to the name, it would have no meaning. But then the sentence "Nothung has a sharp blade" would contain a word that had no meaning, and hence

Nun hat er aber Sinn; also muß den Wörtern, aus denen er besteht, immer etwas entsprechen. Also muß das Wort "Nothung" bei der Analyse des Sinnes verschwinden und statt seiner müssen Wörter eintreten, die Einfaches benennen. Diese Wörter werden wir billigerweise die eigentlichen Namen nennen.

40. Laß uns zuerst über *den* Punkt dieses Gedankengangs reden: daß das Wort keine Bedeutung hat, wenn ihm nichts entspricht. — Es ist wichtig, festzustellen, daß das Wort "Bedeutung" sprachwidrig gebraucht wird, wenn man damit das Ding bezeichnet, das dem Wort 'entspricht'. Dies heißt, die Bedeutung eines Namens verwechseln mit dem *Träger* des Namens. Wenn Herr N. N. stirbt, so sagt man, es sterbe der Träger des Namens, nicht, es sterbe die Bedeutung des Namens. Und es wäre unsinnig, so zu reden, denn hörte der Name auf, Bedeutung zu haben, so hätte es keinen Sinn, zu sagen "Herr N. N. ist gestorben".

41. Im §15 haben wir in die Sprache (8) Eigennamen eingeführt. Nimm nun an, das Werkzeug mit dem Namen "N" sei zerbrochen. A weiß es nicht und gibt dem B das Zeichen "N". Hat dieses Zeichen nun Bedeutung, oder hat es keine? — Was soll B tun, wenn er dieses Zeichen erhält? — Wir haben darüber nichts vereinbart. Man könnte fragen: was *wird* er tun? Nun, er wird vielleicht ratlos dastehen, oder A die Stücke zeigen. Man *könnte* hier sagen: "N" sei bedeutungslos geworden; und dieser Ausdruck würde besagen, daß für das Zeichen "N" in unserm Sprachspiel nun keine Verwendung mehr ist (es sei denn, wir gäben ihm eine neue). "N" könnte auch dadurch bedeutungslos werden, daß man, aus welchem Grund immer, dem Werkzeug eine andere Bezeichnung gibt und das Zeichen "N" im Sprachspiel nicht weiter verwendet. — Wir können uns aber auch eine Abmachung denken, nach der B, wenn ein Werkzeug zerbrochen ist und A das Zeichen dieses Werkzeugs gibt, als Antwort darauf den Kopf zu schütteln hat. — Damit, könnte man sagen, ist der Befehl "N", auch wenn dieses Werkzeug nicht mehr existiert, in das Sprachspiel aufgenommen worden, und das Zeichen "N" habe Bedeutung, auch wenn sein Träger zu existieren aufhört.

42. Aber haben etwa auch Namen in jenem Spiel Bedeutung, die *nie* für ein Werkzeug verwendet worden sind? —— Nehmen wir also an, "X" sei so ein Zeichen, und A gäbe dieses Zeichen dem B — nun, es könnten auch solche Zeichen in das Sprachspiel aufgenommen werden, und B hätte etwa auch sie mit einem Kopfschütteln zu beantworten. (Man könnte sich dies als eine Art Belustigung der Beiden denken.)

the sentence would be nonsense. But it does have a sense; so there must still be something corresponding to the words of which it consists. So the word "Nothung" must disappear when the sense is |20| analysed and its place be taken by words which name simples. It will be reasonable to call these words the real names.

40. Let us first discuss the following point in the argument: that a word has no meaning if nothing corresponds to it. — It is important to note that it is a solecism to use the word "meaning" to signify the thing that 'corresponds' to a word. That is to confound the meaning of a name with the *bearer* of the name. When Mr N.N. dies, one says that the bearer of the name dies, not that the meaning dies. And it would be nonsensical to say this, for if the name ceased to have meaning, it would make no sense to say "Mr N.N. is dead".

41. In §15 we introduced proper names into language (8). Now suppose that the tool with the name "N" is broken. Not knowing this, A gives B the sign "N". Has this sign a meaning now, or not? — What is B to do when he is given it? — We haven't settled anything about this. One might ask: what *will* he do? Well, perhaps he will stand there at a loss, or show A the pieces. Here one *might* say: "N" has become meaningless; and this expression would mean that the sign "N" no longer had a use in our language-game (unless we gave it a new one). "N" might also become meaningless because, for whatever reason, the tool was given another name, and the sign "N" no longer used in the language-game. — But we could also imagine a convention whereby B has to shake his head in reply if A gives the sign for a tool that is broken. — In this way, the command "N" might be said to be admitted into the language-game even when the tool no longer exists, and the sign "N" to have meaning even when its bearer ceases to exist.

42. But have even names that have *never* been used for a tool got a meaning in that game? —— Let's assume that "X" is such a sign, and that A gives this sign to B — well, even such signs could be admitted into the language-game, and B might have to answer them with a shake of the head. (One could imagine this as a kind of amusement for them.)

43. Man kann für eine *große* Klasse von Fällen der Benützung des Wortes
"Bedeutung" — wenn auch nicht für *alle* Fälle seiner Benützung — dieses
Wort so erklären: Die Bedeutung eines Wortes ist sein Gebrauch in der
Sprache.

Und die *Bedeutung* eines Namens erklärt man manchmal dadurch,
daß man auf seinen *Träger* zeigt.

44. Wir sagten: der Satz "Nothung hat eine scharfe Schneide" habe Sinn,
auch wenn Nothung schon zerschlagen ist. Nun, das ist so, weil in diesem
Sprachspiel ein Name auch in der Abwesenheit seines Trägers
gebraucht wird. Aber wir können uns ein Sprachspiel mit Namen
denken (d. h. mit Zeichen, die wir gewiß auch "Namen" nennen werden) in welchem diese nur in der Anwesenheit des Trägers gebraucht
werden; also *immer* ersetzt werden können durch das hinweisende
Fürwort mit der hinweisenden Gebärde.

45. Das hinweisende "dieses" kann nie trägerlos werden. Man könnte
sagen: "Solange es ein *Dieses* gibt, solange hat das Wort 'dieses' auch
Bedeutung, ob *dieses* nun einfach oder zusammengesetzt ist." —— Aber
das macht das Wort eben nicht zu einem Namen. Im Gegenteil; denn
ein Name wird nicht mit der hinweisenden Geste verwendet, sondern
nur durch sie erklärt.

46. Was hat es nun für eine Bewandtnis damit, daß Namen eigentlich
das Einfache bezeichnen? —

Sokrates (im Theätetus): "Täusche ich mich nämlich nicht, so habe
ich von Etlichen gehört: für die *Urelemente* — um mich so auszudrücken
— aus denen wir und alles übrige zusammengesetzt sind, gebe es keine
Erklärung; denn alles, was an und für sich ist, könne man nur mit Namen
bezeichnen; eine andere Bestimmung sei nicht möglich, weder die, es
sei, noch die, es *sei nicht* . . . Was aber an und für sich ist, müsse man
. . . ohne alle anderen Bestimmungen benennen. Somit aber sei es
unmöglich, von irgend einem Urelement erklärungsweise zu reden;
denn für dieses gebe es nichts, als die bloße Benennung; es habe ja nur
seinen Namen. Wie aber das, was aus diesen Urelementen sich zusammensetzt, selbst ein verflochtenes Gebilde sei, so seien auch seine
Benennungen in dieser Verflechtung zur erklärenden Rede geworden; denn
deren Wesen sei die Verflechtung von Namen."

Diese Urelemente waren auch Russell's 'individuals', und auch meine
'Gegenstände' (Log. Phil. Abh.).

47. Aber welches sind die einfachen Bestandteile, aus denen sich die
Realität zusammensetzt? — Was sind die einfachen Bestandteile eines

43. For a *large* class of cases of the employment of the word "meaning" — though not for *all* — this word can be explained in this way: the meaning of a word is its use in the language. |21|

And the *meaning* of a name is sometimes explained by pointing to its *bearer*.

44. We said that the sentence "Nothung has a sharp blade" has a sense even when Nothung is already shattered. Well, this is so because in this language-game a name is also used in the absence of its bearer. But we can imagine a language-game with names (that is, with signs which we would certainly call "names"), in which they are used only in the presence of the bearer, and so could *always* be replaced by a demonstrative pronoun and a pointing gesture.

45. The demonstrative "this" can never be without a bearer. It might be said: "So long as there is a *this*, the word 'this' has a meaning too, whether *this* is simple or complex." —— But that does not make the word into a name. On the contrary: for a name is not used with, but only explained by means of, a pointing gesture.

46. What lies behind the idea that names really signify simples? —

 *   Socrates says in the *Theaetetus*: "If I am not mistaken, I have heard some people say this: there is no explanation of the *primary elements* — so to speak — out of which we and everything else are composed; for everything that exists in and of itself can be *signified* only by names; no other determination is possible, either that it *is* or that it *is not* . . . But what exists in and of itself has to be . . . named without any other determination. In consequence, it is impossible to give an explanatory account of any primary element, since for it, there is nothing other than mere naming; after all, its name is all it has. But just as what is composed of the primary elements is itself an interwoven structure, so the correspondingly interwoven names become explanatory language; for the essence of the latter is the interweaving of names."

 *   Both Russell's 'individuals' and my 'objects' (*Tractatus Logico-Philosophicus*) were likewise such primary elements.

47. But what are the simple constituent parts of which reality is composed? — What are the simple constituent parts of a chair? — The pieces

Sessels? — Die Stücke Holz, aus denen er zusammengefügt ist? Oder die Moleküle, oder die Atome? — "Einfach" heißt: nicht zusammengesetzt. Und da kommt es darauf an: in welchem Sinne 'zusammengesetzt'? Es hat gar keinen Sinn von den 'einfachen Bestandteilen des Sessels schlechtweg' zu reden.

Oder: Besteht mein Gesichtsbild dieses Baumes, dieses Sessels, aus Teilen? und welches sind seine einfachen Bestandteile? Mehrfarbigkeit ist *eine* Art der Zusammengesetztheit; eine andere ist, z. B., die einer gebrochenen Kontur aus geraden Stücken. Und ein Kurvenstück kann man zusammengesetzt nennen aus einem aufsteigenden und einem absteigenden Ast.

Wenn ich jemandem ohne weitere Erklärung sage "Was ich jetzt vor mir sehe, ist zusammengesetzt", so wird er mit Recht fragen: "Was meinst du mit 'zusammengesetzt'? Das kann ja alles Mögliche heißen!" — Die Frage "Ist, was du siehst, zusammengesetzt?" hat wohl Sinn, wenn bereits feststeht, um welche Art des Zusammengesetztseins — d. h., um welchen besonderen Gebrauch dieses Wortes — es sich handeln soll. Wäre festgelegt worden, das Gesichtsbild eines Baumes solle "zusammengesetzt" heißen, wenn man nicht nur einen Stamm, sondern auch Äste sieht, so hätte die Frage "Ist das Gesichtsbild dieses Baumes einfach oder zusammengesetzt?" und die Frage "Welches sind seine einfachen Bestandteile?" einen klaren Sinn — eine klare Verwendung. Und auf die zweite Frage ist die Antwort natürlich nicht "Die Äste" (dies wäre eine Antwort auf die *grammatische* Frage: "Was *nennt* man hier die 'einfachen Bestandteile'?") sondern etwa eine Beschreibung der einzelnen Äste.

Aber ist z. B. nicht ein Schachbrett offenbar und schlechtweg zusammengesetzt? — Du denkst wohl an die Zusammensetzung aus 32 weißen und 32 schwarzen Quadraten. Aber könnten wir z. B. nicht auch sagen, es sei aus den Farben Weiß, Schwarz und dem Schema des Quadratnetzes zusammengesetzt? Und wenn es hier ganz verschiedene Betrachtungsweisen gibt, willst du dann noch sagen, das Schachbrett sei 'zusammengesetzt' schlechtweg? — *Außerhalb* eines bestimmten Spiels zu fragen "Ist dieser Gegenstand zusammengesetzt?", das ist ähnlich dem, was einmal ein kleiner Junge tat, der angeben sollte, ob die Zeitwörter in gewissen Satzbeispielen in der aktiven, oder in der passiven Form gebraucht seien, und der sich nun darüber den Kopf zerbrach, ob z. B. das Zeitwort "schlafen" etwas Aktives, oder etwas Passives bedeute.

Das Wort "zusammengesetzt" (und also das Wort "einfach") wird von uns in einer Unzahl verschiedener, in verschiedenen Weisen mit einander verwandten, Arten benützt. (Ist die Farbe eines Schachfeldes einfach, oder besteht sie aus reinem Weiß und reinem Gelb? Und ist

of wood from which it is assembled? Or the molecules, or the atoms? — "Simple" means: not composite. And here the point is: in what sense 'composite'? It makes no sense at all to speak absolutely of the 'simple parts of a chair'. |22|

* Again: Does my visual image of this tree, of this chair, consist of parts? And what are its simple constituent parts? Multi-colouredness is *one* kind of compositeness; another is, for example, that of an open curve composed of straight bits. And a continuous curve may be said to be composed of an ascending and a descending segment.

If I tell someone without any further explanation, "What I see before me now is composite", he will legitimately ask, "What do you mean by 'composite'? For there are all sorts of things it may mean!" — The question "Is what you see composite?" makes good sense if it is already established what kind of compositeness — that is, which particular use of this word — is in question. If it had been laid down that the visual image of a tree was to be called "composite" if one saw not just a trunk, but also branches, then the question "Is the visual image of this tree simple or composite?" and the question "What are its simple constituent parts?" would have a clear sense — a clear use. And of course the answer to the second question is not "The branches" (that would be an answer to the *grammatical* question: "What are here *called* 'simple constituent parts'?"), but rather a description of the individual branches.

But isn't a chessboard, for instance, obviously, and absolutely composite? — You're probably thinking of its being composed of 32 white and 32 black squares. But couldn't we also say, for instance, that it was composed of the colours black and white and the schema of squares? And if there are quite different ways of looking at it, do you still want to say that the chessboard is absolutely 'composite'? — Asking "Is this object composite?" *outside* a particular game is like what a boy once did when he had to say whether the verbs in certain sentences were in the active or passive voice, and who racked his brains over the question whether the verb "to sleep", for example, meant something active or passive.

We use the word "composite" (and therefore the word "simple") in an enormous number of different and differently related ways. (Is the colour of a square on a chessboard simple, or does it consist of pure white and pure yellow? And is the white simple, or does it consist of

das Weiß einfach, oder besteht es aus den Farben des Regenbogens? —
Ist diese Strecke von 2 cm einfach, oder besteht sie aus zwei
Teilstrecken von je 1 cm? Aber warum nicht aus einem Stück von 3 cm
Länge und einem, in negativem Sinn angesetzten, Stück von 1 cm?)

Auf die *philosophische* Frage: "Ist das Gesichtsbild dieses Baumes
zusammengesetzt, und welches sind seine Bestandteile?" ist die richtige
Antwort: "Das kommt drauf an, was du unter 'zusammengesetzt' verstehst." (Und das ist natürlich keine Beantwortung, sondern eine
Zurückweisung der Frage.)

48. Laß uns die Methode des §2 auf die Darstellung im Theätetus anwen-
den. Betrachten wir ein Sprachspiel, wofür diese Darstellung wirklich
gilt. Die Sprache diene dazu, Kombinationen farbiger Quadrate auf einer
Fläche darzustellen. Die Quadrate bilden einen schachbrettförmigen
Komplex. Es gibt rote, grüne, weiße und schwarze Quadrate. Die
Wörter der Sprache seien (entsprechend): "R", "G", "W", "S", und ein
Satz ist eine Reihe dieser Wörter. Sie beschreiben eine Zusammen-
stellung von Quadraten in der Reihenfolge

1	2	3
4	5	6
7	8	9

Der Satz "RRSGGGRWW" beschreibt also z. B. eine Zusammensetzung
dieser Art:

Hier ist der Satz ein Komplex von Namen, dem ein Komplex von
Elementen entspricht. Die Urelemente sind die farbigen Quadrate.
"Aber sind diese einfach?" — Ich wüßte nicht, was ich in diesem
Sprachspiel natürlicher das "Einfache" nennen sollte. Unter anderen
Umständen aber würde ich ein einfärbiges Quadrat "zusammenge-
setzt" nennen, etwa aus zwei Rechtecken, oder aus den Elementen Farbe
und Form. Aber der Begriff der Zusammensetzung könnte auch so gedehnt
werden, daß die kleinere Fläche 'zusammengesetzt' genannt wird aus

the colours of the rainbow? — Is this length of 2 cm simple, or does it consist of two parts, each 1 cm long? But why not of one bit 3 cm long, and one bit 1 cm long measured in the opposite direction?)

To the *philosophical* question "Is the visual image of this tree |23| composite, and what are its constituent parts?" the correct answer is: "That depends on what you understand by 'composite'." (And that, of course, is not an answer to, but a rejection of, the question.)

48. Let us apply the method of §2 to the account in the *Theaetetus*. Consider a language-game for which this account is really valid. The language serves to represent combinations of coloured squares on a surface. The squares form a chessboard-like complex. There are red, green, white and black squares. The words of the language are (correspondingly) "R", "G", "W", "B", and a sentence is a sequence of these words. Such sequences describe an arrangement of squares in the order

1	2	3
4	5	6
7	8	9

And so, for instance, the sentence "RRBGGGRWW" describes an arrangement of this sort:

Here the sentence is a complex of names, to which a complex of elements corresponds. The primary elements are the coloured squares. "But are these simple?" — I wouldn't know what I could more naturally call a 'simple' in this language-game. But under other circumstances, I'd call a monochrome square, consisting perhaps of two rectangles or of the elements colour and shape, "composite". But the concept of compositeness might also be extended so that a smaller area was said to be

einer größeren und einer von ihr subtrahierten. Vergleiche 'Zusammensetzung' der Kräfte, 'Teilung' einer Strecke durch einen Punkt außerhalb;
diese Ausdrücke zeigen, daß wir unter Umständen auch geneigt sind,
das Kleinere als Resultat der Zusammensetzung von Größerem aufzufassen, und das Größere als ein Resultat der Teilung des Kleineren.

Aber ich weiß nicht, ob ich nun sagen soll, die Figur, die unser Satz
beschreibt, bestehe aus vier Elementen oder aus neun! Nun, besteht
jener Satz aus vier Buchstaben oder aus neun? — Und welches sind
seine Elemente: die Buchstabentypen, oder die Buchstaben? Ist es nicht
gleichgültig, welches wir sagen? wenn wir nur im besonderen Fall
Mißverständnisse vermeiden!

49. Was heißt es aber, daß wir diese Elemente nicht erklären (d. h.
beschreiben) sondern nur benennen können? Das könnte etwa sagen,
daß die Beschreibung eines Komplexes, wenn er, in einem Grenzfall, nur
aus *einem* Quadrat besteht, einfach der Name des Farbquadrates ist.

Man könnte hier sagen — obwohl dies leicht zu allerlei philosophi-
schem Aberglauben führt — ein Zeichen "R", oder "S", etc., könne einmal Wort und einmal Satz sein. Ob es aber 'Wort oder Satz ist', hängt
von der Situation ab, in der es ausgesprochen oder geschrieben wird.
Soll z. B. A dem B Komplexe von Farbquadraten beschreiben und
gebraucht er hier das Wort "R" *allein*, so werden wir sagen können,
das Wort sei eine Beschreibung — ein Satz. Memoriert er aber etwa die
Wörter und ihre Bedeutungen, oder lehrt er einen Andern den Gebrauch
der Wörter und spricht sie beim hinweisenden Lehren aus, so werden
wir nicht sagen, sie seien hier Sätze. In dieser Situation ist das Wort
"R" z. B. keine Beschreibung; man *benennt* damit ein Element —— aber
darum wäre es hier seltsam zu sagen, das Element könne man *nur* benennen! Benennen und Beschreiben stehen ja nicht auf *einer* Ebene: Das
Benennen ist eine Vorbereitung zur Beschreibung. Das Benennen ist noch
gar kein Zug im Sprachspiel, — so wenig, wie das Aufstellen einer
Schachfigur ein Zug im Schachspiel. Man kann sagen: Mit dem
Benennen eines Dings ist noch *nichts* getan. Es *hat* auch keinen Namen,
außer im Spiel. Das war es auch, was Frege damit meinte: ein Wort habe
nur im Satzzusammenhang Bedeutung.

50. Was heißt es nun, von den Elementen zu sagen, daß wir ihnen weder
Sein noch Nichtsein beilegen können? — Man könnte sagen: Wenn
alles, was wir "Sein" und "Nichtsein" nennen, im Bestehen und
Nichtbestehen von Verbindungen zwischen den Elementen liegt, dann
hat es keinen Sinn vom Sein (Nichtsein) eines Elements zu sprechen;
sowie, wenn alles, was wir "zerstören" nennen, in der Trennung von

'composed' of a greater area and another one subtracted from it. Compare the 'composition' of |24| forces, the 'division' of a line by a point outside it; these expressions show that we are sometimes even inclined to conceive the smaller as the result of a composition of greater parts, and the greater as the result of a division of the smaller.

But I do not know whether to say that the figure described by our sentence consists of four or of nine elements! Well, does the sentence consist of four letters or of nine? — And which are its elements, the types of letter, or the letters? Does it matter which we say, so long as we avoid misunderstandings in any particular case?

49. But what does it mean to say that we cannot explain (that is, describe) these elements, but only name them? Well, it could mean, for instance, that when in a limiting case a complex consists of only *one* square, its description is simply the name of the coloured square.

* Here one might say — though this easily leads to all kinds of philosophical superstition — that a sign "R" or "B", etc., may sometimes be a word and sometimes a sentence. But whether it 'is a word or a sentence' depends on the situation in which it is uttered or written. For instance, if A has to describe complexes of coloured squares to B, and he uses the word "R" *by itself*, we'll be able to say that the word is a description — a sentence. But if he is memorizing the words and their meanings, or if he is teaching someone else the use of the words and uttering them in the course of ostensive teaching, we'll not say that they are sentences. In this situation the word "R", for instance, is not a description; one *names* an element with it —— but that is why it would be strange to say here that an element can *only* be named! For naming and describing do not stand on the *same* level: naming is a preparation for describing. Naming is not yet a move in a language-game — any more than putting a piece in its place on the board is a move in chess. One may say: with the mere naming of a thing, nothing has yet been done. Nor *has* it a name except in a game. This was what Frege meant too when he said that a word has a meaning only in the context of a sentence.

50. What does it mean to say that we can attribute neither being nor non-being to the elements? — One might say: if everything that we call "being" and "non-being" consists in the obtaining and non-obtaining of connections between elements, it makes no sense to speak of the being (non-being) of an element; just as it makes no sense to speak of the

Elementen liegt, es keinen Sinn hat, vom Zerstören eines Elements zu reden.

Aber man möchte sagen: Man kann dem Element nicht Sein beilegen, denn *wäre* es nicht, so könnte man es auch nicht einmal nennen und also gar nichts von ihm aussagen. — Betrachten wir doch einen analogen Fall! Man kann von *einem* Ding nicht aussagen, es sei 1 m lang, noch, es sei nicht 1 m lang, und das ist das Urmeter in Paris. — Damit haben wir aber diesem natürlich nicht irgend eine merkwürdige Eigenschaft zugeschrieben, sondern nur seine eigenartige Rolle im Spiel des Messens mit dem Metermaß gekennzeichnet. — Denken wir uns auf ähnliche Weise wie das Urmeter auch die Muster von Farben in Paris aufbewahrt. So erklären wir: "Sepia" heiße die Farbe des dort unter Luftabschluß aufbewahrten Ur-Sepia. Dann wird es keinen Sinn haben, von diesem Muster auszusagen, es habe diese Farbe, noch, es habe sie nicht.

Wir können das so ausdrücken: Dieses Muster ist ein Instrument der Sprache, mit der wir Farbaussagen machen. Es ist in diesem Spiel nicht Dargestelltes, sondern Mittel der Darstellung. — Und eben das gilt von einem Element im Sprachspiel (48), wenn wir, es benennend, das Wort "R" aussprechen: wir haben damit diesem Ding eine Rolle in unserm Sprachspiel gegeben; es ist nun *Mittel* der Darstellung. Und zu sagen "*Wäre* es nicht, so könnte es keinen Namen haben" sagt nun so viel, und so wenig, wie: gäbe es dieses Ding nicht, so könnten wir es in unserem Spiel nicht verwenden. — Was es, scheinbar, geben *muß*, gehört zur Sprache. Es ist in unserem Spiel ein Paradigma; etwas, womit verglichen wird. Und dies feststellen, kann heißen, eine wichtige Feststellung machen; aber es ist dennoch eine Feststellung unser Sprachspiel — unsere Darstellungsweise — betreffend.

51. In der Beschreibung des Sprachspiels (48) sagte ich, den Farben der Quadrate entsprächen die Wörter "R", "S", etc. Worin aber besteht diese Entsprechung; inwiefern kann man sagen, diesen Zeichen entsprächen gewisse Farben der Quadrate? Die Erklärung in (48) stellte ja nur einen Zusammenhang zwischen diesen Zeichen und gewissen Wörtern unserer Sprache her (den Farbnamen). — Nun, es war vorausgesetzt, daß der Gebrauch der Zeichen im Spiel anders, und zwar durch Hinweisen auf Paradigmen, gelehrt würde. Wohl; aber was heißt es nun, zu sagen, in der *Praxis der Sprache* entsprächen den Zeichen gewisse Elemente? — Liegt es darin, daß der, welcher die Komplexe von Farbquadraten beschreibt, hierbei immer "R" sagt, wo ein rotes Quadrat steht; "S", wo ein schwarzes steht, etc.? Aber wie, wenn er sich bei der Beschreibung irrt und, fälschlich, "R" sagt, wo er ein schwarzes

destruction of an element, if everything that we call "destruction" lies in the separation of elements. |25|

One would like to say, however, that being cannot be attributed to an element, for if it did not *exist*, one could not even name it, and so one could state nothing at all about it. — But let us consider an analogous case. There is *one* thing of which one can state neither that it is 1 metre long, nor that it is not 1 metre long, and that is the standard metre in Paris. — But this is, of course, not to ascribe any remarkable property to it, but only to mark its peculiar role in the game of measuring with a metre-rule. — Suppose that samples of colour were preserved in Paris like the standard metre. So we explain that "sepia" means the colour of the standard sepia which is kept there hermetically sealed. Then it will make no sense to state of this sample either that it is of this colour or that it is not.

We can put it like this: This sample is an instrument of the language, by means of which we make colour statements. In this game, it is not something that is represented, but is a means of representation. — And the same applies to an element in language-game (48) when we give it a name by uttering the word "R" — in so doing we have given that object a role in our language-game; it is now a *means* of representation. And to say "If it did not exist, it could have no name" is to say as much and as little as: if this thing did not exist, we could not use it in our language-game. — What looks as if it *had* to exist is part of the language. It is a paradigm in our game; something with which comparisons are made. And this may be an important observation; but it is none the less an observation about our language-game — our mode of representation.

51. In describing language-game (48), I said that the words "R", "B", etc. corresponded to the colours of the squares. But what does this correspondence consist in? In what sense can one say that certain colours of squares correspond to these signs? After all, the explanation in (48) merely set up a connection between those signs and certain words of our language (colour names). — Well, it was assumed that the use of the signs in the game would be taught in a different way — by pointing to paradigms. Very well; but what does it mean to say that in the *practice of the language* certain elements correspond to the signs? — Is it that the person who is describing the complexes of coloured squares always says "R" where there is a red square, "B" where there is a black one, and so on? But what if he goes wrong in the description and mistakenly says "R" where he sees a black square —— what is the

Quadrat sieht —— was ist hier das Kriterium dafür, daß dies ein *Fehler* war? — Oder besteht, daß "R" ein rotes Quadrat bezeichnet, darin, daß den Menschen, die die Sprache gebrauchen, immer ein rotes Quadrat im Geist vorschwebt, wenn sie das Zeichen "R" gebrauchen?

Um klarer zu sehen, müssen wir hier, wie in unzähligen ähnlichen Fällen, die Einzelheiten der Vorgänge ins Auge fassen; was vorgeht *aus der Nähe betrachten.*

52. Wenn ich dazu neige, anzunehmen, daß eine Maus durch Urzeugung aus grauen Fetzen und Staub entsteht, so wird es gut sein, diese Fetzen genau daraufhin zu untersuchen, wie eine Maus sich in ihnen verstecken konnte, wie sie dort hin kommen konnte, etc. Bin ich aber überzeugt, daß eine Maus aus diesen Dingen nicht entstehen kann, dann wird diese Untersuchung vielleicht überflüssig sein.

Was es aber ist, das sich in der Philosophie einer solchen Betrachtung der Einzelheiten entgegensetzt, müssen wir erst verstehen lernen.

53. Es gibt nun *verschiedene* Möglichkeiten für unser Sprachspiel (48), verschiedene Fälle, in denen wir sagen würden, ein Zeichen benenne in dem Spiel ein Quadrat von der und der Farbe. Wir würden dies z. B. sagen, wenn wir wüßten, daß den Menschen, die diese Sprache gebrauchen, der Gebrauch der Zeichen auf die und die Art beigebracht wurde. Oder, wenn es schriftlich, etwa in Form einer Tabelle, niedergelegt wäre, daß diesem Zeichen dieses Element entspricht, und wenn diese Tabelle beim Lehren der Sprache benützt und in gewissen Streitfällen zur Entscheidung herangezogen würde.

Wir können uns aber auch denken, daß eine solche Tabelle ein Werkzeug im Gebrauch der Sprache ist. Die Beschreibung eines Komplexes geht dann so vor sich: Der den Komplex beschreibt, führt eine Tabelle mit sich und sucht in ihr jedes Element des Komplexes auf und geht von ihm in der Tabelle zum Zeichen über (und es kann auch der, dem die Beschreibung gegeben wird, die Worte derselben durch eine Tabelle in die Anschauung von färbigen Quadraten übersetzen). Man könnte sagen, diese Tabelle übernehme hier die Rolle, die in anderen Fällen Gedächtnis und Assoziation spielen. (Wir werden den Befehl "Bring mir eine rote Blume!" für gewöhnlich nicht so ausführen, daß wir die Farbe Rot in einer Farbentabelle aufsuchen und dann eine Blume bringen von der Farbe, die wir in der Tabelle finden; aber wenn es sich darum handelt, einen bestimmten Ton von Rot zu wählen, oder zu mischen, dann geschieht es, daß wir uns eines Musters, oder einer Tabelle bedienen.)

criterion here for this being a *mistake?* — Or does "R"'s signifying a red square consist in this, that the |26| people who use the language always have a red square come before their mind when they use the sign "R"?

*   In order to see more clearly, here as in countless similar cases, we must look at what really happens *in detail*, as it were from close up.

52. If I am inclined to suppose that a mouse comes into being by spontaneous generation out of grey rags and dust, it's a good idea to examine those rags very closely to see how a mouse could have hidden in them, how it could have got there, and so on. But if I am convinced that a mouse cannot come into being from these things, then this investigation will perhaps be superfluous.

But what it is in philosophy that resists such an examination of details, we have yet to come to understand.

53. Our language-game (48) has *various* possibilities. There is a variety of cases in which we would say that a sign in the game was the name of a square of such-and-such a colour. We'd say so, for example, if we knew that the people who used the language were taught the use of the signs in such-and-such a way. Or if it were laid down somewhere, say in the form of a chart, that this element corresponded to this sign, and if the chart were used in teaching the language and were appealed to in deciding certain disputed cases.

We can, however, also imagine such a chart's being a tool in the use of the language. Describing a complex is then done like this: the person who describes the complex has a chart with him and looks up each element of the complex in it and passes from the element to the sign (and the person to whom the description is given may also translate its words into a picture of coloured squares by the use of a chart). This chart might be said to take over here the role that memory and association play in other cases. (We don't usually carry out the order "Bring me a red flower" by looking up the colour red in a colour chart and then bringing a flower of the colour that we find in the chart; but when it is a question of choosing or mixing a particular shade of red, we do sometimes make use of a sample or chart.)

Nennen wir eine solche Tabelle den Ausdruck einer Regel des Sprachspiels, so kann man sagen, daß dem, was wir Regel eines Sprachspiels
nennen, sehr verschiedene Rollen im Spiel zukommen können.

54. Denken wir doch daran, in was für Fällen wir sagen, ein Spiel werde
nach einer bestimmten Regel gespielt!
    Die Regel kann ein Behelf des Unterrichts im Spiel sein. Sie wird dem
Lernenden mitgeteilt und ihre Anwendung eingeübt. — Oder sie ist
ein Werkzeug des Spieles selbst. — Oder: Eine Regel findet weder im
Unterricht noch im Spiel selbst Verwendung; noch ist sie in einem
Regelverzeichnis niedergelegt. Man lernt das Spiel, indem man zusieht,
wie Andere es spielen. Aber wir sagen, es werde nach den und den Regeln
gespielt, weil ein Beobachter diese Regeln aus der Praxis des Spiels able-
sen kann, — wie ein Naturgesetz, dem die Spielhandlungen folgen. ——
Wie aber unterscheidet der Beobachter in diesem Fall zwischen einem
Fehler der Spielenden und einer richtigen Spielhandlung? — Es gibt dafür
Merkmale im Benehmen der Spieler. Denke an das charakteristische
Benehmen dessen, der ein Versprechen korrigiert. Es wäre möglich,
zu erkennen, daß Einer dies tut, auch wenn wir seine Sprache nicht
verstehen.

55. "Was die Namen der Sprache bezeichnen, muß unzerstörbar sein:
denn man muß den Zustand beschreiben können, in dem alles, was zer-
störbar ist, zerstört ist. Und in dieser Beschreibung wird es Wörter geben;
und was ihnen entspricht, darf dann nicht zerstört sein, denn sonst hätten die Wörter keine Bedeutung." Ich darf mir nicht den Ast absägen,
auf welchem ich sitze.
    Man könnte nun freilich gleich einwenden, daß ja die Beschreibung
selbst sich von der Zerstörung ausnehmen müsse. — Aber das, was den
Wörtern der Beschreibung entspricht und also nicht zerstört sein darf,
wenn sie wahr ist, ist, was den Wörtern ihre Bedeutung gibt, — ohne
welches sie keine Bedeutung hätten. — Aber dieser Mensch ist ja doch
in einem Sinne das, was seinem Namen entspricht. Er aber ist zerstör-
bar; und sein Name verliert seine Bedeutung nicht, wenn der Träger
zerstört wird. — Das, was dem Namen entspricht, und ohne dem er
keine Bedeutung hätte, ist, z. B., ein Paradigma, das im Sprachspiel in
Verbindung mit dem Namen gebraucht wird.

56. Aber wie, wenn kein solches Muster zur Sprache gehört, wenn wir
uns, z. B., die Farbe, die ein Wort bezeichnet, *merken*? —— "Und wenn
wir sie uns merken, so tritt sie also vor unser geistiges Auge, wenn wir
etwa das Wort aussprechen. Sie muß also an sich unzerstörbar sein, wenn

If we call such a chart the expression of a rule of the language-game, it can be said that what we call a rule of a language-game may have very different roles in the game.

54. Just think of the kinds of case where we say that a game is played according to a particular rule. |27|

*   The rule may be an aid in teaching the game. The learner is told it and given practice in applying it. — Or it is a tool of the game itself. — Or a rule is employed neither in the teaching nor in the game itself; nor is it set down in a list of rules. One learns the game by watching how others play it. But we say that it is played according to such-and-such rules because an observer can read these rules off from the way the game is played — like a natural law governing the play. —— But how does the observer distinguish in this case between players' mistakes and correct play? — There are characteristic signs of it in the players' behaviour. Think of the behaviour characteristic of someone correcting a slip of the tongue. It would be possible to recognize that someone was doing so even without knowing his language.

55. "What the names in language signify must be indestructible; for it must be possible to describe the state of affairs in which everything destructible is destroyed. And this description will contain words; and what corresponds to these cannot in that case be destroyed, for otherwise the words would have no meaning." I must not saw off the branch on which I am sitting.

Now one might, of course, object at once that this description would have to exempt itself from the destruction. — But what corresponds to the words of the description, and so cannot be destroyed if it is true, is what gives the words their meaning — that without which they would have no meaning. —— In a sense, however, this man is surely what corresponds to his name. But he is destructible, and his name does not lose its meaning when its bearer is destroyed. — A paradigm that is used in conjunction with a name in a language-game — that would be an example of something which corresponds to a name and without which it would have no meaning.

56. But what if no such sample is part of the language, and we *bear in mind* the colour (for instance) that a word signifies? —— "And if we bear it in mind, then it comes before our mind's eye when we utter the word. So, if it is supposed to be possible for us to remember it

die Möglichkeit bestehen soll, daß wir uns jederzeit an sie erinnern."
—— Aber was sehen wir denn als das Kriterium dafür an, daß wir uns
richtig an sie erinnern? — Wenn wir mit einem Muster statt mit unserm
Gedächtnis arbeiten, so sagen wir unter Umständen, das Muster habe
seine Farbe verändert und beurteilen dies mit dem Gedächtnis. Aber können wir nicht unter Umständen auch von einem Nachdunkeln (z. B.)
unseres Erinnerungsbildes reden? Sind wir dem Gedächtnis nicht
ebenso ausgeliefert, wie einem Muster? (Denn es könnte Einer sagen
wollen: "Wenn wir kein Gedächtnis hätten, wären wir einem Muster
ausgeliefert.") — Oder etwa einer chemischen Reaktion. Denke, du solltest eine bestimmte Farbe "F" malen, und es ist die Farbe, welche man
sieht, wenn sich die chemischen Substanzen X und Y miteinander
verbinden. — Nimm an, die Farbe käme dir an einem Tag heller vor als
an einem andern; würdest du da nicht unter Umständen sagen: "Ich muß
mich irren, die Farbe ist gewiß die gleiche, wie gestern"? Das zeigt, daß
wir uns dessen, was das Gedächtnis sagt, nicht immer als des obersten,
inappellabeln, Schiedsspruchs bedienen.

57. "Etwas Rotes kann zerstört werden, aber Rot kann nicht zerstört
werden, und darum ist die Bedeutung des Wortes 'rot' von der Existenz
eines roten Dinges unabhängig." — Gewiß, es hat keinen Sinn, zu sagen,
die Farbe Rot (color, nicht pigmentum) werde zerrissen, oder zer-
stampft. Aber sagen wir nicht, "Die Röte verschwindet"? Und
klammre dich nicht daran, daß wir sie uns vors geistige Auge rufen können, auch wenn es nichts Rotes mehr gibt! Dies ist nicht anders, als
wolltest du sagen, daß es dann immer noch eine chemische Reaktion
gäbe, die eine rote Flamme erzeugt. — Denn wie, wenn du dich nicht
mehr an die Farbe erinnern kannst? — Wenn wir vergessen, welche Farbe
es ist, die diesen Namen hat, so verliert er seine Bedeutung für uns; d. h.,
wir können ein bestimmtes Sprachspiel nicht mehr mit ihm spielen. Und
die Situation ist dann der zu vergleichen, daß das Paradigma, welches
ein Mittel unserer Sprache war, verloren gegangen ist.

58. "Ich will 'Name' nur das nennen, was nicht in der Verbindung 'X
existiert' stehen kann. — Und so kann man nicht sagen 'Rot existiert',
weil, wenn es Rot nicht gäbe, von ihm überhaupt nicht geredet werden
könnte." — Richtiger: Wenn "X existiert" soviel besagen soll, wie: "X"
habe Bedeutung, — dann ist es kein Satz, der von X handelt, sondern
ein Satz über unsern Sprachgebrauch, nämlich den Gebrauch des
Wortes "X".

whenever we want, the colour in itself must be indestructible." —— But what do we regard as the criterion for remembering it right? — If we use a sample instead of our memory, there are circumstances in which we might say that the sample has changed colour, and we judge whether this is so by memory. But can't we sometimes speak of a darkening (for example) of our memory-image? Aren't we as much at the mercy of memory as of a sample? (For someone might feel like saying: "If we |28| had no memory, we would be at the mercy of a sample.") — Or perhaps of some chemical reaction. Imagine that you were supposed to paint a particular colour "C", which was the colour that appeared when the chemical substances X and Y combined. — Suppose that the colour struck you as brighter on one day than on another; would you perhaps not say: "I must be wrong, the colour is surely the same as yesterday"? This shows that we do not always resort to what memory tells us as the verdict of the highest court of appeal.

57. "Something red can be destroyed, but red cannot be destroyed, and that is why the meaning of the word 'red' is independent of the existence of a red thing." — Certainly it makes no sense to say that the colour red (as opposed to the pigment) is torn up or pounded to bits. But don't we say "The red is vanishing"? And don't cling to the idea of our always being able to bring red before our mind's eye even when there is nothing red any more! That is just as if you were to say that there would still always be a chemical reaction producing a red flame. — For what if you cannot remember the colour any more? — If we forget which colour this is the name of, the name loses its meaning for us; that is, we're no longer able to play a particular language-game with it. And then the situation is comparable to that in which we've lost a paradigm which was an instrument of our language.

58. "I want to restrict the term 'name' to what cannot occur in the combination 'X exists'. — And so one cannot say 'Red exists', because if there were no red, it could not be spoken of at all." — More correctly: If "X exists" amounts to no more than "X" has a meaning — then it is not a sentence which treats of X, but a sentence about our use of language, that is, about the use of the word "X".

Es erscheint uns, als sagten wir damit etwas über die Natur von Rot: daß die Worte "Rot existiert" keinen Sinn ergeben. Es existiere eben 'an und für sich'. Die gleiche Idee, — daß dies eine metaphysische Aussage über Rot ist, — drückt sich auch darin aus, daß wir etwa sagen, Rot sei zeitlos, und vielleicht noch stärker im Wort "unzerstörbar".

Aber eigentlich *wollen* wir eben nur "Rot existiert" auffassen als Aussage: das Wort "Rot" hat Bedeutung. Oder vielleicht richtiger: "Rot existiert nicht" als " 'Rot' hat keine Bedeutung". Nur wollen wir nicht sagen, daß jener Ausdruck das *sagt*, sondern daß er *das* sagen müßte, *wenn* er einen Sinn hätte. Daß er sich aber beim Versuch, das zu sagen, selbst widerspricht — da eben Rot 'an und für sich' sei. Während ein Widerspruch nur etwa darin liegt, daß der Satz aussieht, als rede er von der Farbe, während er etwas über den Gebrauch des Wortes "rot" sagen soll. — In Wirklichkeit aber sagen wir sehr wohl, eine bestimmte Farbe existiere; und das heißt soviel wie: es existiere etwas, was diese Farbe hat. Und der erste Ausdruck ist nicht weniger exakt, als der zweite; besonders dort nicht, wo 'das, was die Farbe hat', kein physikalischer Gegenstand ist.

59. "*Namen* bezeichnen nur das, was *Element* der Wirklichkeit ist. Was sich nicht zerstören läßt; was in allem Wandel gleichbleibt." — Aber was ist das? — Während wir den Satz sagten, schwebte es uns ja schon vor! Wir sprachen schon eine ganz bestimmte Vorstellung aus. Ein bestimmtes Bild, das wir verwenden wollen. Denn die Erfahrung zeigt uns diese Elemente ja nicht. Wir sehen *Bestandteile* von etwas Zusammengesetztem (eines Sessels z. B.). Wir sagen, die Lehne ist ein Teil des Sessels, aber selbst wieder zusammengesetzt aus verschiedenen Hölzern; während ein Fuß ein einfacher Bestandteil ist. Wir sehen auch ein Ganzes, was sich ändert (zerstört wird) während seine Bestandteile unverändert bleiben. Dies sind die Materialien, aus denen wir jenes Bild der Wirklichkeit anfertigen.

60. Wenn ich nun sage: "Mein Besen steht in der Ecke", — ist dies eigentlich eine Aussage über den Besenstiel und die Bürste des Besens? Jedenfalls könnte man doch die Aussage ersetzen durch eine, die die Lage des Stiels und die Lage der Bürste angibt. Und diese Aussage ist doch nun eine weiter analysierte Form der ersten. — Warum aber nenne ich sie "weiter analysiert"? — Nun, wenn der Besen sich dort befindet, so heißt das doch, es müssen Stiel und Bürste dort sein und in bestimmter Lage zueinander; und dies war früher gleichsam im Sinn des Satzes verborgen, und im analysierten Satz ist es *ausgesprochen*. Also meint der,

It looks to us as if we were saying something about the nature of red in saying that the words "Red exists" do not make sense. Namely, that red exists 'in and of itself'. The same idea — that this is a metaphysical statement about red — finds expression again when we say such a thing as that red is timeless, and perhaps still more strongly in the word "indestructible".

But what we really *want* is simply to take "Red exists" as the statement: the word "red" has a meaning. Or, perhaps more correctly, "Red does not exist" as " 'Red' has no meaning". Only we do not want to say that that expression *says* this, but that *this* is what it would have to be saying *if* it made sense — that the expression actually contradicts itself in the attempt |29| to say that just because red exists 'in and of itself'. Whereas the only contradiction lies in something like this: the sentence looks as if it were about the colour, while it is supposed to be saying something about the use of the word "red". — In reality, however, we quite readily say that a particular colour exists, and that is as much as to say that something exists that has that colour. And the first expression is no less accurate than the second; particularly where 'what has the colour' is not a physical object.

59. "A *name* signifies only what is an *element* of reality — what cannot be destroyed, what remains the same in all changes." — But what is that? — Even as we uttered the sentence, that's what we already had in mind! We already gave expression to a quite specific idea, a particular picture that we wanted to use. For experience certainly does not show us these elements. We see *constituent parts* of something composite (a chair, for instance). We say that the back is part of the chair, but that it itself is composed of different pieces of wood; whereas a leg is a simple constituent part. We also see a whole which changes (is destroyed) while its constituent parts remain unchanged. These are the materials from which we construct that picture of reality.

60. When I say "My broom is in the corner", is this really a statement about the broomstick and the brush? Well, it could at any rate be replaced by a statement giving the position of the stick and the position of the brush. And this statement is surely a further analysed form of the first one. — But why do I call it "further analysed"? — Well, if the broom is there, that surely means that the stick and brush must be there, and in a particular relation to one another; and previously this was, as it were, hidden in the sense of the first sentence, and is *articulated* in the analysed sentence. Then does someone who says that the broom is in

der sagt, der Besen stehe in der Ecke, eigentlich: der Stiel sei dort und die Bürste, und der Stiel stecke in der Bürste? — Wenn wir jemand fragten, ob er das meint, würde er wohl sagen, daß er gar nicht an den Besenstiel besonders, oder an die Bürste besonders, gedacht habe. Und das wäre die *richtige* Antwort, denn er wollte weder vom Besenstiel, noch von der Bürste besonders reden. Denke, du sagtest jemandem statt "Bring mir den Besen!" — "Bring mir den Besenstiel und die Bürste, die an ihm steckt!" — Ist die Antwort darauf nicht: "Willst du den Besen haben? Und warum drückst du das so sonderbar aus?" —— Wird er den weiter analysierten Satz also besser verstehen? — Dieser Satz, könn-te man sagen, leistet dasselbe, wie der gewöhnliche, aber auf einem umständlicheren Wege. — Denk dir ein Sprachspiel, in dem jemandem Befehle gegeben werden, gewisse, aus mehreren Teilen zusammengesetz-te, Dinge zu bringen, zu bewegen, oder dergleichen. Und zwei Arten es zu spielen: in der einen (a) haben die zusammengesetzten Dinge (Besen, Stühle, Tische, etc.) Namen, wie in (15); in der anderen (b) erhalten nur die Teile Namen und das Ganze wird mit ihrer Hilfe beschrieben. — Inwiefern ist denn ein Befehl des zweiten Spiels eine analysierte Form eines Befehls des ersten? Steckt denn jener in diesem und wird nun durch Analyse herausgeholt? — Ja, der Besen wird zerlegt, wenn man Stiel und Bürste trennt; aber besteht darum auch der Befehl, den Besen zu brin-gen, aus entsprechenden Teilen?

61. "Aber du wirst doch nicht leugnen, daß ein bestimmter Befehl in (a) das Gleiche sagt, wie einer in (b); und wie willst du denn den zweiten nennen, wenn nicht eine analysierte Form des ersten?" — Freilich, ich würde auch sagen, ein Befehl in (a) habe den gleichen Sinn, wie einer in (b); oder, wie ich es früher ausgedrückt habe: sie leisten dasselbe. Und das heißt: Wenn mir etwa ein Befehl in (a) gezeigt und die Frage gestellt würde "Welchem Befehl in (b) ist dieser gleichsinnig?", oder auch "Welchen Befehlen in (b) widerspricht er?", so werde ich die Frage so und so beantworten. Aber damit ist nicht gesagt, daß wir uns über die Verwendung des Ausdrucks "den gleichen Sinn haben", oder "dasselbe leisten" *im Allgemeinen* verständigt haben. Man kann nämlich fragen: In welchem Fall sagen wir "Das sind nur zwei verschiedene Formen des-selben Spiels"?

62. Denke etwa, der, dem die Befehle in (a) und (b) gegeben werden, habe in einer Tabelle, welche Namen und Bilder einander zuordnet, nachzusehen, ehe er das Verlangte bringt. Tut er nun *dasselbe*, wenn er einen Befehl in (a) und den entsprechenden in (b) ausführt? — Ja und nein. Du kannst sagen: "Der *Witz* der beiden Befehle ist der gleiche."

the corner really mean: the broomstick is there, and so is the brush, and the broomstick is fixed in the brush? — If we were to ask anyone if he meant this, he would probably say that he had not specially thought of either the broomstick or the brush. And that would be the *right* answer, for he did not mean to speak either of the stick or of the brush in particular. Suppose that, instead of telling someone "Bring me the broom!", you said "Bring me the broomstick and the brush which is fitted on to it!" — Isn't the answer: "Do you want the broom? Why do you put it so oddly?" —— Is he going to understand the further analysed sentence better? — This sentence, one might say, comes to the same thing as the ordinary one, but in a more roundabout way. |30| Imagine a language-game in which someone is ordered to bring certain objects which are composed of several parts, to move them about, or something else of the kind. And two ways of playing it: in one (a) the composite objects (brooms, chairs, tables, etc.) have names, as in (15); in the other (b) only the parts are given names, and the wholes are described by means of them. — In what sense is an order in the second game an analysed form of an order in the first? Does the former lie concealed in the latter, and is it now brought out by analysis? — True, the broom is taken to pieces when one separates broomstick and brush; but does it follow that the order to bring the broom also consists of corresponding parts?

61. "But surely you won't deny that a particular order in (a) says the same as one in (b); and what would you call the second one, if not an analysed form of the first?" — Certainly I too would say that an order in (a) had the same sense as one in (b), or, as I expressed it earlier, they come to the same thing. And this means that if I were shown an order in (a) and asked, "Which order in (b) has the same sense as this?", or again, "Which orders in (b) does this contradict?", I would give such-and-such an answer. But that is not to say that we have come to a *general* agreement about the use of the expression "to have the same sense" or "to come to the same thing". For one may ask: in what cases do we say "These are merely two different forms of the same game"?

62. Suppose, for example, that the person who is given the orders in (a) and (b) has to look up a table co-ordinating names and pictures before bringing what is required. Does he do *the same* when he carries out an order in (a) and the corresponding one in (b)? — Yes and no. You may say: "The *point* of the two orders is the same." I would say

Ich würde hier dasselbe sagen. — Aber es ist nicht überall klar, was man den 'Witz' des Befehls nennen soll. (Ebenso kann man von gewissen Dingen sagen: ihr Zweck ist der und der. Das Wesentliche ist, daß das eine *Lampe* ist, zur Beleuchtung dient —— daß sie das Zimmer schmückt, einen leeren Raum füllt, etc., ist nicht wesentlich. Aber nicht immer sind wesentlich und unwesentlich klar getrennt.)

63. Der Ausdruck aber, ein Satz in (b) sei eine 'analysierte' Form eines in (a), verführt uns leicht dazu, zu meinen, jene Form sei die fundamentalere; sie zeige erst, was mit der andern gemeint sei, etc. Wir denken etwa: Wer nur die unanalysierte Form besitzt, dem geht die Analyse ab; wer aber die analysierte Form kennt, der besitze damit alles. — Aber kann ich nicht sagen, daß *diesem* ein Aspekt der Sache verloren geht, so wie jenem?

64. Denken wir uns das Spiel (48) dahin abgeändert, daß in ihm Namen nicht einfärbige Quadrate bezeichnen, sondern Rechtecke, die aus je zwei solchen Quadraten bestehen. Ein solches Rechteck, halb rot, halb grün, heiße "U"; ein Rechteck, halb grün, halb weiß, heiße "V", etc. Könnten wir uns nicht Menschen denken, die für solche Farbenkombinationen Namen hätten, aber nicht für die einzelnen Farben? Denk an die Fälle, in denen wir sagen: "Diese Farbenzusammenstellung (die französische Tricolore etwa) hat einen ganz besonderen Charakter."
Inwiefern sind die Zeichen dieses Sprachspiels einer Analyse bedürftig? Ja, inwieweit *kann* das Spiel durch (48) ersetzt werden? — Es ist eben ein *anderes* Sprachspiel; wenn auch mit (48) verwandt.

65. Hier stoßen wir auf die große Frage, die hinter allen diesen Betrachtungen steht. — Denn man könnte mir nun einwenden: "Du machst dir's leicht! Du redest von allen möglichen Sprachspielen, hast aber nirgends gesagt, was denn das Wesentliche des Sprachspiels, und also der Sprache, ist. Was allen diesen Vorgängen gemeinsam ist und sie zur Sprache, oder zu Teilen der Sprache macht. Du schenkst dir also gerade den Teil der Untersuchung, der dir selbst seinerzeit das meiste Kopfzerbrechen gemacht hat, nämlich den, die *allgemeine Form des Satzes* und der Sprache betreffend."
Und das ist wahr. — Statt etwas anzugeben, was allem, was wir Sprache nennen, gemeinsam ist, sage ich, es ist diesen Erscheinungen gar nicht Eines gemeinsam, weswegen wir für alle das gleiche Wort verwenden, — sondern sie sind mit einander in vielen verschiedenen Weisen *verwandt*. Und dieser Verwandtschaft, oder dieser Verwandtschaften wegen nennen wir sie alle "Sprachen". Ich will versuchen, dies zu erklären.

so too. — But it is not clear everywhere what should be called the 'point' of an order. (Similarly, one may say of certain objects that they have this or that purpose. The essential thing is that this is a *lamp*, that it serves to give light —— what is not essential is that it is an ornament to the room, fills an empty space, and so on. But there is not always a clear boundary between essential and inessential.)

63. To say, however, that a sentence in (b) is an 'analysed' form of one in (a) readily seduces us into thinking that the former is the more fundamental form, that it alone shows what is meant by the other, and so on. We may think: someone who has only the unanalysed form lacks the analysis; but he who knows the analysed form |31| has got it all. — But can't I say that an aspect of the matter is lost to the latter no less than to the former?

64. Let's imagine language-game (48) altered so that names signify not monochrome squares but rectangles each consisting of two such squares. Let such a rectangle which is half red, half green, be called "U"; a half green, half white one "V"; and so on. Could we not imagine people who had names for such combinations of colour, but not for the individual colours? Think of cases where we say, "This arrangement of colours (say the French tricolor) has a quite special character".

In what way do the symbols of this language-game stand in need of analysis? How far is it even *possible* to replace this game by (48)? — It is just a *different* language-game; even though it is related to (48).

* 65. Here we come up against the great question that lies behind all these considerations. — For someone might object against me: "You make things easy for yourself! You talk about all sorts of language-games, but have nowhere said what is essential to a language-game, and so to language: what is common to all these activities, and makes them into language or parts of language. So you let yourself off the very part of the investigation that once gave you the most headache, the part about the *general form of the proposition* and of language."

And this is true. — Instead of pointing out something common to all that we call language, I'm saying that these phenomena have no one thing in common in virtue of which we use the same word for all — but there are many different kinds of *affinity* between them. And on account of this affinity, or these affinities, we call them all "languages". I'll try to explain this.

66. Betrachte z. B. einmal die Vorgänge, die wir "Spiele" nennen. Ich meine Brettspiele, Kartenspiele, Ballspiele, Kampfspiele, u. s. w. Was ist allen diesen gemeinsam? — Sag nicht: "Es *muß* ihnen etwas gemeinsam sein, sonst hießen sie nicht 'Spiele'" — sondern *schau*, ob ihnen allen etwas gemeinsam ist. — Denn, wenn du sie anschaust, wirst du zwar nicht etwas sehen, was *allen* gemeinsam wäre, aber du wirst Ähnlichkeiten, Verwandtschaften, sehen, und zwar eine ganze Reihe. Wie gesagt: denk nicht, sondern schau! — Schau z. B. die Brettspiele an, mit ihren mannigfachen Verwandtschaften. Nun geh zu den Kartenspielen über: hier findest du viele Entsprechungen mit jener ersten Klasse, aber viele gemeinsame Züge verschwinden, andere treten auf. Wenn wir nun zu den Ballspielen übergehen, so bleibt manches Gemeinsame erhalten, aber vieles geht verloren. — Sind sie alle '*unterhaltend*'? Vergleiche Schach mit dem Mühlfahren. Oder gibt es überall ein Gewinnen und Verlieren, oder eine Konkurrenz der Spielenden? Denk an die Patiencen. In den Ballspielen gibt es Gewinnen und Verlieren; aber wenn ein Kind den Ball an die Wand wirft und wieder auffängt, so ist dieser Zug verschwunden. Schau, welche Rolle Geschick und Glück spielen. Und wie verschieden ist Geschick im Schachspiel und Geschick im Tennisspiel. Denk nun an die Reigenspiele: Hier ist das Element der Unterhaltung, aber wie viele der anderen Charakterzüge sind verschwunden! Und so können wir durch die vielen, vielen anderen Gruppen von Spielen gehen. Ähnlichkeiten auftauchen und verschwinden sehen.

Und das Ergebnis dieser Betrachtung lautet nun: Wir sehen ein kompliziertes Netz von Ähnlichkeiten, die einander übergreifen und kreuzen. Ähnlichkeiten im Großen und Kleinen.

67. Ich kann diese Ähnlichkeiten nicht besser charakterisieren, als durch das Wort "Familienähnlichkeiten"; denn so übergreifen und kreuzen sich die verschiedenen Ähnlichkeiten, die zwischen den Gliedern einer Familie bestehen: Wuchs, Gesichtszüge, Augenfarbe, Gang, Temperament, etc. etc. — Und ich werde sagen: die 'Spiele' bilden eine Familie.

Und ebenso bilden z. B. die Zahlenarten eine Familie. Warum nennen wir etwas "Zahl"? Nun etwa, weil es eine — direkte — Verwandtschaft mit manchem hat, was man bisher Zahl genannt hat; und dadurch, kann man sagen, erhält es eine indirekte Verwandtschaft zu anderem, was wir auch *so* nennen. Und wir dehnen unseren Begriff der Zahl aus, wie wir beim Spinnen eines Fadens Faser an Faser drehen. Und die Stärke des Fadens liegt nicht darin, daß irgend eine Faser durch seine ganze Länge läuft, sondern darin, daß viele Fasern einander übergreifen.

* 66. Consider, for example, the activities that we call "games". I mean
board-games, card-games, ball-games, athletic games, and so on. What
is common to them all? — Don't say: "They *must* have something
in common, or they would not be called 'games'" — but *look and
see* whether there is anything common to all. — For if you look at
them, you won't see something that is common to *all*, but similarities,
affinities, and a whole series of them at that. To repeat: don't think,
but look! — Look, for example, at board-games, with their various affinities. Now pass to card-games; here you find many correspondences with
the first group, but many common |32| features drop out, and others
appear. When we pass next to ball-games, much that is common is
retained, but much is lost. — Are they all *'entertaining'*? Compare chess
with noughts and crosses. Or is there always winning and losing, or
competition between players? Think of patience. In ball-games, there
is winning and losing; but when a child throws his ball at the wall and
catches it again, this feature has disappeared. Look at the parts played
by skill and luck, and at the difference between skill in chess and skill
in tennis. Think now of singing and dancing games; here we have the
element of entertainment, but how many other characteristic features
have disappeared! And we can go through the many, many other
groups of games in the same way, can see how similarities crop up
and disappear.

And the upshot of these considerations is: we see a complicated net-
work of similarities overlapping and criss-crossing: similarities in the
large and in the small.

67. I can think of no better expression to characterize these similarities than "family resemblances"; for the various resemblances between
members of a family — build, features, colour of eyes, gait, temperament, and so on and so forth — overlap and criss-cross in the same
way. — And I shall say: 'games' form a family.

And likewise the kinds of number, for example, form a family. Why
do we call something a "number"? Well, perhaps because it has a —
direct — affinity with several things that have hitherto been called "number"; and this can be said to give it an indirect affinity with other things
that we also call "numbers". And we extend our concept of number,
as in spinning a thread we twist fibre on fibre. And the strength of the
thread resides not in the fact that some one fibre runs through its whole
length, but in the overlapping of many fibres.

Wenn aber Einer sagen wollte: "Also ist allen diesen Gebilden etwas gemeinsam, — nämlich die Disjunktion aller dieser Gemeinsamkeiten" — so würde ich antworten: Hier spielst du nur mit einem Wort. Ebenso könnte man sagen: es läuft ein Etwas durch den ganzen Faden, — nämlich das lückenlose Übergreifen dieser Fasern.

68. "Gut; so ist also der Begriff der Zahl für dich erklärt als die logische Summe jener einzelnen mit einander verwandten Begriffe: Kardinalzahl, Rationalzahl, reelle Zahl, etc.; und gleicherweise der Begriff des Spiels als logische Summe entsprechender Teilbegriffe." — Dies muß nicht sein. Denn ich *kann* so dem Begriff 'Zahl' feste Grenzen geben, d. h. das Wort "Zahl" zur Bezeichnung eines fest begrenzten Begriffs gebrauchen, aber ich kann es auch so gebrauchen, daß der Umfang des Begriffs *nicht* durch eine Grenze abgeschlossen ist. Und so verwenden wir ja das Wort "Spiel". Wie ist denn der Begriff des Spiels abgeschlossen? Was ist noch ein Spiel und was ist keines mehr? Kannst du die Grenzen angeben? Nein. Du kannst welche *ziehen*: denn es sind noch keine gezogen. (Aber das hat dich noch nie gestört, wenn du das Wort "Spiel" angewendet hast.)

"Aber dann ist ja die Anwendung des Wortes nicht geregelt; das 'Spiel', welches wir mit ihm spielen, ist nicht geregelt." —— Es ist nicht überall von Regeln begrenzt; aber es gibt ja auch keine Regel dafür z. B., wie hoch man im Tennis den Ball werfen darf, oder wie stark, aber Tennis ist doch ein Spiel und es hat auch Regeln.

69. Wie würden wir denn jemandem erklären, was ein Spiel ist? Ich glaube, wir werden ihm *Spiele* beschreiben, und wir könnten der Beschreibung hinzufügen: "das, *und Ähnliches*, nennt man 'Spiele' ". Und wissen wir selbst denn mehr? Können wir etwa nur dem Andern nicht genau sagen, was ein Spiel ist? — Aber das ist nicht Unwissenheit. Wir kennen die Grenzen nicht, weil keine gezogen sind. Wie gesagt, wir können — für einen besondern Zweck — eine Grenze ziehen. Machen wir dadurch den Begriff erst brauchbar? Durchaus nicht! Es sei denn, für diesen besondern Zweck. So wenig, wie der das Längenmaß '1 Schritt' brauchbar machte, der die Definition gab: 1 Schritt = 75 cm. Und wenn du sagen willst "Aber vorher war es doch kein exaktes Längenmaß", so antworte ich: gut, dann war es ein unexaktes. — Obgleich du mir noch die Definition der Exaktheit schuldig bist.

70. "Aber wenn der Begriff 'Spiel' auf diese Weise unbegrenzt ist, so weißt du ja eigentlich nicht, was du mit 'Spiel' meinst." —— Wenn ich

But if someone wanted to say, "So there is something common to all these constructions — namely, the disjunction of all their common properties" — I'd reply: Now you are only playing with a word. One might as well say, "There is a Something that runs through the whole thread — namely, the continuous overlapping of these fibres".

68. "Right; so in your view the concept of number is explained as the logical sum of those individual interrelated concepts: cardinal numbers, rational numbers, real numbers, and so forth; and in the same way, the concept of a game as the logical sum of corresponding sub-concepts."
—— This need not be so. For I *can* give the concept of number rigid boundaries |33| in this way, that is, use the word "number" for a rigidly bounded concept; but I can also use it so that the extension of the concept is *not* closed by a boundary. And this is how we do use the word "game". For how is the concept of a game bounded? What still counts as a game, and what no longer does? Can you say where the boundaries are? No. You can *draw* some, for there aren't any drawn yet. (But this never bothered you before when you used the word "game".)
"But then the use of the word is unregulated — the 'game' we play with it is unregulated." —— It is not everywhere bounded by rules; but no more are there any rules for how high one may throw the ball in tennis, or how hard, yet tennis is a game for all that, and has rules too.

69. How would we explain to someone what a game is? I think that we'd describe *games* to him, and we might add to the description: "This *and similar things* are called 'games'." And do we know any more ourselves? Is it just that we can't tell others exactly what a game is? — But this is not ignorance. We don't know the boundaries because none have been drawn. To repeat, we can draw a boundary — for a special purpose. Does it take this to make the concept usable? Not at all! Except perhaps for that special purpose. No more than it took the definition: 1 pace = 75 cm to make the measure of length 'one pace' usable. And if you want to say "But still, before that it wasn't an exact measure of length", then I reply: all right, so it was an inexact one. — Though you still owe me a definition of exactness.

70. "But if the concept 'game' is without boundaries in this way, you don't really know what you mean by a 'game'." —— When I give the

die Beschreibung gebe: "Der Boden war ganz mit Pflanzen bedeckt", —
willst du sagen, ich weiß nicht, wovon ich rede, ehe ich nicht eine
Definition der Pflanze geben kann?

Eine Erklärung dessen, was ich meine, wäre etwa eine Zeichnung und
die Worte "So ungefähr hat der Boden ausgesehen". Ich sage vielleicht
auch: "*genau* so hat er ausgesehen". — Also waren genau *diese* Gräser
und Blätter, in diesen Lagen, dort? Nein, das heißt es nicht. Und kein
Bild würde ich, in *diesem* Sinne, als das genaue anerkennen.

> Jemand sagt mir: "Zeige den Kindern ein Spiel!" Ich lehre sie, um
> Geld würfeln, und der Andere sagt mir "Ich habe nicht so ein Spiel
> gemeint". Mußte ihm da, als er mir den Befehl gab, der
> Ausschluß des Würfelspiels vorschweben?

71. Man kann sagen, der Begriff 'Spiel' ist ein Begriff mit verschwommenen Rändern. — "Aber ist ein verschwommener Begriff
überhaupt ein *Begriff*?" — Ist eine unscharfe Photographie überhaupt
ein Bild eines Menschen? Ja, kann man ein unscharfes Bild immer mit
Vorteil durch ein scharfes ersetzen? Ist das unscharfe nicht oft gerade
das, was wir brauchen?

Frege vergleicht den Begriff mit einem Bezirk und sagt: einen unklar
begrenzten Bezirk könne man überhaupt keinen Bezirk nennen. Das heißt
wohl, wir können mit ihm nichts anfangen. — Aber ist es sinnlos zu
sagen: "Halte dich ungefähr hier auf!"? Denk dir, ich stünde mit einem
Andern auf einem Platz und sagte dies. Dabei werde ich nicht einmal
irgend eine Grenze ziehen, sondern etwa mit der Hand eine zeigende
Bewegung machen — als zeigte ich ihm einen bestimmten *Punkt*. Und
gerade so erklärt man etwa, was ein Spiel ist. Man gibt Beispiele und
will, daß sie in einem gewissen Sinne verstanden werden. — Aber mit
diesem Ausdruck meine ich nicht: er solle nun in diesen Beispielen das
Gemeinsame sehen, welches ich — aus irgend einem Grunde — nicht
aussprechen konnte. Sondern: er solle diese Beispiele nun in bestimmter
Weise *verwenden*. Das Exemplifizieren ist hier nicht ein *indirektes*
Mittel der Erklärung, — in Ermanglung eines Bessern. Denn, mißverstanden kann auch jede allgemeine Erklärung werden. *So spielen wir
eben das Spiel.* (Ich meine das Sprachspiel mit dem Worte "Spiel".)

72. *Das Gemeinsame sehen.* Nimm an, ich zeige jemand verschiedene
bunte Bilder, und sage: "Die Farbe, die du in allen siehst, heißt

description "The ground was quite covered with plants", do you want to say that I don't know what I'm talking about until I can give a definition of a plant?

An explanation of what I meant would be, say, a drawing and the words "The ground looked roughly like this". Perhaps I even say: "It looked *exactly* like this." — Then were just *these* blades of grass and *these* leaves there, arranged just like this? No, that is not what it means. And I wouldn't accept any picture as the exact one in *this* sense. |34|

---

* Someone says to me, "Show the children a game." I teach them gambling with dice, and the other says, "I didn't mean that sort of game". In that case, must he have had the exclusion of the game with dice before his mind when he gave me the order? |p. 33 n.|

---

71. One can say that the concept of a game is a concept with blurred edges. — "But is a blurred concept a *concept* at all?" — Is a photograph that is not sharp a picture of a person at all? Is it even always an advantage to replace a picture that is not sharp by one that is? Isn't one that isn't sharp often just what we need?

* Frege compares a concept to a region, and says that a region without clear boundaries can't be called a region at all. This presumably means that we can't do anything with it. — But is it senseless to say "Stay roughly here"? Imagine that I were standing with someone in a city square and said that. As I say it, I do not bother drawing any boundary, but just make a pointing gesture — as if I were indicating a particular spot. And this is just how one might explain what a game is. One gives examples and intends them to be taken in a particular way. — I do not mean by this expression, however, that he is supposed to see in those examples that common feature which I — for some reason — was unable to formulate, but that he is now to employ those examples in a particular way. Here giving examples is not an *indirect* way of explaining — in default of a better one. For any general explanation may be misunderstood too. *This*, after all, is how we play the game. (I mean the language-game with the word "game".)

72. *Seeing what is in common.* Suppose I show someone various multi-coloured pictures, and say: "The colour you see in all these is called

'Ocker'." — Das ist eine Erklärung, die verstanden wird, indem der Andere aufsucht und sieht, was jenen Bildern gemeinsam ist. Er kann dann auf das Gemeinsame blicken, darauf zeigen.

Vergleiche damit: Ich zeige ihm Figuren verschiedener Form, alle in der gleichen Farbe gemalt und sage: "Was diese mit einander gemein haben, heißt 'Ocker'."

Und vergleiche damit: Ich zeige ihm Muster verschiedener Schattierungen von Blau und sage: "Die Farbe, die allen gemeinsam ist, nenne ich 'Blau' ".

73. Wenn Einer mir die Namen der Farben erklärt, indem er auf Muster zeigt und sagt "Diese Farbe heißt 'Blau', diese 'Grün', . . .", so kann dieser Fall in vieler Hinsicht dem verglichen werden, daß er mir eine Tabelle an die Hand gibt, in der unter den Mustern von Farben die Wörter stehen. — Wenn auch dieser Vergleich in mancher Weise irreführen kann. — Man ist nun geneigt, den Vergleich auszudehnen: Die Erklärung verstanden haben, heißt, einen Begriff des Erklärten im Geiste besitzen, und d. i. ein Muster, oder Bild. Zeigt man mir nun verschiedene Blätter und sagt "Das nennt man 'Blatt' ", so erhalte ich einen Begriff der Blattform, ein Bild von ihr im Geiste. — Aber wie schaut denn das Bild eines Blattes aus, das keine bestimmte Form zeigt, sondern 'das, was allen Blattformen gemeinsam ist'? Welchen Farbton hat das 'Muster in meinem Geiste' der Farbe Grün — dessen, was allen Tönen von Grün gemeinsam ist?

"Aber könnte es nicht solche 'allgemeine' Muster geben? Etwa ein Blattschema, oder ein Muster von *reinem* Grün?" — Gewiß! Aber, daß dieses Schema als *Schema* verstanden wird, und nicht als die Form eines bestimmten Blattes, und daß ein Täfelchen von reinem Grün als Muster alles dessen verstanden wird, was grünlich ist, und nicht als Muster für reines Grün — das liegt wieder in der Art der Anwendung dieser Muster.

Frage dich: Welche *Gestalt* muß das Muster der Farbe Grün haben? Soll es viereckig sein? oder würde es dann das Muster für grüne Vierecke sein? — Soll es also 'unregelmäßig' geformt sein? Und was verhindert uns, es dann nur als Muster der unregelmäßigen Form anzusehen — d. h. zu verwenden?

74. Hierher gehört auch der Gedanke, daß der, welcher dieses Blatt als Muster 'der Blattform im allgemeinen' ansieht, es anders *sieht*, als der, welcher es etwa als Muster für diese bestimmte Form betrachtet. Nun, das könnte ja so sein — obwohl es nicht so ist —, denn es würde nur besagen, daß erfahrungsgemäß der, welcher das Blatt in bestimmter Weise *sieht*,

'yellow ochre'." — This is an explanation that another person will come to understand by looking for, and seeing, what is common to the pictures. Then he can look at, can point to, the common feature.

Compare with this a case in which I show him figures of different shapes, all painted the same colour, and say: "What these have in common is called 'yellow ochre'."

And compare this case: I show him samples of different shades of blue, and say: "The colour that is common to all these is what I call 'blue'."

73. When someone explains the names of colours to me by pointing at samples and saying "This colour is called 'blue', this 'green' . . .", this case can be compared in many respects to handing me a chart with the words written under the colour samples. — Though this comparison may mislead in various ways. — One is now inclined to extend the comparison: to have understood the explanation means to have in one's mind an idea of the thing explained, and that is a sample or picture. So if I'm shown various leaves and told |35| "This is called a 'leaf'", I get an idea of the shape of a leaf, a picture of it in my mind. — But what does the picture of a leaf look like when it does not show us any particular shape, but rather 'what is common to all shapes of leaf'? What shade is the 'sample in my mind' of the colour green — the sample of what is common to all shades of green?

"But might there not be such 'general' samples? Say a schematic leaf, or a sample of *pure* green?" — Certainly! But for such a schema to be understood as a *schema*, and not as the shape of a particular leaf, and for a snippet of pure green to be understood as a sample of all that is greenish, and not as a sample of pure green — this in turn resides in the way the samples are applied.

Ask yourself, what *shape* must the sample of the colour green be? Should it be rectangular? Or would it then be the sample of green rectangles? — So should it be 'irregular' in shape? And what is then to prevent us from viewing it — that is, from using it — only as a sample of irregularity of shape?

74. Here also belongs the idea that someone who views this leaf as a sample of 'leaf shape in general' will *see* it differently from someone who views it as, say, a sample of this particular shape. Well, this might be so — though it is not so — for it would only amount to saying that, as a matter of experience, someone who *sees* the leaf in a particular

es dann so und so, oder den und den Regeln gemäß, verwendet. Es gibt natürlich ein *so* und *anders* Sehen; und es gibt auch Fälle, in denen der, der ein Muster *so* sieht, es im allgemeinen in *dieser* Weise verwenden wird, und wer es anders sieht, in anderer Weise. Wer, z. B., die schematische Zeichnung eines Würfels als ebene Figur sieht, bestehend aus einem Quadrat und zwei Rhomben, der wird den Befehl "Bringe mir so etwas!" vielleicht anders ausführen, als der, welcher das Bild räumlich sieht.

75. Was heißt es: wissen, was ein Spiel ist? Was heißt es, es wissen und es nicht sagen können? Ist dieses Wissen irgendein Äquivalent einer nicht ausgesprochenen Definition? So daß, wenn sie ausgesprochen würde, ich sie als den Ausdruck meines Wissens anerkennen könnte? Ist nicht mein Wissen, mein Begriff vom Spiel, ganz in den Erklärungen ausgedrückt, die ich geben könnte? Nämlich darin, daß ich Beispiele von Spielen verschiedener Art beschreibe; zeige, wie man nach Analogie dieser auf alle möglichen Arten andere Spiele konstruieren kann; sage, daß ich das und das wohl kaum mehr ein Spiel nennen würde; und dergleichen mehr.

76. Wenn Einer eine scharfe Grenze zöge, so könnte ich sie nicht als die anerkennen, die ich auch schon immer ziehen wollte, oder im Geist gezogen habe. Denn ich wollte gar keine ziehen. Man kann dann sagen: sein Begriff ist nicht der gleiche wie der meine, aber ihm verwandt. Und die Verwandtschaft ist die zweier Bilder, deren eines aus unscharf begrenzten Farbflecken, das andere aus ähnlich geformten und verteilten, aber scharf begrenzten, besteht. Die Verwandtschaft ist dann ebenso unleugbar, wie die Verschiedenheit.

77. Und wenn wir diesen Vergleich noch etwas weiter führen, so ist es klar, daß der Grad, bis zu welchem das scharfe Bild dem verschwommenen ähnlich sein *kann*, vom Grade der Unschärfe des zweiten abhängt. Denn denk dir, du solltest zu einem verschwommenen Bild ein ihm 'entsprechendes' scharfes entwerfen. In jenem ist ein unscharfes rotes Rechteck; du setzt dafür ein scharfes. Freilich — es ließen sich ja mehrere solche scharfe Rechtecke ziehen, die dem unscharfen entsprächen. — Wenn aber im Original die Farben ohne die Spur einer Grenze ineinanderfließen, — wird es dann nicht eine hoffnungslose Aufgabe werden, ein dem verschwommenen entsprechendes scharfes Bild zu zeichnen? Wirst du dann nicht sagen müssen: "Hier könnte ich ebenso gut einen Kreis, wie ein Rechteck, oder eine Herzform zeichnen; es fließen ja alle Farben durcheinander. Es stimmt alles — und nichts." — Und in dieser Lage befindet sich z. B. der, der in der Ästhetik, oder Ethik nach Definitionen sucht, die unseren Begriffen entsprechen.

way will then use it in such-and-such a way or according to such-and-such rules. Of course, there is such a thing as seeing in *this* way or *that*; and there are also cases where whoever sees a sample like *this* will in general use it in this way, and whoever sees it otherwise in another way. For example, someone who sees the schematic drawing of a cube as a plane figure consisting of a square and two rhombi will perhaps carry out the order "Bring me something like this!" differently from someone who sees the picture three-dimensionally.

75. What does it mean to know what a game is? What does it mean to know it and not be able to say it? Is this knowledge somehow equivalent to an unformulated definition? So that if it were formulated, I'd be able to recognize it as the expression of my knowledge? Isn't my knowledge, my concept of a game, completely expressed in the explanations that I could give? That is, in my describing examples of various kinds of game, showing how all sorts of other games can be constructed on the analogy of these, saying that I would hardly call this or that a game, and so on. |36|

76. If someone were to draw a sharp boundary, I couldn't acknowledge it as the one that I too always wanted to draw, or had drawn in my mind. For I didn't want to draw one at all. It can then be said: his concept is not the same as mine, but akin to it. The affinity is that of two pictures, one of which consists of colour patches with blurred boundaries and the other of patches similarly shaped and distributed but with sharp boundaries. The affinity is just as undeniable as the difference.

77. And if we carry this comparison a little further, it is clear that the degree to which the sharp picture *can* resemble the blurred one depends on the degree to which the latter lacks sharpness. For imagine having to draw a sharp picture 'corresponding' to a blurred one. In the latter there is a blurred red rectangle; you replace it with a sharp one. Of course — several such sharply delineated rectangles could be drawn to correspond to the blurred one. — But if the colours in the original shade into one another without a hint of any boundary, won't it become a hopeless task to draw a sharp picture corresponding to the blurred one? Won't you then have to say: "Here I might just as well draw a circle as a rectangle or a heart, for all the colours merge. Anything — and nothing — is right." —— And this is the position in which, for example, someone finds himself in ethics or aesthetics when he looks for definitions that correspond to our concepts.

Frage dich in dieser Schwierigkeit immer: Wie haben wir denn die Bedeutung dieses Wortes ("gut" z. B.) *gelernt*? An was für Beispielen; in welchen Sprachspielen? Du wirst dann leichter sehen, daß das Wort eine Familie von Bedeutungen haben muß.

78. Vergleiche: *wissen* und *sagen*:

wieviele m hoch der Mont-Blanc ist —
wie das Wort "Spiel" gebraucht wird —
wie eine Klarinette klingt.

Wer sich wundert, daß man etwas wissen könne, und nicht sagen, denkt vielleicht an einen Fall wie den ersten. Gewiß nicht an einen, wie den dritten.

79. Betrachte dieses Beispiel: Wenn man sagt "Moses hat nicht existiert", so kann das Verschiedenerlei bedeuten. Es kann heißen: die Israeliten haben nicht *einen* Führer gehabt, als sie aus Ägypten auszogen —— oder: ihr Führer hat nicht Moses geheißen —— oder: es hat keinen Menschen gegeben, der alles das vollbracht hat, was die Bibel von Moses berichtet —— oder etc. etc. — Nach Russell können wir sagen: der Name "Moses" kann durch verschiedene Beschreibungen definiert werden. Z. B. als: "der Mann, welcher die Israeliten durch die Wüste geführt hat", "der Mann, welcher zu dieser Zeit und an diesem Ort gelebt hat und damals 'Moses' genannt wurde", "der Mann, welcher als Kind von der Tochter Pharaos aus dem Nil gezogen wurde", etc. Und je nachdem wir die eine, oder die andere Definition annehmen, bekommt der Satz "Moses hat existiert" einen andern Sinn, und ebenso jeder andere Satz, der von Moses handelt. — Und wenn man uns sagt "N hat nicht existiert", fragen wir auch: "Was meinst du? Willst du sagen, daß . . . , oder daß . . . , etc.?"
Aber wenn ich nun eine Aussage über Moses mache, — bin ich immer bereit, irgend *eine* dieser Beschreibungen für "Moses" zu setzen? Ich werde etwa sagen: Unter "Moses" verstehe ich den Mann, der getan hat, was die Bibel von Moses berichtet, oder doch vieles davon. Aber wievieles? Habe ich mich entschieden, wieviel sich als falsch erweisen muß, damit ich meinen Satz als falsch aufgebe? Hat also der Name "Moses" für mich einen festen und eindeutig bestimmten Gebrauch in allen möglichen Fällen? — Ist es nicht so, daß ich sozusagen eine ganze Reihe von Stützen in Bereitschaft habe, und bereit bin, mich auf eine zu stützen, wenn mir die andere entzogen werden sollte, und umgekehrt? —— Betrachte noch einen andern Fall. Wenn ich sage "N

In this sort of predicament, always ask yourself: How did we *learn* the meaning of this word ("good", for instance)? From what sort of examples? In what language-games? Then it will be easier for you to see that the word must have a family of meanings.

78. Compare *knowing* and *saying*:

how many metres high Mont Blanc is —
how the word "game" is used —
how a clarinet sounds.

Someone who is surprised that one can know something and not be able to say it is perhaps thinking of a case like the first. Certainly not of one like the third.

79. Consider this example: if one says "Moses did not exist", this may mean various things. It may mean: the Israelites did not have a single leader when they came out of Egypt —— or: their leader was not called Moses —— or: there wasn't anyone who accomplished all that the Bible relates of Moses —— or: ... — According to Russell, we may say: the name "Moses" can be defined by |37| means of various descriptions. For example, as "the man who led the Israelites through the wilderness", "the man who lived at that time and place and was then called 'Moses'", "the man who as a child was taken out of the Nile by Pharaoh's daughter", and so on. And according as we accept one definition or another, the sentence "Moses did exist" acquires a different sense, and so does every other sentence about Moses. — And if we are told "N did not exist", we do ask: "What do you mean? Do you want to say ... or ... and so on?"

*   But if I make a statement about Moses, am I always ready to substitute some *one* of these descriptions for "Moses"? I shall perhaps say: By "Moses" I mean the man who did what the Bible relates of Moses, or at any rate much of it. But how much? Have I decided how much must turn out to be false for me to give up my proposition as false? So is my use of the name "Moses" fixed and determined for all possible cases? — Isn't it like this, that I have, so to speak, a whole series of props in readiness, and am ready to lean on one if another should be taken from under me, and vice versa? —— Consider yet another case. If I say "N is dead", then something like the following may hold for

ist gestorben", so kann es mit der Bedeutung des Namens "N" etwa diese Bewandtnis haben: Ich glaube, daß ein Mensch gelebt hat, den ich (1) dort und dort gesehen habe, der (2) so und so ausgeschaut hat (Bilder), (3) das und das getan hat und (4) in der bürgerlichen Welt diesen Namen "N" führt. — Gefragt, was ich unter "N" verstehe, würde ich alles das, oder einiges davon, und bei verschiedenen Gelegenheiten Verschiedenes, aufzählen. Meine Definition von "N" wäre also etwa: "der Mann, von dem alles das stimmt". — Aber wenn sich nun etwas davon als falsch erwiese! — Werde ich bereit sein, den Satz "N ist gestorben" für falsch zu erklären, — auch wenn nur etwas mir nebensächlich Scheinendes sich als falsch herausstellt? Wo aber ist die Grenze des Nebensächlichen? — Hätte ich in so einem Fall eine Erklärung des Namens gegeben, so wäre ich nun bereit, sie abzuändern.

Und das kann man so ausdrücken: Ich gebrauche den Namen "N" ohne *feste* Bedeutung. (Aber das tut seinem Gebrauch so wenig Eintrag, wie dem eines Tisches, daß er auf vier Beinen ruht, statt auf dreien, und daher unter Umständen wackelt.)

Soll man sagen, ich gebrauche ein Wort, dessen Bedeutung ich nicht kenne, rede also Unsinn? — Sage, was du willst, solange dich das nicht verhindert, zu sehen, wie es sich verhält. (Und wenn du das siehst, wirst du Manches nicht sagen.)

(Das Schwanken wissenschaftlicher Definitionen: Was heute als erfahrungsmäßige Begleiterscheinung des Phänomens A gilt, wird morgen zur Definition von "A" benützt.)

80. Ich sage: "Dort steht ein Sessel". Wie, wenn ich hingehe und ihn holen will und er entschwindet plötzlich meinem Blick? —— "Also war es kein Sessel, sondern irgend eine Täuschung." —— Aber in ein paar Sekunden sehen wir ihn wieder und können ihn angreifen, etc. —— "Also war der Sessel doch da und sein Verschwinden war irgend eine Täuschung." —— Aber nimm an, nach einer Zeit verschwindet er wieder, — oder scheint zu verschwinden. Was sollen wir nun sagen? Hast du für solche Fälle Regeln bereit, — die sagen, ob man so etwas noch "Sessel" nennen darf? Aber gehen sie uns beim Gebrauch des Wortes "Sessel" ab; und sollen wir sagen, daß wir mit diesem Wort eigentlich keine Bedeutung verbinden, da wir nicht für alle Möglichkeiten seiner Anwendung mit Regeln ausgerüstet sind?

81. F. P. Ramsey hat einmal im Gespräch mit mir betont, die Logik sei eine 'normative Wissenschaft'. Genau welche Idee ihm dabei vorschwebte, weiß ich nicht; sie war aber zweifellos eng verwandt mit der, die mir erst später aufgegangen ist: daß wir nämlich in der

the meaning of the name "N": I believe that a human being has lived, whom (1) I have seen in such-and-such places, who (2) looked like this (pictures), (3) has done such-and-such things, and (4) bore the name "N" in civic life. — Asked what I mean by "N", I'd enumerate all or some of these points, and different ones on different occasions. So my definition of "N" would perhaps be "the man of whom all this is true". — But if some point were now to turn out to be false? — Would I be prepared to declare the proposition "N is dead" false — even if what has turned out to be false is only something which strikes me as insignificant? But where are the boundaries of what is insignificant? — If I had given an explanation of the name in such a case, I'd now be ready to alter it.

And this can be expressed as follows: I use the name "N" without a *fixed* meaning. (But that impairs its use as little as the use of a table is impaired by the fact that it stands on four legs instead of three and so sometimes wobbles.)

Should it be said that I'm using a word whose meaning I don't know, and so am talking nonsense? — Say what you please, so long as it does not prevent you from seeing how things are. (And when you see that, there will be some things that you won't say.)

(The fluctuation of scientific definitions: what today counts as an |38| observed concomitant of phenomenon A will tomorrow be used to define "A".)

80. I say, "There is a chair over there". What if I go to fetch it, and it suddenly disappears from sight? —— "So it wasn't a chair, but some kind of illusion." —— But a few seconds later, we see it again and are able to touch it, and so on. —— "So the chair was there after all, and its disappearance was some kind of illusion." —— But suppose that after a time it disappears again — or seems to disappear. What are we to say now? Have you rules ready for such cases — rules saying whether such a thing is still to be called a "chair"? But do we miss them when we use the word "chair"? And are we to say that we do not really attach any meaning to this word, because we are not equipped with rules for every possible application of it?

* 81. F. P. Ramsey once emphasized in conversation with me that logic was a 'normative science'. I do not know exactly what idea he had in mind, but it was doubtless closely related to one that dawned on me only later: namely, that in philosophy we often *compare* the use of words

Philosophie den Gebrauch der Wörter oft mit Spielen, Kalkülen nach festen Regeln, *vergleichen*, aber nicht sagen können, wer die Sprache gebraucht, *müsse* ein solches Spiel spielen. —— Sagt man nun aber, daß unser sprachlicher Ausdruck sich solchen Kalkülen *nur nähert*, so steht man damit unmittelbar am Rande eines Mißverständnisses. Denn so kann es scheinen, als redeten wir in der Logik von einer *idealen* Sprache. Als wäre unsre Logik eine Logik, gleichsam, für den luftleeren Raum. — Während die Logik doch nicht von der Sprache — bzw. vom Denken — handelt in dem Sinne, wie eine Naturwissenschaft von einer Naturerscheinung, und man höchstens sagen kann, wir *konstruierten* ideale Sprachen. Aber hier wäre das Wort "ideal" irreführend, denn das klingt, als wären diese Sprachen besser, vollkommener, als unsere Umgangssprache; und als brauchte es den Logiker, damit er den Menschen endlich zeigt, wie ein richtiger Satz ausschaut.

All das kann aber erst dann im rechten Licht erscheinen, wenn man über die Begriffe des Verstehens, Meinens und Denkens größere Klarheit gewonnen hat. Denn dann wird es auch klar werden, was uns dazu verleiten kann (und mich verleitet hat) zu denken, daß, wer einen Satz ausspricht und ihn *meint*, oder *versteht*, damit einen Kalkül betreibt nach bestimmten Regeln.

82. Was nenne ich 'die Regel, nach der er vorgeht'? — Die Hypothese, die seinen Gebrauch der Worte, den wir beobachten, zufriedenstellend beschreibt; oder die Regel, die er beim Gebrauch der Zeichen nachschlägt; oder, die er uns zur Antwort gibt, wenn wir ihn nach seiner Regel fragen? — Wie aber, wenn die Beobachtung keine Regel klar erkennen läßt, und die Frage keine zu Tage fördert? — Denn er gab mir zwar auf meine Frage, was er unter "N" verstehe, eine Erklärung, war aber bereit, diese Erklärung zu widerrufen und abzuändern. — Wie soll ich also die Regel bestimmen, nach der er spielt? Er weiß sie selbst nicht. — Oder richtiger: Was soll der Ausdruck "Regel, nach welcher er vorgeht" hier noch besagen?

83. Steckt uns da nicht die Analogie der Sprache mit dem Spiel ein Licht auf? Wir können uns doch sehr wohl denken, daß sich Menschen auf einer Wiese damit unterhielten, mit einem Ball zu spielen, so zwar, daß sie verschiedene bestehende Spiele anfingen, manche nicht zu Ende spielten, dazwischen den Ball planlos in die Höhe würfen, einander im Scherz mit dem Ball nachjagen und bewerfen, etc. Und nun sagt Einer: Die ganze Zeit hindurch spielen die Leute ein Ballspiel, und richten sich daher bei jedem Wurf nach bestimmten Regeln.

with games, calculi with fixed rules, but cannot say that someone who is using language *must* be playing such a game. —— But if someone says that our languages only *approximate* to such calculi, he is standing on the very brink of a misunderstanding. For then it may look as if what we are talking about in logic were an *ideal* language. As if our logic were, so to speak, a logic for a vacuum. — Whereas logic does not treat of language — or of thought — in the sense in which a natural science treats of a natural phenomenon, and the most that can be said is that we *construct* ideal languages. But here the word "ideal" is liable to mislead, for it sounds as if these languages were better, more perfect, than our everyday language; and as if it took a logician to show people at last what a proper sentence looks like.

All this, however, can appear in the right light only when one has attained greater clarity about the concepts of understanding, meaning something, and thinking. For it will then also become clear what may mislead us (and did mislead me) into thinking that if anyone utters a sentence and *means* or *understands* it, he is thereby operating a calculus according to definite rules.

* 82. What do I call 'the rule according to which he proceeds'? — The hypothesis that satisfactorily describes his use of words, which we observe; or the rule which he looks up when he uses signs; or the one which he |39| gives us in reply if we ask him what his rule is? — But what if observation does not clearly reveal any rule, and the question brings none to light? — For he did indeed give me an explanation when I asked him what he meant by "N", but he was prepared to withdraw this explanation and alter it. — So how am I to determine the rule according to which he is playing? He does not know it himself. — Or, more correctly, what is left for the expression "the rule according to which he proceeds" to say?

83. Doesn't the analogy between language and games throw light here? We can easily imagine people amusing themselves in a field by playing with a ball like this: starting various existing games, but playing several without finishing them, and in between throwing the ball aimlessly into the air, chasing one another with the ball, throwing it at one another for a joke, and so on. And now someone says: The whole time they are playing a ball-game and therefore are following definite rules at every throw.

Und gibt es nicht auch den Fall, wo wir spielen und — 'make up the rules as we go along'? Ja auch den, in welchem wir sie abändern — as we go along.

84. Ich sagte von der Anwendung eines Wortes: sie sei nicht überall von Regeln begrenzt. Aber wie schaut denn ein Spiel aus, das überall von Regeln begrenzt ist? dessen Regeln keinen Zweifel eindringen lassen; ihm alle Löcher verstopfen. — Können wir uns nicht eine Regel denken, die die Anwendung der Regel regelt? Und einen Zweifel, den *jene* Regel behebt, — und so fort?

Aber das sagt nicht, daß wir zweifeln, weil wir uns einen Zweifel *denken* können. Ich kann mir sehr wohl denken, daß jemand jedesmal vor dem Öffnen seiner Haustüre zweifelt, ob sich hinter ihr nicht ein Abgrund aufgetan hat, und daß er sich darüber vergewissert, eh' er durch die Tür tritt (und es kann sich einmal erweisen, daß er recht hatte) — aber deswegen zweifle ich im gleichen Falle doch nicht.

85. Eine Regel steht da, wie ein Wegweiser. — Läßt er keinen Zweifel offen über den Weg, den ich zu gehen habe? Zeigt er, in welche Richtung ich gehen soll, wenn ich an ihm vorbei bin; ob der Straße nach, oder dem Feldweg, oder querfeldein? Aber wo steht, in welchem Sinne ich ihm zu folgen habe; ob in der Richtung der Hand, oder (z. B.) in der entgegengesetzten? — Und wenn statt eines Wegweisers eine geschlossene Kette von Wegweisern stünden, oder Kreidestriche auf dem Boden liefen, — gibt es für sie nur *eine* Deutung? — Also kann ich sagen, der Wegweiser läßt doch einen Zweifel offen. Oder vielmehr: er läßt manchmal einen Zweifel offen, manchmal nicht. Und dies ist nun kein philosophischer Satz mehr, sondern ein Erfahrungssatz.

86. Ein Sprachspiel wie (2), werde mit Hilfe einer Tabelle gespielt. Die Zeichen, die A dem B gibt, seien nun Schriftzeichen. B hat eine Tabelle; in der ersten Spalte stehen die Schriftzeichen, die im Spiel gebraucht werden, in der zweiten, Bilder von Bausteinformen. A zeigt dem B ein solches Schriftzeichen; B sucht es in der Tabelle auf, blickt auf das gegenüberliegende Bild, etc. Die Tabelle ist also eine Regel, nach der er sich beim Ausführen der Befehle richtet. — Das Aufsuchen des Bildes in der Tabelle lernt man durch Abrichtung, und ein Teil dieser Abrichtung besteht etwa darin, daß der Schüler lernt, in der Tabelle mit dem Finger horizontal von links nach rechts zu fahren; also lernt, sozusagen eine Reihe horizontaler Striche zu ziehen.

Denk dir, es würden nun verschiedene Arten eingeführt, eine Tabelle zu lesen; nämlich einmal, wie oben, nach dem Schema:

And is there not also the case where we play, and make up the rules as we go along? And even where we alter them — as we go along.

84. Speaking of the application of a word, I said that it is not everywhere bounded by rules. But what does a game look like that is everywhere bounded by rules? whose rules never let a doubt creep in, but stop up all the gaps where it might? — Can't we imagine a rule regulating the application of a rule; and a doubt which *it* removes — and so on?

But that is not to say that we are in doubt because it is possible for us to *imagine* a doubt. I can easily imagine someone always doubting before he opened his front door whether an abyss did not yawn behind it, and making sure about it before he went through the door (and he might on some occasion prove to be right) — but for all that, I do not doubt in such a case.

* 85. A rule stands there like a signpost. — Does the signpost leave no doubt about the way I have to go? Does it show which direction I am to take when I have passed it, whether along the road or the footpath or cross-country? But where does it say which way I am to follow it; whether in the direction of its finger or (for example) in the opposite one? — And if there were not a single signpost, but a sequence of signposts or chalk marks on the ground — is there only *one* way of interpreting them? — So I can say that the signpost does after all |40| leave room for doubt. Or rather, it sometimes leaves room for doubt, and sometimes not. And now this is no longer a philosophical proposition, but an empirical one.

86. Imagine a language-game like (2) played with the help of a chart. The signs A gives to B are now written ones. B has a chart; in the first column are the signs used in the game, in the second, pictures of different shapes of building stones. A shows B such a written sign; B looks it up in the chart, looks at the picture opposite, and so on. So the chart is a rule which he follows in carrying out orders. — One learns to look up the picture in the chart by being trained, and part of this training may well consist in the pupil's learning to pass with his finger horizontally from left to right; and so, as it were, to draw a series of horizontal lines on the chart.

Suppose different ways of reading a chart were now introduced; one time, as above, according to the schema:

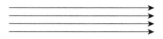

ein andermal nach diesem Schema:

oder einem andern. — So ein Schema werde der Tabelle beigefügt als
Regel, wie sie zu gebrauchen sei.

Können wir uns nun nicht weitere Regeln zur Erklärung *dieser*
vorstellen? und war anderseits jene erste Tabelle unvollständig ohne das
Schema der Pfeile? Und sind es die andern Tabellen ohne ihr Schema?

87. Nimm an, ich erkläre: "Unter 'Moses' verstehe ich den Mann, wenn
es einen solchen gegeben hat, der die Israeliten aus Ägypten geführt hat,
wie immer er damals geheißen hat und was immer er sonst getan, oder
nicht getan haben mag." — Aber über die Wörter dieser Erklärung sind
ähnliche Zweifel möglich, wie die über den Namen "Moses" (was nennst
du "Ägypten", wen "die Israeliten", etc.?). Ja, diese Fragen kommen
auch nicht zu einem Ende, wenn wir bei Wörtern wie "rot", "dunkel",
"süß", angelangt wären. — "Aber wie hilft mir dann eine Erklärung
zum Verständnis, wenn sie doch nicht die letzte ist? Die Erklärung ist
dann ja nie beendet; ich verstehe also noch immer nicht, und nie, was
er meint!" — Als hinge eine Erklärung, gleichsam, in der Luft, wenn
nicht eine andere sie stützte. Während eine Erklärung zwar auf einer
andern, die man gegeben hat, ruhen kann, aber keine einer anderen
bedarf — es sei denn, daß *wir* sie benötigen, um ein Mißverständnis
zu vermeiden. Man könnte sagen: Eine Erklärung dient dazu, ein
Mißverständnis zu beseitigen, oder zu verhüten —— also eines, das ohne
die Erklärung eintreten würde; aber nicht: jedes, welches ich mir
vorstellen kann.

Es kann leicht so scheinen, als *zeigte* jeder Zweifel nur eine vorhan-
dene Lücke im Fundament; so daß ein sicheres Verständnis nur dann
möglich ist, wenn wir zuerst an allem zweifeln, woran gezweifelt werden *kann*, und dann alle diese Zweifel beheben.

Der Wegweiser ist in Ordnung, — wenn er, unter normalen
Verhältnissen, seinen Zweck erfüllt.

another time according to this schema:

or some other one. — Such a schema is added to the chart as a rule for its use.

Can we not now imagine further rules to explain *this* one? And, on the other hand, was that first chart incomplete without the schema of arrows? And are the other charts incomplete without their schemata?

87. Suppose I give this explanation: "I take 'Moses' to mean the man, if there was such a man, who led the Israelites out of Egypt, whatever he was called then and whatever he may or may not have done besides." — But similar doubts to those about the name "Moses" are possible about the words of this explanation (what are you calling "Egypt", whom the "Israelites", and so forth?). These questions would not even come to an end when we got down to words like "red", "dark", "sweet". — "But then how does an explanation help me to understand, |41| if, after all, it is not the final one? In that case the explanation is never completed; so I still don't understand what he means, and never shall!" — As though an explanation, as it were, hung in the air unless supported by another one. Whereas an explanation may indeed rest on another one that has been given, but none stands in need of another — unless *we* require it to avoid a misunderstanding. One might say: an explanation serves to remove or to prevent a misunderstanding —— one, that is, that would arise if not for the explanation, but not every misunderstanding that I can imagine.

It may easily look as if every doubt merely *revealed* a gap in the foundations; so that secure understanding is possible only if we first doubt everything that *can* be doubted, and then remove all these doubts.

The signpost is in order — if, under normal circumstances, it fulfils its purpose.

88. Wenn ich Einem sage "Halte dich ungefähr hier auf!" — kann denn diese Erklärung nicht vollkommen funktionieren? Und kann jede andere nicht auch versagen?

"Aber ist die Erklärung nicht doch unexakt?" — Doch; warum soll man sie nicht "unexakt" nennen? Verstehen wir aber nur, was "unexakt" bedeutet! Denn es bedeutet nun nicht "unbrauchbar". Und überlegen wir uns doch, was wir, im Gegensatz zu dieser Erklärung, eine "exakte" Erklärung nennen! Etwa das Abgrenzen eines Bezirks durch einen Kreidestrich? Da fällt uns gleich ein, daß der Strich eine Breite hat. Exakter wäre also eine Farbgrenze. Aber hat denn diese Exaktheit hier noch eine Funktion; läuft sie nicht leer? Und wir haben ja auch noch nicht bestimmt, was als Überschreiten dieser scharfen Grenze gelten soll; wie, mit welchen Instrumenten, es festzustellen ist. U. s. w.

Wir verstehen, was es heißt: eine Taschenuhr auf die genaue Stunde stellen, oder, sie richten, daß sie genau geht. Wie aber, wenn man fragte: Ist diese Genauigkeit eine ideale Genauigkeit, oder wie weit nähert sie sich ihr? — Wir können freilich von Zeitmessungen reden, bei welchen es eine andere und, wie wir sagen würden, größere Genauigkeit gibt, als bei der Zeitmessung mit der Taschenuhr. Wo die Worte "die Uhr auf die genaue Stunde stellen" eine andere, wenn auch verwandte, Bedeutung haben, und 'die Uhr ablesen' ein anderer Vorgang ist, etc. — Wenn ich nun jemandem sage: "Du solltest pünktlicher zum Essen kommen; du weißt, daß es genau um ein Uhr anfängt" — ist hier von *Genauigkeit* eigentlich nicht die Rede? weil man sagen kann: "Denk an die Zeitbestimmung im Laboratorium, oder auf der Sternwarte; *da* siehst du, was 'Genauigkeit' bedeutet."

"Unexakt", das ist eigentlich ein Tadel, und "exakt" ein Lob. Und das heißt doch: das Unexakte erreicht sein Ziel nicht so vollkommen, wie das Exaktere. Da kommt es also auf das an, was wir "das Ziel" nennen. Ist es unexakt, wenn ich den Abstand der Sonne von uns nicht auf 1 m genau angebe; und dem Tischler die Breite des Tisches nicht auf 0,001 mm?

Ein Ideal der Genauigkeit ist nicht vorgesehen; wir wissen nicht, was wir uns darunter vorstellen sollen — es sei denn, du selbst setzt fest, was so genannt werden soll. Aber es wird dir schwer werden, so eine Festsetzung zu treffen; eine, die dich befriedigt.

89. Wir stehen mit diesen Überlegungen an dem Ort, wo das Problem steht: Inwiefern ist die Logik etwas Sublimes?

Denn es schien, daß ihr eine besondere Tiefe — allgemeine Bedeutung — zukomme. Sie liege, so schien es, am Grunde aller Wissenschaften.

88. If I tell someone "Stay roughly here" — may this explanation not work perfectly? And may not any other one fail too?

*   "But still, isn't it an inexact explanation?" — Yes, why shouldn't one call it "inexact"? Only let's understand what "inexact" means! For it does not mean "unusable". And let's consider what we call an "exact" explanation in contrast to this one. Perhaps like drawing a boundary-line around a region with chalk? Here it strikes us at once that the line has breadth. So a colour edge would be more exact. But has this exactness still got a function here: isn't it running idle? Moreover, we haven't yet laid down what is to count as overstepping this sharp boundary; how, with what instruments, it is to be ascertained. And so on.

We understand what it means to set a pocket-watch to the exact time, or to regulate it to be exact. But what if it were asked: Is this exactness ideal exactness? Or: How nearly does it approach the ideal? — Of course we can speak of measurements of time in which there is a different, and as we should say a greater, exactness than in the measurement of time by a pocket-watch; in which the words "to set the clock to the exact time" have a different, though related, meaning and 'to tell the time' is a different process, and so on. — Now, if I tell someone: "You should come to dinner more punctually; you know it begins at one o'clock exactly" — is there really no question of *exactness* here? After all, one can say: "Think of the determination of time in the laboratory or the observatory; *there* you see what 'exactness' means." |42|

"Inexact" is really a reproach, and "exact" is praise. And that is to say that what is inexact attains its goal less perfectly than does what is more exact. So it all depends on what we call "the goal". Is it inexact when I don't give our distance from the sun to the nearest metre, or tell a joiner the width of a table to the nearest thousandth of a millimetre?

No single ideal of exactness has been envisaged; we do not know what we are to make of this idea — unless you yourself stipulate what is to be so called. But you'll find it difficult to make such a stipulation — one that satisfies you.

*   89. With these considerations we find ourselves facing the problem: In what way is logic something sublime?

*   For logic seemed to have a peculiar depth — a universal significance. Logic lay, it seemed, at the foundation of all the sciences. — For logical

— Denn die logische Betrachtung erforscht das Wesen aller Dinge. Sie will den Dingen auf den Grund sehen, und soll sich nicht um das So oder So des tatsächlichen Geschehens kümmern. —— Sie entspringt nicht einem Interesse für Tatsachen des Naturgeschehens, noch dem Bedürfnisse, kausale Zusammenhänge zu erfassen. Sondern einem Streben, das Fundament, oder Wesen, alles Erfahrungsmäßigen zu verstehen. Nicht aber, als sollten wir dazu neue Tatsachen aufspüren: es ist vielmehr für unsere Untersuchung wesentlich, daß wir nichts *Neues* mit ihr lernen wollen. Wir wollen etwas *verstehen*, was schon offen vor unsern Augen liegt. Denn *das* scheinen wir, in irgend einem Sinne, nicht zu verstehen.

Augustinus (Conf. XI/14): "quid est ergo tempus? si nemo ex me quaerat scio; si quaerenti explicare velim, nescio." — Dies könnte man nicht von einer Frage der Naturwissenschaft sagen (etwa der nach dem spezifischen Gewicht des Wasserstoffs). Das, was man weiß, wenn uns niemand fragt, aber nicht mehr weiß, wenn wir es erklären sollen, ist etwas, worauf man sich *besinnen* muß. (Und offenbar etwas, worauf man sich aus irgendeinem Grunde schwer besinnt.)

90. Es ist uns, als müßten wir die Erscheinungen *durchschauen*: unsere Untersuchung aber richtet sich nicht auf die *Erscheinungen*, sondern, wie man sagen könnte, auf die 'Möglichkeiten' der Erscheinungen. Wir besinnen uns, heißt das, auf die *Art der Aussagen*, die wir über die Erscheinungen machen. Daher besinnt sich auch Augustinus auf die verschiedenen Aussagen, die man über die Dauer von Ereignissen, über ihre Vergangenheit, Gegenwart, oder Zukunft macht. (Dies sind natürlich nicht *philosophische* Aussagen über die Zeit, Vergangenheit, Gegenwart und Zukunft.)

Unsere Betrachtung ist daher eine grammatische. Und diese Betrachtung bringt Licht in unser Problem, indem sie Mißverständnisse wegräumt. Mißverständnisse, die den Gebrauch von Worten betreffen; hervorgerufen, unter anderem, durch gewisse Analogien zwischen den Ausdrucksformen in verschiedenen Gebieten unserer Sprache. — Manche von ihnen lassen sich beseitigen, indem man eine Ausdrucksform durch eine andere ersetzt; dies kann man ein "Analysieren" unsrer Ausdrucksformen nennen, denn der Vorgang hat manchmal Ähnlichkeit mit einem Zerlegen.

91. Nun aber kann es den Anschein gewinnen, als gäbe es so etwas, wie eine letzte Analyse unserer Sprachformen, also *eine* vollkommen zerlegte Form des Ausdrucks. D. h.: als seien unsere gebräuchlichen Ausdrucksformen, wesentlich, noch unanalysiert; als sei in ihnen etwas verborgen, was ans Licht zu befördern ist. Ist dies geschehen, so sei der Ausdruck damit vollkommen geklärt und unsre Aufgabe gelöst.

investigation explores the essence of all things. It seeks to see to the foundation of things, and shouldn't concern itself whether things actually happen in this or that way. —— It arises neither from an interest in the facts of nature, nor from a need to grasp causal connections, but from an urge to understand the foundations, or essence, of everything empirical. Not, however, as if to this end we had to hunt out new facts; it is, rather, essential to our investigation that we do not seek to learn anything *new* by it. We want to *understand* something that is already in plain view. For *this* is what we seem in some sense not to understand.

*   Augustine says in *Confessions* XI. 14, "quid est ergo tempus? si nemo ex me quaerat scio; si quaerenti explicare velim, nescio". — This could not be said about a question of natural science ("What is the specific gravity of hydrogen?", for instance). Something that one knows when nobody asks one, but no longer knows when one is asked to explain it, is something that has to be *called to mind*. (And it is obviously something which, for some reason, it is difficult to call to mind.)

*   90. We feel as if we had to *see right into* phenomena: yet our investigation is directed not towards *phenomena*, but rather, as one might say, towards the '*possibilities*' of phenomena. What that means is that we call to mind the *kinds of statement* that we make about phenomena. So too, Augustine calls to mind the different statements that are made about the duration of events, about their being past, present or future. (These are, of course, not *philosophical* statements about time, the past, the present and the future.) |43|

Our inquiry is therefore a grammatical one. And this inquiry sheds light on our problem by clearing misunderstandings away. Misunderstandings concerning the use of words, brought about, among other things, by certain analogies between the forms of expression in different regions of our language. — Some of them can be removed by substituting one form of expression for another; this may be called 'analysing' our forms of expression, for sometimes this procedure resembles taking a thing apart.

91. But now it may come to look as if there were something like a final analysis of our linguistic expressions, and so a single completely analysed form of every expression. That is, as if our usual forms of expression were, essentially, still unanalysed; as if there were something hidden in them that had to be brought to light. As if, when this is done, the expression is completely clarified and our task accomplished.

Man kann das auch so sagen: Wir beseitigen Mißverständnisse, indem wir unsern Ausdruck exakter machen: aber es kann nun so scheinen, als ob wir einem bestimmten Zustand, der vollkommenen Exaktheit, zustreben; und als wäre das das eigentliche Ziel unserer Untersuchung.

92. Dies drückt sich aus in der Frage nach dem *Wesen* der Sprache, des Satzes, des Denkens. — Denn wenn wir auch in unsern Untersuchungen das Wesen der Sprache — ihre Funktion, ihren Bau — zu verstehen trachten, so ist es doch nicht *das*, was diese Frage im Auge hat. Denn sie sieht in dem Wesen nicht etwas, was schon offen zutage liegt und was durch Ordnen *übersichtlich* wird. Sondern etwas, was *unter* der Oberfläche liegt. Etwas, was im Innern liegt, was wir sehen, wenn wir die Sache durchschauen, und was eine Analyse hervorgraben soll.

'*Das Wesen ist uns verborgen*': das ist die Form, die unser Problem nun annimmt. Wir fragen: "*Was ist* die Sprache?", "*Was ist* der Satz?". Und die Antwort auf diese Fragen ist ein für allemal zu geben; und unabhängig von jeder künftigen Erfahrung.

93. Einer könnte sagen "Ein Satz, das ist das Alltäglichste von der Welt", und der Andre: "Ein Satz — das ist etwas sehr Merkwürdiges!" —— Und dieser kann nicht: einfach nachschaun, wie Sätze funktionieren. Weil die Formen unserer Ausdrucksweise, die Sätze und das Denken betreffend, ihm im Wege stehen.

Warum sagen wir, der Satz sei etwas Merkwürdiges? Einerseits, wegen der ungeheuren Bedeutung, die ihm zukommt. (Und das ist richtig.) Andererseits verführt uns diese Bedeutung und ein Mißverstehen der Sprachlogik dazu, daß wir meinen, der Satz müsse etwas Außerordentliches, ja Einzigartiges, leisten. — Durch ein *Mißverständnis* erscheint es uns, als *tue* der Satz etwas Seltsames.

94. 'Der Satz, ein merkwürdiges Ding!': darin liegt schon die Sublimierung der ganzen Darstellung. Die Tendenz, ein reines Mittelwesen anzunehmen zwischen dem Satz*zeichen* und den Tatsachen. Oder auch, das Satzzeichen selber reinigen, sublimieren, zu wollen. — Denn, daß es mit gewöhnlichen Dingen zugeht, das zu sehen, verhindern uns auf mannigfache Weise unsere Ausdrucksformen, indem sie uns auf die Jagd nach Chimären schicken.

95. "Denken muß etwas Einzigartiges sein." Wenn wir sagen, *meinen*, daß es sich so und so verhält, so halten wir mit dem, was wir meinen,

It may also be put like this: we eliminate misunderstandings by making our expressions more exact; but now it may look as if we were aiming at a particular state, a state of complete exactness, and as if this were the real goal of our investigation.

* 92. This finds expression in the question of the *essence* of language, of propositions, of thought. — For although we, in our investigations, are trying to understand the nature of language — its function, its structure — yet *this* is not what that question has in view. For it sees the essence of things not as something that already lies open to view, and that becomes *surveyable* through a process of ordering, but as something that lies *beneath* the surface. Something that lies within, which we perceive when we see *right into* the thing, and which an analysis is supposed to unearth.

* '*The essence is hidden from us*': this is the form our problem now assumes. We ask: "*What is* language?", "*What is* a proposition?" And the answer to these questions is to be given once for all, and independently of any future experience.

93. One person might say, "A proposition is the most ordinary thing in the world", and another, "A proposition — that's something very remarkable!" —— And the latter is unable simply to look and see how propositions work. For the forms of the expressions we use in talking about propositions and thought stand in his way.

Why do we say that a proposition is something remarkable? On the one hand, because of the enormous importance attaching to it. (And that is correct.) On the other hand, this importance, together with a misunderstanding |44| of the logic of language, seduces us into thinking that something extraordinary, even unique, must be achieved by propositions. — A *misunderstanding* makes it look to us as if a proposition *did* something strange.

* 94. 'Remarkable things, propositions!' Here we already have the sublimation of our whole account of logic. The tendency to assume a pure intermediary between the propositional *sign* and the facts. Or even to try to purify, to sublimate, the sign itself. — For our forms of expression, which send us in pursuit of chimeras, prevent us in all sorts of ways from seeing that nothing extraordinary is involved.

* 95. "Thinking must be something unique." When we say, *mean*, that such-and-such is the case, then, with what we mean, we do not

nicht irgendwo vor der Tatsache: sondern meinen, daß *das und das —
so und so — ist*. — Man kann aber dieses Paradox (welches ja die Form
einer Selbstverständlichkeit hat) auch so ausdrücken: Man kann
denken, was nicht der Fall ist.

96. Der besondern Täuschung, die hier gemeint ist, schließen sich, von
verschiedenen Seiten, andere an. Das Denken, die Sprache, erscheint uns
nun als das einzigartige Korrelat, Bild, der Welt. Die Begriffe: Satz,
Sprache, Denken, Welt, stehen in einer Reihe hintereinander, jeder dem
andern äquivalent. (Wozu aber sind diese Wörter nun zu brauchen? Es
fehlt das Sprachspiel, worin sie anzuwenden sind.)

97. Das Denken ist mit einem Nimbus umgeben. — Sein Wesen, die Logik,
stellt eine Ordnung dar, und zwar die Ordnung a priori der Welt, d. i.
die Ordnung der *Möglichkeiten*, die Welt und Denken gemeinsam sein
muß. Diese Ordnung aber, scheint es, muß *höchst einfach* sein. Sie ist
vor aller Erfahrung; muß sich durch die ganze Erfahrung hindurchziehen;
ihr selbst darf keine erfahrungsmäßige Trübe oder Unsicherheit anhaften.
—— Sie muß vielmehr vom reinsten Kristall sein. Dieser Kristall aber
erscheint nicht als eine Abstraktion; sondern als etwas Konkretes, ja als
das Konkreteste, gleichsam *Härteste*. (Log. Phil. Abh. 5.5563.)
    Wir sind in der Täuschung, das Besondere, Tiefe, das uns Wesentliche
unserer Untersuchung liege darin, daß sie das unvergleichliche Wesen
der Sprache zu begreifen trachtet. D. i., die Ordnung, die zwischen den
Begriffen des Satzes, Wortes, Schließens, der Wahrheit, der Erfahrung,
u. s. w. besteht. Diese Ordnung ist eine *Über*-Ordnung zwischen —
sozusagen — *Über*-Begriffen. Während doch die Worte "Sprache",
"Erfahrung", "Welt", wenn sie eine Verwendung haben, eine so
niedrige haben müssen, wie die Worte "Tisch", "Lampe", "Tür".

98. Einerseits ist klar, daß jeder Satz unsrer Sprache 'in Ordnung ist,
wie er ist'. D. h., daß wir nicht ein Ideal *anstreben*: Als hätten unsere
gewöhnlichen, vagen Sätze noch keinen ganz untadelhaften Sinn und
eine vollkommene Sprache wäre von uns erst zu konstruieren. —
Andererseits scheint es klar: Wo Sinn ist, muß vollkommene Ordnung sein.
—— Also muß die vollkommene Ordnung auch im vagsten Satze
stecken.

99. Der Sinn des Satzes — möchte man sagen — kann freilich dies oder
das offen lassen, aber der Satz muß doch *einen* bestimmten Sinn haben.
Ein unbestimmter Sinn, — das wäre eigentlich *gar kein* Sinn. — Das ist

stop anywhere short of the fact, but mean: *such-and-such — is — thus-and-so.* — But this paradox (which indeed has the form of a truism) can also be expressed in this way: one can *think* what is not the case.

96. Other illusions come from various quarters to join the particular one spoken of here. Thought, language, now appear to us as the unique correlate, picture, of the world. These concepts: proposition, language, thought, world, stand in line one behind the other, each equivalent to each. (But what are these words to be used for now? The language-game in which they are to be applied is missing.)

*   97. Thinking is surrounded by a nimbus. — Its essence, logic, presents an order: namely, the a priori order of the world; that is, the order of *possibilities*, which the world and thinking must have in common. But this order, it seems, must be *utterly simple.* It is *prior* to all experience, must run through all experience; no empirical cloudiness or uncertainty may attach to it. —— It must rather be of the purest crystal. But this crystal does not appear as an abstraction, but as something concrete, indeed, as the most concrete, as it were the *hardest* thing there is (*Tractatus Logico-Philosophicus* 5.5563).

We are under the illusion that what is peculiar, profound and essential to us in our investigation resides in its trying to grasp the incomparable essence of language. That is, the order existing between the concepts of proposition, word, inference, truth, experience, and so forth. This order is a *super*-order between — so to speak — *super*-concepts. Whereas, in fact, if the words "language", "experience", "world" have a use, it must be as humble a one as that of the words "table", "lamp", "door". |45|

*   98. On the one hand, it is clear that every sentence in our language 'is in order as it is'. That is to say, we are not *striving after* an ideal, as if our ordinary vague sentences had not yet got a quite unexceptionable sense, and a perfect language still had to be constructed by us. — On the other hand, it seems clear that where there is sense, there must be perfect order. —— So there must be perfect order even in the vaguest sentence.

99. The sense of a sentence — one would like to say — may, of course, leave this or that open, but the sentence must nevertheless have a determinate sense. An indeterminate sense — that would really not be a sense

wie: Eine unscharfe Begrenzung, das ist eigentlich gar keine Begrenzung. Man denkt da etwa so: Wenn ich sage "ich habe den Mann fest im Zimmer eingeschlossen — nur *eine* Tür ist offen geblieben" — so habe ich ihn eben gar nicht eingeschlossen. Er ist nur zum Schein eingeschlossen. Man wäre geneigt, hier zu sagen: "Also hast du damit gar nichts getan." Eine Umgrenzung, die ein Loch hat, ist so gut, wie *gar keine*. — Aber ist das denn wahr?

100. "Es ist doch kein Spiel, wenn es eine Vagheit *in den Regeln* gibt." — Aber *ist* es dann kein Spiel? — "Ja, vielleicht wirst du es Spiel nennen, aber es ist doch jedenfalls kein vollkommenes Spiel." D. h.: es ist doch dann verunreinigt, und ich interessiere mich nun für dasjenige, was hier verunreinigt wurde. — Aber ich will sagen: Wir mißverstehen die Rolle, die das Ideal in unsrer Ausdrucksweise spielt. D. h.: auch wir würden es ein Spiel nennen, nur sind wir vom Ideal geblendet und sehen daher nicht deutlich die wirkliche Anwendung des Wortes "Spiel".

101. Eine Vagheit in der Logik — wollen wir sagen — kann es nicht geben. Wir leben nun in der Idee: das Ideal '*müsse*' sich in der Realität finden. Während man noch nicht sieht, *wie* es sich darin findet, und nicht das Wesen dieses "muß" versteht. Wir glauben: es muß in ihr stecken; denn wir glauben es schon in ihr zu sehen.

102. Die strengen und klaren Regeln des logischen Satzbaues erscheinen uns als etwas im Hintergrund, — im Medium des Verstehens versteckt. Ich sehe sie schon jetzt (wenn auch durch ein Medium hindurch), da ich ja das Zeichen verstehe, etwas mit ihm meine.

103. Das Ideal, in unsern Gedanken, sitzt unverrückbar fest. Du kannst nicht aus ihm heraustreten. Du mußt immer wieder zurück. Es gibt gar kein Draußen; draußen fehlt die Lebensluft. — Woher dies? Die Idee sitzt gleichsam als Brille auf unsrer Nase, und was wir ansehen, sehen wir durch sie. Wir kommen gar nicht auf den Gedanken, sie abzunehmen.

104. Man prädiziert von der Sache, was in der Darstellungsweise liegt. Die Möglichkeit des Vergleichs, die uns beeindruckt, nehmen wir für die Wahrnehmung einer höchst allgemeinen Sachlage.

(Faraday "The Chemical History of a Candle"): "Water is one individual thing — it never changes."

at all. — This is similar to: a boundary which is not sharply defined is not really a boundary at all. Here one thinks something like this: if I say "I have locked the man up in the room — there is only one door left open" — then I simply haven't locked him up at all; his being locked up is a sham. One would be inclined to say here: "So you haven't accomplished anything at all." An enclosure with a hole in it is as good as *none.* — But is that really true?

*   100. "Still, it isn't a game at all, if there is some vagueness *in the rules.*" But is it really not a game, then? — "Well, perhaps you'll call it a game, but at any rate it isn't a perfect game." This means: then it has been contaminated, and what I am interested in now is what it was that was contaminated. — But I want to say: we misunderstand the role played by the ideal in our language. That is to say: we too would call it a game, only we are dazzled by the ideal, and therefore fail to see the actual application of the word "game" clearly.

101. We want to say that there can't be any vagueness in logic. The idea now absorbs us that the ideal *'must'* occur in reality. At the same time, one doesn't as yet see *how* it occurs there, and doesn't understand the nature of this "must". We think the ideal must be in reality; for we think we already see it there.

102. The strict and clear rules for the logical construction of a proposition appear to us as something in the background — hidden in the medium of understanding. I already see them (even though through a medium), for I do understand the sign, I mean something by it.

103. The ideal, as we conceive of it, is unshakable. You can't step outside it. You must always turn back. There is no outside; outside you cannot breathe. — How come? The idea is like a pair of glasses on our nose through which we see whatever we look at. It never occurs to us to take them off. |46|

104. One predicates of the thing what lies in the mode of representation. We take the possibility of comparison, which impresses us, as the perception of a highly general state of affairs.

---

*   Faraday in *The Chemical History of a Candle*: "Water is one individual thing — it never changes." |p. 46 n.|

105. Wenn wir glauben, jene Ordnung, das Ideal, in der wirklichen Sprache finden zu müssen, werden wir nun mit dem unzufrieden, was man im gewöhnlichen Leben "Satz", "Wort", "Zeichen" nennt.

Der Satz, das Wort, von dem die Logik handelt, soll etwas Reines und Scharfgeschnittenes sein. Und wir zerbrechen uns nun über das Wesen des *eigentlichen* Zeichens den Kopf. — Ist es etwa die *Vorstellung* vom Zeichen? oder die Vorstellung im gegenwärtigen Augenblick?

106. Hier ist es schwer, gleichsam den Kopf oben zu behalten, — zu sehen, daß wir bei den Dingen des alltäglichen Denkens bleiben müssen, und nicht auf den Abweg zu geraten, wo es scheint, als müßten wir die letzten Feinheiten beschreiben, die wir doch wieder mit unsern Mitteln gar nicht beschreiben könnten. Es ist uns, als sollten wir ein zerstörtes Spinnennetz mit unsern Fingern in Ordnung bringen.

107. Je genauer wir die tatsächliche Sprache betrachten, desto stärker wird der Widerstreit zwischen ihr und unsrer Forderung. (Die Kristallreinheit der Logik hatte sich mir ja nicht *ergeben*; sondern sie war eine Forderung.) Der Widerstreit wird unerträglich; die Forderung droht nun zu etwas Leerem zu werden. — Wir sind aufs Glatteis geraten, wo die Reibung fehlt, also die Bedingungen in gewissem Sinne ideal sind, aber wir eben deshalb auch nicht gehen können. Wir wollen gehen; dann brauchen wir die *Reibung*. Zurück auf den rauhen Boden!

108. Wir erkennen, daß, was wir "Satz", "Sprache", nennen, nicht die formelle Einheit ist, die ich mir vorstellte, sondern die Familie mehr oder weniger mit einander verwandter Gebilde. —— Was aber wird nun aus der Logik? Ihre Strenge scheint hier aus dem Leim zu gehen. — Verschwindet sie damit aber nicht ganz? — Denn wie kann die Logik ihre Strenge verlieren? Natürlich nicht dadurch, daß man ihr etwas von ihrer Strenge abhandelt. — Das *Vorurteil* der Kristallreinheit kann nur so beseitigt werden, daß wir unsere ganze Betrachtung drehen. (Man könnte sagen: Die Betrachtung muß gedreht werden, aber um unser eigentliches Bedürfnis als Angelpunkt.)

105. When we believe that we have to find that order, the ideal, in our actual language, we become dissatisfied with what are ordinarily called "sentences", "words", "signs".

The sentence and the word that logic deals with are supposed to be something pure and clear-cut. And now we rack our brains over the nature of the *real* sign. — Is it perhaps the *idea* of the sign? Or the idea at the present moment?

106. Here it is difficult to keep our heads above water, as it were, to see that we must stick to matters of everyday thought, and not to get on the wrong track where it seems that we have to describe extreme subtleties, which again we are quite unable to describe with the means at our disposal. We feel as if we had to repair a torn spider's web with our fingers.

107. The more closely we examine actual language, the greater becomes the conflict between it and our requirement. (For the crystalline purity of logic was, of course, not something I had *discovered*: it was a requirement.) The conflict becomes intolerable; the requirement is now in danger of becoming vacuous. — We have got on to slippery ice where there is no friction, and so, in a certain sense, the conditions are ideal; but also, just because of that, we are unable to walk. We want to walk: so we need *friction*. Back to the rough ground!

108. We see that what we call "proposition", "language", has not the formal unity that I imagined, but is a family of structures more or less akin to one another. —— But what becomes of logic now? Its rigour seems to be giving way here. — But in that case doesn't logic altogether disappear? — For how can logic lose its rigour? Of course not by our bargaining any of its rigour out of it. — The *preconception* of crystalline purity can only be removed by turning our whole inquiry around. (One might say: the inquiry must be turned around, but on the pivot of our real need. |47|

Die Philosophie der Logik redet in keinem andern Sinn von
Sätzen und Wörtern, als wir es im gewöhnlichen Leben tun, wenn
wir etwa sagen "hier steht ein chinesischer Satz aufgeschrieben",
oder "nein, das sieht nur aus wie Schriftzeichen, ist aber ein
Ornament", etc.

Wir reden von dem räumlichen und zeitlichen Phänomen der
Sprache; nicht von einem unräumlichen und unzeitlichen Unding.
[Nur kann man sich in verschiedener Weise für ein Phänomen inter-
essieren.] Aber wir reden von ihr so, wie von den Figuren des
Schachspiels, indem wir Spielregeln für sie angeben, nicht ihre
physikalischen Eigenschaften beschreiben.

Die Frage "Was ist eigentlich ein Wort?" ist analog der "Was
ist eine Schachfigur?"

109. Richtig war, daß unsere Betrachtungen nicht wissenschaftliche
Betrachtungen sein durften. Die Erfahrung, 'daß sich das oder das denken
lasse, entgegen unserm Vorurteil' — was immer das heißen mag — konnte uns nicht interessieren. (Die pneumatische Auffassung des Denkens.)
Und wir dürfen keinerlei Theorie aufstellen. Es darf nichts Hypothe-
tisches in unsern Betrachtungen sein. Alle *Erklärung* muß fort, und nur
Beschreibung an ihre Stelle treten. Und diese Beschreibung empfängt
ihr Licht, d. i. ihren Zweck, von den philosophischen Problemen.
Diese sind freilich keine empirischen, sondern sie werden durch eine
Einsicht in das Arbeiten unserer Sprache gelöst, und zwar so, daß dieses
erkannt wird: *entgegen* einem Trieb, es mißzuverstehen. Die Probleme
werden gelöst, nicht durch Beibringen neuer Erfahrung, sondern
durch Zusammenstellung des längst Bekannten. Die Philosophie ist ein
Kampf gegen die Verhexung unsres Verstandes durch die Mittel unserer
Sprache.

110. "Die Sprache (oder das Denken) ist etwas Einzigartiges" — das
erweist sich als ein Aberglaube (nicht Irrtum!) hervorgerufen selbst durch
grammatische Täuschungen.

Und auf diese Täuschungen, auf die Probleme, fällt nun das Pathos
zurück.

111. Die Probleme, die durch ein Mißdeuten unserer Sprachformen entstehen, haben den Charakter der *Tiefe*. Es sind tiefe Beunruhigungen; sie

*

> The sense in which philosophy of logic speaks of sentences and
> words is no different from that in which we speak of them in ordi-
> nary life when we say, for example, "What is written here is a
> Chinese sentence", or "No, that only looks like writing; it's actu-
> ally just ornamental", and so on.
>
> We're talking about the spatial and temporal phenomenon of
> language, not about some non-spatial, atemporal non-entity.
> [Only it is possible to be interested in a phenomenon in a variety
> of ways]. But we talk about it as we do about the pieces in chess
> when we are stating the rules for their moves, not describing their
> physical properties.
>
> The question "What is a word really?" is analogous to "What
> is a piece in chess?" |§108(b)–(d)|

* 109. It was correct that our considerations must not be scientific ones.
The feeling 'that it is possible, contrary to our preconceived ideas, to
think this or that' — whatever that may mean — could be of no interest to us. (The pneumatic conception of thinking.) And we may not
advance any kind of theory. There must not be anything hypothetical
in our considerations. All *explanation* must disappear, and description
alone must take its place. And this description gets its light — that is
to say, its purpose — from the philosophical problems. These are, of
course, not empirical problems; but they are solved through an insight
into the workings of our language, and that in such a way that these
workings are recognized — *despite* an urge to misunderstand them. The
problems are solved, not by coming up with new discoveries, but by
assembling what we have long been familiar with. Philosophy is a struggle against the bewitchment of our understanding by the resources of
our language.

110. "Language (or thinking) is something unique" — this proves to be
a superstition (not a mistake!), itself produced by grammatical illusions.

And now the impressiveness retreats to these illusions, to the
problems.

111. The problems arising through a misinterpretation of our forms of
language have the character of *depth*. They are deep disquietudes; they

wurzeln so tief in uns, wie die Formen unserer Sprache, und ihre Bedeutung ist so groß, wie die Wichtigkeit unserer Sprache. —— Fragen wir uns: Warum empfinden wir einen grammatischen Witz als *tief*? (Und das ist ja die philosophische Tiefe.)

112. Ein Gleichnis, das in die Formen unserer Sprache aufgenommen ist, bewirkt einen falschen Schein; der beunruhigt uns: "Es ist doch nicht *so*!" — sagen wir. "Aber es muß doch *so sein*!"

113. "Es ist doch *so* — — —" sage ich wieder und wieder vor mich hin. Es ist mir, als müßte ich das Wesen der Sache erfassen, wenn ich meinen Blick nur *ganz scharf* auf dies Faktum einstellen, es in den Brennpunkt rücken könnte.

114. Log. Phil. Abh. (4.5): "Die allgemeine Form des Satzes ist: Es verhält sich so und so." —— Das ist ein Satz von jener Art, die man sich unzählige Male wiederholt. Man glaubt, wieder und wieder der Natur nachzufahren, und fährt nur der Form entlang, durch die wir sie betrachten.

115. Ein *Bild* hielt uns gefangen. Und heraus konnten wir nicht, denn es lag in unsrer Sprache, und sie schien es uns nur unerbittlich zu wiederholen.

116. Wenn die Philosophen ein Wort gebrauchen — "Wissen", "Sein", "Gegenstand", "Ich", "Satz", "Name" — und das *Wesen* des Dings zu erfassen trachten, muß man sich immer fragen: Wird denn dieses Wort in der Sprache, in der es seine Heimat hat, je tatsächlich so gebraucht? —

Wir führen die Wörter von ihrer metaphysischen, wieder auf ihre alltägliche Verwendung zurück.

117. Man sagt mir: "Du verstehst doch diesen Ausdruck? Nun also, — in der Bedeutung, die du kennst, gebrauche auch ich ihn." — Als wäre die Bedeutung ein Dunstkreis, den das Wort mitbringt und in jederlei Verwendung hinübernimmt.

(Wenn z. B. Einer sagt, der Satz "Dies ist hier" (wobei er vor sich hin auf einen Gegenstand zeigt) habe für ihn Sinn, so möge er sich fragen, unter welchen besonderen Umständen man diesen Satz tatsächlich verwendet. In diesen hat er dann Sinn.)

are as deeply rooted in us as the forms of our language, and their sig-nificance is as great as the importance of our language. —— Let's ask ourselves: why do we feel a grammatical joke to be *deep*? (And that is what the depth of philosophy is.)

112. A simile that has been absorbed into the forms of our language produces a false appearance which disquiets us. "But *this* isn't how it is!" — we say. "Yet *this* is how it *has to be*!" |48|

113. "But *this* is how it is — — —", I say to myself over and over again. I feel as though, if only I could fix my gaze *absolutely sharply* on this fact and get it into focus, I could not but grasp the essence of the matter.

114. *Tractatus Logico-Philosophicus* (4.5): "The general form of propositions is: This is how things are." —— That is the kind of pro-position one repeats to oneself countless times. One thinks that one is tracing nature over and over again, and one is merely tracing round the frame through which we look at it.

115. A *picture* held us captive. And we couldn't get outside it, for it lay in our language, and language seemed only to repeat it to us inexorably.

116. When philosophers use a word — "knowledge", "being", "object", "I", "proposition/sentence", "name" — and try to grasp the *essence* of the thing, one must always ask oneself: is the word ever actually used in this way in the language in which it is at home? —

What *we* do is to bring words back from their metaphysical to their everyday use.

117. I am told: "You understand this expression, don't you? Well then — I'm using it with the meaning you're familiar with." As if the mean-ing were an aura the word brings along with it and retains in every kind of use.

(If, for example, someone says that the sentence "This is here" (say-ing which he points to an object in front of him) makes sense to him, then he should ask himself in what special circumstances this sentence is actually used. There it does make sense.)

118. Woher nimmt die Betrachtung ihre Wichtigkeit, da sie doch nur alles Interessante, d. h. alles Große und Wichtige, zu zerstören scheint? (Gleichsam alle Bauwerke; indem sie nur Steinbrocken und Schutt übrig läßt.) Aber es sind nur Luftgebäude, die wir zerstören, und wir legen den Grund der Sprache frei, auf dem sie standen.

119. Die Ergebnisse der Philosophie sind die Entdeckung irgend eines schlichten Unsinns und Beulen, die sich der Verstand beim Anrennen an die Grenze der Sprache geholt hat. Sie, die Beulen, lassen uns den Wert jener Entdeckung erkennen.

120. Wenn ich über Sprache (Wort, Satz, etc.) rede, muß ich die Sprache des Alltags reden. Ist diese Sprache etwa zu grob, materiell, für das, was wir sagen wollen? *Und wie wird denn eine andere gebildet?* — Und wie merkwürdig, daß wir dann mit der unsern überhaupt etwas anfangen können!

Daß ich bei meinen Erklärungen, die Sprache betreffend, schon die volle Sprache (nicht etwa eine vorbereitende, vorläufige) anwenden muß, zeigt schon, daß ich nur Äußerliches über die Sprache vorbringen kann.

Ja, aber wie können uns diese Ausführungen dann befriedigen? — Nun, deine Fragen waren ja auch schon in dieser Sprache abgefaßt; mußten in dieser Sprache ausgedrückt werden, wenn etwas zu fragen war!

Und deine Skrupel sind Mißverständnisse.

Deine Fragen beziehen sich auf Wörter; so muß ich von Wörtern reden.

Man sagt: Es kommt nicht aufs Wort an, sondern auf seine Bedeutung; und denkt dabei an die Bedeutung, wie an eine Sache von der Art des Worts, wenn auch vom Wort verschieden. Hier das Wort, hier die Bedeutung. Das Geld und die Kuh, die man dafür kaufen kann. (Anderseits aber: das Geld, und sein Nutzen.)

121. Man könnte meinen: wenn die Philosophie vom Gebrauch des Wortes "Philosophie" redet, so müsse es eine Philosophie zweiter Ordnung geben. Aber es ist eben nicht so; sondern der Fall entspricht dem der Rechtschreibelehre, die es auch mit dem Wort "Rechtschreibelehre" zu tun hat, aber dann nicht eine solche zweiter Ordnung ist.

122. Es ist eine Hauptquelle unseres Unverständnisses, daß wir den Gebrauch unserer Wörter nicht *übersehen*. — Unserer Grammatik fehlt es an Übersichtlichkeit. — Die übersichtliche Darstellung vermittelt das Verständnis, welches eben darin besteht, daß wir die 'Zusammenhänge sehen'. Daher die Wichtigkeit des Findens und des Erfindens von *Zwischengliedern*.

118. Where does this investigation get its importance from, given that it seems only to destroy everything interesting: that is, all that is great and important? (As it were, all the buildings, leaving behind only bits of stone and rubble.) But what we are destroying are only houses of cards, and we are clearing up the ground of language on which they stood.

119. The results of philosophy are the discovery of some piece of plain nonsense and the bumps that the understanding has got by running up against the limits of language. They — these bumps — make us see the value of that discovery.

120. When I talk about language (word, sentence, etc.), I must speak the language of every day. So is this language too coarse, too material, for what we want to say? *Well then, how is another one to be |49| constructed?* — And how extraordinary that we should be able to do anything at all with the one we have!

In giving explanations, I already have to use language full-blown (not some sort of preparatory, provisional one); this is enough to show that I can come up only with externalities about language.

Yes, but then how can these observations satisfy us? — Well, your very questions were framed in this language; they had to be expressed in this language, if there was anything to ask!

And your scruples are misunderstandings.

Your questions refer to words; so I have to talk about words.

People say: it's not the word that counts, but its meaning, thinking of the meaning as a thing of the same kind as the word, even though different from the word. Here the word, there the meaning. The money, and the cow one can buy with it. (On the other hand, however: money, and what can be done with it.)

121. One might think: if philosophy speaks of the use of the word "philosophy", there must be a second-order philosophy. But that's not the way it is; it is, rather, like the case of orthography, which deals with the word "orthography" among others without then being second-order.

*   122. A main source of our failure to understand is that we don't have *an overview* of the use of our words. — Our grammar is deficient in surveyability. — A surveyable representation produces precisely that kind of understanding which consists in 'seeing connections'. Hence the importance of finding and inventing *intermediate links*.

Der Begriff der übersichtlichen Darstellung ist für uns von grundlegender Bedeutung. Er bezeichnet unsere Darstellungsform, die Art, wie wir die Dinge sehen. (Ist dies eine 'Weltanschauung'?)

123. Ein philosophisches Problem hat die Form: "Ich kenne mich nicht aus."

124. Die Philosophie darf den tatsächlichen Gebrauch der Sprache in keiner Weise antasten, sie kann ihn am Ende also nur beschreiben.
    Denn sie kann ihn auch nicht begründen.
    Sie läßt alles wie es ist.
    Sie läßt auch die Mathematik wie sie ist, und keine mathematische Entdeckung kann sie weiterbringen. Ein "führendes Problem der mathematischen Logik" ist für uns ein Problem der Mathematik, wie jedes andere.

125. Es ist nicht Sache der Philosophie, den Widerspruch durch eine mathematische, logisch-mathematische, Entdeckung zu lösen. Sondern den Zustand der Mathematik, der uns beunruhigt, den Zustand *vor* der Lösung des Widerspruchs, übersehbar zu machen. (Und damit geht man nicht etwa einer Schwierigkeit aus dem Wege.)
    Die fundamentale Tatsache ist hier: daß wir Regeln, eine Technik, für ein Spiel festlegen, und daß es dann, wenn wir den Regeln folgen, nicht so geht, wie wir angenommen hatten. Daß wir uns also gleichsam in unsern eigenen Regeln verfangen.
    Dieses Verfangen in unsern Regeln ist, was wir verstehen, d. h. übersehen wollen.
    Es wirft ein Licht auf unsern Begriff des Meinens. Denn es kommt also in jenen Fällen anders, als wir es gemeint, vorausgesehen, hatten. Wir sagen eben, wenn, z. B., der Widerspruch auftritt: "So hab' ich's nicht gemeint."
    Die bürgerliche Stellung des Widerspruchs, oder seine Stellung in der bürgerlichen Welt: das ist das philosophische Problem.

126. Die Philosophie stellt eben alles bloß hin, und erklärt und folgert nichts. — Da alles offen daliegt, ist auch nichts zu erklären. Denn, was etwa verborgen ist, interessiert uns nicht.
    "Philosophie" könnte man auch das nennen, was *vor* allen neuen Entdeckungen und Erfindungen möglich ist.

127. Die Arbeit des Philosophen ist ein Zusammentragen von Erinnerungen zu einem bestimmten Zweck.

The concept of a surveyable representation is of fundamental significance for us. It characterizes the way we represent things, how we look at matters. (Is this a 'Weltanschauung'?)

123. A philosophical problem has the form: "I don't know my way about."

124. Philosophy must not interfere in any way with the actual use of language, so it can in the end only describe it.

For it cannot justify it either.

It leaves everything as it is.

* It also leaves mathematics as it is, and no mathematical discovery can advance it. A "leading problem of mathematical logic" is for us a problem of mathematics like any other. |50|

125. It is not the business of philosophy to resolve a contradiction by means of a mathematical or logico-mathematical discovery, but to render surveyable the state of mathematics that troubles us — the state of affairs *before* the contradiction is resolved. (And in doing this one is not sidestepping a difficulty.)

Here the fundamental fact is that we lay down rules, a technique, for playing a game, and that then, when we follow the rules, things don't turn out as we had assumed. So that we are, as it were, entangled in our own rules.

This entanglement in our rules is what we want to understand: that is, to survey.

It throws light on our concept of meaning something. For in those cases, things turn out otherwise than we had meant, foreseen. That is just what we say when, for example, a contradiction appears: "That's not the way I meant it."

The civic status of a contradiction, or its status in civic life — that is the philosophical problem.

126. Philosophy just puts everything before us, and neither explains nor deduces anything. — Since everything lies open to view, there is nothing to explain. For whatever may be hidden is of no interest to us.

The name "philosophy" might also be given to what is possible *before* all new discoveries and inventions.

* 127. The work of the philosopher consists in marshalling recollections for a particular purpose.

128. Wollte man *Thesen* in der Philosophie aufstellen, es könnte nie über sie zur Diskussion kommen, weil Alle mit ihnen einverstanden wären.

129. Die für uns wichtigsten Aspekte der Dinge sind durch ihre Einfachheit und Alltäglichkeit verborgen. (Man kann es nicht bemerken, — weil man es immer vor Augen hat.) Die eigentlichen Grundlagen seiner Forschung fallen dem Menschen gar nicht auf. Es sei denn, daß ihm *dies* einmal aufgefallen ist. — Und das heißt: das, was, einmal gesehen, das Auffallendste und Stärkste ist, fällt uns nicht auf.

130. Unsere klaren und einfachen Sprachspiele sind nicht Vorstudien zu einer künftigen Reglementierung der Sprache, — gleichsam erste Annäherungen, ohne Berücksichtigung der Reibung und des Luftwiderstands. Vielmehr stehen die Sprachspiele da als *Vergleichsobjekte*, die durch Ähnlichkeit und Unähnlichkeit ein Licht in die Verhältnisse unsrer Sprache werfen sollen.

131. Nur so nämlich können wir der Ungerechtigkeit, oder Leere unserer Behauptungen entgehen, indem wir das Vorbild als das, was es ist, als Vergleichsobjekt — sozusagen als Maßstab — hinstellen; und nicht als Vorurteil, dem die Wirklichkeit entsprechen *müsse*. (Der Dogmatismus, in den wir beim Philosophieren so leicht verfallen.)

132. Wir wollen in unserm Wissen vom Gebrauch der Sprache eine Ordnung herstellen: eine Ordnung zu einem bestimmten Zweck; eine von vielen möglichen Ordnungen; nicht *die* Ordnung. Wir werden zu diesem Zweck immer wieder Unterscheidungen *hervorheben*, die unsre gewöhnlichen Sprachformen leicht übersehen lassen. Dadurch kann es den Anschein gewinnen, als sähen wir es als unsre Aufgabe an, die Sprache zu reformieren.

So eine Reform für bestimmte praktische Zwecke, die Verbesserung unserer Terminologie zur Vermeidung von Mißverständnissen im praktischen Gebrauch, ist wohl möglich. Aber das sind nicht die Fälle, mit denen wir es zu tun haben. Die Verwirrungen, die uns beschäftigen, entstehen gleichsam, wenn die Sprache leerläuft, nicht wenn sie arbeitet.

133. Wir wollen nicht das Regelsystem für die Verwendung unserer Worte in unerhörter Weise verfeinern oder vervollständigen.

Denn die Klarheit, die wir anstreben, ist allerdings eine *vollkommene*. Aber das heißt nur, daß die philosophischen Probleme *vollkommen* verschwinden sollen.

128. If someone were to advance *theses* in philosophy, it would never be possible to debate them, because everyone would agree to them.

129. The aspects of things that are most important for us are hidden because of their simplicity and familiarity. (One is unable to notice something — because it is always before one's eyes.) The real foundations of their inquiry do not strike people at all. Unless *that* fact has at some time struck them. — And this means: we fail to be struck by what, once seen, is most striking and most powerful.

130. Our clear and simple language-games are not preliminary studies for a future regimentation of language — as it were, first approximations, ignoring friction and air resistance. Rather, the language-games stand there as *objects of comparison* which, through similarities and dissimilarities, are meant to throw light on features of our language. |51|

131. For we can avoid unfairness or vacuity in our assertions only by presenting the model as what it is, as an object of comparison — as a sort of yardstick; not as a preconception to which reality *must* conform. (The dogmatism into which we fall so easily in doing philosophy.)

132. We want to establish an order in our knowledge of the use of language: an order for a particular purpose, one out of many possible orders, not *the* order. For this purpose we shall again and again *emphasize* distinctions which our ordinary forms of language easily make us overlook. This may make it appear as if we saw it as our task to reform language.

Such a reform for particular practical purposes, an improvement in our terminology designed to prevent misunderstandings in practice, may well be possible. But these are not the cases we are dealing with. The confusions which occupy us arise when language is, as it were, idling, not when it is doing work.

133. We don't want to refine or complete the system of rules for the use of our words in unheard-of ways.

For the clarity that we are aiming at is indeed *complete* clarity. But this simply means that the philosophical problems should *completely* disappear.

Die eigentliche Entdeckung ist die, die mich fähig macht, das Philosophieren abzubrechen, wann ich will. — Die die Philosophie zur Ruhe bringt, so daß sie nicht mehr von Fragen gepeitscht wird, die *sie selbst* in Frage stellen. — Sondern es wird nun an Beispielen eine Methode gezeigt, und die Reihe dieser Beispiele kann man abbrechen. —— Es werden Probleme gelöst (Schwierigkeiten beseitigt), nicht *ein* Problem.

Es gibt nicht *eine* Methode der Philosophie, wohl aber gibt es Methoden, gleichsam verschiedene Therapien.

134. Betrachten wir den Satz: "Es verhält sich so und so" — wie kann ich sagen, dies sei die allgemeine Form des Satzes? — Es ist vor allem *selbst* ein Satz, ein deutscher Satz, denn es hat Subjekt und Prädikat. Wie aber wird dieser Satz angewendet — in unsrer alltäglichen Sprache nämlich? Denn nur *daher* habe ich ihn ja genommen.

Wir sagen z. B.: "Er erklärte mir seine Lage, sagte, es verhalte sich so und so und er brauche daher einen Vorschuß." Man kann also insofern sagen, jener Satz stünde für irgendwelche Aussagen. Er wird als Satz*schema* verwendet; aber das *nur*, weil er den Bau eines deutschen Satzes hat. Man könnte statt seiner ohneweiters auch sagen: "das und das ist der Fall", oder "so und so liegen die Sachen", etc. Man könnte auch, wie in der symbolischen Logik, bloß einen Buchstaben, eine Variable gebrauchen. Aber den Buchstaben "p" wird doch niemand die allgemeine Form eines Satzes nennen. Wie gesagt: "Es verhält sich so und so" war dies nur dadurch, daß es selbst das ist, was man einen deutschen Satz nennt. Aber obschon es ein Satz ist, so hat es doch nur als Satzvariable Verwendung. Zu sagen, dieser Satz stimme mit der Wirklichkeit überein (oder nicht überein) wäre offenbar Unsinn und er illustriert also dies, daß *ein* Merkmal unseres Satzbegriffes der *Satzklang* ist.

135. Aber haben wir denn nicht einen Begriff davon, was ein Satz ist, was wir unter "Satz" verstehen? — Doch; sofern wir auch einen Begriff davon haben, was wir unter "Spiel" verstehen. Gefragt, was ein Satz ist — ob wir nun einem Andern antworten sollen, oder uns selbst — werden wir Beispiele angeben und unter diesen auch, was man induktive Reihen von Sätzen nennen kann; nun, auf *diese* Weise haben wir einen Begriff vom Satz. (Vergleiche den Begriff des Satzes mit dem Begriff der Zahl.)

The real discovery is the one that enables me to break off philosophizing when I want to. — The one that gives philosophy peace, so that
it is no longer tormented by questions which bring *itself* in question.
— Instead, a method is now demonstrated by examples, and the series
of examples can be broken off. —— Problems are solved (difficulties eliminated), not a *single* problem.

---

*   There is not a single philosophical method, though there are
     indeed methods, different therapies, as it were. |§133d|

---

*   134. Let's examine the sentence "This is how things are". — How can
I say that this is the general form of propositions? — It is first and fore-
most *itself* a sentence, an English sentence, for it has a subject and a
predicate. But how is this sentence applied — that is, in our everyday
language? For I got it from *there*, and nowhere else.
   We say, for example, "He explained his position to me, said that this
was how things were, and that therefore he needed an advance". So
far, then, one can say that this sentence stands for some statement or
other. It is employed as a propositional *schema*, but *only* because it has
the |52| construction of an English sentence. One could easily say
instead "such-and-such is the case", "things are thus-and-so", and so
on. One could also simply use a letter, a variable, as in symbolic logic.
But surely no one is going to call the letter "p" the general form of
propositions. To repeat: "This is how things are" had that role only
because it is itself what one calls an English sentence. But though it is
a sentence, still it gets used as a propositional variable. To say that it
agrees (or does not agree) with reality would be obvious nonsense, and
so it illustrates the fact that one feature of our concept of a proposition is *sounding* like one.

135. But haven't we got a concept of what a proposition is, of what
we understand by "proposition"? — Indeed, we do; just as we also have
a concept of what we understand by "game". Asked what a proposition is — whether it is another person or ourselves that we have to answer
— we'll give examples, and these will include what one may call an induc-
tive series of propositions. So, it is in *this* way that we have a concept
of a proposition. (Compare the concept of a proposition with the concept of number.)

136. Im Grunde ist die Angabe von "Es verhält sich so und so" als allgemeine Form des Satzes das gleiche, wie die Erklärung: ein Satz sei
alles, was wahr oder falsch sein könne. Denn, statt "Es verhält sich
. . ." hätte ich auch sagen können: "Das und das ist wahr." (Aber auch:
"Das und das ist falsch.") Nun ist aber

'p' ist wahr = p
'p' ist falsch = nicht-p.

Und zu sagen, ein Satz sei alles, was wahr oder falsch sein könne, kommt
darauf hinaus: Einen Satz nennen wir das, worauf wir *in unserer
Sprache* den Kalkül der Wahrheitsfunktionen anwenden.

Es scheint nun, als bestimmte die Erklärung — Satz sei dasjenige, was
wahr oder falsch sein könne — was ein Satz ist, indem sie sage: Was
zum Begriff 'wahr' paßt, oder, worauf der Begriff 'wahr' paßt, das ist
ein Satz. Es ist also so, als hätten wir einen Begriff von wahr und falsch,
mit dessen Hilfe wir nun bestimmen können, was ein Satz ist und was
keiner. Was in den Begriff der Wahrheit *eingreift* (wie in ein Zahnrad),
das ist ein Satz.

Aber das ist ein schlechtes Bild. Es ist, als sagte man "Schachkönig
ist *die* Figur, der man Schach ansagen kann." Aber das kann doch nur
heißen, daß wir in unserm Schachspiel nur dem König Schach geben.
So wie der Satz, daß nur ein *Satz* wahr sein könne, nur sagen kann,
daß wir "wahr" und "falsch" nur von dem prädizieren, was wir einen
Satz nennen. Und was ein Satz ist, ist in *einem* Sinne bestimmt durch
die Regeln des Satzbaus (der deutschen Sprache z. B.), in einem andern
Sinne durch den Gebrauch des Zeichens im Sprachspiel. Und der
Gebrauch der Wörter "wahr" und "falsch" kann auch ein Bestandteil
dieses Spiels sein; und dann *gehört* er für uns zum Satz, aber er '*paßt*'
nicht zu ihm. Wie wir auch sagen können, das Schachgeben *gehöre* zu
unserm Begriff vom Schachkönig (gleichsam als ein Bestandteil dessel-
ben). Zu sagen, das Schachgeben *passe* nicht auf unsern Begriff von den
Bauern, würde heißen, daß ein Spiel, in welchem den Bauern Schach
gegeben wird, in welchem etwa der verliert, der seine Bauern verliert,
— daß ein solches Spiel uninteressant wäre, oder dumm, oder zu kom-
pliziert, oder dergleichen.

137. Wie ist es denn, wenn wir das Subjekt im Satz bestimmen lernen
durch die Frage "Wer oder was . . .?"? — Hier gibt es doch ein '*Passen*'
des Subjekts zu dieser Frage; denn wie erführen wir sonst durch die Frage,
was das Subjekt ist? Wir erfahren es in ähnlicher Weise, wie wir

136. At bottom, giving "This is how things are" as the general form of propositions is the same as giving the explanation: a proposition is whatever can be true or false. For instead of "This is how things are", I could just as well have said "Such-and-such is true". (Or again, "Such-and-such is false".) But

$$\text{'p' is true} = \text{p}$$
$$\text{'p' is false} = \text{not-p.}$$

And to say that a proposition is whatever can be true or false amounts to saying: we call something a proposition if *in our language* we apply the calculus of truth functions to it.

Now it looks as if the explanation — a proposition is whatever can be true or false — determined what a proposition was, by saying: what fits the concept 'true', or what the concept 'true' fits, is a proposition. So it is as if we had a concept of true and false, which we could use to ascertain what is, and what is not, a proposition. What *engages* with the concept of truth (as with a cog-wheel) is a proposition.

But this is a bad picture. It is as if one were to say "The chess king is *the* piece that one puts in check". But this can mean no more than that in our game of chess only the king is put in check. Just as the proposition that only a *proposition* can be true can say no more than |53| that we predicate "true" and "false" only of what we call a proposition. And what a proposition is, is in *one* sense determined by the rules of sentence formation (in English, for example), and in another sense by the use of the sign in the language-game. And the use of the words "true" and "false" may also be a constituent part of this game; and we treat it as *belonging* to our concept 'proposition', but it doesn't '*fit*' it. As we might also say, check *belongs* to our concept of the chess king (as, so to speak, a constituent part of it). To say that check did not *fit* our concept of the pawns would mean that a game in which pawns were checked, in which, say, the player who lost his pawns lost the game, would be uninteresting or stupid or too complicated or something of the kind.

137. What about learning to determine the subject of a sentence by means of the question "Who or what . . . ?" — Here, surely, there is such a thing as the subject's '*fitting*' this question; for otherwise how should we find out what the subject was by means of the question? We find it

erfahren, welcher Buchstabe im Alphabet nach dem 'K' kommt, indem
wir uns das Alphabet bis zum 'K' hersagen. Inwiefern paßt nun das 'L'
zu jener Buchstabenreihe? — Und insofern könnte man auch sagen,
"wahr" und "falsch" passe zum Satz; und man könnte ein Kind lehren,
Sätze von andern Ausdrücken zu unterscheiden, indem man ihm sagt:
"Frag dich, ob du danach sagen kannst 'ist wahr'. Wenn diese Worte
passen, so ist es ein Satz." (Und ebenso hätte man sagen können: Frage
dich, ob du davor die Worte "Es verhält sich *so*:" setzen kannst.)

138. Kann denn aber nicht die Bedeutung eines Worts, die ich verstehe,
zum Sinn des Satzes, den ich verstehe, passen? Oder die Bedeutung eines
Worts zur Bedeutung eines andern? —— Freilich, wenn die Bedeutung
der *Gebrauch* ist, den wir vom Worte machen, dann hat es keinen Sinn,
von so einem Passen zu reden. Nun *verstehen* wir aber die Bedeutung
eines Wortes, wenn wir es hören, oder aussprechen; wir erfassen sie mit
einem Schlage; und was wir so erfassen, ist doch etwas Andres, als der
in der Zeit ausgedehnte 'Gebrauch'!

Muß ich *wissen*, ob ich ein Wort verstehe? Geschieht es nicht auch,
daß ich mir *einbilde*, ein Wort zu verstehen (nicht anders, als eine
Rechnungsart zu verstehen) und nun darauf komme, daß ich es
nicht verstanden habe? ("Ich habe geglaubt, ich weiß, was 'rela-
tive' und 'absolute' Bewegung heißt, aber ich sehe, ich weiß es
nicht.")

139. Wenn mir jemand z. B. das Wort "Würfel" sagt, so weiß ich, was
es bedeutet. Aber kann mir denn die ganze *Verwendung* des Wortes
vorschweben, wenn ich es so *verstehe*?

Ja, wird aber anderseits die Bedeutung des Worts nicht auch durch
diese Verwendung bestimmt? Und können sich diese Bestimmungen nun
widersprechen? Kann, was wir so *mit einem Schlage* erfassen, mit einer
Verwendung übereinstimmen, zu ihr passen, oder nicht zu ihr passen?
Und wie kann das, was uns in einem Augenblicke gegenwärtig ist, was
uns in einem Augenblick vorschwebt, zu einer *Verwendung* passen?

Was ist es denn eigentlich, was uns vorschwebt, wenn wir ein Wort
verstehen? — Ist es nicht etwas, wie ein Bild? Kann es nicht ein Bild *sein*?

Nun, nimm an, beim Hören des Wortes "Würfel" schwebt dir ein
Bild vor. Etwa die Zeichnung eines Würfels. Inwiefern kann dies Bild

out much as we find out which letter of the alphabet comes after 'K' by saying the alphabet up to 'K' to ourselves. Now in what sense does 'L' fit this series of letters? — In *that* sense "true" and "false" could be said to fit propositions; and a child might be taught to distinguish propositions from other expressions by being told "Ask yourself if you can say 'is true' after it. If these words fit, it's a proposition". (And in the same way one might have said: Ask yourself if you can put the words "*This* is how things are:" in front of it.)

138. But can't the meaning of a word that I understand fit the sense of a sentence that I understand? Or the meaning of one word fit the meaning of another? —— Of course, if the meaning is the *use* we make of the word, it makes no sense to speak of such fitting. But we *understand* the meaning of a word when we hear or say it; we grasp the meaning at a stroke, and what we grasp in this way is surely something different from the 'use' which is extended in time! |54|

---

*

Must I *know* whether I understand a word? Don't I also sometimes *think* I understand a word (as I may think I understand a method of calculation) and then realize that I did not understand it? ("I thought I knew what 'relative' and 'absolute' motion meant, but I see that I don't know.") |p. 53 n.|

---

139. When someone says the word "cube" to me, for example, I know what it means. But can the whole *use* of the word come before my mind when I *understand* it in this way?

Yes; but on the other hand, isn't the meaning of the word also determined by this use? And can these ways of determining meaning conflict? Can what we grasp *at a stroke* agree with a use, fit or fail to fit it? And how can what is present to us in an instant, what comes before our mind in an instant, fit a *use*?

What really comes before our mind when we *understand* a word? — Isn't it something like a picture? Can't it *be* a picture?

Well, suppose that a picture does come before your mind when you hear the word "cube", say the drawing of a cube. In what way can this

zu einer Verwendung des Wortes "Würfel" passen, oder nicht zu ihr passen? — Vielleicht sagst du: "das ist einfach; — wenn mir dieses Bild vorschwebt und ich zeige z. B. auf ein dreieckiges Prisma und sage, dies sei ein Würfel, so paßt diese Verwendung nicht zum Bild." — Aber paßt sie nicht? Ich habe das Beispiel absichtlich so gewählt, daß es ganz leicht ist, sich eine *Projektionsmethode* vorzustellen, nach welcher das Bild nun doch paßt.

Das Bild des Würfels *legte* uns allerdings eine gewisse Verwendung *nahe*, aber ich konnte es auch anders verwenden.

a) "Ich glaube, das richtige Wort in diesem Fall ist . . .". Zeigt das nicht, daß die Bedeutung des Worts ein Etwas ist, das uns vorschwebt, und das gleichsam das genaue Bild ist, welches wir hier brauchen wollen? Denke, ich wählte zwischen den Wörtern "stattlich", "würdevoll", "stolz", "Achtung gebietend"; ist es nicht, als ob ich zwischen den Zeichnungen in einer Mappe wählte? — Nein; daß man vom *treffenden Wort* redet, *zeigt* nicht die Existenz eines Etwas, welches etc. Vielmehr ist man geneigt, von jenem bildartigen Etwas zu sprechen, weil man ein Wort als treffend empfinden kann; zwischen Worten oft, wie zwischen ähnlichen, aber doch nicht gleichen Bildern, wählt; weil man Bilder oft statt Wörtern, oder zur Illustration von Wörtern gebraucht; etc.

b) Ich sehe ein Bild: es stellt einen alten Mann dar, der auf einen Stock gestützt einen steilen Weg aufwärts geht. — Und wie das? Konnte es nicht auch so aussehen, wenn er in dieser Stellung die Straße hinunterrutschte? Ein Marsbewohner würde das Bild vielleicht so beschreiben. Ich brauche nicht zu erklären, warum *wir* es nicht so beschreiben.

140. Welcher Art war dann aber mein Irrtum; der, welchen man so ausdrücken möchte: ich hätte geglaubt, das Bild zwinge mich nun zu einer bestimmten Verwendung? Wie konnte ich denn das glauben? Was *habe* ich da geglaubt? Gibt es denn ein Bild, oder etwas einem Bild Ähnliches, das uns zu einer bestimmten Anwendung zwingt, und war mein Irrtum also eine Verwechslung? — Denn wir könnten geneigt sein, uns auch so auszudrücken: wir seien höchstens unter einem psychologischen Zwang, aber unter keinem logischen. Und da scheint es ja völlig, als kennten wir zweierlei Fälle.

picture fit or fail to fit a use of the word "cube"? — Perhaps you say: "It's quite simple; if that picture occurs to me and I point to a triangular prism for instance, and say it is a cube, then this use of the word doesn't fit the picture." — But doesn't it fit? I have purposely so chosen the example that it is quite easy to imagine *a method of projection* according to which the picture does fit after all.

The picture of the cube did indeed *suggest* a certain use to us, but it was also possible for me to use it differently. |55|

(*a*) "I believe the right word in this case is. . . ." Doesn't this show that the meaning of a word is a Something that we have in our mind and which is, as it were, the exact picture we want to use here? Suppose I were choosing between the words "stately", "dignified", "proud", "imposing"; isn't it as though I were choosing between drawings in a portfolio? — No; the fact that one speaks of the *apt word* does not *show* the existence of a Something that . . . One is inclined, rather, to speak of this picture-like Something because one can find a word apt; because one often chooses between words as between similar but not identical pictures; because pictures are often used instead of words, or to illustrate words, and so on.

(*b*) I see a picture; it represents an old man walking up a steep path leaning on a stick. — How? Might it not have looked just the same if he had been sliding downhill in that position? Perhaps a Martian would describe the picture so. I don't need to explain why *we* don't describe it so. |p. 54 n.|

---

140. Then what was the nature of my mistake — the mistake one would like to express by saying "I thought the picture forced a particular use on me?" How could I think that? What *did* I think? Is there a picture, or something like a picture, that forces a particular application on us; so that my mistake amounted to a confusion? — For we might also be inclined to express ourselves like this: we're at most under a psychological, not a logical, compulsion. And now, indeed, it looks as if we knew of two kinds of case.

Was tat denn mein Argument? Es machte darauf aufmerksam (erinnerte uns daran), daß wir unter Umständen bereit wären, auch einen andern Vorgang "Anwendung des Würfelbilds" zu nennen, als nur den, an welchen wir ursprünglich gedacht hatten. Unser 'Glaube, das Bild zwinge uns zu einer bestimmten Anwendung', bestand also darin, daß uns nur der eine Fall und kein andrer einfiel. "Es gibt auch eine andere Lösung" heißt: es gibt auch etwas Anderes, was ich bereit bin "Lösung" zu nennen; worauf ich bereit bin, das und das Bild, die und die Analogie anzuwenden, etc.

Und das Wesentliche ist nun, daß wir sehen, daß uns das Gleiche beim Hören des Wortes vorschwebt, und seine Anwendung doch eine andere sein kann. Und hat es dann beide Male die *gleiche* Bedeutung? Ich glaube, das werden wir verneinen.

141. Aber wie, wenn uns nicht einfach das Bild des Würfels, sondern dazu auch die Projektionsmethode vorschwebt? —— Wie soll ich mir das denken? — Etwa so, daß ich ein Schema der Projektionsart vor mir sehe. Ein Bild etwa, das zwei Würfel zeigt durch Projektionsstrahlen miteinander verbunden. — Aber bringt mich denn das wesentlich weiter? Kann ich mir nun nicht auch verschiedene Anwendungen dieses Schemas denken? —— Ja aber kann mir denn also nicht eine *Anwendung vorschweben*? — Doch; nur müssen wir uns über unsre Anwendung *dieses* Ausdrucks klarer werden. Nimm an, ich setze jemandem verschiedene Projektionsmethoden auseinander, damit er sie dann anwende; und fragen wir uns, in welchem Falle wir sagen werden, es schwebe ihm *die* Projektionsmethode vor, welche ich meine.

Wir erkennen dafür nun offenbar zweierlei Kriterien an: Einerseits das Bild (welcher Art immer es sei), welches ihm zu irgendeiner Zeit vorschwebt; anderseits die Anwendung, die er — im Laufe der Zeit — von dieser Vorstellung macht. (Und ist es hier nicht klar, daß es durchaus unwesentlich ist, daß dieses Bild ihm in der Phantasie vorschwebt, und nicht vielmehr als eine Zeichnung vor ihm liegt, oder als Modell; oder auch von ihm als Modell hergestellt wird?)

Können nun Bild und Anwendung kollidieren? Nun, sie können insofern kollidieren, als uns das Bild eine andere Verwendung erwarten läßt; weil die Menschen im allgemeinen von *diesem* Bild *diese* Anwendung machen.

Ich will sagen: Es gibt hier einen *normalen* Fall und abnormale Fälle.

142. Nur in normalen Fällen ist der Gebrauch der Worte uns klar vorgezeichnet; wir wissen, haben keinen Zweifel, was wir in diesem oder jenem Fall zu sagen haben. Je abnormaler der Fall, desto zweifelhafter

What was the effect of my argument? It called our attention to (reminded us of) the fact that there are other processes, besides the one we originally thought of, which we should sometimes be prepared to call "applying the picture of a cube". So our 'belief that the picture forced a particular application upon us' consisted in the fact that only the one case and no other occurred to us. "There is another solution as well" means: there is something else that I'm also prepared to call a "solution", to which I'm prepared to apply such-and-such a picture, such-and-such an analogy, and so on.

What is essential now is to see that the same thing may be in our minds when we hear the word and yet the application still be different. Has it the *same* meaning both times? I think we would deny that.

141. But what if not just the picture of the cube, but also the method of projection, comes before our mind? —— How am I to imagine this? — Perhaps I see before me a schema showing the method of projection: say, a picture of two cubes connected by lines of projection. — But does this really get me any further? Can't I now imagine different applications of this schema too? —— Well, yes, but can't an *application come before my mind*? — It can: only we need to become clearer about our application of *this* expression. Suppose I explain various methods of projection to someone, so that he may go on to apply them; let's ask ourselves in what case we'd say that the method I mean comes before his mind.

Now evidently we accept two different kinds of criteria for this: on the one hand, the picture (of whatever kind) that he visualizes at some time or other; on the other, the application which — in the course of time — he makes of this image. (And isn't it obvious here that it is absolutely inessential that this picture be in his imagination, rather than in front of him as a drawing or model; or again, as something that he himself constructs as a model?) |56|

Can there be a clash between picture and application? Well, they can clash in so far as the picture makes us expect a different use; because people in general apply *this* picture like *this*.

I want to say: we have here a *normal* case and abnormal cases.

142. It is only in normal cases that the use of a word is clearly laid out in advance for us; we know, are in no doubt, what we have to say in this or that case. The more abnormal the case, the more doubtful it

wird es, was wir nun hier sagen sollen. Und verhielten sich die Dinge ganz anders, als sie sich tatsächlich verhalten —— gäbe es z. B. keinen charakteristischen Ausdruck des Schmerzes, der Furcht, der Freude; würde, was Regel ist, Ausnahme und was Ausnahme, zur Regel; oder würden beide zu Erscheinungen von ungefähr gleicher Häufigkeit —— so verlören unsere normalen Sprachspiele damit ihren Witz. — Die Prozedur, ein Stück Käse auf die Waage zu legen und nach dem Ausschlag der Waage den Preis zu bestimmen, verlöre ihren Witz, wenn es häufiger vorkäme, daß solche Stücke ohne offenbare Ursache plötzlich anwüchsen, oder einschrumpften. Diese Bemerkung wird klarer werden, wenn wir über Dinge, wie das Verhältnis des Ausdrucks zum Gefühl und Ähnliches reden werden.

Was wir zur Erklärung der Bedeutung, ich meine der Wichtigkeit, eines Begriffs sagen müssen, sind oft außerordentlich allgemeine Naturtatsachen. Solche, die wegen ihrer großen Allgemeinheit kaum je erwähnt werden.

143. Betrachten wir nun diese Art von Sprachspiel: B soll auf den Befehl des A Reihen von Zeichen niederschreiben nach einem bestimmten Bildungsgesetz.

Die erste dieser Reihen soll die sein der natürlichen Zahlen im Dezimalsystem. — Wie lernt er dieses System verstehen? — Zunächst werden ihm Zahlenreihen vorgeschrieben und er wird angehalten, sie nachzuschreiben. (Stoß dich nicht an dem Wort "Zahlenreihen", es ist hier nicht unrichtig verwendet!) Und schon hier gibt es eine normale und eine abnormale Reaktion des Lernenden. — Wir führen ihm etwa zuerst beim Nachschreiben der Reihe 0 bis 9 die Hand; dann aber wird die *Möglichkeit der Verständigung* daran hängen, daß er nun selbständig weiterschreibt. — Und hier können wir uns, z. B., denken, daß er nun zwar selbständig Ziffern kopiert, aber nicht nach der Reihe, sondern regellos einmal die, einmal die. Und dann hört *da* die Verständigung auf. — Oder aber er macht 'Fehler' in der Reihenfolge. — Der Unterschied zwischen diesem und dem ersten Fall ist natürlich einer der Häufigkeit. — Oder: er macht einen *systematischen* Fehler, er schreibt z. B. immer nur jede zweite Zahl nach; oder er kopiert die Reihe 0, 1, 2, 3, 4, 5, . . . so: 1, 0, 3, 2, 5, 4, . . . Hier werden wir beinahe versucht sein zu sagen, er habe uns *falsch* verstanden.

Aber merke: Es gibt keine scharfe Grenze zwischen einem regellosen und einem systematischen Fehler. D. h., zwischen dem, was du einen "regellosen", und dem, was du einen "systematischen Fehler" zu nennen geneigt bist.

becomes what we are to say. And if things were quite different from what they actually are —— if there were, for instance, no characteristic expression of pain, of fear, of joy; if rule became exception, and exception rule; or if both became phenomena of roughly equal frequency —— our normal language-games would thereby lose their point. — The procedure of putting a lump of cheese on a balance and fixing the price by the turn of the scale would lose its point if it frequently happened that such lumps suddenly grew or shrank with no obvious cause. This remark will become clearer when we discuss such things as the relation of expression to feeling, and similar topics.

---

*

> What we have to mention in order to explain the significance, I mean the importance, of a concept are often extremely general facts of nature: such facts as are hardly ever mentioned because of their great generality. |p. 56 n.|

---

143. Let's now examine the following kind of language-game: when A gives an order, B has to write down series of signs according to a certain formation rule.

Let the first of these series be that of the natural numbers in the decimal system. — How does he come to understand this system? First of all, series of numbers are written down for him, and he is required to copy them. (Don't balk at the expression "series of numbers"; it is not being used wrongly here.) And here already there is a normal and an abnormal learner's reaction. — At first, perhaps, we guide his hand in writing out the series 0 to 9; but then the *possibility of communication* will depend on his going on to write it down by himself. — And here we may imagine, for example, that he does copy the figures by himself, but not in the right order: he writes sometimes one, sometimes another, at random. And at *that* point communication stops. — Or again, he makes '*mistakes*' |57| in the order. — The difference between this and the first case will of course be one of frequency. — Or he makes a *systematic* mistake; for example, he copies every other number, or he copies the series 0, 1, 2, 3, 4, 5, . . . like this: 1, 0, 3, 2, 5, 4, ... Here we shall almost be tempted to say that he has understood us *wrongly*.

Notice, however, that there is no sharp distinction between a random and a systematic mistake. That is, between what you are inclined to call a "random" and what a "systematic" one.

Man kann ihm nun vielleicht den systematischen Fehler abgewöhnen (wie eine Unart). Oder, man läßt seine Art des Kopierens gelten und trachtet, ihm die normale Art als eine Abart, Variation, der seinigen beizubringen. — Und auch hier kann die Lernfähigkeit unseres Schülers abbrechen.

144. Was meine ich denn, wenn ich sage "hier *kann* die Lernfähigkeit des Schülers abbrechen"? Teile ich das aus meiner Erfahrung mit? Natürlich nicht. (Auch wenn ich so eine Erfahrung gemacht hätte.) Und was tue ich denn mit jenem Satz? Ich möchte doch, daß du sagst: "Ja, es ist wahr, das könnte man sich auch denken, das könnte auch geschehen!" — Aber wollte ich Einen darauf aufmerksam machen, daß er imstande ist, sich dies vorzustellen? —— Ich wollte dies Bild vor seine Augen stellen, und seine *Anerkennung* dieses Bildes besteht darin, daß er nun geneigt ist, einen gegebenen Fall anders zu betrachten: nämlich ihn mit *dieser* Bilderreihe zu vergleichen. Ich habe seine *Anschauungsweise* geändert. [Indische Mathematiker: "Sieh dies an!"]

145. Der Schüler schreibe nun die Reihe 0 bis 9 zu unsrer Zufriedenheit. — Und dies wird nur der Fall sein, wenn ihm dies *oft* gelingt, nicht, wenn er es einmal unter hundert Versuchen richtig macht. Ich führe ihn nun weiter in der Reihe und lenke seine Aufmerksamkeit auf die Wiederkehr der ersten Reihe in den Einern; dann auf diese Wiederkehr in den Zehnern. (Was nur heißt, daß ich gewisse Betonungen anwende, Zeichen unterstreiche, in der und der Weise untereinander schreibe, und dergleichen.) — Und nun setzt er einmal die Reihe selbständig fort, — oder er tut es nicht. — Aber warum sagst du das; *das* ist selbstverständlich! — Freilich; ich wollte nur sagen: die Wirkung jeder weiteren *Erklärung* hänge von seiner *Reaktion* ab.

Aber nehmen wir nun an, er setzt, nach einigen Bemühungen des Lehrers, die Reihe richtig fort, d. h. so, wie wir es tun. Nun können wir also sagen: er beherrscht das System. — Aber wie weit muß er die Reihe richtig fortsetzen, damit wir das mit Recht sagen können? Es ist klar: du kannst hier keine Begrenzung angeben.

146. Wenn ich nun frage: "Hat er das System verstanden, wenn er die Reihe hundert Stellen weit fortsetzt?" Oder — wenn ich in unserm primitiven Sprachspiel nicht von 'verstehen' reden soll: Hat er das System inne, wenn er die Reihe bis *dorthin* richtig fortsetzt? — Da wirst du vielleicht sagen: Das System innehaben (oder auch, verstehen) kann nicht darin bestehen, daß man die Reihe bis zu *dieser*, oder bis zu *jener* Zahl fortsetzt; *das* ist nur die Anwendung des Verstehens. Das Verstehen selbst ist ein Zustand, *woraus* die richtige Verwendung entspringt.

Perhaps it is possible to wean him from the systematic mistake (as from a bad habit). Or perhaps one accepts his way of copying and tries to teach him the normal one as an offshoot, a variant of his. — And here too, our pupil's ability to learn may come to an end.

* 144. What do I mean when I say "the pupil's ability to learn *may* come to an end here"? Do I report this from my own experience? Of course not. (Even if I have had such experience.) Then what am I doing with that remark? After all, I'd like you to say: "Yes, it's true, one could imagine that too, that might happen too!" — But was I trying to draw someone's attention to the fact that he is able to imagine that? —— I wanted to put that picture before him, and his *acceptance* of the picture consists in his now being inclined to regard a given case differently: that is, to compare it with *this* sequence of pictures. I have changed his *way of looking at things*. (Indian mathematicians: "Look at this!")

145. Suppose the pupil now writes the series 0 to 9 to our satisfaction. — And this will be the case only if he is *often* successful, not if he does it right once in a hundred attempts. Now I continue to guide him through the series and draw his attention to the recurrence of the first series in the units; and then to its recurrence in the tens. (Which means only that I use particular emphases, underline figures, write them one under another in such-and-such ways, and similar things.) — And now at some point he continues the series by himself — or he does not. — But why do you say that? *That* much is obvious! — Of course; I only wished to say: the effect of any further *explanation* depends on his *reaction*.

Now, however, let us suppose that after some efforts on the teacher's part he continues the series correctly, that is, as we do it. So now we can say that he has mastered the system. — But how far does he have to continue |58| the series correctly for us to be able rightly to say that? Clearly, you cannot state a limit here.

146. Suppose I now ask: "Has he understood the system if he continues the series to the hundredth place?" Or, if I shouldn't speak of 'understanding' in our primitive language-game: has he got the system if he continues the series correctly up to *this* point? — Perhaps you will say here: to have got the system (or again, to understand it) can't consist in continuing the series up to *this* or *that* number: *that* is only applying one's understanding. Understanding itself is a state which is the *source* of the correct use.

Und an was denkt man da eigentlich? Denkt man nicht an das Ableiten einer Reihe aus ihrem algebraischen Ausdruck? Oder doch an etwas Analoges? — Aber da waren wir ja schon einmal. Wir können uns ja eben mehr als *eine* Anwendung eines algebraischen Ausdrucks denken; und jede Anwendungsart kann zwar wieder algebraisch niedergelegt werden, aber dies führt uns selbstverständlich nicht weiter. — Die Anwendung bleibt ein Kriterium des Verständnisses.

147. "Aber wie kann sie das sein? Wenn *ich* sage, ich verstehe das Gesetz einer Reihe, so sage ich es doch nicht auf Grund der *Erfahrung*, daß ich bis jetzt den algebraischen Ausdruck so und so angewandt habe! Ich weiß doch von mir selbst jedenfalls, daß ich die und die Reihe meine; gleichgültig, wie weit ich sie tatsächlich entwickelt habe." —
Du meinst also: du weißt die Anwendung des Gesetzes der Reihe, auch ganz abgesehen von einer Erinnerung an die tatsächlichen Anwendungen auf bestimmte Zahlen. Und du wirst vielleicht sagen: "Selbstverständlich! denn die Reihe ist ja unendlich und das Reihenstück, das ich entwickeln konnte, endlich."

148. Worin aber besteht dies Wissen? Laß mich fragen: *Wann* weißt du diese Anwendung? Immer? Tag und Nacht? oder nur während du gerade an das Gesetz der Reihe denkst? D. h.: Weißt du sie, wie du auch das ABC und das Einmaleins weißt; oder nennst du 'Wissen' einen Bewußtheitszustand oder Vorgang — etwa ein An-etwas-denken, oder dergleichen?

149. Wenn man sagt, das Wissen des ABC sei ein Zustand der Seele, so denkt man an den Zustand eines Seelenapparats (etwa unsres Gehirns), mittels welches wir die *Äußerungen* dieses Wissens erklären. Einen solchen Zustand nennt man eine Disposition. Es ist aber nicht einwandfrei, hier von einem Zustand der Seele zu reden, insofern es für den Zustand zwei Kriterien geben sollte; nämlich ein Erkennen der Konstruktion des Apparates, abgesehen von seinen Wirkungen. (Nichts wäre hier verwirrender, als der Gebrauch der Wörter "bewußt" und "unbewußt" für den Gegensatz von Bewußtseinszustand und Disposition. Denn jenes Wortpaar verhüllt einen grammatischen Unterschied.)

What is one really thinking of here? Isn't one thinking of the derivation of a series from its algebraic formula? Or at least of something analogous? — But this is where we were before. We can indeed think of more than *one* application of an algebraic formula; and while every mode of application can in turn be formulated algebraically, this, of course, does not get us any further. — The application is still a criterion of understanding.

147. "But how can it be? When *I* say I understand the rule of a series, I'm surely not saying so on the basis of the *experience* of having applied the algebraic formula in such-and-such a way! In my own case at any rate, I surely know that I mean such-and-such a series, no matter how far I've actually developed it." —

So you mean that you know the application of the rule of the series quite apart from remembering actual applications to particular numbers. And you'll perhaps say: "Of course! For the series is infinite, and the bit of it that I could develop finite."

148. But what does this knowledge consist in? Let me ask: *When* do you know that application? Always? Day and night? Or only while you are actually thinking of the rule of the series? Do you know it, that is, in the same way as you know the alphabet and the multiplication table? Or is what you call 'knowledge' a state of consciousness or a process — say a thinking-of-something, or the like?

149. If one says that knowing the ABC is a state of the mind, one is thinking of a state of an apparatus of the mind (perhaps a state of the brain) by means of which we explain the *manifestations* of that knowledge. Such a state is called a disposition. But it is not unobjectionable to speak |59| of a state of the mind here, inasmuch as there would then have to be two different criteria for this: finding out the structure of the apparatus, as distinct from its effects. (Nothing would be more confusing here than to use the words "conscious" and "unconscious" for the contrast between a state of consciousness and a disposition. For this pair of terms covers up a grammatical difference.)

a) 'Ein Wort verstehen', ein Zustand. Aber ein *seelischer* Zustand?
— Betrübnis, Aufregung, Schmerzen, nennen wir seelische Zustände.
Mache diese grammatische Betrachtung: Wir sagen
    "Er war den ganzen Tag betrübt"
    "Er war den ganzen Tag in großer Aufregung"
    "Er hatte seit gestern ununterbrochen Schmerzen". —
Wir sagen auch "Ich verstehe dieses Wort seit gestern". Aber "ununter-
brochen"? — Ja, man kann von einer Unterbrechung des
Verstehens reden. Aber in welchen Fällen? Vergleiche: "Wann
haben deine Schmerzen nachgelassen?" und "Wann hast du
aufgehört, das Wort zu verstehen?".

b) Wie, wenn man fragte: Wann *kannst* du Schach spielen?
Immer? oder während du einen Zug machst? Und während jedes
Zuges das ganze Schach? — Und wie seltsam, daß Schachspie-
lenkönnen so kurze Zeit braucht, und eine Partie so viel länger.

150. Die Grammatik des Wortes "wissen" ist offenbar eng verwandt
der Grammatik der Worte "können", "imstande sein". Aber auch eng
verwandt der des Wortes "verstehen". (Eine Technik 'beherrschen'.)

151. Nun gibt es aber auch *diese* Verwendung des Wortes "wissen": Wir
sagen "Jetzt weiß ich's!" — und ebenso "Jetzt kann ich's!" und "Jetzt
versteh ich's!".

    Stellen wir uns dieses Beispiel vor: A schreibt Reihen von Zahlen an;
B sieht ihm zu und trachtet, in der Zahlenfolge ein Gesetz zu finden.
Ist es ihm gelungen, so ruft er: "Jetzt kann ich fortsetzen!" —— Diese
Fähigkeit, dieses Verstehen ist also etwas, was in einem Augenblick ein-
tritt. Schauen wir also nach: Was ist es, was hier eintritt? — A habe die
Zahlen 1, 5, 11, 19, 29 hingeschrieben; da sagt B, jetzt wisse er weiter.
Was geschah da? Es konnte verschiedenerlei geschehen sein; z. B.:
Während A langsam eine Zahl nach der andern hinsetzte, ist B damit
beschäftigt, verschiedene algebraische Formeln an den angeschriebenen
Zahlen zu versuchen. Als A die Zahl 19 geschrieben hatte, versuchte B
die Formel $a_n = n^2 + n - 1$; und die nächste Zahl bestätigte seine Annahme.

    Oder aber: B denkt nicht an Formeln. Er sieht mit einem gewissen
Gefühl der Spannung zu, wie A seine Zahlen hinschreibt; dabei
schwimmen ihm allerlei unklare Gedanken im Kopf. Endlich fragt er
sich "Was ist die Reihe der Differenzen?". Er findet: 4, 6, 8, 10 und
sagt: Jetzt kann ich weiter.

*

(a) "Understanding a word": a state. But a *mental* state? — We call dejection, excitement, pain, mental states. Carry out a grammatical investigation as follows: we say

"He felt dejected the whole day"

"He was in great excitement the whole day"

"He has been in pain uninterruptedly since yesterday". —
We also say, "Since yesterday I have understood this word."
'Uninterruptedly', though? — To be sure, one can speak of an interruption of understanding. But in what cases? Compare: "When did your pains get less?" and "When did you stop understanding that word?"

(b) What if one asked: When *can* you play chess? All the time? Or just while you are making a move? And the whole of chess during each move? — And how odd that being able to play chess should take such a short time, and a game so much longer! |p. 59 n.|

150. The grammar of the word "know" is evidently closely related to the grammar of the words "can", "is able to". But also closely related to that of the word "understand". (To have 'mastered' a technique.)

151. But there is also *this* use of the word "know": we say "Now I know!" — and similarly, "Now I can do it!" and "Now I understand!"

Let us imagine the following example: A writes down series of numbers; B watches him and tries to find a rule for the number series. If he succeeds, he exclaims: "Now I can go on!" —— So this ability, this understanding, is something that occurs in a moment. So let us have a look: what is it that occurs here? — A has written down the numbers 1, 5, 11, 19, 29; at this point B says he knows how to go on. What happened here? Various things may have happened; for example, while A was slowly writing down one number after another, B was busy trying out various algebraic formulae on the numbers which had been written down. After A had written the number 19, B tried the formula $a_n = n^2 + n - 1$; and the next number confirmed his supposition. |60|

Or again, B does not think of formulae. He watches, with a certain feeling of tension, how A writes his numbers down, while all sorts of vague thoughts float through his head. Finally he asks himself, "What is the series of differences?" He finds: 4, 6, 8, 10, and says: "Now I can go on."

Oder er sieht hin und sagt: "Ja, *die* Reihe kenn' ich" — und setzt sie
fort; wie er's etwa auch getan hätte, wenn A die Reihe 1, 3, 5, 7, 9
hingeschrieben hätte. — Oder er sagt gar nichts und schreibt bloß die
Reihe weiter. Vielleicht hatte er eine Empfindung, die man "das ist leicht!"
nennen kann. (Eine solche Empfindung ist z. B. die eines leichten, schnellen
Einziehens des Atems, ähnlich wie bei einem gelinden Schreck.)

152. Aber sind denn diese Vorgänge, die ich da beschrieben habe, das
Verstehen?
    "B versteht das System der Reihe" heißt doch nicht einfach: B fällt
die Formel "$a_n = \ldots$" ein! Denn es ist sehr wohl denkbar, daß ihm die
Formel einfällt und er doch nicht versteht. "Er versteht" muß mehr bein-
halten als: ihm fällt die Formel ein. Und ebenso auch mehr, als irgendeiner jener, mehr oder weniger charakteristischen, *Begleitvorgänge*, oder
Äußerungen, des Verstehens.

153. Wir versuchen nun, den seelischen Vorgang des Verstehens, der sich,
scheint es, hinter jenen gröbern und uns daher in die Augen fallenden
Begleiterscheinungen versteckt, zu erfassen. Aber das gelingt nicht.
Oder, richtiger gesagt: es kommt gar nicht zu einem wirklichen
Versuch. Denn auch angenommen, ich hätte etwas gefunden, was in allen
jenen Fällen des Verstehens geschähe, — warum sollte *das* nun das
Verstehen sein? Ja, wie konnte denn der Vorgang des Verstehens ver-
steckt sein, wenn ich doch sagte "Jetzt verstehe ich", *weil* ich verstand?!
Und wenn ich sage, er ist versteckt, — wie weiß ich denn, wonach ich
zu suchen habe? Ich bin in einem Wirrwarr.

154. Aber halt! — wenn "jetzt verstehe ich das System" nicht das
Gleiche sagt, wie "mir fällt die Formel . . . ein" (oder "ich spreche die
Formel aus", "ich schreibe sie auf", etc.) — folgt daraus, daß ich den
Satz "jetzt verstehe ich . . .", oder "jetzt kann ich fortsetzen", als
Beschreibung eines Vorgangs verwende, der hinter, oder neben dem des
Aussprechens der Formel besteht?
    Wenn etwas 'hinter dem Aussprechen der Formel' stehen muß, so sind
es *gewisse Umstände*, die mich berechtigen, zu sagen, ich könne fort-
setzen, — wenn mir die Formel einfällt.
    Denk doch einmal gar nicht an das Verstehen als 'seelischen
Vorgang'! — Denn *das* ist die Redeweise, die dich verwirrt. Sondern frage
dich: in was für einem Fall, unter was für Umständen sagen wir denn
"Jetzt weiß ich weiter"? ich meine, wenn mir die Formel eingefallen
ist. —

Or he watches and says, "Yes, I know *that* series" — and continues it, just as he would have done if A had written down the series 1, 3, 5, 7, 9. — Or he says nothing at all and simply continues the series. Perhaps he had what may be called the feeling "That's easy!" (Such a feeling is, for example, that of a light quick intake of breath, as when one is slightly startled.)

152. But are the processes which I've described here *understanding*?

"B understands the system behind the series" surely doesn't mean simply: the formula "$a_n = \ldots$" occurs to B. For it is perfectly conceivable that the formula should occur to him and that he should nevertheless not understand. "He understands" must have more to it than: the formula occurs to him. And equally, more than any of those more or less characteristic *concomitant processes* or manifestations of understanding.

153. Now we try to get hold of the mental process of understanding which seems to be hidden behind those coarser, and therefore more readily visible, concomitant phenomena. But it doesn't work; or, more correctly, it does not get as far as a real attempt. For even supposing I had found something that happened in all those cases of understanding, why should *that* be the understanding? Indeed, how can the process of understanding have been hidden, given that I said "Now I understand" because I *did* understand? And if I say it is hidden — then how do I know what I have to look for? I am in a muddle.

154. But wait! — if "Now I understand the system" does not mean the same as "The formula . . . occurs to me" (or "I utter the formula", "I write it down", etc.) — does it follow from this that I employ the sentence "Now I understand" or "Now I can go on" as a description of a process occurring behind or side by side that of uttering the formula?

If something has to stand 'behind the utterance of the formula', it is *particular circumstances*, which warrant my saying that I can go on — if the formula occurs to me. |61|

Just for once, don't think of understanding as a 'mental process' at all! — For *that* is the way of talking which confuses you. Instead, ask yourself: in what sort of case, in what kind of circumstances, do we say "Now I know how to go on"? I mean, if the formula has occurred to me. —

In dem Sinne, in welchem es für das Verstehen charakteristische
Vorgänge (auch seelische Vorgänge) gibt, ist das Verstehen kein seelischer Vorgang.

(Das Ab- und Zunehmen einer Schmerzempfindung, das Hören einer
Melodie, eines Satzes: seelische Vorgänge.)

155. Ich wollte also sagen: Wenn er plötzlich weiter wußte, das System
verstand, so hatte er vielleicht ein besonderes Erlebnis — welches er etwa
beschreiben wird, wenn man ihn fragt "Wie war das, was ging da vor,
als du das System plötzlich begriffst?", ähnlich wie wir es oben
beschrieben haben —— das aber, was ihn für uns berechtigt, in so einem
Fall zu sagen, er verstehe, er wisse weiter, sind die *Umstände*, unter denen
er ein solches Erlebnis hatte.

156. Dies wird klarer werden, wenn wir die Betrachtung eines andern
Wortes einschalten, nämlich des Wortes "*lesen*". Zuerst muß ich
bemerken, daß ich zum 'Lesen', in dieser Betrachtung, nicht das
Verstehen des Sinns des Gelesenen rechne; sondern Lesen ist hier die
Tätigkeit, Geschriebenes oder Gedrucktes in Laute umzusetzen; auch aber,
nach Diktat zu schreiben, Gedrucktes abzuschreiben, nach Noten zu spielen und dergleichen.

Der Gebrauch dieses Worts unter den Umständen unsres gewöhnlichen
Lebens ist uns natürlich ungemein wohl bekannt. Die Rolle aber, die
das Wort in unserm Leben spielt, und damit das Sprachspiel, in dem
wir es verwenden, wäre schwer auch nur in groben Zügen darzustellen.
Ein Mensch, sagen wir ein Deutscher, ist in der Schule, oder zu Hause,
durch eine der bei uns üblichen Unterrichtsarten gegangen, er hat in
diesem Unterricht seine Muttersprache lesen gelernt. Später liest er Bücher,
Briefe, die Zeitung, u. a.

Was geht nun vor sich, wenn er, z. B., die Zeitung liest? — Seine
Augen gleiten — wie wir sagen — den gedruckten Wörtern entlang, er
spricht sie aus, — oder sagt sie nur zu sich selbst; und zwar gewisse
Wörter, indem er ihre Druckform als Ganzes erfaßt, andere, nachdem
sein Aug die ersten Silben erfaßt hat, einige wieder liest er Silbe für Silbe,
und das eine oder andre vielleicht Buchstabe für Buchstabe. — Wir würden auch sagen, er habe einen Satz gelesen, wenn er während des Lesens
weder laut noch zu sich selbst spricht, aber danach imstande ist, den
Satz wörtlich oder annähernd wiederzugeben. — Er kann auf das
achten, was er liest, oder auch — wie wir sagen könnten — als bloße
Lesemaschine funktionieren, ich meine, laut und richtig lesen, ohne auf
das, was er liest, zu achten; vielleicht während seine Aufmerksamkeit
auf etwas ganz anderes gerichtet ist (so daß er nicht imstande ist, zu
sagen, was er gelesen hat, wenn man ihn gleich darauf fragt).

In the sense in which there are processes (including mental processes) which are characteristic of understanding, understanding is not
a mental process.

(A pain's increasing or decreasing, listening to a tune or a sentence
— mental processes.)

155. So, what I wanted to say was: if he suddenly knew how to go on,
if he understood the system, then he may have had a distinctive experience — and if he is asked: "What was it? What took place when you
suddenly grasped the system?", perhaps he will describe it much as we
described it above —— but for us it is the *circumstances* under which he
had such an experience that warrant him saying in such a case that he
understands, that he knows how to go on.

156. This will become clearer if we interpolate an examination of
another word: namely, *"reading"*. First I must note that I'm not count-
ing the understanding of what is read as part of 'reading' for purposes
of this examination: reading is here the activity of rendering out loud
what is written or printed; but also of writing from dictation, copying
something printed, playing from sheet music, and so on.

The use of this word in the circumstances of our ordinary life is
of course extremely familiar to us. But the part the word plays in
our life, and so too the language-game in which we employ it, would
be difficult to describe even in rough outline. A person, let's say an
Englishman, has received at school or at home one of the kinds of instruction usual among us, and in the course of it has learned to read
his native language. Later he reads books, letters, newspapers, and so
forth.

Now what goes on when, say, he reads a newspaper? —— His
eye passes — as we say — along the printed words; he says them out
loud — or only to himself; that is, he reads certain words by taking
in their printed shapes as wholes, others when his eye has taken in
the first syllables; others again he reads syllable by syllable, and an
occasional one perhaps letter by letter. — We would also say that he
had read a sentence if he spoke neither aloud nor to himself during
the reading, but was afterwards able to repeat the sentence word for
word or nearly so. — He may attend to what he reads, or again — as
we |62| might put it — function as a mere reading-machine: I mean, read
aloud and correctly without attending to what he is reading; perhaps
with his attention on something quite different (so that he is unable
to say what he has been reading if he is asked about it immediately
afterwards).

Vergleiche nun mit diesem Leser einen Anfänger. Er liest die Wörter, indem er sie mühsam buchstabiert. — Einige Wörter aber errät er aus dem Zusammenhang; oder er weiß das Lesestück vielleicht zum Teil schon auswendig. Der Lehrer sagt dann, daß er die Wörter nicht wirklich *liest* (und in gewissen Fällen, daß er nur vorgibt, sie zu lesen).

Wenn wir an *dieses* Lesen, an das Lesen des Anfängers, denken und uns fragen, worin *Lesen* besteht, werden wir geneigt sein, zu sagen: es sei eine besondere bewußte geistige Tätigkeit.

Wir sagen von dem Schüler auch: "Nur er weiß natürlich, ob er wirklich liest, oder die Worte bloß auswendig sagt." (Über diese Sätze "Nur *er* weiß, . . ." muß noch geredet werden.)

Ich will aber sagen: Wir müssen zugeben, daß — was das Aussprechen irgend *eines* der gedruckten Wörter betrifft — im Bewußtsein des Schülers, der 'vorgibt' es zu lesen, das Gleiche stattfinden kann, wie im Bewußtsein des geübten Lesers, der es 'liest'. Das Wort "lesen" wird *anders* angewandt, wenn wir vom Anfänger, und wenn wir vom geübten Leser sprechen. —— Wir möchten nun freilich sagen: Was im geübten Leser und was im Anfänger vor sich geht, wenn sie das Wort aussprechen, *kann* nicht das Gleiche sein. Und wenn kein Unterschied in dem wäre, was ihnen gerade bewußt ist, so im unbewußten Arbeiten ihres Geistes; oder auch im Gehirn. — Wir möchten also sagen: Hier sind jedenfalls zwei verschiedene Mechanismen! Und was in ihnen vorgeht, muß Lesen von Nichtlesen unterscheiden. — Aber diese Mechanismen sind doch nur Hypothesen; Modelle zur Erklärung, zur Zusammenfassung dessen, was du wahrnimmst.

157. Überlege dir folgenden Fall: Menschen, oder andere Wesen, würden von uns als Lesemaschinen benützt. Sie werden zu diesem Zweck abgerichtet. Der, welcher sie abrichtet, sagt von Einigen, sie können schon lesen, von Andern, sie könnten es noch nicht. Nimm den Fall eines Schülers, der bisher nicht mitgetan hat: zeigt man ihm ein geschriebenes Wort, so wird er manchmal irgendwelche Laute hervorbringen, und hie und da geschieht es dann 'zufällig', daß sie ungefähr stimmen. Ein Dritter hört diesen Schüler in so einem Fall und sagt "Er liest". Aber der Lehrer sagt: "Nein, er liest nicht; es war nur ein Zufall." — Nehmen wir aber an, dieser Schüler, wenn ihm nun weitere Wörter vorgelegt werden, reagiert auf sie fortgesetzt richtig. Nach einiger Zeit sagt der Lehrer: "Jetzt kann er lesen!" — Aber wie war es mit jenem ersten Wort? Soll der Lehrer sagen: "Ich hatte mich geirrt, er hat es *doch* gelesen" — oder: "Er hat erst später angefangen, wirklich zu lesen"? — Wann hat er angefangen, zu lesen? Welches ist das

Now compare a beginner with this reader. The beginner reads the words by laboriously spelling them out. — Some words, however, he guesses from the context, or perhaps he already partly knows the passage by heart. Then his teacher says that he is not really *reading* the words (and in certain cases that he is only pretending to read them).

If we think of *this* sort of reading, the reading of a beginner, and ask ourselves what *reading* consists in, we'll be inclined to say: it is a distinctive conscious mental activity.

We also say of the pupil: "Of course, only he knows if he is really reading or merely saying the words off by heart." (We've yet to discuss these propositions: "Only *he* knows . . .")

But I want to say: we have to admit that — as far as concerns uttering any one of the printed words — the same thing may take place in the mind of the pupil who is 'pretending' to read as in that of a practised reader who is 'reading' it. The word "read" is applied *differently* when we are speaking of the beginner and of the practised reader. —— Now we would, of course, like to say: What goes on in the practised reader and in the beginner when they utter the word *can't* be the same. And if there is no difference in what they are currently conscious of, there must be one in the unconscious workings of their minds, or, again, in the brain. — So we'd like to say: There are, at any rate, two different mechanisms here! And what goes on in them must distinguish reading from not reading. — But these mechanisms are only hypotheses, models to explain, to sum up, what you observe.

157. Consider the following case: we use human beings, or creatures of some other kind, as reading-machines. They are trained for this purpose. The trainer says of some that they can already read, of others that they cannot yet do so. Take the case of a pupil who has so far not participated in the training: if he is shown a written word, he will sometimes produce random sounds, and now and again the sounds will 'accidentally' come out roughly right. A third person hears this pupil on such an occasion and says, "He is reading". But the teacher says, "No, he isn't reading; that was just an accident". — But let's suppose that this pupil continues to react correctly to further words |63| that are put before him. After a while, the teacher says, "Now he can read!" — But what of that first word? Is the teacher to say, "I was wrong, he *did* read it after all" — or, "He only began really to read later on"? — When did he begin to read? Which was the first word that he *read*? This

erste Wort, das er *gelesen* hat? Diese Frage ist hier sinnlos. Es sei denn, wir erklärten: "Das erste Wort, das Einer 'liest', ist das erste Wort der ersten Reihe von 50 Wörtern, die er richtig liest" (oder dergl.).

Verwenden wir dagegen "Lesen" für ein gewisses Erlebnis des Übergangs vom Zeichen zum gesprochenen Laut, dann hat es wohl Sinn, von einem *ersten* Wort zu sprechen, das er wirklich gelesen hat. Er kann dann etwa sagen: "Bei diesem Worte hatte ich zum ersten Male das Gefühl: 'jetzt lese ich'."

Oder aber in dem hievon verschiedenen Fall einer Lesemaschine, die, etwa nach Art eines Pianolas, Zeichen in Laute übersetzt, könnte man sagen: "Erst nachdem dies und dies an der Maschine geschehen war — die und die Teile durch Drähte verbunden worden waren — hat die Maschine *gelesen*; das erste Zeichen, welches sie gelesen hat, war . . ."

Im Falle aber der lebenden Lesemaschine hieß "lesen": so und so auf Schriftzeichen reagieren. Dieser Begriff war also ganz unabhängig von dem eines seelischen, oder andern Mechanismus. — Der Lehrer kann hier auch vom Abgerichteten nicht sagen: "Vielleicht hat er dieses Wort schon gelesen." Denn es ist ja kein Zweifel über das, was er getan hat. — Die Veränderung, als der Schüler zu lesen anfing, war eine Veränderung seines *Verhaltens*; und von einem 'ersten Wort im neuen Zustand' zu reden, hat hier keinen Sinn.

158. Aber liegt dies nicht nur an unserer zu geringen Kenntnis der Vorgänge im Gehirn und im Nervensystem? Wenn wir diese genauer kennten, würden wir sehen, welche Verbindungen durch das Abrichten hergestellt worden waren, und wir könnten dann, wenn wir ihm ins Gehirn sähen, sagen: "Dieses Wort hat er jetzt *gelesen*, jetzt war die Leseverbindung hergestellt." —— Und das *muß* wohl so sein — denn wie könnten wir sonst so sicher sein, daß es eine solche Verbindung gibt? Das ist wohl a priori so — oder ist es nur wahrscheinlich? Und wie wahrscheinlich ist es? Frag dich doch: was *weißt* du denn von diesen Sachen? —— Ist es aber a priori, dann heißt das, daß es eine uns sehr einleuchtende Darstellungsform ist.

159. Aber wir sind, wenn wir darüber nachdenken, versucht zu sagen: das einzig wirkliche Kriterium dafür, daß Einer *liest*, ist der bewußte Akt des Lesens, des Ablesens der Laute von den Buchstaben. "Ein Mensch weiß doch, ob er liest, oder nur vorgibt, zu lesen!" — Angenommen, A will den B glauben machen, er könne cyrillische Schrift lesen. Er lernt einen russischen Satz auswendig und sagt ihn dann, indem er die gedruckten Wörter ansieht, als läse er sie. Wir werden hier gewiß sagen, A wisse, daß er nicht liest, und er empfinde, während er zu lesen

question makes no sense here. Unless, indeed, we stipulate: "The first word that a person 'reads' is the first word of the first series of 50 words that he reads correctly" (or something of the sort).

If, on the other hand, we use "reading" to stand for a certain experience of transition from marks to spoken sounds, then it certainly makes sense to speak of the *first* word that he really read. He can then say, for example, "At this word, for the first time, I had the feeling: 'now I am reading'."

Or again, in the different case of a reading-machine which translated marks into sounds, perhaps as a pianola does, it would be possible to say: "The machine *read* only after such-and-such had happened to it — after such-and-such parts had been connected by wires; the first word that it read was . . ."

But in the case of the live reading-machine, "reading" meant: reacting to written signs in such-and-such ways. So this concept was quite independent of that of a mental or other mechanism. — Nor can the teacher here say of the trainee, "Perhaps he was already reading when he said that word". For there is no doubt about what he did. — The change when the pupil began to read was a change in his *behaviour*; and it makes no sense here to speak of 'a first word in his new state'.

158. But isn't that only because of our too slight acquaintance with what goes on in the brain and the nervous system? If we had a more accurate knowledge of these things, we would see what connections were established by the training, and then when we looked into his brain, we would be able to say: "Now he has *read* this word, now the reading connection has been set up." —— And it presumably *must* be like that — for otherwise how could we be so sure that there was such a connection? That it is so is presumably a priori — or is it only probable? And how probable is it? Now, ask yourself: what do you *know* about these things? —— But if it is a priori, that means that it is a form of representation which is very appealing to us.

159. But when we think the matter over, we're tempted to say: the one real criterion for anybody's *reading* is the conscious act of reading, the act of reading the sounds off from the letters. "A man |64| surely knows whether he is reading or only pretending to read!" — Suppose A wants to make B believe that he can read Cyrillic script. He learns a Russian sentence by heart and utters it while looking at the printed words as if he were reading them. Here we'll surely say that A knows he is not

vorgibt, eben dies. Denn es gibt natürlich eine Menge für das Lesen eines Satzes im Druck mehr oder weniger charakteristische Empfindungen; es ist nicht schwer, sich solche ins Gedächtnis zu rufen: denke an Empfindungen des Stockens, genauern Hinsehens, Verlesens, der größeren und geringeren Geläufigkeit der Wortfolgen, u. a. Und ebenso gibt es charakteristische Empfindungen für das Aufsagen von etwas Auswendiggelerntem. Und A wird in unserm Fall keine von den Empfindungen haben, die für das Lesen charakteristisch sind, und er wird etwa eine Reihe von Empfindungen haben, die für das Schwindeln charakteristisch sind.

160. Denke dir aber diesen Fall: Wir geben Einem, der fließend lesen kann, einen Text zu lesen, den er nie zuvor gesehen hat. Er liest ihn uns vor — aber mit der Empfindung, als sage er etwas Auswendiggelerntes (dies könnte die Wirkung irgendeines Giftes sein). Würden wir in einem solchen Falle sagen, er lese das Stück nicht wirklich? Würden wir hier also seine Empfindungen als Kriterium dafür gelten lassen, ob er liest oder nicht?

Oder aber: Wenn man einem Menschen, der unter dem Einfluß eines bestimmten Giftes steht, eine Reihe von Schriftzeichen vorlegt, die keinem existierenden Alphabet anzugehören brauchen, so spreche er nach der Anzahl der Zeichen Wörter aus, so als wären die Zeichen Buchstaben, und zwar mit allen äußeren Merkmalen und Empfindungen des Lesens. (Ähnliche Erfahrungen haben wir in Träumen; nach dem Aufwachen sagt man dann etwa: "Es kam mir vor, als läse ich die Zeichen, obwohl es gar keine Zeichen waren.") In so einem Fall würden Manche geneigt sein, zu sagen, der Mensch *lese* diese Zeichen. Andere, er lese sie nicht. — Angenommen, er habe auf diese Weise eine Gruppe von vier Zeichen als OBEN gelesen (oder gedeutet) — nun zeigen wir ihm die gleichen Zeichen in umgekehrter Reihenfolge und er liest NEBO, und so behält er in weiteren Versuchen immer die gleiche Deutung der Zeichen bei: hier wären wir wohl geneigt, zu sagen, er lege sich ad hoc ein Alphabet zurecht und lese dann danach.

161. Bedenke nun auch, daß es eine kontinuierliche Reihe von Übergängen gibt zwischen dem Falle, in welchem jemand das auswendig hersagt, was er lesen soll, und dem, in welchem er jedes Wort Buchstabe für Buchstabe liest, ohne jede Hilfe des Erratens aus dem Zusammenhang, oder des Auswendigwissens.

Mach diesen Versuch: sag die Zahlenreihe von 1 bis 12. Nun schau auf das Zifferblatt deiner Uhr und *lies* diese Reihe. — Was hast du in diesem Falle "lesen" genannt? Das heißt: was hast du getan, um es zum *Lesen* zu machen?

reading, and has a sense of just this while pretending to read. For there are, of course, many feelings more or less characteristic of reading a printed sentence; it is not difficult to recall such feelings: think of feelings of hesitating, of looking more closely, of misreading, of words following on one another in a more or less familiar fashion, and so on. And equally, there are feelings characteristic of reciting something one has learnt by heart. In our example, A will have none of the feelings that are characteristic of reading, and will perhaps have various feelings characteristic of cheating.

160. But imagine the following case: we give someone who can read fluently a text that he has never seen before. He reads it to us — but with the feeling of saying something he has learnt by heart (this might be the effect of some drug). Would we say in such a case that he was not really reading the passage? That is, would we here allow his feelings to count as a criterion for his reading or not reading?

Or again, suppose that a man who is under the influence of a certain drug is presented with a series of written signs (which need not belong to any existing alphabet). He utters words corresponding to the number of the signs, as if they were letters, and does so with all the outward characteristics and feelings of reading. (We have experiences like this in dreams; after waking up in such a case, one says perhaps: "It seemed to me as if I were reading signs, though they weren't really signs at all.") In such a case, some people would be inclined to say the man was *reading* those signs. Others, that he was not. — Suppose he has in this way read (or interpreted) a set of five signs as A B O V E — and now we show him the same signs in the reverse order and he reads E V O B A; and in further tests he always retains the same interpretation of the signs: here we may well be inclined to say that he was making up an alphabet for himself *ad hoc* and then reading accordingly.

161. Remember too that there is a continuous series of transitional cases between that in which a person repeats from memory what he is supposed to be reading and that in which he spells out every word without being helped at all by guessing from the context or knowing by heart. |65|

Try this experiment: say the numbers from 1 to 12. Now look at the dial of your watch and *read* them. — What was it that you called "reading" in the latter case? That is to say, what did you do, to make it into *reading*?

162. Versuchen wir diese Erklärung: Jemand liest, wenn er die Repro-
duktion von der Vorlage *ableitet*. Und 'Vorlage' nenne ich den Text,
welchen er liest, oder abschreibt; das Diktat, nach welchem er schreibt;
die Partitur, die er spielt; etc. etc. — Wenn wir nun z. B. jemand das
cyrillische Alphabet gelehrt hätten und wie jeder Buchstabe auszusprechen
sei, — wenn wir ihm dann ein Lesestück vorlegen und er liest es, indem
er jeden Buchstaben so ausspricht, wie wir es ihn gelehrt haben, — dann
werden wir wohl sagen, er leite den Klang eines Wortes vom Schriftbild
mit Hilfe der Regel, die wir ihm gegeben haben, ab. Und dies ist auch
ein klarer Fall des *Lesens*. (Wir könnten sagen, wir haben ihn die 'Regel
des Alphabets' gelehrt.)

Aber warum sagen wir, er habe die gesprochenen Worte von den
gedruckten *abgeleitet*? Wissen wir mehr, als daß wir ihn gelehrt haben,
wie jeder Buchstabe auszusprechen sei, und daß er dann die Worte laut
gelesen habe? Wir werden vielleicht antworten: der Schüler zeige, daß
er den Übergang vom Gedruckten zum Gesprochenen mit Hilfe der Regel
macht, die wir ihm gegeben haben. — Wie man dies *zeigen* könne, wird
klarer, wenn wir unser Beispiel dahin abändern, daß der Schüler, statt
den Text vorzulesen, ihn abzuschreiben hat, die Druckschrift in Schreib-
schrift zu übertragen hat. Denn in diesem Fall können wir ihm die Regel
in Form einer Tabelle geben; in einer Spalte stehen die Druckbuchstaben,
in der andern die Kursivbuchstaben. Und daß er die Schrift vom
Gedruckten ableitet, zeigt sich darin, daß er in der Tabelle nachsieht.

163. Aber wie, wenn er dies täte, und dabei ein A immer in ein b, ein
B in ein c, ein C in ein d umschriebe, u. s. f., und ein Z in ein a? —
Auch das würden wir doch ein Ableiten nach der Tabelle nennen. — Er
gebraucht sie nun, könnten wir sagen, nach dem zweiten Schema im
§86, statt nach dem ersten.

Auch das wäre wohl noch ein Ableiten nach der Tabelle, das durch
ein Pfeilschema ohne alle einfache Regelmäßigkeit wiedergegeben würde.

Aber nimm an, er bleibe nicht bei *einer* Art des Transkribierens; sondern ändere sie nach einer einfachen Regel: Hat er einmal ein A in ein
n umgeschrieben, so schreibt er das nächste A in ein o, das nächste in
ein p um, u. s. w. — Aber wo ist die Grenze zwischen diesem Vorgehen
und einem regellosen?

Aber heißt das nun, das Wort "ableiten" habe eigentlich keine Bedeutung, da es ja scheint, daß diese, wenn wir ihr nachgehen, in nichts zerfließt?

164. Im Falle (162) stand die Bedeutung des Wortes "ableiten" klar vor
uns. Aber wir sagten uns, dies sei nur ein ganz spezieller Fall des Ableitens,

162. Let us try the following explanation: someone is reading if he *derives* the reproduction from the original. And what I call the 'original' is the text which he reads or copies, the dictation from which he writes, the score from which he plays, and so on. — Now suppose, for example, that we have taught someone the Cyrillic alphabet and how to pronounce each letter. Next we put a passage before him and he reads it, pronouncing every letter as we have taught him. In this case, we'll probably say that he derives the sound of a word from the written pattern by the rule that we have given him. And this too is a clear case of *reading*. (We might say that we had taught him the 'rule of the alphabet'.)

But why do we say that he has *derived* the spoken from the printed words? Do we know anything more than that we taught him how each letter should be pronounced, and that he then read the words out loud? Perhaps our reply will be: the pupil shows that he is using the rule we have given him to take the step from the printed to the spoken words. — How this can be *shown* becomes clearer if we change our example to one in which the pupil has to copy out the text instead of reading it out, has to go from print to handwriting. For in this case, we can give him the rule in the form of a table with printed letters in one column and cursive letters in the other. And that he is deriving his writing from print is shown by his consulting the table.

163. But suppose that when he did this, he always wrote b for A, c for B, d for C, and so on, and a for Z? — Surely we'd call this too a derivation by means of the table. — He is using it now, we might say, according to the second schema in §86 instead of the first.

It would still be a case of derivation according to the table, even if it were represented by a schema of arrows without any simple regularity.

Suppose, however, that he does not stick to a single way of transcribing, but alters it according to a simple rule: if he has once written n for A, then he writes o for the next A, p for the next, and so on. — But where is the boundary between this procedure and a random one? |66|

But does this mean that the word "derive" really has no meaning, since the meaning seems to dissolve into nothing when we follow it through?

164. In case (162) the meaning of the word "derive" stood out clearly. But we told ourselves that this was only a quite special case of deriving:

eine ganz spezielle Einkleidung; diese mußte ihm abgestreift werden, wenn
wir das Wesen des Ableitens erkennen wollten. Nun streiften wir ihm
die besonderen Hüllen ab; aber da verschwand das Ableiten selbst. —
Um die eigentliche Artischocke zu finden, hatten wir sie ihrer Blätter
entkleidet. Denn es war freilich (162) ein spezieller Fall des Ableitens,
aber das Wesentliche des Ableitens war nicht unter dem Äußeren dieses
Falls versteckt, sondern dieses 'Äußere' war ein Fall aus der Familie der
Fälle des Ableitens.

Und so verwenden wir auch das Wort "Lesen" für eine Familie von
Fällen. Und wir wenden unter verschiedenen Umständen verschiedene
Kriterien an dafür, daß Einer liest.

165. Aber lesen — möchten wir sagen — ist doch ein ganz bestimmter
Vorgang! Lies eine Druckseite, dann kannst du's sehen; es geht da etwas
Besonderes vor und etwas höchst Charakteristisches. —— Nun, was geht
denn vor, wenn ich den Druck lese? Ich sehe gedruckte Wörter und spreche
Wörter aus. Aber das ist natürlich nicht alles; denn ich könnte
gedruckte Wörter sehen und Wörter aussprechen, und es wäre doch nicht
Lesen. Auch dann nicht, wenn die Wörter, die ich spreche, die sind, die
man, zufolge einem bestehenden Alphabet, von jenen gedruckten ablesen *soll*. — Und wenn du sagst, das Lesen sei ein bestimmtes Erlebnis,
so spielt es ja gar keine Rolle, ob du nach einer von Menschen allgemein anerkannten Regel des Alphabets liest, oder nicht. — Worin
besteht also das Charakteristische am Erlebnis des Lesens? — Da möchte
ich sagen: "Die Worte, die ich ausspreche, *kommen* in besonderer Weise."
Nämlich sie kommen nicht so, wie sie kämen, wenn ich sie z. B. ersänne.
— Sie kommen von selbst. — Aber auch das ist nicht genug; denn es
können mir ja Wortklänge *einfallen*, während ich auf die gedruckten
Worte schaue, und ich habe damit diese doch nicht gelesen. — Da könnte
ich noch sagen, daß mir die gesprochenen Wörter auch nicht so einfallen,
als erinnerte mich, z. B., etwas an sie. Ich möchte z. B. nicht sagen: das
Druckwort "nichts" erinnert mich immer an den Laut "nichts". —
Sondern die gesprochenen Wörter schlüpfen beim Lesen gleichsam
herein. Ja, ich kann ein deutsches gedrucktes Wort gar nicht ansehen,
ohne einen eigentümlichen Vorgang des innern Hörens des Wortklangs.

Die Grammatik des Ausdrucks: "eine ganz bestimmte" (Atmosphäre).
Man sagt "Dieses Gesicht hat einen ganz *bestimmten* Ausdruck",
und sucht etwa nach Worten, die ihn charakterisieren.

deriving in quite special clothing, which had to be stripped from it if we wanted to see the essence of deriving. So we stripped off those particular coverings; but then deriving itself disappeared. In order to find the real artichoke, we divested it of its leaves. For (162) was, to be sure, a special case of deriving; what is essential to deriving, however, was not hidden here beneath the exterior, but this 'exterior' was one case out of the family of cases of deriving.

And in the same way, we also use the word "read" for a family of cases. And in different circumstances we apply different criteria for a person's reading.

165. But surely — we'd like to say — reading is a quite particular process! Read a page of print, and you can see that; there is something special going on, something highly characteristic. —— Well, what does go on when I read the page? I see printed words, and I utter words. But, of course, that is not all, for I might see printed words and utter words, and still not be reading. Even if the words which I utter are those which, according to an existing alphabet, are *supposed* to be read off from the printed ones. — And if you say that reading is a particular experience, then it becomes quite unimportant whether or not you read according to some generally recognized alphabetical rule. — So what does the characteristic thing about the experience of reading consist in? — Here I'd like to say: "The words that I utter *come* in a distinctive way." That is, they do not come as they would if I were, for example, making them up. — They come of themselves. — But even that is not enough; for the sounds of words may *occur* to me while I am looking at printed words, but that does not mean that I have read them. — In addition, I might say here, neither do the spoken words occur to me as if, say, something reminded me of them. I should, for example, not wish to say: the printed word "nothing" always reminds me of the sound "nothing". Rather, the spoken words, as it were, slip in as one |67| reads. Indeed, I can't even look at a printed English word without that peculiar process occurring of inwardly hearing the sound of the word.

---

* The grammar of the expression "a quite particular" (atmosphere). One says "This face has a quite *particular* expression," and perhaps looks for words to characterize it. |p. 66 n.|

166. Ich sagte, die gesprochenen Worte beim Lesen kämen 'in besonderer Weise'; aber in welcher Weise? Ist dies nicht eine Fiktion? Sehen
wir uns einzelne Buchstaben an und geben Acht, in welcher Weise der
Laut des Buchstabens kommt. Lies den Buchstaben A. — Nun, wie kam
der Laut? — Wir wissen gar nichts darüber zu sagen. —— Nun schreib
ein kleines lateinisches a! — Wie kam die Handbewegung beim
Schreiben? Anders als der Laut im vorigen Versuch? — Ich habe auf den
Druckbuchstaben gesehen und schrieb den Kursivbuchstaben; mehr
weiß ich nicht. —— Nun schau auf das Zeichen und laß dir dabei
einen Laut einfallen; sprich ihn aus. Mir fiel der Laut 'U' ein; aber ich
könnte nicht sagen, es war ein wesentlicher Unterschied in der Art und
Weise, wie dieser Laut *kam*. Der Unterschied lag in der etwas andern
Situation: Ich hatte mir vorher gesagt, ich solle mir einen Laut einfallen
lassen; es war eine gewisse Spannung da, ehe der Laut kam. Und ich
sprach nicht automatisch den Laut 'U', wie beim Anblick des Buchstaben
U. Auch war mir jenes Zeichen nicht *vertraut*, wie die Buchstaben. Ich
sah es gleichsam gespannt, mit einem gewissen Interesse für seine Form
an; ich dachte dabei an ein umgekehrtes Sigma. —— Stell dir vor, du
müßtest nun dieses Zeichen regelmäßig als Buchstaben benützen; du
gewöhnst dich also daran, bei seinem Anblick einen bestimmten Laut
auszusprechen, etwa den Laut 'sch'. Können wir mehr sagen, als daß
nach einiger Zeit dieser Laut automatisch kommt, wenn wir das
Zeichen ansehen? D. h.: ich frage mich bei seinem Anblick nicht mehr
"Was ist das für ein Buchstabe?" — auch sage ich mir natürlich nicht "Ich
will bei diesem Zeichen den Laut 'sch' aussprechen" — noch auch "Dieses
Zeichen erinnert mich irgendwie an den Laut 'sch'."

(Vergleiche damit die Idee: das Gedächtnisbild unterscheide sich von
andern Vorstellungsbildern durch ein besonderes Merkmal.)

167. Was ist nun an dem Satz, das Lesen sei doch 'ein ganz bestimmter
Vorgang'? Das heißt doch wohl, beim Lesen finde immer *ein* bestimmter Vorgang statt, den wir wiedererkennen. — Aber wenn ich nun
einmal einen Satz im Druck lese und einandermal nach Morsezeichen
schreibe, — findet hier wirklich der gleiche seelische Vorgang statt? ——
Dahingegen ist aber freilich eine Gleichförmigkeit in dem Erlebnis des
Lesens einer Druckseite. Denn der Vorgang ist ja ein gleichförmiger. Und
es ist ja leicht verständlich, daß sich dieser Vorgang unterscheidet von
dem etwa, sich Wörter beim Anblick beliebiger Striche einfallen zu lassen.
— Denn schon der bloße Anblick einer gedruckten Zeile ist ja ungemein
charakteristisch, d. h., ein ganz spezielles Bild: Die Buchstaben alle
von ungefähr der gleichen Größe, auch der Gestalt nach verwandt,
immer wiederkehrend; die Wörter, die zum großen Teil sich ständig

166. I said that when one reads, the spoken words come 'in a distinctive way': but in what way? Isn't this a fiction? Let's look at individual letters and attend to the way the sound of the letter comes. Read the letter A. — Now, how did the sound come? — We have no idea what to say about it. —— Now write a small Roman a! — How did the movement of the hand come as you wrote? Differently from the way the sound came when you tried previously? — I looked at the printed letter and wrote the cursive letter; that's all I know. —— Now look at the sign ↺ , and let a sound occur to you as you do so; then utter it. The sound 'U' occurred to me; but I could not claim that there was any essential difference in the kind of way that sound *came*. The difference lay in the somewhat different situation. I told myself previously that I was to think of a sound; there was a certain tension present before the sound came. And I did not say 'U' automatically as I do when I look at the letter U. Further, that mark was not *familiar* to me in the way the letters of the alphabet are. I looked at it, as it were, expectantly, with a certain interest in its shape; as I looked, I thought of a reversed sigma. —— Imagine having to use this mark regularly as a letter; so that you get used to uttering a particular sound at the sight of it, say the sound "sh". Can we say anything but that, after a while, this sound comes automatically when we look at the sign? That is to say, I no longer ask myself on seeing it, "What sort of letter is that?" — nor, of course, do I tell myself, "At this sign I'll utter the sound 'sh' ", nor yet "This sign somehow reminds me of the sound 'sh' ".

(Compare with this the idea that memory-images are distinguished from other mental images by some special characteristic.)

167. Now what is there in the claim that reading is 'a quite particular process'? It presumably means that whenever we read, *one* particular process takes place, which we recognize. — But suppose that I at one time read a sentence from print and at another write it from Morse code — is the mental process really the same? —— On the other hand, there is surely some uniformity in the experience of reading a page of print. For the process is a uniform one. And it is quite easy to understand that there is a difference between this process and one of, say, coming up with words at the sight of arbitrary signs. — For the mere look of a printed line is itself extremely |68| characteristic — it presents, that is, a quite special appearance, the letters all roughly the same size, akin in shape too, and always recurring; most of the words constantly

wiederholen und uns unendlich wohlvertraut sind, ganz wie wohlver-
traute Gesichter. — Denke an das Unbehagen, das wir empfinden, wenn
die Rechtschreibung eines Wortes geändert wird. (Und an die noch tieferen
Gefühle, die Fragen der Schreibung von Wörtern aufgeregt haben.)
Freilich, nicht jede Zeichenform hat sich uns *tief* eingeprägt. Ein Zeichen
z. B. in der Algebra der Logik kann durch ein beliebiges anderes ersetzt
werden, ohne daß tiefe Gefühle in uns aufgeregt würden. —
    Bedenke, daß das gesehene Wortbild uns in ähnlichem Grade vertraut
ist, wie das gehörte.

168. Auch gleitet der Blick anders über die gedruckte Zeile, als über
eine Reihe beliebiger Haken und Schnörkel. (Ich rede hier aber nicht
von dem, was durch Beobachtung der Augenbewegung des Lesenden
festgestellt werden kann.) Der Blick gleitet, möchte man sagen, besonders widerstandslos, ohne hängen zu bleiben; und doch *rutscht* er nicht.
Und dabei geht ein unwillkürliches Sprechen in der Vorstellung vor sich.
Und so verhält es sich, wenn ich Deutsch und andere Sprachen lese;
gedruckt, oder geschrieben, und in verschiedenen Schriftformen. — Was
aber von dem allen ist für das Lesen als solches wesentlich? Nicht ein
Zug, der in allen Fällen des Lesens vorkäme! (Vergleiche mit dem Vorgang
beim Lesen der gewöhnlichen Druckschrift das Lesen von Worten, die
ganz in Großbuchstaben gedruckt sind, wie manchmal die Auflösungen
von Rätseln. Welch anderer Vorgang! — Oder das Lesen unserer Schrift
von rechts nach links.)

169. Aber empfinden wir nicht, wenn wir lesen, eine Art Verursachung
unseres Sprechens durch die Wortbilder? —— Lies einen Satz! — und nun
schau der Reihe

entlang und sprich dabei einen Satz. Ist es nicht fühlbar, daß im ersten
Fall das Sprechen mit dem Anblick der Zeichen *verbunden* war und im
zweiten ohne Verbindung neben dem Sehen der Zeichen herläuft?
    Aber warum sagst du, wir fühlten eine Verursachung? Verursachung
ist doch das, was wir durch Experimente feststellen; indem wir, z. B.,
das regelmäßige Zusammentreffen von Vorgängen beobachten. Wie könnte ich denn sagen, daß ich das, was so durch Versuche festgestellt wird,
fühle? (Es ist wohl wahr, daß wir Verursachung nicht nur durch die
Beobachtung eines regelmäßigen Zusammentreffens feststellen.) Eher noch
könnte man sagen, ich fühle, daß die Buchstaben der *Grund* sind, warum
ich so und so lese. Denn, wenn mich jemand fragt: "Warum liest du
so?" — so begründe ich es durch die Buchstaben, welche da stehen.

repeated and immensely familiar to us, like well-known faces. — Think
of the uneasiness we feel when the spelling of a word is changed. (And
of the still deeper feelings that questions about the spelling of words
have aroused.) Of course, not every kind of sign has made a *deep* impression on us. A sign in the algebra of logic, for instance, can be replaced
by any other one without exciting deep feelings in us. —

Remember that the look of a word is familiar to us in much the same
way as its sound.

168. Again, our eye passes over printed lines differently from the way
it passes over arbitrary pothooks and squiggles. (But I am not speaking here of what can be found out by observing the movement of
the eyes of a reader.) The glance slides, one would like to say, entirely
unimpeded, without becoming snagged, and yet it doesn't *skid*. And at
the same time involuntary speech goes on in the imagination. That is
how it is when I read English and other languages, printed or written,
and in various letterings. — But what in all this is essential to reading
as such? Not any one feature that occurs in all cases of reading.
(Compare what goes on while reading ordinary print with reading words
which are printed entirely in capital letters, as solutions of puzzles
sometimes are. How different it is! — Or reading our script from right
to left.)

* 169. But when we read, don't we feel the look of the words somehow
causing our utterance? —— Read a sentence. — And now look along
the following sequence

and utter a sentence as you do so. Can't one feel that in the first case
the utterance was *connected* with seeing the signs and in the second
went on side by side with the seeing without any connection?

But why do you say that we felt a causing? Causation is surely something established by experiments, by observing a regular concurrence
of events, for example. So how could I say that I *feel* something which
is found out in this way by experiment? (It is indeed true that observation of regular concurrence is not the only way we establish causation.) One might rather say, I feel that the letters are the *reason* why I
read such-and-such. For if someone asks me, "Why |69| do you read it
this way?" — I justify it by the letters which are there.

Aber was soll es heißen, diese Begründung, die ich ausgesprochen, gedacht, habe, zu *fühlen*? Ich möchte sagen: Ich fühle beim Lesen einen gewissen *Einfluß* der Buchstaben auf mich —— aber nicht einen Einfluß jener Reihe beliebiger Schnörkel auf das, was ich rede. — Vergleichen wir wieder einen einzelnen Buchstaben mit einem solchen Schnörkel! Würde ich auch sagen, ich fühle den Einfluß von "i", wenn ich diesen Buchstaben lese? Es ist natürlich ein Unterschied, ob ich beim Anblicken von "i" den i-Laut sage, oder beim Anblick von "𝄞". Der Unterschied ist etwa, daß beim Anblick des Buchstabens das innere Hören des i-Lauts automatisch, ja gegen meinen Willen, vor sich geht; und wenn ich den Buchstaben laut lese, sein Aussprechen anstrengungsloser ist, als beim Anblick von "𝄞". Das heißt — es verhält sich so, wenn ich den *Versuch* mache; aber natürlich nicht, wenn ich, zufällig auf das Zeichen "𝄞" blickend, etwa ein Wort ausspreche, in welchem der i-Laut vorkommt.

170. Wir wären ja nie auf den Gedanken gekommen, wir *fühlten den Einfluß* der Buchstaben auf uns beim Lesen, wenn wir nicht den Fall der Buchstaben mit dem beliebiger Striche verglichen hätten. Und hier merken wir allerdings einen *Unterschied*. Und diesen Unterschied deuten wir als Einfluß, und Fehlen des Einflusses.

Und zwar sind wir zu dieser Deutung dann besonders geneigt, wenn wir absichtlich langsam lesen, — etwa um zu sehen, was denn beim Lesen geschieht. Wenn wir uns sozusagen recht absichtlich von den Buchstaben *führen* lassen. Aber dieses 'mich führen lassen' besteht wieder nur darin, daß ich mir die Buchstaben gut anschaue, — etwa, gewisse andere Gedanken ausschalte.

Wir bilden uns ein, wir nähmen durch ein Gefühl, quasi, einen verbindenden Mechanismus wahr zwischen dem Wortbild und dem Laut, den wir sprechen. Denn wenn ich vom Erlebnis des Einflusses, der Verursachung, des Geführtwerdens rede, so soll das ja heißen, daß ich sozusagen die Bewegung der Hebel fühle, die den Anblick der Buchstaben mit dem Sprechen verbinden.

171. Ich hätte mein Erlebnis beim Lesen eines Wortes auf verschiedene Weise treffend durch Worte ausdrücken können. So könnte ich sagen, daß das Geschriebene mir die Laute *eingebe*. — Aber auch dies, daß Buchstabe und Laut beim Lesen eine *Einheit* bilden — gleichsam eine Legierung. (Eine ähnliche Verschmelzung gibt es z. B. zwischen den Gesichtern berühmter Männer und dem Klang ihrer Namen. Es kommt uns vor, dieser Name sei der einzig richtige Ausdruck für dieses Gesicht.) Wenn ich diese Einheit fühle, könnte ich sagen: ich sehe, oder höre den Laut in dem geschriebenen Wort. —

But what is it supposed to mean: to *feel* the justification that I uttered or thought? I'd like to say: when I read, I feel a certain *influence* of the letters on me —— but I feel no influence on what I say from that series of arbitrary squiggles. — Let's once more compare an individual letter with such a squiggle. Would I also say I feel the influence of "i" when I read it? It does of course make a difference whether I say "i" when I see "i" or when I see "𝔥". The difference is, roughly, that when I see the letter, it's automatic for me inwardly to hear the sound "i", even against my will, and that I pronounce the letter with less effort when I read it than when I am looking at "𝔥". That is to say: this is how it is when I *try*; but of course it is not so if I happen to be looking at the mark "𝔥" and at the same time pronounce a word in which the sound "i" occurs.

170. We'd never have hit on the idea that we *felt the influence* of the letters on us when reading had we not compared the case of letters with that of arbitrary marks. And here we do indeed notice a *difference*. And we interpret it as the difference between influence and absence of influence.

And we're especially inclined towards this interpretation when we make a point of reading slowly — perhaps in order to see what does happen when we read. When we, so to speak, more or less deliberately let ourselves be *guided* by the letters. But this 'letting myself be guided' in turn consists only in my looking carefully at the letters — and perhaps excluding certain other thoughts.

We imagine that a feeling enables us to perceive, as it were, a connecting mechanism between the look of the word and the sound that we utter. For when I speak of the experiences of being influenced, of causation, of being guided, that is really supposed to mean that I, so to say, feel the movement of the levers which connect the appearance of the letters with speaking.

171. I might have used various words to hit off the experience I have when I read a word. So I might say that the written word *intimates* the sound to me. — Or again, that when one reads, letter and sound form a *unity* — as it were an alloy. (A similar fusion occurs, for example, between the faces of famous men and the sound of their names. |70| It seems to us that this name is the only right one for this face.) Once I feel this unity, I might say that I see or hear the sound in the written word. —

Aber jetzt lies einmal ein paar Sätze im Druck, so wie du's gewöhnlich tust, wenn du nicht an den Begriff des Lesens denkst; und frage
dich, ob du beim Lesen solche Erlebnisse der Einheit, des Einflusses,
etc. gehabt hast. — Sag nicht, du habest sie unbewußt gehabt! Auch
lassen wir uns nicht durch das Bild verleiten, 'beim nähern Hinsehen'
zeigten sich diese Erscheinungen! Wenn ich beschreiben soll, wie ein
Gegenstand aus der Ferne ausschaut, so wird diese Beschreibung nicht
genauer dadurch, daß ich sage, was bei näherem Hinsehen an ihm zu
bemerken ist.

172. Denken wir an das Erlebnis des Geführtwerdens! Fragen wir
uns: Worin besteht dieses Erlebnis, wenn wir z. B. einen *Weg* geführt
werden? — Stelle dir diese Fälle vor:
   Du bist auf einem Spielplatz, etwa mit verbundenen Augen, und wirst
von jemand an der Hand geleitet, bald links, bald rechts; du mußt immer
des Zuges seiner Hand gewärtig sein, auch Acht geben, daß du bei einem
unerwarteten Zug nicht stolperst.
   Oder aber: du wirst von jemandem an der Hand mit Gewalt geführt,
wohin du nicht willst.
   Oder: du wirst im Tanz von einem Partner geführt; du machst dich
so rezeptiv wie möglich, um seine Absicht zu erraten und dem leises-
ten Drucke zu folgen.
   Oder: jemand führt dich einen Spazierweg; ihr geht im Gespräch; wo
immer er geht, gehst du auch.
   Oder: du gehst einen Feldweg entlang, läßt dich von ihm führen.
   Alle diese Situationen sind einander ähnlich; aber was ist allen den
Erlebnissen gemeinsam?

173. "Aber Geführtwerden ist doch ein bestimmtes Erlebnis!" — Die
Antwort darauf ist: Du *denkst* jetzt an ein bestimmtes Erlebnis des
Geführtwerdens.
   Wenn ich mir das Erlebnis desjenigen vergegenwärtigen will, der in
einem der früheren Beispiele durch den gedruckten Text und die
Tabelle beim Schreiben geführt wird, so stelle ich mir das 'gewis-
senhafte' Nachsehen, etc., vor. Ich nehme dabei sogar einen bestimmten
Gesichtsausdruck an (den z. B. eines gewissenhaften Buchhalters). An
diesem Bild ist z. B. die *Sorgfalt* sehr wesentlich; an einem andern wieder
das Ausschalten jedes eigenen Willens. (Denke dir aber, daß jemand Dinge,
die der gewöhnliche Mensch mit den Zeichen der Unachtsamkeit tut,
mit dem Ausdruck — und warum nicht mit den Empfindungen? — der
Sorgfalt begleitet. — Ist er nun sorgfältig? Stell dir etwa vor, der Diener

But now, just read a few sentences in print as you usually do when you are not thinking about the concept of reading, and ask yourself whether you had such experiences of unity, of being influenced, and so on, as you read. — Don't say you had them unconsciously! Nor should we be misled by the picture of these phenomena coming forth 'on closer inspection'. If I'm supposed to describe how an object looks from far off, I don't make the description more accurate by saying what can be noticed about the object on closer inspection.

172. Let's consider the experience of being guided, and ask ourselves: what does this experience consist in when, for example, our steps are guided? — Imagine the following cases:

You're in a playground with your eyes blindfolded, and someone leads you by the hand, sometimes left, sometimes right; you have constantly to be ready for the tug of his hand, and must also take care not to stumble when he gives an unexpected tug.

Or again, someone leads you by the hand where you are unwilling to go, by force.

Or you're guided by a partner in a dance; you make yourself as receptive as possible, in order to guess his intention and obey the slightest pressure.

Or someone leads you along a footpath; you're having a conversation; you go wherever he does.

Or you walk along a track in a field, letting yourself be guided by it.

All these situations are similar to one another; but what is common to all the experiences?

173. "But being guided is surely a particular experience!" — The answer to this is: you're now *thinking* of a particular experience of being guided.

If I want to picture to myself the experience of the person in one of the earlier examples, whose writing is guided by the printed text and the table, I imagine his 'conscientious' looking-up, and so on. As I do this, I even assume a particular facial expression (say, that of a conscientious bookkeeper). *Carefulness* is a most essential part of this picture; in another, the exclusion of every volition of one's own would be essential. (But take something that normal people do with all the signs of carelessness, and imagine someone accompanying it with the expression — and why not the |71| feelings? — of great carefulness. — Is he then careful? Imagine a servant dropping the tea-tray and everything

lasse das Teebrett mit allem was darauf ist, mit den äußeren Zeichen der Sorgfalt, zu Boden fallen.) Vergegenwärtige ich mir so ein bestimmtes Erlebnis, so erscheint es mir als *das* Erlebnis des Geführtwerdens (oder Lesens). Nun aber frage ich mich: Was tust du? — Du schaust auf jedes Zeichen, du machst dieses Gesicht dazu, du schreibst die Buchstaben mit Bedacht (u. dergl.). — Das ist also das Erlebnis des Geführtwerdens? —— Da möchte ich sagen: "Nein, das ist es nicht; es ist etwas Innerlicheres, Wesentlicheres." — Es ist, als ob zuerst all diese mehr oder weniger unwesentlichen Vorgänge in eine bestimmte Atmosphäre gekleidet wären, die sich nun verflüchtigt, wenn ich genau hinschaue.

174. Frage dich, wie du '*mit Bedacht*' eine Strecke parallel zu einer gegebenen Strecke ziehst, — ein andermal mit Bedacht in einem Winkel zu ihr. Was ist das Erlebnis des Bedachts? Da fällt dir gleich eine bestimmte Miene, eine Gebärde ein, — und dann möchtest du sagen: "Und es ist eben ein *bestimmtes* inneres Erlebnis." (Womit du natürlich gar nichts mehr gesagt hast.)

(Es ist da ein Zusammenhang mit der Frage nach dem Wesen der Absicht, des Willens.)

175. Mach einen beliebigen Fahrer auf dem Papier. —— Und nun zeichne ihn daneben nach, laß dich von ihm führen. —— Ich möchte sagen: "Gewiß! ich habe mich jetzt führen lassen. Aber was dabei Charakteristisches geschehen ist? — Wenn ich sage, was geschehen ist, so kommt es mir nicht mehr charakteristisch vor."

Aber nun merke dies: *Während* ich mich führen lasse, ist alles ganz einfach, ich merke nichts *Besonderes*; aber danach, wenn ich mich frage, was damals geschehen ist, so scheint es etwas Unbeschreibbares gewesen zu sein. *Danach* genügt mir keine Beschreibung. Ich kann, sozusagen, nicht glauben, daß ich bloß hingeschaut, dieses Gesicht gemacht, den Strich gezogen habe. — Aber *erinnere* ich mich denn an etwas anderes? Nein; und doch kommt mir vor, als müsse etwas anderes gewesen sein; und zwar dann, wenn ich mir dabei das Wort "*führen*", "*Einfluß*" und derlei, vorsage. "Denn ich bin doch *geführt* worden", sage ich mir. — Dann erst tritt die Idee jenes ätherischen, ungreifbaren Einflusses auf.

176. Ich habe, wenn ich nachträglich an das Erlebnis denke, das Gefühl, daß das Wesentliche an ihm ein 'Erlebnis eines Einflusses', einer Verbindung, ist — im Gegensatz zu irgendeiner bloßen Gleichzeitigkeit von Phänomenen: Zugleich aber möchte ich kein erlebtes Phänomen "Erlebnis des Einflusses" nennen. (Hier liegt die Idee: der Wille ist keine

on it with all the outward signs of carefulness.) If I picture to myself such a particular experience, it seems to me to be *the* experience of being guided (or of reading). But now I ask myself: what are you doing? — You look at every letter, you make this face, you write the letters deliberately (and so on). — So that is the experience of being guided? —— Here I should like to say: "No, it isn't that; it is something more inward, more essential." — It is as if at first all these more or less inessential processes were shrouded in a particular atmosphere, which dissipates when I look closely.

174. Ask yourself how you '*deliberately*' draw a line parallel to a given one — and another time, deliberately, one at an angle to it. What is the experience of doing something *deliberately*? Here a particular look, a gesture, at once occur to you — and then you would like to say: "And it just is a *particular* inner experience." (And by this, of course, you say nothing at all.)

(There is here a connection with the inquiry into the nature of intention, of the will.)

175. Make some arbitrary doodle on a bit of paper. —— And now make a copy next to it, let yourself be guided by it. —— I'd like to say: "Sure enough, I let myself be guided here. But what was characteristic in what happened? — If I say what happened, it no longer seems to me to be characteristic."

But now notice this: *while* I let myself be guided, everything is quite simple, I notice nothing *special*; but afterwards, when I ask myself what it was that happened, it seems to have been something indescribable. *Afterwards* no description satisfies me. It's as if I couldn't believe that I merely looked, made such-and-such a face, and drew a line. But do I *remember* anything else? No; and yet I feel as if there must have been something else; in particular when I say "*guidance*", "*influence*", and other such words to myself. "For surely", I tell myself, "I was being *guided*." — Only then does the idea of that ethereal, intangible influence arise.

176. When I look back on the experience, I have the feeling that what is essential about it is an 'experience of being influenced', of connection — as opposed to any mere simultaneity of phenomena: but at the same time, I'd not be willing to call any experience of a phenomenon the "experience of being influenced". |72| (Hence the idea that the will

Erscheinung.) Ich möchte sagen, ich hätte das 'Weil' erlebt; und doch will ich keine Erscheinung "Erlebnis des Weil" nennen.

177. Ich möchte sagen: "Ich erlebe das Weil". Aber nicht, weil ich mich an dieses Erlebnis erinnere; sondern, weil ich beim Nachdenken darüber, was ich in so einem Fall erlebe, dies durch das Medium des Begriffes 'weil' (oder 'Einfluß', oder 'Ursache', oder 'Verbindung') anschaue. — Denn es ist freilich richtig, zu sagen, ich habe diese Linie unter dem Einfluß der Vorlage gezogen: dies liegt aber nicht einfach in dem, was ich beim Ziehen der Linie empfinde — sondern, unter Umständen, z. B. darin, daß ich sie der andern parallel ziehe; obwohl auch das wieder für das Geführtwerden nicht allgemein wesentlich ist. —

178. Wir sagen auch: "Du *siehst* ja, daß ich mich von ihr führen lasse" — und was sieht der, der das sieht?

Wenn ich zu mir selbst sage: "Ich werde doch geführt" — so mache ich etwa eine Handbewegung dazu, die das Führen ausdrückt. — Mach eine solche Handbewegung, gleichsam als leitetest du jemand entlang, und frage dich dann, worin das *Führende* dieser Bewegung besteht. Denn du hast hier ja niemand geführt. Und doch möchtest du die Bewegung eine 'führende' nennen. Also war in dieser Bewegung, und Empfindung, nicht das Wesen des Führens enthalten und doch drängte es dich, diese Bezeichnung zu gebrauchen. Es ist eben *eine Erscheinungsform* des Führens, die uns diesen Ausdruck aufdrängt.

179. Kehren wir zu unserm Fall (151) zurück. Es ist klar: wir würden nicht sagen, B habe ein Recht, die Worte "Jetzt weiß ich weiter" zu sagen, weil ihm die Formel eingefallen ist, — wenn nicht erfahrungsmäßig ein Zusammenhang bestünde zwischen dem Einfallen — Aussprechen, Anschreiben — der Formel und dem tatsächlichen Fortsetzen der Reihe. Und so ein Zusammenhang besteht ja offenbar. — Und nun könnte man meinen, der Satz "Ich kann fortsetzen" sage soviel wie: "Ich habe ein Erlebnis, welches erfahrungsgemäß zum Fortsetzen der Reihe führt." Aber meint das B, wenn er sagt, er könne fortsetzen? Schwebt ihm jener Satz dabei im Geiste vor, oder ist er bereit, ihn als Erklärung dessen, was er meint, zu geben?

Nein. Die Worte "Jetzt weiß ich weiter" waren richtig angewandt, wenn ihm die Formel eingefallen war: nämlich unter gewissen Umständen. Z. B., wenn er Algebra gelernt, solche Formeln schon früher benützt hatte. — Das heißt aber nicht, jene Aussage sei nur eine Abkürzung für die Beschreibung sämtlicher Umstände, die den Schauplatz unseres

is not a *phenomenon*.) I'd like to say that I had experienced the *'because'*, and yet I don't want to call any phenomenon an "experience of the because".

177. I'd like to say, "I experience the because". Not because I remember such an experience, but because when I reflect on what I experience in such a case, I look at it through the medium of the concept 'because' (or 'influence' or 'cause' or 'connection'). — For it is, of course, correct to say that I drew the line under the influence of the original: this, however, does not consist simply in my feelings as I drew the line — rather, under certain circumstances, it may consist in my drawing it parallel to the other — even though this in turn is not in general essential to being guided. —

178. We also say, "You can *see* that I let myself be guided by it" — and what does someone who sees this see?

When I say to myself, "Surely I *am* guided", I make, say, a movement with my hand that expresses guidance. — Make such a movement of the hand as if you were guiding someone along, and then ask yourself what the *guiding* character of this movement consists in. For you were not guiding anyone. But you still want to call the movement one of 'guiding'. So this movement, and feeling, did not contain the essence of guiding, and yet you were impelled to use this word. It is precisely through its being *one form* of guidance that the expression forces itself on us.

179. Let us return to our case (151). It is clear that we wouldn't say that B had a right to say the words "Now I know how to go on" just because the formula occurred to him — unless experience showed that there was a connection between the formula's occurring to him (his saying it, writing it down) and his actually continuing the series. And obviously such a connection does exist. — And now one might think that the sentence "I can go on" meant "I have an experience which is empirically known to lead to continuing the series". But does B mean that when he says he can continue? Does that sentence come to his mind, or is he ready to produce it in explanation of what he means?

No. The words "Now I know how to go on" were correctly used when the formula occurred to him: namely, under certain circumstances. For example, if he had learnt algebra, had used such formulae before. — But that does not mean that his statement is only short for a description of all the circumstances which set the stage for our language-game.

Sprachspiels bilden. — Denke daran, wie wir jene Ausdrücke, "jetzt weiß ich weiter", "jetzt kann ich fortsetzen", u. a., gebrauchen lernen; in welcher Familie von Sprachspielen wir ihren Gebrauch lernen.

Wir können uns auch den Fall vorstellen, daß im Geist des B gar nichts anderes vorfiel, als daß er plötzlich sagte "Jetzt weiß ich weiter" — etwa mit einem Gefühl der Erleichterung; und daß er nun die Reihe tatsächlich fortrechnet, ohne die Formel zu benützen. Und auch in diesem Falle würden wir — unter gewissen Umständen — sagen, er habe weiter gewußt.

180. *So werden diese Worte gebraucht.* Es wäre, in diesem letzteren Fall z. B., ganz irreleitend, die Worte eine "Beschreibung eines seelischen Zustandes" zu nennen. — Eher könnte man sie hier ein "Signal" nennen; und ob es richtig angewendet war, beurteilen wir nach dem, was er weiter tut.

181. Um dies zu verstehen, müssen wir uns auch folgendes überlegen: Angenommen, B sagt, er wisse weiter — wenn er aber nun fortsetzen will, stockt er und kann es nicht: Sollen wir dann sagen, er habe mit Unrecht gesagt, er könne fortsetzen, oder aber: er hätte damals fortsetzen können, nur jetzt könne er es nicht? — Es ist klar, daß wir in verschiedenen Fällen Verschiedenes sagen werden. (Überlege dir beide Arten von Fällen.)

182. Die Grammatik von "passen", "können" und "verstehen". Aufgaben: 1) Wann sagt man, ein Zylinder Z passe in einen Hohlzylinder H? Nur solange Z in H steckt? 2) Man sagt manchmal: Z hat um die und die Zeit aufgehört, in H zu passen. Welche Kriterien verwendet man in so einem Fall dafür, daß es um diese Zeit geschah? 3) Was betrachtet man als Kriterien dafür, daß ein Körper sein Gewicht um eine bestimmte Zeit geändert hat, wenn er damals nicht auf der Waage lag? 4) Gestern wußte ich das Gedicht auswendig; heute weiß ich's nicht mehr. In was für Fällen hat die Frage Sinn: "Wann habe ich aufgehört, es auswendig zu wissen"? 5) Jemand fragt mich: "Kannst du dieses Gewicht heben?" Ich antworte "Ja". Nun sagt er "Tu's!" — da kann ich es nicht. Unter was für Umständen würde man die Rechtfertigung gelten lassen: "Als ich antwortete 'Ja', da *konnte* ich's, nur jetzt kann ich's nicht"?

Die Kriterien, die wir für das 'Passen', 'Können', 'Verstehen' gelten lassen, sind viel kompliziertere, als es auf den ersten Blick scheinen möchte. D. h., das Spiel mit diesen Worten, ihre Verwendung im sprachlichen Verkehr, dessen Mittel sie sind, ist verwickelter — die Rolle dieser Wörter in unsrer Sprache eine andere, als wir versucht sind, zu glauben.

— Think how we learn to use the expressions "Now I know how to go |73| on", "Now I can go on", and others; in what family of language-games we learn their use.

We can also imagine the case where nothing at all occurred in B's mind except that he suddenly said "Now I know how to go on" — perhaps with a feeling of relief; and that he did in fact go on working out the series without using the formula. And in this case too we should say — in certain circumstances — that he did know how to go on.

180. *This is how these words are used*. It would be quite misleading, in this last case, for instance, to call the words a "description of a mental state". Rather, one could here call them a "signal"; and we judge whether it was rightly applied by what he goes on to do.

181. In order to understand this, we need also to consider the following: suppose B says he knows how to go on — but when he wants to go on, he hesitates and can't do it. Are we then to say that it was wrong of him to say he could go on; or rather, that he was able to go on then, only now is not? — Clearly, we shall say different things in different cases. (Consider both kinds of case.)

182. The grammar of "to fit", "to be able" and "to understand". Exercises: (1) When is a cylinder C said to fit into a hollow cylinder H? Only as long as C is inside H? (2) Sometimes one says that: C has ceased to fit into H at such-and-such a time. What criteria are used in such a case for its having happened at that time? (3) What does one regard as criteria for a body's having changed its weight at a particular time, if it was not actually on the balance at that time? (4) Yesterday I knew the poem by heart; today I no longer know it. In what kind of case does it make sense to ask, "When did I stop knowing it by heart?" (5) Someone asks me, "Can you lift this weight?" I answer, "Yes". Now he says, "Do it!" — and I can't. In what kind of circumstances would one accept the excuse "When I answered 'yes' I *could* do it, only now I can't"?

The criteria which we accept for 'fitting', 'being able to', 'understanding', are much more complicated than might appear at first sight. That is, the game with these words, their use in the linguistic intercourse that is carried on by their means, is more involved — the role of these words in our language is other than we are tempted to think.

(Diese Rolle ist es, die wir verstehen müssen, um philosophische Paradoxe aufzulösen. Und darum genügt dazu gewöhnlich nicht eine Definition; und schon erst recht nicht die Feststellung, ein Wort sei 'undefinierbar'.)

183. Wie aber, — hat nun der Satz "Jetzt kann ich fortsetzen" im Fall (151) das Gleiche geheißen, wie "Jetzt ist mir die Formel eingefallen", oder etwas anderes? Wir können sagen, daß dieser Satz, unter diesen Umständen, den gleichen Sinn habe (das Gleiche leiste) wie jener. Aber auch, daß, *allgemein*, diese beiden Sätze nicht den gleichen Sinn haben. Wir sagen auch: "Jetzt kann ich fortsetzen, ich meine, ich weiß die Formel"; wie wir sagen: "Ich kann gehen, d. h., ich habe Zeit"; aber auch: "Ich kann gehen, d. h., ich bin schon stark genug"; oder: "Ich kann gehen, was den Zustand meines Beins anbelangt", wenn wir nämlich *diese* Bedingung des Gehens andern Bedingungen entgegensetzen. Hier müssen wir uns aber hüten, zu glauben, es gebe, entsprechend der Natur des Falles, eine *Gesamtheit* aller Bedingungen (z. B. dafür, daß Einer geht) so daß er, sozusagen, nicht anders als gehen *könnte*, wenn sie alle erfüllt sind.

184. Ich will mich an eine Melodie erinnern und sie fällt mir nicht ein; plötzlich sage ich "Jetzt weiß ich's!", und singe sie. Wie war es, als ich sie plötzlich wußte? Sie konnte mir doch nicht in diesem Moment *ganz* eingefallen sein! — Du sagst vielleicht: "Es ist ein bestimmtes Gefühl, als wäre sie jetzt *da*" — aber *ist* sie jetzt da? Wie, wenn ich nun anfange, sie zu singen und stecken bleibe? —— Ja aber konnte ich nicht doch in diesem Moment *sicher* sein, daß ich sie wüßte? Sie war also eben doch in irgendeinem Sinne *da*! —— Aber in welchem Sinne? Du sagst wohl, die Melodie sei da, wenn er sie etwa durchsingt, oder von Anfang zu Ende vor dem innern Ohr hört. Ich leugne natürlich nicht, daß der Aussage, die Melodie sei da, auch ein ganz anderer Sinn gegeben werden kann — z. B. der, ich hätte einen Zettel, auf dem sie aufgeschrieben steht. — Und worin besteht es denn, daß er 'sicher' ist, er wisse sie? — Man kann natürlich sagen: Wenn jemand mit Überzeugung sagt, jetzt wisse er die Melodie, so steht sie in diesem Augenblick (irgendwie) ganz vor seinem Geist —— und dies ist eine Erklärung der Worte: "Die Melodie steht ganz vor seinem Geist".

185. Gehen wir nun zu unserm Beispiel (143) zurück. Der Schüler beherrscht jetzt — nach den gewöhnlichen Kriterien beurteilt — die Grundzahlenreihe. Wir lehren ihn nun auch andere Reihen von Kardinalzahlen anschreiben und bringen ihn dahin, daß er z. B. auf Befehle von der Form "+n" Reihen der Form

(This role is what we need to understand in order to resolve philosophical paradoxes. And that's why definitions usually aren't enough to |74| resolve them; and even less so the statement that a word is 'indefinable'.)

183. Now then, did the sentence "Now I can go on" in case (151) mean the same as "Now the formula has occurred to me", or something different? We may say that in these circumstances the one sentence has the same sense (comes to the same thing) as the other. But also that *in general*, these two sentences do not have the same sense. We do say, "Now I can go on, I mean I know the formula," as we say "I can walk, I mean I have time"; but also "I can walk, I mean I am already strong enough"; or "I can walk, as far as the state of my leg is concerned", that is, when we are contrasting *this* condition for walking with others. But here we must be on our guard against thinking that there is some *totality* of conditions corresponding to the nature of each case (for example, for a person's walking) so that, as it were, he *could not but* walk if they were all fulfilled.

184. I want to remember a tune, and it escapes me; suddenly I say, "Now I know it", and I sing it. What was it like suddenly to know it? Surely it can't have occurred to me *in its entirety* in that moment! — Perhaps you will say: "It's a particular feeling, as if it were now *there*" — but *is* it now there? Suppose I then begin to sing it and get stuck? —— But may I not have been *certain* at that moment that I knew it? So in some sense or other it was *there* after all! —— But in what sense? Perhaps you would say that the tune was there if, for example, someone sang it through, or rehearsed it in his imagination from beginning to end. I am not, of course, denying that the statement that the tune is there can also be given a quite different sense — for example, that I have a bit of paper on which it is written. — And what does his being 'certain' he knows it consist in? — Of course, one can say: if someone says with conviction that now he knows the tune, then it is (somehow) present to his mind in its entirety at that moment —— and this is an explanation of the words "the tune is present to his mind in its entirety".

185. Let us return to our example (143). Now, judged by the usual criteria, the pupil has mastered the series of natural numbers. Next we teach him to write down other series of cardinal numbers and get him to the point of writing down, say, series of the form

0, n, 2n, 3n, etc.

anschreibt; auf den Befehl "+ 1" also die Grundzahlreihe. — Wir hätten unsre Übungen und Stichproben seines Verständnisses im Zahlenraum bis 1000 gemacht.

Wir lassen nun den Schüler einmal eine Reihe (etwa "+ 2") über 1000 hinaus fortsetzen, — da schreibt er: 1000, 1004, 1008, 1012.

Wir sagen ihm: "Schau, was du machst!" — Er versteht uns nicht. Wir sagen: "Du solltest doch *zwei* addieren; schau, wie du die Reihe begonnen hast!" — Er antwortet: "Ja! Ist es denn nicht richtig? Ich dachte, so *soll* ich's machen." —— Oder nimm an, er sagte, auf die Reihe weisend: "Ich bin doch auf die gleiche Weise fortgefahren!" — Es würde uns nun nichts nützen, zu sagen "Aber siehst du denn nicht . . . ?" — und ihm die alten Erklärungen und Beispiele zu wiederholen. — Wir könnten in so einem Falle etwa sagen: Dieser Mensch versteht von Natur aus jenen Befehl, auf unsre Erklärungen hin, so, wie *wir* den Befehl: "Addiere bis 1000 immer 2, bis 2000 4, bis 3000 6, etc."

Dieser Fall hätte Ähnlichkeit mit dem, als reagierte ein Mensch auf eine zeigende Gebärde der Hand von Natur damit, daß er in der Richtung von der Fingerspitze zur Handwurzel blickt, statt in der Richtung zur Fingerspitze.

186. "Was du sagst, läuft also darauf hinaus, es sei zum richtigen Befolgen des Befehls '+ n' auf jeder Stufe eine neue Einsicht — Intuition — nötig." — Zur richtigen Befolgung! Wie wird denn entschieden, welches an einem bestimmten Punkt der richtige Schritt ist? — "Der richtige Schritt ist der, welcher mit dem Befehl — wie er *gemeint* war — übereinstimmt." — Du hast also zur Zeit, als du den Befehl "+ 2" gabst, gemeint, er solle auf 1000 1002 schreiben — und hast du damals auch gemeint, er solle auf 1866 1868 schreiben, und auf 100034 100036, u. s. f. — eine unendliche Anzahl solcher Sätze? — "Nein; ich habe gemeint, er solle nach *jeder* Zahl, die er schreibt, die zweitnächste schreiben; und daraus folgen ihres Orts alle jene Sätze." — Aber es ist ja gerade die Frage, was, an irgend einem Ort, aus jenem Satz folgt. Oder auch — was wir an irgend einem Ort "Übereinstimmung" mit jenem Satz nennen sollen (und auch mit der *Meinung*, die du damals dem Satz gegeben hast, — worin immer diese bestanden haben mag). Richtiger, als zu sagen, es sei an jedem Punkt eine Intuition nötig, wäre beinah, zu sagen: es sei an jedem Punkt eine neue Entscheidung nötig.

187. "Ich habe aber doch auch damals, als ich den Befehl gab, schon gewußt, daß er auf 1000 1002 schreiben soll!" — Gewiß; und du kannst

0, n, 2n, 3n, etc.

at an order of the form "+ n"; so at the order "+ 1" he writes |75| down
the series of natural numbers. — Let's suppose we have done exercises,
and tested his understanding up to 1000.

Then we get the pupil to continue one series (say "+ 2") beyond 1000
— and he writes 1000, 1004, 1008, 1012.

We say to him, "Look what you're doing!" — He doesn't understand.
We say, "You should have added *two*: look how you began the series!"
— He answers, "Yes, isn't it right? I thought that was how I *had* to do
it." —— Or suppose he pointed to the series and said, "But I did go on
in the same way". — It would now be no use to say, "But can't you
see . . . ?" — and go over the old explanations and examples for him
again. In such a case, we might perhaps say: this person finds it natural, once given our explanations, to understand our order as *we* would
understand the order "Add 2 up to 1000, 4 up to 2000, 6 up to 3000,
and so on".

This case would have similarities to that in which it comes naturally
to a person to react to the gesture of pointing with the hand by looking in the direction from fingertip to wrist, rather than from wrist to
fingertip.

186. "What you are saying, then, comes to this: a new insight — intuition — is needed at every step to carry out the order '+ n' correctly."
— To carry it out correctly! How is it decided what is the right step to
take at any particular point? — "The right step is the one that is in
accordance with the order — as it was *meant*." — So when you gave
the order "+ 2", you meant that he was to write 1002 after 1000 — and
did you then also mean that he should write 1868 after 1866, and 100036
after 100034, and so on — an infinite number of such sentences? — "No;
what I meant was, that he should write the next but one number after
every number that he wrote; and from this, stage by stage, all those
sentences follow." — But that is just what is in question: what, at any
stage, does follow from that sentence. Or, again, what at any stage we
are to call "being in accordance" with it (and with how you then *meant*
it — whatever your meaning it may have consisted in). It would almost
be more correct to say, not that an intuition was needed at every point,
but that a new decision was needed at every point.

187. "But I already knew, at the time when I gave the order, that he
should write 1002 after 1000." — Certainly; and you may even say you

sogar sagen, du habest es damals *gemeint*; nur sollst du dich nicht von der Grammatik der Wörter "wissen" und "meinen" irreführen lassen. Denn du meinst ja nicht, daß du damals an den Übergang von 1000 auf 1002 gedacht hast — und wenn auch an diesen Übergang, so doch an andre nicht. Dein "Ich habe damals schon gewußt . . . " heißt etwa: "Hätte man mich damals gefragt, welche Zahl er nach 1000 schreiben soll, so hätte ich geantwortet '1002'." Und daran zweifle ich nicht. Es ist das eine Annahme etwa von der Art dieser: "Wenn er damals ins Wasser gefallen wäre, so wäre ich ihm nachgesprungen." — Worin lag nun das Irrige deiner Idee?

188. Da möchte ich zuerst sagen: Deine Idee sei die gewesen, jenes Meinen des Befehls habe auf seine Weise alle jene Übergänge doch schon gemacht: deine Seele fliege beim Meinen, gleichsam, voraus und mache alle Übergänge, ehe du körperlich bei dem oder jenem angelangt bist.

Du warst also zu Ausdrücken geneigt, wie: "Die Übergänge sind *eigentlich* schon gemacht; auch ehe ich sie schriftlich, mündlich, oder in Gedanken mache." Und es schien, als wären sie in einer *einzigartigen* Weise vorausbestimmt, antizipiert — wie nur das Meinen die Wirklichkeit antizipieren könne.

189. "Aber sind die Übergänge also durch die algebraische Formel *nicht* bestimmt?" — In der Frage liegt ein Fehler.

Wir verwenden den Ausdruck: "die Übergänge sind durch die Formel . . . bestimmt". *Wie* wird er verwendet? — Wir können etwa davon reden, daß Menschen durch Erziehung (Abrichtung) dahin gebracht werden, die Formel $y = x^2$ so zu verwenden, daß Alle, wenn sie die gleiche Zahl für x einsetzen, immer die gleiche Zahl für y herausrechnen. Oder wir können sagen: "Diese Menschen sind so abgerichtet, daß sie alle auf den Befehl '+ 3' auf der gleichen Stufe den gleichen Übergang machen." Wir könnten dies so ausdrücken: "Der Befehl '+ 3' bestimmt für diese Menschen jeden Übergang von einer Zahl zur nächsten völlig." (Im Gegensatz zu andern Menschen, die auf diesen Befehl nicht wissen, was sie zu tun haben; oder die zwar mit völliger Sicherheit, aber ein jeder in anderer Weise, auf ihn reagieren.)

Wir können anderseits verschiedene Arten von Formeln, und zu ihnen gehörige verschiedene Arten der Verwendung (verschiedene Arten der Abrichtung) einander entgegensetzen. Wir *nennen* dann Formeln einer bestimmten Art (und der dazugehörigen Verwendungsweise) "Formeln, welche eine Zahl y für ein gegebenes x bestimmen", und Formeln anderer Art solche, "die die Zahl y für ein gegebenes x nicht bestimmen". ($y = x^2$ wäre von der ersten Art, $y \neq x^2$ von der zweiten.)

meant it then; only you shouldn't let yourself be misled by the grammar of the words "know" and "mean". For you don't |76| mean that you thought of the step from 1000 to 1002 at that time — and even if you did think of this step, still, you didn't think of other ones. Your "I already knew at the time . . ." amounts to something like: "If I had then been asked what number he should write after 1000, I would have replied '1002'." And that I don't doubt. This is an assumption of much the same sort as "If he had fallen into the water then, I would have jumped in after him". — Now, what was wrong with your idea?

188. Here I'd like to say first of all: your idea was that this *meaning the order* had in its own way already taken all those steps: that in meaning it, your mind, as it were, flew ahead and took all the steps before you physically arrived at this or that one.

So you were inclined to use such expressions as "The steps are *really* already taken, even before I take them in writing or in speech or in thought". And it seemed as if they were in some *unique* way predetermined, anticipated — in the way that only meaning something could anticipate reality.

189. "But are the steps then *not* determined by the algebraic formula?" — The question contains a mistake.

We use the expression "The steps are determined by the formula . . .". *How* is the expression used? — We may perhaps mention that people are brought by their education (training) so to use the formula $y = x^2$, that they all work out the same number for y when they substitute the same number for x. Or we may say: "These people are so trained that they all take the same step at the same point when they receive the order '+3'." We might express this by saying "For these people the order '+3' completely determines every step from one number to the next". (By contrast with other people who do not know what they are to do on receiving this order, or who react to it with perfect certainty, but each one in a different way.)

On the other hand, we may contrast different kinds of formula, and the different kinds of use (different kinds of training) appropriate to them. Then we *call* formulae of a particular kind (with the appropriate method of use) "formulae which determine a number y for a given value of x", and formulae of another kind, ones which "do not determine the number y for a given value of x". ($y = x^2$ would be of the first kind, $y \neq x^2$ of the second.) The sentence "The formula . . .

Der Satz "Die Formel . . . bestimmt eine Zahl y" ist dann eine Aussage über die Form der Formel — und es ist nun zu unterscheiden ein Satz wie dieser: "Die Formel, die ich hingeschrieben habe, bestimmt y" oder "Hier steht eine Formel, die y bestimmt" — von einem Satz der Art: "Die Formel y = x^2 bestimmt die Zahl y für ein gegebenes x." Die Frage "Steht dort eine Formel, die y bestimmt?" heißt dann dasselbe wie: "Steht dort eine Formel dieser Art, oder jener Art?" — was wir aber mit der Frage anfangen sollen "Ist y = x^2 eine Formel, die y für ein gegebenes x bestimmt?" ist nicht ohne Weiteres klar. Diese Frage könnte man etwa an einen Schüler richten, um zu prüfen, ob er die Verwendung des Wortes "bestimmen" versteht; oder es könnte eine mathematische Aufgabe sein, in einem bestimmten System zu beweisen, daß x nur ein Quadrat besitzt.

190. Man kann nun sagen: "Wie die Formel gemeint wird, das bestimmt, welche Übergänge zu machen sind." Was ist das Kriterium dafür, wie die Formel gemeint ist? Etwa die Art und Weise, wie wir sie ständig gebrauchen, wie uns gelehrt wurde, sie zu gebrauchen.

Wir sagen z. B. Einem, der ein uns unbekanntes Zeichen gebraucht: "Wenn du mit 'x!2' meinst x^2, so erhältst du *diesen* Wert für y, wenn du 2x damit meinst, *jenen*." — Frage dich nun: Wie macht man es, mit "x!2" das eine, oder das andere *meinen*?

So kann also das Meinen die Übergänge zum Voraus bestimmen.

191. "Es ist, als könnten wir die ganze Verwendung des Wortes mit einem Schlage erfassen." — Wie *was* z. B.? — *Kann* man sie nicht — in gewissem Sinne — mit einem Schlag erfassen? Und in *welchem* Sinne kannst du dies nicht? — Es ist eben, als könnten wir sie in einem noch viel direkteren Sinne 'mit einem Schlag erfassen'. — Aber hast du dafür ein Vorbild? Nein. Es bietet sich uns nur diese Ausdrucksweise an. Als das Resultat sich kreuzender Bilder.

192. Du hast kein Vorbild dieser übermäßigen Tatsache, aber du wirst dazu verführt, einen Über-Ausdruck zu gebrauchen. (Man könnte das einen philosophischen Superlativ nennen.)

193. Die Maschine als Symbol ihrer Wirkungsweise: Die Maschine — könnte ich zuerst sagen — scheint ihre Wirkungsweise schon in sich zu haben. Was heißt das? — Indem wir die Maschine kennen, scheint alles Übrige, nämlich die Bewegungen, welche sie machen wird, schon ganz bestimmt zu sein.

determines a number y" will then be a statement about |77| the form of the formula — and now a sentence such as "The formula which I have written down determines y", or "Here is a formula which determines y", is to be distinguished from a sentence of the following kind: "The formula $y = x^2$ determines the number y for a given value of x." The question "Is the formula written down there one that determines y?" will then mean the same as "Is what is there a formula of this kind or that?" — but it is not clear offhand what we are to make of the question "Is $y = x^2$ a formula which determines y for a given x?" One might address this question to a pupil in order to test whether he understands the use of the word "to determine"; or it might be a mathematical problem to prove in a particular system that x has only one square.

190. One may then say: "How the formula is meant determines which steps are to be taken." What is the criterion for how the formula is meant? It is, for example, the kind of way we always use it, were taught to use it.

We say, for instance, to someone who uses a sign unknown to us: "If by '$x!2$' you mean x^2, then you get *this* value for y, if you mean $2x$, *that* one." — Now ask yourself: how does one do it — *mean* the one thing or the other by "$x!2$"?

In *this* way, then, meaning something can determine the steps in advance.

191. "It is as if we could grasp the whole use of the word at a stroke." Like *what*, for example? — *Can't* the use — in a certain sense — be grasped at a stroke? And in *what* sense can't it? — It is indeed as if we could 'grasp it at a stroke' in a much more direct sense. — But have you a model for this? No. It is just that this mode of expression suggests itself to us. As a result of the crossing of different pictures.

192. You have no model of this inordinate fact, but you are seduced into using a super-expression. (It might be called a philosophical superlative.)

193. A machine as a symbol of its mode of operation. The machine, I might say for a start, seems already to contain its own mode of operation. What does that mean? — If we know the machine, everything else — that is the movements it will make — seem to be already completely determined.

Wir reden so, als könnten sich diese Teile nur so bewegen, als könnten sie nichts anderes tun. Wie ist es — vergessen wir also die Möglichkeit, daß sie sich biegen, abbrechen, schmelzen, etc.? Ja; wir denken in vielen Fällen gar nicht daran. Wir gebrauchen eine Maschine, oder das Bild einer Maschine, als Symbol für eine bestimmte Wirkungsweise. Wir teilen z. B. Einem dieses Bild mit und setzen voraus, daß er die Erscheinungen der Bewegung der Teile aus ihm ableitet. (So wie wir jemand eine Zahl mitteilen können, indem wir sagen, sie sei die fünfundzwanzigste der Reihe 1, 4, 9, 16, . . .)

"Die Maschine scheint ihre Wirkungsweise schon in sich zu haben" heißt: wir sind geneigt, die künftigen Bewegungen der Maschine in ihrer Bestimmtheit mit Gegenständen zu vergleichen, die schon in einer Lade liegen und nun von uns herausgeholt werden. —— So aber reden wir nicht, wenn es sich darum handelt, das wirkliche Verhalten einer Maschine vorauszusagen. Da vergessen wir, im allgemeinen, nicht die Möglichkeit der Deformation der Teile, etc. —— Wohl aber, wenn wir uns darüber wundern, wie wir denn die Maschine als Symbol einer Bewegungsweise verwenden können, — da sie sich doch auch ganz *anders* bewegen kann.

Wir könnten sagen, die Maschine, oder ihr Bild, sei der Anfang einer Reihe von Bildern, die wir aus diesem Bild abzuleiten gelernt haben.

Wenn wir aber bedenken, daß sich die Maschine auch anders hätte bewegen können, so kann es nun scheinen, als müßte in der Maschine, als Symbol, ihre Bewegungsart noch viel bestimmter enthalten sein, als in der wirklichen Maschine. Es genüge da nicht, daß dies die erfahrungsmäßig vorausbestimmten Bewegungen seien, sondern sie müßten eigentlich — in einem mysteriösen Sinne — bereits *gegenwärtig* sein. Und es ist ja wahr: die Bewegung des Maschinensymbols ist in anderer Weise vorausbestimmt, als die einer gegebenen wirklichen Maschine.

194. Wann denkt man denn: die Maschine habe ihre möglichen Bewegungen schon in irgendeiner mysteriösen Weise in sich? — Nun, wenn man philosophiert. Und was verleitet uns, das zu denken? Die Art und Weise, wie wir von der Maschine reden. Wir sagen z. B., die Maschine *habe* (besäße) diese Bewegungsmöglichkeiten; wir sprechen von der ideal starren Maschine, die sich nur so und so bewegen *könne*. —— Die Bewegungs*möglichkeit*, was ist sie? Sie ist nicht die *Bewegung*; aber sie scheint auch nicht die bloße physikalische Bedingung der Bewegung zu sein — etwa, daß zwischen Lager und Zapfen ein Spielraum ist, der Zapfen nicht zu streng ins Lager paßt. Denn dies ist zwar erfahrungsmäßig die Bedingung der Bewegung, aber man könnte sich die Sache auch anders vorstellen. Die Bewegungsmöglichkeit soll eher

We talk as if these parts could only move in this way, as if they could not do anything else. Is this how it is? Do we forget the possibility of their bending, breaking off, melting, and so on? Yes; in many cases |78| we don't think of that at all. We use a machine, or a picture of a machine, as a symbol of a particular mode of operation. For instance, we give someone such a picture and assume that he will derive the successive movements of the parts from it. (Just as we can give someone a number by telling him that it is the twenty-fifth in the series 1, 4, 9, 16, . . .)

"The machine seems already to contain its own mode of operation" means: we are inclined to compare the future movements of the machine in their definiteness to objects which have been lying in a drawer and which we now take out. —— But we don't say this kind of thing when it is a matter of predicting the actual behaviour of a machine. Then we do not in general forget the possibility of a distortion of the parts and so on. —— We *do* talk like that, however, when we are wondering at the way we can use a machine as a symbol of some way of moving — since it can, after all, also move quite differently.

We might say that a machine, or a picture of it, is the first of a series of pictures which we have learnt to derive from this one.

But when we reflect that the machine could also have moved differently, it may now look as if the way it moves must be contained in the machine *qua* symbol still more determinately than in the actual machine. As if it were not enough for the movements in question to be empirically predetermined, but they had to be really — in a mysterious sense — already *present*. And it is quite true: the movement of the machine *qua* symbol is predetermined in a different way from how the movement of any given actual machine is.

194. When does one have the thought that a machine already contains its possible movements in some mysterious way? — Well, when one is doing philosophy. And what lures us into thinking that? The kind of way in which we talk about the machine. We say, for example, that the machine *has* (possesses) such-and-such possibilities of movement; we speak of an ideally rigid machine which *can* move only thus-and-so. —— The *possibility* of movement — what is it? It is not the *movement*, but it does not seem to be a mere physical condition for moving either — such as there being play between socket and pin, the pin's not fitting too tight in the socket. For while this is empirically a condition for movement, one could also imagine things to be otherwise. The possibility of a movement is supposed, rather, to be like a shadow of the movement

wie ein Schatten der Bewegung selber sein. Aber kennst du so einen Schatten? Und unter Schatten verstehe ich nicht irgend ein Bild der Bewegung, — denn dies Bild müßte ja nicht das Bild gerade *dieser* Bewegung sein. Aber die Möglichkeit dieser Bewegung muß die Möglichkeit gerade dieser Bewegung sein. (Sieh, wie hoch die Wellen der Sprache hier gehen!)

Die Wellen legen sich, sowie wir uns fragen: Wie gebrauchen wir denn, wenn wir von einer Maschine reden, das Wort "Möglichkeit der Bewegung"? —— Woher kamen aber dann die seltsamen Ideen? Nun, ich zeige dir die Möglichkeit der Bewegung, etwa durch ein *Bild* der Bewegung: 'also ist die Möglichkeit etwas der Wirklichkeit Ähnliches'. Wir sagen: "es bewegt sich noch nicht, aber es hat schon die Möglichkeit, sich zu bewegen" —— 'also ist die Möglichkeit etwas der Wirklichkeit sehr Nahes'. Wir mögen zwar bezweifeln, ob die und die physikalische Bedingung diese Bewegung möglich macht, aber wir diskutieren nie, ob *dies* die Möglichkeit dieser, oder jener Bewegung sei: 'also steht die Möglichkeit der Bewegung zur Bewegung selbst in einer einzigartigen Relation; enger, als die des Bildes zu seinem Gegenstand'; denn es kann bezweifelt werden, ob dies das Bild dieses, oder jenes Gegenstandes ist. Wir sagen "Die Erfahrung wird lehren, ob dies dem Zapfen diese Bewegungsmöglichkeit gibt", aber wir sagen nicht "Die Erfahrung wird lehren, ob dies die Möglichkeit dieser Bewegung ist": 'also ist es nicht Erfahrungstatsache, daß diese Möglichkeit die Möglichkeit gerade dieser Bewegung ist'.

Wir achten auf unsere eigene Ausdrucksweise, diese Dinge betreffend, verstehen sie aber nicht, sondern mißdeuten sie. Wir sind, wenn wir philosophieren, wie Wilde, primitive Menschen, die die Ausdrucksweise zivilisierter Menschen hören, sie mißdeuten und nun die seltsamsten Schlüsse aus ihrer Deutung ziehen.

195. "Aber ich meine nicht, daß, was ich jetzt (beim Erfassen) tue, die künftige Verwendung *kausal* und erfahrungsmäßig bestimmt, sondern daß, in einer *seltsamen* Weise, diese Verwendung selbst in irgend einem Sinne gegenwärtig ist." — Aber 'in *irgend* einem Sinne' ist sie es ja! Eigentlich ist an dem, was du sagst, falsch nur der Ausdruck "in seltsamer Weise". Das Übrige ist richtig; und seltsam erscheint der Satz nur, wenn man sich zu ihm ein anderes Sprachspiel vorstellt, als das, worin wir ihn tatsächlich verwenden. (Jemand sagte mir, er habe sich als Kind darüber gewundert, daß der Schneider '*ein Kleid nähen*' könne — er dachte, dies heiße, es werde durch bloßes Nähen ein Kleid erzeugt, indem man Faden an Faden näht.)

itself. But do you know of any such shadow? And by a shadow I do not mean some picture of the movement — for such a |79| picture would not have to be a picture of just *this* movement. But the possibility of this movement must be the possibility of just this movement. (See how high the seas of language run here!)

The waves subside as soon as we ask ourselves: how do we use the phrase "possibility of movement" when we are talking about a given machine? —— But then where did these strange ideas come from? Well, I show you the possibility of a movement, say by means of a *picture* of the movement, 'So possibility is something which is similar to reality'. We say, "It isn't moving yet, but it already has the possibility of moving" —— 'so possibility is something very near reality'. Though we may doubt whether such-and-such a physical condition makes this movement possible, we never discuss whether *this* is the possibility of this or of that movement: 'so the possibility of the movement stands in a unique relation to the movement itself; closer than that of a picture to its subject'; for it can be doubted whether a picture is the picture of this or that subject. We say, "Experience will show whether this gives the pin this possibility of movement", but we do not say, "Experience will show whether this is the possibility of this movement"; 'so it is not a matter of experience that this possibility is the possibility of just this movement'.

Though we do pay attention to the way we talk about these matters, we don't understand it, but misinterpret it. When we do philosophy, we are like savages, primitive people, who hear the way in which civilized people talk, put a false interpretation on it, and then draw the oddest conclusions from this.

195. "But I don't mean that what I do now (in grasping the whole use of a word) determines the future use *causally* and as a matter of experience, but that, in a *strange* way, the use itself is in some sense present." — But of course it is, 'in *some* sense'! Really, the only thing wrong with what you say is the expression "in an odd way". The rest is right; and the sentence seems odd only when one imagines it to belong to a different language-game from the one in which we actually use it. (Someone once told me that as a child he had been amazed that a tailor could 'sew a dress' — he thought this meant that a dress was produced by sewing alone, by sewing one thread on to another.)

196. Die unverstandene Verwendung des Wortes wird als Ausdruck eines seltsamen *Vorgangs* gedeutet. (Wie man sich die Zeit als seltsames Medium, die Seele als seltsames Wesen denkt.)

197. "Es ist, als könnten wir die ganze Verwendung des Wortes mit einem Schlag erfassen." — Wir sagen ja, daß wir es tun. D. h., wir beschreiben ja manchmal, was wir tun, mit diesen Worten. Aber es ist an dem, was geschieht, nichts Erstaunliches, nichts Seltsames. Seltsam wird es, wenn wir dazu geführt werden, zu denken, daß die künftige Entwicklung auf irgend eine Weise schon im Akt des Erfassens gegenwärtig sein muß und doch nicht gegenwärtig ist. — Denn wir sagen, es sei kein Zweifel, daß wir dies Wort verstehen, und anderseits liegt seine Bedeutung in seiner Verwendung. Es ist kein Zweifel, daß ich jetzt Schach spielen will; aber das Schachspiel ist dies Spiel durch alle seine Regeln (u. s. f.). Weiß ich also nicht, was ich spielen wollte, ehe ich gespielt *habe*? oder aber, sind alle Regeln in meinem Akt der Intention enthalten? Ist es nun Erfahrung, die mich lehrt, daß auf diesen Akt der Intention für gewöhnlich diese Art des Spielens folgt? kann ich also doch nicht sicher sein, was zu tun ich beabsichtigte? Und wenn dies Unsinn ist, — welcherlei über-starre Verbindung besteht zwischen dem Akt der Absicht und dem Beabsichtigten? —— Wo ist die Verbindung gemacht zwischen dem Sinn der Worte "Spielen wir eine Partie Schach!" und allen Regeln des Spiels? — Nun, im Regelverzeichnis des Spiels, im Schachunterricht, in der täglichen Praxis des Spielens.

198. "Aber wie kann mich eine Regel lehren, was ich an *dieser* Stelle zu tun habe? Was immer ich tue, ist doch durch irgend eine Deutung mit der Regel zu vereinbaren." — Nein, so sollte es nicht heißen. Sondern so: Jede Deutung hängt, mitsamt dem Gedeuteten, in der Luft; sie kann ihm nicht als Stütze dienen. Die Deutungen allein bestimmen die Bedeutung nicht.

"Also ist, was immer ich tue, mit der Regel vereinbar?" — Laß mich so fragen: Was hat der Ausdruck der Regel — sagen wir, der Wegweiser — mit meinen Handlungen zu tun? Was für eine Verbindung besteht da? — Nun, etwa diese: ich bin zu einem bestimmten Reagieren auf dieses Zeichen abgerichtet worden, und so reagiere ich nun.

Aber damit hast du nur einen kausalen Zusammenhang angegeben, nur erklärt, wie es dazu kam, daß wir uns jetzt nach dem Wegweiser richten; nicht, worin dieses Dem-Zeichen-Folgen eigentlich besteht. Nein; ich habe auch noch angedeutet, daß sich Einer nur insofern nach einem Wegweiser richtet, als es einen ständigen Gebrauch, eine Gepflogenheit, gibt.

196. In misunderstanding the use of the word, one takes it to signify an odd *process*. (As one thinks of time as a strange medium, of the mind as an odd kind of being.) |80|

197. "It's as if we could grasp the whole use of a word at a stroke." — Well, that is just what we say we do. That is, we sometimes describe what we do in these words. But there is nothing astonishing, nothing strange, about what happens. It becomes strange when we are led to think that the future development must in some way already be present in the act of grasping the use and yet isn't present. — For we say that there isn't any doubt that we understand the word, and on the other hand that its meaning lies in its use. There is no doubt that I now want to play chess, but chess is the game it is in virtue of all its rules (and so on). Don't I know, then, which game I want to play until I *have* played it? Or is it, rather, that all the rules are contained in my act of intending? Is it experience that tells me that this sort of game usually follows such an act of intending? So can't I actually be sure what I intended to do? And if that is nonsense — what kind of super-rigid connection obtains between the act of intending and the thing intended? — — Where is the connection effected between the sense of the words "Let's play a game of chess" and all the rules of the game? — Well, in the list of rules of the game, in the teaching of it, in the everyday practice of playing.

198. "But how can a rule teach me what I have to do at *this* point? After all, whatever I do can, on some interpretation, be made compatible with the rule." — No, that's not what one should say. Rather, this: every interpretation hangs in the air together with what it interprets, and cannot give it any support. Interpretations by themselves do not determine meaning.

"So is whatever I do compatible with the rule?" — Let me ask this: what has the expression of a rule — say a signpost — got to do with my actions? What sort of connection obtains here? — Well, this one, for example: I have been trained to react in a particular way to this sign, and now I do so react to it.

But with this you have pointed out only a causal connection; only explained how it has come about that we now go by the signpost; not what this following-the-sign really consists in. Not so; I have further indicated that a person goes by a signpost only in so far as there is an established usage, a custom.

199. Ist, was wir "einer Regel folgen" nennen, etwas, was nur *ein* Mensch, nur *einmal* im Leben, tun könnte? — Und das ist natürlich eine Anmerkung zur *Grammatik* des Ausdrucks "der Regel folgen".

Es kann nicht ein einziges Mal nur ein Mensch einer Regel gefolgt sein. Es kann nicht ein einziges Mal nur eine Mitteilung gemacht, ein Befehl gegeben, oder verstanden worden sein, etc. — Einer Regel folgen, eine Mitteilung machen, einen Befehl geben, eine Schachpartie spielen sind *Gepflogenheiten* (Gebräuche, Institutionen).

Einen Satz verstehen, heißt, eine Sprache verstehen. Eine Sprache verstehen, heißt eine Technik beherrschen.

200. Es ist natürlich denkbar, daß in einem Volke, das Spiele nicht kennt, zwei Leute sich an ein Schachbrett setzen und die Züge einer Schachpartie ausführen; ja auch mit allen seelischen Begleiterscheinungen. Und sähen *wir* dies, so würden wir sagen, sie spielten Schach. Aber nun denk dir eine Schachpartie nach gewissen Regeln in eine Reihe von Handlungen übersetzt, die wir nicht gewöhnt sind, mit einem *Spiel* zu assoziieren, — etwa ein Ausstoßen von Schreien und Stampfen mit den Füßen. Und jene Beiden sollen nun, statt die uns geläufige Form des Schach zu spielen, schreien und stampfen; und zwar so, daß diese Vorgänge sich nach geeigneten Regeln in eine Schachpartie übersetzen ließen. Wären wir nun noch geneigt, zu sagen, sie spielten ein Spiel; und mit welchem Recht könnte man das sagen?

201. Unser Paradox war dies: eine Regel könnte keine Handlungsweise bestimmen, da jede Handlungsweise mit der Regel in Übereinstimmung zu bringen sei. Die Antwort war: Ist jede mit der Regel in Übereinstimmung zu bringen, dann auch zum Widerspruch. Daher gäbe es hier weder Übereinstimmung noch Widerspruch.

Daß da ein Mißverständnis ist, zeigt sich schon darin, daß wir in diesem Gedankengang Deutung hinter Deutung setzen; als beruhige uns eine jede wenigstens für einen Augenblick, bis wir an eine Deutung denken, die wieder hinter dieser liegt. Dadurch zeigen wir nämlich, daß es eine Auffassung einer Regel gibt, die *nicht* eine *Deutung* ist; sondern sich, von Fall zu Fall der Anwendung, in dem äußert, was wir "der Regel folgen", und was wir "ihr entgegenhandeln" nennen.

Darum besteht eine Neigung, zu sagen: jedes Handeln nach der Regel sei ein Deuten. "Deuten" aber sollte man nur nennen: einen Ausdruck der Regel durch einen anderen ersetzen.

202. Darum ist 'der Regel folgen' eine Praxis. Und der Regel zu folgen *glauben* ist nicht: der Regel folgen. Und darum kann man nicht der Regel

199. Is what we call "following a rule" something that it would be possible for only *one* person, only *once* in a lifetime, to do? — And this is, of course, a gloss on the *grammar* of the expression "to follow a rule". |81|

It is not possible that there should have been only one occasion on which only one person followed a rule. It is not possible that there should have been only one occasion on which a report was made, an order given or understood, and so on. — To follow a rule, to make a report, to give an order, to play a game of chess, are *customs* (routines, institutions).

To understand a sentence means to understand a language. To understand a language means to have mastered a technique.

200. It is, of course, imaginable that two people belonging to a tribe unacquainted with games should sit at a chessboard and go through the moves of a game of chess; and even with all the mental accompaniments. And if *we* were to see it, we'd say that they were playing chess. But now imagine a game of chess translated according to certain rules into a series of actions which we do not ordinarily associate with a *game* — say into yells and stamping of feet. And now suppose those two people to yell and stamp instead of playing the form of chess that we are used to; and this in such a way that what goes on is translatable by suitable rules into a game of chess. Would we still be inclined to say that they were playing a game? And with what right could one say so?

201. This was our paradox: no course of action could be determined by a rule, because every course of action can be brought into accord with the rule. The answer was: if every course of action can be brought into accord with the rule, then it can also be brought into conflict with it. And so there would be neither accord nor conflict here.

That there is a misunderstanding here is shown by the mere fact that in this chain of reasoning we place one interpretation behind another, as if each one contented us at least for a moment, until we thought of yet another lying behind it.(For what we thereby show is that there is a way of grasping a rule which is *not* an interpretation, but which, from case to case of application, is manifest in what we call "following the rule" and "going against it".)

That's why there is an inclination to say: every action according to a rule is an interpretation.(But one should speak of interpretation only when one expression of a rule is substituted for another.)

202. That's why 'following a rule' is a practice. And to *think* one is following a rule is not to follow a rule. And that's why it's not possible

'privatim' folgen, weil sonst der Regel zu folgen glauben dasselbe wäre, wie der Regel folgen.

203. Die Sprache ist ein Labyrinth von Wegen. Du kommst von *einer* Seite und kennst dich aus; du kommst von einer andern zur selben Stelle, und kennst dich nicht mehr aus.

204. Ich kann etwa, wie die Sachen stehen, ein Spiel erfinden, das nie von jemandem gespielt wird. — Wäre aber auch dies möglich: Die Menschheit habe nie Spiele gespielt; einmal aber hat Einer ein Spiel erfunden, — das dann allerdings nie gespielt wurde?

205. "Das ist ja das Merkwürdige an der *Intention*, am seelischen Vorgang, daß für ihn das Bestehen der Gepflogenheit, der Technik, nicht nötig ist. Daß es z. B. denkbar ist, zwei Leute spielten in einer Welt, in der sonst nicht gespielt wird, eine Schachpartie, ja auch nur den Anfang einer Schachpartie, — und würden dann gestört."

Ist aber das Schachspiel nicht durch seine Regeln definiert? Und wie sind diese Regeln im Geist dessen gegenwärtig, der beabsichtigt, Schach zu spielen?

206. Einer Regel folgen, das ist analog dem: einen Befehl befolgen. Man wird dazu abgerichtet und man reagiert auf ihn in bestimmter Weise. Aber wie, wenn nun der Eine *so*, der Andere *anders* auf Befehl und Abrichtung reagiert? Wer hat dann Recht?

Denke, du kämst als Forscher in ein unbekanntes Land mit einer dir gänzlich fremden Sprache. Unter welchen Umständen würdest du sagen, daß die Leute dort Befehle geben, Befehle verstehen, befolgen, sich gegen Befehle auflehnen, u. s. w.?

Die gemeinsame menschliche Handlungsweise ist das Bezugssystem, mittels welches wir uns eine fremde Sprache deuten.

207. Denken wir uns, die Leute in jenem Land verrichteten gewöhnliche menschliche Tätigkeiten und bedienen sich dabei, wie es scheint, einer artikulierten Sprache. Sieht man ihrem Treiben zu, so ist es verständlich, erscheint uns 'logisch'. Versuchen wir aber, ihre Sprache zu erlernen, so finden wir, daß es unmöglich ist. Es besteht nämlich bei ihnen kein regelmäßiger Zusammenhang des Gesprochenen, der Laute, mit den Handlungen; dennoch aber sind diese Laute nicht überflüssig; denn knebeln wir z. B. einen dieser Leute, so hat dies die gleichen Folgen, wie bei uns: ohne jene Laute geraten ihre Handlungen in Verwirrung — wie ich mich ausdrücken will.

to follow a rule 'privately'; otherwise, thinking one was following a rule would be the same thing as following a rule. |82|

203. Language is a labyrinth of paths. You approach from *one* side and know your way about; you approach the same place from another side and no longer know your way about.

204. As things are, I can, for example, invent a game that is never played by anyone. — But would the following be possible too: mankind has never played any games; once though, someone invented a game — which, however, was never played?

205. "But that is just what is remarkable about *intention*, about the mental process, that the existence of a custom, of a technique, is not necessary to it. That, for example, it is imaginable that two people should play a game of chess, or even only the beginning of a game of chess, in a world in which otherwise no games existed — and then be interrupted."
   But isn't chess defined by its rules? And how are these rules present in the mind of someone who intends to play chess?

206. Following a rule is analogous to obeying an order. One is trained to do so, and one reacts to an order in a particular way. But what if one person reacts to the order and training *thus*, and another *otherwise*? Who is right, then?
   Suppose you came as an explorer to an unknown country with a language quite unknown to you. In what circumstances would you say that the people there gave orders, understood them, obeyed them, rebelled against them, and so on?
   Shared human behaviour is the system of reference by means of which we interpret an unknown language.

207. Let's imagine that the people in that country carried on usual human activities and in the course of them employed, apparently, an articulate language. If we watch their activities, we find them intelligible, they seem 'logical'. But when we try to learn their language, we find it impossible to do so. For there is no regular connection between what they say, the sounds they make, and their activities; but still these sounds are not superfluous, for if, for example, we gag one of these people, this has the same consequences as with us: without those sounds their actions fall into confusion — as I feel like putting it.

Sollen wir sagen, diese Leute hätten eine Sprache; Befehle, Mitteilungen, u. s. w.?

Zu dem, was wir "Sprache" nennen, fehlt die Regelmäßigkeit.

208. So erkläre ich also, was "Befehl" und was "Regel" heißt, durch "Regelmäßigkeit"? — Wie erkläre ich jemandem die Bedeutung von "regelmäßig", "gleichförmig", "gleich"? — Einem der, sagen wir, nur Französisch spricht, werde ich diese Wörter durch die entsprechenden französischen erklären. Wer aber diese *Begriffe* noch nicht besitzt, den werde ich die Worte durch *Beispiele* und durch *Übung* gebrauchen lehren. — Und dabei teile ich ihm nicht weniger mit, als ich selber weiß.

Ich werde ihm also in diesem Unterricht gleiche Farben, gleiche Längen, gleiche Figuren zeigen, ihn sie finden und herstellen lassen, u. s. w. Ich werde ihn etwa dazu anleiten, Reihenornamente auf einen Befehl hin 'gleichmäßig' fortzusetzen. — Und auch dazu, Progressionen fortzusetzen. Also etwa auf . .. ... so fortzufahren: ....
. . . .

Ich mach's ihm vor, er macht es mir nach; und ich beeinflusse ihn durch Äußerungen der Zustimmung, der Ablehnung, der Erwartung, der Aufmunterung. Ich lasse ihn gewähren, oder halte ihn zurück; u. s. w.

Denke, du wärest Zeuge eines solchen Unterrichts. Es würde darin kein Wort durch sich selbst erklärt, kein logischer Zirkel gemacht.

Auch die Ausdrücke "und so weiter" und "und so weiter ad infinitum" werden in diesem Unterricht erklärt werden. Es kann dazu unter anderem auch eine Gebärde dienen. Die Gebärde, die bedeutet "fahr so fort!", oder "und so weiter" hat eine Funktion, vergleichbar der des Zeigens auf einen Gegenstand, oder auf einen Ort.

Es ist zu unterscheiden: das "u. s. w.", das eine Abkürzung der Schreibweise ist, von demjenigen, welches dies *nicht* ist. Das "u. s. w. ad inf." ist *keine* Abkürzung der Schreibweise. Daß wir nicht alle Stellen von π anschreiben können, ist nicht eine menschliche Unzulänglichkeit, wie Mathematiker manchmal glauben.

Ein Unterricht, der bei den vorgeführten Beispielen stehen bleiben will, unterscheidet sich von einem, der über sie 'hinausweist'.

209. "Aber reicht denn nicht das Verständnis weiter, als alle Beispiele?" — Ein sehr merkwürdiger Ausdruck, und ganz natürlich! —

Aber ist das *alles*? Gibt es nicht eine noch tiefere Erklärung; oder muß nicht doch das *Verständnis* der Erklärung tiefer sein? — Ja, habe ich denn selbst ein tieferes Verständnis? *Habe* ich mehr, als ich in der Erklärung gebe? — Woher aber dann das Gefühl, ich hätte mehr?

Are we to say that these people have a language: orders, reports, and so on?

The regularity for what we call "language" is lacking.

208. Then am I explaining what "order" and "rule" mean in terms of "regularity"? — How do I explain the meaning of "regular", "uniform", |83| "same" to anyone? — I'll explain these words to someone who, say, speaks only French by means of the corresponding French words. But if a person has not yet got the *concept*s, I'll teach him to use the words by means of *examples* and by *exercises*. — And when I do this, I do not communicate less to him than I know myself.

In the course of this teaching, I'll show him the same colours, the same lengths, the same shapes; I'll make him find them and produce them; and so on. For example, I'll teach him to continue an ornamental pattern 'uniformly' when told to do so. — And also to continue progressions. That is, for example, when given: . .. ... to go on:
. . . .

I do it, he does it after me; and I influence him by expressions of agreement, rejection, expectation, encouragement. I let him go his way, or hold him back; and so on.

Imagine witnessing such teaching. None of the words would be explained by means of itself; there would be no logical circle.

The expressions "and so on", "and so on *ad infinitum*", are also explained in this teaching. A gesture, among other things, might serve this purpose. The gesture that means "go on like this" or "and so on" has a function comparable to that of pointing to an object or a place.

A distinction is to be drawn between the "and so on" which is and the "and so on" which *is not* an abbreviated notation. "And so on *ad inf.*" is *not* such an abbreviation. The fact that we cannot write down all the digits of π is not a human shortcoming, as mathematicians sometimes think.

Teaching which is not meant to apply to anything but the examples given is different from that which '*points beyond*' them.

209. "But then doesn't our understanding reach beyond all examples?" — A very curious expression, and a quite natural one! —

But is that *all*? Isn't there a deeper explanation; or at least, mustn't the *understanding* of the explanation be deeper? — Well, have I myself a deeper understanding? Have I *got* more than I give in the explanation? — But then, whence the feeling that I have more?

Ist es, wie wenn ich das nicht Begrenzte als Länge deute, die über jede Länge hinausreicht?

210. "Aber erklärst du ihm wirklich, was du selber verstehst? Läßt du ihn das Wesentliche nicht *erraten*? Du gibst ihm Beispiele, — er aber muß ihre Tendenz erraten, also deine Absicht." — Jede Erklärung, die ich mir selbst geben kann, gebe ich auch ihm. — "Er errät, was ich meine" würde heißen: ihm schweben verschiedene Deutungen meiner Erklärung vor, und er rät auf eine von ihnen. Er könnte also in diesem Falle fragen; und ich könnte, und würde, ihm antworten.

211. "Wie immer du ihn im Fortführen des Reihenornaments unterrichtest, — wie kann er *wissen*, wie er selbständig fortzusetzen hat?" — Nun, wie weiß *ich's*? —— Wenn das heißt "Habe ich Gründe?", so ist die Antwort: die Gründe werden mir bald ausgehen. Und ich werde dann, ohne Gründe, handeln.

212. Wenn jemand, den ich fürchte, mir den Befehl gibt, die Reihe fortzusetzen, so werde ich schleunig, mit völliger Sicherheit, handeln, und das Fehlen der Gründe stört mich nicht.

213. "Aber dieser Reihenanfang konnte offenbar verschieden gedeutet werden (z. B. durch algebraische Ausdrücke) und du mußtest also erst *eine* solche Deutung wählen." — Durchaus nicht! Es war, unter Umständen, ein Zweifel möglich. Aber das sagt nicht, daß ich gezweifelt habe, oder auch nur zweifeln konnte. (Damit steht im Zusammenhang, was über die psychologische 'Atmosphäre' eines Vorgangs zu sagen ist.)
Nur Intuition konnte diesen Zweifel heben? — Wenn sie eine innere Stimme ist, — wie weiß ich, *wie* ich ihr folgen soll? Und wie weiß ich, daß sie mich nicht irreleitet? Denn, kann sie mich richtig leiten, dann kann sie mich auch irreleiten.
((Die Intuition eine unnötige Ausrede.))

214. Ist eine Intuition zum Entwickeln der Reihe 1 2 3 4 ... nötig, dann auch zum Entwickeln der Reihe 2 2 2 2 ...

215. Aber ist nicht wenigstens gleich: *gleich*?
Für die Gleichheit scheinen wir ein unfehlbares Paradigma zu haben in der Gleichheit eines Dinges mit sich selbst. Ich will sagen: "Hier kann es doch nicht verschiedene Deutungen geben. Wenn er ein Ding vor sich sieht, so sieht er auch Gleichheit."

Is it like the case where I interpret what is not limited as a length that reaches beyond every length?

210. "But do you really explain to the other person what you yourself understand? Don't you leave it to him to *guess* the essential thing? You give him examples — but he has to guess their drift, to guess your |84| intention." — Every explanation which I can give myself I give to him too. — "He guesses what I mean" would amount to: "various interpretations of my explanation come to his mind, and he picks one of them". So in this case he could ask; and I could and would answer him.

211. "No matter how you instruct him in continuing the ornamental pattern, how can he *know* how he is to continue it by himself?" — Well, how do *I* know? —— If that means "Have I reasons?", the answer is: my reasons will soon give out. And then I shall act, without reasons.

212. When someone of whom I am afraid orders me to continue a series, I act quickly, with perfect assurance, and the lack of reasons does not trouble me.

213. "But this initial segment of a series could obviously be variously interpreted (for example, by means of algebraic expressions), so you must first have chosen *one* such interpretation." — Not at all! A doubt was possible in certain circumstances. But that is not to say that I did doubt, or even could doubt. (What is to be said about the psychological 'atmosphere' of a process is connected with that.)

Only intuition could have removed this doubt? — If intuition is an inner voice — how do I know *how* I am to follow it? And how do I know that it doesn't mislead me? For if it can guide me right, it can also guide me wrong.

((Intuition an unnecessary evasion.))

214. If an intuition is necessary for continuing the series 1 2 3 4 . . . , then also for continuing the series 2 2 2 2 . . .

215. But isn't at least the same *the same*?

For identity we seem to have an infallible paradigm: namely, in the identity of a thing with itself. I feel like saying: "Here at any rate there can't be different interpretations. If someone sees a thing, he sees identity too."

Also sind zwei Dinge gleich, wenn sie so sind, wie *ein* Ding? Und wie soll ich nun das, was mir das *eine* Ding zeigt, auf den Fall der zwei anwenden?

216. "Ein Ding ist mit sich selbst identisch." — Es gibt kein schöneres Beispiel eines nutzlosen Satzes, der aber doch mit einem Spiel der Vorstellung verbunden ist. Es ist, als legten wir das Ding, in der Vorstellung, in seine eigene Form hinein, und sähen, daß es paßt.

Wir könnten auch sagen: "Jedes Ding paßt in sich selbst." — Oder anders: "Jedes Ding paßt in seine eigene Form hinein." Man schaut dabei ein Ding an und stellt sich vor, daß der Raum dafür ausgespart war und es nun genau hineinpaßt.

'Paßt' dieser Fleck ♠ in seine weiße Umgebung? — *Aber genau so würde es aussehen*, wenn statt seiner erst ein Loch gewesen wäre und er nun hineinpaßte. Mit dem Ausdruck "er paßt" wird eben nicht einfach dies Bild beschrieben. Nicht einfach diese *Situation*.

"Jeder Farbfleck paßt genau in seine Umgebung" ist ein etwas spezialisierter Satz der Identität.

217. "Wie kann ich einer Regel folgen?" — wenn das nicht eine Frage nach den Ursachen ist, so ist es eine nach der Rechtfertigung dafür, daß ich *so* nach ihr handle.

Habe ich die Begründungen erschöpft, so bin ich nun auf dem harten Felsen angelangt, und mein Spaten biegt sich zurück. Ich bin dann geneigt, zu sagen: "So handle ich eben."

(Erinnere dich, daß wir manchmal Erklärungen fordern nicht ihres Inhalts wegen, sondern der Form der Erklärung wegen. Unsere Forderung ist eine architektonische; die Erklärung eine Art Scheingesims, das nichts trägt.)

218. Woher die Idee, es wäre die angefangene Reihe ein sichtbares Stück unsichtbar bis ins Unendliche gelegter Geleise? Nun, statt der Regel könnten wir uns Geleise denken. Und der nicht begrenzten Anwendung der Regel entsprechen unendlich lange Geleise.

219. "Die Übergänge sind eigentlich alle schon gemacht" heißt: ich habe keine Wahl mehr. Die Regel, einmal mit einer bestimmten Bedeutung gestempelt, zieht die Linien ihrer Befolgung durch den ganzen Raum. —— Aber wenn so etwas wirklich der Fall wäre, was hülfe es mir?

Nein; meine Beschreibung hatte nur Sinn, wenn sie symbolisch zu verstehen war. — *So kommt es mir vor* — sollte ich sagen.

Then are two things the same when they are what *one* thing is? And how am I to apply what the one thing shows me to the case of two things?

216. "A thing is identical with itself." — There is no finer example of a useless sentence, which nevertheless is connected with a certain play of the imagination. It is as if in our imagination we put a thing into its own shape and saw that it fitted. |85|

We might also say: "Every thing fits into itself." — Or again: "Every thing fits into its own shape." While saying this, one looks at a thing and imagines that there was a space left for it and that now it fits into it exactly.

Does this spot ♣ '*fit*' into its white surrounding? — *But that is just how it would look* if there had at first been a hole in its place and it then fitted into the hole. So when we say "it fits", we are describing not simply this picture, not simply this *situation*.

"Every coloured patch fits exactly into its surrounding" is a somewhat specialized form of the law of identity.

217. "How am I able to follow a rule?" — If this is not a question about causes, then it is about the justification for my acting in *this* way in complying with the rule.

Once I have exhausted the justifications, I have reached bedrock, and my spade is turned. Then I am inclined to say: "This is simply what I do."

(Remember that we sometimes demand explanations for the sake not of their content, but of their form. Our requirement is an architectural one; the explanation a kind of sham corbel that supports nothing.)

218. Whence the idea that the beginning of a series is a visible section of rails invisibly laid to infinity? Well, we might imagine rails instead of a rule. And infinitely long rails correspond to the unlimited application of a rule.

219. "All the steps are really already taken" means: I no longer have any choice. The rule, once stamped with a particular meaning, traces the lines along which it is to be followed through the whole of space. —— But if something of this sort really were the case, how would it help me?

No; my description made sense only if it was to be understood symbolically. — I should say: *This is how it strikes me.*

Wenn ich der Regel folge, wähle ich nicht.
Ich folge der Regel *blind*.

220. Welchen Zweck hat aber jener symbolische Satz? Er sollte einen Unterschied hervorheben zwischen kausaler Bedingtheit und logischer Bedingtheit.

221. Mein symbolischer Ausdruck war eigentlich eine mythologische Beschreibung des Gebrauchs einer Regel.

222. "Die Linie gibt's mir ein, wie ich gehen soll." — Aber das ist natürlich nur ein Bild. Und urteile ich, sie gebe mir, gleichsam verantwortungslos, dies oder das ein, so würde ich nicht sagen, ich folgte ihr als einer Regel.

223. Man fühlt nicht, daß man immer des Winkes (der Einflüsterung) der Regel gewärtig sein muß. Im Gegenteil. Wir sind nicht gespannt darauf, was sie uns wohl jetzt sagen wird, sondern sie sagt uns immer dasselbe, und wir tun, was sie uns sagt.
  Man könnte dem, den man abrichtet, sagen: "Sieh, ich tue immer das Gleiche: ich . . ."

224. Das Wort "Übereinstimmung" und das Wort "Regel" sind miteinander *verwandt*, sie sind Vettern. Lehre ich Einen den Gebrauch des einen Wortes, so lernt er damit auch den Gebrauch des andern.

225. Die Verwendung des Wortes "Regel" ist mit der Verwendung des Wortes "gleich" verwoben. (Wie die Verwendung von "Satz" mit der Verwendung von "wahr".)

226. Nimm an, Einer folgt der Reihe 1, 3, 5, 7, . . . indem er die Reihe der 2x - 1 hinschreibt. Und er fragte sich: "aber tue ich auch immer das Gleiche, oder jedesmal etwas anderes?"
  Wer von einem Tag auf den andern verspricht "Morgen will ich dich besuchen" — sagt der jeden Tag das Gleiche; oder jeden Tag etwas anderes?

227. Hätte es einen Sinn zu sagen: "Wenn er jedesmal etwas *anderes* täte, würden wir nicht sagen: er folge einer Regel"? Das hat *keinen* Sinn.

228. "Eine Reihe hat für uns *ein* Gesicht!" — Wohl; aber welches? Nun doch das algebraische, und das eines Stücks der Entwicklung. Oder hat sie sonst noch eins? — "Aber in dem liegt doch schon alles!" — Aber das ist keine Feststellung über das Reihenstück, oder über etwas, was

When I follow the rule, I do not choose.
I follow the rule *blindly*.

220. But what is the purpose of that symbolical sentence? It was supposed to highlight a difference between causal and logical dependence.

221. My symbolical expression was really a mythological description of the use of a rule. |86|

222. "The line intimates to me the way I am to go." — But that is, of course, only a picture. And if I judged that it intimated this or that, as it were, irresponsibly, I wouldn't say that I was following it like a rule.

223. One does not feel that one has always got to wait upon the nod (the prompt) of the rule. On the contrary, we are not on tenterhooks about what it will tell us next, but it always tells us the same, and we do what it tells us.
    One might say to the person one was training: "Look, I always do the same thing: I . . ."

224. The word "accord" and the word "rule" are *related* to one another; they are cousins. If I teach anyone the use of the one word, he learns the use of the other with it.

225. The use of the word "rule" and the use of the word "same" are interwoven. (As are the use of "proposition" and the use of "true".)

* 226. Suppose someone continues the sequence 1, 3, 5, 7, . . . in expanding the series $2x - 1$. And now he asks himself, "But am I always doing the same thing, or something different every time?"
    If, from one day to the next, someone promises: "Tomorrow I'll come to see you" — is he saying the same thing every day, or every day something different?

227. Would it make sense to say: "If he did something *different* every time, we wouldn't say he was following a rule"? That makes *no* sense.

* 228. "A series presents us with *one* face!" — All right, but which one? Well, surely, the algebraic one, with a segment of the expansion. Or does it have yet another face? — "But surely everything is already contained in this one!" — But that is not an observation about the segment

wir darin erblicken; sondern der Ausdruck dafür, daß wir nur auf den Mund der Regel schauen und *tun*, und an keine weitere Anleitung appellieren.

229. Ich glaube, im Reihenstück ganz fein eine Zeichnung wahrzunehmen, einen charakteristischen Zug, der nur noch des "u. s. w." bedarf, um in die Unendlichkeit zu reichen.

230. "Die Linie gibt's mir ein, wie ich gehen soll": das paraphrasiert nur: sie sei meine *letzte* Instanz dafür, wie ich gehen soll.

231. "Aber du siehst doch . . . !" Nun, das ist eben die charakteristische Äußerung Eines, der von der Regel gezwungen ist.

232. Nimm an, eine Regel gebe mir ein, wie ich ihr folgen soll; d. h., wenn ich der Linie mit den Augen nachgehe, so sagt mir nun eine innere Stimme: "Zieh *so*!" — Was ist der Unterschied zwischen diesem Vorgang, einer Art Inspiration zu folgen, und dem, einer Regel zu folgen? Denn sie sind doch nicht das Gleiche. In dem Fall der Inspiration *warte* ich auf die Anweisung. Ich werde einen Andern nicht meine 'Technik' lehren können, der Linie zu folgen. Es sei denn, ich lehrte ihn eine Art des Hinhorchens, der Rezeptivität. Aber dann kann ich natürlich nicht verlangen, daß er der Linie so folge, wie ich.

Dies sind nicht meine Erfahrungen vom Handeln nach einer Inspiration und nach einer Regel; sondern grammatische Anmerkungen.

233. Man könnte sich auch so einen Unterricht in einer Art von Arithmetik denken. Die Kinder können dann, ein jedes auf seine Weise, rechnen, — solange sie nur auf die innere Stimme horchen und ihr folgen. Dieses Rechnen wäre wie ein Komponieren.

234. Aber könnten wir nicht auch rechnen, wie wir rechnen (Alle übereinstimmend, etc.), und doch bei jedem Schritt das Gefühl haben, von den Regeln wie von einem Zauber geleitet zu werden; erstaunt darüber vielleicht, daß wir übereinstimmen? (Der Gottheit etwa für diese Übereinstimmung dankend.)

235. Daraus siehst du nur, was alles zu der Physiognomie desjenigen gehört, was wir im alltäglichen Leben "einer Regel folgen" nennen!

236. Die Kunstrechner, die zum richtigen Resultat gelangen, aber nicht sagen können, wie. Sollen wir sagen, sie rechnen nicht? (Eine Familie von Fällen.)

of the series, or about anything that we notice in it; it gives expression to the fact that all we do is read the lips of the rule and *act*, without appealing to anything else for guidance.

229. I believe that I faintly perceive a pattern in the segment of the series, a characteristic feature, which needs only an "and so on" in order to reach to infinity.

230. "The line intimates to me the way I'm to go" is only a paraphrase of: it is my *final* court of appeal for the way I'm to go.

231. "But, surely you can see . . . !" That's precisely the characteristic exclamation of someone who is compelled by a rule. |87|

232. Suppose that a rule intimates to me how I'm to follow it; that is, as my eye travels along the line, an inner voice tells me "Draw *this* way!' — What's the difference between this process of following a kind of inspiration and that of following a rule? For they surely aren't the same. In the case of inspiration, I *await* direction. I won't be able to teach anyone else my 'technique' of following the line. Unless, indeed, I teach him some way of listening, some kind of receptivity. But then, of course, I can't expect him to follow the line in the same way as I do.

These aren't the experiences I have gained from acting from inspiration and from acting according to a rule; they're grammatical remarks.

233. One might also imagine such instruction in a certain kind of arithmetic. Children could then calculate, each in their own way — as long as they listened to their inner voice and followed it. Calculating in this way would resemble a sort of composing.

234. Wouldn't it be possible for us, however, to calculate as we actually do (all agreeing, and so on), and still at every step to have a feeling of being guided by the rules as by a spell, astonished perhaps at the fact that we agreed? (Perhaps giving thanks to the Deity for this agreement.)

235. From this you can see how much there is to the physiognomy of what we call "following a rule" in everyday life.

236. Calculating prodigies who arrive at the correct result but can't say how. Are we to say that they do not calculate? (A family of cases.)

237. Denke dir, Einer folgte einer Linie als Regel auf diese Weise: Er hält einen Zirkel, dessen eine Spitze er der Regel-Linie entlang führt, während die andre Spitze die Linie zieht, welche der Regel folgt. Und während er so der Regel entlang fährt, verändert er die Öffnung des Zirkels, wie es scheint mit großer Genauigkeit, wobei er immer auf die Regel schaut, als bestimme sie sein Tun. Wir nun, die ihm zusehen, sehen keinerlei Regelmäßigkeit in diesem Öffnen und Schließen des Zirkels. Wir können seine Art, der Linie zu folgen, von ihm nicht lernen. Wir würden hier vielleicht wirklich sagen: "Die Vorlage scheint ihm *einzugeben*, wie er zu gehen hat. Aber sie ist keine Regel."

238. Damit es mir erscheinen kann, als hätte die Regel alle ihre Folgesätze zum Voraus erzeugt, müssen sie mir *selbstverständlich* sein. So selbstverständlich, wie es mir ist, diese Farbe "blau" zu nennen. (Kriterien dafür, daß dies mir 'selbstverständlich' ist.)

239. Wie soll er wissen, welche Farbe er zu wählen hat, wenn er "rot" hört? — Sehr einfach: er soll die Farbe nehmen, deren Bild ihm beim Hören des Wortes einfällt. — Aber wie soll er wissen, welche Farbe das ist, 'deren Bild ihm einfällt'? Braucht es dafür ein weiteres Kriterium? (Es gibt allerdings einen Vorgang: die Farbe wählen, die einem beim Wort . . . einfällt.)

"'Rot' bedeutet die Farbe, die mir beim Hören des Wortes 'rot' einfällt" — wäre eine *Definition*. Keine Erklärung des *Wesens* der Bezeichnung durch ein Wort.

240. Es bricht kein Streit darüber aus (etwa zwischen Mathematikern), ob der Regel gemäß vorgegangen wurde, oder nicht. Es kommt darüber z. B. nicht zu Tätlichkeiten. Das gehört zu dem Gerüst, von welchem aus unsere Sprache wirkt (z. B. eine Beschreibung gibt).

241. "So sagst du also, daß die Übereinstimmung der Menschen entscheide, was richtig und was falsch ist?" — Richtig und falsch ist, was Menschen *sagen*; und in der *Sprache* stimmen die Menschen überein. Dies ist keine Übereinstimmung der Meinungen, sondern der Lebensform.

242. Zur Verständigung durch die Sprache gehört nicht nur eine Übereinstimmung in den Definitionen, sondern (so seltsam dies klingen mag) eine Übereinstimmung in den Urteilen. Dies scheint die Logik aufzuheben; hebt sie aber nicht auf. — Eines ist, die Meßmethode zu beschreiben, ein Anderes, Messungsergebnisse zu finden und auszusprechen.

237. Imagine someone following a line that serves him as a rule in this way: he holds a pair of compasses, and guides one of its points along the line that is the 'rule', while the other one draws the line that follows the rule. And while he moves along the rule, he alters the opening of the compasses, apparently with great precision, looking at the rule the whole time as if it determined what he did. And watching him, we see no regularity of any kind in this opening and shutting of the compasses. We can't learn his way of following the line from him. Here perhaps we really would say: "The original seems to *intimate* to him how he has to go. But it is not a rule."

238. The rule can only seem to me to produce all its consequences in advance if I draw them as *a matter of course*. As much as it is a matter |88| of course for me to call this colour "blue". (Criteria for 'its being a matter of course' for me.)

239. How is he to know what colour he is to pick out when he hears "red"? — Quite simple: he is to take the colour whose image occurs to him when he hears the word. — But how is he to know which colour it is 'whose image occurs to him'? Is a further criterion needed for that? (There is indeed such a procedure as choosing the colour which occurs to one when one hears the word ". . .".)

" 'Red' means the colour that occurs to me when I hear the word 'red' " — would be a *definition*. Not an explanation of what signifying something by a word *essentially* is.

240. Disputes do not break out (among mathematicians, say) over the question of whether or not a rule has been followed. People don't come to blows over it, for example. This belongs to the scaffolding from which our language operates (for example, yields descriptions).

241. "So you are saying that human agreement decides what is true and what is false?" — What is true or false is what human beings *say*; and it is in their *language* that human beings agree. This is agreement not in opinions, but rather in form of life.

242. It is not only agreement in definitions, but also (odd as it may sound) agreement in judgements that is required for communication by means of language. This seems to abolish logic, but does not do so. — It is one thing to describe methods of measurement, and another to obtain

Aber was wir "messen" nennen, ist auch durch eine gewisse Konstanz der Messungsergebnisse bestimmt.

243. Ein Mensch kann sich selbst ermutigen, sich selbst befehlen, gehorchen, tadeln, bestrafen, eine Frage vorlegen und auf sie antworten. Man könnte sich also auch Menschen denken, die nur monologisch sprächen. Ihre Tätigkeiten mit Selbstgesprächen begleiteten. — Einem Forscher, der sie beobachtet und ihre Reden belauscht, könnte es gelingen, ihre Sprache in die unsre zu übersetzen. (Er wäre dadurch in den Stand gesetzt, Handlungen dieser Leute richtig vorherzusagen, denn er hört sie auch Vorsätze und Entschlüsse fassen.)

Wäre aber auch eine Sprache denkbar, in der Einer seine inneren Erlebnisse — seine Gefühle, Stimmungen, etc. — für den eigenen Gebrauch aufschreiben, oder aussprechen könnte? —— Können wir denn das in unserer gewöhnlichen Sprache nicht tun? — Aber so meine ich's nicht. Die Wörter dieser Sprache sollen sich auf das beziehen, wovon nur der Sprechende wissen kann; auf seine unmittelbaren, privaten, Empfindungen. Ein Anderer kann diese Sprache also nicht verstehen.

244. Wie *beziehen* sich Wörter auf Empfindungen? — Darin scheint kein Problem zu liegen; denn reden wir nicht täglich von Empfindungen, und benennen sie? Aber wie wird die Verbindung des Namens mit dem Benannten hergestellt? Die Frage ist die gleiche, wie die: Wie lernt ein Mensch die Bedeutung der Namen von Empfindungen? Z. B. des Wortes "Schmerz". Dies ist eine Möglichkeit: Es werden Worte mit dem ursprünglichen, natürlichen, Ausdruck der Empfindung verbunden und an dessen Stelle gesetzt. Ein Kind hat sich verletzt, es schreit; und nun sprechen ihm die Erwachsenen zu und bringen ihm Ausrufe und später Sätze bei. Sie lehren das Kind ein neues Schmerzbenehmen.

"So sagst du also, daß das Wort 'Schmerz' eigentlich das Schreien bedeute?" — Im Gegenteil; der Wortausdruck des Schmerzes ersetzt das Schreien und beschreibt es nicht.

245. Wie kann ich denn mit der Sprache noch zwischen die Schmerz-äußerung und den Schmerz treten wollen?

246. Inwiefern sind nun meine Empfindungen *privat*? — Nun, nur ich kann wissen, ob ich wirklich Schmerzen habe; der Andere kann es nur vermuten. — Das ist in einer Weise falsch, in einer andern unsinnig. Wenn wir das Wort "wissen" gebrauchen, wie es normalerweise gebraucht wird (und wie sollen wir es denn gebrauchen!) dann wissen es Andre sehr häufig, wenn ich Schmerzen habe. — Ja, aber doch nicht mit der

and state results of measurement. But what we call "measuring" is in part determined by a certain constancy in results of measurement.

243. A human being can encourage himself, give himself orders, obey, blame and punish himself; he can ask himself a question and answer it. So one could imagine human beings who spoke only in monologue, who accompanied their activities by talking to themselves. — An explorer who watched them and listened to their talk might succeed in translating their language into ours. (This would enable him to predict these people's actions correctly, for he also hears them making resolutions and decisions.)

But is it also conceivable that there be a language in which a person could write down or give voice to his inner experiences — his feelings, moods, and so on — for his own use? —— Well, can't we do so in our ordinary language? — But that is not what I mean. The |89| words of this language are to refer to what only the speaker can know — to his immediate private sensations. So another person cannot understand the language.

244. How do words *refer* to sensations? — There doesn't seem to be any problem here; don't we talk about sensations every day, and name them? But how is the connection between the name and the thing named set up? This question is the same as: How does a human being learn the meaning of names of sensations? For example, of the word "pain". Here is one possibility: words are connected with the primitive, natural, expressions of sensation and used in their place. A child has hurt himself and he cries; then adults talk to him and teach him exclamations and, later, sentences. They teach the child new pain-behaviour.

"So you are saying that the word 'pain' really means crying?" — On the contrary: the verbal expression of pain replaces crying, it does not describe it.

245. How can I even attempt to interpose language between the expression of pain and the pain?

246. In what sense are my sensations *private*? — Well, only I can know whether I am really in pain; another person can only surmise it. — In one way this is false, and in another nonsense. If we are using the word "know" as it is normally used (and how else are we to use it?), then other people very often know if I'm in pain. — Yes, but all the same,

Sicherheit, mit der ich selbst es weiß! — Von mir kann man überhaupt nicht sagen (außer etwa im Spaß) ich *wisse*, daß ich Schmerzen habe. Was soll es denn heißen — außer etwa, daß ich Schmerzen *habe*?

Man kann nicht sagen, die Andern lernen meine Empfindung *nur* durch mein Benehmen, — denn von mir kann man nicht sagen, ich lernte sie. Ich *habe* sie.

Das ist richtig: es hat Sinn, von Andern zu sagen, sie seien im Zweifel darüber, ob ich Schmerzen habe; aber nicht, es von mir selbst zu sagen.

247. "Nur du kannst wissen, ob du die Absicht hattest." Das könnte man jemandem sagen, wenn man ihm die Bedeutung des Wortes "Absicht" erklärt. Es heißt dann nämlich: *so* gebrauchen wir es.

(Und "wissen" heißt hier, daß der Ausdruck der Ungewißheit sinnlos ist.)

248. Der Satz "Empfindungen sind privat" ist vergleichbar dem: "Patience spielt man allein."

249. Sind wir vielleicht voreilig in der Annahme, daß das Lächeln des Säuglings nicht Verstellung ist? — Und auf welcher Erfahrung beruht unsre Annahme?

(Das Lügen ist ein Sprachspiel, das gelernt sein will, wie jedes andre.)

250. Warum kann ein Hund nicht Schmerzen heucheln? Ist er zu ehrlich? Könnte man einen Hund Schmerzen heucheln lehren? Man kann ihm vielleicht beibringen, bei bestimmten Gelegenheiten wie im Schmerz aufzuheulen, ohne daß er Schmerzen hat. Aber zum eigentlichen Heucheln fehlte diesem Benehmen noch immer die richtige Umgebung.

251. Was bedeutet es, wenn wir sagen: "Ich kann mir das Gegenteil davon nicht vorstellen", oder: "Wie wäre es denn, wenn's anders wäre?" — Z. B., wenn jemand gesagt hat, daß meine Vorstellungen privat seien; oder, daß nur ich selbst wissen kann, ob ich einen Schmerz empfinde; und dergleichen.

"Ich kann mir das Gegenteil nicht vorstellen" heißt hier natürlich nicht: meine Vorstellungskraft reicht nicht hin. Wir wehren uns mit diesen Worten gegen etwas, was uns durch seine Form einen Erfahrungssatz vortäuscht, aber in Wirklichkeit ein grammatischer Satz ist.

Aber warum sage ich "Ich kann mir das Gegenteil nicht vorstellen"? Warum nicht: "Ich kann mir, was du sagst, nicht vorstellen"?

not with the certainty with which I know it myself! — It can't be said of me at all (except perhaps as a joke) that I *know* I'm in pain. What is it supposed to mean — except perhaps that I *am* in pain?

Other people cannot be said to learn of my sensations *only* from my behaviour — for I cannot be said to learn of them. I *have* them.

This much is true: it makes sense to say about other people that they doubt whether I am in pain; but not to say it about myself.

247. "Only you can know if you had that intention." One might tell someone this when explaining the meaning of the word "intention" to him. For then it means: *that* is how we use it.

(And here "know" means that the expression of uncertainty is sense-less.) |90|

248. The sentence "Sensations are private" is comparable to "One plays patience by oneself".

249. Are we perhaps over-hasty in our assumption that the smile of a baby is not pretence? — And on what experience is our assumption based?

(Lying is a language-game that needs to be learned like any other one.)

250. Why can't a dog simulate pain? Is it too honest? Could one teach a dog to simulate pain? Perhaps it is possible to teach it to howl on particular occasions as if it were in pain, even when it isn't. But the right surroundings for this behaviour to be real simulation would still be missing.

251. What does it mean when we say, "I can't imagine the opposite of this" or "What would it be like if it were otherwise?" — For example, when someone has said that my mental images are private; or that only I myself can know whether I am feeling pain; and so forth.

Of course, here "I can't imagine the opposite" doesn't mean: my powers of imagination are unequal to the task. We use these words to fend off something whose form produces the illusion of being an empirical proposition, but which is really a grammatical one.

But why do I say: "I can't imagine the opposite"? Why not: "I can't imagine what you say"?

Beispiel: "Jeder Stab hat eine Länge." Das heißt etwa: wir nennen etwas (oder *dies*) "die Länge eines Stabes" — aber nichts "die Länge einer Kugel". Kann ich mir nun vorstellen, daß 'jeder Stab eine Länge hat'? Nun, ich stelle mir eben einen Stab vor; und das ist alles. Nur spielt dieses Bild in Verbindung mit diesem Satz eine ganz andere Rolle, als ein Bild in Verbindung mit dem Satz "Dieser Tisch hat die gleiche Länge wie der dort". Denn hier verstehe ich, was es heißt, sich ein Bild vom Gegenteil zu machen (und es muß kein Vorstellungsbild sein).

Das Bild aber zum grammatikalischen Satz konnte nur etwa zeigen, was man "Länge eines Stabes" nennt. Und was sollte davon das entgegengesetzte Bild sein?

((Bemerkung über die Verneinung eines Satzes a priori.))

252. Wir könnten auf den Satz "Dieser Körper hat eine Ausdehnung" antworten: "Unsinn!" — neigen aber dazu, zu antworten: "Freilich!" — Warum?

253. "Der Andre kann nicht meine Schmerzen haben." — Welches sind *meine* Schmerzen? Was gilt hier als Kriterium der Identität? Überlege, was es möglich macht, im Falle physikalischer Gegenstände von "zwei genau gleichen" zu sprechen. Z. B. zu sagen: "Dieser Sessel ist nicht derselbe, den du gestern hier gesehen hast, aber er ist ein genau gleicher."

Soweit es *Sinn* hat, zu sagen, mein Schmerz sei der gleiche, wie seiner, soweit können wir auch beide den gleichen Schmerz haben. (Ja es wäre auch denkbar, daß zwei Menschen an der gleichen — nicht nur homologen — Stelle Schmerz empfänden. Bei siamesischen Zwillingen, z. B., könn-te das der Fall sein.)

Ich habe gesehen, wie jemand in einer Diskussion über diesen Gegenstand sich an die Brust schlug und sagte: "Aber der Andre kann doch nicht DIESEN Schmerz haben!" — Die Antwort darauf ist, daß man durch das emphatische Betonen des Wortes "diesen" kein Kriterium der Identität definiert. Die Emphase spiegelt uns vielmehr nur den Fall vor, daß ein solches Kriterium uns geläufig ist, wir aber daran erinnert werden müssen.

254. Auch das Ersetzen des Wortes "gleich" durch "identisch" (z. B.) ist ein typisches Auskunftsmittel in der Philosophie. Als redeten wir von Abschattungen der Bedeutung und es handle sich nur darum, mit unsern Worten die richtige Nuance zu treffen. Und darum handelt sich's beim Philosophieren nur dort, wo es unsre Aufgabe ist, die Versuchung, eine bestimmte Ausdrucksweise zu gebrauchen, psychologisch genau darzustellen. Was wir in so einem Fall 'zu sagen versucht

Example: "Every rod has a length." That means something like: we call something (or *this*) "the length of a rod" — but nothing "the length of a sphere". Now can I imagine 'every rod having a length'? Well, I just imagine a rod; and that is all. Only this picture, in connection with this proposition, has a quite different role from one used in connection with the proposition "This table has the same length as the one over there". For here I understand what it means to have a picture of the opposite (and it doesn't have to be a mental picture either).

But the picture that goes together with the grammatical proposition could only show, say, what is called "the length of a rod". And what should the opposite picture be?

((Remark about the negation of an a priori proposition.))

252. "This body has extension." To these words we could respond by saying: "Nonsense!" — but are inclined to reply "Of course!" — Why?
|91|

253. "Another person can't have my pains." — *My* pains — what pains are they? What counts as a criterion of identity here? Consider what makes it possible in the case of physical objects to speak of "two exactly the same": for example, to say, "This chair is not the one you saw here yesterday, but is exactly the same as it".

In so far as it makes *sense* to say that my pain is the same as his, it is also possible for us both to have the same pain. (And it would also be conceivable that two people feel pain in the same — not just the corresponding — place. That might be the case with Siamese twins, for instance.)

I have seen a person in a discussion on this subject strike himself on the breast and say: "But surely another person can't have THIS pain!" — The answer to this is that one does not define a criterion of identity by emphatically enunciating the word "this". Rather, the emphasis merely creates the illusion of a case in which we are conversant with such a criterion of identity, but have to be reminded of it.

254. The substitution of "identical" for "the same" (for example) is another typical expedient in philosophy. As if we were talking about shades of meaning, and all that were in question were to find words to hit on the correct nuance. And that is in question in philosophy only where we have to give a psychologically accurate account of the temptation to use a particular mode of expression. What we are 'tempted

sind', ist natürlich nicht Philosophie; sondern es ist ihr Rohmaterial. Was also ein Mathematiker, z. B., über Objektivität und Realität der mathematischen Tatsachen zu sagen geneigt ist, ist nicht eine Philosophie der Mathematik, sondern etwas, was Philosophie zu *behandeln* hätte.

255. Der Philosoph behandelt eine Frage; wie eine Krankheit.

256. Wie ist es nun mit der Sprache, die meine innern Erlebnisse beschreibt und die nur ich selbst verstehen kann? *Wie* bezeichne ich meine Empfindungen mit Worten? — So wie wir's gewöhnlich tun? Sind also meine Empfindungsworte mit meinen natürlichen Empfindungsäußerungen verknüpft? — In diesem Falle ist meine Sprache nicht 'privat'. Ein Anderer könnte sie verstehen, wie ich. — Aber wie, wenn ich keine natürlichen Äußerungen der Empfindung, sondern nur die Empfindung besäße? Und nun *assoziiere* ich einfach Namen mit den Empfindungen und verwende diese Namen in einer Beschreibung. —

257. "Wie wäre es, wenn die Menschen ihre Schmerzen nicht äußerten (nicht stöhnten, das Gesicht nicht verzögen, etc.)? Dann könnte man einem Kind nicht den Gebrauch des Wortes 'Zahnschmerzen' beibringen." — Nun, nehmen wir an, das Kind sei ein Genie und erfinde selbst einen Namen für die Empfindung! — Aber nun könnte es sich freilich mit diesem Wort nicht verständlich machen. — Also versteht es den Namen, kann aber seine Bedeutung niemand erklären? — Aber was heißt es denn, daß er 'seinen Schmerz benannt hat'? — Wie hat er das gemacht: den Schmerz benennen?! Und, was immer er getan hat, was hat es für einen Zweck? — Wenn man sagt "Er hat der Empfindung einen Namen gegeben", so vergißt man, daß schon viel in der Sprache vorbereitet sein muß, damit das bloße Benennen einen Sinn hat. Und wenn wir davon reden, daß Einer dem Schmerz einen Namen gibt, so ist die Grammatik des Wortes "Schmerz" hier das Vorbereitete; sie zeigt den Posten an, an den das neue Wort gestellt wird.

258. Stellen wir uns diesen Fall vor. Ich will über das Wiederkehren einer gewissen Empfindung ein Tagebuch führen. Dazu assoziiere ich sie mit dem Zeichen "E" und schreibe in einem Kalender zu jedem Tag, an dem ich die Empfindung habe, dieses Zeichen. —— Ich will zuerst bemerken, daß sich eine Definition des Zeichens nicht aussprechen läßt. — Aber ich kann sie doch mir selbst als eine Art hinweisende Definition geben! — Wie? kann ich auf die Empfindung zeigen? — Nicht im gewöhnlichen Sinne. Aber ich spreche, oder schreibe das Zeichen, und dabei konzentriere ich meine Aufmerksamkeit auf die Empfindung — zeige also gleichsam im Innern auf sie. — Aber wozu diese Zeremonie? denn nur

to say' in such a case is, of course, not philosophy; but it is its raw material. So, for example, what a mathematician is inclined to say about the objectivity and reality of mathematical facts is not a philosophy of mathematics, but something for philosophical *treatment*.

255. The philosopher treats a question; like an illness.

256. Now, what about the language which describes my inner experiences and which only I myself can understand? *How* do I use words to signify my sensations? — As we ordinarily do? Then are my words for sensations tied up with my natural expressions of sensation? In that case my language is not a 'private' one. Someone else might understand it as well as I. — But suppose I didn't have any natural expression of sensation, but only had sensations? And now I simply *associate* names with sensations, and use these names in descriptions. — |92|

257. "What would it be like if human beings did not manifest their pains (did not groan, grimace, etc.)? Then it would be impossible to teach a child the use of the word 'toothache'." — Well, let's assume that the child is a genius and invents a name for the sensation by himself! — But then, of course, he couldn't make himself understood when he used the word. — So does he understand the name, without being able to explain its meaning to anyone? — But what does it mean to say that he has 'named his pain'? — How has he managed this naming of pain? And whatever he did, what was its purpose? — When one says "He gave a name to his sensation", one forgets that much must be prepared in the language for mere naming to make sense. And if we speak of someone's giving a name to a pain, the grammar of the word "pain" is what has been prepared here; it indicates the post where the new word is stationed.

258. Let's imagine the following case. I want to keep a diary about the recurrence of a certain sensation. To this end I associate it with the sign "S" and write this sign in a calendar for every day on which I have the sensation. —— I first want to observe that a definition of the sign cannot be formulated. — But all the same, I can give one to myself as a kind of ostensive definition! — How? Can I point to the sensation? — Not in the ordinary sense. But I speak, or write the sign down, and at the same time I concentrate my attention on the sensation — and so, as it were, point to it inwardly. — But what is this ceremony for? For that

eine solche scheint es zu sein! Eine Definition dient doch dazu, die Bedeutung eines Zeichens festzulegen. — Nun, das geschieht eben durch das Konzentrieren der Aufmerksamkeit; denn dadurch präge ich mir die Verbindung des Zeichens mit der Empfindung ein. — "Ich präge sie mir ein" kann doch nur heißen: dieser Vorgang bewirkt, daß ich mich in Zukunft *richtig* an die Verbindung erinnere. Aber in unserm Falle habe ich ja kein Kriterium für die Richtigkeit. Man möchte hier sagen: richtig ist, was immer mir als richtig erscheinen wird. Und das heißt nur, daß hier von 'richtig' nicht geredet werden kann.

259. Sind die Regeln der privaten Sprache *Eindrücke* von Regeln? — Die Waage, auf der man die Eindrücke wägt, ist nicht der *Eindruck* von einer Waage.

260. "Nun, ich *glaube*, daß dies wieder die Empfindung E ist." — Du *glaubst* es wohl zu glauben!

So hätte sich also, der das Zeichen in den Kalender eintrug, *gar nichts* notiert? — Sieh's nicht als selbstverständlich an, daß Einer sich etwas notiert, wenn er Zeichen — in einen Kalender z. B. — einträgt. Eine Notiz hat ja eine Funktion; und das "E" hat, soweit, noch keine.

(Man kann zu sich selber reden. — Spricht Jeder zu sich selbst, der redet, wenn niemand anderer zugegen ist?)

261. Welchen Grund haben wir, "E" das Zeichen für eine *Empfindung* zu nennen? "Empfindung" ist nämlich ein Wort unserer allgemeinen, nicht mir allein verständlichen, Sprache. Der Gebrauch dieses Worts bedarf also einer Rechtfertigung, die Alle verstehen. — Und es hülfe auch nichts, zu sagen: es müsse keine *Empfindung* sein; wenn er "E" schreibe, habe er *Etwas* — und mehr könnten wir nicht sagen. Aber "haben" und "etwas" gehören auch zur allgemeinen Sprache. — So gelangt man beim Philosophieren am Ende dahin, wo man nur noch einen unartikulierten Laut ausstoßen möchte. — Aber ein solcher Laut ist ein Ausdruck nur in einem bestimmten Sprachspiel, das nun zu beschreiben ist.

262. Man könnte sagen: Wer sich eine private Worterklärung gegeben hat, der muß sich nun im Innern *vornehmen*, das Wort so und so zu gebrauchen. Und wie nimmt er sich das vor? Soll ich annehmen, daß er die Technik dieser Anwendung erfindet; oder daß er sie schon fertig vorgefunden hat?

is all it seems to be! A definition serves to lay down the meaning of a sign, doesn't it? — Well, that is done precisely by concentrating my attention; for in this way I commit to memory the connection between the sign and the sensation. — But "I commit it to memory" can only mean: this process brings it about that I remember the connection *correctly* in the future. But in the present case, I have no criterion of correctness. One would like to say: whatever is going to seem correct to me is correct. And that only means that here we can't talk about 'correct'.

259. Are the rules of the private language *impressions* of rules? — The balance on which impressions are weighed is not the *impression* of a balance.

260. "Well, I *believe* that this is the sensation S again." — Perhaps you *believe* that you believe it!

Then did the man who made the entry in the calendar make a note |93| of *nothing whatever*? — Don't consider it a matter of course that a person is making a note of something when he makes a mark — say in a calendar. For a note has a function, and this "S" so far has none.

(One can talk to oneself. — Is everyone who speaks when no one else is present talking to himself?)

261. What reason have we for calling "S" the sign for a *sensation*? For "sensation" is a word of our common language, which is not a language intelligible only to me. So the use of this word stands in need of a justification which everybody understands. — And it would not help either to say that it need not be a *sensation*; that when he writes "S" he has *Something* — and that is all that can be said. But "has" and "something" also belong to our common language. — So in the end, when one is doing philosophy, one gets to the point where one would like just to emit an inarticulate sound. — But such a sound is an expression only in a particular language-game, which now has to be described.

262. One might say: someone who has given himself a private explanation of a word must inwardly *resolve* to use the word in such-and-such a way. And how does he resolve that? Should I assume that he invents the technique of applying the word; or that he found it ready-made?

263. "Ich kann mir (im Innern) doch vornehmen, in Zukunft DAS 'Schmerz' zu nennen." — "Aber hast du es dir auch gewiß vorgenommen? Bist du sicher, daß es dazu genug war, die Aufmerksamkeit auf dein Gefühl zu konzentrieren?" — Seltsame Frage. —

264. "Wenn du einmal weißt, *was* das Wort bezeichnet, verstehst du es, kennst seine ganze Anwendung."

265. Denken wir uns eine Tabelle, die nur in unsrer Vorstellung existiert; etwa ein Wörterbuch. Mittels eines Wörterbuchs kann man die Übersetzung eines Wortes X durch ein Wort Y rechtfertigen. Sollen wir es aber auch eine Rechtfertigung nennen, wenn diese Tabelle nur in der Vorstellung nachgeschlagen wird? — "Nun, es ist dann eben eine subjektive Rechtfertigung." — Aber die Rechtfertigung besteht doch darin, daß man an eine unabhängige Stelle appelliert. — "Aber ich kann doch auch von einer Erinnerung an eine andre appellieren. Ich weiß (z. B.) nicht, ob ich mir die Abfahrzeit des Zuges richtig gemerkt habe und rufe mir zur Kontrolle das Bild der Seite des Fahrplans ins Gedächtnis. Haben wir hier nicht den gleichen Fall?" – Nein; denn dieser Vorgang muß nun wirklich die *richtige* Erinnerung hervorrufen. Wäre das Vorstellungsbild des Fahrplans nicht selbst auf seine Richtigkeit zu *prüfen*, wie könnte es die Richtigkeit der ersten Erinnerung bestätigen? (Als kaufte Einer mehrere Exemplare der heutigen Morgenzeitung, um sich zu vergewissern, daß sie die Wahrheit schreibt.)

In der Vorstellung eine Tabelle nachschlagen ist so wenig ein Nachschlagen einer Tabelle, wie die Vorstellung des Ergebnisses eines vorgestellten Experiments das Ergebnis eines Experiments ist.

266. Ich kann auf die Uhr schaun, um zu sehen, wieviel Uhr es ist. Aber ich kann auch, um zu *raten*, wieviel Uhr es ist, auf das Zifferblatt einer Uhr sehen; oder zu diesem Zweck die Zeiger einer Uhr verstellen, bis mir die Stellung richtig vorkommt. So kann das Bild der Uhr auf mehr als eine Weise dazu dienen, die Zeit zu bestimmen. (In der Vorstellung auf die Uhr schaun.)

267. Angenommen, ich wollte die Dimensionierung einer Brücke, die in meiner Vorstellung gebaut wird, dadurch rechtfertigen, daß ich zuerst in der Vorstellung Zerreißproben mit dem Material der Brücke mache. Dies wäre natürlich die Vorstellung von dem, was man die Rechtfertigung der Dimensionierung einer Brücke nennt. Aber würden wir es auch eine Rechtfertigung der Vorstellung einer Dimensionierung nennen?

263. "Surely I can (inwardly) resolve to call THIS 'pain' in the future."
— "But is it certain that you have resolved this? Are you sure that it
was enough for this purpose to concentrate your attention on your feeling?" — An odd question. —

264. "Once you know *what* the word signifies, you understand it, you
know its whole application."

265. Let us imagine a table, something like a dictionary, that exists only
in our imagination. A dictionary can be used to justify the translation
of a word X by a word Y. But are we also to call it a justification if
such a table is to be looked up only in the imagination? — "Well, yes;
then it is a subjective justification." — But justification consists in
appealing to an independent authority — "But surely I can appeal from
one memory to another. For example, I don't know if I have remembered the time of departure of a train correctly, and to check it I call
to mind how a page of the timetable looked. Isn't this the same sort of
case?" No; for this procedure must now actually call forth |94| the *cor-
rect* memory. If the mental image of the timetable could not itself be
tested for correctness, how could it confirm the correctness of the first
memory? (As if someone were to buy several copies of today's morning paper to assure himself that what it said was true.)
    Looking up a table in the imagination is no more looking up a table
than the image of the result of an imagined experiment is the result of
an experiment.

266. I can look at a clock to see what time it is. But I can also look at
the dial of a clock in order to *guess* what time it is; or for the same
purpose move the hands of a clock till their position strikes me as right.
So the look of a clock may serve to determine the time in more than
one way. (Looking at a clock in one's imagination.)

267. Suppose I wanted to justify the choice of dimensions for a bridge
which I imagine being built, by first imagining making loading tests on
the material of the bridge. This would, of course, be to imagine what
is called justifying the choice of dimensions for a bridge. But would we
also call it justifying an imagined choice of dimensions?

268. Warum kann meine rechte Hand nicht meiner linken Geld schenken? — Meine rechte Hand kann es in meine linke geben. Meine rechte Hand kann eine Schenkungsurkunde schreiben und meine linke eine Quittung. — Aber die weitern praktischen Folgen wären nicht die einer Schenkung. Wenn die linke Hand das Geld von der rechten genommen hat, etc., wird man fragen: "Nun, und was weiter?" Und das Gleiche könnte man fragen, wenn Einer sich eine private Worterklärung gegeben hätte; ich meine, wenn er sich ein Wort vorgesagt und dabei seine Aufmerksamkeit auf eine Empfindung gerichtet hat.

269. Erinnern wir uns daran, daß es gewisse Kriterien des Benehmens dafür gibt, daß Einer ein Wort nicht versteht: daß es ihm nichts sagt, er nichts damit anzufangen weiß. Und Kriterien dafür, daß er das Wort 'zu verstehen glaubt', eine Bedeutung mit ihm verbindet, aber nicht die richtige. Und endlich Kriterien dafür, daß er das Wort richtig versteht. Im zweiten Falle könnte man von einem subjektiven Verstehen reden. Und eine "private Sprache" könnte man Laute nennen, die kein Andrer versteht, ich aber 'zu verstehen scheine'.

270. Denken wir uns nun eine Verwendung des Eintragens des Zeichens "E" in mein Tagebuch. Ich mache folgende Erfahrung: Wenn immer ich eine bestimmte Empfindung habe, zeigt mir ein Manometer, daß mein Blutdruck steigt. So werde ich in den Stand gesetzt, ein Steigen meines Blutdrucks ohne Zuhilfenahme eines Apparats anzusagen. Dies ist ein nützliches Ergebnis. Und nun scheint es hier ganz gleichgültig zu sein, ob ich die Empfindung *richtig* wiedererkannt habe, oder nicht. Nehmen wir an, ich irre mich beständig bei ihrer Identifizierung, so macht es gar nichts. Und das zeigt schon, daß die Annahme dieses Irrtums nur ein Schein war. (Wir drehten, gleichsam, an einem Knopf, der aussah, als könnte man mit ihm etwas an der Maschine einstellen; aber er war ein bloßes Zierrat, mit dem Mechanismus gar nicht verbunden.)

Und welchen Grund haben wir hier, "E" die Bezeichnung einer Empfindung zu nennen? Vielleicht die Art und Weise, wie dies Zeichen in diesem Sprachspiel verwendet wird. — Und warum eine "bestimmte Empfindung", also jedesmal die gleiche? Nun, wir nehmen ja an, wir schrieben jedesmal "E".

271. "Denke dir einen Menschen, der es nicht im Gedächtnis behalten könnte, *was* das Wort 'Schmerz' bedeutet — und der daher immer wieder etwas Anderes so nennt — das Wort aber dennoch in Übereinstimmung mit den gewöhnlichen Anzeichen und Voraussetzungen des Schmerzes verwendete!" — der es also verwendet, wie wir Alle. Hier möchte ich sagen: das Rad gehört nicht zur Maschine, das man drehen kann, ohne daß Anderes sich mitbewegt.

268. Why can't my right hand give my left hand money? — My right hand can put it into my left hand. My right hand can write a deed of gift, and my left hand a receipt. — But the further practical consequences would not be those of a gift. When the left hand has taken the money from the right, and so forth, one will ask, "Well, and now what?" And the same could be asked if a person had given himself a private explanation of a word; I mean, if he has said the word to himself and at the same time has directed his attention to a sensation.

269. Let us remember that there are certain criteria in a man's behaviour for his not understanding a word: that it means nothing to him, that he can do nothing with it. And criteria for his 'thinking he understands', attaching some meaning to the word, but not the right one. And lastly, criteria for his understanding the word correctly. In the second case, one might speak of a subjective understanding. And sounds which no one else understands but which I *appear to understand* might be called a "private language".

270. Let us now imagine a use for the entry of the sign "S" in my diary. I find out the following from experience: whenever I have a particular sensation, a manometer |95| shows that my blood pressure is rising. This puts me in a position to declare my blood pressure is rising without using any apparatus. This is a useful result. And now it seems quite indifferent whether I've recognized the sensation *correctly* or not. Suppose that I regularly make a mistake in identifying it, this does not make any difference at all. And this alone shows that the supposition of this mistake was merely sham. (We, as it were, turned a knob which looked as if it could be used to adjust something in the machine; but it was a mere ornament not connected with the mechanism at all.)

And what reason do we have here for calling "S" the name of a sensation? Perhaps the kind of way this sign is employed in this language-game. — And why a "particular sensation", that is, the same one every time? Well, we're supposing, aren't we, that we write "S" every time.

271. "Imagine a person who could not remember *what* the word 'pain' meant — so that he constantly called different things by that name — but nevertheless used it in accordance with the usual symptoms and pre-suppositions of pain" — in short, he uses it as we all do. Here I'd like to say: a wheel that can be turned though nothing else moves with it is not part of the mechanism.

272. Das Wesentliche am privaten Erlebnis ist eigentlich nicht, daß Jeder sein eigenes Exemplar besitzt, sondern, daß Keiner weiß, ob der Andere auch *dies* hat, oder etwas anderes. Es wäre also die Annahme möglich — obwohl nicht verifizierbar — ein Teil der Menschheit habe *eine* Rotempfindung, ein anderer Teil eine andere.

273. Wie ist es nun mit dem Worte "rot" — soll ich sagen, dies bezeichne etwas 'uns Allen Gegenüberstehendes', und Jeder sollte eigentlich außer diesem Wort noch eines haben zur Bezeichnung seiner *eigenen* Empfindung von Rot? Oder ist es so: das Wort "rot" bezeichnet etwas uns gemeinsam Bekanntes; und für Jeden, außerdem, etwas nur ihm Bekanntes? (Oder vielleicht besser: es *bezieht* sich auf etwas nur ihm Bekanntes.)

274. Es hilft uns natürlich nichts zum Begreifen der Funktion von "rot", zu sagen, es "*beziehe* sich auf", statt "es bezeichne" das Private; aber es ist der psychologisch treffendere Ausdruck für ein bestimmtes Erlebnis beim Philosophieren. Es ist, als werfe ich beim Aussprechen des Worts einen Seitenblick auf die eigene Empfindung, gleichsam um mir zu sagen: ich wisse schon, was ich damit meine.

275. Schau auf das Blau des Himmels, und sag zu dir selbst "Wie blau der Himmel ist!". — Wenn du es spontan tust — nicht mit philosophischen Absichten — so kommt es dir nicht in den Sinn, dieser Farbeneindruck gehöre nur *dir*. Und du hast kein Bedenken, diesen Ausruf an einen Andern zu richten. Und wenn du bei den Worten auf etwas zeigst, so ist es der Himmel. Ich meine: Du hast nicht das Gefühl des In-dich-selber-Zeigens, das oft das 'Benennen der Empfindung' begleitet, wenn man über die 'private Sprache' nachdenkt. Du denkst auch nicht, du solltest eigentlich nicht mit der Hand, sondern nur mit der Aufmerksamkeit auf die Farbe zeigen. (Überlege, was es heißt, "mit der Aufmerksamkeit auf etwas zeigen".)

276. "Aber *meinen* wir denn nicht wenigstens etwas ganz Bestimmtes, wenn wir auf eine Farbe hinschauen und den Farbeindruck benennen?" Es ist doch förmlich, als lösten wir den Farb*eindruck*, wie ein Häutchen, von dem gesehenen Gegenstand ab. (Dies sollte unsern Verdacht erregen.)

277. Aber wie ist es überhaupt möglich, daß man in Versuchung ist, zu glauben, man *meine* einmal mit einem Wort die Allen bekannte Farbe, — einmal: den 'visuellen Eindruck', den *ich jetzt* erhalte? Wie kann hier auch nur eine Versuchung bestehen? —— Ich wende in diesen Fällen der

* 272. The essential thing about private experience is really not that each person possesses his own specimen, but that nobody knows whether other people also have *this* or something else. The assumption would thus be possible — though unverifiable — that one section of mankind had one visual impression of red, and another section another.

* 273. What about the word "red"? — Am I to say that it signifies something 'confronting us all', and that everyone should really have another word, besides this one, to signify his *own* impression of red? Or is it like this: the word "red" signifies something known to us all; and in addition, for each person, it signifies something known only to him? (Or perhaps, rather: it *refers* to something known only to him.)

* 274. Of course, saying that the word "red" "*refers* to" rather than "signifies" something private does not help us in the least to grasp its function; but it is the more psychologically apt expression for a particular experience in doing philosophy. It is as if, when I uttered the word, I cast a sidelong glance at my own colour impression, as it were, in order to say to myself: I know all right what I mean by the word. |96|

275. Look at the blue of the sky and say to yourself, "How blue the sky is!" — When you do it spontaneously — without philosophical purposes — the idea never crosses your mind that this impression of colour belongs only to *you*. And you have no qualms about exclaiming thus to another. And if you point at anything as you say the words, it is at the sky. I mean: you don't have the pointing-into-yourself feeling that often accompanies 'naming sensations' when one is thinking about the 'private language'. Nor do you think that really you ought to point at the colour not with your hand, but with your attention. (Consider what "to point at something with one's attention" means.)

276. "But don't we at least *mean* something quite definite when we look at a colour and name our colour impression?" It is virtually as if we detached the colour *impression* from the object, like a membrane. (This ought to arouse our suspicions.)

277. But how is it even possible for one to be tempted to think that one uses a word to *mean* at one time the colour known to everyone — and at another time the 'visual impression' which *I* am getting *now*? How can there be so much as a temptation here? —— I don't turn the

Farbe nicht die gleiche Art der Aufmerksamkeit zu. Meine ich (wie ich sagen möchte) den mir zu eigen gehörenden Farbeindruck, so vertiefe ich mich in die Farbe — ungefähr so, wie wenn ich mich an einer Farbe 'nicht sattsehen kann'. Daher ist es leichter, dieses Erlebnis zu erzeugen, wenn man auf eine leuchtende Farbe sieht, oder auf eine Farbenzusammenstellung, die sich uns einprägt.

278. "Ich weiß, wie *mir* die Farbe Grün erscheint" — nun, das hat doch Sinn! — Gewiß; welche Verwendung des Satzes denkst du dir?

279. Denke dir Einen, der sagte: "Ich weiß doch, wie hoch ich bin!" und dabei die Hand als Zeichen auf seinen Scheitel legt!

280. Einer malt ein Bild, um zu zeigen, wie er sich, etwa, eine Szene auf dem Theater vorstellt. Und nun sage ich: "Dies Bild hat eine doppelte Funktion; es teilt Andern etwas mit, wie Bilder oder Worte eben etwas mitteilen —— aber für den Mitteilenden ist es noch eine Darstellung (oder Mitteilung?) anderer Art: für ihn ist es das Bild seiner Vorstellung, wie es das für keinen Andern sein kann. Sein privater Eindruck des Bildes sagt ihm, was er sich vorgestellt hat; in einem Sinne, in welchem es das Bild für die Andern nicht kann." — Und mit welchem Recht rede ich in diesem zweiten Falle von Darstellung, oder Mitteilung, — wenn diese Worte im *ersten* Falle richtig angewandt waren?

281. "Aber kommt, was du sagst, nicht darauf hinaus, es gebe, z. B., keinen Schmerz ohne *Schmerzbenehmen*?" — Es kommt darauf hinaus: man könne nur vom lebenden Menschen, und was ihm ähnlich ist, (sich ähnlich benimmt) sagen, es habe Empfindungen; es sähe; sei blind; höre; sei taub; sei bei Bewußtsein, oder bewußtlos.

282. "Aber im Märchen kann doch auch der Topf sehen und hören!" (Gewiß; aber er *kann* auch sprechen.)
    "Aber das Märchen erdichtet doch nur, was nicht der Fall ist; es spricht doch nicht *Unsinn*." — So einfach ist es nicht. Ist es Unwahrheit, oder Unsinn, zu sagen, ein Topf rede? Macht man sich ein klares Bild davon, unter welchen Umständen wir von einem Topf sagen würden, er rede? (Auch ein Unsinn-Gedicht ist nicht Unsinn in der Weise, wie etwa das Lallen eines Kindes.)
    Ja; wir sagen von Leblosem, es habe Schmerzen: im Spiel mit Puppen z. B. Aber diese Verwendung des Schmerzbegriffs ist eine sekundäre. Stellen wir uns doch den Fall vor, Leute sagten *nur* von Leblosem, es

same kind of attention on the colour in the two cases. When I mean the colour impression that (as I should like to say) belongs to me alone, I immerse myself in the colour — rather like when I 'can't get my fill of a colour'. That's why it is easier to produce this experience when one is looking at a bright colour, or at a colour scheme which sticks in our memory.

278. "I know how the colour green looks to *me*" — surely that makes sense! — Certainly; what use of the sentence are you thinking of?

279. Imagine someone saying, "But I know how tall I am!" and laying his hand on top of his head to indicate it!

280. Someone paints a picture in order to show, for example, how he imagines a stage set. And now I say: "This picture has a double function: it informs others, as pictures or words do —— but for the informant it is in addition a representation (or piece of information?) of another kind: for him it is the picture of his image, as it can't be for anyone else. His private impression of the picture tells him what he imagined, in a sense in which the picture can't do this for others." — And what right have I to speak in this second |97| case of a representation or piece of information — if these words were correctly used in the *first* case?

281. "But doesn't what you say amount to this: that there is no pain, for example, without *pain-behaviour*?" — It amounts to this: that only of a living human being and what resembles (behaves like) a living human being can one say: it has sensations; it sees; is blind; hears; is deaf; is conscious or unconscious.

282. "But in a fairy tale a pot too can see and hear!" (Certainly; but it *can* also talk.)

"But a fairy tale only invents what is not the case; it does not talk *nonsense*, does it?" — It's not as simple as that. Is it untrue or nonsensical to say that a pot talks? Does one have a clear idea of the circumstances in which we'd say of a pot that it talked? (Even a nonsense poem is not nonsense in the same way as the babble of a baby.)

We do indeed say of an inanimate thing that it is in pain: when playing with dolls, for example. But this use of the concept of pain is a secondary one. Imagine a case in which people said *only* of inanimate things

habe Schmerzen; bedauerten *nur* Puppen! (Wenn Kinder Eisenbahn spielen, hängt ihr Spiel mit ihrer Kenntnis der Eisenbahn zusammen. Es könnten aber Kinder eines Volksstammes, dem die Eisenbahn unbekannt ist, dies Spiel von andern übernommen haben, und es spielen, ohne zu wissen, daß damit etwas nachgeahmt wird. Man könnte sagen, das Spiel habe für sie nicht den gleichen *Sinn*, wie für uns.)

283. Woher kommt uns *auch nur der Gedanke*: Wesen, Gegenstände, könnten etwas fühlen?

Meine Erziehung hätte mich darauf geführt, indem sie mich auf die Gefühle in mir aufmerksam machte, und nun übertrage ich die Idee auf Objekte außer mir? Ich erkenne, es ist da (in mir) etwas, was ich, ohne mit dem Wortgebrauch der Andern in Widerspruch zu geraten, "Schmerzen" nennen kann? — Auf Steine und Pflanzen, etc. übertrage ich meine Idee nicht.

Könnte ich mir nicht denken, ich hätte fürchterliche Schmerzen und würde, während sie andauern, zu einem Stein? Ja, wie weiß ich, wenn ich die Augen schließe, ob ich nicht zu einem Stein geworden bin? — Und wenn das nun geschehen ist, inwiefern wird *der Stein* Schmerzen haben? Inwiefern wird man es vom Stein aussagen können? Ja warum soll der Schmerz hier überhaupt einen Träger haben?!

Und kann man von dem Stein sagen, er habe eine Seele und *die* hat Schmerzen? Was hat eine Seele, was haben Schmerzen, mit einem Stein zu tun?

Nur von dem, was sich benimmt wie ein Mensch, kann man sagen, daß es Schmerzen *hat*.

Denn man muß es von einem Körper sagen, oder, wenn du willst, von einer Seele, die ein Körper *hat*. Und wie kann ein Körper eine Seele *haben*?

284. Schau einen Stein an und denk dir, er hat Empfindungen! — Man sagt sich: Wie konnte man auch nur auf die Idee kommen, einem *Ding* eine *Empfindung* zuzuschreiben? Man könnte sie ebensogut einer Zahl zuschreiben! — Und nun schau auf eine zappelnde Fliege, und sofort ist diese Schwierigkeit verschwunden und der Schmerz scheint hier *angreifen* zu können, wo vorher alles gegen ihn, sozusagen, *glatt* war.

Und so scheint uns auch ein Leichnam dem Schmerz gänzlich unzugänglich. — Unsere Einstellung zum Lebenden ist nicht die zum Toten. Alle unsre Reaktionen sind verschieden. — Sagt Einer: "Das kann nicht einfach daran liegen, daß das Lebendige sich so und so bewegt und das Tote nicht" — so will ich ihm bedeuten, hier liege ein Fall des Übergangs 'von der Quantität zur Qualität' vor.

that they are in pain; pitied *only* dolls! (When children play trains, their game is connected with their acquaintance with trains. It would nevertheless be possible for the children of a tribe unacquainted with trains to learn this game from others, and to play it without knowing that it was imitating anything. One could say that the game did not make the same kind of *sense* to them as to us.)

283. What gives us *so much as the idea* that beings, things, can feel?

Is it that my education has led me to it by drawing my attention to feelings in myself, and now I transfer the idea to objects outside myself? That I recognize that there is something there (in me) which I can call "pain" without getting into conflict with other people's usage? — I do not transfer my idea to stones, plants, and so on.

Couldn't I imagine having frightful pains and, while they were going on, turning to stone? Indeed, how do I know, if I shut my eyes, whether I have not turned into a stone? — And if that has happened, in what sense will *the stone* have pains? In what sense will they be ascribable to a stone? Why indeed should the pain here have a bearer at all?!

And can one say of the stone that it has a mind, and *that* is what has the pain? What has a mind, what have pains, to do with a stone? |98|

Only of what behaves like a human being can one say that it *has* pains.

For one has to say it of a body, or, if you like, of a mind which some body *has*. And how can a body *have* a mind?

284. Look at a stone and imagine it having sensations. — One says to oneself: How could one so much as get the idea of ascribing a *sensation* to a *thing*? One might as well ascribe it to a number! — And now look at a wriggling fly, and at once these difficulties vanish, and pain seems able to get *a foothold* here, where before everything was, so to speak, too *smooth* for it.

And so, too, a corpse seems to us quite inaccessible to pain. — Our attitude to what is alive and to what is dead is not the same. All our reactions are different. — If someone says, "That cannot simply come from the fact that living beings move in such-and-such ways and dead ones don't", then I want to suggest to him that this is a case of the transition 'from quantity to quality'.

285. Denk an das Erkennen des *Gesichtsausdrucks*. Oder an die Beschreibung des Gesichtsausdrucks, — die nicht darin besteht, daß man die Maße des Gesichts angibt! Denke auch daran, wie man das Gesicht eines Menschen nachahmen kann, ohne das eigene dabei im Spiegel zu sehen.

286. Aber ist es nicht absurd, von einem *Körper* zu sagen, er habe Schmerzen? —— Und warum fühlt man darin eine Absurdität? Inwiefern fühlt meine Hand nicht Schmerzen; sondern ich in meiner Hand?

Was ist das für eine Streitfrage: Ist es der *Körper*, der Schmerzen fühlt? — Wie ist sie zu entscheiden? Wie macht es sich geltend, daß es *nicht* der Körper ist? — Nun, etwa so: Wenn Einer in der Hand Schmerzen hat, so sagt's die *Hand* nicht (außer sie schreibt's), und man spricht nicht der Hand Trost zu, sondern dem Leidenden; man sieht ihm in die Augen.

287. Wie bin ich von Mitleid *für diesen Menschen* erfüllt? Wie zeigt es sich, welches Objekt das Mitleid hat? (Das Mitleid, kann man sagen, ist eine Form der Überzeugung, daß ein Andrer Schmerzen hat.)

288. Ich erstarre zu Stein und meine Schmerzen dauern an. — Und wenn ich mich nun irrte und es nicht mehr *Schmerzen* wären! —— Aber ich kann mich doch hier nicht irren; es heißt doch nichts, zu zweifeln, ob ich Schmerzen habe! — D. h.: wenn Einer sagte "Ich weiß nicht, ist das ein Schmerz, was ich habe, oder ist es etwas anderes?", so dächten wir etwa, er wisse nicht, was das deutsche Wort "Schmerz" bedeute und würden's ihm erklären. — Wie? Vielleicht durch Gebärden, oder indem wir ihn mit einer Nadel stächen und sagten "Siehst du, das ist Schmerz". Er könnte diese Worterklärung, wie jede andere, richtig, falsch, oder gar nicht verstehen. Und welches er tut, wird er im Gebrauch des Wortes zeigen, wie es auch sonst geschieht.

Wenn er nun z. B. sagte: "Oh, ich weiß, was 'Schmerz' heißt, aber ob *das* Schmerzen sind, was ich jetzt hier habe, das weiß ich nicht" — da würden wir bloß die Köpfe schütteln und müßten seine Worte für eine seltsame Reaktion ansehen, mit der wir nichts anzufangen wissen. (Es wäre etwa, wie wenn wir jemand im Ernste sagen hörten: "Ich erinnere mich deutlich, einige Zeit vor meiner Geburt geglaubt zu haben, . . .")

Jener Ausdruck des Zweifels gehört nicht zu dem Sprachspiel; aber wenn nun der Ausdruck der Empfindung, das menschliche Benehmen, ausgeschlossen ist, dann scheint es, ich *dürfe* wieder zweifeln. Daß ich hier versucht bin, zu sagen, man könne die Empfindung für etwas andres halten, als was sie ist, kommt daher: Wenn ich das normale Sprachspiel mit dem Ausdruck der Empfindung abgeschafft denke, brauche ich nun ein Kriterium der Identität für sie; und dann bestünde auch die Möglichkeit des Irrtums.

285. Think of the recognition of *facial expressions*. Or of the description of facial expressions — which does not consist in giving the measurements of the face! Think, too, how one can imitate a man's face without seeing one's own in a mirror.

286. But isn't it absurd to say of a *body* that it has pain? —— And why does one feel an absurdity in that? In what sense does my hand not feel pain, but I in my hand?

What sort of issue is this: Is it the *body* that feels pain? — How is it to be decided? How does it become clear that it is *not* the body? — Well, something like this: if someone has a pain in his hand, then the *hand* does not say so (unless it writes it), and one does not comfort the hand, but the sufferer: one looks into his eyes.

287. How am I filled with pity *for this human being*? How does it come out what the object of my pity is? (Pity, one may say, is one form of being convinced that someone else is in pain.)

288. I turn to stone, and my pain goes on. — What if I were mistaken, and it was no longer *pain*? —— But surely I can't be mistaken here; it means nothing to doubt whether I am in pain! — That is, if someone said "I don't know if what I have is a pain or something else", we would think, perhaps, that he does not know what the |99| English word "pain" means; and we'd explain it to him. — How? Perhaps by means of gestures, or by pricking him with a pin and saying, "See, that's pain!" This explanation of a word, like any other, he might understand rightly, wrongly, or not at all. And he will show which by his use of the word, in this as in other cases.

If he now said, for example, "Oh, I know what 'pain' means; what I don't know is whether *this*, that I have now, is pain" — we'd merely shake our heads and have to regard his words as a strange reaction which we can't make anything of. (It would be rather as if we heard someone say seriously, "I distinctly remember that sometime before I was born I believed . . .")

That expression of doubt has no place in the language-game; but if expressions of sensation — human behaviour — are excluded, it looks as if I might then *legitimately* begin to doubt. My temptation to say that one might take a sensation for something other than what it is arises from this: if I assume the abrogation of the normal language-game with the expression of a sensation, I need a criterion of identity for the sensation; and then the possibility of error also exists.

289. "Wenn ich sage 'Ich habe Schmerzen', bin ich jedenfalls *vor mir selbst* gerechtfertigt." — Was heißt das? Heißt es: "Wenn ein Anderer wissen könnte, was ich 'Schmerzen' nenne, würde er zugeben, daß ich das Wort richtig verwende"?

Ein Wort ohne Rechtfertigung gebrauchen, heißt nicht, es zu Unrecht gebrauchen.

290. Ich identifiziere meine Empfindung freilich nicht durch Kriterien, sondern ich gebrauche den gleichen Ausdruck. Aber damit *endet* ja das Sprachspiel nicht; damit fängt es an.

Aber fängt es nicht mit der Empfindung an, — die ich beschreibe? — Das Wort "beschreiben" hat uns da vielleicht zum Besten. Ich sage "Ich beschreibe meinen Seelenzustand" und "Ich beschreibe mein Zimmer". Man muß sich die Verschiedenheiten der Sprachspiele ins Gedächtnis rufen.

291. Was wir "*Beschreibungen*" nennen, sind Instrumente für besondere Verwendungen. Denke dabei an eine Maschinenzeichnung, einen Schnitt, einen Aufriß mit den Maßen, den der Mechaniker vor sich hat. Wenn man an eine Beschreibung als ein Wortbild der Tatsachen denkt, so hat das etwas Irreführendes: Man denkt etwa nur an Bilder, wie sie an unsern Wänden hängen; die schlechtweg abzubilden scheinen, wie ein Ding aussieht, wie es beschaffen ist. (Diese Bilder sind gleichsam müßig.)

292. Glaub nicht immer, daß du deine Worte von Tatsachen abliest; diese nach Regeln in Worte abbildest! Denn die Anwendung der Regel im besondern Fall müßtest du ja doch ohne Führung machen.

293. Wenn ich von mir selbst sage, ich wisse nur vom eigenen Fall, was das Wort "Schmerz" bedeutet, — muß ich *das* nicht auch von den Andern sagen? Und wie kann ich denn den *einen* Fall in so unverantwortlicher Weise verallgemeinern?

Nun, ein Jeder sagt es mir von sich, er wisse nur von sich selbst, was Schmerzen seien! —— Angenommen, es hätte Jeder eine Schachtel, darin wäre etwas, was wir "Käfer" nennen. Niemand kann je in die Schachtel des Andern schaun; und Jeder sagt, er wisse nur vom Anblick *seines* Käfers, was ein Käfer ist. — Da könnte es ja sein, daß Jeder ein anderes Ding in seiner Schachtel hätte. Ja, man könnte sich vorstellen, daß sich ein solches Ding fortwährend veränderte. — Aber wenn nun das Wort "Käfer" dieser Leute doch einen Gebrauch hätte? — So wäre er nicht der der Bezeichnung eines Dings. Das Ding in der Schachtel gehört überhaupt nicht zum Sprachspiel; auch nicht einmal als ein *Etwas*: denn die Schachtel könnte auch leer sein. — Nein, durch dieses Ding in der Schachtel kann 'gekürzt werden'; es hebt sich weg, was immer es ist.

289. "When I say 'I am in pain', I am at any rate justified *before myself*."
— What does that mean? Does it mean: "If someone else could know what I am calling 'pain', he would admit that I was using the word correctly"?

To use a word without a justification does not mean to use it wrongfully.

290. It is not, of course, that I identify my sensation by means of criteria; it is, rather, that I use the same expression. But it is not as if the language-game *ends* with this; it begins with it.

But doesn't it begin with the sensation — which I describe? — Perhaps this word "describe" tricks us here. I say "I describe my state of mind" and "I describe my room". One needs to call to mind the differences between the language-games.

291. What we call *"descriptions"* are instruments for particular uses. Think of a machine-drawing, a cross-section, an elevation with measurements, which an engineer has before him. Thinking of a description as a word-picture of the facts has something misleading about it: one tends to think only of such pictures as hang on our walls, which seem simply to depict how a thing looks, what it is like. (These pictures are, as it were, idle.) |100|

292. Don't always think that you read off what you say from the facts; that you depict these in words according to rules! For you would still have to apply the rule in the particular case without guidance.

293. If I say of myself that it is only from my own case that I know what the word "pain" means — must I not say *that* of other people too? And how can I generalize the *one* case so irresponsibly?

Well, everyone tells me that he knows what pain is only from his own case! —— Suppose that everyone had a box with something in it which we call a "beetle". No one can ever look into anyone else's box, and everyone says he knows what a beetle is only by looking at *his* beetle. — Here it would be quite possible for everyone to have something different in his box. One might even imagine such a thing constantly changing. — But what if these people's word "beetle" had a use nonetheless? — If so, it would not be as the name of a thing. The thing in the box doesn't belong to the language-game at all; not even as a *Something*: for the box might even be empty. — No, one can 'divide through' by the thing in the box; it cancels out, whatever it is.

Das heißt: Wenn man die Grammatik des Ausdrucks der Empfindung nach dem Muster von 'Gegenstand und Bezeichnung' konstruiert, dann fällt der Gegenstand als irrelevant aus der Betrachtung heraus.

294. Wenn du sagst, er sähe ein privates Bild vor sich, das er beschreibe, so hast du immerhin eine Annahme gemacht über das, was er vor sich hat. Und das heißt, daß du es näher beschreiben kannst, oder beschreibst. Gibst du zu, daß du gar keine Ahnung hast, von welcher Art, was er vor sich hat, sein könnte, — was verführt dich dann dennoch zu sagen, er habe etwas vor sich? Ist das nicht, als sagte ich von Einem: "Er *hat* etwas. Aber ob es Geld, oder Schulden, oder eine leere Kasse ist, weiß ich nicht."

295. Und was soll "Ich weiß nur vom *eigenen* Fall . . ." überhaupt für ein Satz sein? Ein Erfahrungssatz? Nein. — Ein grammatischer?
    Ich denke mir also: Jeder sage von sich selbst, er wisse nur vom eigenen Schmerz, was Schmerz sei. — Nicht, daß die Menschen das wirklich sagen, oder auch nur bereit sind, zu sagen. Aber *wenn* nun Jeder es sagte —— es könnte eine Art Ausruf sein. Und wenn er auch als Mitteilung nichtssagend ist, so ist er doch ein Bild; und warum sollten wir uns so ein Bild nicht vor die Seele rufen wollen? Denke dir statt der Worte ein gemaltes allegorisches Bild.
    Ja, wenn wir beim Philosophieren in uns schauen, bekommen wir oft gerade so ein Bild zu sehen. Förmlich, eine bildliche Darstellung unsrer Grammatik. Nicht Fakten; sondern gleichsam illustrierte Redewendungen.

296. "Ja, aber es ist doch da ein Etwas, was meinen Ausruf des Schmerzes begleitet! Und um dessentwillen ich ihn mache. Und dieses Etwas ist das, was wichtig ist, — und schrecklich." — Wem teilen wir das nur mit? Und bei welcher Gelegenheit?

297. Freilich, wenn das Wasser im Topf kocht, so steigt der Dampf aus dem Topf und auch das Bild des Dampfes aus dem Bild des Topfes. Aber wie, wenn man sagen wollte, im Bild des Topfes müsse auch etwas kochen?

298. Daß wir so gerne sagen möchten "Das Wichtige ist *das*" — indem wir für uns selbst auf die Empfindung deuten, — zeigt schon, wie sehr wir geneigt sind, etwas zu sagen, was keine Mitteilung ist.

That is to say, if we construe the grammar of the expression of sensation on the model of 'object and name', the object drops out of consideration as irrelevant.

294. If you say that he sees a private picture before him, which he is describing, you have at any rate made an assumption about what he has before him. And this means that you can describe it or do describe it more closely. If you admit that you have no idea what kind of thing it might be that he has before him — then what seduces you into saying, in spite of that, that he has something before him? Isn't it as if I were to say of someone: "He *has* something. But I don't know whether it is money, or debts, or an empty till."

295. "I know . . . only from my *own* case" — what kind of proposition is this meant to be? An empirical one? No. — A grammatical one?

So this is what I imagine: everyone says of himself that he knows what pain is only from his own pain. — Not that people really say that, or are even prepared to say it. But *if* everybody said it —— it might be a kind of exclamation. And even if it gives no information, still, it is a picture; and why should we not want to call such a picture before our mind? Imagine an allegorical painting instead of the words.

Indeed, when we look into ourselves as we do philosophy, we often get to |101| see just such a picture. Virtually a pictorial representation of our grammar. Not facts; but, as it were, illustrated turns of speech.

296. "Right; but there is a Something there all the same, which accompanies my cry of pain! And it is on account of this that I utter it. And this Something is what is important — and frightful." — Only to whom are we telling this? And on what occasion?

297. Of course, if water boils in a pot, steam comes out of the pot, and also a picture of steam comes out of a picture of the pot. But what if one insisted on saying that there must also be something boiling in the picture of the pot?

298. The very fact that we'd so much like to say "*This* is the important thing" — while we point for ourselves to the sensation — is enough to show how much we are inclined to say something which is not informative.

299. Nicht umhin können — wenn wir uns philosophischen Gedanken hingeben — das und das zu sagen, unwiderstehlich dazu neigen, dies zu sagen, heißt nicht, zu einer *Annahme* gezwungen sein, oder einen Sachverhalt unmittelbar einsehen, oder wissen.

300. Zu dem Sprachspiel mit den Worten "er hat Schmerzen" gehört — möchte man sagen — nicht nur das Bild des Benehmens, sondern auch das Bild des Schmerzes. Oder: nicht nur das Paradigma des Benehmens, sondern auch das des Schmerzes. — Zu sagen "Das Bild des Schmerzes tritt ins Sprachspiel mit dem Worte 'Schmerz' ein", ist ein Mißverständnis. Die Vorstellung des Schmerzes ist kein Bild, und *diese* Vorstellung ist im Sprachspiel auch nicht durch etwas ersetzbar, was wir ein Bild nennen würden. — Wohl tritt die Vorstellung des Schmerzes in einem Sinn ins Sprachspiel ein; nur nicht als Bild.

301. Eine Vorstellung ist kein Bild, aber ein Bild kann ihr entsprechen.

302. Wenn man sich den Schmerz des Andern nach dem Vorbild des eigenen vorstellen muß, dann ist das keine so leichte Sache: da ich mir nach den Schmerzen, die ich *fühle*, Schmerzen vorstellen soll, die ich *nicht fühle*. Ich habe nämlich in der Vorstellung nicht einfach einen Übergang von einem Ort des Schmerzes zu einem andern zu machen. Wie von Schmerzen in der Hand zu Schmerzen im Arm. Denn ich soll mir nicht vorstellen, daß ich an einer Stelle seines Körpers Schmerz empfinde. (Was auch möglich wäre.)

Das Schmerzbenehmen kann auf eine schmerzhafte Stelle deuten, — aber die leidende Person ist die, welche Schmerz äußert.

303. "Ich kann nur *glauben*, daß der Andre Schmerzen hat, aber ich *weiß* es, wenn ich sie habe." — Ja; man kann sich dazu entschließen, zu sagen "Ich glaube, er hat Schmerzen" statt "Er hat Schmerzen". Aber das ist alles. —— Was hier wie eine Erklärung, oder Aussage über die seelischen Vorgänge ausschaut, ist in Wahrheit ein Vertauschen einer Redeweise für eine andere, die, während wir philosophieren, uns die treffendere scheint.

Versuch einmal — in einem wirklichen Fall — die Angst, die Schmerzen des Andern zu bezweifeln!

304. "Aber du wirst doch zugeben, daß ein Unterschied ist, zwischen Schmerzbenehmen mit Schmerzen und Schmerzbenehmen ohne Schmerzen." — Zugeben? Welcher Unterschied könnte größer sein! — "Und doch gelangst du immer wieder zum Ergebnis, die Empfindung selbst sei ein

299. Being unable — when we indulge in philosophical thought — to help saying something or other, being irresistibly inclined to say it — does not mean being forced into an *assumption*, or having an immediate insight into, or knowledge of, a state of affairs.

300. It is, one would like to say, not merely the picture of the behaviour that belongs to the language-game with the words "he is in pain", but also the picture of the pain. Or, not merely the paradigm of the behaviour, but also that of the pain. — It is a misunderstanding to say "The picture of pain enters into the language-game with the word 'pain'". Pain in the imagination is not a picture, and *it* is not replaceable in the language-game by anything that we'd call a picture. — Imagined pain certainly enters into the language-game in a sense; only not as a picture.

301. What is in the imagination is not a picture, but a picture can correspond to it.

302. If one has to imagine someone else's pain on the model of one's own, this is none too easy a thing to do: for I have to imagine pain which I *don't feel* on the model of pain which I *do feel*. That is, what I have to do is not simply to make a transition in the imagination from pain in one place to pain in another. As from pain in the hand to pain in the arm. For it is not as if I had to imagine that I feel pain in some part of his body. (Which would also be possible.)

Pain-behaviour can indicate a painful place — but the person who is suffering is the person who manifests pain. |102|

303. "I can only *believe* that someone else is in pain, but I *know* it if I am." — Yes: one can resolve to say "I believe he is in pain" instead of "He is in pain". But that's all. —— What looks like an explanation here, or like a statement about a mental process, in truth just exchanges one way of talking for another which, while we are doing philosophy, seems to us the more apt.

Just try — in a real case — to doubt someone else's fear or pain!

304. "But you will surely admit that there is a difference between pain-behaviour with pain and pain-behaviour without pain." — Admit it? What greater difference could there be? — "And yet you again and again reach the conclusion that the sensation itself is a Nothing." — Not at

Nichts." — Nicht doch. Sie ist kein Etwas, aber auch nicht ein Nichts! Das Ergebnis war nur, daß ein Nichts die gleichen Dienste täte, wie ein Etwas, worüber sich nichts aussagen läßt. Wir verwarfen nur die Grammatik, die sich uns hier aufdrängen will.

Das Paradox verschwindet nur dann, wenn wir radikal mit der Idee brechen, die Sprache funktioniere immer auf *eine* Weise, diene immer dem gleichen Zweck: Gedanken zu übertragen — seien diese nun Gedanken über Häuser, Schmerzen, Gut und Böse, oder was immer.

305. "Aber du kannst doch nicht leugnen, daß, z. B., beim Erinnern ein innerer Vorgang stattfindet." — Warum macht es denn den Eindruck, als wollten wir etwas leugnen? Wenn man sagt "Es findet doch dabei ein innerer Vorgang statt" — so will man fortsetzen: "Du *siehst* es doch." Und es ist doch dieser innere Vorgang, den man mit dem Wort "sich erinnern" meint. — Der Eindruck, als wollten wir etwas leugnen, rührt daher, daß wir uns gegen das Bild vom 'innern Vorgang' wenden. Was wir leugnen, ist, daß das Bild vom innern Vorgang uns die richtige Idee von der Verwendung des Wortes "erinnern" gibt. Ja wir sagen, daß dieses Bild mit seinen Ramifikationen uns verhindert, die Verwendung des Wortes zu sehen, wie sie ist.

306. Warum soll ich denn leugnen, daß ein geistiger Vorgang da ist?! Nur heißt "Es hat jetzt in mir der geistige Vorgang der Erinnerung an . . . stattgefunden" nichts andres als: "Ich habe mich jetzt an . . . erinnert." Den geistigen Vorgang leugnen, hieße, das Erinnern leugnen; leugnen, daß irgend jemand sich je an etwas erinnert.

307. "Bist du nicht doch ein verkappter Behaviourist? Sagst du nicht doch, im Grunde, daß alles Fiktion ist, außer dem menschlichen Benehmen?" — Wenn ich von einer Fiktion rede, dann von einer *grammatischen* Fiktion.

308. Wie kommt es nur zum philosophischen Problem der seelischen Vorgänge und Zustände und des Behaviourism? —— Der erste Schritt ist der ganz unauffällige. Wir reden von Vorgängen und Zuständen, und lassen ihre Natur unentschieden! Wir werden vielleicht einmal mehr über sie wissen — meinen wir. Aber eben dadurch haben wir uns auf eine bestimmte Betrachtungsweise festgelegt. Denn wir haben einen bestimmten Begriff davon, was es heißt: einen Vorgang näher kennen zu lernen. (Der entscheidende Schritt im Taschenspielerkunststück ist getan, und gerade er schien uns unschuldig.) — Und nun zerfällt der Vergleich, der uns unsere Gedanken hätte begreiflich machen sollen. Wir müssen also

all. It's not a Something, but not a Nothing either! The conclusion was only that a Nothing would render the same service as a Something about which nothing could be said. We've only rejected the grammar which tends to force itself on us here.

The paradox disappears only if we make a radical break with the idea that language always functions in one way, always serves the same purpose: to convey thoughts — which may be about houses, pains, good and evil, or whatever.

305. "But you surely can't deny that, for example, in remembering, an inner process takes place." — What gives the impression that we want to deny anything? When one says, "Still, an inner process does take place here" — one wants to go on: "After all, you *see* it." And it is this inner process that one means by the word "remembering". — The impression that we wanted to deny something arises from our setting our face against the picture of an 'inner process'. What we deny is that the picture of an inner process gives us the correct idea of the use of the word "remember". Indeed, we're saying that this picture, with its ramifications, stands in the way of our seeing the use of the word as it is.

306. Why ever should I deny that there is a mental process? It is only that "There has just taken place in me the mental process of remembering . . ." means nothing more than "I have just remembered . . ." To deny the mental process would mean to deny the remembering; to deny that anyone ever remembers anything.

307. "Aren't you nevertheless a behaviourist in disguise? Aren't you nevertheless basically saying that everything except human behaviour is |103| a fiction?" — If I speak of a fiction, then it is of a *grammatical* fiction.

308. How does the philosophical problem about mental processes and states and about behaviourism arise? —— The first step is the one that altogether escapes notice. We talk of processes and states, and leave their nature undecided. Sometime perhaps we'll know more about them — we think. But that's just what commits us to a particular way of looking at the matter. For we have a certain conception of what it means to learn to know a process better. (The decisive movement in the conjuring trick has been made, and it was the very one that seemed to us quite innocent.) — And now the analogy which was to make us understand our thoughts falls to pieces. So we have to deny the as yet

den noch unverstandenen Prozeß im noch unerforschten Medium leugnen. Und so scheinen wir also die geistigen Vorgänge geleugnet zu haben. Und wollen sie doch natürlich nicht leugnen!

309. Was ist dein Ziel in der Philosophie? — Der Fliege den Ausweg aus dem Fliegenglas zeigen.

310. Ich sage jemandem, ich habe Schmerzen. Seine Einstellung zu mir wird nun die des Glaubens sein; des Unglaubens; des Mißtrauens; u. s. w.

Nehmen wir an, er sagt: "Es wird nicht so schlimm sein." — Ist das nicht der Beweis dafür, daß er an etwas glaubt, das hinter der Schmerz-äußerung steht? —— Seine Einstellung ist ein Beweis seiner Einstellung. Denke dir nicht nur den Satz "Ich habe Schmerzen", sondern auch die Antwort "Es wird nicht so schlimm sein" durch Naturlaute und Gebärden ersetzt!

311. "Welcher Unterschied könnte größer sein!" — Im Falle der Schmerzen glaube ich, ich könne mir diesen Unterschied privatim vor-führen. Den Unterschied aber zwischen einem abgebrochenen und einem nicht abgebrochenen Zahn kann ich Jedem vorführen. — Aber zu der privaten Vorführung brauchst du dir gar nicht Schmerzen her-vorzurufen, sondern es genügt, wenn du dir sie *vorstellst*, — z. B. ein wenig das Gesicht verziehst. Und weißt du, daß, was du dir so vorführst, Schmerzen sind, und nicht z. B. ein Gesichtsausdruck? Wie weißt du auch, was du dir vorführen sollst, ehe du dir's vorführst? Diese *private* Vorführung ist eine Illusion.

312. Aber sind die Fälle des Zahnes und der Schmerzen nicht doch wieder ähnlich? Denn der Gesichtsempfindung im einen entspricht die Schmerzempfindung im andern. Die Gesichtsempfindung kann ich mir so wenig vorführen, oder so gut, wie die Schmerzempfindung.

Denken wir uns diesen Fall: Die Oberflächen der Dinge unsrer Umgebung (Steine, Pflanzen, etc. etc.) hätten Flecken und Zonen, die unsrer Haut bei der Berührung Schmerz verursachten. (Etwa durch die chemische Beschaffenheit dieser Oberflächen. Aber das brauchen wir nicht zu wissen.) Wir würden nun, wie heute von einem rotgefleckten Blatt einer bestimmten Pflanze, von einem Blatt mit Schmerzflecken reden. Ich denke mir, daß die Wahrnehmung dieser Flecken und ihrer Gestalt für uns von Nutzen wäre, daß wir aus ihr Schlüsse auf wichtige Eigenschaften der Dinge ziehen könnten.

uncomprehended process in the as yet unexplored medium. And now it looks as if we had denied mental processes. And naturally we don't want to deny them.

309. What is your aim in philosophy? — To show the fly the way out of the fly-bottle.

310. I tell someone I'm in pain. His attitude to me will then be that of belief, disbelief, suspicion, and so on.

Let's suppose he says, "It's not so bad". — Doesn't that prove that he believes in something behind my utterance of pain? —— His attitude is proof of his attitude. Imagine not merely the words "I'm in pain", but also the reply "It's not so bad", replaced by instinctive noises and gestures.

311. "What greater difference could there be?" — In the case of pain, I believe that I can privately give myself an exhibition of the difference. But the difference between a broken and an unbroken tooth I can exhibit to anyone. — For the private exhibition, however, you don't have to give yourself actual pain; it is enough to *imagine* it — for instance, you screw up your face a bit. And do you know that what you are exhibiting to yourself in this way is pain and not, for example, a facial expression? And how do you know what you are to exhibit to yourself before you do it? This *private* exhibition is an illusion.

* 312. But again, *aren't* the cases of the tooth and the pain similar? For the visual impression in the one corresponds to the sensation of pain in the other. I can exhibit the visual impression to myself as little or as well as the sensation of pain. |104|

Let's imagine the following. The surfaces of the things around us (stones, plants, etc.) have patches and regions which cause pain in our skin when we touch them. (Perhaps through the chemical composition of these surfaces. But we needn't know that.) In this case, we'd speak of pain-patches on the leaf of a particular plant, just as at present we speak of red patches. I'm supposing that it is useful to us to notice these patches and their shapes; that we can infer important properties of the objects from them.

313. Ich kann Schmerzen vorführe, wie ich Rot vorführe, und wie ich Gerade und Krumm und Baum und Stein vorführe. — *Das nennen* wir eben "vorführen".

314. Es zeigt ein fundamentales Mißverständnis an, wenn ich meinen gegenwärtigen Zustand der Kopfschmerzen zu betrachten geneigt bin, um über das philosophische Problem der Empfindung ins Klare zu kommen.

315. Könnte der das Wort "Schmerz" verstehen, der *nie* Schmerz gefühlt hat? — Soll die Erfahrung mich lehren, ob es so ist oder nicht? — Und wenn wir sagen "Einer kann sich Schmerzen nicht vorstellen, außer er hat sie einmal gefühlt" — woher wissen wir das? Wie läßt sich entscheiden, ob das wahr ist?

316. Um über die Bedeutung des Wortes "denken" klar zu werden, schauen wir uns selbst beim Denken zu: Was wir da beobachten, werde das sein, was das Wort bedeutet! — Aber so wird dieser Begriff eben nicht gebraucht. (Es wäre ähnlich, wenn ich, ohne Kenntnis des Schachspiels, durch genaues Beobachten des letzten Zuges einer Schachpartie herausbringen wollte, was das Wort "mattsetzen" bedeutet.)

317. Irreführende Parallele: Der Schrei, ein Ausdruck des Schmerzes — der Satz, ein Ausdruck des Gedankens!
   Als wäre es der Zweck des Satzes, Einen wissen zu lassen, wie es dem Andern zu Mute ist: Nur, sozusagen, im Denkapparat und nicht im Magen.

318. Wenn wir denkend sprechen, oder auch schreiben — ich meine, wie wir es gewöhnlich tun — so werden wir, im allgemeinen, nicht sagen, wir dächten schneller, als wir sprechen; sondern der Gedanke erscheint hier vom Ausdruck *nicht abgelöst.* Anderseits aber redet man von der Schnelle des Gedankens; wie ein Gedanke uns blitzartig durch den Kopf geht, wie Probleme uns mit einem Schlage klar werden, etc. Da liegt es nahe, zu fragen: Geschieht beim blitzartigen Denken das gleiche, wie beim nicht gedankenlosen Sprechen, — nur äußerst beschleunigt? So daß also im ersten Fall das Uhrwerk gleichsam mit einem Ruck abläuft, im zweiten aber, durch die Worte gehemmt, Schritt für Schritt.

319. Ich kann in demselben Sinn blitzartig einen Gedanken ganz vor mir sehen, oder verstehen, wie ich ihn mit wenigen Worten, oder Strichen notieren kann.
   Was macht diese Notiz zu einer Zusammenfassung dieses Gedankens?

313. I can exhibit pain, as I exhibit red, and as I exhibit straight and crooked and trees and stones. — *That* is what we *call* "exhibiting".

314. It indicates a fundamental misunderstanding, if I'm inclined to study my current headache in order to get clear about the philosophical problem of sensation.

315. Could someone who had *never* felt pain understand the word "pain"? — Is experience to teach me whether this is so or not? — And if we say "A man could not imagine pain without having sometime felt it", how do we know? How can it be decided whether it's true?

316. In order to get clear about the meaning of the word "think", we watch ourselves thinking; what we observe will be what the word means! — But that's just *not* how this concept is used. (It would be as if without knowing how to play chess, I were to try to make out what the word "checkmate" meant by close observation of the last move of a game of chess.)

317. Misleading parallel: a cry, an expression of a pain — a sentence, an expression of a thought.
   As if the purpose of a sentence were to convey to one person how it is with another: only, so to speak, in his thinking apparatus, and not in his stomach.

318. When we speak, or write, with thought — I mean, as we normally do — we wouldn't, by and large, say that we think more quickly than we talk; rather, the thought seems *not to be detached* from the expression. On the other hand, however, one does speak of the speed of thought, of how a thought goes through one's head like lightning, of how problems become clear to us at a stroke, and so on. So it is natural to ask whether the same thing happens in lightning-like thought as in speech that is not thoughtless — only extremely accelerated. So that in the |105| first case the clockwork, as it were, runs down all at once, but in the second bit by bit, braked by the words.

319. I can see, or understand, a thought complete before my mind's eye in a flash, in the same sense in which I can make a note of it in a few words or a few pencilled dashes.
   What makes this note into an epitome of this thought?

320. Der blitzartige Gedanke kann sich zum ausgesprochenen verhalten, wie die algebraische Formel zu einer Zahlenfolge, die ich aus ihr entwickle.

Wird mir z. B. eine algebraische Funktion gegeben, so bin ich SICHER, ich werde ihre Werte für die Argumente 1, 2, 3, bis 10 berechnen können. Man wird diese Sicherheit 'wohlbegründet' nennen, denn ich habe gelernt, solche Funktionen zu berechnen, u. s. w. In andern Fällen wird sie nicht begründet sein, — aber durch den Erfolg dennoch gerechtfertigt.

321. "Was geschieht, wenn ein Mensch plötzlich versteht?" — Die Frage ist schlecht gestellt. Fragt sie nach der Bedeutung des Ausdrucks "plötzlich verstehen", so ist die Antwort nicht das Hinweisen auf einen Vorgang, den wir so nennen. — Die Frage könnte bedeuten: Was sind Anzeichen dafür, daß Einer plötzlich versteht; welches sind die charakteristischen psychischen Begleiterscheinungen des plötzlichen Verstehens?

(Es ist kein Grund, anzunehmen, daß ein Mensch die Ausdrucksbewegungen seines Gesichts, z. B., oder die für eine Gemütsbewegung charakteristischen Veränderungen in seiner Atmung, fühle. Auch wenn er sie fühlt, sobald er seine Aufmerksamkeit auf sie lenkt.) ((Positur.))

322. Daß die Antwort auf die Frage nach der Bedeutung des Ausdrucks mit dieser Beschreibung nicht gegeben ist, verleitet dann zu der Folgerung, das Verstehen sei eben ein spezifisches, undefinierbares, Erlebnis. Man vergißt aber, daß, was uns interessieren muß, die Frage ist: Wie *vergleichen* wir diese Erlebnisse; was *legen wir fest* als Kriterium der Identität des Geschehnisses?

323. "Jetzt weiß ich weiter!" ist ein Ausruf; er entspricht einem Naturlaut, einem freudigen Aufzucken. Aus meiner Empfindung folgt natürlich nicht, daß ich nicht stecken bleibe, sowie ich versuche, weiterzugehen. — Es gibt da Fälle, in denen ich sagen werde: "Als ich sagte, ich wisse weiter, da *war* es so." Das wird man z. B. sagen, wenn eine unvorhergesehene Störung eingetreten ist. Aber das Unvorhergesehene durfte nicht einfach das sein, daß ich steckenblieb.

Es wäre auch denkbar, daß Einer immer wieder Scheinerleuchtungen hätte, — ausriefe "Jetzt hab ich's!" und es dann nie durch die Tat rechtfertigen könnte. — Es könnte ihm scheinen, als vergäße er augenblicklich wieder die Bedeutung des Bildes, das ihm vorschwebte.

324. Wäre es richtig zu sagen, es handle sich hier um Induktion, und ich sei so sicher, daß ich die Reihe werde fortsetzen können, wie ich es bin, daß dieses Buch zur Erde fallen wird, wenn ich es auslasse; und

320. A lightning-like thought may stand to a spoken thought as an algebraic formula to a sequence of numbers which I develop from it.

When, for example, I am given an algebraic function, I am CERTAIN that I shall be able to work out its values for the arguments 1, 2, 3 . . . up to 10. This certainty will be called 'well-grounded', for I have learnt to compute such functions, and so on. In other cases, there will be no grounds — but it will nonetheless be justified by success.

321. "What happens when a man suddenly understands?" — The question is badly framed. If it is a question about the meaning of the expression "sudden understanding", the answer is not to point to a process to which we give this name. — The question might mean: what are the symptoms of sudden understanding; what are its characteristic mental accompaniments?

(There is no reason to think that a man feels his expressive facial movements, for example, or alterations in his breathing that are characteristic of some emotion. Even if he feels them as soon as he directs his attention towards them.) ((Posture.))

322. The question what the expression means is not answered by such a description; and this tempts us to conclude that understanding is a specific, indefinable experience. But one forgets that the question which should be our concern is: how do we *compare* these experiences; what criterion of identity *do we stipulate* for their occurrence?

323. "Now I know how to go on!" is an exclamation; it corresponds to an instinctive sound, a glad start. Of course, it does not follow from my feeling that I won't find I'm stuck when I do try to go on. — Here there are cases in which I'd say: "When I said I knew how to go on, I *did* know." One will say that if, for example, an unforeseen interruption occurs. But what is unforeseen must not simply be that I get stuck. |106|

One could also imagine a case in which light was constantly seeming to dawn on someone — he exclaims "Now I have it!", and then can never substantiate this in practice. — It might seem to him as if in the twinkling of an eye he forgot again the meaning of the picture that occurred to him.

324. Would it be correct to say that this is a matter of induction, and that I am as certain that I'll be able to continue the series as I am that this book will drop to the ground when I let it go; and that I'd be no

ich wäre nicht erstaunter, wenn ich plötzlich ohne offenbare Ursache im Entwickeln der Reihe steckenbliebe, als ich es wäre, wenn das Buch, statt zu fallen, in der Luft schweben bliebe? — Darauf will ich antworten, daß wir eben auch zu *dieser* Sicherheit keiner Gründe bedürfen. Was könnte die Sicherheit *mehr* rechtfertigen, als der Erfolg?

325. "Die Gewißheit, daß ich werde fortsetzen können, nachdem ich dies Erlebnis gehabt habe — z. B. diese Formel gesehen habe — gründet sich einfach auf Induktion." Was heißt das? — "Die Gewißheit, daß das Feuer mich brennen wird, gründet sich auf Induktion." Heißt dies, daß ich bei mir schließe "Ich habe mich immer an einer Flamme verbrannt, also wird es auch jetzt geschehen"? Oder ist die frühere Erfahrung die *Ursache* meiner Gewißheit, nicht ihr Grund? Ist die frühere Erfahrung die Ursache der Gewißheit — das kommt auf das System von Hypothesen, Naturgesetzen an, in welchem wir das Phänomen der Gewißheit betrachten.

Ist die Zuversicht gerechtfertigt? — Was die Menschen als Rechtfertigung gelten lassen, — zeigt, wie sie denken und leben.

326. Wir erwarten *dies* und werden von *dem* überrascht; aber die Kette der Gründe hat ein Ende.

327. "Kann man denken, ohne zu reden?" — Und was ist *Denken*? — Nun, denkst du nie? Kannst du dich nicht beobachten und sehen, was da vorgeht? Das sollte doch einfach sein. Du mußt ja darauf nicht, wie auf ein astronomisches Ereignis warten und dann etwa in Eile deine Beobachtung machen.

328. Nun, was nennt man noch "denken"? Wofür hat man gelernt, das Wort zu benützen? — Wenn ich sage, ich habe gedacht, — muß ich da immer recht haben? — Was für eine *Art* des Irrtums gibt es da? Gibt es Umstände, unter denen man fragen würde: "War, was ich da getan habe, wirklich ein Denken; irre ich mich nicht?" Wenn jemand, im Verlauf eines Gedankengangs, eine Messung ausführt: hat er das Denken unterbrochen, wenn er beim Messen nicht zu sich selbst spricht?

329. Wenn ich in der Sprache denke, so schweben mir nicht neben dem sprachlichen Ausdruck noch 'Bedeutungen' vor; sondern die Sprache selbst ist das Vehikel des Denkens.

330. Ist Denken eine Art Sprechen? Man möchte sagen, es ist das, was denkendes Sprechen vom gedankenlosen Sprechen unterscheidet.

less astonished if I suddenly, and for no obvious reason, got stuck in working out the series than I would be if the book remained hanging in the air instead of falling? — To that I'll reply that we don't need any grounds for *this* certainty either. What could justify the certainty *better* than success?

325. "The certainty that I'll be able to go on after I've had this experience — seen this formula, for example — is simply based on induction." What does this mean? — "The certainty that fire will burn me is based on induction." Does it mean that I reason to myself: "Fire has always burned me, so it will happen now too"? Or is the previous experience the *cause* of my certainty, not its reason? Whether the earlier experience is the cause of the certainty depends on the system of hypotheses, of natural laws, in terms of which we are considering the phenomenon of certainty.

Is such confidence justified? — What people accept as a justification shows how they think and live.

326. We expect *this*, and are surprised at *that*. But the chain of reasons has an end.

327. "Can one think without speaking?" — And what is *thinking*? Well, don't you ever think? Can't you observe yourself and see what is going on? It should be quite simple. You don't have to wait for it as for an astronomical event, and then perhaps make your observation in a hurry.

328. Well, what does one call 'thinking'? What has one learnt to use this word for? — If I say I've thought — need I always be right? — What *kind* of mistake is there room for here? Are there circumstances in which one would ask, "Was what I was doing then really thinking; aren't I making a mistake?" Suppose someone takes a measurement in the middle of a train of thought: has he interrupted the thinking if he doesn't say anything to himself while measuring? |107|

329. When I think in words, I don't have 'meanings' in my mind in addition to the verbal expressions; rather, language itself is the vehicle of thought.

330. Is thinking a kind of speaking? One would like to say that it is what distinguishes speech with thought from talking without thought.

— Und da scheint es eine Begleitung des Sprechens zu sein. Ein Vorgang, der vielleicht auch etwas anderes begleiten, oder selbständig ablaufen kann.

Sprich die Zeile: "Die Feder ist wohl stumpf. Nu, nu, sie geht." Einmal denkend; dann gedankenlos; dann denk nur den Gedanken, aber ohne die Worte. — Nun, ich könnte, im Laufe einer Handlung, die Spitze meiner Feder prüfen, mein Gesicht verziehen, — dann mit einer Gebärde der Resignation weiterschreiben. — Ich könnte auch, mit irgendwelchen Messungen beschäftigt, so handeln, daß, wer mir zusieht, sagen würde, ich habe — ohne Worte — gedacht: Sind zwei Größen einer dritten gleich, so sind sie untereinander gleich. — Aber was hier das Denken ausmacht, ist nicht ein Vorgang, der die Worte begleiten muß, wenn sie nicht gedankenlos ausgesprochen sein sollen.

331. Stell dir Menschen vor, die nur laut denken könnten! (Wie es Menschen gibt, die nur laut lesen können.)

332. "Denken" nennen wir wohl manchmal, den Satz mit einem seelischen Vorgang begleiten, aber "Gedanke" nennen wir nicht jene Begleitung. —— Sprich einen Satz und denke ihn; sprich ihn mit Verständnis! — Und nun sprich ihn nicht, und tu nur das, womit du ihn beim verständnisvollen Sprechen begleitet hast! — (Sing dies Lied mit Ausdruck! Und nun sing es nicht, aber wiederhole den Ausdruck! — Und man könnte auch hier etwas wiederholen; z. B. Schwingungen des Körpers, langsameres und schnelleres Atmen, etc.)

333. "Das kann nur Einer sagen, der davon *überzeugt* ist." — Wie hilft ihm die Überzeugung, wenn er es sagt? — Ist sie dann neben dem gesprochenen Ausdruck vorhanden? (Oder wird sie von diesem zugedeckt, wie ein leiser Ton von einem lauten, so daß sie gleichsam nicht mehr gehört werden kann, wenn man sie laut ausdrückt?) Wie, wenn Einer sagte: "Damit man eine Melodie nach dem Gedächtnis singen kann, muß man sie im Geiste hören und sie nachsingen"?

334. "Du wolltest also eigentlich sagen . . ." — Mit dieser Redeweise leiten wir Jemand von einer Ausdrucksform zu einer andern. Man ist versucht, das Bild zu gebrauchen: das, was er eigentlich 'sagen wollte', was er 'meinte', sei, noch ehe wir es aussprachen, in seinem Geist vorhanden gewesen. Was uns dazu bewegt, einen Ausdruck aufzugeben und an seiner Stelle einen andern anzunehmen, kann von mannigfacher Art sein. Das zu verstehen, ist es nützlich, das Verhältnis zu betrachten, in welchem Lösungen mathematischer Probleme zum Anlaß und Ursprung ihrer Fragestellung stehen. Der Begriff 'Dreiteilung des Winkels mit Lineal

— And so it seems to be an accompaniment of speech. A process which may accompany something else or go on by itself.

Say: "Yes, this pen is blunt. Oh well, it'll do." First, with thought; then without thought; then just think the thought without the words. — Well, while writing, I might test the point of my pen, make a face — and then go on writing with a gesture of resignation. — So too I might, while taking various measurements, act in such a way that an onlooker would say that I had wordlessly thought: if two magnitudes are equal to a third, they are equal to one another. — But what constitutes thought here is not some process which has to accompany the words if they are not to be spoken without thought.

331. Imagine people who could think only aloud. (As there are people who can read only aloud.)

332. True, we sometimes call accompanying a sentence by a mental process "thinking"; nonetheless, that accompaniment is not what we call a "thought". —— Utter a sentence, and think it; utter it with understanding. — And now don't utter it, and just do what you accompanied it with when you uttered it with understanding! — (Sing this song with expression! And now don't sing it, but repeat its expression! — And here too there is something one might repeat: for example, swaying of the body, slower and faster breathing, and so on.)

333. "Only someone who is *convinced* can say that." — How does the conviction help him when he says it? — Is it present alongside the spoken expression? (Or is it masked by it, as a soft sound by a loud one, so that it can, as it were, no longer be heard when one expresses it out loud?) What if someone were to say, "In order to be able to sing a tune from memory, one has to hear it in one's mind and sing from that"?

334. "So you really wanted to say . . ." — We use this phrase in order to lead someone from one form of expression to another. One is tempted to use the following picture: what he really 'wanted to say', what he 'meant', was already present in his mind even |108| before we articulated it. Various kinds of thing may persuade us to give up one expression and to adopt another in its place. To understand this, it's useful to consider the relation in which solutions of mathematical problems stand to their occasion, and the original setting in which they were posed: the concept of trisecting an angle with ruler and compass,

und Zirkel', wenn Einer nach der Dreiteilung sucht, und anderseits, wenn bewiesen ist, daß es sie nicht gibt.

335. Was geschieht, wenn wir uns bemühen — etwa beim Schreiben eines Briefes — den richtigen Ausdruck für unsere Gedanken zu finden? — Diese Redeweise vergleicht den Vorgang dem einer Übersetzung, oder Beschreibung: Die Gedanken sind da (etwa schon vorher) und wir suchen nur noch nach ihrem Ausdruck. Dieses Bild trifft für verschiedene Fälle mehr, oder weniger zu. — Aber was kann hier nicht alles geschehen! — Ich gebe mich einer Stimmung hin, und der Ausdruck *kommt*. Oder: es schwebt mir ein Bild vor, das ich zu beschreiben trachte. Oder: es fiel mir ein englischer Ausdruck ein, und ich will mich auf den entsprechenden deutschen besinnen. Oder: ich mache eine Gebärde, und frage mich: "Welches sind die Worte, die dieser Gebärde entsprechen?" Etc.

Wenn man nun fragte "Hast du den Gedanken, ehe du den Ausdruck hattest?" — was müßte man da antworten? Und was auf die Frage: "Worin bestand der Gedanke, wie er vor dem Ausdruck vorhanden war?"

336. Es liegt hier ein Fall vor, ähnlich dem, wenn jemand sich vorstellt, man könne einen Satz mit der merkwürdigen Wortstellung der deutschen oder lateinischen Sprache nicht einfach denken, wie er dasteht. Man müsse ihn zuerst denken, und dann bringt man die Wörter in jene seltsame Ordnung. (Ein französischer Politiker schrieb einmal, es sei eine Eigentümlichkeit der französischen Sprache, daß in ihr die Worte in der Ordnung stehen, in welcher man sie denkt.)

337. Aber habe ich nicht die Gesamtform des Satzes, z. B., schon an seinem Anfang beabsichtigt? Also war er mir doch schon im Geiste, ehe er noch ausgesprochen war! — Wenn er mir im Geiste war, dann, im allgemeinen, nicht mit anderer Wortstellung. Aber wir machen uns hier wieder ein irreführendes Bild vom 'Beabsichtigen'; d. h., vom Gebrauch dieses Worts. Die Absicht ist eingebettet in der Situation, den menschlichen Gepflogenheiten und Institutionen. Gäbe es nicht die Technik des Schachspiels, so könnte ich nicht beabsichtigen, eine Schachpartie zu spielen. Soweit ich die Satzform im voraus beabsichtige, ist dies dadurch ermöglicht, daß ich deutsch sprechen kann.

338. Man kann doch nur etwas sagen, wenn man sprechen gelernt hat. Wer also etwas sagen *will*, muß dazu auch gelernt haben, eine Sprache beherrschen; und doch ist es klar, daß er beim Sprechenwollen nicht sprechen mußte. Wie er auch beim Tanzenwollen nicht tanzt.

when people are trying to do it, and, on the other hand, when it has been proved that there's no such thing.

335. What happens when we make an effort — say in writing a letter — to find the right expression for our thoughts? — This way of speaking compares the process to one of translating or describing: the thoughts are already there (perhaps were there in advance), and we merely look for their expression. This picture is more or less appropriate in different cases. — But can't all sorts of things happen here? — I surrender to a mood, and the expression *comes*. Or I have a picture before my mind, and I try to describe it. Or an English expression occurs to me, and I try to recollect the corresponding German one. Or I make a gesture, and ask myself: "What words correspond to this gesture?" And so on.

  Now if it were asked, "Do you have the thought before finding the expression?", what would one have to reply? And what to the question "What did the thought, as it existed before its expression, consist in?"

*   336. This case is similar to the one in which someone imagines that one could not think a sentence with the curious word order of German or Latin just as it stands. One first has to think it, and then one arranges the words in that strange order. (A French politician once wrote that it was a peculiarity of the French language that in it words occur in the order in which one thinks them.)

337. But didn't I already intend the whole construction of the sentence (for example) at its beginning? So surely it already existed in my mind before I uttered it out loud! — If it was in my mind, still it would not normally be there in some different word order. But here again, we are forming a misleading picture of 'intending': that is, of the use of this word. An intention is embedded in a setting, in human customs and institutions. If the technique of the game of chess did not exist, I could not intend to play a game of chess. To the extent that I do intend the construction of an English sentence in advance, that is made possible by the fact that I can speak English. |109|

338. After all, one can only say something if one has learned to talk. Therefore, in order to *want* to say something, one must also have mastered a language; and yet it is clear that one can want to speak without speaking. Just as one can want to dance without dancing.

Und wenn man darüber nachdenkt, so greift der Geist nach der *Vorstellung* des Tanzens, Redens, etc.

339. Denken ist kein unkörperlicher Vorgang, der dem Reden Leben und Sinn leiht, und den man vom Reden ablösen könnte, gleichsam wie der Böse den Schatten Schlemihls vom Boden abnimmt. —— Aber wie: "kein unkörperlicher Vorgang"? Kenne ich also unkörperliche Vorgänge, das Denken aber ist nicht einer von ihnen? Nein; das Wort "unkörperlicher Vorgang" nahm ich mir zu Hilfe, in meiner Verlegenheit, da ich die Bedeutung des Wortes "denken" auf primitive Weise erklären wollte.

Man könnte aber sagen "Denken ist ein unkörperlicher Vorgang", wenn man dadurch die Grammatik des Wortes "denken" von der des Wortes "essen", z. B., unterscheiden will. Nur erscheint dadurch der Unterschied der Bedeutungen *zu gering*. (Ähnlich ist es, wenn man sagt: die Zahlzeichen seien wirkliche, die Zahlen nicht-wirkliche Gegenstände.) Eine unpassende Ausdrucksweise ist ein sicheres Mittel, in einer Verwirrung stecken zu bleiben. Sie verriegelt gleichsam den Ausweg aus ihr.

340. Wie ein Wort funktioniert, kann man nicht erraten. Man muß seine Anwendung *ansehen* und daraus lernen.

Die Schwierigkeit aber ist, das Vorurteil zu beseitigen, das diesem Lernen entgegensteht. Es ist kein *dummes* Vorurteil.

341. Gedankenloses und nicht gedankenloses Sprechen ist zu vergleichen dem gedankenlosen und nicht gedankenlosen Spielen eines Musikstücks.

342. William James, um zu zeigen, daß Denken ohne Sprechen möglich ist, zitiert die Erinnerung eines Taubstummen, Mr. Ballard, welcher schreibt, er habe in seiner frühen Jugend, noch ehe er sprechen konnte, sich über Gott und die Welt Gedanken gemacht. — Was das wohl heißen mag! — Ballard schreibt: "It was during those delightful rides, some two or three years before my initiation into the rudiments of written language, that I began to ask myself the question: how came the world into being?" — Bist du sicher, daß dies die richtige Übersetzung deiner wortlosen Gedanken in Worte ist? — möchte man fragen. Und warum reckt diese Frage — die doch sonst gar nicht zu existieren scheint — hier ihren Kopf hervor? Will ich sagen, es täusche den Schreiber sein Gedächtnis? — Ich weiß nicht einmal, ob ich *das* sagen würde. Diese Erinnerungen sind ein seltsames Gedächtnisphänomen — und ich weiß nicht, welche Schlüsse auf die Vergangenheit des Erzählers man aus ihnen ziehen kann!

And when one thinks about this, the mind reaches for the *idea* of dancing, speaking, etc.

* 339. Thinking is not an incorporeal process which lends life and sense to speaking, and which it would be possible to detach from speaking, rather as the Devil took the shadow of Schlemihl from the ground. —— But in what way "not an incorporeal process"? Am I acquainted with incorporeal processes, then, only thinking is not one of them? No; in my predicament, I helped myself to the expression "an incorporeal process" as I was trying to explain the meaning of the word "thinking" in a primitive way.

* One could, however, say "Thinking is an incorporeal process" if one were using this to distinguish the grammar of the word "think" from that of, say, the word "eat". Only that makes the difference between the meanings look *too slight*. (It is like saying: numerals are actual, and numbers are non-actual objects.) An inappropriate expression is a sure means of remaining stuck in confusion. It, as it were, bars the way out.

340. One cannot guess how a word functions. One has to *look* at its application and learn from that.

But the difficulty is to remove the prejudice which stands in the way of doing so. It is not a *stupid* prejudice.

341. Speech with and without thought is to be compared to playing a piece of music with and without thought.

* 342. William James, in order to show that thought is possible without speech, quotes the reminiscences of a deaf-mute, Mr Ballard, who wrote that in his early youth, even before he could speak, he had had thoughts about God and the world. — What could that mean!? — Ballard writes: "It was during those delightful rides, some two or three years before my initiation into the rudiments of written language, that I began to ask myself the question: how came the world into being?" — Are you sure — one would like to ask — that this is the correct translation of your wordless thoughts into words? And why does this question — which otherwise seems not to exist — arise here? Do I want to say that the writer's memory deceives |110| him? — I don't even know if I'd say *that*. These recollections are a strange memory phenomenon — and I don't know what conclusions one can draw from them about the narrator's past!

343. Die Worte, mit denen ich meine Erinnerung ausdrücke, sind meine Erinnerungsreaktion.

344. Wäre es denkbar, daß Menschen nie eine hörbare Sprache sprächen, wohl aber eine im Innern, in der Vorstellung, zu sich selber?

"Wenn die Menschen immer nur in ihrem Innern zu sich selbst sprächen, so täten sie schließlich nur dasjenige *beständig*, was sie auch heute *manchmal* tun." — Es ist also ganz leicht, sich dies vorzustellen; man braucht nur den leichten Übergang von Einigen zu Allen zu machen. (Ähnlich: "Eine unendlich lange Baumreihe ist einfach eine, die *nicht* zu einem Ende kommt.") Unser Kriterium dafür, daß Einer zu sich selbst spricht, ist das, was er uns sagt, und sein übriges Verhalten; und wir sagen nur von dem, er spräche zu sich selbst, der, im gewöhnlichen Sinne, *sprechen kann*. Und wir sagen es auch nicht von einem Papagei; und nicht von einem Grammophon.

345. "Was manchmal geschieht, könnte immer geschehen" — was wäre das für ein Satz? Ein ähnlicher, wie dieser: Wenn "F(a)" Sinn hat, hat "(x).F(x)" Sinn.

"Wenn es vorkommen kann, daß Einer in einem Spiel falsch zieht, so könnte es sein, daß alle Menschen in allen Spielen nichts als falsche Züge machten." — Wir sind also in der Versuchung, hier die Logik unsrer Ausdrücke mißzuverstehen, den Gebrauch unsrer Worte unrichtig darzustellen.

Befehle werden manchmal nicht befolgt. Wie aber würde es aussehen, wenn Befehle *nie* befolgt würden? Der Begriff 'Befehl' hätte seinen Zweck verloren.

346. Aber könnten wir uns nicht vorstellen, daß Gott einem Papagei plötzlich Verstand schenkte, und dieser nun zu sich selbst redete? — Aber hier ist es wichtig, daß ich zu dieser Vorstellung die Vorstellung von einer Gottheit zu Hilfe nahm.

347. "Aber ich weiß doch von mir selbst, was es heißt 'zu sich selbst sprechen'. Und würde ich der Organe des lauten Sprechens beraubt, so könnte ich dennoch in mir Selbstgespräche führen."

Weiß ich's nur von mir selbst, dann weiß ich also nur, was *ich* so nenne, nicht, was ein Andrer so nennt.

348. "Diese Taubstummen haben alle nur eine Gebärdensprache gelernt, Jeder aber spricht zu sich selbst im Innern eine Lautsprache." — Nun, verstehst du das nicht? — Wie weiß ich nur, ob ich's verstehe?! — Was

343. The words with which I express my memory are my memory reaction.

344. Is it conceivable that people should never speak an audible language, but should nevertheless talk to themselves inwardly, in the imagination?

"If people talked only inwardly, to themselves, then they would merely be doing *always* what, as it is, they do *sometimes*." — So it is quite easy to imagine this; one need only make the easy transition from some to all. (Similarly, "An infinitely long row of trees is simply one that does *not* come to an end.") Our criterion for someone's saying something to himself is what he tells us, as well as the rest of his behaviour; and we say that someone talks to himself only if, in the ordinary sense of the words, he *can talk*. And we do not say it of a parrot; or of a gramophone.

345. "What sometimes happens might always happen." — What kind of proposition is that? It is similar to this one: If "F(a)" makes sense, "(x).F(x)" makes sense.

"If it is possible for someone to make a false move in some game, then it could be that everybody made nothing but false moves in every game." — So we're tempted to misunderstand the logic of our expressions here, to give an incorrect account of the use of our words.

Orders are sometimes not obeyed. But what would it be like if no orders were *ever* obeyed? The concept of an order would have lost its purpose.

346. But couldn't we imagine God's suddenly giving a parrot reason, and its now saying things to itself? — But here it is important that, in order to arrive at this idea, I had recourse to the notion of a deity.

347. "But at least I know from my own case what it means 'to say things to oneself'. And if I were deprived of the organs of speech, I could still conduct internal monologues."

If I know it only from my own case, then I know only what *I* call that, not what anyone else does.

348. "All these deaf-mutes have learned only a sign-language, but each of them talks to himself inwardly in a vocal language." — Well, |111| don't you understand that? — How should I know whether I

kann ich mit dieser Mitteilung (wenn's eine ist) anfangen? Die ganze
Idee des Verstehens erhält hier einen verdächtigen Geruch. Ich weiß nicht,
ob ich sagen soll, ich versteh's, oder ich versteh's nicht. Ich möchte
antworten: "Es ist ein deutscher Satz; *scheinbar* ganz in Ordnung, —
ehe man nämlich mit ihm arbeiten will; er steht mit andern Sätzen in
einem Zusammenhang, der es uns schwer macht, zu sagen, man wisse
eigentlich nicht, was er uns mitteilt; Jeder, der nicht durch Philosophieren
empfindungslos geworden ist, merkt, daß hier etwas nicht stimmt."

349. "Aber diese Annahme hat doch gewiß einen guten Sinn!" — Ja;
diese Worte und dies Bild haben unter gewöhnlichen Umständen eine
uns geläufige Anwendung. — Nehmen wir aber einen Fall an, in
welchem diese Anwendung wegfällt, so werden wir uns nun gleichsam
zum ersten Male der Nacktheit der Worte und des Bildes bewußt.

350. "Aber wenn ich annehme, Einer habe Schmerzen, so nehme ich
einfach an, er habe dasselbe, was ich so oft gehabt habe." — Das führt
uns nicht weiter. Es ist, als sagte ich: "Du weißt doch, was es heißt 'Es
ist hier 5 Uhr'; dann weißt du auch, was es heißt, es sei 5 Uhr auf der
Sonne. Es heißt eben, es sei dort ebensoviel Uhr, wie hier, wenn es hier
5 Uhr ist." — Die Erklärung mittels der *Gleichheit* funktioniert hier nicht.
Weil ich zwar weiß, daß man 5 Uhr hier "die gleiche Zeit" nennen kann,
wie 5 Uhr dort, aber eben nicht weiß, in welchem Falle man von
Zeitgleichheit hier und dort sprechen soll.
  Geradeso ist es keine Erklärung, zu sagen: die Annahme, er habe
Schmerzen, sei eben die Annahme, er habe das Gleiche wie ich. Denn
dieser Teil der Grammatik ist mir wohl klar: daß man nämlich sagen
werde, der Ofen habe das gleiche Erlebnis wie ich, *wenn* man sagt: er
habe Schmerzen und ich habe Schmerzen.

351. Wir möchten doch immer sagen: "Schmerzgefühl ist Schmerzgefühl
— ob *er* es hat, oder *ich* es habe; und wie immer ich erfahre, ob er eines
hat oder nicht." — Damit könnte ich mich einverstanden erklären. —
Und wenn du mich fragst: "Weißt du denn nicht, was ich meine, wenn
ich sage, der Ofen habe Schmerzen?" — so kann ich antworten: Diese
Worte können mich zu allerlei Vorstellungen führen; aber weiter geht
ihr Nutzen nicht. Und ich kann mir auch etwas bei den Worten
vorstellen "Es war gerade 5 Uhr nachmittag auf der Sonne" — nämlich
etwa eine Pendeluhr, die auf 5 zeigt. — Noch besser wäre aber das Beispiel
der Anwendung von "oben" und "unten" auf die Erdkugel. Hier haben
wir alle eine ganz deutliche Vorstellung davon, was "oben" und "unten"

understand it?! — What can I do with this information (if that's what it is)? The whole idea of understanding smells fishy here. I don't know whether I am to say I understand it, or I don't understand it. I'm inclined to answer "It's an English sentence; *apparently* quite in order — that is, until one wants to do something with it; it has a connection with other sentences, which makes it difficult for us to say that one doesn't really know what it tells us. Anyone who has not become insensitive by doing philosophy notices that there is something wrong here."

349. "But this assumption surely makes good sense!" — Yes; in ordinary circumstances these words and this picture have an application with which we are familiar. — But if we suppose a case in which this application does not exist, we become aware for the first time of the nakedness, as it were, of the words and the picture.

350. "But if I suppose that someone has a pain, then I am simply supposing that he has just the same as I have so often had." — That gets us no further. It is as if I were to say, "You surely know what 'It's 5 o'clock here' means; so you also know what 'It's 5 o'clock on the sun' means. It means simply that it is just the same time there as it is here when it is 5 o'clock here." — The explanation by means of *sameness* does not work here. For I know well enough that one can call 5 o'clock here and 5 o'clock there "the same time", but do not know in what cases one is to speak of its being the same time here and there.

In exactly the same way, it is no explanation to say: the supposition that he has a pain is simply the supposition that he has the same as I. For what's surely clear to me is *this* part of grammar: that one will say that the stove has the same experience as I *if* one says: it's in pain and I'm in pain.

* 351. Yet we keep wanting to say: "A sensation of pain is a sensation of pain — whether *he* has it, or *I* have it, no matter how I come to know whether he has a pain or not." — I might go along with that. — And when you ask me, "Don't you know, then, what I mean when I say that the stove is in pain?", I can reply: "These words may lead me to imagine all sorts of things; but their usefulness goes no further." And I can also imagine something in connection with the words: "Just now it was 5 o'clock in the afternoon on the sun" — such as a grandfather clock which shows 5. — But a still better example would be that of the application of "above" and "beneath" to the globe. Here we all have a quite clear idea of what |112| "above" and "beneath" mean. I see well

bedeutet. Ich sehe doch, daß ich oben bin; die Erde ist doch unter mir!
(Lächle ja nicht über dieses Beispiel. Es wird uns zwar schon in der
Volksschule beigebracht, daß es dumm ist, so etwas zu sagen. Aber es
ist eben viel leichter, ein Problem zuzuschütten, als es zu lösen.) Und
erst eine Überlegung zeigt uns, daß in diesem Fall "oben" und "unten"
nicht auf die gewohnte Weise zu gebrauchen sind. (Daß wir z. B. von
den Antipoden als den Menschen 'unter' unserem Erdteil reden könn-
en, es aber nun für richtig anerkennen müssen, wenn sie auf uns den
gleichen Ausdruck anwenden.)

352. Hier geschieht es nun, daß uns unser Denken einen seltsamen Streich
spielt. Wir wollen nämlich das Gesetz vom ausgeschlossenen Dritten
zitieren und sagen: "Entweder es schwebt ihm ein solches Bild vor, oder
nicht; ein Drittes gibt es nicht!" — Dieses seltsame Argument treffen
wir auch in andern Gebieten der Philosophie. "In der unendlichen
Entwicklung von π kommt einmal die Gruppe "7777" vor, oder nicht
— ein Drittes gibt es nicht." D. h.: Gott sieht es — aber wir wissen es
nicht. Was bedeutet das aber? — Wir gebrauchen ein Bild; das Bild einer
sichtbaren Reihe, die der Eine übersieht, der Andre nicht. Der Satz vom
ausgeschlossenen Dritten sagt hier: Es muß entweder *so* ausschaun, oder
so. Er sagt also eigentlich — und das ist ja selbstverständlich — gar nichts,
sondern gibt uns ein Bild. Und das Problem soll nun sein: ob die
Wirklichkeit mit dem Bild übereinstimme, oder nicht. Und dies Bild *scheint*
nun, was wir zu tun, wie und wonach wir zu suchen haben, zu bestimmen — tut es aber nicht, weil wir eben nicht wissen, wie es zu
applizieren ist. Wenn wir hier sagen "Es gibt kein Drittes", oder "Es
gibt doch kein Drittes!" — so drückt sich darin aus, daß wir den Blick
von diesem Bild nicht wenden können, — das ausschaut, als müßte in
ihm schon das Problem und seine Lösung liegen, während wir doch
fühlen, daß es nicht der Fall ist.
    Ebenso, wenn man sagt "Entweder hat er diese Empfindung, oder er
hat sie nicht!" — so schwebt uns dabei vor allem ein Bild vor, das schon
den Sinn der Aussagen *unmißverständlich* zu bestimmen scheint. "Du
weißt jetzt, worum es sich handelt" — möchte man sagen. Und gerade
das weiß er damit noch nicht.

353. Die Frage nach der Art und Möglichkeit der Verifikation eines Satzes
ist nur eine besondere Form der Frage "Wie meinst du das?" Die Antwort
ist ein Beitrag zur Grammatik des Satzes.

354. Das Schwanken in der Grammatik zwischen Kriterien und Sym-
ptomen läßt den Schein entstehen, als gäbe es überhaupt nur Symptome.

enough that I am on top; the earth is surely beneath me! (And don't smile at this example. We are indeed all taught at elementary school that it is stupid to talk like that. But it is much easier to bury a problem than to solve it.) And it is only reflection that shows us that in this case "above" and "beneath" cannot be used in the customary way. (That we might, for instance, say that the people at the antipodes are 'beneath' our part of the earth, but must then also recognize it as right for them to use the same expression about us.)

352. At this point, our thinking plays us a strange trick. That is, we want to quote the law of excluded middle and say: "Either such an image floats before his mind, or it does not; there is no third possibility!" — We encounter this curious argument also in other regions of philosophy. "In the infinite expansion of π either the group '7777' occurs, or it does not — there is no third possibility." That is to say: God sees — but we don't know. But what does that mean? — We use a picture: the picture of a visible series, the whole of which one person can survey and another can't. Here the law of excluded middle says: it must look either like *this* or like *that*. So really — and this is surely obvious — it says nothing at all, but gives us a picture. And the problem is now supposed to be: does reality accord with the picture or not? And this picture *seems* to determine what we have to do, what to look for, and how — but it does not, precisely because we do not know how it is to be applied. Here, saying "There is no third possibility" or "There really isn't a third possibility!" expresses our inability to turn our eyes away from this picture — a picture which looks as if it must already contain both the problem and its solution, while all the time we *feel* that it is not so.

   Similarly, when it is said "Either he has this sensation, or he doesn't", what primarily occurs to us is a picture which already seems to determine the sense of the statements *unequivocally*: "Now you know what is in question", one would like to say. And that's just what it does not tell you.

353. Asking whether and how a proposition can be verified is only a special form of the question "How do you mean?" The answer is a contribution to the grammar of the proposition.

354. The fluctuation in grammar between criteria and symptoms makes it look as if there were nothing at all but symptoms. We say,

Wir sagen etwa: "Die Erfahrung lehrt, daß es regnet, wenn das Barometer fällt, aber sie lehrt auch, daß es regnet, wenn wir bestimmte Gefühle der Nässe und Kälte haben, oder den und den Gesichtseindruck." Als Argument dafür gibt man dann an, daß diese Sinneseindrücke uns täuschen können. Aber man bedenkt dabei nicht, daß die Tatsache, daß sie uns gerade den Regen vortäuschen, auf einer Definition beruht.

355. Nicht darum handelt es sich, daß unsre Sinneseindrücke uns belügen können, sondern, daß wir ihre Sprache verstehen. (Und diese Sprache beruht, wie jede andere, auf Übereinkunft.)

356. Man ist geneigt zu sagen: "Es regnet, oder es regnet nicht — wie ich das weiß, wie mich die Kunde davon erreicht hat, ist eine andere Sache." Aber stellen wir also die Frage so: Was nenne ich "eine Kunde davon, daß es regnet"? (Oder habe ich auch von dieser Kunde nur Kunde erhalten?) Und was kennzeichnet denn diese 'Kunde' als Kunde von etwas? Leitet uns da nicht die Form unseres Ausdrucks irre? Ist das eben nicht eine irreführende Metapher: "Mein Auge gibt mir Kunde davon, daß dort ein Sessel stehe"?

357. Wir sagen nicht, ein Hund spräche *möglicherweise* zu sich selber. Ist das, weil wir seine Seele so genau kennen? Nun, man könnte so sagen: Wenn man das Benehmen des Lebewesens sieht, sieht man seine Seele. — Aber sage ich auch von mir, ich spreche zu mir selber, weil ich mich so und so benehme? — Ich sage es *nicht* auf die Beobachtung meines Benehmens hin. Aber es hat nur Sinn, weil ich mich so benehme. — So hat es also nicht darum Sinn, weil ich es *meine*?

358. Aber ist es nicht unser *Meinen*, das dem Satz Sinn gibt? (Und dazu gehört natürlich: Sinnlose Wortreihen kann man nicht meinen.) Und das Meinen ist etwas im seelischen Bereich. Aber es ist auch etwas Privates! Es ist das ungreifbare Etwas; vergleichbar nur dem Bewußtsein selbst.
Wie könnte man das lächerlich finden! es ist ja, gleichsam, ein Traum unserer Sprache.

359. Könnte eine Maschine denken? —— Könnte sie Schmerzen haben? — Nun, soll der menschliche Körper so eine Maschine heißen? Er kommt doch am nächsten dazu, so eine Maschine zu sein.

360. Aber eine Maschine kann doch nicht denken! — Ist das ein Erfahrungssatz? Nein. Wir sagen nur vom Menschen, und was ihm

|113| for example, "Experience teaches that there is rain when the barometer falls, but it also teaches that there is rain when we have certain feelings of wet and cold, or such-and-such visual impressions." As an argument in support of this, one says that these sense impressions can deceive us. But here one overlooks the fact that their deceiving us precisely *about rain* rests on a definition.

355. The point here is not that our sense impressions can lie to us, but that we understand their language. (And this language, like any other, rests on convention.)

356. One is inclined to say: "Either it is raining, or it isn't — how I know, how the message has reached me, is another matter." But then let's put the question like this: What do I call "a message that it is raining"? (Or have I only word of this message too?) And what gives this 'message' the character of a message about something? Doesn't the form of our expression mislead us here? For isn't it a misleading metaphor to say, "My eyes send me the message that there is a chair over there"?

357. We do not say that *possibly* a dog talks to itself. Is that because we are so minutely acquainted with its mind? Well, one might say this: if one sees the behaviour of a living being, one sees its mind. — But do I also say in my own case that I am talking to myself, because I am behaving in such-and-such a way? — I do *not* say it from observation of my behaviour. But it makes sense only because I do behave in this way. — So isn't it because I *mean* it that it makes sense?

358. But isn't it our *meaning* it that gives sense to the sentence? (And here, of course, belongs the fact that one cannot mean a senseless sequence of words.) And meaning something lies within the domain of the mind. But it is also something private! It is the intangible Something; comparable only to consciousness itself.

How *could* one find this ludicrous? After all, it is, as it were, a dream of our language.

359. Could a machine think? —— Could it be in pain? — Well, is the human body to be called such a machine? It surely comes as close as possible to being such a machine.

360. But surely a machine cannot think! — Is that an empirical statement? No. We say only of a human being and what is like one that it

ähnlich ist, es denke. Wir sagen es auch von Puppen und wohl auch von Geistern. Sieh das Wort "denken" als Instrument an!

361. Der Sessel denkt bei sich selber: . . .

Wo? In einem seiner Teile? Oder außerhalb seines Körpers; in der Luft um ihn? Oder gar nicht *irgendwo*? Aber was ist dann der Unterschied zwischen dem inneren Sprechen dieses Sessels und eines andern, der daneben steht? — Aber wie ist es dann mit dem Menschen: Wo spricht *er* zu sich selber? Wie kommt es, daß diese Frage sinnlos scheint; und keine Ortsbestimmung nötig ist, außer der, daß eben dieser Mensch zu sich selbst spricht? Während die Frage, *wo* der Sessel mit sich selbst spreche, eine Antwort zu verlangen scheint. — Der Grund ist: Wir wollen wissen, *wie* der Sessel hier einem Menschen gleichen soll; ob der Kopf z. B. am obern Ende der Lehne ist, u. s. w.

Wie ist das, wenn man im Innern zu sich selbst spricht; was geht da vor? — Wie soll ich's erklären? Nun, nur so, wie du Einen die Bedeutung des Ausdrucks "zu sich selbst sprechen" lehren kannst. Und als Kinder lernen wir ja diese Bedeutung. — Nur, daß niemand sagen wird, wer sie uns lehrt, sage uns, 'was da vorgeht'.

362. Vielmehr scheint es uns, als ob der Lehrer in diesem Falle dem Schüler die Bedeutung *beibringe* — ohne sie ihm direkt zu sagen; daß aber der Schüler endlich dazu gebracht wird, sich selbst die richtige hinweisende Erklärung zu geben. Und hierin liegt unsre Illusion.

363. "Wenn ich mir etwas vorstelle, so *geschieht* doch wohl etwas!" Nun, es geschieht etwas — und wozu mache ich dann einen Lärm? Wohl dazu, was geschieht, mitzuteilen. — Aber wie teilt man denn überhaupt etwas mit? Wann sagt man, etwas werde mitgeteilt? — Was ist das Sprachspiel des Mitteilens?

Ich möchte sagen: du siehst es für viel zu selbstverständlich an, daß man Einem etwas mitteilen kann. Das heißt: Wir sind so sehr an die Mitteilung durch Sprechen, im Gespräch, gewöhnt, daß es uns scheint, als läge der ganze Witz der Mitteilung darin, daß ein Andrer den Sinn meiner Worte — etwas Seelisches — auffaßt, sozusagen in seinen Geist aufnimmt. Wenn er dann auch noch etwas damit anfängt, so gehört das nicht mehr zum unmittelbaren Zweck der Sprache.

Man möchte sagen "Die Mitteilung bewirkt, daß er *weiß*, daß ich Schmerzen habe; sie bewirkt dies geistige Phänomen; alles Andere ist der Mitteilung unwesentlich." Was dieses merkwürdige Phänomen des

thinks. We also say it of dolls; and perhaps even of ghosts. Regard the word "to think" as an instrument! |114|

361. The chair is thinking to itself . . .

WHERE? In one of its parts? Or outside its body; in the air around it? Or not *anywhere* at all? But then what is the difference between this chair's talking silently to itself and another one's doing so, next to it? — But then how is it with man: where does *he* talk to himself? How come that this question seems senseless; and that no specification of a place is necessary, except just that this man is talking silently to himself? Whereas the question of *where* the chair talks silently to itself seems to demand an answer. — The reason is: we want to know *how* the chair is supposed to be like a human being; whether, for instance, its head is at the top of the back, and so on.

What is it like to talk silently to oneself; what goes on there? — How am I to explain it? Well, only in the way in which you can teach someone the meaning of the expression "to talk silently to oneself". And we *do* learn the meaning of that as children. — Only no one is going to say that the person who teaches it to us tells us 'what goes on here'.

362. Rather, it seems to us as though, in this case, the instructor *conveyed* the meaning to the pupil — without telling him directly; but in the end, the pupil is brought to the point of giving himself the correct ostensive definition. And this is where our illusion lies.

363. "But when I imagine something, something *goes on*, doesn't it?" Well, something goes on — and then I make a noise. What for? Presumably in order to communicate what went on. — But how, in general, does one communicate something? When does one say that something is being communicated? — What is the language-game of communicating something?

I'd like to say: you regard it much too much as a matter of course that one can communicate anything to anyone. That is to say, we are so much accustomed to communicating in speech, in conversation, that it looks to us as if the whole point of communicating lay in this: that someone else grasps the sense of my words — which is something mental — that he, as it were, takes it into his own mind. If he then does something further with it as well, that is no part of the immediate purpose of language.

One would like to say "It is through my communicating it that he comes to *know* that I am in pain; it produces this mental phenomenon; everything else is immaterial to the communicating". As for what this

Wissens ist — damit läßt man sich Zeit. Seelische Vorgänge sind eben merkwürdig. (Es ist, als sagte man: "Die Uhr zeigt uns die Zeit an. *Was* die Zeit ist, ist noch nicht entschieden. Und *wozu* man die Zeit abliest — das gehört nicht hieher.")

364. Jemand macht eine Berechnung im Kopf. Das Ergebnis verwendet er, sagen wir, beim Bauen einer Brücke, oder Maschine. — Willst du sagen, er habe diese Zahl *eigentlich* nicht durch Berechnung gefunden? Sie sei ihm etwa, nach einer Art Träumerei, in den Schoß gefallen? Es mußte doch da gerechnet werden, und ist gerechnet worden. Denn er *weiß*, daß, und wie, er gerechnet hat; und das richtige Resultat wäre ohne Rechnung nicht erklärbar. —— Wie aber, wenn ich sagte: "Es *kommt ihm vor*, er habe gerechnet. Und warum soll sich das richtige Resultat erklären lassen? Ist es nicht unverständlich genug, daß er ohne ein Wort, oder Schriftzeichen, RECHNEN konnte?" —

Ist das Rechnen in der Vorstellung in gewissem Sinne unwirklicher, als das auf dem Papier? Es ist das *wirkliche* — Kopfrechnen. — Ist es ähnlich dem Rechnen auf dem Papier? — Ich weiß nicht, ob ich es ähnlich nennen soll. Ist ein Stück weißes Papier mit schwarzen Strichen drauf einem menschlichen Körper ähnlich?

365. Spielen Adelheid und der Bischof eine *wirkliche* Schachpartie? — Freilich. Sie geben nicht bloß vor, eine zu spielen — wie es doch in einem Theaterstücke auch geschehen könnte. — Aber diese Partie hat doch z. B. keinen Anfang! — Doch; sonst wäre es ja keine Schachpartie. —

366. Ist das Rechnen im Kopf unwirklicher, als das Rechnen auf dem Papier? — Man ist vielleicht geneigt, so etwas zu sagen; kann sich aber auch zur gegenteiligen Ansicht bringen, indem man sich sagt: Papier, Tinte, etc. seien nur logische Konstruktionen aus unsern Sinnesdaten.

"Ich habe die Multiplikation . . . im Kopfe ausgeführt" — *glaube* ich etwa so eine Aussage nicht? — Aber war es wirklich eine Multiplikation? Es war nicht bloß 'eine' Multiplikation, sondern *diese* — im Kopfe. Dies ist der Punkt, an dem ich irregehe. Denn ich will jetzt sagen: Es war irgend ein, dem Multiplizieren auf dem Papier *entsprechender*, geistiger Vorgang. So daß es Sinn hätte, zu sagen: "*Dieser* Vorgang im Geiste entspricht *diesem* Vorgang auf dem Papier." Und es hätte dann Sinn, von einer Methode der Abbildung zu reden, nach welcher die Vorstellung des Zeichens das Zeichen selbst darstellt.

367. Das Vorstellungsbild ist das Bild, das beschrieben wird, wenn Einer seine Vorstellung beschreibt.

remarkable phenomenon of knowledge is — that can be taken care of later. Mental processes just are strange. (It is as if one said, "The clock shows us the time. *What* time is, is not yet settled. And as regards the point of telling the time — that doesn't come in here.") |115|

364. Someone does a calculation in his head. He uses the result, let's say, for building a bridge or a machine. — Do you want to say that it wasn't *really* by a calculation that he arrived at this number? That it has, say, just dropped into his lap, after some sort of reverie? There surely must have been calculation going on, and there was. For he *knows* that, and how, he calculated; and the correct result he got would be inexplicable without calculation. —— But what if I said: "It *seems to him* just as if he had calculated. And why should the correct result be explicable? Is it not incomprehensible enough, that without saying a word, without making a note, he was able to CALCULATE?" —

Is calculating in the imagination in some sense less real than calculating on paper? It is *real* — calculating-in-the-head. — Is it similar to calculating on paper? — I don't know whether to call it similar. Is a bit of white paper with black lines on it similar to a human body?

* 365. Do Adelheid and the Bishop play a *real* game of chess? — Of course. They are not merely pretending to do so — which would also be possible as part of a play. — But the game, for example, has no beginning! — Of course it has; otherwise it would not be a game of chess. —

366. Is calculating in the head less real than calculating on paper? — One is, perhaps, inclined to say some such thing; but one can get oneself to think the opposite as well by telling oneself: paper, ink, and so on are only logical constructions out of our sense-data.

"I have done the multiplication . . . in my head" — don't I *believe* such a statement? — But was it really a multiplication? It was not merely 'a' multiplication, but *this* one — in the head. This is the point at which I go wrong. For I now want to say: it was some mental process *corresponding* to the multiplication on paper. So it would make sense to say: "*This* process in the mind corresponds to *this* process on paper." And then it would make sense to talk of a method of projection according to which the mental image of the sign was a representation of the sign itself.

367. A mental image is the image which is described when someone describes what he imagines.

368. Ich beschreibe Einem ein Zimmer, und lasse ihn dann, zum Zeichen, daß er meine Beschreibung verstanden hat, ein *impressionistisches* Bild nach dieser Beschreibung malen. — Er malt nun die Stühle, die in meiner Beschreibung grün hießen, dunkelrot; wo ich "gelb" sagte, malt er blau. — Das ist der Eindruck, den er von diesem Zimmer erhielt. Und nun sage ich: "Ganz richtig; so sieht es aus."

369. Man möchte fragen: "Wie ist das — was geht da vor — wenn Einer im Kopfe rechnet?" — Und im besondern Fall kann die Antwort sein: "Ich addiere zuerst 17 und 18, dann subtrahiere ich 39 . . ." Aber das ist nicht die Antwort auf unsre Frage. Was im Kopfe rechnen heißt, wird auf *solche* Weise nicht erklärt.

370. Nicht, was Vorstellungen sind, oder was da geschieht, wenn man sich etwas vorstellt, muß man fragen, sondern: wie das Wort "Vorstellung" gebraucht wird. Das heißt aber nicht, daß ich nur von Worten reden will. Denn soweit in meiner Frage vom Wort "Vorstellung" die Rede ist, ist sie's auch in der Frage nach dem Wesen der Vorstellung. Und ich sage nur, daß diese Frage nicht durch ein Zeigen — weder für den Vorstellenden, noch für den Andern, zu erklären ist; noch durch die Beschreibung irgend eines Vorgangs. Nach einer Worterklärung fragt auch die erste Frage; aber sie lenkt unsre Erwartung auf eine falsche Art der Antwort.

371. Das *Wesen* ist in der Grammatik ausgesprochen.

372. Überlege: "Das einzige Korrelat in der Sprache zu einer Naturnotwendigkeit ist eine willkürliche Regel. Sie ist das Einzige, was man von dieser Naturnotwendigkeit in einen Satz abziehen kann."

373. Welche Art von Gegenstand etwas ist, sagt die Grammatik. (Theologie als Grammatik.)

374. Die große Schwierigkeit ist hier, die Sache nicht so darzustellen, als *könne* man etwas nicht. Als wäre da wohl ein Gegenstand, von dem ich die Beschreibung abziehe, aber ich wäre nicht im Stande, ihn jemandem zu zeigen. —— Und das Beste, was ich vorschlagen kann, ist wohl, daß wir der Versuchung, dies Bild zu gebrauchen, nachgeben: aber nun untersuchen, wie die *Anwendung* dieses Bildes aussieht.

375. Wie lehrt man jemand, leise für sich selbst lesen? Wie weiß man, wenn er's kann? Wie weiß er selbst, daß er tut, was man von ihm verlangt?

368. I describe a room to someone, and then get him to paint an *impressionistic* picture from this description to show that he has understood it. — Now he paints the chairs which I described as green, dark red; where I said "yellow", he paints blue. — That is the impression |116| which he got of that room. And now I say: "Quite right! That's what it looks like."

369. One is inclined to ask: "What is it like — what goes on — when one calculates in one's head?" — And in a particular case, the answer may be "First I add 17 and 18, then I subtract 39 . . ." But that is not the answer to our question. What is called calculating in one's head is not explained in *this* way.

* 370. One ought to ask, not what images are or what goes on when one imagines something, but how the word "imagination" is used. But that does not mean that I want to talk only about words. For the question of what imagination essentially is, is as much about the word "imagination" as my question. And I am only saying that this question is not to be clarified — neither for the person who does the imagining, nor for anyone else — by pointing; nor yet by a description of some process. The first question also asks for the clarification of a word; but it makes us expect a wrong kind of answer.

* 371. *Essence* is expressed in grammar.

372. Consider: "The only correlate in language to an objective necessity is an arbitrary rule. It is the only thing which one can milk out of this objective necessity into a proposition."

* 373. Grammar tells what kind of object anything is. (Theology as grammar.)

374. The great difficulty here is not to present the matter as if there were something one *couldn't* do. As if there really were an object, from which I extract a description, which I am not in a position to show anyone. —— And the best that I can propose is that we yield to the temptation to use this picture, but then investigate what the *application* of the picture looks like.

375. How does one teach someone to read silently to himself? How does one know when he can do so? How does he himself know that he is doing what is required of him?

376. Wenn ich mir im Innern das ABC vorsage, was ist das Kriterium dafür, daß ich das Gleiche tue, wie ein Andrer, der es sich im Stillen vorsagt? Es könnte gefunden werden, daß in meinem Kehlkopf und in seinem das Gleiche dabei vorgeht. (Und ebenso, wenn wir beide an das Gleiche denken, das Gleiche wünschen, etc.) Aber lernten wir denn die Verwendung der Worte "sich im Stillen das und das vorsagen", indem auf einen Vorgang im Kehlkopf, oder im Gehirn, hingewiesen wurde? Ist es nicht auch wohl möglich, daß meiner Vorstellung vom Laute a und seiner verschiedene physiologische Vorgänge entsprechen? Die Frage ist: *Wie vergleicht* man Vorstellungen?

377. Ein Logiker denkt vielleicht: Gleich ist gleich — es ist eine psychologische Frage, wie ein Mensch sich von der Gleichheit überzeugt. (Höhe ist Höhe — es gehört in die Psychologie, daß der Mensch sie manchmal *sieht*, manchmal *hört*.)

Was ist das Kriterium der Gleichheit zweier Vorstellungen? — Was ist das Kriterium der Röte einer Vorstellung? Für mich, wenn der Andre sie hat: was er sagt und tut. Für mich, wenn ich sie habe: gar nichts. Und was für "rot" gilt, gilt auch für "gleich".

378. "Ehe ich urteile, daß zwei meiner Vorstellungen gleich sind, muß ich sie doch als gleich erkennen." Und wenn das geschehen ist, wie werde ich dann wissen, daß das Wort "gleich" meine Erkenntnis beschreibt? Nur dann, wenn ich diese Erkenntnis auf andere Weise ausdrücken, und ein Andrer mich lehren kann, daß hier "gleich" das richtige Wort ist.

Denn, bedarf ich einer Berechtigung dafür, ein Wort zu gebrauchen, dann muß es eine auch für den Andern sein.

379. Ich erkenne es erst als *das*; und nun erinnere ich mich daran, wie das genannt wird. — Bedenke: In welchen Fällen kann man dies mit Recht sagen?

380. Wie erkenne ich, daß dies rot ist? — "Ich sehe, daß es *dies* ist; und nun weiß ich, daß dies so heißt." Dies? — Was?! Welche Art der Antwort hat auf diese Frage Sinn?

(Du steuerst immer wieder auf eine innere hinweisende Erklärung hin.)

Auf den *privaten* Übergang von dem Gesehenen zum Wort könnte ich keine Regeln anwenden. Hier hingen die Regeln wirklich in der Luft; da die Institution ihrer Anwendung fehlt.

381. Wie erkenne ich, daß diese Farbe Rot ist? — Eine Antwort wäre: "Ich habe Deutsch gelernt."

376. When I say the ABC silently to myself, what is the criterion that shows that I am doing the same as someone else who silently repeats it to himself? It might be found that the same thing goes on in my larynx and in his. (And similarly when we both think of the same thing, wish the same, and so on.) But then did we learn the use of the words "to |117| say such-and-such silently to oneself" by someone's pointing to a process in the larynx or the brain? Is it not also perfectly possible that my auditory image of the sound *a* and his correspond to different physiological processes? The question is: How does one *compare* images?

377. A logician will perhaps think: The same is the same — how a person satisfies himself of sameness is a psychological question. (High is high — it is a matter of psychology that one sometimes *sees*, and sometimes *hears* it.)

What is the criterion for the sameness of two images? — What is the criterion for the redness of an image? For me, when it's someone else's image: what he says and does. — For myself, when it's my image: nothing. And what goes for "red" also goes for "same".

378. "Before I judge that two images which I have are the same, surely I must recognize them as the same." And when that has happened, how am I to know that the word "same" describes what I recognize? Only if I can express my recognition in some other way, and if it is possible for someone else to teach me that "same" is the correct word here.

For if I need a warrant for using a word, it must also be a warrant for someone else.

379. First I recognize it as *this*; and then I remember what it is called. — Consider: in what cases can one rightly say this?

380. How do I recognize that this is red? — "I see that it is *this*; and then I know that that is what this is called." This? — What?! What kind of answer to this question makes sense?

(You keep on steering towards an inner ostensive explanation.)

I could not apply any rules to a *private* transition from what is seen to words. Here the rules really would hang in the air; for the institution of their application is lacking.

381. How do I recognize that this colour is red? — One answer would be: "I have learnt English."

382. Wie kann ich es *rechtfertigen*, daß ich mir auf diese Worte hin diese Vorstellung mache?

Hat mir jemand die Vorstellung der blauen Farbe gezeigt, und gesagt, daß *sie* es sei?

Was bedeuten die Worte "*diese* Vorstellung"? Wie zeigt man auf eine Vorstellung? Wie zeigt man zweimal auf die gleiche Vorstellung?

383. Wir analysieren nicht ein Phänomen (z. B. das Denken), sondern einen Begriff (z. B. den des Denkens), und also die Anwendung eines Worts. So kann es scheinen, als wäre, was wir treiben, Nominalismus. Nominalisten machen den Fehler, daß sie alle Wörter als *Namen* deuten, also ihre Verwendung nicht wirklich beschreiben, sondern sozusagen nur eine papierene Anweisung auf so eine Beschreibung geben.

384. Den *Begriff* 'Schmerz' hast du mit der Sprache gelernt.

385. Frage dich: Wäre es denkbar, daß Einer im Kopfe rechnen lernte, ohne je schriftlich oder mündlich zu rechnen? — "Es lernen" heißt wohl: dazu gebracht werden, daß man's kann. Und es fragt sich nur, was als Kriterium dafür gelten wird, daß jemand dies kann. —— Ist aber auch dies möglich, daß einem Volksstamm nur das Kopfrechnen bekannt ist, und kein andres? Hier muß man sich fragen "Wie wird das aussehen?" — Man wird sich dies also als einen Grenzfall ausmalen müssen. Und es wird sich dann fragen, ob wir hier noch den Begriff des 'Kopfrechnens' anwenden wollen — oder ob er unter solchen Umständen seinen Zweck eingebüßt hat; weil die Erscheinungen nun zu einem andern Vorbild hin gravitieren.

386. "Aber warum traust du dir selbst so wenig? Du weiß doch sonst immer, was 'rechnen' heißt. Wenn du also sagst, du habest in der Vorstellung gerechnet, so wird es eben so sein. Hättest du *nicht* gerechnet, so würdest du's nicht sagen. Ebenso: wenn du sagst, du sähest etwas Rotes in der Vorstellung, so wird es eben rot *sein*. Du weißt ja sonst, was 'rot' ist. — Und weiter: du verläßt dich ja nicht immer auf die Übereinstimmung mit den Andern; denn oft berichtest du, du habest etwas gesehen, was niemand Andrer gesehen hat." —— Aber ich traue mir ja — ich sage ja ohne Bedenken, ich habe dies im Kopf gerechnet, diese Farbe mir vorgestellt. Nicht das ist die Schwierigkeit, daß ich zweifle, ob ich mir wirklich etwas Rotes vorgestellt habe. Sondern *dies*: daß wir so ohne weiteres zeigen oder beschreiben können, welche Farbe wir uns vorgestellt haben, daß uns das Abbilden der Vorstellung in die Wirklichkeit gar keine Schwierigkeit bereitet. Sehen sie sich denn zum

382. How can I *justify* forming this image in response to this word?

   Has anyone shown me the image of the colour blue and told me that *it* is the image of blue?

   What is the meaning of the words "*this* image"? How does one point at an image? How does one point twice at the same image? |118|

383. We do not analyse a phenomenon (for example, thinking) but a concept (for example, that of thinking), and hence the application of a word. So it may look as if what we were doing were nominalism. Nominalists make the mistake of interpreting all words as *names*, and so of not really describing their use, but only, so to speak, giving a paper draft on such a description.

384. You learned the *concept* 'pain' in learning language.

385. Ask yourself: Is it conceivable that someone learn to calculate in his head without ever calculating aloud or on paper? — "Learning it" presumably means: being brought to the point of being able to do it. Only the question arises, what will count as a criterion for being able to do it? —— But is it also possible for some tribe to be acquainted only with calculation in the head, and with no other kind? Here one has to ask oneself: "What will that look like?" — And so one will have to depict it as a limiting case. And the question will then arise whether we still want to apply the concept of calculating in the head here — or whether in such circumstances it has lost its purpose, because the phenomena now gravitate towards another paradigm.

386. "But why have you so little confidence in yourself? Ordinarily you know perfectly well what is called 'calculating'. So if you say that you have calculated in the imagination, then you will have done so. If you had *not* calculated, you would not have said you had. Equally, if you say that you see something red in the imagination, then it will *be* red. You know what 'red' is elsewhere. — And further: you don't always rely on agreement with other people; for you often report that you have seen something no one else has." —— But I do have confidence in myself — I say without hesitation that I have done this calculation in my head, have imagined this colour. The difficulty is not that I doubt whether I really imagined anything red. But it is *this*: that we should be able, just like that, to point out or describe the colour we have imagined, that mapping the image into reality presents no difficulty at all. Do they then

Verwechseln ähnlich? — Aber ich kann ja auch ohne weiteres einen Menschen nach einer Zeichnung erkennen. — Aber kann ich denn fragen "Wie schaut eine richtige Vorstellung dieser Farbe aus?", oder "Wie ist sie beschaffen?"; kann ich dies *lernen*?

(Ich kann sein Zeugnis nicht annehmen, weil es kein *Zeugnis* ist. Es sagt mir nur, was er zu sagen *geneigt* ist.)

387. Der *tiefe* Aspekt entschlüpft leicht.

388. "Ich sehe zwar hier nichts Violettes, aber wenn du mir einen Farbkasten gibst, so kann ich's dir darin zeigen." Wie kann man *wissen*, daß man es zeigen kann, wenn . . ., daß man es also erkennen kann, wenn man es sieht?

Wie weiß ich von meiner *Vorstellung* her, wie die Farbe wirklich ausschaut?

Wie weiß ich, daß ich etwas werde tun können? d. h., daß der Zustand, in welchem ich jetzt bin, der ist: jenes tun zu können?

389. "Die Vorstellung muß ihrem Gegenstand ähnlicher sein, als jedes Bild: Denn wie ähnlich ich auch das Bild dem mache, was es darstellen soll, es kann immer noch das Bild von etwas anderm sein. Aber die Vorstellung hat es in sich, daß sie die Vorstellung von *diesem*, und von nichts anderem, ist." Man könnte so dahin kommen, die Vorstellung als ein Über-Bildnis anzusehen.

390. Könnte man sich vorstellen, daß ein Stein Bewußtsein hätte? Und wenn's Einer kann — warum soll das nicht bloß beweisen, daß diese Vorstellerei für uns kein Interesse hat?

391. Ich kann mir vielleicht auch vorstellen (obwohl es nicht leicht ist), jeder der Leute, die ich auf der Straße sehe, habe furchtbare Schmerzen, verberge sie aber kunstvoll. Und es ist wichtig, daß ich mir hier ein kunstvolles Verbergen vorstellen muß. Daß ich mir also nicht einfach sage: "Nun, seine Seele hat Schmerzen; aber was hat das mit seinem Leib zu tun!", oder "das muß sich schließlich am Leib nicht zeigen!" — Und wenn ich mir das nun vorstelle, — was tue ich; was sage ich zu mir selbst; wie sehe ich die Leute an? Ich schaue etwa Einen an und denke mir "Das muß schwer sein, zu lachen, wenn man solche Schmerzen hat", und vieles dergleichen. Ich spiele gleichsam eine Rolle, *tue so*, als hätten die Andern Schmerzen. Wenn ich das tue, sagt man etwa, ich stelle mir vor, . . .

look so alike that one might mix them up? — But I can also recognize a man from a drawing straight off. — Well, but can I ask: "What does an actual mental image of this colour look like?" or "What sort of thing is it?"; can I *learn* this?

(I cannot accept his testimony, because it is not *testimony*. It tells me only what he is *inclined* to say.)

387. The *deep* aspect readily eludes us. |119|

388. "I don't see anything violet here, but I can show it you if you give me a paint box." How can one *know* that one can show it if . . . , in other words, that one can recognize it if one sees it?

How do I know from my *mental image*, what the colour really looks like?

How do I know that I'll be able to do something? That is, that the state I am in now is that of being able to do that thing?

389. "A mental image must be more like its object than any picture. For however similar I make the picture to what it is supposed to represent, it may still be the picture of something else. But it is an intrinsic feature of a mental image that it is the image of *this* and of nothing else." That is how one might come to regard a mental image as a super-likeness.

390. Could one imagine a stone's having consciousness? And if someone can — why should that not prove merely that such image-mongery is of no interest to us?

391. I can perhaps even imagine (though it is not easy) that each of the people whom I see in the street is in frightful pain, but is adroitly concealing it. And it is important that I have to imagine adroit concealment here. That I do not simply say to myself: "Well, his mind is in pain: but what has that to do with his body?" or "After all, it need not show in his body". — And if I imagine this — what do I do? What do I say to myself? How do I look at the people? Perhaps I look at one and think, "It must be difficult to laugh when one is in such pain", and much else of the same kind. I, as it were, play a part, *act* as if the others were in pain. When I do this, one might say that I am imagining . . .

392. "Wenn ich mir vorstelle, er habe Schmerzen, geht eigentlich nur . . . in mir vor." Ein Andrer sagt dann: "Ich glaube, ich kann es mir auch vorstellen, *ohne* dabei . . . zu denken." ("Ich glaube, ich kann denken, ohne zu reden.") Das führt zu nichts. Die Analyse schillert zwischen einer naturwissenschaftlichen und einer grammatischen.

393. "Wenn ich mir vorstelle, daß Einer, der lacht, in Wirklichkeit Schmerzen hat, so stelle ich mir doch kein Schmerzbenehmen vor, denn ich sehe eben das Gegenteil. *Was* stelle ich mir also vor?" — Ich habe es schon gesagt. Und ich stelle mir dazu nicht notwendigerweise vor, daß *ich* Schmerzen fühle. —— "Aber wie geht es also vor sich: sich dies vorstellen?" —— Wo (außerhalb der Philosophie) verwenden wir denn die Worte "Ich kann mir vorstellen, daß er Schmerzen hat", oder "Ich stelle mir vor, daß . . .", oder "Stell dir vor, daß . . . !"?

Man sagt z. B. dem, der eine Theaterrolle zu spielen hat: "Du mußt dir hier vorstellen, daß dieser Mensch Schmerzen hat, die er verbirgt" — und wir geben ihm nun keine Anweisung, sagen ihm nicht, was er *eigentlich* tun soll. Darum ist auch jene Analyse nicht zur Sache. — Wir schaun nun dem Schauspieler zu, der sich diese Situation vorstellt.

394. Unter was für Umständen würden wir jemand fragen: "Was ist da eigentlich in dir vorgegangen, wie du dir dies vorgestellt hast?" — Und was für eine Antwort erwarten wir uns da?

395. Es besteht Unklarheit darüber, welche Rolle *Vorstellbarkeit* in unserer Untersuchung spielt. Inwiefern sie nämlich den Sinn eines Satzes sicherstellt.

396. Es ist so wenig für das Verständnis eines Satzes wesentlich, daß man sich bei ihm etwas vorstelle, als daß man nach ihm eine Zeichnung entwerfe.

397. Statt "Vorstellbarkeit" kann man hier auch sagen: Darstellbarkeit in einem bestimmten Mittel der Darstellung. Und von einer solchen Darstellung *kann* allerdings ein sicherer Weg zur weitern Verwendung führen. Anderseits kann sich uns ein Bild aufdrängen und gar nichts nützen.

398. "Aber wenn ich mir etwas vorstelle, oder auch wirklich Gegenstände *sähe*, so *habe* ich doch etwas, was mein Nachbar nicht hat." — Ich verstehe dich. Du willst um dich schaun und sagen: "Nur *ich* habe doch dieses." — Wozu diese Worte? Sie taugen zu nichts. — Ja, kann man nicht auch sagen "Es ist hier von einem 'Sehen' — und daher

392. "When I imagine he's in pain, all that really goes on in me is . . ." Then someone else says: "I believe I can also imagine it *without* thinking . . ." ("I believe I can think without words.") That comes to nothing. The analysis oscillates between natural science and grammar.

393. "When I imagine that someone who is laughing is really in pain, I don't imagine any pain-behaviour, for I see just the opposite. So *what* do I imagine?" — I have already said what. And for that, I do not necessarily have to imagine that *I* feel pain. —— "But then what is the process of imagining it?" —— Well, where (outside philosophy) do we use the |120| words "I can imagine that he is in pain", or "I imagine that . . .", or "Imagine that . . ."?

One says, for example, to someone who has to play a part on-stage: "Here you must imagine that this man is in pain and is concealing this" — and now we give him no directions, don't tell him what he is *actually* to do. For this reason too, the suggested analysis is not to the point. — We now watch the actor, who is imagining this situation.

394. In what sort of circumstances would we ask someone: "What actually went on in you as you imagined this?" — And what sort of answer do we expect?

395. There is a lack of clarity about the role of *imaginability* in our investigation. Namely, about the extent to which it ensures that a sentence makes sense.

396. It is no more essential to the understanding of a sentence that one should imagine something in connection with it than that one should make a sketch from it.

397. Instead of "imaginability", one can also say here: representability in a particular medium of representation. And such a representation *may* indeed safely point a way to a further use of a sentence. On the other hand, a picture may obtrude itself upon us and be of no use at all.

398. "But when I imagine something, or even actually *see* objects, surely I have *got* something which my neighbour has not." — I understand you. You want to look about you and say: "At any rate only *I* have got THIS." — What are these words for? They serve no purpose. — Indeed, can't one add: "There is here no question of a 'seeing' — and therefore

auch von einem 'Haben' — und von einem Subjekt, also auch vom Ich, nicht die Rede"? Könnte ich nicht fragen: Das, wovon du redest und sagst, nur du habest es, — inwiefern *hast* du es denn? Besitzt du es? Du *siehst* es nicht einmal. Ja, müßtest du nicht davon sagen, niemand habe es? Es ist ja auch klar: wenn du logisch ausschließt, daß ein Andrer etwas hat, so verliert es auch seinen Sinn, zu sagen, du habest es.

Aber was ist dann das, wovon du redest? Ich sagte ja, ich wisse in meinem Innern, was du meinst. Aber das hieß: ich weiß, wie man diesen Gegenstand aufzufassen, zu sehen, wie man ihn sozusagen durch Blick und Gesten zu bezeichnen meint. Ich weiß, in welcher Weise man in diesem Fall vor sich und um sich schaut, — und anderes. Ich glaube, man kann sagen: Du redest (wenn du z. B. im Zimmer sitzt) vom 'visuellen Zimmer'. Das, was keinen Besitzer hat, ist das 'visuelle Zimmer'. Ich kann es so wenig besitzen, als ich darin umhergehen, oder es anschaun, oder darauf zeigen kann. Es gehört insofern nicht mir an, als es niemand anderm angehören kann. Oder: es gehört insofern nicht mir an, als ich ja darauf die gleiche Ausdrucksform anwenden will, wie auf das materielle Zimmer selbst, in dem ich sitze. Die Beschreibung des letztern braucht keinen Besitzer zu erwähnen, es muß ja auch keinen Besitzer haben. Dann aber *kann* das visuelle Zimmer keinen haben. "Denn es hat keinen Herrn außer sich und keinen in sich" — könnte man sagen.

Denk dir ein Landschaftsbild, eine Phantasielandschaft, und in ihr ein Haus — und jemand fragte "Wem gehört das Haus?" — Es könnte übrigens die Antwort darauf sein: "Dem Bauer, der auf der Bank davor sitzt." Aber dieser kann sein Haus dann, z. B., nicht betreten.

399. Man könnte auch sagen: der Besitzer des visuellen Zimmers müßte doch wesensgleich mit ihm sein; aber er befindet sich nicht in ihm, noch gibt es ein Außen.

400. Was der, der gleichsam das 'visuelle Zimmer' entdeckt zu haben schien, — was der gefunden hatte, war eine neue Sprechweise, ein neuer Vergleich; und man könnte auch sagen, eine neue Empfindung.

401. Du deutest die neue Auffassung als das Sehen eines neuen Gegenstands. Du deutest eine grammatische Bewegung, die du gemacht hast: als quasi-physikalische Erscheinung, die du beobachtest. (Denk z. B. an die Frage "Sind Sinnesdaten der Baustoff des Universums?")

Aber mein Ausdruck ist nicht einwandfrei: Du habest eine 'grammatische' Bewegung gemacht. Du hast vor allem eine neue Auffassung gefunden. So, als hättest du eine neue Malweise erfunden; oder auch ein neues Metrum, oder eine neue Art von Gesängen. —

none of a 'having' — nor of a subject, nor therefore of the I either"? Couldn't I ask: In what sense have you *got* what you are talking about and saying that only you have got it? Do you possess it? You do not even *see* it. Don't you really have to say that no one has got it? And indeed, it's clear: if you logically exclude other people's having something, it loses its sense to say that you have it.

But what are you then talking about? It's true I said that I knew deep down what you meant. But that meant that I knew how one thinks to conceive this object, to see it, to gesture at it, as it were, by looking and pointing. I know how one stares ahead and looks about |121| one in this case — and the rest. I think one can say: you are talking (if, for example, you are sitting in a room) of the 'visual room'. That which has no owner is the 'visual room'. I can as little own it as I can walk about it, or look at it, or point at it. In so far as it cannot belong to anyone else, it doesn't belong to me either. Or again, in so far as I want to apply the same form of expression to it as to the material room in which I sit, it doesn't belong to me. A description of the latter need not mention an owner. Indeed, the material room need not have an owner. But then the visual room *cannot* have an owner. "For" — one might say — "it has no master outside it, and none inside it either."

Think of a picture of a landscape, an imaginary landscape with a house in it. — Someone asks "Whose house is that?" — The answer, by the way, might be "It belongs to the farmer who is sitting on the bench in front of it". But then he cannot, for example, step into his house.

399. One could also say: surely the owner of the visual room has to be of the same nature as it; but he isn't inside it, and there is no outside.

* 400. The visual room seemed like a discovery, as it were; but what its discoverer really found was a new way of speaking, a new comparison, and, one could even say, a new experience.

401. You interpret the new conception as the seeing of a new object. You interpret a grammatical movement that you have made as a quasi-physical phenomenon which you are observing. (Remember, for example, the question "Are sense-data the stuff of which the universe is made?")

But my expression "You have made a 'grammatical' movement" is not unobjectionable. Above all, you have found a new conception. As if you had invented a new way of painting; or, again, a new metre, or a new kind of song. —

402. "Ich sage zwar 'Ich habe jetzt die und die Vorstellung', aber die Worte 'ich habe' sind nur ein Zeichen für den *Andern*; die Vorstellungswelt ist *ganz* in der Beschreibung der Vorstellung dargestellt." — Du meinst: das "Ich habe" ist wie ein "Jetzt Achtung!" Du bist geneigt, zu sagen, es sollte eigentlich anders ausgedrückt werden. Etwa einfach, indem man mit der Hand ein Zeichen gibt und dann beschreibt. — Wenn man, wie hier, mit den Ausdrücken unsrer gewöhnlichen Sprache (die doch ihre Schuldigkeit tun) nicht einverstanden ist, so sitzt uns ein Bild im Kopf, das mit dem der gewöhnlichen Ausdrucksweise streitet. Während wir versucht sind, zu sagen, unsre Ausdrucksweise beschreibe die Tatsachen nicht so, wie sie wirklich sind. Als ob (z. B.) der Satz "Er hat Schmerzen" noch auf andre Weise falsch sein könnte, als dadurch, daß dieser Mensch *nicht* Schmerzen hat. Als sage die Ausdrucksform etwas Falsches, auch wenn der Satz, zur Not, etwas Richtiges behauptet.

Denn *so* sehen ja die Streitigkeiten zwischen Idealisten, Solipsisten und Realisten aus. Die Einen greifen die normale Ausdrucksform an, so als griffen sie eine Behauptung an; die Andern verteidigen sie, als konstatierten sie Tatsachen, die jeder vernünftige Mensch anerkennt.

403. Wenn ich das Wort "Schmerz" ganz für dasjenige in Anspruch nähme, was ich bis dahin "meinen Schmerz" genannt habe, und was Andre "den Schmerz des L.W." genannt haben, so geschähe den Andern damit kein Unrecht, solange nur eine Notation vorgesehen wäre, in der der Ausfall des Wortes "Schmerz" in anderen Verbindungen irgendwie ersetzt würde. Die Andern werden dann dennoch bedauert, vom Arzt behandelt, u. s. w. Es wäre natürlich auch *kein* Einwand gegen diese Ausdrucksweise, zu sagen: "Aber die Andern haben ja genau dasselbe, was du hast!"

Aber was hätte ich dann von dieser neuen Art der Darstellung? Nichts. Aber der Solipsist *will* ja auch keine praktischen Vorteile, wenn er seine Anschauung vertritt!

404. "Wenn ich sage 'ich habe Schmerzen', weise ich nicht auf eine Person, die die Schmerzen hat, da ich in gewissem Sinne gar nicht weiß, *wer* sie hat." Und das läßt sich rechtfertigen. Denn vor allem: Ich sagte ja nicht, die und die Person habe Schmerzen, sondern "ich habe . . .". Nun, damit nenne ich ja keine Person. So wenig, wie dadurch, daß ich vor Schmerz *stöhne*. Obwohl der Andre aus dem Stöhnen ersieht, wer Schmerzen hat.

Was heißt es denn: wissen, *wer* Schmerzen hat? Es heißt, z. B., wissen, welcher Mensch in diesem Zimmer Schmerzen hat: also, der dort sitzt, oder, der in dieser Ecke steht, der Lange mit den blonden Haaren

* 402. "It's true that I say 'I now have such-and-such a visual image', but the words 'I have' are merely a sign for *others*; the visual world is described *completely* by the description of the visual image." — You mean: the words "I have" are like "Attention please!" You're inclined to say that it should really have been expressed differently. Perhaps simply by making a sign with one's hand and then giving a description. — When, as in this case, one disapproves of the expressions of ordinary language (which, after all, do their duty), we have got a picture in our heads which conflicts with the picture of our ordinary |122| way of speaking. At the same time, we're tempted to say that our way of speaking does not describe the facts as they really are. As if, for example, the proposition "he has pains" could be false in some other way than by that man's *not* having pains. As if the form of expression were saying something false, even when the proposition *faute de mieux* asserted something true.

For *this* is what disputes between idealists, solipsists and realists look like. The one party attacks the normal form of expression as if they were attacking an assertion; the others defend it, as if they were stating facts recognized by every reasonable human being.

403. If I were to reserve the word "pain" solely for what I had previously called "my pain", and others "L.W.'s pain", I'd do other people no injustice, so long as a notation were provided in which the loss of the word "pain" in other contexts were somehow made good. Other people would still be pitied, treated by doctors, and so on. It would, of course, be *no* objection to this way of talking to say "But look here, other people have just the same as you!"

But what would I gain from this new mode of representation? Nothing. But then the solipsist does not *want* any practical advantage when he advances his view either!

404. "When I say 'I am in pain', I don't point to a person who is in pain, since in a certain sense I don't know *who* is." And this can be given a justification. For the main point is: I didn't say that such-and-such a person was in pain, but "I am . . .". Now, in saying this, I don't name any person. Just as I don't name anyone when I *groan* with pain. Though someone else sees who is in pain from the groaning.

What does it mean to know *who* is in pain? It means, for example, to know which man in this room is in pain: for instance, that it's the one who is sitting over there, or the one who is standing in that corner, the tall one over there with the fair hair, and so on. — What am I

dort, etc. — Worauf will ich hinaus? Darauf, daß es sehr verschiedene Kriterien der '*Identität*' der Person gibt.

Nun, welches ist es, das mich bestimmt, zu sagen, '*ich*' habe Schmerzen? Gar keins.

405. "Aber du willst doch jedenfalls, wenn du sagst 'ich habe Schmerzen', die Aufmerksamkeit der Andern auf eine bestimmte Person lenken." — Die Antwort könnte sein: Nein; ich will sie nur auf *mich* lenken. —

406. "Aber du willst doch durch die Worte 'Ich habe . . .' zwischen *dir* und *dem Andern* unterscheiden." — Kann man das in allen Fällen sagen? Auch, wenn ich bloß stöhne? Und auch wenn ich zwischen mir und dem Andern 'unterscheiden will' — will ich damit zwischen den Personen L. W. und N. N. unterscheiden?

407. Man könnte sich denken, daß jemand stöhnte: "Irgend jemand hat Schmerzen — ich weiß nicht wer!" — worauf man ihm, dem Stöhnenden, zu Hilfe eilte.

408. "Du zweifelst doch nicht, ob du die Schmerzen, oder der Andere sie hat!" — Der Satz "Ich weiß nicht, ob ich, oder der Andere Schmerzen hat" wäre ein logisches Produkt, und einer seiner Faktoren: "Ich weiß nicht, ob ich Schmerzen habe oder nicht" — und dies ist kein sinnvoller Satz.

409. Denke, mehrere Leute stehen in einem Kreis, darunter auch ich. Irgend einer von uns, einmal der, einmal jener, wird mit den Polen einer Elektrisiermaschine verbunden, ohne daß wir es sehen können. Ich beobachte die Gesichter der Andern und trachte zu erkennen, welcher von uns jetzt gerade elektrisiert wird. — Einmal sage ich: "Jetzt *weiß* ich, welcher es ist; *ich* bin's nämlich." In diesem Sinne könnte ich auch sagen: "Jetzt weiß ich, wer die Schläge spürt; ich nämlich." Dies wäre eine etwas seltsame Ausdrucksweise. — Nehme ich aber hier an, daß ich Schläge auch dann fühlen kann, wenn Andre elektrisiert werden, dann wird nun die Ausdrucksweise "Jetzt weiß ich, wer . . ." ganz unpassend. Sie gehört nicht zu diesem Spiel.

410. "Ich" benennt keine Person, "hier" keinen Ort, "dieses" ist kein Name. Aber sie stehen mit Namen in Zusammenhang. Namen werden mittels ihrer erklärt. Es ist auch wahr, daß die Physik dadurch charakterisiert ist, daß sie diese Wörter nicht verwendet.

getting at? At the fact that there is a great variety of criteria for the *'identity'* of a person.

Now, which of them leads me to say that *I* am in pain? None.

405. "But at any rate when you say 'I'm in pain', you want to draw the attention of others to a particular person." — The answer could be: No, I just want to draw their attention to *myself*. — |123|

406. "But surely what you want to do with the words 'I am . . .' is to distinguish between *yourself* and *other* people." — Can this be said in every case? Even when I merely groan? And even when I 'want to distinguish' between myself and other people — do I want to distinguish between the person L.W. and the person N.N.?

407. It would be possible to imagine someone groaning out: "Someone is in pain — I don't know who!" — whereupon people would hurry to help him, the one who groaned.

408. "But you aren't in doubt whether it is you or someone else who is in pain!" — The proposition "I don't know whether I or someone else is in pain" would be a logical product, and one of its factors would be: "I don't know whether I am in pain or not" — and that is not a significant sentence.

409. Imagine several people standing in a circle, myself among them. One of us, sometimes this one, sometimes that, is connected to the poles of an electrostatic generator without our being able to see this. I observe the faces of the others and try to see which of us has just been given an electric shock. — At one point I say: "Now I know who it is — it's me." In this sense I could also say: "Now I know who is feeling the shocks — it's me." This would be a rather odd way of speaking. — But if I suppose that I can feel an electric shock even when someone else is being given one, then the form of expression "Now I know who . . ." becomes quite inappropriate. It does not belong to this game.

410. "I" doesn't name a person, nor "here" a place, and "this" is not a name. But they are connected with names. Names are explained by means of them. It is also true that it is characteristic of physics not to use these words.

411. Überlege: Wie können diese Fragen angewendet, und wie entschieden werden:

1) "Sind diese Bücher *meine* Bücher?"
2) "Ist dieser Fuß *mein* Fuß?"
3) "Ist dieser Körper *mein* Körper?"
4) "Ist diese Empfindung *meine* Empfindung?"

Jede dieser Fragen hat praktische (unphilosophische) Anwendungen.

Zu 2): Denk an Fälle, in denen mein Fuß anästhesiert oder gelähmt ist. Unter gewissen Umständen könnte die Frage dadurch entschieden werden, daß festgestellt wird, ob ich in diesem Fuß Schmerzen empfinde.

Zu 3): Dabei könnte man auf ein Bild im Spiegel weisen. Unter gewissen Umständen aber könnte man einen Körper betasten und die Frage stellen. Unter andern Umständen bedeutet sie das gleiche, wie: "Sieht *so* mein Körper aus?"

Zu 4): Welche ist denn *diese* Empfindung? D. h.: wie verwendet man hier das hinweisende Fürwort? Doch anders, als z. B. im ersten Beispiel! Verirrungen entstehen hier wieder dadurch, daß man sich einbildet, man zeige auf eine Empfindung, indem man seine Aufmerksamkeit auf sie richtet.

412. Das Gefühl der Unüberbrückbarkeit der Kluft zwischen Bewußtsein und Gehirnvorgang: Wie kommt es, daß das in die Betrachtungen des gewöhnlichen Lebens nicht hineinspielt? Die Idee dieser Artverschiedenheit ist mit einem leisen Schwindel verbunden, — der auftritt, wenn wir logische Kunststücke ausführen. (Der gleiche Schwindel erfaßt uns bei gewissen Theoremen der Mengenlehre.) Wann tritt, in unserm Fall, dieses Gefühl auf? Nun, wenn ich z. B. meine Aufmerksamkeit in bestimmter Weise auf mein Bewußtsein lenke und mir dabei staunend sage: DIES solle durch einen Gehirnvorgang erzeugt werden! — indem ich mir gleichsam an die Stirne greife. — Aber was kann das heißen: "meine Aufmerksamkeit auf mein Bewußtsein lenken"? Es ist doch nichts merkwürdiger, als daß es so etwas gibt! Was ich so nannte (denn diese Worte werden ja im gewöhnlichen Leben nicht gebraucht) war ein Akt des Schauens. Ich schaute steif vor mich hin — aber *nicht* auf irgend einen bestimmten Punkt, oder Gegenstand. Meine Augen waren weit offen, meine Brauen nicht zusammengezogen (wie sie es meistens sind, wenn ein bestimmtes Objekt mich interessiert). Kein solches Interesse war dem Schauen vorangegangen. Mein Blick war 'vacant'; oder *ähnlich* dem eines Menschen, der die Beleuchtung des Himmels bewundert und das Licht eintrinkt.

411. Consider how the following questions can be applied, and how decided:

(1) "Are these books *my* books?"
(2) "Is this foot *my* foot?"
(3) "Is this body *my* body?"
(4) "Is this sensation *my* sensation?"

Each of these questions has practical (non-philosophical) applications.

For (2): Think of cases in which my foot is anaesthetized or paralysed. Under certain circumstances, the question could be settled by finding out whether I can feel pain in this foot. |124|

For (3): Here one might be pointing to a reflection in a mirror. But in certain circumstances, one might touch a body and ask the question. In others, it means the same as "Does my body look like *that*?"

For (4): But which sensation is *this* one? That is, how is one using the demonstrative pronoun here? Certainly otherwise than in, say, the first example. Here, again, one goes astray, because one imagines that by directing one's attention to a sensation, one is pointing at it.

412. The feeling of an unbridgeable gulf between consciousness and brain process: how come that this plays no role in reflections of ordinary life? This idea of a difference in kind is accompanied by slight giddiness — which occurs when we are doing logical tricks. (The same giddiness attacks us when dealing with certain theorems in set theory.) When does this feeling occur in the present case? It is when I, for example, turn my attention in a particular way on to my own consciousness and, astonished, say to myself: "THIS is supposed to be produced by a process in the brain!" — as it were clutching my forehead. — But what can it mean to speak of "turning my attention on to my own consciousness"? There is surely nothing more extraordinary than that there should be any such thing! What I described with these words (which are not used in this way in ordinary life) was an act of gazing. I gazed fixedly in front of me — but *not* at any particular point or object. My eyes were wide open, brows not contracted (as they mostly are when I am interested in a particular object). No such interest preceded this gazing. My glance was vacant; or again, *like* that of someone admiring the illumination of the sky and drinking in the light.

Bedenk nun, daß an dem Satz, den ich als Paradox aussprach (DIES werde durch einen Gehirnvorgang erzeugt!) gar nichts Paradoxes war. Ich hätte ihn während eines Experiments aussprechen können, dessen Zweck es war zu zeigen, der Beleuchtungseffekt, den ich sehe, werde durch die Erregung einer bestimmten Gehirnpartie erzeugt. — Aber ich sprach den Satz nicht in der Umgebung aus, in welcher er einen alltäglichen und nicht-paradoxen Sinn gehabt hätte. Und meine Aufmerksamkeit war nicht von der Art, die dem Experiment gemäß gewesen wäre. (Mein Blick wäre 'intent', nicht 'vacant' gewesen.)

413. Hier haben wir einen Fall von Introspektion; nicht unähnlich derjenigen, durch welche William James herausbrachte, das 'Selbst' bestehe hauptsächlich aus 'peculiar motions in the head and between the head and throat'. Und was die Introspektion James' zeigte, war nicht die Bedeutung des Wortes "Selbst" (sofern dies etwas Ähnliches bedeutet, wie "Person", "Mensch", "er selbst", "ich selbst"), noch eine Analyse eines solchen Wesens, sondern der Aufmerksamkeitszustand eines Philosophen, der sich das Wort "Selbst" vorspricht und seine Bedeutung analysieren will. (Und daraus ließe sich vieles lernen.)

414. Du denkst, du muß doch einen Stoff weben: weil du vor einem — wenngleich leeren — Webstuhl sitzt und die Bewegungen des Webens machst.

415. Was wir liefern, sind eigentlich Bemerkungen zur Naturgeschichte des Menschen; aber nicht kuriose Beiträge, sondern Feststellungen, an denen niemand gezweifelt hat, und die dem Bemerktwerden nur entgehen, weil sie ständig vor unsern Augen sind.

416. "Die Menschen sagen übereinstimmend: sie sehen, hören, fühlen, etc. (wenn auch Mancher blind und Mancher taub ist). Sie bezeugen also von sich, sie haben *Bewußtsein*." — Aber wie merkwürdig! wem mache ich eigentlich eine Mitteilung, wenn ich sage "Ich habe Bewußtsein"? Was ist der Zweck, mir das zu sagen, und wie kann der Andre mich verstehen? — Nun, Sätze wie "Ich sehe", "Ich höre", "Ich bin bei Bewußtsein" haben ja wirklich ihren Gebrauch. Dem Arzt sage ich "Jetzt höre ich wieder auf diesem Ohr"; dem, der mich ohnmächtig glaubt, sage ich "Ich bin wieder bei Bewußtsein", u. s. w.

417. Beobachte ich mich also und nehme wahr, daß ich sehe, oder bei Bewußtsein bin? Und wozu überhaupt von Beobachtung reden! Warum nicht einfach sagen "Ich nehme wahr, daß ich bei Bewußtsein bin"? — Aber wozu hier die Worte "Ich nehme wahr" — warum nicht sagen "Ich

Note that the sentence which I uttered as a paradox ("THIS is produced by a brain process!") has nothing paradoxical about it. I could
have said it in the course of an experiment whose purpose was to show
that an effect of light which I see is produced by stimulation of a particular part of the brain. — But I did not utter the sentence in the surroundings in which it would have had an everyday and unparadoxical
sense. And my attention was not such as would have been in keeping
with that experiment. (If it had been, my gaze would have been intent,
not vacant.)

413. Here we have a case of introspection, not unlike that which gave
William James the idea that the 'self' consisted mainly of 'peculiar motions
in the head and between the head and throat'. |125| And James's intro-
spection showed, not the meaning of the word "self" (so far as it means
something like "person", "human being", "he himself", "I myself"), or
any analysis of such a being, but the state of a philosopher's attention
when he says the word "self" to himself and tries to analyse its meaning. (And much could be learned from this.)

414. You think that after all you must be weaving a piece of cloth: because
you are sitting at a loom — even if it is empty — and going through
the motions of weaving.

415. What we are supplying are really remarks on the natural history
of human beings; not curiosities, however, but facts that no one has
doubted, which have escaped notice only because they are always
before our eyes.

416. "Human beings agree in saying that they see, hear, feel, and so on
(even though some are blind and some are deaf). So they are their own
witnesses that they have *consciousness*." — But how strange this is! Whom
do I really inform if I say "I have consciousness"? What is the purpose
of saying this to myself, and how can another person understand me?
— Now, sentences like "I see", "I hear", "I am conscious" really have
their uses. I tell a doctor "Now I can hear with this ear again", or I
tell someone who believes I am in a faint "I am conscious again", and
so on.

417. Do I observe myself, then, and perceive that I am seeing or conscious? And why talk about observation at all? Why not simply say "I
perceive I am conscious"? — But what are the words "I perceive" for

bin bei Bewußtsein"? — Aber zeigen die Worte "Ich nehme wahr" hier nicht an, daß ich auf mein Bewußtsein aufmerksam bin? — was doch gewöhnlich nicht der Fall ist. — Wenn es so ist, dann sagt der Satz "Ich nehme wahr, daß . . ." nicht, daß ich bei Bewußtsein bin, sondern, daß meine Aufmerksamkeit so und so eingestellt sei.

Aber ist es denn nicht eine bestimmte Erfahrung, die mich veranlaßt, zu sagen "Ich bin wieder bei Bewußtsein"? — *Welche* Erfahrung? In welcher Situation sagen wir es?

418. Ist, daß ich Bewußtsein habe, eine Erfahrungstatsache? —

Aber sagt man nicht vom Menschen, er habe Bewußtsein; vom Baum, oder Stein aber, sie haben keines? — Wie wäre es, wenn's anders wäre? — Wären die Menschen alle bewußtlos? — Nein; nicht im gewöhnlichen Sinn des Worts. Aber ich, z. B., hätte nicht Bewußtsein —— wie ich's jetzt tatsächlich habe.

419. Unter welchen Umständen werde ich sagen, ein Stamm habe einen *Häuptling*? Und der Häuptling muß doch *Bewußtsein* haben. Er darf doch nicht ohne Bewußtsein sein!

420. Aber kann ich mir nicht denken, die Menschen um mich her seien Automaten, haben kein Bewußtsein, wenn auch ihre Handlungsweise die gleiche ist, wie immer? — Wenn ich mir's jetzt — allein in meinem Zimmer — vorstelle, sehe ich die Leute mit starrem Blick (etwa wie im Trance) ihren Verrichtungen nachgehen — die Idee ist vielleicht ein wenig unheimlich. Aber nun versuch einmal im gewöhnlichen Verkehr, z. B. auf der Straße, an dieser Idee festzuhalten! Sag dir etwa: "Die Kinder dort sind bloße Automaten; alle ihre Lebendigkeit ist bloß automatisch." Und diese Worte werden dir entweder gänzlich nichtssagend werden; oder du wirst in dir etwa eine Art unheimliches Gefühl, oder dergleichen, erzeugen.

Einen lebenden Menschen als Automaten sehen, ist analog dem, irgend eine Figur als Grenzfall, oder Variation einer andern zu sehen, z. B. ein Fensterkreuz als Swastika.

421. Es scheint uns paradox, daß wir in *einem* Bericht Körper- und Bewußtseinszustände kunterbunt durcheinander mischen: "Er litt große Qualen und warf sich unruhig umher." Das ist ganz gewöhnlich; warum erscheint es uns also paradox? Weil wir sagen wollen, der Satz handle von Greifbarem und Ungreifbarem. — Aber findest du etwas dabei, wenn ich sage: "Diese 3 Stützen geben dem Bau Festigkeit"? Sind Drei und Festigkeit greifbar? —— Sieh den Satz als Instrument an, und seinen Sinn als seine Verwendung!

here — why not say "I am conscious"? But don't the words "I perceive" here show that I am attending to my consciousness? — which is ordinarily not the case. — If so, then the sentence "I perceive I am conscious" does not say that I am conscious, but that my attention is focused in such-and-such a way.

But isn't it a particular experience that occasions my saying "I am conscious again"? — *What* experience? In what situations do we say it?

418. Is my having consciousness a fact of experience? –

But doesn't one say that human beings have consciousness, and that trees or stones do not? — What would it be like if it were otherwise? — Would human beings all be unconscious? — No; not in the ordinary sense of the word. But I, for instance, would not have consciousness —— as I now in fact have it. |126|

419. In what circumstances shall I say that a tribe has a *chief*? And the chief must surely have *consciousness*. Surely he mustn't be without consciousness!

420. But can't I imagine that people around me are automata, lack consciousness, even though they behave in the same way as usual? — If I imagine it now — alone in my room — I see people with fixed looks (as in a trance) going about their business — the idea is perhaps a little uncanny. But just try to hang on to this idea in the midst of your ordinary intercourse with others — in the street, say! Say to yourself, for example: "The children over there are mere automata; all their liveliness is mere automatism." And you will either find these words becoming quite empty; or you will produce in yourself some kind of uncanny feeling, or something of the sort.

Seeing a living human being as an automaton is analogous to seeing one figure as a limiting case or variant of another; the cross-pieces of a window as a swastika, for example.

421. It seems paradoxical to us that in a single report we should make such a medley, mixing physical states and states of consciousness up together: "He suffered great torments and tossed about restlessly." It is quite usual; so why does it seem paradoxical to us? Because we want to say that the sentence is about both tangibles and intangibles. — But does it worry you if I say: "These three struts give the building stability?" Are three and stability tangible? —— Regard the sentence as an instrument, and its sense as its employment.

422. Woran glaube ich, wenn ich an eine Seele im Menschen glaube?
Woran glaube ich, wenn ich glaube, diese Substanz enthalte zwei Ringe
von Kohlenstoffatomen? In beiden Fällen ist ein Bild im Vordergrund,
der Sinn aber weit im Hintergrund; d. h., die Anwendung des Bildes
nicht leicht zu übersehen.

423. *Gewiß*, in dir geschehen alle diese Dinge. — Und nun laß mich nur
den Ausdruck verstehen, den wir gebrauchen. — Das Bild ist da. Und
seine Gültigkeit im besondern Falle bestreite ich nicht. — Nur laß mich
jetzt noch die Anwendung des Bildes verstehen.

424. Das Bild ist *da*; und ich bestreite seine *Richtigkeit* nicht. Aber *was*
ist seine Anwendung? Denke an das Bild der Blindheit als einer
Dunkelheit in der Seele oder im Kopf des Blinden.

425. Während wir nämlich in unzähligen Fällen uns bemühen, ein Bild
zu finden, und ist dieses gefunden, die Anwendung sich gleichsam von
selbst macht, so haben wir hier bereits ein Bild, das sich uns auf Schritt
und Tritt aufdrängt, — uns aber nicht aus der Schwierigkeit hilft, die
nun erst anfängt.
   Frage ich z. B.: "Wie soll ich es mir vorstellen, daß *dieser* Mechanismus
in *dieses* Gehäuse geht?" — so kann als Antwort etwa eine Zeichnung
in verkleinertem Maßstab dienen. Man kann mir dann sagen "Siehst
du, *so* geht er hinein"; oder vielleicht auch: "Warum wundert es dich?
So, wie du es *hier* siehst, so geht es auch dort." — Das letztere erklärt
freilich nichts mehr, sondern fordert mich nur auf, nun die Anwendung
von dem Bild, das man mir gegeben hat, zu machen.

426. Ein Bild wird heraufbeschworen, das *eindeutig* den Sinn zu bestimmen scheint. Die wirkliche Verwendung scheint etwas Verunreinigtes
der gegenüber, die das Bild uns vorzeichnet. Es geht hier wieder, wie in der
Mengenlehre: Die Ausdrucksweise scheint für einen Gott zugeschnitten
zu sein, der weiß, was wir nicht wissen können; er sieht die ganzen
unendlichen Reihen und sieht in das Bewußtsein des Menschen hinein.
Für uns freilich sind diese Ausdrucksformen quasi ein Ornat, das wir
wohl anlegen, mit dem wir aber nicht viel anfangen können, da uns die
reale Macht fehlt, die dieser Kleidung Sinn und Zweck geben würde.
   In der wirklichen Verwendung der Ausdrücke machen wir gleichsam
Umwege, gehen durch Nebengassen; während wir wohl die gerade breite Straße vor uns sehen, sie aber freilich nicht benützen können, weil
sie permanent gesperrt ist.

422. What do I believe in when I believe that man has a soul? What do I believe in when I believe that this substance contains two carbon rings? In both cases, there is a picture in the foreground, but the sense lies far in the background; that is, the application of the picture is not easy to survey.

423. *Certainly* all these things happen in you. — And now just let me understand the expression we use. — The picture is there. And I am not disputing its validity in particular cases. — Only let me now understand its application.

424. The picture is there; and I do not dispute its *correctness*. But *what* is its application? Think of the picture of blindness as a darkness in the mind or in the head of a blind person.

425. While in innumerable cases we exert ourselves to find a picture, and once it is found, the application, as it were, comes about automatically, |127| here we already have a picture which obtrudes itself on us at every turn — but does not help us out of the difficulty, which begins only now.

If I ask, for example, "How am I to imagine *this* mechanism fitting into *this* casing?" — perhaps a drawing reduced in scale may serve to answer me. Then I can be told: "You see, it fits like *this*." Or perhaps even: "Why are you surprised? See how it works *here*; well, it is the same there." — Of course, the latter no longer explains anything: it merely invites me to apply the picture I was given.

426. A picture is conjured up which seems to fix the sense unambiguously. The actual use, compared with that traced out by the picture, seems like something muddied. Here again, what is going on is the same as in set theory: the form of expression seems to have been tailored for a god, who knows what we cannot know; he sees all of those infinite series, and he sees into the consciousness of human beings. For us, however, these forms of expression are like vestments, which we may put on, but cannot do much with, since we lack the effective power that would give these trappings point and purpose.

In the actual use of these expressions we, as it were, make detours, go by side roads. We see the straight highway before us, but of course cannot use it, because it is permanently closed.

427. "Während ich zu ihm sprach, wußte ich nicht, was hinter seiner Stirn vorging." Dabei denkt man nicht an Gehirnvorgänge, sondern an Denkvorgänge. Das Bild ist ernst zu nehmen. Wir möchten wirklich hinter diese Stirne schauen. Und doch meinen wir nur das, was wir auch sonst mit den Worten meinen: wir möchten wissen, was er denkt. Ich will sagen: wir haben das lebhafte Bild — und denjenigen Gebrauch, der dem Bild zu widersprechen scheint, und das Psychische ausdrückt.

428. "Der Gedanke, dieses seltsame Wesen" — aber er kommt uns nicht seltsam vor, wenn wir denken. Der Gedanke kommt uns nicht geheimnisvoll vor, während wir denken, sondern nur, wenn wir gleichsam retrospektiv sagen: "Wie war das möglich?" Wie war es möglich, daß der Gedanke von diesem Gegenstand *selbst* handelte? Es scheint uns, als hätten wir mit ihm die Realität eingefangen.

429. Die Übereinstimmung, Harmonie, von Gedanke und Wirklichkeit liegt darin, daß, wenn ich fälschlich sage, etwas sei *rot*, es doch immerhin nicht *rot* ist. Und wenn ich jemandem das Wort "rot" im Satze "Das ist nicht rot" erklären will, ich dazu auf etwas Rotes zeige.

430. "Lege einen Maßstab an diesen Körper an; er sagt nicht, daß der Körper so lang ist. Vielmehr ist er an sich — ich möchte sagen — tot, und leistet nichts von dem, was der Gedanke leistet." — Es ist, als hätten wir uns eingebildet, das Wesentliche am lebenden Menschen sei die äußere Gestalt, und hätten nun einen Holzblock von dieser Gestalt hergestellt und sähen mit Beschämung den toten Klotz, der auch keine Ähnlichkeit mit einem Lebewesen hat.

431. "Zwischen dem Befehl und der Ausführung ist eine Kluft. Sie muß durch das Verstehen geschlossen werden."
     "Erst im Verstehen heißt es, daß wir DAS zu tun haben. Der *Befehl* —— das sind ja nur Laute, Tintenstriche. —"

432. Jedes Zeichen scheint *allein* tot. *Was* gibt ihm Leben? — Im Gebrauch *lebt* es. Hat es da den lebenden Atem in sich? — Oder ist der *Gebrauch* sein Atem?

433. Wenn wir einen Befehl geben, so kann es scheinen, als ob das Letzte, was der Befehl wünscht, unausgedrückt bleiben muß, da immer noch eine Kluft zwischen dem Befehl und seiner Befolgung bleibt. Ich wünsche etwa, daß Einer eine bestimmte Bewegung macht, etwa den Arm

427. "While I was speaking to him, I did not know what was going on in his head." In saying this, one is not thinking of brain processes, but of thought processes. This picture should be taken seriously. We really would like to see into his head. And yet we only mean what we ordinarily mean by saying that we would like to know what he is thinking. I want to say: we have this vivid picture — and that use, apparently contradicting the picture, which expresses something mental.

428. "A thought — what a strange thing!" — but it does not strike us as strange when we are thinking. A thought does not strike us as mysterious while we are thinking, but only when we say, as it were retrospectively, "How was that possible?" How was it possible for a thought to deal with *this very* object? It seems to us as if we had captured reality with the thought.

429. The agreement, the harmony, between thought and reality consists in this: that if I say falsely that something is *red*, then all the same, it is *red* that it isn't. |128| And in this: that if I want to explain the word "red" to someone, in the sentence "That is not red", I do so by pointing to something that *is* red.

430. "Put a ruler against this object; it does not say that the object is so-and-so long. Rather, it is in itself — I am tempted to say — dead, and achieves nothing of what a thought can achieve." — It is as if we had imagined that the essential thing about a living human being was the outward form. Then we made a lump of wood into that form and were abashed to see the lifeless block, lacking any similarity to a living creature.

431. "There is a gap between an order and its execution. It has to be closed by the process of understanding."

"Only in the process of understanding does the order mean that we are to do THIS. The *order* —— why, that is nothing but sounds, inkmarks. —"

432. Every sign *by itself* seems dead. *What* gives it life? — In use it *lives*. Is it there that it has living breath within it? — Or is the *use* its breath?

433. When we give an order, it may look as if the ultimate thing sought by the order had to remain unexpressed, as there is still a gap between an order and its execution. Say I want someone to make a particular movement: for example, to raise his arm. To make my order quite clear,

hebt. Damit es ganz deutlich wird, mache ich ihm die Bewegung vor. Dieses Bild scheint unzweideutig; bis auf die Frage: wie weiß er, daß *er diese Bewegung machen soll*? — Wie weiß er überhaupt, wie er die Zeichen, welche immer ich ihm gebe, gebrauchen soll? — Ich werde nun etwa trachten, den Befehl durch weitere Zeichen zu ergänzen, indem ich von mir auf den Andern deute, Gebärden der Aufmunterung mache, etc. Hier scheint es, als finge der Befehl zu stammeln an.

Als trachtete das Zeichen mit unsichern Mitteln in uns ein Verständnis hervorzurufen. — Aber wenn wir es nun verstehen, in welchen Zeichen tun wir das?

434. Die Gebärde *versucht* vorzubilden — möchte man sagen — aber kann es nicht.

435. Wenn man fragt "Wie macht der Satz das, daß er darstellt?" — so könnte die Antwort sein: "Weißt du es denn nicht? Du siehst es doch, wenn du ihn benützt." Es ist ja nichts verborgen.

Wie macht der Satz das? — Weißt du es denn nicht? Es ist ja nichts versteckt.

Aber auf die Antwort "Du weißt ja, wie es der Satz macht, es ist ja nichts verborgen" möchte man erwidern: "Ja, aber es fließt alles so rasch vorüber, und ich möchte es gleichsam breiter auseinander gelegt sehen."

436. Hier ist es leicht, in jene Sackgasse des Philosophierens zu geraten, wo man glaubt, die Schwierigkeit der Aufgabe liege darin, daß schwer erhaschbare Erscheinungen, die schnell entschlüpfende gegenwärtige Erfahrung oder dergleichen, von uns beschrieben werden sollen. Wo die gewöhnliche Sprache uns zu roh erscheint, und es scheint, als hätten wir es nicht mit den Phänomenen zu tun, von denen der Alltag redet, sondern "mit den leicht entschwindenden, die mit ihrem Auftauchen und Vergehen jene ersteren annähernd erzeugen".

(Augustinus: Manifestissima et usitatissima sunt, et eadem rursus nimis latent, et nova est inventio eorum.)

437. Der Wunsch scheint schon zu wissen, was ihn erfüllen wird, oder würde; der Satz, der Gedanke, was ihn wahr macht, auch wenn es gar nicht da ist! Woher dieses *Bestimmen*, dessen, was noch nicht da ist? Dieses despotische Fordern? ("Die Härte des logischen Muß".)

438. "Der Plan ist als Plan etwas Unbefriedigtes." (Wie der Wunsch, die Erwartung, die Vermutung, u. s. f.)

I demonstrate the movement to him. This picture seems unambiguous until the question is raised: how does he know that *he is to make that movement?* — How does he know at all what he is to do with the signs I give him, whatever they are? — Perhaps I shall now try to supplement the order with further signs, by pointing from myself to him, by making encouraging gestures, and so forth. Here it looks as if the order were beginning to stammer.

As if the sign were precariously trying to induce understanding in us. — But if we now understand it, in what signs do we do so?

434. The gesture — one would like to say — tries to prefigure, but can't do so.

435. If it is asked, "How does a sentence manage to represent?" — the answer might be: "Don't you know? Surely you see it, when you use one." After all, nothing is concealed.

How does a sentence do it? — Don't you know? After all, nothing is hidden.

But when given the answer "But you know how a sentence does it, after all, nothing is concealed", one would like to retort, "Yes, but it all goes by so quickly, and I should like to see it, as it were, more fully laid out." |129|

* 436. Here it is easy to get into that dead end in philosophizing where one believes that the difficulty of the problem consists in our having to describe phenomena that evade our grasp, the present experience that slips quickly by, or something akin — where we find ordinary language too crude, and it looks as if we were dealing not with the phenomena of everyday conversation, but with ones that "are evanescent, and, in their coming to be and passing away, tend to produce those others".

* (Augustine: Manifestissima et usitatissima sunt, et eadem rursus nimis latent, et nova est inventio eorum.)

* 437. A wish seems already to know what will or would satisfy it; a proposition, a thought, to know what makes it true — even when there is nothing there! Whence this determining of what is not yet there? This despotic demand? ("The hardness of the logical must".)

438. "A plan, as such, is something unsatisfied." (Like a wish, an expectation, a conjecture, and so on.)

Und hier meine ich: die Erwartung ist unbefriedigt, weil sie die Erwartung von etwas ist; der Glaube, die Meinung, unbefriedigt, weil sie die Meinung ist, daß etwas der Fall ist, etwas Wirkliches, etwas außerhalb dem Vorgang des Meinens.

439. Inwiefern kann man den Wunsch, die Erwartung, den Glauben, etc. "unbefriedigt" nennen? Was ist unser Urbild der Unbefriedigung? Ist es ein Hohlraum? Und würde man von einem solchen sagen, er sei unbefriedigt? Wäre das nicht auch eine Metapher? — Ist es nicht ein Gefühl, was wir Unbefriedigung nennen, — etwa den Hunger?

Wir können in einem bestimmten System des Ausdrucks einen Gegenstand mittels der Worte "befriedigt" und "unbefriedigt" beschreiben. Wenn wir z. B. festsetzen, den Hohlzylinder einen "unbefriedigten Zylinder" zu nennen, und den ihn ergänzenden Vollzylinder "seine Befriedigung".

440. Zu sagen "Ich habe Lust auf einen Apfel" heißt nicht: Ich glaube, ein Apfel wird mein Gefühl der Unbefriedigung stillen. *Dieser* Satz ist keine Äußerung des Wunsches, sondern der Unbefriedigung.

441. Wir sind von Natur und durch eine bestimmte Abrichtung, Erziehung, so eingestellt, daß wir unter bestimmten Umständen Wunschäußerungen machen. (Ein solcher 'Umstand' ist natürlich nicht der *Wunsch*.) Eine Frage, ob ich weiß, was ich wünsche, ehe mein Wunsch erfüllt ist, kann in diesem Spiele gar nicht auftreten. Und daß ein Ereignis meinen Wunsch zum Schweigen bringt, bedeutet nicht, daß es den Wunsch erfüllt. Ich wäre vielleicht nicht befriedigt, wäre mein Wunsch befriedigt worden.

Anderseits wird auch das Wort "wünschen" so gebraucht: "Ich weiß selbst nicht, was ich mir wünsche." ("Denn die Wünsche verhüllen uns selbst das Gewünschte.")

Wie, wenn man fragte: "Weiß ich, wonach ich lange, ehe ich es erhalte?" Wenn ich sprechen gelernt habe, so weiß ich's.

442. Ich sehe, wie Einer das Gewehr anlegt, und sage: "Ich erwarte mir einen Knall." Der Schuß fällt. — Wie, das hast du dir erwartet; war also dieser Knall irgendwie schon in deiner Erwartung? Oder stimmt deine Erwartung nur in anderer Hinsicht mit dem Eingetretenen überein; war dieser Lärm nicht in deiner Erwartung enthalten und kam nur als Accidens hinzu, als die Erwartung erfüllt wurde? — Aber nein, wenn der Lärm nicht eingetreten wäre, so wäre meine Erwartung nicht erfüllt worden;

Here I mean: expectation is unsatisfied, because it is an expectation of something; a belief, an opinion, is unsatisfied, because it is an opinion that something is the case, something real, something outside the process of believing.

439. In what sense can one call wishes, expectations, beliefs, etc. "unsatisfied"? What is our prototype of non-satisfaction? Is it a hollow space? And would one call that "unsatisfied"? Wouldn't this be a metaphor too? — Isn't what we call non-satisfaction — say, hunger — a feeling?

In a particular system of expressions we can describe an object by means of the words "satisfied" and "unsatisfied". For example, if we stipulate that a hollow cylinder is to be called "an unsatisfied cylinder", and the solid cylinder that fills it "its satisfaction".

440. Saying "I'd like an apple" does not mean: I believe an apple will quell my feeling of non-satisfaction. *This* utterance is an expression not of a wish but of non-satisfaction.

441. By nature and by a particular training, a particular education, we are predisposed to express wishes in certain circumstances. (A wish is, of course, not such a 'circumstance'.) In this game, a question as to whether I know what I wish before my wish is |130| fulfilled cannot arise at all. And the fact that some event stops my wishing does not mean that it fulfils it. Perhaps I wouldn't have been satisfied if my wish had been satisfied.

*   On the other hand, the word "wish" is also used in this way: "I don't know myself what I wish for." ("For wishes themselves are a veil between us and the thing wished for.")

*   Suppose someone asked, "Do I know what I long for before I get it?" If I have learned to talk, then I do.

442. I see someone aiming a gun and say "I expect a bang". The shot is fired. — What! — was that what you expected? So did that bang somehow already exist in your expectation? Or is it just that your expectation agrees in some other respect with what occurred; that that noise was not contained in your expectation, and merely supervened as an accidental property when the expectation was being fulfilled? — But no, if the noise had not occurred, my expectation would not have been

der Lärm hat sie erfüllt; er trat nicht zur Erfüllung hinzu, wie ein zweiter Gast zu dem einen, den ich erwartet hatte. — War das am Ereignis, was nicht auch in der Erwartung war, ein Accidens, eine Beigabe der Schickung? — Aber was war denn dann *nicht* Beigabe? Kam denn irgend etwas von diesem Schuß schon in meiner Erwartung vor? — Und was *war* denn Beigabe, — denn hatte ich mir nicht den ganzen Schuß erwartet?

"Der Knall war nicht so laut, als ich ihn erwartet hatte." — "Hat es also in deiner Erwartung lauter geknallt?"

443. "Das Rot, das du dir vorstellst, ist doch gewiß nicht Dasselbe (nicht dieselbe Sache) wie das, was du vor dir siehst; wie kannst du dann sagen, es sei das, was du dir vorgestellt hattest?" — Aber verhält es sich nicht analog in den Sätzen "Hier ist ein roter Fleck" und "Hier ist kein roter Fleck"? In beiden kommt das Wort "rot" vor; also kann dieses Wort nicht das Vorhandensein von etwas Rotem anzeigen.

444. Man hat vielleicht das Gefühl, daß man sich im Satz "Ich erwarte, daß er kommt" der Worte "er kommt" in anderer Bedeutung bedient, als in der Behauptung "Er kommt". Aber wäre es so, wie könnte ich davon reden, daß meine Erwartung in Erfüllung gegangen ist? Wollte ich die beiden Wörter "er" und "kommt" erklären, etwa durch hinweisende Erklärungen, so würden die gleichen Erklärungen dieser Wörter für beide Sätze gelten.

Nun könnte man aber fragen: Wie schaut das aus, wenn er kommt? — Es geht die Tür auf, jemand tritt herein, etc. — Wie schaut das aus, wenn ich erwarte, daß er kommt? — Ich gehe im Zimmer auf und ab, sehe zuweilen auf die Uhr, etc. — Aber der eine Vorgang hat ja mit dem andern nicht die geringste Ähnlichkeit! Wie kann man dann dieselben Worte zu ihrer Beschreibung gebrauchen? — Aber nun sage ich vielleicht beim auf und ab Gehen: "Ich erwarte, daß er hereinkommt." — Nun ist eine Ähnlichkeit vorhanden. Aber welcher Art ist sie?!

445. In der Sprache berühren sich Erwartung und Erfüllung.

446. Komisch wäre es, zu sagen: "Ein Vorgang sieht anders aus, wenn er geschieht, als wenn er nicht geschieht." Oder: "Ein roter Fleck sieht anders aus, wenn er da ist, als wenn er nicht da ist — aber die Sprache abstrahiert von diesem Unterschied, denn sie spricht von einem roten Fleck, ob er da ist, oder nicht."

447. Das Gefühl ist, als müßte der verneinende Satz, um einen Satz zu verneinen, ihn erst in gewissem Sinne wahr machen.

fulfilled; the noise fulfilled it; it was not an accompaniment of the fulfilment like a second guest accompanying the one I expected. Was the feature of the event that was not also in the expectation something accidental, an extra provided by fate? — But then, what was *not* an extra? Did something of the shot already occur in my expectation? — Then what *was* extra? for wasn't I expecting the whole shot?

"The bang was not as loud as I had expected." — "Then was there a louder bang in your expectation?"

443. "The red which you imagine is surely not the same (not the same thing) as the red which you see in front of you; so how can you say that it is what you imagined?" — But haven't we an analogous case with the sentences "Here is a red patch" and "Here there isn't a red patch". The word "red" occurs in both; so this word can't indicate the presence of something red.

444. One may have the feeling that in the sentence "I expect he is coming" one is using the words "he is coming" in a different sense from the one they have in the assertion "He is coming". But if that were so, how could I say that my expectation had been fulfilled? If I wanted to explain the words "he" and "is coming", say by means of ostensive explanations, the same explanations of these words would go for both sentences.

But now one might ask: what does his coming look like? — The door opens, someone walks in, and so on. — What does my expecting him |131| to come look like? — I walk up and down the room, look at the clock now and then, and so on. — But the one sequence of events has not the slightest similarity to the other! So how can one use the same words in describing them? — But then perhaps I say, as I walk up and down: "I expect he'll come in." — Now there is a similarity here. But of what kind?!

445. It is in language that an expectation and its fulfilment make contact.

446. It would be odd to say: "A process looks different when it happens from when it doesn't happen." Or: "A red patch looks different when it is there from when it isn't there — but language abstracts from this difference, for it speaks of a red patch whether it is there or not."

447. The feeling is as if the negation of a proposition had first, in a certain sense, to make it true, in order to be able to negate it.

(Die Behauptung des verneinenden Satzes enthält den verneinten Satz, aber nicht dessen Behauptung.)

448. "Wenn ich sage, ich habe heute nacht *nicht* geträumt, so muß ich doch wissen, wo nach dem Traum zu suchen wäre; d. h.: der Satz 'Ich habe geträumt' darf, auf die tatsächliche Situation angewendet, falsch, aber nicht unsinnig sein." — Heißt das also, daß du doch etwas gespürt hast, sozusagen die Andeutung eines Traums, die dir die Stelle bewußt macht, an der ein Traum gestanden hätte?

Oder: wenn ich sage "Ich habe keine Schmerzen im Arm", heißt das, daß ich einen Schatten eines Schmerzgefühls habe, der gleichsam die Stelle andeutet, in die der Schmerz eintreten könnte?

Inwiefern enthält der gegenwärtige schmerzlose Zustand die Möglichkeit der Schmerzen?

Wenn Einer sagt: "Damit das Wort 'Schmerzen' Bedeutung habe, ist es notwendig, daß man Schmerzen als solche erkennt, wenn sie auftreten" — so kann man antworten: "Es ist nicht notwendiger, als daß man das Fehlen der Schmerzen erkennt."

449. "Aber muß ich nicht wissen, wie es wäre, wenn ich Schmerzen hätte?" — Man kommt nicht davon weg, daß die Benützung des Satzes darin besteht, daß man sich bei jedem Wort etwas vorstelle.

Man bedenkt nicht, daß man mit den Worten *rechnet*, operiert, sie mit der Zeit in dies oder jenes Bild überführt. — Es ist, als glaubte man, daß etwa die schriftliche Anweisung auf eine Kuh, die mir Einer ausfolgen soll, immer von einer Vorstellung einer Kuh begleitet sein müsse, damit diese Anweisung nicht ihren Sinn verliere.

450. Wissen, wie jemand ausschaut: es sich vorstellen können — aber auch: es *nachmachen* können. Muß man sich's vorstellen, um es nachzumachen? Und ist, es nachmachen, nicht ebenso stark, als es sich vorstellen?

451. Wie ist es, wenn ich Einem den Befehl gebe "Stell dir hier einen roten Kreis vor!" — und ich sage nun: den Befehl verstehen heiße, wissen, wie es ist, wenn er ausgeführt wurde — oder gar: sich vorstellen können, wie es ist . . . ?

452. Ich will sagen: "Wenn Einer die Erwartung, den geistigen Vorgang, sehen könnte, müßte er sehen, *was* erwartet wird." — Aber so ist es ja auch: Wer den Ausdruck der Erwartung sieht, sieht, was erwartet wird. Und wie könnte man es auf andere Weise, in anderem Sinne, sehen?

(The assertion of the negating proposition contains the proposition which is negated, but not the assertion of it.)

448. "If I say I did *not* dream last night, still I must know where to look for a dream; that is, 'I dreamt', applied to this actual situation, may be false, but mustn't be nonsense." — Does that mean, then, that you did, after all, feel something, as it were the hint of a dream, which made you aware of the place which a dream would have occupied?

Again, if I say "I have no pain in my arm", does that mean that I have a shadow of a sensation of pain, which, as it were, indicates the place where a pain could have been?

In what sense does my present painless state contain the possibility of pain?

If someone says, "For the word 'pain' to have a meaning, it is necessary that pain should be recognized as such when it occurs" — one can reply: "It is not more necessary than that the absence of pain should be recognized."

449. "But mustn't I know what it would be like if I were in pain?" — One can't shake oneself free of the idea that using a sentence consists in imagining something for every word.

One fails to bear in mind the fact that one *calculates*, operates, with words, and in due course transforms them into this or that picture. — It is as if one believed that a written order for a |132| cow, which someone is to hand over to me, always had to be accompanied by a mental image of a cow if the order was not to lose its sense.

450. Knowing what someone looks like: being able to imagine it — but also: being able to *mimic* it. Need one imagine it in order to mimic it? And isn't mimicking it just as good as imagining it?

451. What if I give someone the order "Imagine a red circle here" — and now I say: understanding the order means knowing what it is like for it to have been carried out — or even: being able to imagine what it is like . . . ?

452. I want to say: "If someone could see an expectation, the mental process, then he'd surely see *what* was being expected." — But that's just how it is: anyone who sees the expression of an expectation will see what is being expected. And in what other way, in what other sense, could one see it?

453. Wer mein Erwarten wahrnähme, müßte unmittelbar wahrnehmen, *was* erwartet wird. D. h.: nicht aus dem wahrgenommenen Vorgang darauf *schließen*! — Aber zu sagen, Einer nehme die Erwartung wahr, *hat keinen Sinn*. Es sei denn etwa den: er nehme den Ausdruck der Erwartung wahr. Vom Erwartenden zu sagen, er nähme die Erwartung wahr, statt, er erwarte, wäre blödsinnige Verdrehung des Ausdrucks.

454. "Es liegt alles schon in . . ." Wie kommt es, daß der Pfeil »———→ *zeigt*? Scheint er nicht schon etwas außerhalb seiner selbst in sich zu tragen? — "Nein, es ist nicht der tote Strich; nur das Psychische, die Bedeutung, kann dies." — Das ist wahr und falsch. Der Pfeil zeigt nur in der Anwendung, die das Lebewesen von ihm macht.
    Dieses Zeigen ist *nicht* ein Hokuspokus, welches nur die Seele vollziehen kann.

455. Wir wollen sagen: "Wenn wir meinen, so ist hier kein totes Bild (welcher Art immer), sondern es ist, als gingen wir auf jemand zu." Wir gehen auf das Gemeinte zu.

456. "Wenn man meint, so meint man selber"; so bewegt man sich selber. Man stürmt selber vor und kann daher das Vorstürmen nicht auch beobachten. Gewiß nicht.

457. Ja; meinen ist, wie wenn man auf jemanden zugeht.

458. "Der Befehl befiehlt seine Befolgung." So kennt er seine Befolgung, schon ehe sie da ist? — Aber dies war ein grammatischer Satz und er sagt: Wenn ein Befehl lautet "Tu das und das!", dann nennt man "das und das tun" das Befolgen des Befehls.

459. Wir sagen "Der Befehl befiehlt *dies* —" und tun es; aber auch: "Der Befehl befiehlt dies: ich soll . . ." Wir übertragen ihn einmal in einen Satz, einmal in eine Demonstration, und einmal in die Tat.

460. Könnte die Rechtfertigung einer Handlung als Befolgung eines Befehls so lauten: "Du hast gesagt 'Bring mir eine gelbe Blume' und diese hier hat mir daraufhin ein Gefühl der Befriedigung gegeben, darum habe ich sie gebracht"? Müßte man da nicht antworten: "Ich habe dir doch nicht geschafft, mir die Blume zu bringen, die dir auf meine Worte hin ein solches Gefühl geben wird!"?

453. Anyone who perceived my expecting should perceive directly *what* was expected — that is, not *infer* it from the process he perceived! — But to say that someone perceives an expectation *makes no sense*. Unless it means something like: he perceives the manifestations of expectation. To say of an expectant person that he perceives his expectation, instead of saying "he expects" would be an idiotic distortion of the words.

* 454. "Everything is already there in . . ." How does it come about that this arrow »——→ *points*? Doesn't it seem to carry within it something extraneous to itself? — "No, not the dead line on paper; only a mental thing, the meaning, can do that." — That is both true and false. The arrow points only in the application that a living creature makes of it.

This pointing is *not* a hocus-pocus that can be performed only by the mind.

455. We are inclined to say: "When we mean something, there is no dead picture here (no matter of what kind), but, rather, it's like going towards someone." We go towards the thing we mean.

456. "When one means something, it is oneself that means"; so one sets oneself in motion. One rushes ahead, and so cannot also observe one's rushing ahead. Indeed not. |133|

457. Yes, meaning something is like going towards someone.

* 458. "An order orders its own execution." So it knows its execution before it is even there? — But that was a grammatical proposition, and it says: if an order runs "Do such-and-such", then *doing such-and-such* is called "executing the order".

459. We say "The order orders *this* —", and do it; but also: "The order orders this: I am to . . ." We translate it at one time into a sentence, at another into a demonstration, and at another into action.

460. Could a justification of an action as the execution of an order run like this: "You said 'Bring me a yellow flower', whereupon this flower gave me a feeling of satisfaction; that's why I've brought it"? Wouldn't one have to reply: "But I didn't tell you to bring me a flower that would give you that sort of feeling in response to my words!"?

461. Inwiefern antizipiert denn der Befehl die Ausführung? — Dadurch, daß er *das* jetzt befiehlt, was später ausgeführt wird? — Aber es müßte ja heißen: "was später ausgeführt, oder auch nicht ausgeführt wird". Und das sagt nichts.

"Aber wenn auch mein Wunsch nicht bestimmt, was der Fall sein wird, so bestimmt er doch sozusagen das Thema einer Tatsache; ob die nun den Wunsch erfüllt, oder nicht." Wir wundern uns — gleichsam — nicht darüber, daß Einer die Zukunft weiß; sondern darüber, daß er überhaupt prophezeien kann (richtig oder falsch).

Als nähme die bloße Prophezeiung, gleichgültig ob richtig oder falsch, schon einen Schatten der Zukunft voraus; während sie über die Zukunft nichts weiß, und weniger als nichts nicht wissen kann.

462. Ich kann ihn suchen, wenn er nicht da ist, aber ihn nicht hängen, wenn er nicht da ist.

Man könnte sagen wollen: "Da muß er doch auch dabei sein, wenn ich ihn suche." — Dann muß er auch dabei sein, wenn ich ihn nicht finde, und auch, wenn es ihn gar nicht gibt.

463. "*Den* hast du gesucht? Du konntest ja nicht einmal wissen, ob er da ist!" — Dieses Problem aber entsteht *wirklich* beim Suchen in der Mathematik. Man kann z. B. die Frage stellen: Wie war es möglich, nach der Dreiteilung des Winkels auch nur zu *suchen*?

464. Was ich lehren will, ist: von einem nicht offenkundigen Unsinn zu einem offenkundigen übergehen.

465. "Eine Erwartung ist so gemacht, daß, was immer kommt, mit ihr übereinstimmen muß oder nicht."

Wenn man nun fragt: Ist also die Tatsache durch die Erwartung auf ja und nein bestimmt, oder nicht, — d. h., ist es bestimmt, in welchem Sinne die Erwartung durch ein Ereignis — welches immer eintreffen mag — beantwortet werden wird; so muß man antworten "Ja; es sei denn, daß der Ausdruck der Erwartung unbestimmt ist, daß er etwa eine Disjunktion verschiedener Möglichkeiten enthält."

466. Wozu denkt der Mensch? wozu ist es nütze? — Wozu *berechnet* er Dampfkessel und überläßt ihre Wandstärke nicht dem Zufall? Es ist doch nur Erfahrungstatsache, daß Kessel, die so berechnet wurden, nicht so oft explodieren! Aber so, wie er alles eher täte, als die Hand ins Feuer stecken, das ihn früher gebrannt hat, so wird er alles eher tun, als den

461. In what sense does an order anticipate its fulfilment? — By now ordering *just that* which later on is carried out? — But this would surely have to run: "which later on is carried out, or again is not carried out". And that says nothing.

"But even if my wish does not determine what is going to be the case, still it does, so to speak, determine the theme of a fact, no matter whether such a fact fulfils the wish or not." We are, as it were, surprised, not at someone's knowing the future, but at his being able to prophesy at all (right or wrong).

As if the mere prophecy, no matter whether true or false, foreshadowed the future; whereas it knows nothing of the future and cannot know less than nothing.

462. I can look for him when he is not there, but not hang him when he is not there.

One might want to say: "But he must be around, if I am looking for him." — Then he must also be around if I don't find him, and even if he doesn't exist at all.

463. "You were looking for *him*? You couldn't even have known if he was there!" — But this problem *really does* arise when one looks for something in mathematics. One can ask, for example, how was it possible so much as to *look* for the trisection of an angle?

464. What I want to teach is: to pass from unobvious nonsense to obvious nonsense. |134|

465. "An expectation is so made that whatever happens has to accord with it, or not."

If someone now asks: then is what is the case determined, give or take a yes or no, by an expectation or not — that is, is it determined in what sense the expectation would be satisfied by an event, no matter what happens? — then one has to reply: "Yes, unless the expression of the expectation is indefinite, for example, if it contains a disjunction of different possibilities."

466. What does man reason for? What is it good for? — Why does he make boilers according to *calculations*, and not leave the thickness of their walls to chance? After all, it is only a fact of experience that boilers made according to these calculations do not explode so often. But, just as having once been burnt, he would do anything rather than put

Kessel nicht berechnen. — Da uns Ursachen aber nicht interessieren, — werden wir sagen: Die Menschen denken tatsächlich: sie gehen, z. B., auf diese Weise vor, wenn sie einen Dampfkessel bauen. — Kann nun ein so erzeugter Kessel nicht explodieren? O doch.

467. Denkt der Mensch also, weil Denken sich bewährt hat? — Weil er denkt, es sei vorteilhaft, zu denken?
   (Erzieht er seine Kinder, weil es sich bewährt hat?)

468. Wie wäre herauszubringen: *warum* er denkt?

469. Und doch kann man sagen, das Denken habe sich bewährt. Es seien jetzt weniger Kesselexplosionen als früher, seit etwa die Wandstärken nicht mehr nach dem Gefühl bestimmt, sondern auf die und die Weise berechnet werden. Oder, seit man jede Berechnung eines Ingenieurs durch einen zweiten kontrollieren läßt.

470. *Manchmal* also denkt man, weil es sich bewährt hat.

471. Wenn wir die Frage "warum" unterdrücken, werden wir oft erst die wichtigen *Tatsachen* gewahr; die dann in unseren Untersuchungen zu einer Antwort führen.

472. Die Natur des Glaubens an die Gleichförmigkeit des Geschehens wird vielleicht am klarsten im Falle, in dem wir Furcht vor dem Erwarteten empfinden. Nichts könnte mich dazu bewegen, meine Hand in die Flamme zu stecken, — obwohl ich mich doch *nur in der Vergangenheit* verbrannt habe.

473. Der Glaube, daß mich das Feuer brennen wird, ist von der Art der Furcht, daß es mich brennen wird.

474. Daß mich das Feuer brennen wird, wenn ich die Hand hineinstecke: das ist Sicherheit.
   D. h., da sehen wir, was Sicherheit bedeutet. (Nicht nur, was das Wort "Sicherheit" bedeutet, sondern auch, was es mit ihr auf sich hat.)

475. Nach den Gründen zu einer Annahme gefragt, *besinnt* man sich auf diese Gründe. Geschieht hier dasselbe, wie, wenn man darüber nachdenkt, was die Ursachen eines Ereignisses gewesen sein mögen?

his hand into a fire, so too he would do anything rather than not calculate for a boiler. — However, since we are not interested in causes,
we shall say: human beings do in fact reason: this is how they proceed,
for example, when they make a boiler. — Now, can't a boiler produced
in this way explode? Oh, yes.

467. Does man reason, then, because reasoning has proved itself? —
Because he thinks it advantageous to reason?
     (Does he bring his children up because bringing them up pays?)

468. How could one find out *why* he reasons?

469. And yet one may say that reasoning has proved itself. That there
are fewer boiler explosions than there used to be, now that we no longer
go by hunches in deciding the thickness of the walls, but make such-
and-such calculations instead. Or, ever since each calculation done by
one engineer got checked by another.

470. So *sometimes* one reasons because reasoning has proved itself.

471. Often it is only when we suppress the question "Why?" that we
become aware of those important facts, which then, in the course of
our investigations, lead to an answer.

472. The character of the belief in the uniformity of nature can
perhaps be seen most clearly in the case in which what is expected is
something we fear. Nothing could induce me to put my hand into a
flame — even though it is *only in the past* that I have burnt myself.

473. The belief that fire will burn me is of the same kind as the fear
that it will burn me. |135|

474. I shall get burnt if I put my hand in the fire — that is certainty.
     That is to say, here we see what certainty means. (Not just the mean-
ing of the word "certainty" but also what certainty amounts to.)

475. On being asked for the reasons for a supposition, one calls them
to mind. Does the same thing happen here as when one considers what
may have been the causes of an event?

476. Es ist zu unterscheiden zwischen dem Gegenstand der Furcht und der Ursache der Furcht.

So ist das Gesicht, das uns Furcht, oder Entzücken, einflößt (der Gegenstand der Furcht, des Entzückens) darum nicht ihre Ursache, sondern — man könnte sagen — ihre Richtung.

477. "Warum glaubst du, daß du dich an der heißen Herdplatte verbrennen wirst?" — Hast du Gründe für diesen Glauben; und brauchst du Gründe?

478. Was für einen Grund habe ich, anzunehmen, daß mein Finger, wenn er den Tisch berührt, einen Widerstand spüren wird? Was für einen Grund, zu glauben, daß dieser Bleistift sich nicht schmerzlos durch meine Hand wird stecken lassen? — Wenn ich dies frage, melden sich hundert Gründe, die einander kaum zu Wort kommen lassen wollen. "Ich habe es doch selbst unzählige Male erfahren; und ebenso oft von ähnlichen Erfahrungen gehört; wenn es nicht so wäre, würde . . . ; etc."

479. Die Frage "Aus welchen Gründen glaubst du das?" könnte bedeuten: "Aus welchen Gründen leitest du das jetzt ab (hast du es jetzt abgeleitet)?" Aber auch: "Welche Gründe kannst du mir nachträglich für diese Annahme angeben?"

480. Man könnte also unter "Gründen" zu einer Meinung tatsächlich nur das verstehen, was Einer sich vorgesagt hat, ehe er zu der Meinung kam. Die Rechnung, die er tatsächlich ausgeführt hat. Wenn man nun fragte: Wie *kann* aber frühere Erfahrung ein Grund zur Annahme sein, es werde später das und das eintreffen? — so ist die Antwort: Welchen allgemeinen Begriff vom Grund zu solch einer Annahme haben wir denn? Diese Art Angabe über die Vergangenheit nennen wir eben Grund zur Annahme, es werde das in Zukunft geschehen. — Und wenn man sich wundert, daß wir ein solches Spiel spielen, dann berufe ich mich auf die *Wirkung* einer vergangenen Erfahrung (darauf, daß ein gebranntes Kind das Feuer fürchtet).

481. Wer sagte, er sei durch Angaben über Vergangenes nicht davon zu überzeugen, daß irgend etwas in Zukunft geschehen werde, — den würde ich nicht verstehen. Man könnte ihn fragen: Was willst du denn hören? Was für Angaben nennst du Gründe dafür, das zu glauben? Was nennst du denn "überzeugen"? Welche Art des Überzeugens erwartest du dir? — Wenn *das* keine Gründe sind, was sind denn Gründe? — Wenn du sagst, das seien keine Gründe, so mußt du doch angeben können, was der Fall sein müßte, damit wir mit Recht sagen könnten, es seien Gründe für unsre Annahme vorhanden.

476. A distinction should be made between the object of fear and the cause of fear.

So a face which inspires fear or delight (the object of fear or delight) is not on that account its cause, but — one might say — its target.

477. "Why do you believe that you will burn yourself on the hotplate?" — Have you reasons for this belief, and do you need reasons?

478. What kind of reason have I to assume that my finger will feel a resistance when it touches the table? What kind of reason for believing that this pencil will not pierce my hand without hurting it? — When I ask this, a hundred reasons present themselves, each drowning out the voice of the others. "But I have experienced it myself innumerable times, often heard of similar experiences; if it were not so, it would . . . ; and so forth."

479. The question "For what reasons do you believe this?" might mean: "From what reasons are you now deriving it (have you just derived it)?" But it might also mean: "With hindsight, what reasons can you give me for this supposition?"

* 480. So one could actually take "reasons" for a belief to mean only what a person had said to himself before he arrived at the belief — the calculation that he actually carried out. If someone now asks, "But how *can* previous experience be a reason for the supposition that such-and-such will occur later on?", the answer is: What general concept have we of reasons for this kind of supposition? This sort of statement about the past is simply what we call a reason for supposing that this will happen in the future. — And if one is surprised at our playing such a game, I appeal to the *effect* of a past experience (to the fact that a burnt child fears the fire). |136|

481. If anyone said that information about the past couldn't convince him that something would happen in the future, I wouldn't understand him. One might ask him: What do you expect to be told, then? What sort of information do you call a reason for believing this? What do you call "convincing"? In what kind of way do you expect to be convinced? — If *these* are not reasons, then what are reasons? — If you say that these are not reasons, then you must surely be able to state what must be the case for us to be warranted in saying that there are reasons for our supposition.

Denn wohlgemerkt: Gründe sind hier nicht Sätze, aus denen das Geglaubte logisch folgt.

Aber nicht, als ob man sagen könnte: fürs Glauben genügt eben weniger als für das Wissen. — Denn hier handelt es sich nicht um eine Annäherung an das logische Folgen.

482. Wir werden irregeführt durch die Ausdrucksweise: "Dieser Grund ist gut, denn er macht das Eintreffen des Ereignisses wahrscheinlich." Hier ist es, als ob wir nun etwas Weiteres über den Grund ausgesagt hätten, was ihn als Grund rechtfertigt; während mit dem Satz, daß dieser Grund das Eintreffen wahrscheinlich macht, nichts gesagt ist, wenn nicht, daß dieser Grund einem bestimmten Maßstab des guten Grundes entspricht, — der Maßstab aber nicht begründet ist!

483. Ein guter Grund ist einer, der *so* aussieht.

484. Man möchte sagen: "Ein guter Grund ist er nur darum, weil er das Eintreffen *wirklich* wahrscheinlich macht." Weil er sozusagen wirklich einen Einfluß auf das Ereignis hat; also quasi einen erfahrungsmäßigen.

485. Die Rechtfertigung durch die Erfahrung hat ein Ende. Hätte sie keins, so wäre sie keine Rechtfertigung.

486. *Folgt*, daß dort ein Sessel steht, aus den Sinneseindrücken, die ich empfange? — Wie kann denn ein *Satz* aus Sinneseindrücken folgen? Nun, folgt er aus den Sätzen, die die Sinneseindrücke beschreiben? Nein. — Aber schließe ich denn nicht aus den Eindrücken, Sinnesdaten, daß ein Sessel dort steht? — Ich ziehe keinen Schluß! — Manchmal aber doch. Ich sehe z. B. eine Photographie und sage "Es muß also dort ein Sessel gestanden sein", oder auch "Aus dem, was man da sieht, schließe ich, daß ein Sessel dort steht". Das ist ein Schluß; aber keiner der Logik. Ein Schluß ist der Übergang zu einer Behauptung; also auch zu dem der Behauptung entsprechenden Benehmen. 'Ich ziehe die Konsequenzen' nicht nur in Worten, sondern auch in Handlungen.

War ich dazu berechtigt, diese Konsequenzen zu ziehen? Was *nennt* man hier eine Berechtigung? — Wie wird das Wort "Berechtigung" gebraucht? Beschreibe Sprachspiele! Aus ihnen wird sich auch die Wichtigkeit des Berechtigtseins entnehmen lassen.

487. "Ich verlasse das Zimmer, weil du es befiehlst."

"Ich verlasse das Zimmer, aber nicht, weil du es befiehlst."

For note: here reasons are not propositions which logically imply what is believed.

But it is not as if one can say: less is needed for belief than for knowledge. — For this is not a matter of approximating to logical consequence.

482. We are misled by this way of putting it: "This is a good reason, for it makes the occurrence of the event probable." That is as if we had said something further about the reason, something which justified it as a reason; whereas to say that this reason makes the occurrence probable is to say nothing except that this reason comes up to a particular standard of good reasons — but that the standard has no grounds!

483. A good reason is one that looks *like this*.

484. One would like to say: "It is a good reason only because it makes the occurrence *really* probable." Because it, so to speak, really has an influence on the event; as it were an empirical one.

485. Justification by experience comes to an end. If it did not, it would not be justification.

486. Does it *follow* from the sense impressions which I get that there is a chair over there? — How can a *proposition* follow from sense impressions? Well, does it follow from the propositions which describe the sense impressions? No. — But don't I infer that a chair is there from impressions, from sense-data? — I make no inference! — and yet I sometimes do. I see a photograph, for example, and say "So there must have been a chair over there", or again, "From what one can see here, I infer that there is a chair over there". That is an inference; but not one belonging to logic. An inference is a transition to an assertion; and so also to the behaviour that corresponds to the assertion. 'I draw the consequences' not only in words, but also in deeds. |137|

Was I justified in drawing these consequences? What is *called* a justification here? — How is the word "justification" used? Describe language-games! From these you will also be able to see the importance of being justified.

487. "I'm leaving the room because you tell me to."

"I'm leaving the room, but not because you tell me to."

Beschreibt dieser Satz einen Zusammenhang meiner Handlung mit seinem Befehl; oder macht er den Zusammenhang?

Kann man fragen: "Woher weißt du, daß du es deswegen tust, oder nicht deswegen tust?" Und ist die Antwort gar: "Ich fühle es"?

488. Wie beurteile ich, ob es so ist? Nach Indizien?

489. Frage dich: Bei welcher Gelegenheit, zu welchem Zweck, sagen wir das?

Welche Handlungsweisen begleiten diese Worte? (Denk ans Grüßen!) In welchen Szenen werden sie gebraucht; und wozu?

490. Wie weiß ich, daß *dieser Gedankengang* mich zu dieser Handlung geführt hat? — Nun, es ist ein bestimmtes Bild: z. B., in einer experimentellen Untersuchung durch eine Rechnung zu einem weitern Experiment geführt werden. Es sieht *so* aus —— und nun könnte ich ein Beispiel beschreiben.

491. Nicht: "ohne Sprache könnten wir uns nicht miteinander verständigen" — wohl aber: ohne Sprache können wir andre Menschen nicht so und so beeinflussen; können wir nicht Straßen und Maschinen bauen, etc. Und auch: Ohne den Gebrauch der Rede und der Schrift könnten sich Menschen nicht verständigen.

492. Eine Sprache erfinden, könnte heißen, auf Grund von Naturgesetzen (oder in Übereinstimmung mit ihnen) eine Vorrichtung zu bestimmtem Zweck erfinden; es hat aber auch den andern Sinn, dem analog, in welchem wir von der Erfindung eines Spiels reden.

Ich sage hier etwas über die Grammatik des Wortes "Sprache" aus, indem ich sie mit der Grammatik des Wortes "erfinden" in Verbindung bringe.

493. Man sagt: "Der Hahn ruft die Hühner durch sein Krähen herbei" — aber liegt dem nicht schon der Vergleich mit unsrer Sprache zu Grunde? — Wird der Aspekt nicht ganz verändert, wenn wir uns vorstellen, durch irgend eine physikalische Einwirkung setze das Krähen die Hühner in Bewegung?

Wenn aber gezeigt würde, in welcher Weise die Worte "Komm zu mir!" auf den Angesprochenen einwirken, so daß am Schluß unter gewissen Bedingungen seine Beinmuskeln innerviert werden, etc. — würde jener Satz damit für uns den Charakter des Satzes verlieren?

Does this sentence *describe* a connection between my action and his order; or does it make the connection?

Can one ask: "How do you know that you do it because of this, or not because of this?" And is the answer perhaps: "I feel it"?

488. How do I judge whether it is so? By circumstantial evidence?

489. Ask yourself: On what occasion, for what purpose, do we say this?

What kinds of action accompany these words? (Think of a greeting.) In what kinds of setting will they be used; and what for?

490. How do I know that *this train of thought* has led me to this action? — Well, it is a particular picture: for example, of a calculation leading to a further experiment in an experimental investigation. It looks like *this* —— and now I could describe an example.

491. Not: "without language we could not communicate with one another" — but for sure: without language we cannot influence other human beings in such-and-such ways; cannot build roads and machines, and so on. And also: without the use of speech and writing, human beings could not communicate.

492. To invent a language could mean to invent a device for a particular purpose on the basis of the laws of nature (or consistently with them); but it also has the other sense, analogous to that in which we speak of the invention of a game.

Here I am saying something about the grammar of the word "language", by connecting it with the grammar of the word "invent".

493. One says, "The cock calls the hens by crowing" — but isn't all this already based on a comparison with our language? — Don't we see all this quite differently if we imagine the crowing to set the hens in motion by some kind of physical causation?

But if it were shown how the words "Come to me" act on the person addressed so that, finally, given certain conditions, the muscles of his |138| legs are innervated, and so on — would that sentence thereby lose the character of a *sentence* for us?

494. Ich will sagen: Der Apparat unserer gewöhnlichen Sprache, unserer Wortsprache, ist *vor allem* das, was wir "Sprache" nennen; und dann anderes nach seiner Analogie oder Vergleichbarkeit mit ihr.

495. Es ist klar, ich kann durch Erfahrung feststellen, daß ein Mensch (oder Tier) auf ein Zeichen so reagiert, wie ich es will, auf ein anderes nicht. Daß z. B. ein Mensch auf das Zeichen "———▶" hin nach rechts, auf das Zeichen "◀———" nach links geht; daß er aber auf das Zeichen "0———|" nicht so reagiert, wie auf "◀———", etc.

Ja, ich brauche gar keinen Fall zu erdichten, und nur den tatsächlichen betrachten, daß ich einen Menschen, der nur Deutsch gelernt hat, nur mit der deutschen Sprache lenken kann. (Denn das Lernen der deutschen Sprache betrachte ich nun als ein Einstellen des Mechanismus auf eine gewisse Art der Beeinflussung; und es kann uns gleich sein, ob der Andre die Sprache gelernt hat, oder vielleicht schon von Geburt so gebaut ist, daß er auf die Sätze der deutschen Sprache so reagiert, wie der gewöhnliche Mensch, wenn er Deutsch gelernt hat.)

496. Grammatik sagt nicht, wie die Sprache gebaut sein muß, um ihren Zweck zu erfüllen, um so und so auf Menschen zu wirken. Sie beschreibt nur, aber erklärt in keiner Weise, den Gebrauch der Zeichen.

497. Man kann die Regeln der Grammatik "willkürlich" nennen, wenn damit gesagt sein soll, der *Zweck* der Grammatik sei nur der der Sprache.

Wenn Einer sagt "Hätte unsere Sprache nicht diese Grammatik, so könnte sie diese Tatsachen nicht ausdrücken" — so frage man sich, was hier das "*könnte*" bedeutet.

498. Wenn ich sage, der Befehl "Bring mir Zucker!" und "Bring mir Milch!" hat Sinn, aber nicht die Kombination "Milch mir Zucker", so heißt das nicht, daß das Aussprechen dieser Wortverbindung keine Wirkung hat. Und wenn sie nun die Wirkung hat, daß der Andre mich anstarrt und den Mund aufsperrt, so nenne ich sie deswegen nicht den Befehl, mich anzustarren etc., auch wenn ich gerade diese Wirkung hätte hervorbringen wollen.

499. Zu sagen "Diese Wortverbindung hat keinen Sinn" schließt sie aus dem Bereich der Sprache aus und umgrenzt dadurch das Gebiet der Sprache. Wenn man aber eine Grenze zieht, so kann das verschiedenerlei Gründe haben. Wenn ich einen Platz mit einem Zaun, einem Strich, oder sonst irgendwie umziehe, so kann das den Zweck haben, jemand nicht hinaus, oder nicht hinein zu lassen; es kann aber auch zu einem

494. I want to say: it is *above all* the apparatus of our ordinary language, of our word-language, that we call "language"; and then other things by analogy or comparability with it.

495. Clearly, I can establish by experience that a human being (or animal) reacts to one sign as I want him to, and to another not. That, for example, a human being goes to the right at the sign "——→" and goes to the left at the sign "←——"; but does not react to the sign " 0——|" as to "←——", and so on.

I don't even need to make up a case, I just have to consider what is actually so: namely, that I can direct a person who has learned only English, only by using English. (For here I am looking at learning English as adjusting a mechanism to respond to a certain kind of influence; and it may be all one to us whether someone has learned the language, or was perhaps from birth constituted to react to sentences in English like a normal person who has learned English.)

496. Grammar does not tell us how language must be constructed in order to fulfil its purpose, in order to have such-and-such an effect on human beings. It only describes, and in no way explains, the use of signs.

497. The rules of grammar may be called "arbitrary", if that is to mean that the *purpose* of grammar is nothing but that of language.

If someone says, "If our language had not this grammar, it could not express these facts" — it should be asked what "*could*" means here.

498. When I say that the orders "Bring me sugar!" and "Bring me milk!" have a sense, but not the combination "Milk me sugar", this does not mean that the utterance of this combination of words has no effect. And if its effect is that the other person stares at me and gapes, I don't on that account call it an order to stare at me and gape, even if that was precisely the effect that I wanted to produce.

499. To say "This combination of words has no sense" excludes it from the sphere of language, and thereby bounds the domain of language. But when one draws a boundary, it may be for various kinds of reason. If I surround an area with a fence or a line or otherwise, the purpose may be to prevent someone from getting in or out; |139| but it

Spiel gehören und die Grenze soll etwa von den Spielern übersprungen werden; oder es kann andeuten, wo der Besitz eines Menschen aufhört und der des andern anfängt; etc. Ziehe ich also eine Grenze, so ist damit noch nicht gesagt, weshalb ich sie ziehe.

500. Wenn gesagt wird, ein Satz sei sinnlos, so ist nicht, quasi, sein Sinn sinnlos. Sondern eine Wortverbindung wird aus der Sprache ausgeschlossen, aus dem Verkehr gezogen.

501. "Der Zweck der Sprache ist, Gedanken auszudrücken." — So ist es wohl der Zweck jedes Satzes, einen Gedanken auszudrücken. Welchen Gedanken drückt also z. B. der Satz "Es regnet" aus? —

502. Die Frage nach dem Sinn. Vergleiche:
    "Dieser Satz hat Sinn." — "Welchen?"
    "Diese Wortreihe ist ein Satz." — "Welcher?"

503. Wenn ich jemandem einen Befehl gebe, so ist es mir *ganz genug*, ihm Zeichen zu geben. Und ich würde nie sagen: Das sind ja nur Worte, und ich muß hinter die Worte dringen. Ebenso, wenn ich jemand etwas gefragt hätte und er gibt mir eine Antwort (also ein Zeichen) bin ich zufrieden — das war es, was ich erwartete — und wende nicht ein: Das ist ja eine bloße Antwort.

504. Wenn man aber sagt: "Wie soll ich wissen, was er meint, ich sehe ja nur seine Zeichen", so sage ich: "Wie soll *er* wissen, was er meint, er hat ja auch nur seine Zeichen."

505. Muß ich einen Befehl verstehen, ehe ich nach ihm handeln kann? — Gewiß! sonst wüßtest du ja nicht, was du zu tun hast. — Aber vom *Wissen* zum Tun ist ja wieder ein Sprung! —

506. Der Zerstreute, der auf den Befehl "Rechts um!" sich nach links dreht, und nun, an die Stirn greifend, sagt "Ach so — rechts um" und rechts um macht. — Was ist ihm eingefallen? Eine Deutung?

507. "Ich sage das nicht nur, ich meine auch etwas damit." — Wenn man sich überlegt, was dabei in uns vorgeht, wenn wir Worte *meinen* (und nicht nur sagen) so ist es uns, als wäre dann etwas mit diesen Worten gekuppelt, während sie sonst leerliefen. — Als ob sie gleichsam in uns eingriffen.

may also be part of a game and the players are supposed, say, to jump over the boundary; or it may show where the property of one person ends and that of another begins; and so on. So if I draw a boundary-line, that is not yet to say what I am drawing it for.

500. When a sentence is called senseless, it is not, as it were, its sense that is senseless. Rather, a combination of words is being excluded from the language, withdrawn from circulation.

501. "The purpose of language is to express thoughts." — So presumably the purpose of every sentence is to express a thought. Then what thought is expressed, for example, by the sentence "It's raining"? —

502. Asking what the sense is. Compare:
    "This sentence has a sense." — "What sense?"
    "This sequence of words is a sentence." — "What sentence?"

503. If I give anyone an order, I feel it to be *quite enough* to give him signs. And I'd never say: these are just words, and I've got to get behind the words. Equally, when I've asked someone something, and he gives me an answer (that is, a sign), I am content — that's what I expected — and I don't object: but that's a mere answer.

504. But if someone says, "How am I to know what he means — I see only his signs?", then I say, "How is *he* to know what he means, he too has only his signs?"

505. Must I understand an order before I can act on it? — Certainly, otherwise you wouldn't know what you had to do! — But from *knowing* to doing is surely a further step! —

506. The absent-minded man who at the order "Right turn!" turns left, and then, clutching his forehead, says "Oh! right turn", and does a right turn. — What has struck him? An interpretation?

507. "I am not merely saying this, I mean something by it." — When one considers what is going on in us when we *mean* (and don't merely say) words, it seems to us as if there were something coupled to these words, which otherwise would run idle. — As if they, so to speak, engaged with something in us.

508. Ich sage einen Satz: "Das Wetter ist schön"; aber die Worte sind doch willkürliche Zeichen — setzen wir also an ihrer Statt diese: "a b c d". Aber nun kann ich, wenn ich dies lese, mit ihm nicht ohne Weiteres den obigen Sinn verbinden. — Ich bin nicht gewöhnt, könnte ich sagen, statt "das" "a", statt "Wetter" "b" zu sagen, etc. Aber damit meine ich nicht, ich sei nicht gewöhnt, mit "a" sofort das Wort "das" zu assoziieren, sondern ich bin nicht gewöhnt, "a" *an der Stelle* von "das" zu gebrauchen — also in der Bedeutung von "das". (Ich beherrsche diese Sprache nicht.)

(Ich bin nicht gewöhnt, Temperaturen in Fahrenheit-Graden zu messen. Darum 'sagt' mir eine solche Temperaturangabe nichts.)

509. Wie, wenn wir jemanden fragten "Inwiefern sind diese Worte eine Beschreibung dessen, was du siehst?" — und er antwortet: "Ich *meine* das mit diesen Worten." (Er sah etwa auf eine Landschaft.) Warum ist diese Antwort "Ich *meine* das . . ." gar keine Antwort?

Wie *meint* man, was man vor sich sieht, mit Worten?

Denke, ich sagte "a b c d" und meine damit: Das Wetter ist schön. Ich hatte nämlich beim Aussprechen dieser Zeichen das Erlebnis, welches normalerweise nur der hätte, der jahraus jahrein "a" in der Bedeutung von "das", "b" in der Bedeutung von "Wetter", u. s. w., gebraucht hat. — Sagt dann "a b c d": das Wetter ist schön?

Welches soll das Kriterium dafür sein, daß ich *dies* Erlebnis hatte?

510. Mach diesen Versuch: *Sag* "Hier ist es kalt" und *meine* "Hier ist es warm". Kannst du es? — Und was tust du dabei? Und gibt es nur eine Art, das zu tun?

511. Was heißt es denn: "entdecken, daß eine Aussage keinen Sinn hat"? — Und was heißt das: "Wenn ich etwas damit meine, muß es doch Sinn haben"? — Wenn ich etwas damit meine? — Wenn ich *was* damit meine?! — Man will sagen: der sinnvolle Satz ist der, den man nicht nur sagen, sondern den man auch denken kann.

512. Es scheint, als könnte man sagen: "Die Wortsprache läßt unsinnige Wortzusammenstellungen zu, die Sprache der Vorstellung aber nicht unsinnige Vorstellungen." — Also die Sprache der Zeichnung auch nicht unsinnige Zeichnungen? Denke, es wären Zeichnungen, nach denen Körper modelliert werden sollen. Dann haben manche Zeichnungen Sinn, manche keinen. — Wie, wenn ich mir unsinnige Wortzusammenstellungen vorstelle?

508. I utter the sentence "The weather is fine"; but the words are, after all, arbitrary signs — so let's put "a b c d" in their place. But now, when I read this, I can't connect it, without more ado, with the above sense. |140| I am not used, I might say, to saying "a" instead of "the", "b" instead of "weather", and so on. But I don't mean by this that I am not used to making an immediate association between the word "the" and "a"; rather, that I am not used to using "a" *in the place* of "the" — and therefore in the sense of "the". (I don't know this language.)

(I am not used to Fahrenheit measures of temperature. That's why such a specification of temperature '*says*' nothing to me.)

509. What if we asked someone, "In what sense are these words a description of what you see?" — and he answers: "I *mean* this by these words." (Perhaps he was looking at a landscape.) Why is this answer "I *mean* this . . ." no answer at all?

How does one *mean*, with words, what one sees before one?

Suppose I said "a b c d" and meant thereby: the weather is fine. For as I uttered these signs, I had the experience normally had only by someone who, year in, year out, used "a" in the sense of "the", "b" in the sense of "weather", and so on. — Does "a b c d" now say: the weather is fine?

What should be the criterion for my having had *that* experience?

510. Try to do the following: *say* "It's cold here", and *mean* "It's warm here". Can you do it? — And what are you doing as you do it? And is there only one way of doing it?

511. What does "discovering that an utterance doesn't make sense" mean? — And what does it mean to say, "If I mean something by it, surely it must make sense"? — If I mean something by it? — If I mean *what* by it?! — One wants to say: a sentence that makes sense is one which one can not merely say, but also think.

512. It looks as if one could say: "Word-language allows of nonsensical combinations of words, but the language of imagining does not allow us to imagine anything nonsensical." — Hence, too, the language of drawing doesn't allow nonsensical drawings? Suppose they were drawings from which bodies were to be modelled. In this case, some drawings make sense, some not. — What if I imagine nonsensical combinations of words?

513. Betrachte diese Ausdrucksform: "Mein Buch hat soviel Seiten, wie eine Lösung der Gleichung $x^3 + 2x - 3 = 0$ beträgt." Oder: "Die Zahl meiner Freunde ist n und $n^2 + 2n + 2 = 0$." Hat dieser Satz Sinn? Es ist ihm unmittelbar nicht anzukennen. Man sieht an diesem Beispiel, wie es zugehen kann, daß etwas aussieht, wie ein Satz, den wir verstehen, was doch keinen Sinn ergibt.

(Dies wirft ein Licht auf den Begriff 'Verstehen' und 'Meinen'.)

514. Ein Philosoph sagt: er verstehe den Satz "Ich bin hier", meine etwas mit ihm, denke etwas, — auch wenn er sich gar nicht darauf besinnt, wie, bei welcher Gelegenheit, dieser Satz verwendet wird. Und wenn ich sage "Die Rose ist auch im Finstern rot", so siehst du diese Röte im Finstern förmlich vor dir.

515. Zwei Bilder der Rose im Finstern. Das eine ist ganz schwarz; denn die Rose ist unsichtbar. Im andern ist sie in allen Einzelheiten gemalt und von Schwärze umgeben. Ist eines von ihnen richtig, das andere falsch? Reden wir nicht von einer weißen Rose im Finstern und von einer roten Rose im Finstern? Und sagen wir nicht doch, sie ließen sich im Finstern nicht unterscheiden?

516. Es scheint klar: wir verstehen, was die Frage bedeutet "Kommt die Ziffernfolge 7777 in der Entwicklung von π vor?" Es ist ein deutscher Satz; man kann zeigen, was es heißt, 415 komme in der Entwicklung von π vor; und ähnliches. Nun, soweit solche Erklärungen reichen, soweit, kann man sagen, versteht man jene Frage.

517. Es fragt sich: Können wir uns denn darin nicht irren, daß wir eine Frage verstehen?

Denn mancher mathematische Beweis führt uns eben dazu, zu sagen, daß wir uns *nicht* vorstellen können, was wir glaubten, uns vorstellen zu können. (Z. B. die Konstruktion des Siebenecks.) Er führt uns dazu, zu revidieren, was uns als der Bereich des Vorstellbaren galt.

518. Sokrates zu Theaitetos: "Und wer vorstellt, sollte nicht *etwas* vorstellen?" — Th.: "Notwendig." — Sok.: "Und wer etwas vorstellt, nichts Wirkliches?" — Th.: "So scheint es."

Und wer malt, sollte nicht etwas malen — und wer etwas malt, nichts Wirkliches? — Ja, was ist das Objekt des Malens: das Menschenbild (z. B.) oder der Mensch, den das Bild darstellt?

513. Consider the following form of expression: "The number of pages in my book is equal to a solution of the equation $x^3 + 2x - 3 = 0$." Or: "The number of my friends is n, and $n^2 + 2n + 2 = 0$." Does this sentence make sense? This cannot be seen immediately. From this example |141| one can see how it can come about that something looks like a sentence which we understand, and yet makes no sense.

(This throws light on the concepts of understanding and of meaning something.)

514. A philosopher says that he understands the sentence "I am here", that he means something by it, thinks something — even though he doesn't call to mind in the least how, on what occasions, this sentence is used. And if I say "A rose is red in the dark too", you virtually see this red in the dark before you.

515. Two pictures of a rose in the dark. One is quite black; for the rose is not visible. In the other, it is painted in full detail and surrounded by black. Is one of them right, the other wrong? Don't we talk of a white rose in the dark and of a red rose in the dark? And don't we nevertheless say that they can't be distinguished in the dark?

516. It seems clear that we understand the meaning of the question "Does the sequence 7777 occur in the development of π?" It is an English sentence; it can be shown what it means for 415 to occur in the development of π; and similar things. Well, our understanding of that question reaches just so far, one may say, as such explanations reach.

517. The question arises: Can't we be mistaken in thinking that we understand a question?

For some mathematical proofs do lead us to say that we *cannot* imagine something which we believed we could imagine. (For example, the construction of a heptagon.) They lead us to revise what counts as the domain of the imaginable.

* 518. Socrates to Theaetetus: "And if someone imagines, mustn't he imagine *something*?" — Th.: "Yes, he must." — Soc.: "And if he imagines something, mustn't it be something real?" — Th.: "Apparently."

And mustn't someone who is painting be painting something — and someone who is painting something be painting something real? — Well, tell me what the object of painting is: the picture of the man (for example), or the man whom the picture portrays?

519. Man will sagen: ein Befehl sei ein Bild der Handlung, die nach ihm ausgeführt wurde; aber auch, ein Bild der Handlung, die nach ihm ausgeführt werden *soll*.

520. "Wenn man auch den Satz als Bild eines möglichen Sachverhalts auffaßt und sagt, er zeige die Möglichkeit des Sachverhalts, so kann doch der Satz bestenfalls tun, was ein gemaltes, oder plastisches Bild, oder ein Film, tut; und er kann also jedenfalls nicht hinstellen, was nicht der Fall ist. Also hängt es ganz von unserer Grammatik ab, was (logisch) möglich genannt wird, und was nicht, — nämlich eben was sie zuläßt?" — Aber das ist doch willkürlich! — Ist es willkürlich? — Nicht mit jeder satzartigen Bildung wissen wir etwas anzufangen, nicht jede Technik hat eine Verwendung in unserm Leben, und wenn wir in der Philosophie versucht sind, etwas ganz Unnützes unter die Sätze zu zählen, so geschieht es oft, weil wir uns seine Anwendung nicht genügend überlegt haben.

521. Vergleiche 'logisch möglich' mit 'chemisch möglich'. Chemisch möglich könnte man etwa eine Verbindung nennen, für die es eine Strukturformel mit den richtigen Valenzen gibt (etwa H-O-O-O-H). Eine solche Verbindung muß natürlich nicht existieren; aber auch einer Formel HO_2 kann nicht weniger in der Wirklichkeit entsprechen, als keine Verbindung.

522. Wenn wir den Satz mit einem Bild vergleichen, so müssen wir bedenken, ob mit einem Porträt (einer historischen Darstellung) oder mit einem Genrebild. Und beide Vergleiche haben Sinn.

Wenn ich ein Genrebild anschaue, so 'sagt' es mir etwas, auch wenn ich keinen Augenblick glaube (mir einbilde), die Menschen, die ich darin sehe, seien wirklich, oder es habe wirkliche Menschen in dieser Situation gegeben. Denn wie, wenn ich fragte: "*Was* sagt es mir denn?"

523. "Das Bild sagt mir sich selbst" — möchte ich sagen. D. h., daß es mir etwas sagt, besteht in seiner eigenen Struktur, in *seinen* Formen und Farben. (Was hieße es, wenn man sagte "Das musikalische Thema sagt mir sich selbst"?)

524. Sieh es nicht als selbstverständlich an, sondern als ein merkwürdiges Faktum, daß uns Bilder und erdichtete Erzählungen Vergnügen bereiten; unsern Geist beschäftigen.

("Sieh es nicht als selbstverständlich an" — das heißt: Wundere dich darüber so, wie über anderes, was dich beunruhigt. Dann wird das Problematische verschwinden, indem du die eine Tatsache so wie die andere hinnimmst.)

519. One wants to say that an order is a picture of the action that was carried out on the order; but also that it is a picture of the action that *is to be* carried out on the order.

520. "Even if one conceives of a proposition as a picture of a possible state of affairs, and says that it shows the possibility of the state of affairs, |142| still, the most that a proposition can do is what a painting or relief or film does; and so it can, at any rate, not present what is not the case. So does what is, and what is not, called (logically) possible depend wholly on our grammar — that is, on what it permits?" — But surely that is arbitrary! — Is it arbitrary? — It is not every sentence-like formation that we know how to do something with, not every technique that has a use in our life; and when we are tempted in philosophy to count something quite useless as a proposition, that is often because we have not reflected sufficiently on its application.

521. Compare 'logically possible' with 'chemically possible'. One might perhaps call a combination chemically possible if a formula with the right valencies existed (e.g. H - O - O - O - H). Of course, such a combination need not exist; but even the formula HO_2 cannot have less than no combination corresponding to it in reality.

522. If we compare a proposition to a picture, we must consider whether we are comparing it to a portrait (a historical representation) or to a genre-picture. And both comparisons make sense.

When I look at a genre-picture, it 'tells' me something, even though I don't believe (imagine) for a moment that the people I see in it really exist, or that there have really been people in that situation. For suppose I ask, "*What* does it tell me, then?"

523. "A picture tells me itself" is what I'd like to say. That is, its telling me something consists in its own structure, in *its* own forms and colours. (What would it mean to say "A musical theme tells me itself"?)

524. Don't take it as a matter of course, but as a remarkable fact, that pictures and fictitious narratives give us pleasure, absorb us.

("Don't take it as a matter of course" — that means: puzzle over this, as you do over some other things which disturb you. Then what is problematic will disappear, by your accepting the one fact as you do the other.)

((Übergang von einem offenkundigen zu einem nichtoffenkundigen Unsinn.))

525. "Nachdem er das gesagt hatte, verließ er sie wie am vorigen Tage." — Verstehe ich diesen Satz? Verstehe ich ihn ebenso, wie ich es täte, wenn ich ihn im Verlaufe einer Mitteilung hörte? Steht er isoliert da, so würde ich sagen, ich weiß nicht, wovon er handelt. Ich wüßte aber doch, wie man diesen Satz etwa gebrauchen könnte; ich könnte selbst einen Zusammenhang für ihn erfinden.

(Eine Menge wohlbekannter Pfade führen von diesen Worten aus in alle Richtungen.)

526. Was heißt es, ein Bild, eine Zeichnung zu verstehen? Auch da gibt es Verstehen und Nichtverstehen. Und auch da können diese Ausdrücke verschiedenerlei bedeuten. Das Bild ist etwa ein Stilleben; einen Teil davon aber verstehe ich nicht: ich bin nicht fähig, dort Körper zu sehen, sondern sehe nur Farbflecke auf der Leinwand. — Oder ich sehe alles körperlich, aber es sind Gegenstände, die ich nicht kenne (sie schauen aus wie Geräte, aber ich kenne ihren Gebrauch nicht). — Vielleicht aber kenne ich die Gegenstände, verstehe aber, in anderem Sinne — ihre Anordnung nicht.

527. Das Verstehen eines Satzes der Sprache ist dem Verstehen eines Themas in der Musik viel verwandter, als man etwa glaubt. Ich meine es aber so: daß das Verstehen des sprachlichen Satzes näher, als man denkt, dem liegt, was man gewöhnlich Verstehen des musikalischen Themas nennt. Warum sollen sich Stärke und Tempo gerade in *dieser* Linie bewegen? Man möchte sagen: "weil ich weiß, was das alles heißt." Aber was heißt es? Ich wüßte es nicht zu sagen. Zur 'Erklärung' könnte ich es mit etwas anderem vergleichen, was denselben Rhythmus (ich meine, dieselbe Linie) hat. (Man sagt: "Siehst du nicht, das ist, als würde eine Schlußfolgerung gezogen" oder: "Das ist gleichsam eine Parenthese", etc. Wie begründet man solche Vergleiche? — Da gibt es sehr verschiedenartige Begründungen.)

528. Man könnte sich Menschen denken, die etwas einer Sprache nicht ganz Unähnliches besäßen: Lautgebärden, ohne Wortschatz oder Grammatik. ('Mit Zungen reden'.)

529. "Was wäre aber hier die Bedeutung der Laute?" — Was ist sie in der Musik? Wenn ich auch gar nicht sagen will, daß diese Sprache der klanglichen Gebärden mit Musik verglichen werden müßte.

*   ((The transition from obvious nonsense to something which is unobvious nonsense.))

525. "After he had said this, he left her as he did the day before." — Do I understand this sentence? Do I understand it just as I would if I heard it in the course of a report? If it stood alone, |143| I'd say I don't know what it's about. But all the same, I'd know how this sentence might perhaps be used; I could even invent a context for it.

(A multitude of familiar paths lead off from these words in all directions.)

526. What does it mean to understand a picture, a drawing? Here too there is understanding and not understanding. And here too these expressions may mean various kinds of thing. The picture is, say, a still-life; but I don't understand one part of it: I cannot see solid objects there, but only patches of colour on the canvas. — Or I see all the objects, but I am not familiar with them (they look like implements, but I don't know their use). — Perhaps, however, I know the objects, but, in another sense, do not understand the way they are arranged.

527. Understanding a sentence in language is much more akin to understanding a theme in music than one may think. What I mean is that understanding a spoken sentence is closer than one thinks to what is ordinarily called understanding a musical theme. Why is just *this* the pattern of variation in intensity and tempo? One would like to say: "Because I know what it all means." But what does it mean? I'd not be able to say. As an 'explanation', I could compare it with something else which has the same rhythm (I mean the same pattern). (One says, "Don't you see, this is as if a conclusion were being drawn" or "This is, as it were, a parenthesis", and so on. How does one justify such comparisons? — There are very different kinds of justification here.)

528. One might imagine people who had something not altogether unlike a language: vocal gestures, without vocabulary or grammar. ('Speaking with tongues'.)

529. "But what would the meaning of the sounds be in such a case?" — What is it in music? Though I don't at all wish to say that this language of vocal gestures would have to be compared to music.

530. Es könnte auch eine Sprache geben, in deren Verwendung die 'Seele' der Worte keine Rolle spielt. In der uns z. B. nichts daran liegt, ein Wort durch ein beliebig erfundenes neues zu ersetzen.

531. Wir reden vom Verstehen eines Satzes in dem Sinne, in welchem er durch einen andern ersetzt werden kann, der das Gleiche sagt; aber auch in dem Sinne, in welchem er durch keinen andern ersetzt werden kann. (So wenig, wie ein musikalisches Thema durch ein anderes.)

Im einen Fall ist der Gedanke des Satzes, was verschiedenen Sätzen gemeinsam ist; im andern, etwas, was nur diese Worte, in diesen Stellungen, ausdrücken. (Verstehen eines Gedichts.)

532. So hat also "verstehen" hier zwei verschiedene Bedeutungen? — Ich will lieber sagen, diese Gebrauchsarten von "verstehen" bilden seine Bedeutung, meinen *Begriff* des Verstehens.

Denn ich *will* "verstehen" auf alles das anwenden.

533. Wie kann man aber in jenem zweiten Falle den Ausdruck erklären, das Verständnis übermitteln? Frage dich: Wie *führt* man jemand zum Verständnis eines Gedichts, oder eines Themas? Die Antwort darauf sagt, wie man hier den Sinn erklärt.

534. Ein Wort in dieser Bedeutung *hören*. Wie seltsam, daß es so etwas gibt!

So phrasiert, so betont, so gehört, ist der Satz der Anfang eines Übergangs zu *diesen* Sätzen, Bildern, Handlungen.

((Eine Menge wohlbekannter Pfade führen von diesen Worten aus in alle Richtungen.))

535. Was geschieht, wenn wir lernen, den Schluß einer Kirchentonart als Schluß zu *empfinden*?

536. Ich sage: "Dieses Gesicht (das den Eindruck der Furchtsamkeit macht) kann ich mir auch als ein mutiges denken." Damit meinen wir nicht, daß ich mir vorstellen kann, wie jemand mit diesem Gesicht etwa einem Andern das Leben retten kann (das kann man sich natürlich zu jedem Gesicht vorstellen). Ich rede vielmehr von einem Aspekt des Gesichtes selbst. Was ich meine, ist auch nicht, ich könne mir vorstellen, daß dieser Mensch sein Gesicht in ein mutiges, im gewöhn-lichen Sinn, verändern kann; wohl aber, daß es auf ganz bestimmtem Wege in ein solches übergehen kann. Die Umdeutung eines

530. There might also be a language in whose use the 'soul' of the words played no part. In which, for example, we had no objection to replacing one word by a new, arbitrarily invented one.

531. We speak of understanding a sentence in the sense in which it can be replaced by another which says the same; but also in the sense |144| in which it cannot be replaced by any other. (Any more than one musical theme can be replaced by another.)
    In the one case, the thought in the sentence is what is common to different sentences; in the other, something that is expressed only by these words in these positions. (Understanding a poem.)

532. Then has "understanding" two different meanings here? — I would rather say that these kinds of use of "understanding" make up its meaning, make up my *concept* of understanding.
    For I *want* to apply the word "understanding" to all this.

533. But in the second case, how can one explain the expression, communicate what one understands? Ask yourself: How does one *lead* someone to understand a poem or a theme? The answer to this tells us how one explains the sense here.

534. *Hearing* a word as having this meaning. How curious that there should be such a thing!
    Phrased like *this*, emphasized like this, heard in this way, this sentence is the beginning of a transition to *these* sentences, pictures, actions.
*   ((A multitude of familiar paths lead off from these words in all directions.))

535. What happens when we learn to *feel* the ending of a church mode as an ending?

536. I say: "I can think of this face (which gives an impression of timidity) as courageous too." We do not mean by this that I can imagine someone with this face perhaps saving someone's life (that, of course, is imaginable in connection with any face). I am speaking, rather, of an aspect of the face itself. Nor do I mean that I can imagine that this man's face might change so that it looked courageous in the ordinary sense, though I may very well mean that there is a quite definite way in which it can turn into a courageous face. The reinterpretation of a

Gesichtsausdrucks ist zu vergleichen der Umdeutung eines Akkords in der Musik, wenn wir ihn einmal als Überleitung in diese, einmal in jene Tonart empfinden.

537. Man kann sagen "Ich lese die Furchtsamkeit in diesem Gesicht", aber jedenfalls scheint mit dem Gesicht Furchtsamkeit nicht bloß assoziiert, äußerlich verbunden; sondern die Furcht lebt in den Gesichtszügen. Wenn sich die Züge ein wenig ändern, so können wir von einer entsprechenden Änderung der Furcht reden. Würden wir gefragt: "Kannst du dir dieses Gesicht auch als Ausdruck des Mutes denken?" — so wüßten wir, gleichsam, nicht, wie wir den Mut in diesen Zügen unterbringen sollten. Ich sage dann etwa: "Ich weiß nicht was das hieße, wenn dieses Gesicht ein mutiges Gesicht ist." Aber wie sieht die Lösung so einer Frage aus? Man sagt etwa: "Ja, jetzt versteh ich es: das Gesicht ist sozusagen gleichgültig gegen die Außenwelt." Wir haben also Mut hineingedeutet. Der Mut, könnte man sagen, *paßt* jetzt wieder auf das Gesicht. Aber *was* paßt hier *worauf*?

538. Es ist ein verwandter Fall (obwohl es vielleicht nicht so scheinen möchte) wenn wir uns z. B. darüber wundern, daß im Französischen das prädikative Adjektiv mit dem Substantiv im Geschlecht übereinstimmt, und wenn wir uns dies so erklären: Sie meinen "der Mensch ist *ein guter*".

539. Ich sehe ein Bild, das einen lächelnden Kopf darstellt. Was tue ich, wenn ich das Lächeln einmal als ein freundliches, einmal als ein böses auffasse? Stelle ich es mir nicht oft in einer räumlichen und zeitlichen Umgebung vor, die freundlich oder böse ist? So könnte ich mir zu dem Bild vorstellen, daß der Lächelnde auf ein spielendes Kind herunterlächelt, oder aber auf das Leiden eines Feindes.

Daran wird nichts geändert dadurch, daß ich mir auch die auf den ersten Blick liebliche Situation durch eine weitere Umgebung wieder anders deuten kann. — Ein gewisses Lächeln werde ich, wenn keine besondern Umstände meine Deutung umstellen, als freundliches auffassen, ein "freundliches" nennen, entsprechend reagieren.

((Wahrscheinlichkeit, Häufigkeit.))

540. "Ist es nicht eigentümlich, daß ich nicht soll denken können, es werde bald aufhören zu regnen, — auch ohne die Institution der Sprache und ihre ganze Umgebung?" — Willst du sagen, es ist seltsam, daß du dir diese Worte nicht solltest sagen können und sie *meinen* ohne jene Umgebung?

facial expression can be compared to the reinterpretation of a chord in music, when we hear it as a modulation first into this, then into that, key.

* 537. It is possible to say "I read timidity in this face", but, at any rate, the timidity does not seem to be merely associated, outwardly connected, with the face; rather, fear is there, alive, in the features. If the features change slightly, we can speak of a corresponding change in the |145| fear. If we were asked, "Can you think of this face as an expression of courage too?" — we should, as it were, not know how to lodge courage in these features. Then perhaps I say, "I don't know what it would mean if this is a courageous face." But what would an answer to such a question be like? Perhaps one says: "Yes, now I understand: the face is, as it were, indifferent to the outer world." So we have somehow read courage into the face. Now once more, one might say, courage *fits* this face. But *what* fits *what* here?

538. There is a related case (though perhaps it will not seem so) when, for example, we Germans are surprised that in French the predicative adjective agrees with the substantive in gender, and when we explain it to ourselves by saying: they mean "der Mensch ist *ein guter*".

539. I see a picture which represents a smiling face. What do I do if I take the smile now as a kind one, now as malicious? Don't I often imagine it with a spatial and temporal context of kindness or malice? Thus I might, when looking at the picture, imagine it to be of a smiler smiling down on a child at play, or again on the suffering of an enemy.

This is in no way altered by the fact that I can also take the apparently genial situation and interpret it differently by putting it into a wider context. — If no special circumstances reverse my interpretation, I shall conceive a particular smile as kind, call it a "kind" one, react accordingly.

((Probability, frequency.))

540. "Isn't it very peculiar that, without the institution of language and all its surroundings, I shouldn't be able to think that it will soon stop raining?" — Do you want to say that it is strange that you should be unable to say these words to yourself and *mean* them without those surroundings?

Nimm an, jemand rufe, auf den Himmel weisend, eine Reihe unverständlicher Worte aus. Da wir ihn fragen, was er meint, sagt er, das heiße "Gottlob, es wird bald aufhören zu regnen". Ja, er erklärt uns auch, was die einzelnen Wörter bedeuten. — Ich nehme an, er käme gleichsam plötzlich zu sich und sagte: jener Satz sei völliger Unsinn gewesen, sei ihm aber, als er ihn aussprach, als Satz einer ihm geläufigen Sprache erschienen. (Ja sogar wie ein wohlbekanntes Zitat.) — Was soll ich nun sagen? Hat er diesen Satz nicht verstanden, als er ihn sagte? Trug der Satz nicht seine ganze Bedeutung in sich?

541. Aber worin lag jenes Verstehen und die Bedeutung? Er sprach die Lautreihen etwa in erfreutem Tone, indem er auf den Himmel zeigte, während es noch regnete, aber schon lichter wurde; *später* machte er eine Verbindung seiner Worte mit den deutschen Worten.

542. "Aber seine Worte fühlten sich für ihn eben wie die Worte einer ihm wohlbekannten Sprache an." — Ja; ein Kriterium dafür ist, daß er *dies* später sagte. Und nun sag *ja* nicht: "Die Wörter einer uns geläufigen Sprache fühlen sich eben in ganz bestimmter Weise an." (Was ist der *Ausdruck* dieses Gefühls?)

543. Kann ich nicht sagen: der Schrei, das Lachen, seien voll von Bedeutung?
    Und das heißt ungefähr: Es ließe sich viel aus ihnen ablesen.

544. Wenn die Sehnsucht aus mir spricht "Wenn er doch nur käme!", gibt das Gefühl den Worten 'Bedeutung'. Gibt es aber den einzelnen Worten ihre Bedeutungen?
    Man könnte hier aber auch sagen: das Gefühl gebe den Worten *Wahrheit*. Und da siehst du, wie hier die Begriffe ineinander fließen. (Dies erinnert an die Frage: Was ist der *Sinn* eines mathematischen Satzes?)

545. Wenn man aber sagt "Ich *hoffe*, er wird kommen" — gibt das Gefühl nicht dem Worte "hoffen" seine Bedeutung? (Und wie ist es mit dem Satz "Ich hoffe *nicht* mehr, daß er kommen wird"?) Das Gefühl gibt dem Worte "hoffen" vielleicht seinen besondern Klang; d. h., es hat seinen Ausdruck im Klang. — Wenn das Gefühl dem Wort seine Bedeutung gibt, so heißt "Bedeutung" hier: *das, worauf es ankommt*. Warum aber kommt es aufs Gefühl an?
    Ist die Hoffnung ein Gefühl? (Kennzeichen.)

546. So, möchte ich sagen, sind die Worte "Möchte er doch kommen!" mit meinem Wunsche geladen. Und Worte können sich uns entringen, — wie ein Schrei. Worte können *schwer* auszusprechen sein: solche z. B.,

Suppose someone were to point at the sky and come out with a number of unintelligible words. When we ask him what he means, he explains that the words mean "Thank heaven it'll soon stop raining". He even explains to us what the individual words mean. — I am assuming that he will, as it were, suddenly come to himself and say that the sentence was complete nonsense, but that when he uttered it, it had seemed to him like a sentence in a language he knew (perhaps even |146| like a familiar quotation.) — What am I to say now? Didn't he understand the sentence as he was saying it? Wasn't the whole meaning there in the sentence?

541. But what did this understanding, and the meaning, consist in? He uttered the sounds in a cheerful voice perhaps, pointing to the sky while it was still raining but was already beginning to clear up; *later* he made a connection between his words and the English words.

542. "But the point is, the words felt to him like the words of a language he knew well." — Yes; a criterion for it is his later saying just *that*. And now *don't* say: "The feel of the words in a language we know is of a quite particular kind." (What is the *expression* of this feeling?)

543. Can't I say: a cry, a laugh, are full of meaning?
And that means, roughly: much can be gathered from them.

544. When longing makes me exclaim "Oh, if only he'd come!", the feeling gives the words 'meaning'. But does it give the individual words their meanings?
But here one could also say that the feeling gave the words *truth*. And now you see how the concepts here shade into one another. (This recalls the question: what is the *sense* of a mathematical proposition?)

545. But when one says "I *hope* he'll come" — doesn't the feeling give the word "hope" its meaning? (And what about the sentence "I *no* longer hope he'll come"?) The feeling does perhaps give the word "hope" its special ring; that is, it is expressed in that ring. — If the feeling gives the word its meaning, then here "meaning" amounts to: *that which matters*. But why is the feeling what matters?
Is hope a feeling? (Characteristic marks.)

546. In this way, I'd like to say, the words "Oh, if only he'd come!" are charged with my longing. And words can be wrung from us — like

mit denen man auf etwas Verzicht leistet, oder eine Schwäche eingesteht. (Worte sind auch Taten.)

547. Verneinen: eine 'geistige Tätigkeit'. Verneine etwas, und beobachte, was du tust! — Schüttelst du etwa innerlich den Kopf? Und wenn es so ist — ist dieser Vorgang nun unseres Interesses würdiger, als der etwa, ein Verneinungszeichen in einen Satz zu schreiben? Kennst du jetzt das *Wesen* der Negation?

548. Was ist der Unterschied zwischen den beiden Vorgängen: Wünschen, daß etwas geschehe — und wünschen, daß dasselbe *nicht* geschehe?

Will man es bildlich darstellen, so wird man mit dem Bild des Ereignisses verschiedenes vornehmen: es durchstreichen, es abzäunen, und dergleichen. Aber das, kommt uns vor, ist eine *rohe* Methode des Ausdrucks. In der Wortsprache gar verwenden wir das Zeichen "nicht". Dies ist wie ein ungeschickter Behelf. Man meint: im *Denken* geschieht es schon anders.

549. "Wie kann das Wort 'nicht' verneinen?!" — "Das Zeichen 'nicht' deutet an, du sollst, was folgt, negativ auffassen." Man möchte sagen: Das Zeichen der Verneinung ist eine Veranlassung, etwas — möglicherweise sehr Kompliziertes — zu tun. Es ist, als veranlaßte uns das Zeichen der Negation zu etwas. Aber wozu? Das wird nicht gesagt. Es ist, als brauchte es nur angedeutet werden; als wüßten wir es schon. Als sei eine Erklärung unnötig, da wir die Sache ohnehin schon kennen.

a) "Daß drei Verneinungen wieder eine Verneinung ergeben, muß doch schon in der einen Verneinung, die ich jetzt gebrauche, liegen." (Die Versuchung, einen Mythos des "Bedeutens" zu erfinden.)

Es hat den Anschein, als würde aus der Natur der Negation folgen, daß eine doppelte Verneinung eine Bejahung ist. (Und etwas Richtiges ist daran. Was? *Unsere* Natur hängt mit beiden zusammen.)

b) Es kann keine Diskussion darüber geben, ob diese Regeln, oder andere die richtigen für das Wort "nicht" sind (ich meine, ob sie seiner Bedeutung gemäß sind). Denn das Wort hat ohne diese Regeln noch keine Bedeutung; und wenn wir die Regeln ändern, so hat es nun eine andere Bedeutung (oder keine) und wir können dann ebensogut auch das Wort ändern.

a cry. Words can be *hard* to utter: those, for example, with which one renounces something, or confesses a weakness. (Words are also deeds.)

547. Negating: a 'mental activity'. Negate something and observe what you are doing. — Do you perhaps inwardly shake your head? And if you do, is this process more deserving of our interest than, say, |147| that of writing a sign of negation in a sentence? Do you now know the *essence* of negation?

548. What is the difference between the two processes: wishing that something should happen and wishing that the same thing should *not* happen?

If one wanted to represent it pictorially, one might treat the picture of the event in different ways: cross it out, or put a line round it, and so on. But this strikes us as a *crude* method of expression. In word-language we do indeed use the sign "not". This is like a clumsy expedient. One supposes that in *thought* it happens differently.

549. "How can the word 'not' negate?" — "The sign 'not' indicates that you are to take what follows negatively." One would like to say: the sign of negation is our occasion for doing something — possibly something very complicated. It is as if the negation sign prompted us to do something. But what? That is not said. It is as if it only needed to be hinted at; as if we already knew. As if no explanation were needed, since we are already familiar with the matter anyway.

*

(a) "The fact that three negations yield a negation again must already be contained in the single negation that I am using now." (The temptation to invent a myth of 'meaning'.)

It looks as if it followed from the nature of negation that a double negation is an affirmation. (And there is something right about this. What? *Our* nature is connected with both.)

(b) There can be no debate about whether these or other rules are the right ones for the word "not" (I mean, whether they accord with its meaning). For without these rules, the word has as yet no meaning; and if we change the rules, it now has another meaning (or none), and in that case we may just as well change the word too. |p. 147 n.|

550. Die Negation, könnte man sagen, ist eine ausschließende, abweisende, Gebärde. Aber eine solche Gebärde verwenden wir in sehr verschiedenen Fällen!

551. "Ist es die *gleiche* Verneinung: 'Eisen schmilzt nicht bei 100 Grad C' und '2 mal 2 ist nicht 5'?" Soll das durch Introspektion entschieden werden; dadurch, daß wir zu sehen trachten, was wir bei beiden Sätzen *denken*?

552. Wie, wenn ich fragte: Zeigt es sich uns klar, während wir die Sätze aussprechen "Dieser Stab ist 1 m lang" und "Hier steht 1 Soldat", daß wir mit "1" Verschiedenes meinen, daß "1" verschiedene Bedeutungen hat? — Es zeigt sich uns gar nicht. — Sag etwa einen Satz wie "Auf je 1 m steht ein Soldat, auf je 2 m also 2 Soldaten". Gefragt "Meinst du dasselbe mit den beiden Einsern?", würde man etwa antworten: "Freilich meine ich dasselbe: *eins*!" (Dabei hebt man etwa einen Finger in die Höhe.)

553. Hat nun die "1" verschiedene Bedeutung, wenn sie einmal für die Maßzahl, ein andermal für die Anzahl steht? Wird die Frage *so* gestellt, so wird man sie bejahen.

554. Wir können uns leicht Menschen mit einer 'primitiveren' Logik denken, in der es etwas unserer Verneinung Entsprechendes nur für bestimmte Sätze gibt; für solche etwa, die noch keine Verneinung enthalten. Man könnte den Satz "Er geht in das Haus" verneinen, eine Verneinung des negativen Satzes aber wäre sinnlos, oder sie gilt nur als Wiederholung der Verneinung. Denk an andere Mittel, als die unseren, eine Verneinung auszudrücken: etwa durch die Tonhöhe des Satzes. Wie sähe hier eine doppelte Verneinung aus?

555. Die Frage, ob für diese Menschen die Verneinung dieselbe Bedeutung hat, wie für uns, wäre analog der, ob die Ziffer "5" für Menschen, deren Zahlenreihe mit 5 endigt, dasselbe bedeutet, wie für uns.

556. Denk dir eine Sprache mit zwei verschiedenen Worten für die Verneinung, das eine ist "X", das andere "Y". Ein doppeltes "X" gibt eine Bejahung, ein doppeltes "Y" aber eine verstärkte Verneinung. Im übrigen werden die beiden Wörter gleich verwendet. — Haben nun "X" und "Y" die gleiche Bedeutung, wenn sie ohne Wiederholung in Sätzen vorkommen? — Darauf könnte man verschiedenes antworten.

550. Negating, one might say, is a gesture of exclusion, of rejection. But we use such a gesture in a great variety of cases!

551. "Is the negation in 'Iron does not melt at 100 degrees Centigrade' the same as in 'Two times two is not five'?" Is this to be decided by introspection, by trying to see what we are *thinking* as we utter the two sentences?

552. What if I were to ask: does it become evident, while we are uttering the sentences "This rod is 1 metre long" and "Here is 1 soldier", |148| that we mean different things by "1", that "1" has different meanings? — It does not become evident at all. — Say, for example, such a sentence as "1 metre is occupied by 1 soldier, and so 2 metres are occupied by 2 soldiers". Asked, "Do you mean the same by both 'ones'?", one would perhaps answer, "Of course I mean the same: *one!*" (Perhaps raising one finger.)

553. Now has "1" a different meaning when it stands for a measure and when it stands for a number? If the question is framed in *this* way, one will answer affirmatively.

554. We can easily imagine human beings with a 'more primitive' logic, in which something corresponding to our negation is applied only to certain sentences; perhaps to those that do not yet contain any negation. It would be possible to negate the sentence "He is going into the house", but a negation of the negated sentence would be senseless, or would count only as a repetition of the negation. Think of means of expressing negation different from ours: by the pitch of the uttered sentence, for instance. What would a double negation be like there?

555. The question of whether negation had the same meaning to these people as to us would be analogous to the question as to whether the figure "5" meant the same to people whose number series ended at 5 as to us.

556. Imagine a language with two different words for negation, "X" and "Y". Doubling "X" yields an affirmation, doubling "Y" an emphatic negation. Apart from that, the two words are used similarly. — Now have "X" and "Y" the same meaning in sentences where they occur without being repeated? — One might give various answers to this.

a) Die beiden Wörter haben verschiedenen Gebrauch. Also verschiedene Bedeutung. Sätze aber, in denen sie ohne Wiederholung stehen, und die im übrigen gleich lauten, haben gleichen Sinn.

b) Die beiden Wörter haben die gleiche Funktion in Sprachspielen, bis auf die eine Verschiedenheit, die eine unwichtige Sache des Herkommens ist. Der Gebrauch beider Wörter wird auf die gleiche Weise gelehrt, durch die gleichen Handlungen, Gebärden, Bilder, etc.; und der Unterschied in ihrer Gebrauchsweise wird als etwas Nebensächliches, als einer von den kapriziösen Zügen der Sprache, der Erklärung der Wörter hinzugefügt. Darum werden wir sagen: "X" und "Y" haben die gleiche Bedeutung.

c) Mit den beiden Verneinungen verbinden wir verschiedene Vorstellungen. "X" dreht gleichsam den Sinn um 180 Grad. Und *darum* bringen zwei solche Verneinungen den Sinn in seine alte Lage zurück. "Y" ist wie ein Kopfschütteln. Und wie man nicht ein Kopfschütteln durch ein zweites aufhebt, so auch nicht ein "Y" durch ein zweites. Und wenn also auch Sätze mit den beiden Verneinungen praktisch aufs selbe hinauskommen, so drücken "X" und "Y" doch verschiedene Ideen aus.

557. Worin mag das gelegen haben, als ich die doppelte Verneinung aussprach, daß ich sie als verstärkte Verneinung und nicht als Bejahung meinte? Es gibt keine Antwort, die lautet: "Es lag darin, daß . . ." Statt zu sagen "Diese Verdoppelung ist als Verstärkung gemeint" kann ich sie unter gewissen Umständen als Verstärkung *aussprechen*. Statt zu sagen "Die Verdopplung der Verneinung ist als ihre Aufhebung gemeint", kann ich z. B. Klammern setzen. — "Ja, aber diese Klammern selbst können doch verschiedene Rollen spielen; denn wer sagt, daß sie als *Klammern* aufzufassen seien?" Niemand sagt es. Und du hast ja deine Auffassung wieder durch Worte erklärt. Was die Klammern bedeuten, liegt in der Technik ihrer Anwendung. Die Frage ist: Unter welchen Umständen hat es Sinn zu sagen "Ich habe . . . gemeint", und welche Umstände berechtigen mich zu sagen "Er hat . . . gemeint"?

558. Was heißt es, daß im Satze "Die Rose ist rot" das "ist" eine andere Bedeutung hat, als in "zwei mal zwei ist vier"? Wenn man antwortet, es heiße, daß verschiedene Regeln von diesen beiden Wörtern gelten, so ist zu sagen, daß wir hier nur *ein* Wort haben. — Und wenn ich nur auf die grammatischen Regeln achte, so erlauben diese eben die Verwendung des Wortes "ist" in beiderlei Zusammenhängen. — Die Regel aber, welche zeigt, daß das Wort "ist" in diesen Sätzen verschiedene Bedeutung hat, ist die, welche erlaubt, im zweiten Satz das Wort "ist" durch das Gleichheitszeichen zu ersetzen, und die diese Ersetzung im ersten Satz verbietet.

(a) The two words have different uses. So they have different meanings. But sentences in which they occur without being repeated, and which are otherwise the same, have the same sense.

(b) The two words have the same function in language-games, except for this one difference, which is just an unimportant matter of custom. The use of the two words is taught in the same way, by means of the same actions, gestures, pictures, and so on; and in explanations of the words, the difference in the ways they are used is appended as something incidental, as one of the capricious features of the language. That's why we'll say: "X" and "Y" have the same meaning.

(c) We connect different images with the two negations. "X", as it |149| were, turns the sense through 180°. And *that* is why two such negations restore the sense to its former position. "Y" is like shaking one's head. And just as one doesn't annul a shake of the head by shaking it again, so too one doesn't cancel one "Y" by a second one. And so even if in practice sentences with the two signs of negation come to the same thing, still "X" and "Y" express different ideas.

557. When I uttered the double negation, what constituted my meaning it as an emphatic negation and not as an affirmation? There is no answer running: "It consisted in the fact that . . ." In certain circumstances, instead of saying "This reiteration is meant as an emphasis", I can *pronounce* it as an emphasis. Instead of saying "The reiteration of the negation is meant to cancel it", I can, for example, insert brackets. — "Yes, but these brackets may themselves have different roles; for who says that they are to be taken as *brackets*?" No one does. And haven't you explained your own conception in turn by means of words? What the brackets mean lies in the technique of applying them. The question is: under what circumstances does it make sense to say "I meant . . .", and what circumstances warrant my saying "He meant . . ."?

558. What does it mean to say that the "is" in "The rose is red" has a different meaning from the "is" in "Two times two is four"? If it is answered that it means that different rules are valid for these two words, the retort is that we have only *one* word here. — And if I attend only to the grammatical rules, these do allow the use of the word "is" in both kinds of context. — But the rule which shows that the word "is" has different meanings in these sentences is the one allowing us to replace the word "is" in the second sentence by the sign of equality, and forbidding this substitution in the first sentence.

559. Man möchte etwa von der Funktion des Wortes in *diesem* Satz reden. Als sei der Satz ein Mechanismus, in welchem das Wort eine bestimmte Funktion habe. Aber worin besteht diese Funktion? Wie tritt sie zu Tage? Denn es ist ja nichts verborgen, wir sehen ja den ganzen Satz! Die Funktion muß sich im Laufe des Kalküls zeigen. ((Bedeutungskörper.))

560. "Die Bedeutung des Wortes ist das, was die Erklärung der Bedeutung erklärt." D. h.: willst du den Gebrauch des Worts "Bedeutung" verstehen, so sieh nach, was man "Erklärung der Bedeutung" nennt.

561. Ist es nun nicht merkwürdig, daß ich sage, das Wort "ist" werde in zwei verschiedenen Bedeutungen (als Kopula und als Gleichheitszeichen) gebraucht, und nicht sagen möchte, seine Bedeutung sei sein Gebrauch: nämlich als Kopula und Gleichheitszeichen?

Man möchte sagen, diese beiden Arten des Gebrauchs geben nicht *eine* Bedeutung; die Personalunion durch das gleiche Wort sei ein unwesentlicher Zufall.

562. Aber wie kann ich entscheiden, welches ein wesentlicher und welches ein unwesentlicher, zufälliger Zug der Notation ist? Liegt denn eine Realität hinter der Notation, nach der sich ihre Grammatik richtet?

Denken wir an einen ähnlichen Fall im Spiel: im Damespiel wird eine Dame dadurch gekennzeichnet, daß man zwei Spielsteine aufeinanderlegt. Wird man nun nicht sagen, daß es für das Spiel unwesentlich ist, daß eine Dame aus zwei Steinen besteht?

563. Sagen wir: die Bedeutung eines Steines (einer Figur) ist ihre Rolle im Spiel. — Nun werde vor Beginn jeder Schachpartie durch das Los entschieden, welcher der Spieler Weiß erhält. Dazu halte der Eine in jeder geschlossenen Hand einen Schachkönig, der Andre wählt auf gut Glück eine der beiden Hände. Wird man es nun zur Rolle des Schachkönigs im Schachspiel rechnen, daß er so zum Auslosen verwendet wird?

564. Ich bin also geneigt, auch im Spiel zwischen wesentlichen und unwesentlichen Regeln zu unterscheiden. Das Spiel, möchte man sagen, hat nicht nur Regeln, sondern auch einen *Witz*.

565. Wozu das gleiche Wort? Wir machen ja im Kalkül keinen Gebrauch von dieser Gleichheit! — Warum für beide Zwecke die gleichen Spielsteine? — Aber was heißt es hier "von der Gleichheit Gebrauch machen"? Ist es denn nicht ein Gebrauch, wenn wir eben das gleiche Wort gebrauchen?

* 559. One would like to speak of the function of a word in *this* sentence. As if the sentence were a mechanism in which the word had a particular function. But what does this function consist in? How does it come to light? For after all, nothing is hidden — we see the whole sentence! The function must come out in operating the calculus. ((Meaning-bodies.))

* 560. "The meaning of a word is what an explanation of its meaning explains." That is, if you want to understand the use of the word "meaning", look for what one calls "an explanation of meaning". |150|

561. Now isn't it remarkable that I say that the word "is" is used with two different meanings (as copula and as sign of equality), and wouldn't want to say that its meaning is its use; its use, namely, as copula and as sign of equality?

One would like to say that these two kinds of use don't yield a single meaning, that the union under one head, effected by the same word, is an inessential coincidence.

562. But how can I decide what is an essential, and what an inessential, coincidental, feature of the notation? Is there some reality lying behind the notation, to which its grammar conforms?

Let's think of a similar case in a game: in draughts a king is indicated by putting one piece on top of another. Now won't one say that it's inessential to the game for a king to consist of two pieces?

563. Let's say that the meaning of a piece is its role in the game. — Now let it be decided by lot, before a game of chess begins, which of the players gets white. For this, one player holds a king in each closed hand, while the other chooses one of the two hands, trusting to luck. Will it be counted as part of the role of the king in chess that it is used to draw lots in this way?

564. So I am inclined to distinguish between essential and inessential rules in a game too. The game, one would like to say, has not only rules but also a *point*.

565. What's the point of using the same word? In the calculus we don't make use of any such sameness of sign! — Why the same chess piece for both purposes? — But what does it mean here to speak of "making use of the sameness of sign"? For isn't it a single use, if we actually use the same word?

566. Hier scheint es nun, als hätte der Gebrauch des gleichen Worts, des gleichen Steins, einen *Zweck* — wenn die Gleichheit nicht zufällig, unwesentlich, ist. Und als sei der Zweck, daß man den Stein wiedererkennen, und wissen könne, wie man zu spielen hat. — Ist da von einer physischen, oder einer logischen Möglichkeit die Rede? Wenn das Letztere, so gehört eben die Gleichheit der Steine zum Spiel.

567. Das Spiel soll doch durch die Regeln bestimmt sein! Wenn also eine Spielregel vorschreibt, daß zum Auslosen vor der Schachpartie die Könige zu verwenden sind, so gehört das, wesentlich, zum Spiel. Was könnte man dagegen einwenden? Daß man den Witz dieser Vorschrift nicht einsehe. Etwa, wie wenn man auch den Witz einer Regel nicht einsähe, nach der jeder Stein dreimal umzudrehen wäre, ehe man mit ihm zieht. Fänden wir diese Regel in einem Brettspiel, so würden wir uns wundern und Vermutungen über den Zweck der Regel anstellen. ("Sollte diese Vorschrift verhindern, daß man ohne Überlegung zieht?")

568. Wenn ich den Charakter des Spiels richtig verstehe — könnte ich sagen — so gehört das nicht wesentlich dazu.
 ((Die Bedeutung eine Physiognomie.))

569. Die Sprache ist ein Instrument. Ihre Begriffe sind Instrumente. Man denkt nun etwa, es könne keinen *großen* Unterschied machen, *welche* Begriffe wir verwenden. Wie man schließlich mit Fuß und Zoll Physik treiben kann, sowie mit m und cm; der Unterschied sei doch nur einer der Bequemlichkeit. Aber auch das ist nicht wahr, wenn, z. B., Rechnungen in einem Maßsystem mehr Zeit und Mühe erfordern, als wir aufwenden können.

570. Begriffe leiten uns zu Untersuchungen. Sind der Ausdruck unseres Interesses, und lenken unser Interesse.

571. Irreführende Parallele: Psychologie handelt von den Vorgängen in der psychischen Sphäre, wie Physik in der physischen.
 Sehen, Hören, Denken, Fühlen, Wollen sind nicht *im gleichen Sinne* die Gegenstände der Psychologie, wie die Bewegungen der Körper, die elektrischen Erscheinungen, etc., Gegenstände der Physik. Das siehst du daraus, daß der Physiker diese Erscheinungen sieht, hört, über sie nachdenkt, sie uns mitteilt, und der Psychologe die *Äußerungen* (das Benehmen) des Subjekts beobachtet.

566. And now it looks as if the use of the same word or the same piece had a *purpose* — if the sameness is not coincidental, inessential. And as if the purpose were that one should be able to recognize the piece and know how to play. — Are we talking about a physical or a logical possibility here? If the latter, then the sameness of the piece is part of the game.

567. But, after all, the game is supposed to be determined by the rules! So, if a rule of the game prescribes that the kings are to be used for drawing lots before a game of chess, then that is an essential part of the game. What objection might one make to this? That one does not see the point of this prescription. Perhaps as one likewise wouldn't see the point of a rule by which each piece had to be turned round three times |151| before one moved it. If we found this rule in a board-game, we'd be surprised and would speculate about the purpose of the rule. ("Was this prescription meant to prevent one from moving without due consideration?")

568. If I understand the character of the game aright, I might say, then this isn't an essential part of it.
*   ((Meaning — a physiognomy.))

569. Language is an instrument. Its concepts are instruments. Now perhaps one thinks that it can make no *great* difference *which* concepts we employ. As, after all, it is possible to do physics in feet and inches as well as in metres and centimetres; the difference is merely one of convenience. But even this is not true if, for instance, calculations in some system of measurement demand more time and trouble than we can afford.

570. Concepts lead us to make investigations. They are the expression of our interest and direct our interest.

571. A misleading parallel: psychology treats of processes in the mental sphere, as does physics in the physical.
*   Seeing, hearing, thinking, feeling, willing, are not the subject matter of psychology *in the same sense* as that in which the movements of bodies, the phenomena of electricity, and so forth are the subject matter of physics. You can see this from the fact that the physicist sees, hears, thinks about and informs us of these phenomena, and the psychologist observes the *utterances* (the behaviour) of the subject.

572. Erwartung ist, grammatikalisch, ein Zustand; wie: einer Meinung sein, etwas hoffen, etwas wissen, etwas können. Aber um die Grammatik dieser Zustände zu verstehen, muß man fragen: "Was gilt als Kriterium dafür, daß sich jemand in diesem Zustand befindet?" (Zustand der Härte, des Gewichts, des Passens.)

573. Eine Ansicht haben ist ein Zustand. — Ein Zustand wessen? Der Seele? des Geistes? Nun, wovon sagt man, es habe eine Ansicht? Vom Herrn N. N. zum Beispiel. Und das ist die richtige Antwort.

Man darf eben von der Antwort auf die Frage noch keinen Aufschluß erwarten. Fragen, welche tiefer dringen, sind: Was sehen wir, in besondern Fällen, als Kriterien dafür an, daß Einer die und die Meinung hat? Wann sagen wir: er sei damals zu dieser Meinung gekommen? Wann: er habe seine Meinung geändert? U. s. w. Das Bild, welches die Antworten auf diese Fragen uns geben, zeigt, *was* hier grammatisch als *Zustand* behandelt wird.

574. Ein Satz, und daher in anderm Sinne ein Gedanke, kann der 'Ausdruck' des Glaubens, Hoffens, Erwartens, etc., sein. Aber Glauben ist nicht Denken. (Eine grammatische Bemerkung.) Die Begriffe des Glaubens, Erwartens, Hoffens, sind einander weniger artfremd, als sie dem Begriff des Denkens sind.

575. Als ich mich auf diesen Stuhl setzte, glaubte ich natürlich, er werde mich tragen. Ich dachte gar nicht, daß er zusammenbrechen könnte.

Aber: "Trotz allem, was er tat, hielt ich an dem Glauben fest, . . ." Hier wird gedacht, und etwa immer wieder eine bestimmte Einstellung erkämpft.

576. Ich schaue auf die brennende Lunte, folge mit höchster Spannung dem Fortschreiten des Brandes und wie er sich dem Explosivstoff nähert. Ich denke vielleicht überhaupt nichts, oder eine Menge abgerissener Gedanken. Das ist gewiß ein Fall des Erwartens.

577. Wir sagen "Ich erwarte ihn", wenn wir glauben, er werde kommen, sein Kommen uns aber nicht *beschäftigt*. ("Ich erwarte ihn" hieße hier "Ich wäre erstaunt, wenn er nicht käme" — und das wird man nicht die Beschreibung eines Seelenzustands nennen.) Wir sagen aber auch "Ich erwarte ihn", wenn dies heißen soll: Ich harre auf ihn. Wir könnten uns eine Sprache denken, die in diesen Fällen konsequent verschiedene Verben benützt. Und ebenso mehr als ein Verbum dort, wo wir von 'glauben', 'hoffen', u. s. w. reden. Die Begriffe dieser Sprache wären für ein

572. Expectation is, grammatically, a state; like being of an opinion, hoping for something, knowing something, being able to do something. But in order to understand the grammar of these states, it is necessary to ask: "What counts as a criterion for anyone's being in such a state?" (States of hardness, of weight, of fitting.)

573. To have an opinion is a state. — A state of what? Of the soul? Of the mind? Well, what does one say has an opinion? Mr N.N., for example. And that is the correct answer.

One should not expect to be enlightened by the answer to *that* question. Other questions that go deeper are: What, in particular cases, do we regard as criteria for someone's being of such-and-such an opinion? When do we say that he reached this opinion at that time? When that he has altered his opinion? And so on. The picture that the answers to these questions give us shows *what* gets treated grammatically as a *state* here. |152|

574. A sentence, and hence in another sense a thought, can be the 'expression' of belief, hope, expectation, etc. But believing is not thinking. (A grammatical remark.) The concepts of believing, expecting, hoping are less different in kind from one another than they are from the concept of thinking.

575. When I sat down on this chair, of course I believed it would bear me. The thought of its collapsing never crossed my mind.

But: "In spite of everything that he did, I held fast to the belief . . ." Here there is thought, and perhaps a recurrent struggle to maintain an attitude.

576. I look at a burning fuse, excitedly watching the flame approach the explosive. Perhaps I don't think anything at all, or have lots of disjointed thoughts. This is certainly a case of expecting.

577. We say "I'm expecting him" when we believe that he'll come, though his coming does not *occupy* our thoughts. (Here "I'm expecting him" would mean "I'd be surprised if he didn't come" — and that will not be called a description of a state of mind.) But we also say "I'm expecting him" when it is supposed to mean: I'm eagerly awaiting him. We could imagine a language in which different verbs were consistently used in these cases. And similarly, more than one verb where we speak of 'believing', 'hoping', and so on. The concepts of such a language would

Verständnis der Psychologie vielleicht geeigneter, als die Begriffe unsrer Sprache.

578. Frage dich: Was heißt es, den Goldbach'schen Satz *glauben*? Worin besteht dieser Glaube? In einem Gefühl der Sicherheit, wenn wir den Satz aussprechen, hören, oder denken? (Das interessierte uns nicht.) Und was sind die Kennzeichen dieses Gefühls? Ich weiß ja auch nicht, wie weit das Gefühl durch den Satz selbst hervorgerufen sein mag.

Soll ich sagen, der Glaube ist ein Farbton der Gedanken? Woher diese Idee? Nun, es gibt einen Tonfall des Glaubens, wie des Zweifels.

Ich möchte fragen: Wie greift der Glaube in diesen Satz ein? Sehen wir nach, welche Konsequenzen dieser Glaube hat, wozu er uns bringt. "Er bringt mich zum Suchen nach einem Beweis dieses Satzes." — Gut, jetzt sehen wir noch nach, worin dein Suchen eigentlich besteht! dann werden wir wissen, was es mit dem Glauben an den Satz auf sich hat.

579. Das Gefühl der Zuversicht. Wie äußert es sich im Benehmen?

580. Ein 'innerer Vorgang' bedarf äußerer Kriterien.

581. Eine Erwartung ist in einer Situation eingebettet, aus der sie entspringt. Die Erwartung einer Explosion kann z. B. aus einer Situation entspringen, in der eine Explosion *zu erwarten ist*.

582. Wenn Einer, statt zu sagen "Ich erwarte jeden Moment die Explosion", flüstert: "Es wird gleich losgehen", so beschreiben doch seine Worte keine Empfindung; obgleich sie und ihr Ton eine Äußerung seiner Empfindung sein können.

583. "Aber du sprichst ja, als erwartete, hoffte, ich nicht eigentlich *jetzt* — da ich zu hoffen glaube. Als wäre, was *jetzt* geschieht, ohne tiefe Bedeutung." — Was heißt es: "Was jetzt geschieht, hat Bedeutung" oder "hat tiefe Bedeutung"? Was ist eine *tiefe* Empfindung? Könnte Einer eine Sekunde lang innige Liebe oder Hoffnung empfinden, — *was immer* dieser Sekunde voranging, oder ihr folgt? —— Was jetzt geschieht, hat Bedeutung — in dieser Umgebung. Die Umgebung gibt ihm die Wichtigkeit. Und das Wort "hoffen" bezieht sich auf ein Phänomen des menschlichen Lebens. (Ein lächelnder Mund *lächelt* nur in einem menschlichen Gesicht.)

584. Wenn ich nun in meinem Zimmer sitze und hoffe, N. N. werde kommen und mir Geld bringen, und eine Minute dieses Zustands könnte

perhaps be more suitable for understanding psychology than are the concepts of our language.

578. Ask yourself: What does it mean to *believe* Goldbach's conjecture? What does this belief consist in? In a feeling of certainty as we state, hear or think the conjecture? (That would not interest us.) And what are the characteristics of this feeling? Why, I don't even know how far the feeling may be caused by the conjecture itself.

Am I to say that belief is a colour tone of our thoughts? Where does this idea come from? Well, there is a tone of believing, as of doubting.

I should like to ask: how does the belief engage with this conjecture? Let us look and see what are the consequences of this belief, where it takes us. "It makes me search for a proof of the conjecture." — Very well; and now let us look and see what your searching really consists in! Then we shall know what believing the conjecture amounts to. |153|

579. A feeling of confidence. How is it manifested in behaviour?

580. An 'inner process' stands in need of outward criteria.

581. An expectation is embedded in a situation, from which it arises. The expectation of an explosion may, for example, arise from a situation in which an explosion *is to be expected*.

582. If, instead of saying "I expect the explosion any moment now", someone whispered "It'll go off in a moment", then his words do not describe a feeling, although they and their tone may be a manifestation of it.

583. "But you talk as if I weren't really expecting, hoping, *now* — when I thought I was. As if what were happening *now* had no deep significance." — What does it mean to say "What is happening now has significance" or "has deep significance"? What is a *deep* feeling? Could someone have a feeling of ardent love or hope for one second — *no matter what* preceded or followed this second? —— What is happening now has significance — in these surroundings. The surroundings give it its importance. And the word "hope" refers to a phenomenon of human life. (A smiling mouth *smiles* only in a human face.)

584. Now suppose I sit in my room and hope that N.N. will come and bring me some money, and suppose one minute of this state could be

isoliert, aus ihrem Zusammenhang herausgeschnitten werden: wäre, was in ihr geschieht, dann kein Hoffen? — Denke, z. B., an die Worte, die du etwa in dieser Zeit aussprichst. Sie gehören nun nicht mehr dieser Sprache an. Und die Institution des Geldes gibt es in einer andern Umgebung auch nicht.

Eine Königskrönung ist das Bild der Pracht und Würde. Schneide eine Minute dieses Vorgangs aus ihrer Umgebung heraus: dem König im Krönungsmantel wird die Krone aufs Haupt gesetzt. — In einer andern Umgebung aber ist Gold das billigste Metall, sein Glanz gilt als gemein. Das Gewebe des Mantels ist dort billig herzustellen. Die Krone ist die Parodie eines anständigen Huts. Etc.

585. Wenn Einer sagt "Ich hoffe, er wird kommen" — ist das ein *Bericht* über seinen Seelenzustand, oder eine *Äußerung* seiner Hoffnung? — Ich kann es z. B. zu mir selbst sagen. Und mir mache ich doch keinen Bericht. Es kann ein Seufzer sein; aber muß kein Seufzer sein. Sage ich jemandem "Ich kann heute meine Gedanken nicht bei der Arbeit halten; ich denke immer an sein Kommen" — so wird man *das* eine Beschreibung meines Seelenzustandes nennen.

586. "Ich habe gehört, er wird kommen; ich erwarte ihn schon den ganzen Tag." Dies ist ein Bericht darüber, wie ich den Tag verbracht habe. —— Ich komme in einem Gespräch zum Ergebnis, daß ein bestimmtes Ereignis zu erwarten sei, und ziehe diesen Schluß mit den Worten: "Ich muß also jetzt sein Kommen erwarten." Das kann man den ersten Gedanken, den ersten Akt, dieser Erwartung nennen. —— Den Ausruf "Ich erwarte ihn sehnsüchtig!" kann man einen Akt des Erwartens nennen. Ich kann aber dieselben Worte als das Resultat einer Selbstbeobachtung aussprechen, und sie hießen dann etwa: "Also nach allem, was vorgegangen ist, erwarte ich ihn dennoch mit Sehnsucht." Es kommt darauf an: Wie ist es zu diesen Worten gekommen?

587. Hat es Sinn, zu fragen "Woher weißt du, daß du das glaubst?" — und ist die Antwort: "Ich erkenne es durch Introspektion"?

In *manchen* Fällen wird man so etwas sagen können, in den meisten nicht.

Es hat Sinn, zu fragen: "Liebe ich sie wirklich, mache ich mir das nicht nur vor?" und der Vorgang der Introspektion ist das Wachrufen von Erinnerungen; von Vorstellungen möglicher Situationen und der Gefühle, die man hätte, wenn . . .

588. "Ich wälze den Entschluß in mir herum, morgen abzureisen." (Dies kann man eine Beschreibung des Gemützustandes nennen.) —— "Deine Gründe überzeugen mich nicht; ich bin nach wie vor der

isolated, cut out of its context; would what happened in it then not be hoping? — Think, for example, of the words which you may utter in this time. They are no longer part of this language. And in different surroundings the institution of money doesn't exist either.

A coronation is the picture of pomp and dignity. Cut one minute of this proceeding out of its surroundings: the crown is being placed on the head of the king in his coronation robes. — But in different surroundings, gold is the cheapest of metals, its gleam is thought vulgar. There the fabric of the robe is cheap to produce. A crown is a parody of a respectable hat. And so on.

585. When someone says "I hope he'll come", is this a *report* about his state of mind, or a *manifestation* of his hope? — I may, for example, say it to myself. And surely I am not giving myself a report. It may be a sigh; but it need not be. If I tell someone, "I can't keep my mind on my work today; I keep on thinking of his coming" — *this* will be called a description of my state of mind. |154|

586. "I've heard he is coming; I've been expecting him all day." This is a report on how I have spent the day. —— In conversation, I come to the conclusion that a particular event is to be expected, and I draw this conclusion in the words "So now I must expect him to come". This may be called the first thought, the first act, of this expectation. —— The exclamation "I'm expecting him — I'm longing to see him!" may be called an act of expecting. But I can utter the same words as the result of self-observation, and then they might amount to: "So, after all that has happened, I'm still expecting him with longing." It all depends on what led up to these words.

587. Does it make sense to ask "How do you know that you believe that?" — and is the answer: "I find it out by introspection"?

In *some* cases it will be possible to say some such thing, in most not.

It makes sense to ask, "Do I really love her, or am I only fooling myself?", and the process of introspection is the calling up of memories, of imagined possible situations, and of the feelings that one would have if . . .

588. "I'm in two minds whether to go away tomorrow." (This may be called a description of a state of mind.) —— "Your arguments don't convince me; now as before it is my intention to go away tomorrow." Here

Absicht, morgen abzureisen." Hier wird man versucht sein, die Absicht
ein Gefühl zu nennen. Das Gefühl ist das einer gewissen Steifigkeit; des
unabänderlichen Entschlusses. (Aber es gibt auch hier viele verschiedene charakteristische Gefühle, und Haltungen.) —— Man fragt mich:
"Wie lange bleibst du hier?" Ich antworte: "Morgen reise ich ab; meine
Ferien gehen zu Ende." — Dagegen aber: Ich sage am Ende eines Streits
"Nun gut; dann reise ich morgen ab!". Ich fasse einen Entschluß.

589. "Ich habe mich in meinem Herzen dazu entschlossen." Und man
ist dabei auch geneigt, auf die Brust zu zeigen. Diese Redeweise ist psychologisch ernst zu nehmen. Warum sollte sie weniger ernst zu nehmen
sein, als die Aussage, der Glaube sei ein Zustand der Seele? (Luther:
"Der Glaube ist unter der linken Brustzitze.")

590. Es könnte sein, daß jemand die Bedeutung des Ausdrucks "was
man sagt, ernstlich *meinen*" durch ein Zeigen auf das Herz verstehen lerne.
Aber nun muß man fragen "Wie zeigt sich's, daß er es gelernt hat?".

591. Soll ich sagen, wer eine Absicht hat, erlebt eine Tendenz? Es gebe
bestimmte Tendenzerlebnisse? — Erinnere dich an diesen Fall: Wenn man
in einer Diskussion dringend eine Bemerkung, einen Einwurf, machen
will, geschieht es häufig, daß man den Mund öffnet, den Atem einzieht
und anhält; entscheidet man sich dann, den Einwurf zu unterlassen, so
läßt man den Atem aus. Das Erlebnis dieses Vorgangs ist offenbar das
Erlebnis einer Tendenz, zu sprechen. Wer mich beobachtet, wird erkennen, daß ich etwas sagen wollte und mich dann anders besonnen habe.
In *dieser* Situation nämlich. — In einer andern würde er mein
Benehmen so nicht deuten, so charakteristisch es auch in der gegenwärtigen Situation für die Absicht, zu sprechen, ist. Und ist irgend ein
Grund vorhanden, anzunehmen, dieses selbe Erlebnis könnte in einer
ganz andern Situation nicht auftreten, — in der es mit einer Tendenz
nichts zu tun hat?

592. "Aber wenn du sagst 'Ich habe die Absicht, abzureisen', so meinst
du's doch! Es ist eben hier wieder das geistige Meinen, das den Satz
belebt. Sprichst du den Satz bloß einem Andern nach, etwa um seine
Sprechweise zu verspotten, so sprichst du ihn ohne dieses Meinen." —
Wenn wir philosophieren, so kann es manchmal so scheinen. Aber denken
wir uns doch wirklich *verschiedene* Situationen aus, und Gespräche, und
wie jener Satz in ihnen ausgesprochen wird! — "Ich entdecke immer einen
geistigen Unterton; vielleicht nicht immer den *gleichen*." — Und war da

one is tempted to call the intention a feeling. The feeling is one of a certain rigidity, of irrevocable decision. (But here too there are many different characteristic feelings and attitudes.) —— I am asked: "How long are you staying here?" I reply: "Tomorrow I'm going away; it's the end of my holidays." — But, by contrast, I say, at the end of a quarrel, "All right! Then I'll go tomorrow!" — I make a decision.

* 589. "In my heart I've decided it." And one is even inclined to point to one's breast as one says it. Psychologically, this way of speaking should be taken seriously. Why should it be taken less seriously than the statement that faith is a state of the soul? (Luther: "Faith is under the left nipple.")

590. Someone might learn to understand the meaning of the expression "seriously *meaning* what one says" by a gesture of pointing at the heart. But now one must ask: "What shows that he has learnt it?" |155|

591. Am I to say that any one who has an intention has an experience of tending towards something? That there are particular experiences of 'tending'? — Remember this case: if one urgently wants to make some remark, some objection, in a discussion, it often happens that one opens one's mouth, draws a breath, and holds it; if one then decides to let the objection drop, one lets one's breath out. The experience of what goes on here seems to be an experience of a tendency to say something. An observer will realize that I wanted to say something and then thought better of it. In *this* situation, that is. — In a different one, he would not interpret my behaviour in this way, however characteristic of the intention to speak it may be in the present situation. And is there any reason for assuming that this same experience could not occur in some quite different situation in which it has nothing to do with any 'tending'?

592. "But when you say 'I intend to go away', you surely mean it! Here again it just is the mental act of meaning that gives the sentence life. If you merely repeat the sentence after someone else, say in order to mock his way of speaking, then you utter it without this act of meaning." — When we are doing philosophy, it may sometimes look like that. But let's think up really *different* situations and conversations, and the ways in which that sentence is uttered in them. — "I always discover a mental undertone; perhaps not always the *same* one." — And was there no

kein Unterton vorhanden, als du den Satz dem Andern nachsprachst? Und wie nun den 'Unterton' von dem übrigen Erlebnis des Sprechens trennen?

593. Eine Hauptursache philosophischer Krankheiten — einseitige Diät: man nährt sein Denken mit nur einer Art von Beispielen.

594. "Aber die Worte, sinnvoll ausgesprochen, haben doch nicht nur Fläche, sondern auch eine Tiefendimension!" Es findet eben doch etwas anderes statt, wenn sie sinnvoll ausgesprochen werden, als wenn sie bloß ausgesprochen werden. — Wie ich das ausdrücke, darauf kommt's nicht an. Ob ich sage, sie haben im ersten Fall Tiefe; oder, es geht dabei etwas in mir, in meinem Innern, vor; oder, sie haben eine Atmosphäre — es kommt immer aufs gleiche hinaus.
  "Wenn wir nun Alle hierin übereinstimmen, wird es da nicht wahr sein?"
  (Ich kann des Andern Zeugnis nicht annehmen, weil es kein *Zeugnis* ist. Es sagt mir nur, was er zu sagen *geneigt* ist.)

595. Es ist uns natürlich, den Satz in diesem Zusammenhang auszusprechen; und unnatürlich, ihn isoliert zu sagen. Sollen wir sagen: Es gibt ein bestimmtes Gefühl, das das Aussprechen jedes Satzes begleitet, dessen Aussprechen uns natürlich ist?

596. Das Gefühl der 'Bekanntheit' und der 'Natürlichkeit'. Leichter ist es, ein Gefühl der Unbekanntheit und der Unnatürlichkeit aufzufinden. Oder: *Gefühle*. Denn nicht alles, was uns unbekannt ist, macht uns einen Eindruck der Unbekanntheit. Und hier muß man sich überlegen, was wir "unbekannt" nennen. Einen Feldstein, den wir am Weg sehen, erkennen wir als solchen, aber vielleicht nicht als den, der immer da gelegen ist. Einen Menschen etwa als Menschen, aber nicht als Bekannten. Es gibt Gefühle der Wohlvertrautheit; ihre Äußerung ist manchmal ein Blick, oder die Worte "Das alte Zimmer!" (das ich vor vielen Jahren bewohnt habe und nun unverändert wiederfinde). Ebenso gibt es Gefühle der Fremdheit: Ich stutze; sehe den Gegenstand, oder Menschen, prüfend oder mißtrauisch an; sage "Es ist mir alles fremd." — Aber weil es nun dies Gefühl der Fremdheit gibt, kann man nicht sagen: jeder Gegenstand, den wir gut kennen und der uns nicht fremd vorkommt, gebe uns ein Gefühl der Vertrautheit. — Wir meinen, quasi, der Platz, den einmal das Gefühl der Fremdheit einnimmt, müsse doch *irgendwie* besetzt sein. Es ist der Platz für diese Atmosphäre vorhanden, und nimmt ihn nicht die eine ein, dann eine andere.

undertone there when you repeated the sentence after someone else? And how is the 'undertone' now to be separated from the rest of the experience of speaking?

593. A main cause of philosophical diseases — a one-sided diet: one nourishes one's thinking with only one kind of example.

594. "But the words, significantly uttered, have, after all, not only a surface, but also a dimension of depth!" After all, something different does take place when they are uttered significantly from when they are merely uttered. — How I express this is not the point. Whether I say that in the first case they have depth; or that something goes on in me, in my mind, as I utter them; or that they have an atmosphere — it always comes to the same thing.

"Well, if we all agree about that, won't it be true?"

(I cannot accept the other person's testimony, because it is not *testimony*. It only tells me what he is *inclined* to say.)

595. It is natural for us to say a sentence in such-and-such a context, and unnatural to say it in isolation. Are we to say that |156| there is a particular feeling accompanying the utterance of every sentence whose utterance comes naturally to us?

596. The feeling of 'familiarity' and of 'naturalness'. It is easier to come across a feeling of unfamiliarity and of unnaturalness. Or, *feelings*. For not everything that is unfamiliar to us makes an impression of unfamiliarity upon us. And here one has to consider what we call "unfamiliar". If a boulder lies on the road, we know it for a boulder, but perhaps not for the one which has always been lying there. We recognize a man, say, as a man, but not as an acquaintance. There are feelings of long-standing familiarity: they are sometimes manifest in a particular way of looking or by the words "The same old room!" (which I occupied many years before and, now returning, find unchanged). Equally, there are feelings of strangeness: I stop short, look at the object or man questioningly or suspiciously, and say "I find it all strange". — But the existence of this feeling of strangeness does not give us a reason for saying that every object which we know well and which does not seem strange to us gives us a feeling of familiarity. — It is as if we thought that the space once filled by the feeling of strangeness must surely be filled by *something*. The space for these kinds of atmosphere is there, and if one of them is not filling it, then another is.

597. Wie dem Deutschen, der gut Englisch spricht, Germanismen unterlaufen, obgleich er nicht erst den deutschen Ausdruck bildet und ihn dann ins Englische übersetzt; wie er also Englisch spricht, *als übersetze er,* 'unbewußt', aus dem Deutschen, so denken wir oft, als läge unserm Denken ein Denkschema zu Grunde; als übersetzten wir aus einer primitiveren Denkweise in die unsre.

598. Wenn wir philosophieren, möchten wir Gefühle hypostasieren, wo keine sind. Sie dienen dazu, uns unsere Gedanken zu erklären.
    '*Hier* verlangt die Erklärung unseres Denkens ein Gefühl!' Es ist, als ob unsre Überzeugung auf diese Forderung hin ihr nachkäme.

599. In der Philosophie werden nicht Schlüsse gezogen. "Es muß sich doch so verhalten!" ist kein Satz der Philosophie. Sie stellt nur fest, was Jeder ihr zugibt.

600. Macht alles, was uns nicht auffällt, den Eindruck der Unauffälligkeit? Macht uns das Gewöhnliche immer den *Eindruck* der Gewöhnlichkeit?

601. Wenn ich von diesem Tisch rede, — *erinnere* ich mich daran, daß dieser Gegenstand "Tisch" genannt wird?

602. Wenn man mich fragt "Hast du deinen Schreibtisch wiedererkannt, wie du heute morgens in dein Zimmer getreten bist?" — so würde ich wohl sagen "Gewiß!" Und doch wäre es irreführend, zu sagen, es habe sich da ein Wiedererkennen abgespielt. Der Schreibtisch war mir natürlich nicht fremd; ich war nicht überrascht, ihn zu sehen, wie ich es gewesen wäre, wenn ein Anderer da gestanden hätte, oder ein fremdartiger Gegenstand.

603. Niemand wird sagen, daß jedesmal, wenn ich in mein Zimmer komme, in die altgewohnte Umgebung, sich ein Wiedererkennen alles dessen, was ich sehe und hundertmal gesehen habe, abspielt.

604. Von den Vorgängen, die man "Wiedererkennen" nennt, haben wir leicht ein falsches Bild; als bestünde das Wiedererkennen immer darin, daß wir zwei Eindrücke miteinander vergleichen. Es ist, als trüge ich ein Bild eines Gegenstands bei mir und agnoszierte danach einen Gegenstand als den, welchen das Bild darstellt. Unser Gedächtnis scheint uns so einen Vergleich zu vermitteln, indem es uns ein Bild des früher Gesehenen aufbewahrt, oder uns erlaubt (wie durch ein Rohr) in die Vergangenheit zu blicken.

597. Germanisms will creep into the speech of a German who speaks English well, even though he does not first construct the German expression and then translate it into English. This will make him speak English *as if he were translating* 'unconsciously' from German. So too, we often think in a way that makes it seem as if our thinking were grounded in a thought-schema, as if we were translating from a more primitive mode of thought into our own.

598. When we do philosophy, we are inclined to hypostatize feelings where there are none. They serve to explain our thoughts to us.
  "*Here* the explanation of our thinking requires a feeling!" It is as if our conviction answered to this demand.

599. In philosophy no inferences are drawn. "But it must be like this!" is not a philosophical proposition. Philosophy only states what everyone concedes to it.

600. Does everything that we do not find conspicuous make an impression of inconspicuousness? Does what is ordinary always make the *impression* of ordinariness? |157|

601. When I talk about this table — do I *remember* that this object is called a "table"?

602. Asked "Did you recognize your desk when you entered your room this morning?" — I'd no doubt say "Certainly!" And yet it would be misleading to say that any recognizing had occurred. Of course, the desk was not strange to me; I wasn't surprised to see it, as I would have been if another one had been standing there, or some unfamiliar object.

603. No one will say that every time I enter my room, my long familiar surroundings, there occurs an act of recognition of all that I see and have seen hundreds of times before.

604. It is easy to misconceive what is called "recognizing"; as if recognizing always consisted in comparing two impressions with one another. It is as if I carried a picture of an object with me and used it to identify an object as the one represented by the picture. Our memory seems to us to be the agent of such a comparison, by preserving a picture of what has been seen before, or by allowing us to look into the past (as if down a spyglass).

605. Und es ist ja nicht so sehr, als vergliche ich den Gegenstand mit einem neben ihm stehenden Bild, sondern als *deckte* er sich mit dem Bild. Ich sehe also nur Eins und nicht Zwei.

606. Wir sagen "Der Ausdruck seiner Stimme war *echt*". War er unecht, so denken wir uns quasi hinter ihm einen anderen stehen. — Er macht nach außen *dieses* Gesicht, im Innern aber ein anderes. — Das heißt aber nicht, daß, wenn sein Ausdruck *echt* ist, er zwei gleiche Gesichter macht.
        (("Ein ganz bestimmter Ausdruck".))

607. Wie schätzt man, wieviel Uhr es ist? Ich meine aber nicht, nach äußeren Anhaltspunkten, dem Stand der Sonne, der Helligkeit im Zimmer, u. dergl. — Man fragt sich etwa "Wieviel Uhr kann es sein?", hält einen Augenblick inne, stellt sich vielleicht das Zifferblatt vor; und dann spricht man eine Zeit aus. — Oder man überlegt sich mehrere Möglichkeiten; man denkt sich *eine* Zeit, dann eine andre, und bleibt endlich bei einer stehen. So und ähnlich geht es vor sich. —— Aber ist nicht der Einfall von einem Gefühl der Überzeugung begleitet; und heißt das nicht, daß er nun mit einer inneren Uhr übereinstimmt? — Nein, ich lese die Zeit von keiner Uhr ab; ein Gefühl der Überzeugung ist insofern da, als ich mir *ohne* Empfindung des Zweifels, mit Ruhe und Sicherheit, eine Zeit sage. — Aber schnappt nicht etwas bei dieser Zeitangabe ein? — Nichts, das ich wüßte; wenn du nicht das Zur-Ruhe-Kommen der Überlegung, das Stehenbleiben bei einer Zahl so nennst. Ich hätte hier auch nie von einem 'Gefühl der Überzeugung' geredet, sondern gesagt: ich habe eine Weile überlegt und mich dann dafür entschieden, daß es viertel sechs ist. — Wonach aber hab ich mich entschieden? Ich hätte vielleicht gesagt: "bloß nach dem Gefühl"; das heißt nur: ich habe es dem Einfall überlassen. —— Aber du mußtest dich doch wenigstens zum Schätzen der Zeit in einen bestimmten Zustand versetzen; und du nimmst doch nicht jede Vorstellung einer Zeitangabe als Angabe der richtigen Zeit! — Wie gesagt: ich hatte mich *gefragt* "Wieviel Uhr mag es sein?". D. h., ich habe diese Frage nicht, z. B., in einer Erzählung gelesen; noch sie als Ausspruch eines Andern zitiert; noch mich im Aussprechen dieser Wörter geübt; u. s. f. Nicht unter *diesen* Umständen habe ich die Worte gesprochen. — Aber unter *welchen* also? — Ich dachte an mein Frühstück und ob es heute spät damit würde. Solcherart waren die Umstände. — Aber siehst du denn wirklich nicht, daß du doch in einem, wenn auch ungreifbaren, für das Schätzen der Zeit charakteristischen Zustand, gleichsam in einer dafür charakteristischen Atmosphäre warst? — Ja, das Charakteristische war, daß ich mich

605. Indeed, it is not so much as if I were comparing the object with a picture set beside it, but as if the object *coincided* with the picture. So I see only one thing, not two.

606. We say "The expression in his voice was *genuine*". If it was spurious, we think of another one, as it were behind it. — *This* is the face he shows the world; inwardly he has another one. — But this does not mean that when his expression is *genuine*, he has two identical faces.
*   (("A quite particular expression."))

607. How does one guess the time? I don't mean by clues, such as the position of the sun, the brightness of the room, and the like. — One asks oneself, say, "What time can it be?", pauses a moment, perhaps imagines a clock face, and then says a time. — Or one considers various possibilities, thinks first of one time, then of another, and in the end stops at a particular one. That's the sort of thing one does. —— But isn't the hunch accompanied by a feeling of conviction; and doesn't that mean that it now accords with an inner clock? — No, I don't read the time off from any clock; there is a feeling of conviction inasmuch as I say a time to myself *without* a feeling of doubt, with calm assurance. — But doesn't something click as I say [158] the time? — Nothing that I know of; unless this is your word for the calming down of your deliberations, your coming to a halt at some number. And I'd never have spoken of 'a feeling of conviction' here, but would have said: I considered a while and then plumped for its being quarter past five. — But what did I go by? I might perhaps have said "just by feeling", which only means that I relied on a hunch. —— But surely you must at least have put yourself in a particular state of mind in order to guess the time; and you don't take just any old idea of what time it is as giving the correct time! — To repeat: I *asked* myself "I wonder what time it is?" That is, I did not, for example, read this sentence in a story, or quote it as someone else's utterance; nor was I practising the pronunciation of these words; and so on. *These* were not the circumstances of my saying the words. — But then, *what* were the circumstances? — I was thinking about my breakfast, and wondering whether it would be late today. These were the kind of circumstances. — But do you really not see that you were in a state of mind which, though intangible, is characteristic of guessing the time, as if you were surrounded by an atmosphere characteristic of doing so. — Yes; what was characteristic was that I

fragte "Wieviel Uhr mag es sein?" — Und hat dieser Satz eine bestimmte Atmosphäre, — wie soll ich sie von ihm selbst trennen können? Es wäre mir nie eingefallen, der Satz hätte einen solchen Dunstkreis, hätte ich nicht daran gedacht, wie man ihn auch anders — als Zitat, im Scherz, als Sprechübung, etc. — sagen könnte. Und *da* wollte ich auf einmal sagen, da erschien es mir auf einmal, ich müßte die Worte doch irgendwie besonders *gemeint* haben; anders nämlich, als in jenen andern Fällen. Es hatte sich mir das Bild von der besonderen Atmosphäre aufgedrängt; ich sehe sie förmlich vor mir — solange ich nämlich nicht auf das sehe, was nach meiner Erinnerung wirklich gewesen ist.

Und was das Gefühl der Sicherheit anbelangt: so sage ich mir manchmal "Ich bin sicher, es ist ... Uhr", und in mehr oder weniger sicherem Tonfall, etc. Fragst du nach dem *Grund* für diese Sicherheit, so habe ich keinen.

Wenn ich sage: ich lese es auf einer innern Uhr ab, — so ist das ein Bild, dem nur entspricht, daß ich diese Zeitangabe gemacht habe. Und der Zweck des Bildes ist, diesen Fall dem andern anzugleichen. Ich sträube mich, die beiden verschiedenen Fälle anzuerkennen.

608. Von größter Wichtigkeit ist die Idee der Ungreifbarkeit jenes geistigen Zustands beim Schätzen der Zeit. Warum ist er *ungreifbar*? Ist es nicht, weil wir, was an unserm Zustand greifbar ist, uns weigern, zu dem spezifischen Zustand zu rechnen, den wir postulieren?

609. Die Beschreibung einer Atmosphäre ist eine spezielle Sprachanwendung, zu speziellen Zwecken.

((Deuten des 'Verstehens' als Atmosphäre; als seelischer Akt. Man kann zu allem eine Atmosphäre hinzukonstruieren. 'Ein unbeschreiblicher Charakter.'))

610. Beschreib das Aroma des Kaffees! — Warum geht es nicht? Fehlen uns die Worte? Und *wofür* fehlen sie uns? — Woher aber der Gedanke, es müsse doch so eine Beschreibung möglich sein? Ist dir so eine Beschreibung je abgegangen? Hast du versucht, das Aroma zu beschreiben, und es ist nicht gelungen?

((Ich möchte sagen "Diese Töne sagen etwas Herrliches, aber ich weiß nicht was." Diese Töne sind eine starke Geste, aber ich kann ihr nichts Erklärendes an die Seite stellen. Ein tief ernstes Kopfnicken. James: "Es fehlen uns die Worte." Warum führen wir sie dann nicht ein? Was müßte der Fall sein, damit wir es könnten?))

said to myself "I wonder what time it is" — And if this sentence has a particular atmosphere, how am I to separate it from the sentence itself? It would never have occurred to me to think that the sentence had such an aura, if I had not thought of how one might say it differently — as a quotation, as a joke, as practice in elocution, and so on. And *then* all at once I wanted to say — then all at once it seemed to me — that I must after all have *meant* the words somehow specially; differently, that is, from in those other cases. The picture of the special atmosphere forced itself upon me; I virtually see the atmosphere before me — so long, that is, as I do not look at what, according to my memory, really happened.

And as for the feeling of being sure: I sometimes say to myself, "I am sure it's . . . o'clock", and in a more or less confident tone of voice, and so on. If you ask me the *reason* for being sure, I have none.

If I say: I read it off from an inner clock — that is a picture, and all that corresponds to it is that I estimated the time. And the purpose of the picture is to assimilate this case to the other one. I am reluctant to acknowledge two different cases here.

608. The idea of the intangibility of that mental state in estimating the time is of the greatest importance. Why is it *intangible*? Isn't it |159| because we refuse to count what is tangible about our state as part of the specific state which we are postulating?

609. The description of an atmosphere is a special application of language, for special purposes.

* ((Interpreting 'understanding' as atmosphere; as a mental act. One can fabricate an atmosphere apropos anything. 'An indescribable character.'))

610. Describe the aroma of coffee! — Why can't it be done? Do we lack the words? And *for what* are words lacking? — But where do we get the idea that such a description must, after all, be possible? Have you ever felt the lack of such a description? Have you tried to describe the aroma and failed?

* ((I am inclined to say: "These notes say something glorious, but I do not know what." These notes are a powerful gesture, but I cannot put anything side by side with it that will serve as an explanation. A grave nod. James: "We lack the words." Then why don't we introduce new ones? What would have to be the case for us to be able to?))

611. "Das Wollen ist auch nur eine Erfahrung", möchte man sagen (der 'Wille' auch nur 'Vorstellung'). Er kommt, wenn er kommt, und ich kann ihn nicht herbeiführen.

   Nicht herbeiführen? — Wie *was*? Was kann ich denn herbeiführen? Womit vergleiche ich das Wollen, wenn ich dies sage?

612. Von der Bewegung meines Armes, z. B., würde ich nicht sagen, sie komme, wenn sie komme, etc. Und hier ist das Gebiet, in welchem wir sinnvoll sagen, daß uns etwas nicht einfach geschieht, sondern daß wir es *tun*. "Ich brauche nicht abwarten, bis mein Arm sich heben wird, — ich kann ihn heben." Und hier setze ich die Bewegung meines Arms etwa dem entgegen, daß sich das heftige Klopfen meines Herzens legen wird.

613. In dem Sinne, in welchem ich überhaupt etwas herbeiführen kann (etwa Magenschmerzen durch Überessen) kann ich auch das Wollen herbeiführen. In diesem Sinne führe ich das Schwimmen-Wollen herbei, indem ich ins Wasser springe. Ich wollte wohl sagen: ich könnte das Wollen nicht wollen; d. h., es hat keinen Sinn, vom Wollen-Wollen zu sprechen. "Wollen" ist nicht der Name für eine Handlung und also auch für keine willkürliche. Und mein falscher Ausdruck kam daher, daß man sich das Wollen als ein unmittelbares, nichtkausales, Herbeiführen denken will. Dieser Idee aber liegt eine irreführende Analogie zu Grunde; der kausale Nexus erscheint durch einen Mechanismus hergestellt, der zwei Maschinenteile verbindet. Die Verbindung kann auslassen, wenn der Mechanismus gestört wird. (Man denkt nur an die Störungen, denen ein Mechanismus normalerweise ausgesetzt ist; nicht daran, daß etwa die Zahnräder plötzlich weich werden, oder einander durchdringen, etc.)

614. Wenn ich meinen Arm 'willkürlich' bewege, so bediene ich mich nicht eines Mittels, die Bewegung herbeizuführen. Auch mein Wunsch ist nicht ein solches Mittel.

615. "Das Wollen, wenn es nicht eine Art Wünschen sein soll, muß das Handeln selber sein. Es darf nicht vor dem Handeln stehen bleiben." Ist es das Handeln, so ist es dies im gewöhnlichen Sinne des Worts; also: sprechen, schreiben, gehen, etwas heben, sich etwas vorstellen. Aber auch: trachten, versuchen, sich bemühen, — zu sprechen, zu schreiben, etwas zu heben, sich etwas vorzustellen, etc.

616. Wenn ich meinen Arm hebe, so habe ich *nicht* gewünscht, er möge sich heben. Die willkürliche Handlung schließt diesen Wunsch aus. Man kann allerdings sagen: "Ich hoffe, ich werde den Kreis fehlerlos zeichnen." Und damit drückt man einen Wunsch aus, die Hand möge sich so und so bewegen.

* 611. "Willing — wanting — too is merely an experience," one would like to say (the 'will' too only 'idea'). It comes when it comes, and I cannot bring it about.

Not bring it about? — Like *what*? What can I bring about, then? What am I comparing it with when I say this?

612. I wouldn't say of the movement of my arm, for example, that it comes when it comes, and so on. And this is the domain in which it makes sense to say that something doesn't simply happen to us, but that we *do* it. "I don't need to wait for my arm to rise — I can raise it." And here I am making a contrast between the movement of my arm and, say, the fact that the violent thudding of my heart will subside.

613. In the sense in which I can ever bring about anything (such as stomach-ache through overeating), I can also bring about wanting. In this sense, I bring about wanting to swim by jumping into the water. I suppose I was trying to say: I can't want to want; that is, it makes no sense to speak of wanting to want. "Wanting" is not the name of an action, and so not of a voluntary one either. And my use of a wrong expression came from the fact that one is inclined to think of wanting as an immediate non-causal bringing about. But a misleading analogy lies at the root of this idea; the causal |160| nexus seems to be established by a mechanism connecting two parts of a machine. The connection may be disrupted if the mechanism malfunctions. (One thinks only of the normal ways in which a mechanism goes wrong, not, say, of cog-wheels suddenly going soft, or penetrating each other, and so on.)

614. When I raise my arm 'voluntarily', I don't make use of any means to bring the movement about. My wish is not such a means either.

615. "Willing, if it is not to be a sort of wishing, must be the action itself. It mustn't stop anywhere short of the action." If it is the action, then it is so in the ordinary sense of the word; so it is speaking, writing, walking, lifting a thing, imagining something. But it is also striving, trying, making an effort — to speak, to write, to lift a thing, to imagine something, and so on.

616. When I raise my arm, I have *not* wished it to rise. The voluntary action excludes this wish. It is, however, possible to say: "I hope I shall draw the circle faultlessly." And that is to express a wish that one's hand should move in such-and-such a way.

617. Wenn wir unsere Finger in besonderer Weise verschränken, so sind wir manchmal nicht im Stande, einen bestimmten Finger auf Befehl zu bewegen, wenn der Befehlende bloß auf den Finger *zeigt* — ihn bloß unserm Aug zeigt. Wenn er ihn dagegen berührt, so können wir ihn bewegen. Man möchte diese Erfahrung so beschreiben: wir seien nicht im Stande, den Finger bewegen zu *wollen*. Der Fall ist ganz verschieden von dem, wenn wir nicht im Stande sind, den Finger zu bewegen, weil ihn etwa jemand festhält. Man wird nun geneigt sein, den ersten Fall so zu beschreiben: man könne für den Willen keinen Angriff finden, ehe der Finger nicht berührt werde. Erst wenn man ihn fühle, könne der Wille wissen, wo er anzugreifen habe. — Aber diese Ausdrucksweise ist irreführend. Man möchte sagen: "Wie soll ich denn wissen, wo ich mit dem Willen anzupacken habe, wenn das Gefühl nicht die Stelle bezeichnet?" Aber wie weiß man denn, wenn das Gefühl da ist, wohin ich den Willen zu lenken habe?

Daß der Finger in diesem Falle gleichsam gelähmt ist, ehe wir eine Berührung in ihm fühlen, das zeigt die Erfahrung; es war aber nicht a priori einzusehen.

618. Das wollende Subjekt stellt man sich hier als etwas Masseloses (Trägheitsloses) vor; als einen Motor, der in sich selbst keinen Trägheitswiderstand zu überwinden hat. Und also nur Treibendes und nicht Getriebenes ist. D. h.: Man kann sagen "Ich will, aber mein Körper folgt mir nicht" — aber nicht: "Mein Wille folgt mir nicht." (Augustinus)

Aber in dem Sinn, in welchem es mir nicht mißlingen kann, zu wollen, kann ich es auch nicht versuchen.

619. Und man könnte sagen: "Ich kann nur insofern jederzeit *wollen*, als ich nie versuchen kann, zu wollen."

620. *Tun* scheint selbst kein Volumen der Erfahrung zu haben. Es scheint wie ein ausdehnungsloser Punkt, die Spitze einer Nadel. Diese Spitze scheint das eigentliche Agens. Und das Geschehen in der Erscheinung nur Folge dieses Tuns. "Ich *tue*" scheint einen bestimmten Sinn zu haben, abgelöst von jeder Erfahrung.

621. Aber vergessen wir eines nicht: wenn 'ich meinen Arm hebe', hebt sich mein Arm. Und das Problem entsteht: was ist das, was übrigbleibt, wenn ich von der Tatsache, daß ich meinen Arm hebe, die abziehe, daß mein Arm sich hebt?

((Sind nun die kinästhetischen Empfindungen mein Wollen?))

617. If we cross our fingers in a special way, we are sometimes unable to move a particular finger when someone tells us to do so, if he only *points* to the finger — merely shows it to the eye. However, if he touches it, we *can* move it. One would like to describe this experience as follows: we are unable to *will* to move the finger. The case is quite different from that in which we are not able to move the finger because someone is, say, holding it. One is now inclined to describe the former case by saying: one can't find any point of application for the will until the finger is touched. Only when one feels the finger can the will know where it is to engage. — But this way of putting it is misleading. One would like to say: "How am I to know where I am to catch hold with the will, if the feeling does not indicate the place?" But then how do I know to what point I am to direct the will when the feeling *is* there?

It is experience that shows that in this case the finger is, as it were, paralysed until we feel a touch on it; it could not have been known a priori.

* 618. One imagines the willing subject here as something without any mass (without any inertia), as a motor which has no inertia in itself to overcome. And so it is only mover, not moved. That is: |161| one can say "I will, but my body does not obey me" — but not: "My will does not obey me." (Augustine)

But in the sense in which I can't fail to will, I can't try to will either.

619. And one might say: "It is only inasmuch as I can never try to will that I can always will."

620. *Doing* itself seems not to have any experiential volume. It seems like an extensionless point, the point of a needle. This point seems to be the real agent — and what happens in the realm of appearances merely consequences of this doing. "I *do*" seems to have a definite sense, independently of any experience.

621. But there is one thing we shouldn't overlook: when 'I raise my arm', my arm rises. And now a problem emerges: what is left over if I subtract the fact that my arm rises from the fact that I raise my arm?

* ((Are the kinaesthetic sensations my willing?))

622. Wenn ich meinen Arm hebe, *versuche* ich meistens nicht, ihn zu heben.

623. "Ich will unbedingt dieses Haus erreichen." Wenn aber keine Schwierigkeit da ist, — *kann* ich da trachten, unbedingt dies Haus zu erreichen?

624. Im Laboratorium, unter dem Einfluß elektrischer Ströme etwa, sagt Einer mit geschlossenen Augen "Ich bewege meinen Arm auf und ab" — obgleich sich der Arm nicht bewegt. "Er hat also das besondere Gefühl dieser Bewegung" sagen wir. — Beweg mit geschlossenen Augen deinen Arm hin und her. Und nun versuch, während du es tust, dir einzureden, der Arm stehe still und du habest nur gewisse seltsame Empfindungen in Muskeln und Gelenken!

625. "Wie weißt du, daß du deinen Arm gehoben hast?" — "Ich fühle es." Was du also wiedererkennst, ist die Empfindung? Und bist du sicher, daß du sie richtig wiedererkennst? — Du bist sicher, daß du deinen Arm gehoben hast; ist nicht dies das Kriterium, das Maß, des Wiedererkennens?

626. "Wenn ich mit einem Stock diesen Gegenstand abtaste, habe ich die Tastempfindung in der Spitze des Stockes, nicht in der Hand, die ihn hält." Wenn Einer sagt "Ich habe nicht hier in der Hand, sondern im Handgelenk Schmerzen", so ist die Konsequenz, daß der Arzt das Handgelenk untersucht. Welchen Unterschied macht es aber, ob ich sage, ich fühle die Härte des Gegenstands in der Stockspitze, oder in der Hand? Heißt, was ich sage: "Es ist, als hätte ich Nervenenden in der Stockspitze"? *Inwiefern* ist es so? — Nun, ich bin jedenfalls geneigt, zu sagen "Ich fühle die Härte, etc. in der Stockspitze". Und damit geht zusammen, daß ich beim Abtasten nicht auf meine Hand, sondern auf die Stockspitze sehe; daß ich, was ich fühle, mit den Worten beschreibe "Ich fühle dort etwas Hartes, Rundes" — nicht mit den Worten "Ich fühle einen Druck gegen die Fingerspitzen des Daumens, Mittelfingers und Zeigefingers . . .". Wenn mich etwa jemand fragte "Was fühlst du jetzt in den Fingern, die die Sonde halten?", so könnte ich ihm antworten: "Ich weiß nicht —— ich fühle *dort* etwas Hartes, Rauhes."

627. Betrachte diese Beschreibung einer willkürlichen Handlung: "Ich fasse den Entschluß, um 5 Uhr die Glocke zu ziehen; und wenn es 5 schlägt, macht mein Arm nun diese Bewegung." — Ist das die richtige Beschreibung, und nicht *die*: ". . . und wenn es 5 schlägt, hebe ich meinen Arm"? —— Die erste Beschreibung möchte man so ergänzen: "und siehe da! mein Arm hebt sich, wenn es 5 schlägt." Und dies "siehe da" ist

622. When I raise my arm, I don't usually *try* to raise it.

623. "I want to get to that house at all costs." — But if there is no difficulty about it, *can* I strive at all costs to get to the house?

624. In the laboratory, when subjected to an electric current, for example, someone with his eyes shut says "I am moving my arm up and down" — though his arm is not moving. "So", we say, "he has the special feeling of making that movement." — Move your arm to and fro with your eyes shut. And now try, while you do so, to talk yourself into the idea that your arm is staying still and that you are only having certain strange feelings in your muscles and joints!

625. "How do you know that you've raised your arm?" — "I feel it." So what you recognize is the feeling? And are you certain that you recognize it right? — You're certain that you've raised your arm; isn't this the criterion, the measure, of recognizing?

626. "When I touch this object with a stick, I have the sensation of touching in the tip of the stick, not in the hand that holds it." When someone says "The pain isn't here in my hand, but in my wrist", this has the consequence that the doctor examines the wrist. But what difference does it make if I say that I feel the hardness of the |162| object in the tip of the stick or in my hand? Does what I say mean "It's as if I had nerve endings in the tip of the stick?" *In what way* is it like that? — Well, I am at any rate inclined to say, "I feel the hardness and so forth in the tip of the stick". What goes with this is that when I touch the object, I look not at my hand but at the tip of the stick; that I describe what I feel by saying "I feel something hard and round there" — not "I feel a pressure against the tips of my thumb, middle finger, and index finger . . ." If, for example, someone were to ask me, "What are you now feeling in the fingers that hold the probe?", I might reply: "I don't know —— I feel something hard and rough *over there*".

627. Consider the following description of a voluntary action: "I form the decision to pull the bell at 5 o'clock; and when it strikes 5, my arm makes this movement." — Is that the correct description, and not *this* one: ". . . and when it strikes 5, I raise my arm"? —— One would like to supplement the first description: "And lo and behold! my arm goes up when it strikes 5." And this "lo and behold!" is precisely what

gerade, was hier wegfällt. Ich sage *nicht*: "Sieh, mein Arm hebt sich!"
wenn ich ihn hebe.

628. Man könnte also sagen: die willkürliche Bewegung sei durch die
Abwesenheit des Staunens charakterisiert. Und nun will ich nicht, daß
man fragt "Aber *warum* erstaunt man hier nicht?".

629. Wenn Leute über die Möglichkeit eines Vorherwissens der
Zukunft reden, vergessen sie immer die Tatsache des Vorhersagens
der willkürlichen Bewegungen.

630. Betrachte die beiden Sprachspiele:
   a) Einer gibt einem Andern den Befehl, bestimmte Armbewegungen
zu machen, oder Körperstellungen einzunehmen (Turnlehrer und
Schüler). Und eine Variante dieses Sprachspiels ist dies: Der Schüler gibt
sich selbst Befehle und führt sie dann aus.
   b) Jemand beobachtet gewisse regelmäßige Vorgänge — z. B. die
Reaktionen verschiedener Metalle auf Säuren — und macht daraufhin
Vorhersagen über die Reaktionen, die in bestimmten Fällen eintreten
werden.
   Es ist zwischen diesen beiden Sprachspielen eine offenbare Verwandtschaft, und auch Grundverschiedenheit. In beiden könnte man die ausgesprochenen Worte "Voraussagen" nennen. Vergleiche aber die Abrichtung,
die zu der ersten Technik führt, mit der Abrichtung für die zweite!

631. "Ich werde jetzt zwei Pulver einnehmen; eine halbe Stunde darauf
werde ich erbrechen." — Es erklärt nichts, wenn ich sage, im ersten Fall
sei ich das Agens, im zweiten bloß der Beobachter. Oder: im ersten Falle
sähe ich den kausalen Zusammenhang von innen, im zweiten von
außen. Und vieles Ähnliche.
   Es ist auch nicht zur Sache, zu sagen, daß eine Vorhersage der ersten
Art so wenig unfehlbar ist, wie eine der zweiten Art.
   Nicht auf Grund von Beobachtungen meines Verhaltens sagte ich, ich
würde jetzt zwei Pulver einnehmen. Die Antezedentien dieses Satzes waren
andere. Ich meine die Gedanken, Handlungen, etc., die zu ihm hinleiten.
Und es ist nur irreführend, zu sagen: "Die einzige wesentliche Voraussetzung deiner Äußerung war eben dein Entschluß."

632. Ich will nicht sagen: im Falle der Willensäußerung "Ich werde Pulver
einnehmen" sei die Voraussage Ursache — und ihre Erfüllung der Effekt.
(Das könnte vielleicht eine physiologische Untersuchung entscheiden.)
Soviel aber ist wahr: Wir können häufig aus der Äußerung des Entschlusses
die Handlung eines Menschen vorhersagen. Ein wichtiges Sprachspiel.

doesn't belong here. I do *not* say "Look, my arm is going up!" when I raise it.

628. So one might say: voluntary movement is marked by the absence of surprise. And now I don't mean you to ask "But *why* isn't one surprised here?"

629. When people talk about the possibility of foreknowledge of the future, they always overlook the case of predicting one's voluntary movements.

630. Consider these two language-games:

(a) Someone gives someone else the order to make particular movements with his arm, or to assume particular bodily positions (gymnastics instructor and pupil). And a variant of this language-game is this: the pupil gives himself orders and then carries them out.

(b) Someone observes certain regular processes — for example, the reactions of different metals to acids — and thereupon makes predictions about the reactions that will occur in certain cases.

There is an evident kinship between these two language-games, and also a fundamental difference. In both, one might call the spoken words "predictions". But compare the training which leads to the first technique with the training for the second one! |163|

631. "I'm going to take two powders now, and in half an hour I shall be sick." — It explains nothing to say that in the first case I am the agent, in the second merely the observer. Or that in the first case I see the causal connection from inside, in the second from outside. And much else to the same effect.

Nor is it to the point to say that a prediction of the first kind is no more infallible than one of the second kind.

It wasn't on the basis of observations of my behaviour that I said I was going to take two powders. The antecedents of this statement were different. I mean the thoughts, actions, and so on which led up to it. And it can only be misleading to say: "The only essential presupposition of your utterance was precisely your decision."

632. I do not want to say that in the case of the expression of intention "I am going to take two powders" the prediction is a cause — and its fulfilment the effect. (Perhaps a physiological investigation could determine this.) So much, however, is true: we can often predict a man's actions from his expression of a decision. An important language-game.

633. "Du wurdest früher unterbrochen; weißt du noch, was du sagen wolltest?" — Wenn ich's nun weiß und es sage — heißt das, daß ich es schon früher gedacht, und nur nicht gesagt hatte? Nein. Es sei denn, daß du die Sicherheit, mit der ich den unterbrochenen Satz weiterführe, als Kriterium dafür nimmst, daß der Gedanke damals bereits fertig war. — Aber es lag freilich schon alles mögliche in der Situation und in meinen Gedanken, das dem Satz weiterhilft.

634. Wenn ich den unterbrochenen Satz fortsetze und sage, *so* hätte ich ihn damals fortsetzen wollen, so ist das ähnlich, wie wenn ich einen Gedankengang nach kurzen Notizen ausführe.

Und *deute* ich also diese Notizen nicht? War nur *eine* Fortsetzung unter jenen Umständen möglich? Gewiß nicht. Aber ich *wählte* nicht unter diesen Deutungen. Ich *erinnerte* mich: daß ich das sagen wollte.

635. "Ich wollte sagen ..." — Du erinnerst dich an verschiedene Einzelheiten. Aber sie alle zeigen nicht diese Absicht. Es ist, als wäre das Bild einer Szene aufgenommen worden, aber es sind von ihm nur einige verstreute Einzelheiten zu sehen; hier eine Hand, dort ein Stück eines Gesichts, oder ein Hut, — das übrige ist dunkel. Und nun ist es, als wüßte ich doch ganz gewiß, was das ganze Bild darstellt. Als könnte ich das Dunkel lesen.

636. Diese 'Einzelheiten' sind nicht irrelevant in dem Sinne, in welchem andere Umstände, an die ich mich gleichfalls erinnern kann, es sind. Aber wem ich mitteile "Ich wollte für einen Augenblick sagen ...", der erfährt dadurch diese Einzelheiten nicht und muß sie auch nicht erraten. Er muß z. B. nicht wissen, daß ich schon den Mund zum Sprechen geöffnet hatte. Er *kann* sich aber den Vorgang so 'ausmalen'. (Und diese Fähigkeit gehört zum Verstehen meiner Mitteilung.)

637. "Ich weiß genau, was ich sagen wollte!" Und doch hatte ich's nicht gesagt. — Und doch lese ich's nicht von irgend einem andern Vorgang ab, der damals stattfand und mir in der Erinnerung ist.

Und ich *deute* auch nicht die damalige Situation und ihre Vorgeschichte. Denn ich überlege mir sie nicht und beurteile sie nicht.

638. Wie kommt es, daß ich dann trotzdem geneigt bin, ein Deuten darin zu sehen, wenn ich sage "Einen Augenblick lang wollte ich ihn betrügen"?

"Wie kannst du sicher sein, daß du einen Augenblick lang ihn betrügen wolltest? Waren nicht deine Handlungen und Gedanken viel zu rudimentär?"

633. "You were interrupted a while ago; do you still know what you were going to say?" — If I do know now, and say it, does that mean that I had already thought it before, only not said it? No. Unless you take the certainty with which I continue the interrupted sentence as a criterion of the thought's already having been completed at that time. — But, to be sure, the situation and the thoughts I had already contain all sorts of things to help the sentence on.

634. When I continue the interrupted sentence and say that *this* was how I had been going to continue it, this is similar to elaborating a train of thought from brief notes.

Then don't I *interpret* the notes? Was only *one* continuation possible in these circumstances? Of course not. But I didn't *choose* between these interpretations. I *remembered* that I was going to say this.

635. "I was going to say . . ." — You remember various details. But not even all of them together show this intention. It is as if a snapshot of a scene had been taken, but only a few scattered details of it were to be seen: here a hand, there a bit of a face, or a hat — the rest is dark. And now it is as if I knew quite certainly what the whole picture represented. As if I could read the darkness. |164|

636. These 'details' are not irrelevant in the sense in which other circumstances, which I can also remember, are irrelevant. But if I tell someone "For a moment I was going to say . . .", he doesn't learn those details from this, nor need he guess them. He needn't know, for instance, that I had already opened my mouth to speak. But he *can* 'fill out the picture' in this way. (And this ability is part of understanding what I tell him.)

637. "I know exactly what I was going to say!" And yet I didn't say it. — And yet I don't read it off from some other process which took place then and which I remember.

Nor am I *interpreting* that situation and its antecedents, which, after all, I neither consider nor judge.

638. How does it come about that, in spite of this, I am inclined to see an interpretation in saying "For a moment I was going to deceive him"?

"How can you be certain that, for a moment, you were going to deceive him? Weren't your actions and thoughts much too rudimentary?"

Kann denn die Evidenz nicht zu spärlich sein? Ja, wenn man ihr nachgeht, scheint sie außerordentlich spärlich; aber ist das nicht, weil man die Geschichte dieser Evidenz außer Acht läßt? Wenn ich einen Augenblick lang die Absicht hatte, dem Andern Unwohlsein vorzuheucheln, so brauchte es dazu eine Vorgeschichte.

Beschreibt der, der sagt "Für einen Augenblick . . ." wirklich nur einen momentanen Vorgang?

Aber auch die ganze Geschichte war nicht die Evidenz, auf Grund derer ich sagte "Für einen Augenblick . . .".

639. Die Meinung, möchte man sagen, *entwickelt sich*. Aber auch darin liegt ein Fehler.

640. "Dieser Gedanke knüpft an Gedanken an, die ich früher einmal gehabt habe." — Wie tut er das? Durch ein *Gefühl* der Anknüpfung? Aber wie kann das Gefühl die Gedanken wirklich verknüpfen? — Das Wort "Gefühl" ist hier sehr irreleitend. Aber es ist manchmal möglich, mit Sicherheit zu sagen "Dieser Gedanke hängt mit jenen früheren zusammen", ohne daß man doch im Stande ist, den Zusammenhang zu zeigen. Dies gelingt vielleicht später.

641. "Wenn ich die Worte gesagt hätte 'Ich will ihn jetzt betrügen', hätte ich die Absicht nicht gewisser gehabt, als so." — Aber wenn du jene Worte gesagt hättest, mußtest du sie im vollen Ernste gemeint haben? (So ist also der am meisten explizite Ausdruck der Absicht allein keine genügende Evidenz der Absicht.)

642. "Ich habe ihn in diesem Augenblick gehaßt" — was geschah da? Bestand es nicht in Gedanken, Gefühlen und Handlungen? Und wenn ich mir nun diesen Augenblick vorführte, würde ich ein bestimmtes Gesicht machen, dächte an gewisse Geschehnisse, atmete in bestimmter Weise, brächte in mir gewisse Gefühle hervor. Ich könnte ein Gespräch, eine ganze Szene erdenken, in der dieser Haß zum Aufflammen käme. Und ich könnte diese Szene mit Gefühlen spielen, die denen eines wirklichen Vorfalls nahekämen. Dabei wird mir natürlich helfen, daß ich Ähnliches wirklich durchlebt habe.

643. Wenn ich mich nun des Vorfalls schäme, schäme ich mich des Ganzen: der Worte, des giftigen Tones, u. s. w.

644. "Ich schäme mich nicht dessen, was ich damals tat, sondern der Absicht, die ich hatte." — Und lag die Absicht nicht *auch* in dem, was ich tat? Was rechtfertigt die Scham? Die ganze Geschichte des Vorfalls.

For may the evidence not be too scanty? Yes, when one follows it up, it seems extraordinarily scanty; but isn't this because one is taking no account of the background of this evidence? If, for a moment, I intended to pretend to someone that I was unwell, that required an antecedent context.

If someone says "For a moment . . .", is he really only describing a momentary process?

But not even the entire background was my evidence for saying "For a moment . . ."

* 639. Meaning something, one wants to say, *develops*. But there is a mistake in this too.

640. "This thought links up with thoughts which I have had before." — How does it do so? Through a *feeling* of such a link? But how can a feeling really link these thoughts? — The word "feeling" is very misleading here. But it is sometimes possible to say with certainty, "This thought is connected with those earlier ones", even though one is unable to point out the connection. Perhaps one will succeed later.

641. "Even if I had uttered the words 'Now I'm going to deceive him', my intention would have been no more certain than it already was." — But if you had uttered those words, would you necessarily have meant them seriously? (So |165| the most explicit expression of intention is by itself insufficient evidence of intention.)

642. "At that moment I hated him." — What happened here? Didn't it consist in thoughts, feelings and actions? And if I were to rehearse that moment to myself, I'd assume a particular expression, think of certain happenings, breathe in a particular way, arouse certain feelings in myself. I might think up a conversation, a whole scene in which that hatred flared up. And I might act this scene with feelings approximating those of a real incident. That I have actually been through something of the sort will naturally help me to do so.

643. If I now become ashamed of this incident, I am ashamed of the whole thing: of the words, of the poisonous tone, and so on.

644. "I'm not ashamed of what I did then, but of the intention which I had." — And didn't the intention lie *also* in what I did? What justifies the shame? The whole background of the incident.

645. "Einen Augenblick lang wollte ich . . ." D. h., ich hatte ein bestimmtes Gefühl, inneres Erlebnis; und ich erinnere mich dran. —— Und
nun erinnere dich *recht genau*! Da scheint das 'innere Erlebnis' des Wollens
wieder zu verschwinden. Statt dessen erinnert man sich an Gedanken,
Gefühle, Bewegungen, auch an Zusammenhänge mit früheren Situationen.

Es ist, als hätte man die Einstellung eines Mikroskops verändert, und
was jetzt im Brennpunkt liegt, sah man früher nicht.

646. "Nun, das zeigt nur, daß du dein Mikroskop falsch eingestellt hast.
Du solltest eine bestimmte Schicht des Präparats anschaun, und siehst
nun eine andere."

Daran ist etwas richtig. Aber nimm an, ich erinnerte mich (mit einer
bestimmten Einstellung der Linsen) an *eine* Empfindung; wie darf ich
sagen, daß sie das ist, was ich die "Absicht" nenne? Es könnte sein,
daß ein bestimmter Kitzel (z. B.) jede meiner Absichten begleitete.

647. Was ist der natürliche Ausdruck einer Absicht? — Sieh eine Katze
an, wenn sie sich an einen Vogel heranschleicht; oder ein Tier, wenn es
entfliehen will.

((Verbindung mit Sätzen über Empfindungen.))

648. "Ich erinnere mich nicht mehr an meine Worte, aber ich erinnere mich
genau an meine Absicht: ich wollte ihn mit meinen Worten beruhigen."
Was *zeigt* mir meine Erinnerung; was führt sie mir vor die Seele? Nun,
wenn sie nichts täte, als mir diese Worte einzugeben! und vielleicht noch
andere, die die Situation noch genauer ausmalen. — ("Ich erinnere mich
nicht mehr meiner Worte, aber wohl an den Geist meiner Worte.")

649. "So kann also der gewisse Erinnerungen nicht haben, der keine
Sprache gelernt hat?" Freilich, — er kann keine sprachlichen
Erinnerungen, sprachlichen Wünsche oder Befürchtungen, etc. haben.
Und Erinnerungen, etc., in der Sprache sind ja nicht bloß die faden-
scheinigen Darstellungen der *eigentlichen* Erlebnisse; ist denn das
Sprachliche kein Erlebnis?

650. Wir sagen, der Hund fürchtet, sein Herr werde ihn schlagen; aber
nicht: er fürchte, sein Herr werde ihn morgen schlagen. Warum nicht?

651. "Ich erinnere mich, ich wäre damals gerne noch länger
geblieben." — Welches Bild dieses Verlangens tritt mir vor die Seele?
Gar keins. Was ich in der Erinnerung vor mir sehe, läßt keinen Schluß
auf meine Gefühle zu. Und doch erinnere ich mich ganz deutlich daran,
daß sie vorhanden waren.

645. "For a moment I was going to . . ." That is, I had a particular feeling, an inner experience; and I remember it. — And now remember *quite precisely*! Then the 'inner experience' of intending seems to vanish again. Instead, one remembers thoughts, feelings, movements and also connections with earlier situations.

It is as if one had altered the adjustment of a microscope: one did not see before what is now in focus.

646. "Well, that only shows that you have adjusted your microscope wrongly. You were supposed to examine a particular slice of the preparation, and now you are looking at a different one."

There is something right about this. But suppose that (with a certain adjustment of the lenses) I did remember a particular sensation; what allows me to say that it is what I call the "intention"? It might be that (for example) a particular tickle accompanied every one of my intentions.

647. What is the natural expression of an intention? — Look at a cat when it stalks a bird; or a beast when it wants to escape.

((Connection with propositions about sensations.))

648. "I no longer remember the words I used, but I remember my intention precisely; I wanted my words to calm him down." What does my memory *show* me; what does it bring before my mind? Suppose it did |166| nothing but suggest those words to me! — and perhaps others which fill out the picture still more exactly. — ("I don't remember my words any more, but I certainly remember their spirit.")

649. "So if someone has not learned a language, is he unable to have certain memories?" Of course — he cannot have linguistic memories, linguistic wishes or fears, and so on. And memories and suchlike in language are not mere threadbare representations of the *real* experiences; for is what is linguistic not an experience?

650. We say a dog is afraid his master will beat him; but not: he is afraid his master will beat him tomorrow. Why not?

651. "I remember that I would have been glad then to stay still longer." — What picture of this desire comes before my mind? None at all. What I see in my memory allows no conclusion as to my feelings. And yet I remember quite clearly that they were there.

652. "Er maß ihn mit feindseligem Blick und sagte . . ." Der Leser der Erzählung versteht dies; er hat keinen Zweifel in seiner Seele. Nun sagst du: "Wohl, er denkt sich die Bedeutung hinzu, er errät sie." — Im allgemeinen: Nein. Im allgemeinen denkt er sich nichts hinzu, errät nichts. — Es ist aber auch möglich, daß der feindselige Blick und die Worte sich später als Verstellung erweisen, oder daß der Leser im Zweifel darüber erhalten wird, ob sie es sind oder nicht, und daß er also wirklich auf eine mögliche Deutung rät. — Aber dann rät er vor allem auf einen Zusammenhang. Er sagt sich etwa: die Beiden, die hier so feindlich tun, sind in Wirklichkeit Freunde, etc. etc.

(("Wenn du den Satz verstehen willst, mußt du dir die seelische Bedeutung, die Seelenzustände, dazu vorstellen."))

653. Denk dir diesen Fall: Ich sage Einem, ich sei einen gewissen Weg gegangen, einem Plan gemäß, den ich zuvor angefertigt habe. Ich zeige ihm darauf diesen Plan, und er besteht aus Strichen auf einem Papier; aber ich kann nicht erklären, inwiefern diese Striche der Plan meiner Wanderung sind, dem Andern keine Regel sagen, wie der Plan zu deuten ist. Wohl aber bin ich jener Zeichnung mit allen charakteristischen Anzeichen des Kartenlesens nachgegangen. Ich könnte so eine Zeichnung einen 'privaten' Plan nennen; oder die Erscheinung, die ich beschrieben habe: "einem privaten Plan folgen". (Aber dieser Ausdruck wäre natürlich sehr leicht mißzuverstehen.)

Könnte ich nun sagen: "Daß ich damals so und so handeln wollte, lese ich gleichsam wie von einem Plan ab, obgleich kein Plan da ist"? Aber das heißt doch nichts anderes, als: *Ich bin jetzt geneigt, zu sagen*: "Ich lese die Absicht, so zu handeln, in gewissen Seelenzuständen, an die ich mich erinnere."

654. Unser Fehler ist, dort nach einer Erklärung zu suchen, wo wir die Tatsachen als 'Urphänomene' sehen sollten. D. h., wo wir sagen sollten: *dieses Sprachspiel wird gespielt*.

655. Nicht um die Erklärung eines Sprachspiels durch unsre Erlebnisse handelt sich's, sondern um die Feststellung eines Sprachspiels.

656. *Wozu* sage ich jemandem, ich hätte früher den und den Wunsch gehabt? — Sieh auf das Sprachspiel als das *Primäre*! Und auf die Gefühle, etc. als auf eine Betrachtungsweise, eine Deutung, des Sprachspiels!

Man könnte fragen: Wie ist der Mensch je dahin gekommen, eine sprachliche Äußerung zu machen, die wir "Berichten eines vergangenen Wunsches", oder einer vergangenen Absicht, nennen?

652. "He sized him up with a hostile glance and said . . ." The reader of the story understands this; he has no doubt in his mind. Now you say: "Very well, he supplies the meaning, he guesses it." — Generally speaking, no. Generally speaking, he supplies nothing, guesses nothing. — But it is also possible that the hostile glance and the words later prove to have been pretence, or that the reader is kept in doubt whether they are so or not, and so that he really does guess at a possible interpretation. — But then the main thing he guesses is a context. He says to himself, for example: the two men affecting such hostility here are in reality friends, and so forth.

((" If you want to understand the sentence, you have to imagine the psychological significance, the states of mind involved."))

653. Imagine this case: I tell someone that I walked a certain route, going by a map which I had prepared beforehand. Thereupon I show him the map, and it consists of lines on a piece of paper; but I cannot explain how these lines come to be a map of my route, I cannot tell him any rule for interpreting the map. Yet I did follow the drawing with all the characteristic tokens of reading a map. I might call such a drawing a 'private' map; or the phenomenon that I have described, "following a private map". (But this expression would, of course, be very easy to misunderstand.)

Could I now say: "I read off my having then meant to do such-and-|167| such, as if from a map, although there is no map"? That, however, means nothing but: *I am now inclined to say* "I read the intention of acting thus in certain states of mind which I remember".

* 654. Our mistake is to look for an explanation where we ought to regard the facts as 'proto-phenomena'. That is, where we ought to say: *this is the language-game that is being played.*

655. The point is not to explain a language-game by means of our experiences, but to take account of a language-game.

656. What is the *purpose* of telling someone that previously I had such-and-such a wish? — Regard the language-game as the *primary thing*. And regard the feelings, and so forth, as a way of looking at, interpreting, the language-game!

One might ask: how did human beings ever come to make the kind of linguistic utterance which we call "reporting a past wish" or "a past intention"?

657. Denken wir uns, diese Äußerung nehme immer die Form an: "Ich sagte mir: 'wenn ich nur länger bleiben könnte!' " Der Zweck einer solchen Mitteilung könnte sein, den Andern meine Reaktionen kennen zu lehren. (Vergleiche die Grammatik von "meinen" und "vouloir dire".)

658. Denk, wir drückten die Absicht eines Menschen immer so aus, indem wir sagen: "Er sagte gleichsam zu sich selbst 'Ich will . . .'." — Das ist das Bild. Und nun will ich wissen: Wie verwendet man den Ausdruck "etwas gleichsam zu sich selbst sagen"? Denn er bedeutet nicht: etwas zu sich selbst sagen.

659. Warum will ich ihm außer dem, was ich tat, auch noch eine Intention mitteilen? Nicht, weil die Intention auch noch etwas war, was damals vor sich ging. Sondern, weil ich ihm etwas über *mich* mitteilen will, was über das hinausgeht, was damals geschah.

Ich erschließe ihm mein Inneres, wenn ich sage, was ich tun wollte. — Nicht aber auf Grund einer Selbstbeobachtung, sondern durch eine Reaktion (man könnte es auch eine Intuition nennen).

660. Die Grammatik des Ausdrucks "Ich wollte damals sagen . . ." ist verwandt der des Ausdrucks "Ich hätte damals fortsetzen können".

Im einen Fall die Erinnerung an eine Absicht, im andern, an ein Verstehen.

661. Ich erinnere mich, *ihn* gemeint zu haben. Erinnere ich mich eines Vorgangs oder Zustands? — Wann fing er an; wie verlief er; etc.?

662. In einer nur um weniges verschiedenen Situation hätte er, statt stumm mit dem Finger zu winken, jemandem gesagt "Sag dem N., er soll zu mir kommen". Man kann nun sagen, die Worte "Ich wollte, N. solle zu mir kommen" beschreiben den damaligen Zustand meiner Seele, und kann es auch wieder *nicht* sagen.

663. Wenn ich sage "Ich meinte *ihn*", da mag mir wohl ein Bild vorschweben, etwa davon, wie ich ihn ansah, etc.; aber das Bild ist nur wie eine Illustration zu einer Geschichte. Aus ihr allein wäre meistens gar nichts zu erschließen; erst wenn man die Geschichte kennt, weiß man, was es mit dem Bild soll.

664. Man könnte im Gebrauch eines Worts eine 'Oberflächengrammatik' von einer 'Tiefengrammatik' unterscheiden. Das, was sich uns

657. Suppose this sort of utterance always took the form "I said to myself, 'if only I could stay longer!'" The purpose of such a report might be to acquaint someone with my reactions. (Compare the grammar of "mean" and "vouloir dire".)

658. Suppose we always expressed the fact that a man had an intention by saying "He as it were said to himself 'I will . . .'" — That is the picture. And now I want to know: how does one employ the expression "as it were to say something to oneself"? For it doesn't mean: to say something to oneself.

659. Why do I want to tell him about an intention too, over and above telling him what I did? — Not because the intention too was something going on at that time. But because I want to tell him something about *myself*, which goes beyond what happened at that time.

I reveal to him something of myself when I tell him what I was going to do. — Not, however, on grounds of self-observation, but by way of a reaction (it might also be called an intuition).

660. The grammar of the expression "I was then going to say . . ." is related to that of the expression "I could then have gone on".

In the one case I remember an intention, in the other I remember having understood. |168|

661. I remember having meant *him*. Am I remembering a process or a state? — When did it begin, how did it continue; and so on?

662. In an only slightly different situation, instead of silently beckoning, he would have said to someone "Tell N. to come to me". One may now say that the words "I wanted N. to come to me" describe the state of my mind at that time; and again one may *not* say so.

663. If I say "I meant *him*", a picture might come to my mind, perhaps of how I looked at him, and so forth; but the picture is only like an illustration to a story. From it alone, it would mostly be impossible to infer anything at all; only when one knows the story, does one know what the picture is for.

664. In the use of words, one might distinguish 'surface grammar' from 'depth grammar'. What immediately impresses itself upon us about the

am Gebrauch eines Worts unmittelbar einprägt, ist seine Verwendungsweise im *Satzbau*, der Teil seines Gebrauches — könnte man sagen
— den man mit dem Ohr erfassen kann. —— Und nun vergleiche die
Tiefengrammatik, des Wortes "meinen" etwa, mit dem, was seine
Oberflächengrammatik uns würde vermuten lassen. Kein Wunder,
wenn man es schwer findet, sich auszukennen.

665. Denke, jemand zeigte mit dem Gesichtsausdruck des Schmerzes auf
seine Wange und sagte dabei "abrakadabra!". — Wir fragen "Was meinst
du?". Und er antwortet "Ich meinte damit Zahnschmerzen". — Du denkst
dir sofort: Wie kann man denn mit diesem Wort 'Zahnschmerzen'
meinen'? Oder was *hieß* es denn: Schmerzen mit dem Wort *meinen*? Und
doch hättest du, in anderem Zusammenhang, behauptet, daß die
geistige Tätigkeit, das und das zu *meinen*, gerade das Wichtigste beim
Gebrauch der Sprache sei.
  Aber wie, — kann ich denn nicht sagen "Mit 'abrakadabra' meine
ich Zahnschmerzen"? Freilich; aber das ist eine Definition; nicht eine
Beschreibung dessen, was in mir beim Aussprechen des Wortes vorgeht.

666. Denke, du habest Schmerzen und zugleich hörst du, wie nebenan
Klavier gestimmt wird. Du sagst "Es wird bald aufhören". Es ist
doch wohl ein Unterschied, ob du den Schmerz meinst, oder das
Klavierstimmen! — Freilich; aber worin besteht dieser Unterschied? Ich
gebe zu: es wird in vielen Fällen der Meinung eine Richtung der
Aufmerksamkeit entsprechen, sowie auch oft ein Blick, eine Geste, oder ein
Schließen der Augen, das man ein "Nach-Innen-Blicken" nennen könnte.

667. Denke, es simuliert Einer Schmerzen und sagt nun "Es wird bald
nachlassen". Kann man nicht sagen, er meine den Schmerz? und doch
konzentriert er seine Aufmerksamkeit auf keinen Schmerz. — Und wie,
wenn ich endlich sage "Er hat schon aufgehört"?

668. Aber kann man nicht auch so lügen, indem man sagt "Es wird
bald aufhören" und den Schmerz meint, — aber auf die Frage "Was hast
du gemeint?" zur Antwort gibt: "Den Lärm im Nebenzimmer"? In Fällen
dieser Art sagt man etwa: "Ich wollte antworten . . . , habe mir's aber
überlegt und geantwortet . . ."

669. Man kann sich beim Sprechen auf einen Gegenstand beziehen, indem
man auf ihn zeigt. Das Zeigen ist hier ein Teil des Sprachspiels. Und
nun kommt es uns vor, als spreche man von einer Empfindung
dadurch, daß man seine Aufmerksamkeit beim Sprechen auf sie richtet.
Aber wo ist die Analogie? Sie liegt offenbar darin, daß man durch *Schauen*
und *Horchen* auf etwas zeigen kann.

use of a word is the way it is used in the sentence structure, the part of its use — one might say — that can be taken in by the ear. —— And now compare the depth grammar, say of the verb "to mean", with what its surface grammar would lead us to presume. No wonder one finds it difficult to know one's way about.

665. Imagine someone pointing to his cheek with a grimace of pain and saying "abracadabra!" — We ask, "What do you mean?" And he answers, "I meant toothache." — You at once think to yourself: how can one '*mean* toothache' by that word? Or, what did to *mean* pain by that word *amount to*? And yet, in a different context, you would have asserted that the mental activity of *meaning* such-and-such was just what was most important in using language.

But how come? — can't I say "By 'abracadabra', I mean toothache"? Of course I can; but this is a definition, not a description of what goes on in me when I utter the word.

666. Imagine that you were in pain and were simultaneously hearing a piano being tuned in the next room. You say "It'll soon stop". It surely makes quite a difference whether you mean the pain or the piano-tuning! — Of course; but what does this difference consist in? I admit, in many cases some direction of attention will correspond to your meaning one thing or another, just as a look often does, or a gesture, or a way of shutting one's eyes which might be called "looking into oneself". |169|

667. Imagine someone simulating pain, and then saying "It'll get better soon". Can't one say that he means the pain even though he is not concentrating his attention on any pain? — And what about when I finally say "It's stopped now"?

668. But can't one also lie in this way: one says "It'll stop soon", and means pain — but when asked "What did you mean?", one answers "The noise in the next room"? In this sort of case, one perhaps says: "I was going to answer . . . , but thought better of it and answered . . ."

669. When speaking, one can refer to an object by pointing at it. Here pointing is a part of the language-game. And now it seems to us as if one spoke *of* a sensation by directing one's attention to it. But where is the analogy? It evidently lies in the fact that one can point at a thing by *looking* or *listening*.

Aber auch auf den Gegenstand *zeigen*, von dem man spricht, kann ja für das Sprachspiel, für den Gedanken, unter Umständen ganz unwesentlich sein.

670. Denk, du telephonierst jemandem und sagst ihm: "Dieser Tisch ist zu hoch", wobei du mit dem Finger auf den Tisch zeigst. Welche Rolle spielt hier das Zeigen? Kann ich sagen: ich *meine* den betreffenden Tisch, indem ich auf ihn zeige? Wozu dieses Zeigen, und wozu diese Worte und was sonst sie begleiten mag?

671. Und worauf zeige ich denn durch die innere Tätigkeit des Horchens? Auf den Laut, der mir zu Ohren kommt, und auf die Stille, wenn ich *nichts* höre?

Das Horchen *sucht* gleichsam einen Gehörseindruck und kann daher auf ihn nicht zeigen, sondern nur auf den *Ort*, wo es ihn sucht.

672. Wenn die rezeptive Einstellung ein 'Hinweisen' auf etwas genannt wird, — dann nicht auf die Empfindung, die wir dadurch erhalten.

673. Die geistige Einstellung *'begleitet'* das Wort nicht in demselben Sinne, wie eine Gebärde es begleitet. (Ähnlich, wie Einer allein reisen kann, und doch von meinen Wünschen begleitet, und wie ein Raum leer sein kann und doch vom Licht durchflossen.)

674. Sagt man z. B.: "Ich habe jetzt eigentlich nicht meinen Schmerz gemeint; ich habe nicht genügend auf ihn Acht gegeben"? Frage ich mich etwa: "Was habe ich denn jetzt mit diesem Wort gemeint? meine Aufmerksamkeit war zwischen meinem Schmerz und dem Lärm geteilt —"?

675. "Sag mir, was ist in dir vorgegangen, als du die Worte... aussprachst?" — Darauf ist die Antwort nicht "Ich habe gemeint..."!

676. "Ich meinte mit dem Wort *dies*" ist eine Mitteilung, die anders verwendet wird, als die einer Affektion der Seele.

677. Anderseits: "Als du vorhin fluchtest, hast du es wirklich gemeint?" Dies heißt etwa soviel wie: "Warst du dabei wirklich ärgerlich?" — Und die Antwort kann auf Grund einer Introspektion gegeben werden, und ist oft von der Art: "Ich habe es nicht sehr ernst gemeint", "Ich habe es halb im Scherz gemeint" etc. Hier gibt es Gradunterschiede.

Und man sagt allerdings auch: "Ich habe bei diesem Wort halb und halb an ihn gedacht."

But in certain circumstances, even *pointing* at the object one is talking about may be quite inessential to the language-game, to one's thought.

670. Imagine that you were telephoning someone, and you said to him, "This table is too tall", and pointed at the table. What is the role of pointing here? Can I say: I *mean* the table in question by pointing at it? What is this pointing for, or these words, or whatever else may accompany them?

671. And what do I point at by the inner activity of listening? At the sound that comes to my ears, and at the silence when I hear *nothing*?
    Listening, as it were, *searches for* an auditory impression, and so can't point at it, but only at the *place* where it is searching for it.

672. If the receptive attitude is called a kind of 'pointing' at something — then it isn't at the impression we get in that way.

673. A mental attitude doesn't 'accompany' words in the sense in which a gesture accompanies them. (As a man can travel alone, and yet be accompanied by my good wishes; or as a room can be empty, and yet flooded with light.)

674. Does one say, for example, "I didn't really mean my pain just now; my mind wasn't on it enough for that?" Do I ask myself, say, "What did I mean by this word just now? My attention was divided between my pain and the noise —"? |170|

675. "Tell me, what was going on in you when you uttered the words . . . ?" — The answer to this is not "I was meaning . . ."!

676. "I meant *this* by that word" is a statement which is used differently from one about an affection of the mind.

677. On the other hand: "When you were swearing just now, did you really mean it?" This amounts to something like: "Were you really angry?" — And the answer may be given on the basis of introspection, and is often some such thing as "I didn't mean it very seriously", "I meant it half jokingly", and so on. There are differences of degree here.
    And one does indeed also say, "I was half thinking of him when I said that".

678. Worin besteht dieses Meinen (der Schmerzen oder des Klavierstimmens)? Es kommt keine Antwort — denn die Antworten, die sich uns auf den ersten Blick anbieten, taugen nicht. — "Und doch *meinte* ich damals das eine und nicht das andre." Ja, — nun hast du nur einen Satz mit Emphase wiederholt, dem ja niemand widersprochen hat.

679. "Kannst du aber zweifeln, daß du *das* meintest?" — Nein; aber sicher sein, es wissen, kann ich auch nicht.

680. Wenn du mir sagst, du habest geflucht und dabei den N. gemeint, so wird es mir gleichgültig sein, ob du dabei sein Bild angeschaut, ob du dir ihn vorgestellt hast, seinen Namen aussprachst, etc. Die Schlüsse aus dem Faktum, die mich interessieren, haben damit nichts zu tun. Anderseits aber könnte es sein, daß Einer mir erklärt, der Fluch sei nur dann *wirksam*, wenn man sich den Menschen klar vorstellt, oder seinen Namen laut ausspricht. Aber man würde nicht sagen "Es kommt darauf an, wie der Fluchende sein Opfer *meint*".

681. Man fragt natürlich auch nicht: "Bist du sicher, daß du *ihn* verflucht hast, daß die Verbindung mit ihm hergestellt war?"
So ist also wohl diese Verbindung sehr leicht herzustellen, daß man ihrer so sicher sein kann?! Wissen kann, daß sie nicht daneben geht. — Nun, kann es mir passieren, daß ich an den *Einen* schreiben will und tatsächlich an den Andern schreibe? und wie könnte das geschehen?

682. "Du sagtest 'Es wird bald aufhören'. — Hast du an den Lärm gedacht, oder an deine Schmerzen?" Wenn er nun antwortet "Ich habe ans Klavierstimmen gedacht" — konstatiert er, es habe diese Verbindung bestanden, oder schlägt er sie mit diesen Worten? — Kann ich nicht *beides* sagen? Wenn, was er sagte, wahr war, bestand da nicht jene Verbindung — und schlägt er nicht dennoch eine, die nicht bestand?

683. Ich zeichne einen Kopf. Du fragst "Wen soll das vorstellen?" — Ich: "Das soll N. sein." — Du: "Es sieht ihm aber nicht ähnlich; eher noch dem M." — Als ich sagte, es stelle den N. vor, — machte ich einen Zusammenhang, oder berichtete ich von einem? Welcher Zusammenhang hatte denn bestanden?

684. Was ist dafür zu sagen, daß meine Worte einen Zusammenhang, der bestanden hat, beschreiben? Nun, sie beziehen sich auf Verschiedenes, was nicht erst mit ihnen in die Erscheinung trat. Sie sagen, z. B., daß ich damals eine bestimmte Antwort gegeben *hätte*, wenn ich gefragt worden wäre. Und wenn dies auch nur konditional ist, so sagt es doch etwas über die Vergangenheit.

678. What does this meaning (the pain, or the piano-tuning) consist in? No answer comes — for the answers which at first sight suggest themselves are of no use. — "And yet at the time I *meant* the one thing and not the other." Yes — now you have only repeated with emphasis something which no one has contradicted anyway.

679. "But can you doubt that you meant *this*?" — No; but neither can I be certain of it, know it.

680. When you tell me that you cursed and meant N. as you did so, it is all one to me whether you looked at a picture of him, or imagined him, uttered his name, or whatever. The inferences from this fact that interest me have nothing to do with these things. On the other hand, someone might explain to me that cursing was *effective* only when one had a clear image of the man or spoke his name out loud. But one wouldn't say, "It depends on how the man who is cursing *means* his victim".

681. Nor, of course, does one ask: "Are you sure that you cursed *him*, that the link with him was established?"
Then this link is presumably very easy to establish, if one can be so sure of it, can know that it doesn't miss its target! — Well, can it happen to me that I intend to write to one person and in fact write to another? And how might that occur?

682. "You said, 'It'll stop soon'. — Were you thinking of the noise or of your pain?" If he answers, "I was thinking of the piano-tuning" — is he stating that the link existed, or is he making it by means |171| of these words? — Can't I say *both*? If what he said was true, didn't the link exist — and is he not for all that making one which did not exist?

683. I draw a head. You ask, "Whom is that supposed to represent?" — I: "It's supposed to be N." — You: "But it doesn't look like him; if anything, it's rather like M." — When I said it represented N., was I making a connection, or reporting one? And what connection was there?

684. What is there in favour of saying that my words describe an existing connection? Well, they refer to various things which didn't materialize only with the words; they say, for example, that I *would have* given a particular answer then, if I had been asked. And even if this is only conditional, still it does say something about the past.

685. "Suche den A" heißt nicht "Suche den B"; aber ich mag, indem ich die beiden Befehle befolge, genau das gleiche tun.

Zu sagen, es müsse dabei etwas anderes geschehen, wäre ähnlich, als sagte man: die Sätze "Heute ist mein Geburtstag" und "Am 26. April ist mein Geburtstag" müßten sich auf verschiedene Tage beziehen, da ihr Sinn nicht der gleiche sei.

686. "Freilich habe ich den B. gemeint; ich habe gar nicht an A. gedacht!"

"Ich wollte, B. sollte zu mir kommen, damit . . ." — Alles dies deutet auf einen größern Zusammenhang.

687. Statt "Ich habe ihn gemeint" kann man freilich manchmal sagen "Ich habe an ihn gedacht"; manchmal auch "Ja, wir haben von ihm geredet". Also frag dich, worin es besteht 'von ihm reden'!

688. Man kann unter Umständen sagen: "Als ich sprach, empfand ich, ich sagte es *dir*." Aber das würde ich nicht sagen, wenn ich ohnehin mit dir sprach.

689. "Ich denke an N." "Ich rede von N."

Wie rede ich von ihm? Ich sage etwa "Ich muß heute N. besuchen". — Aber das ist doch nicht genug! Mit "N." könnte ich doch verschiedene Personen meinen, die diesen Namen haben. — "Also muß noch eine andere Verbindung meiner Rede mit dem N. bestehen, denn sonst hätte ich *doch* nicht ɪʜɴ gemeint."

Gewiß, eine solche Verbindung besteht. Nur nicht, wie du sie dir vorstellst: nämlich durch einen geistigen *Mechanismus*.

(Man vergleicht "ihn meinen" mit "auf ihn zielen".)

690. Wie, wenn ich einmal eine scheinbar unschuldige Bemerkung mache und sie mit einem verstohlenen Seitenblick auf jemand begleite; ein andermal, vor mich niedersehend, offen über einen Anwesenden rede, indem ich seinen Namen nenne, — denke ich wirklich *eigens* an ihn, wenn ich seinen Namen gebrauche?

691. Wenn ich das Gesicht des N. nach dem Gedächtnis für mich hinzeichne, so kann man doch sagen, ich *meine* ihn mit meiner Zeichnung. Aber von welchem Vorgang, der während des Zeichnens stattfindet (oder vor- oder nachher) könnte ich sagen, er wäre das Meinen?

Denn man möchte natürlich sagen: als er ihn meinte, habe er auf ihn gezielt. Wie aber macht das Einer, wenn er sich das Gesicht des Andern in die Erinnerung ruft?

685. "Look for A" does not mean "Look for B"; but I may do just the same thing in obeying the two orders.

To say that something different must happen in the two cases would be like saying that the sentences "Today is my birthday" and "My birthday is on April 26th" must refer to different days, because their sense is not the same.

686. "Of course I meant B; I didn't think of A at all!"

"I wanted B to come to me, so as to . . ." — All this points to a wider context.

687. Instead of "I meant him", one can, of course, sometimes say, "I thought of him"; sometimes even "Yes, we were speaking of him". So, ask yourself what 'speaking of him' consists in!

688. In certain circumstances, one can say, "As I was speaking, I felt I was saying it *to you*". But I wouldn't say this if I were in any case talking with you.

689. "I am thinking of N." "I am speaking of N."

How do I speak *of* him? I say, for instance, "I must go and see N. today" —— But surely that is not enough! After all, when I say "N.", I might mean various people of this name. — "Then there must surely be a further link between my words and N., for otherwise I would *still* not have meant HIM."

Certainly such a link exists. Only not as you imagine it: namely, by means of a mental *mechanism*.

(One compares "meaning him" with "aiming at him".) |172|

690. What if I at one time make an apparently innocent remark and accompany it with a furtive sidelong glance at someone; and at another time, looking straight ahead, speak openly of somebody present, mentioning his name — am I really thinking *specially* about him when I use his name?

691. When I make myself a sketch of N.'s face from memory, I can surely be said to *mean* him by my drawing. But which of the processes taking place while I draw (or before or afterwards) could I say is meaning him?

For one would, of course, like to say: when he meant him, he aimed at him. But how does someone do that, when he calls the other person's face to mind?

Ich meine, wie ruft er sich IHN ins Gedächtnis?
Wie ruft er ihn?

692. Ist es richtig, wenn Einer sagt: "Als ich dir diese Regel gab, meinte ich, du solltest in diesem Falle . . ."? Auch wenn er, als er die Regel gab, an diesen Fall gar nicht dachte? Freilich ist es richtig. "Es meinen" hieß eben nicht: daran denken. Die Frage ist nun aber: Wie haben wir zu beurteilen, ob Einer dies gemeint hat? — Daß er z. B. eine bestimmte Technik der Arithmetik und Algebra beherrschte und dem Andern den gewöhnlichen Unterricht im Entwickeln einer Reihe gab, ist so ein Kriterium.

693. "Wenn ich Einen die Bildung der Reihe . . . lehre, meine ich doch, er solle an der hundertsten Stelle . . . schreiben." — Ganz richtig: du meinst es. Und offenbar, ohne notwendigerweise auch nur daran zu denken. Das zeigt dir, wie verschieden die Grammatik des Zeitworts "meinen" von der des Zeitworts "denken" ist. Und nichts Verkehrteres, als Meinen eine geistige Tätigkeit nennen! Wenn man nämlich nicht darauf ausgeht, Verwirrung zu erzeugen. (Man könnte auch von einer Tätigkeit der Butter reden, wenn sie im Preise steigt; und wenn dadurch keine Probleme erzeugt werden, so ist es harmlos.)

I mean, how does he call HIM to mind?
How does he call him?

692. Is it correct for someone to say: "When I gave you this rule, I meant that in this case you should . . ."? Even if he did not think of this case at all as he gave the rule? Of course it is correct. For "to mean it" just did not mean: to think of it. But now the question is: How are we to judge whether someone meant such-and-such? — That he has, for example, mastered a particular technique in arithmetic and algebra, and taught someone else the expansion of a series in the usual way, is such a criterion.

693. "When I teach someone the construction of the series . . . , I surely mean him to write . . . at the hundredth place." — Quite right; you mean it. And evidently without necessarily even thinking of it. This shows you how different the grammar of the verb "to mean something" is from that of the verb "to think". And nothing is more wrong-headed than to call meaning something a mental activity! Unless, that is, one is setting out to produce confusion. (Similarly, one might speak of an activity of butter when it rises in price; and if no problems are produced by this, it is harmless.) |173|

Philosophie der Psychologie
— Ein Fragment

Philosophy of Psychology
— A Fragment

[previously known as 'Part II']

1. Man kann sich ein Tier zornig, furchtsam, traurig, freudig, erschrocken vorstellen. Aber hoffend? Und warum nicht?

Der Hund glaubt, sein Herr sei an der Tür. Aber kann er auch glauben, sein Herr werde übermorgen kommen? — Und *was* kann er nun nicht? — Wie mache denn ich's? — Was soll ich darauf antworten?

Kann nur hoffen, wer sprechen kann? Nur der, der die Verwendung einer Sprache beherrscht. D. h., die Erscheinungen des Hoffens sind Modifikationen dieser komplizierten Lebensform. (Wenn ein Begriff auf einen Charakter der menschlichen Handschrift abzielt, dann hat er keine Anwendung auf Wesen, welche nicht schreiben.)

2. "Kummer" beschreibt uns ein Muster, welches im Lebensteppich mit verschiedenen Variationen wiederkehrt. Wenn bei einem Menschen der Körperausdruck des Grames und der Freude, etwa mit dem Ticken einer Uhr, abwechselten, so hätten wir hier nicht den charakteristischen Verlauf des Grammusters, noch des Freudemusters.

3. "Er fühlte für eine Sekunde heftigen Schmerz." — Warum klingt es seltsam: "Er fühlte für eine Sekunde tiefen Kummer"? Nur weil es so selten vorkommt?

4. Aber fühlst du nicht *jetzt* den Kummer? ("Aber spielst du nicht *jetzt* Schach?") Die Antwort kann bejahend sein; aber das macht den Begriff des Kummers nicht ähnlicher einem Empfindungsbegriff. —— Die Frage war ja eigentlich eine zeitliche und persönliche; nicht die logische, die wir stellen wollten.

5. "Du mußt wissen: ich fürchte mich."

"Du mußt wissen: mir graut davor." —

Ja, man kann das auch in *lächelndem* Ton sagen.

Und willst du mir sagen, er spürt das nicht?! Wie *weiß* er's denn sonst? — Aber auch, wenn es eine Mitteilung ist, so lernt er's nicht von seinen Empfindungen.

6. Denn denk dir die Empfindungen hervorgerufen durch die *Gebärden* des Grauens: die Worte "mir graut davor" sind ja auch so eine Gebärde; und wenn ich sie beim Aussprechen höre und fühle, gehört das zu jenen übrigen Empfindungen. Warum soll denn die ungesprochene Gebärde die gesprochene begründen?

1. One can imagine an animal angry, fearful, sad, joyful, startled. But hopeful? And why not?

A dog believes his master is at the door. But can he also believe that his master will come the day after tomorrow? — And *what* can he not do here? — How do I do it? — What answer am I supposed to give to this?

Can only those hope who can talk? Only those who have mastered the use of a language. That is to say, the manifestations of hope are modifications of this complicated form of life. (If a concept points to a characteristic of human handwriting, it has no application to beings that do not write.)

2. "Grief" describes a pattern which recurs, with different variations, in the tapestry of life. If a man's bodily expression of sorrow and of joy alternated, say with the ticking of a clock, here we would not have the characteristic course of the pattern of sorrow or of the pattern of joy.

3. "For a second he felt violent pain." — Why does it sound odd to say: "For a second he felt deep grief"? Only because it so seldom happens?

4. But don't you feel grief *now*? ("But aren't you playing chess *now*?") The answer may be affirmative, but this does not make the concept of grief any more like the concept of sensation. —— The question was really, of course, a temporal and personal one, not the logical question we wanted to ask.

* 5. "I must tell you: I am frightened."

"I must tell you: it horrifies me." — Well, one can say this in a *smiling* tone of voice too.

And do you mean to tell me that he doesn't feel it? How else does he *know* it? — But even if it is a report, he does not learn it from his feelings.

6. Suppose that the feelings are produced by *gestures* of horror: the words "it horrifies me" are themselves such a gesture; and when I hear and feel them as I utter them, this belongs among the rest of those feelings. Now, why should the wordless gesture be the ground of the verbal one?

|175|

7. Mit seinen Worten "Als ich das Wort hörte, bedeutete es für mich . . ." bezieht er sich auf einen *Zeitpunkt* und auf eine *Art der Wortverwendung*. (Was wir nicht begreifen, ist natürlich diese Kombination.)

Und der Ausdruck "Ich wollte damals sagen . . ." bezieht sich auf einen *Zeitpunkt* und auf eine *Handlung*.

Ich rede von den wesentlichen *Bezügen* der Äußerung, um sie von andern Besonderheiten unseres Ausdrucks abzulösen. Und wesentlich sind der Äußerung die Bezüge, die uns veranlassen würden, eine im übrigen uns fremde Art des Ausdrucks in diese bei uns gebräuchliche Form zu übersetzen.

8. Wer nicht im Stande wäre, zu sagen: das Wort "sondern" könne ein Zeitwort und ein Bindewort sein, oder Sätze zu bilden, in denen es einmal dies, einmal jenes ist, der könnte einfache Schulübungen nicht bewältigen. Das aber wird von einem Schüler nicht verlangt: das Wort außerhalb eines Zusammenhangs so, oder so *aufzufassen*, oder zu berichten, wie er's aufgefaßt habe.

9. Die Worte "die Rose ist rot" sind sinnlos, wenn das Wort "ist" die Bedeutung von "ist gleich" hat. — Heißt dies: Wenn du jenen Satz sprichst und "ist" darin als Gleichheitszeichen meinst, so zerfällt dir der Sinn?

Wir nehmen einen Satz und erklären Einem die Bedeutung jedes seiner Wörter; er lernt damit, sie anzuwenden und also auch jenen Satz. Hätten wir statt des Satzes eine Wortreihe ohne Sinn gewählt, so würde er *sie* nicht anwenden lernen. Und erklärt man das Wort "ist" als Gleichheitszeichen, dann lernt er nicht den Satz "die Rose ist rot" verwenden.

Und dennoch hat es auch mit dem 'Zerfallen des Sinnes' seine Richtigkeit. Sie liegt in diesem Beispiel: Man könnte Einem sagen: Wenn du den Ausruf "Ei, ei!" ausdrucksvoll sprechen willst, darfst du nicht an Eier dabei denken!

10. Das Erleben einer Bedeutung und das Erleben eines Vorstellungsbildes. "Man *erlebt* hier und dort," möchte man sagen, "nur etwas Anderes. Ein anderer Inhalt wird dem Bewußtsein dargeboten — steht vor ihm." — Welcher ist der Inhalt des Vorstellungserlebnisses? Die Antwort ist ein Bild, oder eine Beschreibung. Und was ist der Inhalt des Bedeutungserlebnisses? Ich weiß nicht, wie ich antworten soll. — Wenn jene Äußerung irgendeinen Sinn hat, so ist es der, daß die beiden Begriffe sich ähnlich zueinander verhalten, wie die von 'rot' und 'blau'; und das ist falsch.

ii

7. If someone says, "When I heard this word, it meant . . . to me", he is referring to a *point in time* and to a *way of using the word*. (Of course, it is this combination that we fail to grasp.)

And the expression "I was then going to say . . ." refers to a *point in time* and to an *action*.

I speak of the essential *references* of the utterance in order to separate them from other particularities of the expression we use. And the references that are essential to the utterance are the ones which would make us translate an otherwise unfamiliar kind of expression into this, our customary form.

8. Someone who was unable to say that the word "till" can be both a verb and a conjunction or to construct sentences in which it was now the one and now the other, would be unable to manage simple schoolroom exercises. But a schoolboy is not asked to *take* the word in one way or another out of any context, or to report how he has taken it.

* 9. The words "the rose is red" are senseless if the word "is" has the meaning "is identical with". — Does this mean: if you utter this sentence and mean the "is" in it as the sign of identity, the sense disintegrates?

We take a sentence and tell someone the meaning of each of its words; in this way he learns how to apply them, and so how to apply the sentence too. If we had chosen a senseless sequence of words instead of our sentence, he would not learn how to apply *that* sequence. And if one explains the word "is" as the sign of identity, then he doesn't learn how to use the sentence "The rose is red".

And yet there is something right about this 'disintegration of the sense'. You get it in the following example. One might tell someone: if you want to pronounce the salutation "Hail!" expressively, you had better not think of hailstones as you say it.

10. Experiencing a meaning and experiencing a mental image. "In both cases", one would like to say, "one is *experiencing* something, only something different. A different content is presented to — stands before — consciousness." — What is the content of the experience of imagining? The answer is a picture, or a description. And what is the content |176| of the experience of a meaning? I don't know how I should answer. — If there is any sense in the above remark, it is that the two concepts stand to each other as 'red' does to 'blue'; and that is wrong.

11. Kann man das Verstehen einer Bedeutung festhalten wie ein Vorstellungsbild? Wenn mir also plötzlich eine Bedeutung des Wortes einfällt, — kann sie mir auch vor der Seele stehenbleiben?

12. "Der ganze Plan stand mir mit einem Schlage vor der Seele und blieb so fünf Minuten lang stehen." Warum klingt das seltsam? Man möchte glauben: was aufblitzte und was stehen blieb, konnte nicht dasselbe sein.

13. Ich rief aus "Jetzt hab ich's!" — Es war ein plötzliches Aufzucken: dann konnte ich den Plan in seinen Einzelheiten darlegen. Was sollte da stehenbleiben? Ein Bild vielleicht. Aber "Jetzt hab ich's" hieß nicht, ich habe das Bild.

14. Wem eine Bedeutung eines Wortes einfiel, und wer sie nicht wieder *vergaß*, kann nun das Wort in dieser Weise anwenden.

Wem die Bedeutung einfiel, der *weiß* sie nun, und der Einfall war der Anfang des Wissens. Wie ist er dann ähnlich einem Vorstellungserlebnis?

15. Wenn ich sage "Herr Schweizer ist kein Schweizer", so meine ich das erste "Schweizer" als Eigenname, das zweite als Gattungsname. Muß da also beim ersten "Schweizer" etwas anderes in meinem Geiste vorgehen, als beim zweiten? (Es sei denn, daß ich den Satz 'papageienhaft' ausspreche.) —— Versuch, das erste "Schweizer" als Gattungsnamen und das zweite als Eigennamen zu meinen! —— Wie macht man das? Wenn *ich*'s tue, blinzele ich mit den Augen vor Anstrengung, indem ich versuche, mir bei jedem der beiden Worte die richtige Bedeutung vorzuführen. — Aber führe ich mir denn auch beim gewöhnlichen Gebrauch der Wörter ihre Bedeutung vor?

16. Wenn ich den Satz mit den vertauschten Bedeutungen ausspreche, so zerfällt mir der Satzsinn. — Nun, er zerfällt *mir*, aber nicht dem Andern, dem ich die Mitteilung mache. Was schadet es also? —— "Aber es geht eben doch beim gewöhnlichen Aussprechen des Satzes etwas bestimmtes *anderes* vor." — Es geht dabei *nicht* jenes 'Vorführen der Bedeutung' vor sich.

11. Can one keep hold of understanding a meaning as one can keep hold of a mental image? That is, if one meaning of a word suddenly occurs to me — can it also remain there before my mind?

12. "The whole plan came to my mind at a stroke and stayed there like that for five minutes." Why does this sound odd? One would like to think: what struck me and what stayed there in my mind can't have been the same.

13. I exclaimed "Now I've got it!" — I gave a sudden start, and then I was able to present the plan in detail. What is supposed to have stayed in this case? A picture, perhaps. But "Now I've got it" did not mean "I've got a picture".

14. If a meaning of a word has occurred to someone and he has not *forgotten* it, he can now use the word in such-and-such a way.

A person to whom the meaning has occurred now *knows* it, and its occurring to him was the beginning of his knowing it. Then how is this like an experience of imagining something?

15. If I say "Mr Scot is not a Scot", I mean the first "Scot" as a proper name, the second one as a common name. Must what went on in my mind at the first "Scot" differ from what went on at the second? (Unless I'm uttering the sentence 'parrot-wise'.) —— Try to mean the first "Scot" as a common name and the second one as a proper name. —— How does one do it? When *I* do it, I blink with effort as I try to display to myself the right meaning of each of the two words. — But, in their ordinary use, do I also display their meanings to myself?

16. When I utter the sentence with these switched meanings, its sense disintegrates for me. — Well, it disintegrates for *me*, but not for the person I am saying it to. So what harm is done? —— "But still, when one utters the sentence in the usual way, something *else* takes place." — What takes place is *not* this 'displaying the meaning'. |177|

17. Was macht meine Vorstellung von ihm zu einer Vorstellung von *ihm*? Nicht die Ähnlichkeit des Bildes.

Von der Äußerung "Ich sehe ihn jetzt lebhaft vor mir" gilt ja die gleiche Frage, wie von der Vorstellung. Was macht diese Äußerung zu einer Äußerung über *ihn*? — Nichts, was in ihr liegt, oder mit ihr gleichzeitig ist ('hinter ihr steht'). Wenn du wissen willst, wen er gemeint hat, frag ihn!

(Es kann aber auch sein, daß mir ein Gesicht vorschwebt, ja daß ich es zeichnen kann, und weiß nicht, welcher Person es gehört, wo ich es gesehen habe.)

18. Wenn aber jemand beim Vorstellen, oder statt des Vorstellens zeichnete; wenn auch nur mit dem Finger in der Luft. (Man könnte das "motorische Vorstellung" nennen.) Da könnte man fragen "Wen stellt das vor?". Und seine Antwort entschiede. — Es ist ganz so, als hätte er eine Beschreibung in Worten gegeben, und diese kann eben auch *statt* der Vorstellung stehen.

17. What makes my mental image of him into an image of *him*?
Not any pictorial likeness.

The same question applies to the utterance "I see him now vividly before me" as to the image. What makes this utterance into an utterance about *him*? — Nothing in it or simultaneous with it ('behind it'). If you want to know whom he meant, ask him!

(But it is also possible for me to visualize a face, and even to draw it, without my knowing whose it is or where I have seen it.)

18. Suppose that while imagining, or instead of imagining, someone were to draw, even if only in the air with his finger. (This might be called "motor imagery".) Here one might ask: "Whom does that represent?" And his answer would be decisive. — It is just as if he had given a verbal description, which, after all, can also *take the place* of the image. |178|

19. "Ich glaube, daß er leidet." — *Glaube* ich auch, daß er kein Automat ist?

Nur mit Widerstreben könnte ich das Wort in diesen beiden Zusammenhängen aussprechen.

(Oder ist es *so*: ich glaube, daß er leidet; ich bin sicher, daß er kein Automat ist? Unsinn!)

20. Denke, ich sage von einem Freunde: "Er ist kein Automat." — Was wird hier mitgeteilt, und für wen wäre es eine Mitteilung? Für einen *Menschen*, der den Andern unter gewöhnlichen Umständen trifft? Was *könnte* es ihm mitteilen! (Doch höchstens, daß dieser sich immer wie ein Mensch, nicht manchmal wie eine Maschine benimmt.)

21. "Ich glaube, daß er kein Automat ist" hat, so ohne weiteres, noch gar keinen Sinn.

22. Meine Einstellung zu ihm ist eine Einstellung zur Seele. Ich habe nicht die *Meinung*, daß er eine Seele hat.

23. Die Religion lehrt, die Seele könne bestehen, wenn der Leib zerfallen ist. Verstehe ich denn, was sie lehrt? — Freilich verstehe ich's — ich kann mir dabei manches vorstellen. Man hat ja auch Bilder von diesen Dingen gemalt. Und warum sollte so ein Bild nur die unvollkommene Wiedergabe des ausgesprochenen Gedankens sein? Warum soll es nicht den *gleichen* Dienst tun, wie die gesprochene Lehre? Und auf den Dienst kommt es an.

24. Wenn sich uns das Bild vom Gedanken im Kopf aufdrängen kann, warum dann nicht noch viel mehr das vom Gedanken in der Seele?

25. Der menschliche Körper ist das beste Bild der menschlichen Seele.

26. Wie ist es aber mit so einem Ausdruck: "Als du es sagtest, verstand ich es in meinem Herzen"? Dabei deutet man auf's Herz. Und *meint* man diese Gebärde etwa nicht?! Freilich meint man sie. Oder ist man sich bewußt, *nur* ein Bild zu gebrauchen? Gewiß nicht. — Es ist nicht ein Bild unserer Wahl, nicht ein Gleichnis, und doch ein bildlicher Ausdruck.

iv

19. "I believe that he is suffering." —— Do I also *believe* that he isn't an automaton?

Only reluctantly could I use the word in both contexts.

(Or is it like *this*: I believe that he is suffering, but am certain that he is not an automaton? Nonsense!)

20. Suppose I say of a friend: "He isn't an automaton." —— What information is conveyed by this, and to whom would it be information? To a *human being* who meets him in ordinary circumstances? What information *could* it give him? (At the very most, that this man always behaves like a human being, and not occasionally like a machine.)

21. "I believe that he is not an automaton", just like that, so far makes no sense.

22. My attitude towards him is an attitude towards a soul. I am not of the *opinion* that he has a soul.

23. Religion teaches that the soul can exist when the body has disintegrated. Now do I understand what it teaches? — Of course I understand it —— I can imagine various things in connection with it. After all, pictures of these things have even been painted. And why should such a picture be only an imperfect rendering of the idea expressed? Why should it not do the *same* service as the spoken doctrine? And it is the service that counts.

24. If the picture of thoughts in the head can force itself upon us, then why not much more that of thoughts in the mind or soul?

25. The human body is the best picture of the human soul.

26. But how about an expression like this: "When you said that, I understood it in my heart"? In saying which, one points at one's heart. And doesn't one *mean* this gesture? Of course one means it. Or is one aware of using a *mere* picture? Certainly not. — It is not a picture that we choose, not a simile, yet it is a graphic expression. |179|

V

27. Denk dir, wir beobachteten die Bewegung eines Punktes (eines Lichtpunktes auf einem Schirm, z. B.). Wichtige Schlüsse der verschiedensten Art könnten sich aus dem Benehmen dieses Punktes ziehen lassen. Aber wie vielerlei läßt sich an ihm beobachten! — Die Bahn des Punktes und gewisse ihrer Maße (z. B. Amplitude und Wellenlänge), oder die Geschwindigkeit und das Gesetz, wonach sie sich ändert, oder die Anzahl, oder die Lage, der Stellen, an denen sie sich sprungweise ändert, oder die Krümmung der Bahn an diesen Stellen, und Unzähliges. — Und jeder dieser *Züge* des Benehmens könnte der einzige sein, welcher uns interessiert. Es könnte z. B. alles an dieser Bewegung uns gleichgültig sein, außer die Zahl der Schlingen in einer gewissen Zeit. —— Und wenn uns nun nicht nur *ein* solcher Zug interessiert, sondern ihrer mehrere, so mag jeder von ihnen uns einen besondern, seiner Art nach von allen andern verschiedenen Aufschluß geben. Und so ist es mit dem Benehmen des Menschen, mit den verschiedenen Charakteristiken dieses Benehmens, die wir beobachten.

28. So handelt die Psychologie vom Benehmen, nicht von der Seele?

Was berichtet der Psychologe? — Was beobachtet er? Nicht das Benehmen der Menschen, insbesondere ihre Äußerungen? Aber *diese* handeln nicht vom Benehmen.

29. "Ich merkte, er war verstimmt." Ist das ein Bericht über das Benehmen, oder den Seelenzustand? ("Der Himmel sieht drohend aus"; handelt das von der Gegenwart, oder von der Zukunft?) Beides; aber nicht im Nebeneinander; sondern vom einen durch das andere.

30. Der Arzt fragt: "Wie fühlt er sich?" Die Krankenschwester sagt: "Er stöhnt." Ein Bericht über's Benehmen. Aber muß die Frage für die Beiden überhaupt existieren, ob dieses Stöhnen wirklich echt, wirklich der Ausdruck von etwas ist? Könnten sie nicht z. B. den Schluß ziehen "Wenn er stöhnt, so müssen wir ihm noch ein schmerzstillendes Pulver geben" — ohne ein Mittelglied zu verschweigen? Kommt es denn nicht auf den Dienst an, in welchen sie die Beschreibung des Benehmens stellen?

31. "Aber diese machen dann eben eine stillschweigende Voraussetzung." Dann ruht der Vorgang unsres Sprachspiels immer auf einer stillschweigenden Voraussetzung.

V

27. Suppose we were observing the movement of a point (for example, a point of light on a screen). Important inferences of the most varied kinds could be drawn from the behaviour of this point. And what a variety of observations can be made here! — The path of the point and certain of its characteristic measures (amplitude and wavelength for instance), or the velocity and the law according to which it varies, or the number or position of the places at which it changes discontinuously, or the curvature of the path at these places, and innumerable other things. — Any of these features of its behaviour might be the only one to interest us. We might, for example, be indifferent to everything about its path except for the number of loops it made in a certain time. —— And if we were interested, not in just *one* such feature, but in several, each might yield us special information, different in kind from all the rest. This is how it is with the behaviour of man; with the different characteristics that we observe in this behaviour.

28. Then psychology treats of behaviour, not of the mind?

What does a psychologist report? — What does he observe? Isn't it the behaviour of people, in particular their utterances? But *these* are not about their behaviour.

29. "I noticed that he was out of humour." Is this a report about his behaviour or his state of mind? ("The sky looks threatening": is this about the present or the future?) Both; not side by side, however, but about the one via the other.

30. A doctor asks: "How is he feeling?" The nurse says: "He is groaning." A report on his behaviour. But need there be any question, for the two of them, whether the groaning is really genuine, is really the expression of anything? Might they not, for example, draw the conclusion "If he groans, we must give him more analgesic" — without suppressing a middle term? Isn't what counts the service to which they put the description of behaviour?

31. "But then they make a tacit presupposition." Then playing our language-game always rests on a tacit presupposition. |180|

32. Ich beschreibe ein psychologisches Experiment: den Apparat, die Fragen des Experimentators, die Handlungen und Antworten des Subjekts — und nun sage ich, dies sei eine Szene in einem Theaterstück. — Nun hat sich alles geändert. Man wird also erklären: Wenn in einem Buch über Psychologie dieses Experiment in gleicher Weise beschrieben wäre, so würde die Beschreibung des Benehmens eben als Ausdruck von Seelischem verstanden, weil man *voraussetzt*, das Subjekt halte uns nicht zum Besten, habe die Antworten nicht auswendig gelernt, und dergleichen mehr. — Wir machen also eine Voraussetzung?

Würden wir uns wirklich so äußern: "Ich mache natürlich die Voraussetzung, daß . . ."? — Oder nur darum nicht, weil der Andere das schon weiß?

33. Besteht eine Voraussetzung nicht, wo ein Zweifel besteht? Und der Zweifel kann gänzlich fehlen. Das Zweifeln hat ein Ende.

34. Es ist hier wie mit dem Verhältnis: physikalischer Gegenstand und Sinneseindrücke. Wir haben hier zwei Sprachspiele und ihre Beziehungen zueinander sind komplizierter Art. —— Will man diese Beziehungen auf eine *einfache* Formel bringen, so geht man fehl.

*   32. I describe a psychological experiment: the apparatus, the questions of the experimenter, the actions and replies of the subject — and then I say that it is a scene in a play. — Now everything has changed. So one will observe: if this experiment were described in the same way in a book on psychology, then the description of the behaviour would be understood *as* an expression of something mental precisely because it is *presupposed* that the subject is not taking us in, hasn't learnt the replies by heart, and other things of the kind. — So we are making a presupposition?

Would we ever really express ourselves like this: "Naturally I am pre-supposing that . . ."? — Or do we not do so only because the other person already knows that?

33. Doesn't a presupposition exist when a doubt exists? And doubt may be entirely lacking. Doubting has an end.

*   34. There is a similarity here to the way in which 'physical object' and 'sense impressions' stand to each other. We have here two language-games, and their mutual relations are of a complicated kind. —— If one tries to reduce their relations to a *simple* formula, one goes wrong.
|181|

35. Denk dir, Einer sagte: jedes uns wohlbekannte Wort, eines Buchs z. B., habe in unserm Geiste schon einen Dunstkreis, einen 'Hof' schwach angedeuteter Verwendungen in sich. —— So, als wäre auf einem Gemälde jede der Figuren auch von zarten, nebelhaft gezeichneten Szenen, gleichsam in einer anderen Dimension, umgeben, und wir sähen die Figuren hier in andern Zusammenhängen. —— Machen wir nur Ernst mit dieser Annahme! — Da zeigt es sich, daß sie die *Intention* nicht zu erklären vermag.

Wenn es nämlich so ist, daß die Möglichkeiten der Verwendung eines Wortes beim Sprechen, oder Hören uns in Halbtönen vorschweben, — wenn es so ist, so gilt das eben für *uns*. Aber wir verständigen uns mit Andern, ohne zu wissen, ob auch sie diese Erlebnisse haben.

36. Was würden wir denn Einem entgegnen, der uns mitteilte, bei *ihm* sei das Verstehen ein innerer Vorgang? —— Was würden wir ihm entgegnen, wenn er sagte, bei ihm sei das Schachspielenkönnen ein innerer Vorgang? — Daß nichts, was in ihm vorgeht, uns interessiert, wenn wir wissen wollen, ob er Schach spielen kann. — Und wenn er nun darauf antwortet, es interessiere uns eben doch: — nämlich, ob er Schach spielen könne, — da müßten wir ihn auf die Kriterien aufmerksam machen, die uns seine Fähigkeit beweisen würden, und anderseits auf die Kriterien der 'inneren Zustände'.

Auch wenn Einer nur dann, und nur so lange, eine bestimmte Fähigkeit hätte, als er etwas Bestimmtes fühlt, wäre das Gefühl nicht die Fähigkeit.

37. Die Bedeutung ist nicht das Erlebnis beim Hören oder Aussprechen des Wortes, und der Sinn des Satzes nicht der Komplex dieser Erlebnisse. — (Wie setzt sich der Sinn des Satzes "Ich habe ihn noch immer nicht gesehen" aus den Bedeutungen seiner Wörter zusammen?) Der Satz ist aus den Wörtern zusammengesetzt, und das ist genug.

38. Jedes Wort — so möchte man sagen — kann zwar in verschiedenen Zusammenhängen verschiedenen Charakter haben, aber es hat doch immer *einen* Charakter — ein Gesicht. Es schaut uns doch an. —— Aber auch ein *gemaltes* Gesicht schaut uns an.

39. Bist du sicher, daß es *ein* Wenn-Gefühl gibt; nicht vielleicht mehrere? Hast du versucht, das Wort in sehr verschiedenartigen Zusammenhängen auszusprechen? Wenn es z. B. den Hauptton des Satzes trägt, und wenn ihn das nächste Wort trägt.

* 35. Suppose someone said: every familiar word, in a book for example, actually carries an atmosphere with it in our minds, a 'corona' of faintly indicated uses. —— Just as if each figure in a painting were surrounded by delicate shadowy drawings of scenes, as it were in another dimension, and in them we saw the figures in different contexts. —— Let's take this assumption very seriously! — Then it turns out that it cannot explain *intentionality*.

If the possible uses of a word are before our minds in half-tones as we say or hear it — this goes just for *us*. But we communicate with other people without knowing whether they have these experiences too.

36. What would we reply to someone who told us that with *him* understanding was an inner process? —— What would we reply to him if he said that with him knowing how to play chess was an inner process? — We'd say that when we want to know if he can play chess, we aren't interested in anything that goes on inside him. — And if he retorts that this is in fact just what we are interested in, that is, in whether he can play chess — then we should have to draw his attention to the criteria which would demonstrate his ability, and on the other hand to the criteria for 'inner states'.

Even if someone had a particular ability only when, and only as long as, he had a particular feeling, the feeling would not be the ability.

37. The meaning of a word is not the experience one has in hearing or uttering it, and the sense of a sentence is not a complex of these experiences. — (How is the sense of the sentence "I haven't seen him yet" composed of the meanings of its words?) The sentence is composed of the words, and that is enough.

38. Though — one would like to say — every word can have a different character in different contexts, at the same time there is a single character it always has — a face. It looks at us, after all. —— But a face in a painting looks at us too.

39. Are you sure that there is a single if-feeling, and not perhaps several? Have you tried saying the word in a great variety of contexts? For |182| example, when it bears the principal stress of the sentence, and when the following word does.

40. Denk dir, wir fänden einen Menschen, der uns, über seine Wortgefühle, sagt: für ihn hätte "wenn" und "aber" das *gleiche* Gefühl. — Dürften wir ihm das nicht glauben? Es würde uns vielleicht befremden. "Er spielt gar nicht unser Spiel" möchte man sagen. Oder auch: "Das ist ein anderer Typus."

Würden wir von diesem nicht glauben, er verstehe die Worte "wenn" und "aber", so wie wir sie verstehen, wenn er sie so *verwendet*, wie wir?

41. Man schätzt das psychologische Interesse des Wenn-Gefühls falsch ein, wenn man es als selbstverständliches Korrelat einer Bedeutung ansieht; es muß vielmehr in einem andern Zusammenhang gesehen werden, in dem der besondern Umstände, unter denen es auftritt.

42. Hat einer das Wenn-Gefühl nie, wenn er das Wort "wenn" nicht ausspricht? Es ist doch jedenfalls merkwürdig, wenn nur diese Ursache dies Gefühl hervorruft. Und so ist es überhaupt mit der 'Atmosphäre' eines Worts: — warum sieht man es als so selbstverständlich an, daß nur *dies* Wort diese Atmosphäre hat?

43. Das Wenn-Gefühl ist nicht ein Gefühl, das das Wort "wenn" begleitet.

44. Das Wenn-Gefühl müßte zu vergleichen sein dem besondern 'Gefühl', das eine musikalische Phrase uns gibt. (So ein Gefühl beschreibt man manchmal, indem man sagt "Es ist hier, als ob ein Schluß gezogen würde", oder "Ich möchte sagen '*also . . .*' ", oder "ich möchte hier immer eine Geste machen —" und nun macht man sie.)

45. Aber kann man dies Gefühl von der Phrase trennen? Und doch ist es nicht die Phrase selbst; denn Einer kann sie hören ohne dies Gefühl.

46. Ist es darin ähnlich dem 'Ausdruck' mit welchem sie gespielt wird?

47. Wir sagen, diese Stelle gibt uns ein ganz besonderes Gefühl. Wir singen sie uns vor, und machen dabei eine gewisse Bewegung, haben vielleicht auch irgendeine besondere Empfindung. Aber diese Begleitungen — die Bewegung, die Empfindung — würden wir in anderem Zusammenhang gar nicht wiedererkennen. Sie sind ganz leer, außer eben, wenn wir diese Stelle singen.

48. "Ich singe sie mit einem ganz bestimmten Ausdruck." Dieser Ausdruck ist nicht etwas, was man von der Stelle trennen kann. Es ist ein anderer Begriff. (Ein anderes Spiel.)

40. Suppose we found a man who, speaking of how words felt to him, told us that "if" and "but" felt the *same*. — May we not believe him? We might think it strange. "He doesn't play our game at all," one would like to say. Or even: "This is a different kind of human being."

If he *used* the words "if" and "but" as we do, wouldn't we think he understood them as we do?

41. One misjudges the psychological interest of the if-feeling if one regards it as the obvious correlate of a meaning; it needs, rather, to be seen in a different context, in that of the special circumstances in which it occurs.

42. Does a person never have the if-feeling unless he is uttering the word "if"? Surely it is at least curious if this cause is the only one to produce this feeling. And this applies generally to the 'atmosphere' of a word: — why does one regard it so much as a matter of course that only *this* word has this atmosphere?

43. The if-feeling is not a feeling which accompanies the word "if".

44. The if-feeling should be comparable to the special 'feeling' which a musical phrase gives us. (One sometimes describes such a feeling by saying "Here it is as if a conclusion were being drawn", or "I should like to say '*therefore* . . .'", or "Here I should always like to make a gesture —" and then one makes it.)

45. But can this feeling be separated from the phrase? And yet it is not the phrase itself, for someone can hear it without this feeling.

46. Is it in this respect similar to the 'expression' with which the phrase is played?

47. We say this passage gives us a quite special feeling. We sing it to ourselves, and at the same time make a certain movement, and also perhaps have some special feeling. But in a different context we would not recognize these accompaniments — the movement, the feeling — at all. They are quite empty, except just when we are singing this passage. |183|

48. "I sing it with a quite particular expression." This expression is not something that can be separated from the passage. It is a different concept. (A different game.)

49. Das Erlebnis ist diese Stelle, so gespielt (*so*, wie ich es etwa vor-mache; eine Beschreibung könnte es nur *andeuten*).

50. Die vom Ding untrennbare Atmosphäre, — sie ist also keine Atmosphäre.

Was mit einander innig assoziiert ist, assoziiert *wurde*, das scheint zueinander zu passen. Aber wie scheint es das? wie äußert sich's, daß es zu passen scheint? Etwa so: Wir können uns nicht denken, daß der Mann, der diesen Namen, dies Gesicht, diese Schriftzüge hatte, nicht *diese* Werke, sondern etwa ganz andere (die eines anderen großen Mannes) hervorgebracht hat.

Wir können uns das nicht denken? Versuchen wir's denn? —

51. Es könnte so sein: Ich höre, es male jemand ein Bild "Beethoven beim Schreiben der neunten Symphonie". Ich könnte mir leicht vorstellen, was etwa auf so einem Bild zu sehen wäre. Aber wie, wenn Einer darstellen wollte, wie Goethe ausgesehen hätte beim Schreiben der neunten Symphonie? Da wüßte ich mir nichts vorzustellen, was nicht peinlich und lächerlich wäre.

49. The experience is this passage played like *this* (that is, as I am demonstrating, for instance; a description could only *hint* at it).

50. An atmosphere that is inseparable from its object — is no atmosphere.

   Closely associated things, things which *have been* associated, seem to fit one another. But in what way do they seem to fit? How does it come out that they seem to fit? Like this, for example: we cannot imagine the man who had this name, this face, this handwriting, not to have produced *these* works, but perhaps quite different ones instead (those of another great man).

   We cannot imagine it? Do we try? —

51. It might be like this: I hear that someone is painting a picture "Beethoven writing the Ninth Symphony". I could easily imagine the kind of thing such a picture would show us. But suppose someone wanted to represent what Goethe would have looked like writing the Ninth Symphony? Here I could imagine nothing that would not be embarrassing and ridiculous. |184|

52. Leute, die uns nach dem Erwachen gewisse Begebenheiten erzählen (sie seien dort und dort gewesen, etc.). Wir lehren sie nun den Ausdruck "mir hat geträumt", dem die Erzählung folgt. Ich frage sie dann manchmal "hat dir heute nacht etwas geträumt?" und erhalte eine bejahende, oder eine verneinende Antwort, manchmal eine Traumerzählung, manchmal keine. Das ist das Sprachspiel. (Ich habe jetzt angenommen, daß ich selbst nicht träume. Aber ich habe ja auch nie Gefühle einer unsichtbaren Gegenwart und Andere haben sie, und ich kann sie über ihre Erfahrungen befragen.)

Muß ich nun eine Annahme darüber machen, ob die Leute ihr Gedächtnis getäuscht hat, oder nicht; ob sie wirklich während des Schlafs diese Bilder vor sich gesehen haben, oder ob es ihnen nur nach dem Erwachen so vorkommt? Und welchen Sinn hat diese Frage? — Und welches Interesse?! Fragen wir uns das je, wenn uns Einer seinen Traum erzählt? Und wenn nicht, — ist es, weil wir sicher sind, sein Gedächtnis werde ihn nicht getäuscht haben? (Und angenommen, es wäre ein Mensch mit besonders schlechtem Gedächtnis. —)

53. Und heißt das, es sei unsinnig, je die Frage zu stellen: ob der Traum wirklich während des Schlafs vor sich gehe, oder ein Gedächtnisphänomen des Erwachten sei? Es wird auf die Verwendung der Frage ankommen.

54. "Es scheint, der Geist kann dem Wort Bedeutung geben" — ist das nicht, als sagte ich: "Es scheint, daß im Benzol die C-Atome an den Ecken eines Sechsecks liegen"? Das ist doch kein Schein; es ist ein Bild.

55. Die Evolution der höheren Tiere und des Menschen und das Erwachen des Bewußtseins auf einer bestimmten Stufe. Das Bild ist etwa dies: Die Welt ist, trotz aller Ätherschwingungen, die sie durchziehen, dunkel. Eines Tages aber macht der Mensch sein sehendes Auge auf, und es wird hell.

Unsere Sprache beschreibt zuerst einmal ein Bild. Was mit dem Bild zu geschehen hat, wie es zu verwenden ist, bleibt im Dunkeln. Aber es ist ja klar, daß es erforscht werden muß, wenn man den Sinn unserer Aussage verstehen will. Das Bild aber scheint uns dieser Arbeit zu überheben; es deutet schon auf eine bestimmte Verwendung. Dadurch hat es uns zum Besten.

52. People who on waking tell us certain incidents (that they have been in such-and-such places, and so forth). Then we teach them the expression "I dreamt", which is followed by the narrative. Afterwards I sometimes ask them, "Did you dream anything last night?" and am answered Yes or No, sometimes with a dream narrative, sometimes not. That is the language-game. (I have assumed here that I don't dream myself. But then, nor do I ever have feelings of an invisible presence; other people do, and I can question them about their experiences.)

Now must I make an assumption about whether these people are deceived by their memories or not, whether they really had such images while they slept, or whether it merely seems so to them on waking? And what sense does this question have? — And what interest?! Do we ever ask ourselves this when someone is telling us his dream? And if not — is it because we are sure that his memory won't have deceived him? (And suppose it were a man with an exceptionally bad memory. —)

53. Does this mean that it is nonsense ever to raise the question of whether dreams really take place during sleep, or are a memory phenomenon of the awakened? It will depend on how the question is used.

54. "It seems that the mind can give a word meaning" — isn't this as if I were to say "It seems that the carbon atoms in benzene lie at the corners of a hexagon"? But this is no seeming; it is a picture.

55. The evolution of the higher animals and of man, and the awakening of consciousness at a particular stage. The picture is something like this: Though the ether is filled with vibrations, the world is dark. But one day, man opens his seeing eye, and there is light.

In the first place, our language describes a picture. What is to be done with the picture, how it is to be used, is still obscure. Quite clearly, however, it must be explored if we want to understand the sense of our words. But the picture seems to spare us this work: it already points to a particular use. This is how it takes us in. |185|

viii

56. "Meine kinästhetischen Empfindungen belehren mich über die Bewegungen und Lagen meiner Glieder."

Ich lasse meinen Zeigefinger eine leichte pendelnde Bewegung mit kleinem Ausschlag machen. Ich spüre sie kaum, oder gar nicht. Vielleicht ein wenig in der Fingerspitze als ein leichtes Spannen. (Gar nicht im Gelenk.) Und diese Empfindung belehrt mich über die Bewegung? — denn ich kann die Bewegung genau beschreiben.

57. "Du mußt sie eben doch fühlen, sonst wüßtest du nicht (ohne zu schauen), wie sich dein Finger bewegt." Aber, es "wissen", heißt nur: es beschreiben können. — Ich mag die Richtung, aus der ein Schall kommt, nur angeben können, weil er das eine Ohr stärker affiziert als das andere; aber das spüre ich nicht in den Ohren; es bewirkt aber: ich 'weiß', aus welcher Richtung der Schall kommt; ich blicke z. B. in dieser Richtung.

58. So geht es auch mit den Ideen, daß ein Merkmal der Schmerz-empfindung uns über ihren Ort am Körper belehren muß, und ein Merkmal des Erinnerungsbildes über die Zeit, in die es fällt.

59. Eine Empfindung *kann* uns über die Bewegung, oder Lage eines Gliedes belehren. (Wer z. B. nicht, wie der Normale, wüßte, ob sein Arm gestreckt sei, den könnte ein stechender Schmerz im Ellbogen davon überzeugen.) — Und so kann auch der Charakter eines Schmerzes uns über den Sitz der Verletzung belehren. (Und die Vergilbtheit einer Photographie über ihr Alter.)

60. Was ist das Kriterium dafür, daß mich ein Sinneseindruck über die Form und Farbe belehrt?

61. *Welcher* Sinneseindruck? Nun *dieser*; ich beschreibe ihn durch Worte, oder durch ein Bild.

Und nun: was fühlst du, wenn deine Finger in dieser Lage sind? — "Wie soll man ein Gefühl erklären? Es ist etwas Unerklärbares, Besonderes." Aber den Gebrauch der Worte muß man doch lehren können!

62. Ich suche nun nach dem grammatischen Unterschied.

63. Sehen wir einmal vom kinästhetischen Gefühl ab! — Ich will Einem ein Gefühl beschreiben, und sage ihm "Mach's *so*, dann wirst du's haben",

56. "My kinaesthetic sensations apprise me of the movements and positions of my limbs."

I let my index finger make an easy pendulum movement of small amplitude. I either hardly feel it or don't feel it at all. Perhaps a little in the tip of the finger, as a slight tension. (Nothing at all in the joint.) And this sensation apprises me of the movement? — for I can describe the movement exactly.

57. "But still, you must feel it, otherwise you wouldn't know (without looking) how your finger is moving." But "knowing" it only means: being able to describe it. — I may be able to tell the direction from which a sound comes only because it affects one ear more strongly than the other, but I don't feel this in my ears; yet its effect is: I '*know*' the direction from which the sound comes; for instance, I look in that direction.

58. It is the same with the idea that it must be some feature of a pain-sensation that apprises us of its location; and so too with the idea that some feature of a memory-image apprises us of the time to which it refers.

59. A sensation *can* apprise us of the movement or position of a limb. (For example, if someone does not know, as a normal person does, whether his arm is stretched out, a piercing pain in the elbow might convince him.) — In the same way, the character of a pain can apprise us of its location. (And the yellowness of a photograph of its age.)

60. What is the criterion for a sense impression's apprising me of shape and colour?

61. *What* sense impression? Well, *this* one; I describe it by words, or by a picture.

And now: what do you feel when your fingers are in this position? — "How is one to explain a feeling? It is something inexplicable, special." But it must be possible to teach the use of the words!

62. What I am looking for now is the grammatical difference.

63. Let's leave the kinaesthetic feeling out for the moment. —— I want to describe a feeling to someone, and I tell him "Do *this*, and then you'll

dabei halte ich meinen Arm, oder meinen Kopf in bestimmter Lage. Ist das nun eine Beschreibung eines Gefühls, und wann werde ich sagen, er habe verstanden, welches Gefühl ich gemeint habe? — Er wird daraufhin noch eine *weitere* Beschreibung des Gefühls geben müssen. Und welcher Art muß die sein?

64. Ich sage "Mach's *so*, dann wirst du's haben." Kann da nicht ein Zweifel sein? muß nicht einer sein, wenn ein Gefühl gemeint ist?

65. *Das* schaut *so* aus; *das* schmeckt *so*; *das* fühlt sich *so* an. "Das" und "so" müssen verschieden erklärt werden.

66. Ein 'Gefühl' hat für uns ein ganz *bestimmtes* Interesse. Und dazu gehört z. B. der 'Grad des Gefühls', sein 'Ort', die Übertäubbarkeit des einen durch ein anderes. (Wenn die Bewegung sehr schmerzhaft ist, so daß der Schmerz jede andere leise Empfindung an dieser Stelle übertäubt, wird es dadurch unsicher, ob du diese Bewegung wirklich gemacht hast? Könnte es dich etwa dazu bringen, daß du dich mit den Augen davon überzeugst?)

|186| get it", at the same time holding my arm or my head in a particular position. Now is this a description of a feeling? and when shall I say that he has understood what feeling I meant? — He will have to give a *further* description of the feeling afterwards. And what kind of description must it be?

64. I say, "Do *this*, and you'll get it." Can't there be a doubt here? Mustn't there be one, if it is a feeling that is meant?

65. *This* looks *so*; *this* tastes *so*; *this* feels *so*. "This" and "so" must be differently explained.

66. A 'feeling' has for us a quite *particular* interest. And that involves, for instance, the 'degree of intensity of the feeling', its 'location', and the extent to which one feeling can be submerged by another. (When a movement is very painful, so that the pain submerges every other slight sensation in the same place, does this make it uncertain whether you have really made this movement? Could it lead you to make sure by looking?) |187|

67. Wer den eigenen Kummer beobachtet, mit welchen Sinnen beobachtet er ihn? Mit einem besonderen Sinn; mit einem, der den Kummer *fühlt*? So fühlt er ihn *anders*, wenn er ihn beobachtet? Und welchen beobachtet er nun; den, welcher nur da ist, während er beobachtet wird?

'Beobachten' erzeugt nicht das Beobachtete. (Das ist eine begriffliche Feststellung.)

Oder: Ich 'beobachte' nicht *das*, was durch's Beobachten erst entsteht. Das Objekt der Beobachtung ist ein Anderes.

68. Eine Berührung, die gestern noch schmerzhaft war, ist es heute nicht mehr.

Heute fühle ich den Schmerz nur noch, wenn ich an ihn denke. (D. h.: unter gewissen Umständen.)

Mein Kummer ist nicht mehr der gleiche: eine Erinnerung, die mir vor einem Jahr noch unerträglich war, ist es mir heute nicht mehr.

Das ist das Resultat einer Beobachtung.

69. Wann sagt man: jemand beobachte? Ungefähr: Wenn er sich in eine günstige Lage versetzt, gewisse Eindrücke zu erhalten, um (z. B.) was sie ihn lehren, zu beschreiben.

70. Wen man abgerichtet hätte, beim Anblick von etwas Rotem einen bestimmten Laut auszustoßen, beim Anblick von etwas Gelbem einen andern, und so fort für andre Farben, der würde damit noch nicht Gegenstände nach ihren Farben beschreiben. Obwohl er uns zu einer Beschreibung verhelfen könnte. Eine Beschreibung ist eine Abbildung einer Verteilung in einem Raum (der Zeit z. B.).

71. Ich lasse meinen Blick in einem Zimmer umherschweifen, plötzlich fällt er auf einen Gegenstand von auffallender roter Färbung, und ich sage "Rot!" — damit habe ich keine Beschreibung gegeben.

72. Sind die Worte "Ich fürchte mich" eine Beschreibung eines Seelenzustandes?

73. Ich sage "Ich fürchte mich", der Andere fragt mich: "Was war das? Ein Schrei der Angst; oder willst du mir mitteilen, wie dir's zumute ist; oder ist es eine Betrachtung über deinen gegenwärtigen Zustand?" — Könnte ich ihm immer eine klare Antwort geben? könnte ich ihm nie eine geben?

67. If someone observes his own grief, which senses does he use to observe it? With a special sense — one that *feels* grief? Then does he feel it *differently* when he is observing it? And what is the grief that he is observing — one which is there only while being observed?

'Observing' does not produce what is observed. (That is a conceptual statement.)

Again: I do not 'observe' *that* which comes into being only through observation. The object of observation is something else.

68. A touch, which hurt yesterday, no longer does so today.

Today I feel the pain only when I think of it. (That is: under certain circumstances.)

My grief is no longer the same; a memory which was still unbearable to me a year ago is now no longer so.

That is a result of observation.

69. When does one say: someone is observing? Roughly, when he puts himself in a favourable position to receive certain impressions, in order (for example) to describe what they apprise him of.

70. Someone who was trained to emit a particular sound at the sight of something red, another sound at the sight of something yellow, and so on for other colours, would not yet be describing objects by their colours. Though he might help *us* to arrive at a description. A description is a representation of a distribution in a space (in that of time, for instance).

71. I let my gaze wander round a room and suddenly it lights on an object of a striking red colour, and I say "Red!" — I haven't thereby given a description.

72. Are the words "I'm afraid" a description of a state of mind?

73. I say "I'm afraid"; someone else asks me: "What was that? A cry of fear; or did you want to tell me how you feel; or was it an observation On your present state? — Could I always give him a clear answer? Could I never give him one? |188|

74. Man kann sich sehr Verschiedenes vorstellen, z. B.: "Nicht, nicht! Ich fürchte mich!"

"Ich fürchte mich. Ich muß es leider gestehen."

"Ich fürchte mich noch immer ein wenig, aber nicht mehr so, wie früher."

"Ich fürchte mich im Grunde noch immer, obwohl ich mir's nicht gestehen will."

"Ich quäle mich selbst mit allerlei Furchtgedanken."

"Ich fürchte mich, — jetzt, wo ich furchtlos sein sollte!"

Zu jedem dieser Sätze gehört ein besonderer Tonfall, zu jedem ein anderer Zusammenhang.

Man könnte sich Menschen denken, die gleichsam viel bestimmter dächten, als wir, und, wo wir *ein* Wort verwenden, verschiedene verwendeten.

75. Man fragt sich "Was bedeutet 'ich fürchte mich' eigentlich, worauf ziele ich damit?" Und es kommt natürlich keine Antwort, oder eine, die nicht genügt.

Die Frage ist: "In welcher Art Zusammenhang steht es?"

76. Es kommt keine Antwort, wenn ich die Frage "Worauf ziele ich?", "Was denke ich dabei?" dadurch beantworten will, daß ich die Furchtäußerung wiederhole und dabei auf mich achtgebe, aus dem Augenwinkel gleichsam meine Seele beobachte. Ich kann aber allerdings in einem konkreten Fall fragen "Warum habe ich das gesagt, was wollte ich damit?" — und ich könnte die Frage auch beantworten; aber nicht auf Grund der Beobachtung von Begleiterscheinungen des Sprechens. Und meine Antwort würde die frühere Äußerung ergänzen, paraphrasieren.

77. Was ist Furcht? Was heißt "sich fürchten"? Wenn ich's mit *einem* Zeigen erklären wollte — würde ich Furcht *spielen*.

78. Könnte ich Hoffen auch so darstellen? Kaum. Oder gar Glauben?

79. Meinen Seelenzustand (der Furcht etwa) beschreiben, das tue ich in einem bestimmten Zusammenhang. (Wie eine bestimmte Handlung nur in einem bestimmten Zusammenhang ein Experiment ist.)

Ist es denn so erstaunlich, daß ich den gleichen Ausdruck in verschiedenen Spielen verwende? Und manchmal auch, gleichsam, zwischen den Spielen?

80. Und rede ich denn immer mit sehr bestimmter Absicht? — Und ist darum, was ich sage, sinnlos?

74. One can imagine all sorts of things here: for example, "No, no! I'm afraid!"

"I'm afraid. I am sorry to have to admit it."

"I'm still a bit afraid, but no longer as much as before."

"In fact I'm still afraid, though I'm reluctant to admit it to myself."

"I torment myself with all sorts of fearful thoughts."

"Now, just when I should be fearless, I'm afraid!"

To each of these sentences a special tone of voice is appropriate, to each a different context.

It would be possible to imagine people who, as it were, thought much more precisely than we, and used different words where we use only one.

75. One wonders, "What does 'I'm afraid' really mean; what do I aim at when I say it?" And, of course, no answer is forthcoming, or only an inadequate one.

The question is: "In what sort of context does it occur?"

76. No answer is forthcoming if I try to settle the question "What do I aim at?", "What am I thinking when I say it?" by repeating the fear utterance and at the same time attending to myself, as it were observing my mind out of the corner of my eye. In a concrete case, I can indeed ask, "Why did I say that, what was I up to?" — and I could answer the question too; but not on the ground of observing what accompanied the speaking. And my answer would supplement, paraphrase, the earlier utterance.

77. What is fear? What does "being afraid" mean? If I wanted to explain it at a *single* showing — I would *act* fear.

78. Could I also represent hope in this way? Hardly. And what about belief?

79. Describing my state of mind (of fear, say) is something I do in a particular context. (Just as it is only in a particular context that a certain activity is an experiment.)

Is it so surprising that I use the same expression in different games? And sometimes, as it were, even in between the games?

80. And do I always talk with very definite purpose? — And is what I say senseless because I don't? |189|

81. Wenn es in einer Leichenrede heißt "Wir trauern um unsern ...",
so soll das doch der Trauer Ausdruck geben; nicht den Anwesenden etwas
mitteilen. Aber in einem Gebet am Grabe wären diese Worte eine Art
von Mitteilung.

82. Das Problem ist doch dies: Der Schrei, den man keine Beschreibung
nennen kann, der primitiver ist als jede Beschreibung, tut gleichwohl
den Dienst einer Beschreibung des Seelenlebens.

83. Ein Schrei ist keine Beschreibung. Aber es gibt Übergänge. Und die
Worte "Ich fürchte mich" können näher und entfernter von einem Schrei
sein. Sie können ihm ganz nahe liegen, und *ganz* weit von ihm entfernt
sein.

84. Wir sagen doch nicht unbedingt von Einem, er *klage*, weil er sagt,
er habe Schmerzen. Also können die Worte "Ich habe Schmerzen" eine
Klage, und auch etwas anderes sein.

85. Ist aber "Ich fürchte mich" nicht immer, und doch manchmal, etwas
der Klage Ähnliches, warum soll es dann *immer* eine Beschreibung eines
Seelenzustandes sein?

81. When it is said in a funeral oration "We mourn our . . .", this is surely supposed to be an expression of mourning; not to communicate anything to those who are present. But in a prayer at the grave, these words would be a kind of communication.

* 82. Isn't the problem this: a cry, which cannot be called a description, which is more primitive than any description, for all that, does the service of a description of the psychological.

83. A cry is not a description. But there are intermediate cases. And the words "I am afraid" may approximate more, or less, to being a cry. They may come very close to one, and also be *very* far removed from it.

84. We surely do not invariably say that someone is *complaining* because he says he is in pain. So the words "I am in pain" may be a cry of complaint, and may be something else.

85. But if "I'm afraid" is not always similar to a cry of complaint and yet sometimes is, then why should it *always* be a description of a state of mind? |190|

86. Wie ist man je dazu gekommen, einen Ausdruck wie "Ich glaube ..." zu gebrauchen? Ist man einmal auf ein Phänomen (des Glaubens) aufmerksam geworden?

Hatte man sich selbst und die Anderen beobachtet und so das Glauben gefunden?

87. Moore's Paradox läßt sich so aussprechen: Die Äußerung "Ich glaube, es verhält sich so" wird ähnlich verwendet wie die Behauptung "Es verhält sich so"; und doch die *Annahme*, ich glaube, es verhalte sich so, nicht ähnlich wie die Annahme, es verhalte sich so.

88. Da scheint es ja, als wäre die Behauptung "Ich glaube" nicht die Behauptung dessen, was die Annahme "ich glaube" annimmt!

89. Ebenso: Die Aussage "Ich glaube, es wird regnen" hat einen ähnlichen Sinn, d. h., ähnliche Verwendung, wie "Es wird regnen", aber "Ich glaubte damals, es werde regnen" nicht einen ähnlichen, wie "Es hat damals geregnet".

"Aber es muß doch 'Ich glaubte' eben *das* in der Vergangenheit sagen, was 'Ich glaube' in der Gegenwart!" —— Es muß doch $\sqrt{-1}$ eben das für -1 bedeuten, was $\sqrt{1}$ für 1 bedeutet! Das heißt gar nichts.

90. "Im Grunde beschreibe ich mit den Worten 'Ich glaube ...' den eigenen Geisteszustand, — aber diese Beschreibung ist hier indirekt eine Behauptung des geglaubten Tatbestandes selbst." — Wie ich, unter Umständen, eine Photographie beschreibe, um das zu beschreiben, wovon sie eine Aufnahme ist.

Aber dann muß ich noch sagen können, daß die Photographie eine gute Aufnahme ist. Also auch: "Ich glaube, daß es regnet, und mein Glaube ist verläßlich, also verlasse ich mich auf ihn." — Dann wäre mein Glaube eine Art Sinneseindruck.

91. Man kann den eigenen Sinnen mißtrauen, aber nicht dem eigenen Glauben.

92. Gäbe es ein Verbum mit der Bedeutung 'fälschlich glauben', so hätte das keine sinnvolle erste Person im Indikativ des Präsens.

93. Sieh's nicht als selbstverständlich an, sondern als etwas sehr Merkwürdiges, daß die Verben "glauben", "wünschen", "wollen" alle die grammatischen Formen aufweisen, die "schneiden", "kauen", "laufen" auch haben.

86. How did people ever come to use such an expression as "I believe ..."? Did they at some time notice a phenomenon (of believing)?
   Did they observe themselves and others, and so discover believing?

87. Moore's paradox can be put like this: the utterance "I believe that this is the case" is used in a similar way to the assertion "This is the case"; and yet the *supposition* that I believe this is the case is not used like the supposition that this is the case.

88. So it seems as if the assertion "I believe" were not the assertion of what is supposed in the supposition "I believe"!

89. Similarly, the statement "I believe it's going to rain" has a similar sense, that is to say, a similar use, to "It's going to rain", but that of "I believed then that it was going to rain" is not similar to that of "It rained then".
   "But surely 'I believed' must say the very same thing in the past tense as 'I believe' in the present!" —— Surely $\sqrt{-1}$ must mean just the same for -1, as $\sqrt{1}$ means for 1! This signifies nothing at all.

90. "Basically, in using the words 'I believe ...', I describe my own state of mind — but here this description is indirectly an assertion of the fact believed." — As in certain circumstances, I describe a photograph in order to describe what it is a photograph of.
   But then I must be able to go on to say that the photograph is a good one. So also: "I believe it's raining, and my belief is reliable, so I rely on it." — In that case, my belief would be a kind of sense impression.

91. One can mistrust one's own senses, but not one's own belief.

92. If there were a verb meaning 'to believe falsely', it would not have a meaningful first person present indicative.

93. Don't regard it as a matter of course, but as a most remarkable thing, that the verbs "believe", "wish", "want" display all the grammatical forms possessed by "cut", "chew", "run".

94. Das Sprachspiel des Meldens kann so gewendet werden, daß die Meldung den Empfänger nicht über ihren Gegenstand unterrichten soll; sondern über den Meldenden.

So ist es z. B., wenn der Lehrer den Schüler prüft. (Man kann messen, um den Maßstab zu prüfen.)

95. Angenommen, ich führte einen Ausdruck — z. B. den: "Ich glaube" — so ein: Er soll dort der Meldung vorgesetzt werden, wo sie dazu dient, über den Meldenden selbst Auskunft zu geben. (Es braucht dem Ausdruck also keine Unsicherheit anzuhangen. Bedenke, daß die Unsicherheit der Behauptung sich auch unpersönlich ausdrücken läßt: "Er dürfte heute kommen.") — "Ich glaube . . . , und es ist nicht so" wäre ein Widerspruch.

96. "Ich glaube . . ." beleuchtet meinen Zustand. Es lassen sich aus dieser Äußerung Schlüsse auf mein Verhalten ziehen. Also ist hier eine *Ähnlichkeit* mit den Äußerungen der Gemütsbewegung, der Stimmung, etc.

97. Wenn aber "Ich glaube, es sei so" meinen Zustand beleuchtet, dann auch die Behauptung "Es ist so". Denn das Zeichen "Ich glaube" kann's nicht machen; kann es höchstens andeuten.

98. Eine Sprache, in der "Ich glaube, es ist so" nur durch den Ton der Behauptung "Es ist so" ausgedrückt wird. Statt "Er glaubt" heißt es dort "Er ist geneigt, zu sagen . . ." und es gibt auch die Annahme (den Konjunktiv) "Angenommen, ich sei geneigt etc.", aber nicht eine Äußerung: "Ich bin geneigt, zu sagen".

Moore's Paradox gäbe es in dieser Sprache nicht; statt dessen aber ein Verbum, dem eine Form fehlt.

Das aber sollte uns nicht überraschen. Denk daran, daß man die *eigene* künftige Handlung in der Äußerung der Absicht vorhersagen kann.

99. Ich sage vom Andern "Er scheint zu glauben . . ." und Andere sagen es von mir. Nun, warum sage ich's nie von mir, auch dann, wenn es die Andern *mit Recht* von mir sagen? — Sehe und höre ich mich selbst denn nicht? — Man kann es sagen.

100. "Die Überzeugung fühlt man in sich, man schließt nicht auf sie aus den eigenen Worten, oder ihrem Tonfall." — Wahr ist: Man schließt nicht aus den eigenen Worten auf die eigene Überzeugung; oder auf die Handlungen, die dieser entspringen.

94. The language-game of reporting can be given such a turn that a report is meant to inform the hearer not about its subject matter but about the speaker. |191|

It is so when, for instance, a teacher examines a pupil. (One can measure to test a ruler.)

95. Suppose I were to introduce some expression — "I believe", for example — in this way: it is to be prefixed to reports when they serve to give information about the speaker himself. (So no uncertainty need attach to the expression. Remember that the uncertainty of an assertion can be expressed impersonally: "He might come today.") — "I believe . . . , and it isn't so" would be a contradiction.

96. "I believe . . ." throws light on my state. Inferences about my conduct can be drawn from this utterance. So there is a *similarity* here to manifestations of emotion, of mood, and so on.

97. If, however, "I believe it is so" throws light on my state, then so does the assertion "It is so". For the sign "I believe" can't do it, can at the most hint at it.

98. Imagine a language in which "I believe it is so" is expressed only by means of the tone of the assertion "It is so". In this language they say, not "He believes" but "He is inclined to say . . . ," and there exists also the supposition (in the subjunctive) "Suppose I were inclined etc.", but no utterance like "I'm inclined to say".

Moore's paradox wouldn't exist in this language; instead, however, there would be a verb lacking one form.

But this ought not to surprise us. Think of the fact that one can predict one's *own* future action in expressing one's intention.

99. I say of someone else "He seems to believe . . .", and other people say it of me. Now, why do I never say it of myself, not even when others *rightly* say it of me? — Do I not see and hear myself, then? — One might say that.

100. "One feels conviction within oneself, one doesn't infer it from one's own words or their intonation." — What's true is: one does not infer one's own conviction from one's own words, nor yet the actions which arise from that conviction.

101. "Da scheint es ja, als wäre die Behauptung 'Ich glaube' nicht die Behauptung dessen, was die Annahme annimmt." — Ich bin also versucht, nach einer anderen Fortsetzung des Verbums in die erste Person des Indikativ Präsentis auszuschauen.

102. Ich denke so: Glauben ist ein Zustand der Seele. Er dauert an; und unabhängig vom Ablauf seines Ausdrucks in einem Satz, z. B. Er ist also eine Art von Disposition des Glaubenden. Die offenbart mir, im Andern, sein Benehmen; seine Worte. Und zwar ebensowohl eine Äußerung "Ich glaube . . .", wie seine einfache Behauptung. — Wie ist es nun mit mir: wie erkenne ich selbst die eigene Disposition? — Da müßte ich ja wie der Andere auf mich achtgeben, auf meine Worte hören, aus ihnen Schlüsse ziehen können!

103. Ich habe zu meinen eigenen Worten eine ganz andere Einstellung als die Andern.
      Jene Fortsetzung könnte ich finden, wenn ich nur sagen könnte "Ich scheine zu glauben".

104. Horchte ich auf die Rede meines Mundes, so könnte ich sagen, ein Anderer spreche aus meinem Mund.

105. "Nach meiner Äußerung zu urteilen, glaube ich *das*." Nun, es ließen sich Umstände ausdenken, in denen diese Worte Sinn hätten.
      Und dann könnte Einer auch sagen "Es regnet und ich glaube es nicht", oder "Mir scheint, mein Ego glaubt das, aber es ist nicht so." Man müßte sich dazu ein Benehmen ausmalen, das darauf deutet, zwei Wesen sprächen aus meinem Munde.

106. Die Linie liegt schon in der *Annahme* anders, als du denkst.
      In den Worten "Angenommen, ich glaube . . ." setzt du schon die ganze Grammatik des Wortes "glauben" voraus, den gewöhnlichen Gebrauch, den du beherrschst. — Du nimmst nicht einen Stand der Dinge an, der dir, sozusagen, eindeutig durch ein Bild vor Augen steht, so daß du dann eine andere als die gewöhnliche Behauptung an diese Annahme anstückeln kannst. — Du wüßtest gar nicht, was du hier annimmst (d. h., was z. B. aus so einer Annahme folgt), wenn dir nicht schon die Verwendung von "glauben" geläufig wäre.

107. Denk an den Ausdruck "Ich sage . . .", z. B. in "Ich sage, es wird heute regnen", welches einfach der Behauptung "Es wird . . ."

101. "But now, the assertion 'I believe' seems not to be the assertion of what the supposition assumes." — So I am tempted to cast around for a variant first person present indicative in the inflection of the verb.

102. This is how I'm thinking of it: Believing is a state of mind. It persists; and that independently of the process of expressing it in a sentence, for example. So it's a kind of disposition of the believing person. This is revealed to me in the case of someone else by his behaviour; and |192| by his words. And so just as well by the utterance "I believe . . ." as by the simple assertion. — Now what about my own case: how do I myself recognize my own disposition? — Here I would have to be able to do what others do — to attend to myself, listen to myself talking, make inferences from what I say!

103. My attitude to my own words is wholly different from that of others.
    I could find that variant conjugation of the verb, if only I could say "I seem to believe".

104. If I listened to the words issuing from my mouth, then I could say that someone else was speaking out of it.

105. "Judging from my words, *this* is what I believe." Now, it would be possible to think up circumstances in which this made sense.
    And then it would also be possible for someone to say "It is raining and I don't believe it", or "It seems to me that my ego believes this, but it isn't true". One would have to imagine a kind of behaviour suggesting that two beings were speaking through my mouth.

106. Even in the *assumption*, the pattern is not what you think.
    With the words "Assuming I believe . . ." you are presupposing the whole grammar of the word "to believe", the ordinary use, which you have mastered. — You are not assuming some state of affairs which, so to speak, a picture presents unambiguously to you, so that you can tack on to this assumption some assertion other than the ordinary one. — You would not know at all what you were assuming here (that is, what, for example, would follow from such an assumption), if you were not already familiar with the use of "believe".

107. Think of the expression "I say . . .", for example in "I say it will rain today", which simply amounts to the same as the assertion "It will

gleichkommt. "Er sagt, es wird . . ." heißt beiläufig "Er glaubt, es wird
. . .". "Angenommen, ich sage . . ." heißt *nicht*: Angenommen, es
werde heute . . .

108. Verschiedene Begriffe berühren sich hier und laufen ein Stück Wegs
miteinander. Man muß eben nicht glauben, daß die Linien alle *Kreise* seien.

109. Betrachte auch den Unsatz: "Es dürfte regnen; aber es regnet nicht."
   Und hier muß man sich hüten, zu sagen: "Es dürfte regnen" heißt
eigentlich: ich glaube, es wird regnen. — Warum sollte dann nicht
umgekehrt dies jenes heißen?

110. Betrachte nicht die zaghafte Behauptung als Behauptung der
Zaghaftigkeit.

rain today". "He says it will rain today" means roughly "He believes it will rain today". "Assuming I say it will rain today" does *not* mean "Assuming it rains today".

* 108. Different concepts touch here and run side by side for a stretch. One does not have to think that all these lines are *circles*.

109. Consider also the misbegotten sentence: "It's going to rain, but it won't".

And here one should be on one's guard against saying that "It's going to rain" really means "I believe it will rain". — For why not the other way round, why should not the latter mean the former?

110. Don't regard a hesitant assertion as an assertion of hesitancy. |193|

111. Zwei Verwendungen des Wortes "sehen".

Die eine: "Was siehst du dort?" — "Ich sehe *dies*" (es folgt eine Beschreibung, eine Zeichnung, eine Kopie). Die andere: "Ich sehe eine Ähnlichkeit in diesen beiden Gesichtern" — der, dem ich dies mitteile, mag die Gesichter so deutlich sehen, wie ich selbst.

Die Wichtigkeit: Der kategorische Unterschied der beiden 'Objekte' des Sehens.

112. Der Eine könnte die beiden Gesichter genau abzeichnen; der Andere in dieser Zeichnung die Ähnlichkeit bemerken, die der erste nicht sah.

113. Ich betrachte ein Gesicht, auf einmal bemerke ich seine Ähnlichkeit mit einem andern. Ich *sehe*, daß es sich nicht geändert hat; und sehe es doch anders. Diese Erfahrung nenne ich "das Bemerken eines Aspekts".

114. Seine *Ursachen* interessieren den Psychologen.

115. Uns interessiert der Begriff und seine Stellung in den Erfahrungsbegriffen.

116. Man könnte sich denken, daß an mehreren Stellen eines Buches, z. B. eines Lehrbuchs, die Illustration

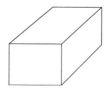

stünde. Im dazugehörigen Text ist jedesmal von etwas anderem die Rede: Einmal von einem Glaswürfel, einmal von einer umgestülpten offenen Kiste, einmal von einem Drahtgestell, das diese Form hat, einmal von drei Brettern, die ein Raumeck bilden. Der Text deutet jedesmal die Illustration.

Aber wir können auch die Illustration einmal als das eine, einmal als das andere Ding *sehen*. — Wir deuten sie also, und *sehen* sie, wie wir sie *deuten*.

117. Da möchte man vielleicht antworten: Die Beschreibung der unmittelbaren Erfahrung, des Seherlebnisses, mittels einer Deutung ist eine

111. Two uses of the word "see".

The one: "What do you see there?" — "I see *this*" (and then a description, a drawing, a copy). The other: "I see a likeness in these two faces" — let the man to whom I tell this be seeing the faces as clearly as I do myself.

What is important is the categorial difference between the two 'objects' of sight.

112. The one man might make an accurate drawing of the two faces, and the other notice in the drawing the likeness which the former did not see.

113. I observe a face, and then suddenly notice its likeness to another. I *see* that it has not changed; and yet I see it differently. I call this experience "noticing an aspect".

114. Its *causes* are of interest to psychologists.

115. We are interested in the concept and its place among the concepts of experience.

116. One could imagine the illustration

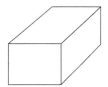

appearing in several places in a book, a textbook for instance. In the accompanying text, something different is in question every time: here a glass cube, there an upturned open box, there a wire frame of that shape, there three boards forming a solid angle. Each time the text supplies the interpretation of the illustration.

But we can also *see* the illustration now as one thing, now as another. — So we interpret it, and *see* it as we *interpret* it.

117. Here perhaps one would like to respond: The description of immediate, visual experience by means of an interpretation is an

indirekte Beschreibung. "Ich sehe die Figur als Kiste" heißt: ich habe ein bestimmtes Seherlebnis, welches mit dem Deuten der Figur als Kiste, oder mit dem Anschauen einer Kiste, erfahrungsgemäß einher geht. Aber wenn es das hieße, dann müßte ich's wissen. Ich müßte mich auf das Erlebnis direkt, und nicht nur indirekt beziehen können. (Wie ich von Rot nicht unbedingt als der Farbe des Blutes reden muß.)

118. Die folgende Figur, welche ich aus Jastrow entnommen habe, wird in meinen Bemerkungen der H-E-Kopf heißen. Man kann ihn als Hasenkopf, oder als Entenkopf sehen.

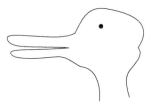

Und ich muß zwischen dem 'stetigen Sehen' eines Aspekts und dem 'Aufleuchten' eines Aspekts unterscheiden.

Das Bild mochte mir gezeigt worden sein, und ich darin nie etwas anderes als einen Hasen gesehen haben.

119. Es ist hier nützlich, den Begriff des Bildgegenstandes einzuführen. Ein 'Bildgesicht' z. B. wäre die Figur

Ich verhalte mich zu ihm in mancher Beziehung wie zu einem menschlichen Gesicht. Ich kann seinen Ausdruck studieren, auf ihn wie auf den Ausdruck des Menschengesichtes reagieren. Ein Kind kann zum Bildmenschen, oder Bildtier reden, sie behandeln, wie es Puppen behandelt.

120. Ich konnte also den H-E-Kopf von vornherein einfach als Bildhasen sehen. D. h.: Gefragt, "Was ist das?", oder "Was siehst du da?", hätte ich geantwortet: "Einen Bildhasen." Hätte man mich weiter gefragt, was das sei, so hätte ich zur Erklärung auf allerlei Hasenbilder, vielleicht auf wirkliche Hasen gezeigt, von dem Leben der Tiere geredet, oder sie nachgemacht.

indirect description. "I see the figure as a box" amounts to: I have a particular visual experience which is empirically found to accompany interpreting the figure as a box, or looking at |194| a box. But if it amounted to this, I ought to know it. I ought to be able to refer to the experience directly, and not only indirectly. (As I can speak of red without necessarily calling it the colour of blood.)

* 118. In my remarks, the following figure, derived from Jastrow, will be called "the duck–rabbit". It can be seen as a rabbit's head or as a duck's.

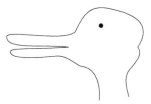

And I must distinguish between the 'continuous seeing' of an aspect and an aspect's 'lighting up'.

The picture might have been shown me, without my ever seeing in it anything but a rabbit.

119. Here it is useful to introduce the concept of a picture-object. For instance, the figure

would be a 'picture-face'.

In some respects, I engage with it as with a human face. I can study its expression, can react to it as to the expression of the human face. A child can talk to a picture-man or picture-animal, can treat them as it treats dolls.

120. I may, then, have seen the duck–rabbit simply as a picture-rabbit from the first. That is to say, if asked "What's that?" or "What do you see there?", I would have replied: "A picture-rabbit." If I had further been asked what that was, I would have explained by pointing to all sorts of pictures of rabbits, would perhaps have pointed to real rabbits, talked about their kind of life, or given an imitation of them.

121. Ich hätte auf die Frage "Was siehst du da?" nicht geantwortet: "Ich sehe das jetzt als Bildhasen." Ich hätte einfach die Wahrnehmung beschrieben; nicht anders, als wären meine Worte gewesen "Ich sehe dort einen roten Kreis". —
    Dennoch hätte ein Anderer von mir sagen können "Er sieht die Figur als Bild-H".

122. Zu sagen "Ich sehe das jetzt als . . .", hätte für mich so wenig Sinn gehabt, als beim Anblick von Messer und Gabel zu sagen: "Ich sehe das jetzt als Messer und Gabel." Man würde diese Äußerung nicht verstehen. — Ebensowenig wie diese: "Das ist jetzt für mich eine Gabel", oder "Das kann auch eine Gabel sein".

123. Man 'hält' auch nicht, was man bei Tisch als Eßbesteck erkennt, für ein Eßbesteck; sowenig wie man, beim Essen, für gewöhnlich den Mund zu bewegen versucht, oder zu bewegen trachtet.

124. Wer sagt "Jetzt ist es für mich ein Gesicht", den kann man fragen: "Auf welche Verwandlung spielst du an?"

125. Ich sehe zwei Bilder; in dem einen den H-E-Kopf umgeben von Hasen, im andern von Enten. Ich bemerke die Gleichheit nicht. *Folgt* daraus, daß ich beide Male etwas andres *sehe*? — Es gibt uns einen Grund, diesen Ausdruck hier zu gebrauchen.

126. "Ich habe es ganz anders gesehen, ich hätte es nie erkannt!" Nun, das ist ein Ausruf. Und er hat auch eine Rechtfertigung.

127. Ich hätte nie daran gedacht, die beiden Köpfe so aufeinander zu legen, sie *so* zu vergleichen. Denn sie legen eine andere Vergleichsweise nahe.
    Der Kopf, *so* gesehen, hat mit dem Kopf, *so* gesehen, auch nicht die leiseste Ähnlichkeit —— obwohl sie kongruent sind.

128. Man zeigt mir einen Bildhasen und fragt mich, was das sei; ich sage "Das ist ein H". Nicht "Das ist jetzt ein H". Ich teile die Wahrnehmung mit. — Man zeigt mir den H-E-Kopf und fragt mich, was das sei; da *kann* ich sagen "Das ist ein H-E-Kopf". Aber ich kann auch ganz anders auf die Frage reagieren. — Die Antwort, es sei der H-E-Kopf, ist wieder die Mitteilung der Wahrnehmung; die Antwort "Jetzt ist es ein H" ist es nicht. Hätte ich gesagt "Es ist ein Hase", so wäre mir die Doppeldeutigkeit entgangen, und ich hätte die Wahrnehmung berichtet.

121. I would not have answered the question "What do you see here?" by saying: "Now I see it as a picture-rabbit." I would simply |195| have described my perception, just as if I had said "I see a red circle over there".

Nevertheless, someone else could have said of me: "He sees the figure as a picture-rabbit."

122. It would have made as little sense for me to say "Now I see it as . . ." as to say at the sight of a knife and fork "Now I see this as a knife and fork". This utterance would not be understood. Any more than: "Now it is a fork for me" or "It can be a fork too".

123. One doesn't 'take' what one knows to be the cutlery at a meal *for* cutlery, any more than one ordinarily tries to move one's mouth as one eats, or strives to move it.

124. If someone says "Now it's a face for me", then one can ask him: "What change are you alluding to?"

125. I see two pictures, with the duck–rabbit surrounded by rabbits in one, by ducks in the other. I don't notice that they are the same. Does it *follow* from this that I *see* something different in the two cases? — It gives us a reason for using this expression here.

126. "I saw it quite differently, I'd never have recognized it!" Now, that is an exclamation. And there is also a justification for it.

127. I'd never have thought of superimposing the heads in this way, of comparing them in *this* way. For they suggest a different mode of comparison.

The head seen in *this* way hasn't even the slightest similarity to the head seen in *that* way —— although they are congruent.

128. I'm shown a picture-rabbit and asked what it is; I say "It's a rabbit". Not "Now it's a rabbit". I'm reporting my perception. — I'm shown the duck–rabbit and asked what it is; I *may* say "It's a duck-rabbit". But I may also react to the question quite differently. — The answer that it is a duck–rabbit is again the report of a perception; the answer "Now it's a rabbit" is not. Had I replied "It's a rabbit", the ambiguity would have escaped me, and I would have been reporting my perception.

129. Der Aspektwechsel. "Du würdest doch sagen, daß sich das Bild jetzt gänzlich geändert hat!"

Aber was ist anders: mein Eindruck? meine Stellungnahme? —— Kann ich's sagen? Ich *beschreibe* die Änderung, wie eine Wahrnehmung; ganz als hätte sich der Gegenstand vor meinen Augen geändert.

130. "Ich sehe ja jetzt *das*", könnte ich sagen (z. B. auf ein anderes Bild deutend). Es ist die Form der Meldung einer neuen Wahrnehmung.

Der Ausdruck des Aspektwechsels ist der Ausdruck einer *neuen* Wahrnehmung, zugleich mit dem Ausdruck der unveränderten Wahrnehmung.

131. Ich sehe auf einmal die Lösung eines Vexierbilds. Wo früher Zweige waren, ist jetzt eine menschliche Gestalt. Mein Gesichtseindruck hat sich geändert, und ich erkenne nun, daß er nicht nur Farbe und Form hatte, sondern auch eine ganz bestimmte 'Organisation'. —— Mein Gesichtseindruck hat sich geändert; — wie war er früher; wie ist er jetzt? —— Stelle ich ihn durch eine genaue Kopie dar — und ist das keine gute Darstellung? — so zeigt sich keine Änderung.

132. Und sag nur ja nicht "Mein Gesichtseindruck ist doch nicht die *Zeichnung*; er ist *dies* —— was ich niemand zeigen kann." — Freilich ist er nicht die Zeichnung, aber auch nichts von der gleichen Kategorie, das ich in mir trage.

133. Der Begriff des 'inneren Bildes' ist irreführend, denn das Vorbild für diesen Begriff ist das '*äußere* Bild'; und doch sind die Verwendungen der Begriffsworte einander nicht ähnlicher, als die von "Zahlzeichen" und "Zahl". (Ja, wer die Zahl das 'ideale Zahlzeichen' nennen wollte, könnte damit eine ähnliche Verwirrung anrichten.)

134. Wer die 'Organisation' des Gesichtseindrucks mit Farben und Formen zusammenstellt, geht vom Gesichtseindruck als einem inneren Gegenstand aus. Dieser Gegenstand wird dadurch freilich ein Unding; ein seltsam schwankendes Gebilde. Denn die Ähnlichkeit mit dem Bild ist nun gestört.

135. Wenn ich weiß, daß es verschiedene Aspekte des Würfelschemas gibt, kann ich den Andern, um zu erfahren, was er sieht, noch außer der Kopie ein Modell des Gesehenen herstellen, oder zeigen lassen; auch wenn *er* gar nicht weiß, wozu ich zwei Erklärungen fordere.

129. The change of aspect. "But surely you'd say that the picture has changed altogether now!"

But what is different: my impression? my attitude? —— Can I say? I *describe* the change like a perception; just as if the object had changed before my eyes. |196|

130. "Ah, now I see *this*", I might say (pointing to another picture, for example). This has the form of a report of a new perception.

The expression of a change of aspect is an expression of a *new* perception and, at the same time, an expression of an unchanged perception.

131. I suddenly see the solution of a puzzle-picture. Where there were previously branches, now there is a human figure. My visual impression has changed, and now I recognize that it has not only shape and colour, but also a quite particular 'organization'. —— My visual impression has changed — what was it like before; what is it like now? —— If I represent it by means of an exact copy — and isn't that a good representation of it? — no change shows up.

132. And above all do not say "Surely, my visual impression isn't the *drawing*; it is *this* —— which I can't show to anyone." Of course it is not the drawing; but neither is it something of the same category, which I carry within myself.

133. The concept of an 'inner picture' is misleading, since the model for this concept is the '*outer* picture'; and yet the uses of these concept-words are no more like one another than the uses of "numeral" and "number". (Indeed, someone who was inclined to call numbers 'ideal numerals' could generate a similar confusion by doing so.)

134. Someone who puts the 'organization' of a visual impression on a level with colours and shapes would be taking it for granted that the visual impression is an inner object. Of course, this makes this object chimerical, a strangely vacillating structure. For the similarity to a picture is now impaired.

135. If I know that the schematic cube has various aspects, and I want to find out what someone else sees, I can get him to make a model of what he sees, in addition to a copy, or to show such a model; even though *he* has no idea of my purpose in demanding two accounts.

Beim Aspektwechsel aber verschiebt sich's. Es wird das der einzig mögliche Erlebnisausdruck, was früher nach der Kopie vielleicht eine unnütze Bestimmung schien, oder auch war.

136. Und das allein tut den Vergleich der 'Organisation' mit Farbe und Form im Gesichtseindruck ab.

137. Wenn ich den H-E-Kopf als H sah, so sah ich: diese Formen und Farben (ich gebe sie genau wieder) — und außerdem noch so etwas: dabei nun zeige ich auf eine Menge verschiedener Hasenbilder. — Dies zeigt die Verschiedenheit der Begriffe.
    Das 'Sehen als . . .' gehört nicht zur Wahrnehmung. Und darum ist es wie ein Sehen und wieder nicht wie ein Sehen.

138. Ich schaue auf ein Tier; man fragt mich: "Was siehst du?" Ich antworte: "Einen Hasen." —— Ich sehe eine Landschaft; plötzlich läuft ein Hase vorbei. Ich rufe aus "Ein Hase!".
    Beides, die Meldung und der Ausruf, ist ein Ausdruck der Wahrnehmung und des Seherlebnisses. Aber der Ausruf ist es in anderem Sinne, als die Meldung. Er entringt sich uns. — Er verhält sich zum Erlebnis ähnlich, wie der Schrei zum Schmerz.

139. Aber da er die Beschreibung einer Wahrnehmung ist, kann man ihn auch Gedankenausdruck nennen. —— Wer den Gegenstand anschaut, muß nicht an ihn denken; wer aber das Seherlebnis hat, dessen Ausdruck der Ausruf ist, der *denkt* auch an das, was er sieht.

140. Und darum erscheint das Aufleuchten des Aspekts halb Seherlebnis, halb ein Denken.

141. Jemand sieht plötzlich eine Erscheinung vor sich, die er nicht erkennt (es mag ein ihm wohlbekannter Gegenstand, aber in ungewöhnlicher Lage, oder Beleuchtung sein); das Nichterkennen dauert vielleicht nur sekundenlang. Ist es richtig: er habe ein anderes Seherlebnis, als der, der den Gegenstand gleich erkannte?

142. Könnte denn Einer die vor ihm auftauchende, ihm unbekannte Form nicht ebenso *genau* beschreiben, wie ich, dem sie vertraut ist? Und ist das nicht die Antwort? — Freilich, im allgemeinen wird es so nicht sein. Auch wird seine Beschreibung ganz anders lauten. (Ich werde z. B. sagen "Das Tier hatte lange Ohren" — er: "Es waren da zwei lange Fortsätze" und nun zeichnet er sie.)

But with a changing aspect, the case is altered. What before perhaps seemed, or even was, a useless specification once there was a copy, now becomes the only possible expression of the experience.

* 136. And this suffices to dispose of the comparison of 'organization' with colour and shape in the visual impression.

137. If I saw the duck–rabbit as a rabbit, then I saw such-and-such shapes and colours (I reproduce them in detail) — and, in addition, I saw something like this: |197| and here I point to a great variety of pictures of rabbits. — This shows the difference between the concepts.
   'Seeing as . . .' is not part of perception. And therefore it is like seeing, and again not like seeing.

138. I look at an animal; someone asks me: "What do you see?" I answer: "A rabbit." —— I see a landscape; suddenly a rabbit runs past. I exclaim: "A rabbit!"
   Both things, both the report and the exclamation, are expressions of perception and of visual experience. But the exclamation is so in a different sense from the report: it is forced from us. — It stands to the experience somewhat as a cry to pain.

139. But since the exclamation is the description of a perception, one can also call it the expression of thought. —— Someone who looks at an object need not think of it; but whoever has the visual experience expressed by the exclamation is also *thinking* of what he sees.

140. And that's why the lighting up of an aspect seems half visual experience, half thought.

141. Someone suddenly sees something which he does not recognize (it may be a familiar object, but in an unusual position or lighting); the lack of recognition perhaps lasts only a few seconds. Is it correct to say that he has a different visual experience from someone who recognized the object straightaway?

142. Couldn't someone describe an unfamiliar shape that appeared before him just as *accurately* as I, to whom it is familiar? And isn't that the answer? — Of course, generally it won't be so. And his description will run quite differently. (I say, for example, "The animal had long ears" — he: "There were two long appendages", and then he draws them.)

143. Ich treffe einen, den ich jahrelang nicht gesehen habe; ich sehe ihn deutlich, erkenne ihn aber nicht. Plötzlich erkenne ich ihn, sehe in seinem veränderten Gesicht sein früheres. Ich glaube, ich würde ihn jetzt anders porträtieren, wenn ich malen könnte.

144. Wenn ich nun meinen Bekannten in der Menschenmenge erkenne, nachdem ich vielleicht schon längere Zeit in seiner Richtung geschaut habe, — ist das ein besonderes Sehen? ist es ein Sehen und Denken? oder eine Verschmelzung der beiden — wie ich beinahe sagen möchte?
   Die Frage ist: *Warum* will man das sagen?

145. Derselbe Ausdruck, der auch Meldung des Gesehenen ist, ist jetzt Ausruf des Erkennens.

146. Was ist das Kriterium des Seherlebnisses? — Was soll das Kriterium sein?
   Die Darstellung dessen, 'was gesehen wird'.

147. Der Begriff der Darstellung des Gesehenen, sowie der Kopie, ist sehr dehnbar, und *mit ihm* der Begriff des Gesehenen. Die beiden hängen innig zusammen. (Und das heißt *nicht*, daß sie ähnlich sind.)

148. Wie merkt man, daß die Menschen räumlich *sehen*? —— Ich frage Einen, wie das Terrain (dort) liegt, das er überschaut. Liegt es *so*? (ich zeige es mit der Hand). —— "Ja." —— "Wie weißt du das?" —— "Es ist nicht neblig, ich sehe es ganz klar." —— Es werden nicht Gründe für die *Vermutung* gegeben. Es ist uns einzig natürlich, das Geschaute räumlich darzustellen; während es für die ebene Darstellung, sei es durch Zeichnung oder durch Worte, besonderer Übung und eines Unterrichts bedarf. (Die Sonderbarkeit der Kinderzeichnungen.)

149. Sieht Einer ein Lächeln, das er nicht als Lächeln erkennt, nicht so versteht, anders, als der es versteht? — Er macht es z. B. anders nach.

150. Halte die Zeichnung eines Gesichts verkehrt und du kannst den Ausdruck des Gesichts nicht erkennen. Vielleicht kannst du sehen, daß es lächelt, aber doch nicht genau, *wie* es lächelt. Du kannst das Lächeln nicht nachahmen, oder seinen Charakter genauer beschreiben.
   Und doch mag das verkehrte Bild das Gesicht eines Menschen höchst genau darstellen.

143. I meet someone whom I have not seen for years; I see him clearly, but fail to recognize him. Suddenly I recognize him, I see his former face in the altered one. I believe that I would portray him differently now if I could paint.

144. Now, when I recognize my acquaintance in a crowd, perhaps after looking in his direction for quite a while — is this a special sort of seeing? Is it a case of both seeing and thinking? Or a fusion of the two — as I would almost like to say?

The question is: *why* does one want to say this? |198|

145. The very expression which is also a report of what is seen is here a cry of recognition.

146. What is the criterion of the visual experience? — What should the criterion be?

A representation of 'what is seen'.

147. The concept of a representation of what is seen, like that of a copy, is very elastic, and so *together with it* is the concept of what is seen. The two are intimately connected. (Which is *not* to say that they are alike.)

148. How does one tell that human beings *see* three-dimensionally? —— I ask someone about the lie of the land (over there) of which he has a view. "Is it like *this*?" (I show him with my hand) —— "Yes." —— "How do you know?" —— "It's not misty, I see it very clearly." —— No reasons are given for the *presumption*. It is altogether natural to us to represent what we see three-dimensionally, whereas special practice and instruction are needed for two-dimensional representation, whether in drawing or in words. (The oddity of children's drawings.)

149. If someone sees a smile and does not recognize it as a smile, does not understand it as such, does he see it differently from someone who understands it? — He mimics it differently, for instance.

150. Hold the drawing of a face upside down and you can't recognize the expression of the face. Perhaps you can see that it is smiling, but not exactly what *kind* of smile it is. You cannot imitate the smile or describe its character more exactly.

And yet the picture which you have turned round may be a most exact representation of a person's face.

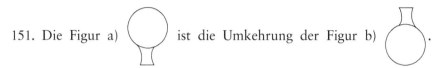

151. Die Figur a) [image] ist die Umkehrung der Figur b) [image] .

Wie die Figur c) *Freude* die Umkehrung von d) *Freude*.

Aber zwischen meinem Eindruck von c und d besteht ein anderer Unterschied — möchte ich sagen — als zwischen dem von a und von b. d sieht z. B. ordentlicher aus als c. (Vergleiche eine Bemerkung von Lewis Carroll.) d ist leicht zu kopieren, c schwer.

152. Denk dir den H-E-Kopf in einem Gewirr von Strichen versteckt. Einmal nun bemerke ich ihn in dem Bild, und zwar einfach als Hasenkopf. Später einmal schaue ich das gleiche Bild an und bemerke die gleiche Linie, aber als Ente, und dabei brauche ich noch nicht zu wissen, daß es beidemale die gleiche Linie war. Wenn ich später nun den Aspekt wechseln sehe, — kann ich sagen, daß dabei die Aspekte H und E ganz anders gesehen werden, als da ich sie einzeln im Gewirr der Striche erkannte? Nein.

   Aber der Wechsel ruft ein Staunen hervor, den das Erkennen nicht hervorrief.

153. Wer in einer Figur (1) nach einer anderen Figur (2) sucht, und sie dann findet, der sieht (1) damit auf neue Weise. Er kann nicht nur eine neue Art der Beschreibung von ihr geben, sondern jenes Bemerken war ein neues Seherlebnis.

154. Aber es muß nicht geschehen, daß er sagen möchte: "Die Figur (1) sieht nun ganz anders aus; sie hat auch keine Ähnlichkeit mit der früheren, obwohl sie mit ihr kongruent ist!"

155. Es gibt hier eine Unmenge miteinander verwandter Erscheinungen und möglicher Begriffe.

156. Ist also die Kopie der Figur eine *unvollkommene* Beschreibung meines Seherlebnisses? Nein. — Es kommt doch auf die Umstände an, ob, und welche, nähere Bestimmungen notwendig sind. — Sie *kann* eine unvollkommene Beschreibung sein; wenn eine Frage übrig bleibt.

157. Man kann natürlich sagen: Es gibt gewisse Dinge, die sowohl unter den Begriff 'Bildhase', als 'Bildente' fallen. Und so ein Ding ist ein Bild, eine Zeichnung. — Aber der *Eindruck* ist nicht zugleich der von einer Bildente und von einem Bildhasen.

*   151. The figure (a) is the reverse of the figure (b)

As (c)  is the reverse of (d) *Pleasure* .

But — I'd like to say — there is another kind of difference between my impressions of (c) and (d) and between those of (a) and (b). (d), for example, looks neater than (c). (Compare a remark of Lewis Carroll's.) (d) is easy, (c) hard to copy. |199|

152. Imagine the duck–rabbit hidden in a tangle of lines. Now I suddenly notice it in the picture, and notice it simply as the head of a rabbit. At some later time, I look at the same picture and notice the same outline, but see it as a duck, without necessarily realizing that it was the same outline both times. If I later see the aspect change — can I say that the duck and rabbit aspects are now seen quite differently from when I recognized them separately in the tangle of lines? No.

But the change produces a surprise not produced by the recognition.

*   153. If someone searches in a certain figure (call it Figure 1) for another figure (call it Figure 2), and then finds it, he sees Figure 1 in a new way. Not only can he give a new kind of description of it, but noticing the second figure was a new visual experience.

154. But he wouldn't necessarily want to say: "Figure 1 looks quite different now; there isn't even any similarity to the figure I saw before, though they are congruent!"

155. Here there is an enormous number of interrelated phenomena and possible concepts.

156. Then is the copy of the figure an *incomplete* description of my visual experience? No. — After all, whether, and what, more detailed specifications are necessary depends on the circumstances. — It *may* be an incomplete description — if some question still remains.

157. Of course one can say: There are certain things which fall both under the concept 'picture-rabbit' and under the concept 'picture-duck'. And a picture, a drawing, is such a thing. — But an *impression* is not simultaneously of a picture-duck and a picture-rabbit.

158. "Was ich eigentlich *sehe*, muß doch das sein, was in mir durch Einwirkung des Objekts zustande kommt." — Das, was in mir zustande kommt, ist dann eine Art Abbild, etwas, was man selbst wieder anschauen, vor sich haben könnte; beinahe so etwas wie eine *Materialisation*.

Und diese Materialisation ist etwas Räumliches und muß sich ganz in räumlichen Begriffen beschreiben lassen. Sie kann z. B. lächeln (wenn sie ein Gesicht ist), aber der Begriff der Freundlichkeit gehört nicht zu ihrer Darstellung, sondern ist dieser Darstellung *fremd* (wenn er ihr auch dienen kann).

159. Fragst du mich, was ich gesehen habe, so werde ich vielleicht eine Skizze herstellen können, die es zeigt; aber daran, wie mein Blick gewandelt ist, werde ich mich in den meisten Fällen überhaupt nicht erinnern.

160. Der Begriff 'sehen' macht einen wirren Eindruck. Nun, so ist er. — Ich sehe in die Landschaft; mein Blick schweift, ich sehe allerlei klare und unklare Bewegung; *dies* prägt sich mir klar ein, *jenes* nur ganz verschwommen. Wie gänzlich zerrissen uns doch erscheinen kann, was wir sehen! Und nun schau an, was "Beschreibung des Gesehenen" heißt! — Aber das ist eben, was man eine Beschreibung des Gesehenen nennt. Es gibt nicht *einen eigentlichen*, ordentlichen Fall so einer Beschreibung — und das Übrige ist eben noch unklar, harrt noch der Klärung, oder muß einfach als Abfall in den Winkel gekehrt werden.

161. Es ist hier für uns die ungeheure Gefahr: feine Unterschiede machen zu wollen. —— Ähnlich ist es, wenn man den Begriff des physikalischen Körpers aus dem 'wirklich Gesehenen' erklären will. — Es ist vielmehr das alltägliche Sprachspiel *hinzunehmen*, und *falsche* Darstellungen sind als dies zu kennzeichnen. Das primitive Sprachspiel, das dem Kind beigebracht wird, bedarf keiner Rechtfertigung; die Versuche der Rechtfertigung bedürfen der Zurückweisung.

162. Betrachte nun als Beispiel die Aspekte des Dreiecks. Das Dreieck

kann gesehen werden: als dreieckiges Loch, als Körper, als geometrische Zeichnung; auf seiner Grundlinie stehend, an seiner Spitze aufgehängt; als Berg, als Keil, als Pfeil oder Zeiger; als ein umgefallener Körper, der (z. B.) auf der kürzeren Kathete stehen sollte, als ein halbes Parallelogramm, und verschiedenes anderes.

158. "What I really *see* must surely be what is produced in me by the object." — Then what is produced in me is a sort of replica, something that in its turn can be looked at, can be before one; almost something like a *materialization*.

And this materialization is something spatial and must be describable in purely spatial terms. For instance, it may be smiling (if it is a face); the concept of friendliness, however, has no place in a description of it, but is *foreign* to such a description (even though it may help it).

159. If you ask me what I saw, perhaps I'll be able to make a sketch which shows it; but how my glance wandered, I'll mostly not recollect at all. |200|

160. The concept of seeing makes a tangled impression. Well, that's how it is. — I look at the landscape; my gaze wanders over it, I see all sorts of distinct and indistinct movement; *this* impresses itself sharply on me, *that* very hazily. How completely piecemeal what we see can appear! And now look at all that can be meant by "description of what is seen"! — But this just is what is called "description of what is seen". There is not *one genuine*, proper case of such description — the rest just being unclear, awaiting clarification, or simply to be swept aside as rubbish.

161. Here we are in enormous danger of wanting to make fine distinctions. —— It is similar when one tries to explain the concept of a physical object in terms of 'what is really seen'. — Rather, the everyday language-game is to be *accepted*, and *false* accounts of it characterized *as* false. The primitive language-game which children are instructed in needs no justification; attempts at justification need to be rejected.

162. Take as an example the aspects of a triangle. This triangle

can be seen as a triangular hole, as a solid, as a geometrical drawing; as standing on its base, as hanging from its apex; as a mountain, as a wedge, as an arrow or pointer, as an overturned object which is meant, for example, to stand on the shorter side of the right angle, as a half parallelogram, and as various other things.

163. "Du kannst dabei einmal an *das* denken, einmal an *das*, einmal es als *das* ansehen, einmal als *das*, und dann wirst du's einmal *so* sehen, einmal *so*." — *Wie* denn? Es gibt ja keine weitere Bestimmung.

164. Wie ist es aber möglich, daß man ein Ding einer *Deutung* gemäß *sieht*? —— Die Frage stellt es als ein seltsames Faktum dar; als wäre hier etwas in eine Form gezwängt worden, was eigentlich nicht hineinpaßt. Aber es ist hier kein Drücken und Zwängen geschehen.

165. Wenn es scheint, es wäre für so eine Form zwischen anderen Formen kein Platz, so mußt du sie in einer anderen Dimension aufsuchen. Wenn hier kein Platz ist, so ist er eben in einer anderen Dimension.
   (In diesem Sinne ist auch auf der reellen Zahlenlinie nicht für imaginäre Zahlen Platz. Und das heißt doch: die Anwendung des imaginären Zahlbegriffs ist unähnlicher der des reellen, als der Anblick der *Rechnungen* es offenbart. Man muß zur Anwendung hinuntersteigen, dann findet jener Begriff einen sozusagen *ungeahnt* verschiedenen Platz.)

166. Wie wäre diese Erklärung: "Ich kann etwas als *das* sehen, wovon es ein Bild sein kann"?
   Das heißt doch: Die Aspekte im Aspektwechsel sind *die*, die die Figur unter Umständen *ständig* in einem Bild haben könnte.

167. Ein Dreieck kann ja wirklich in einem Gemälde *stehen*, in einem anderen hängen, in einem dritten etwas Umgefallenes darstellen. — So zwar, daß ich, der Beschauer nicht sage "Das kann auch etwas Umgefallenes darstellen", sondern "das Glas ist umgefallen und liegt in Scherben". So reagieren wir auf das Bild.

168. Könnte ich sagen, wie ein Bild beschaffen sein muß, um dies zu bewirken? Nein. Es gibt z. B. Malweisen, die mir nichts in dieser unmittelbaren Weise mitteilen, aber doch andern Menschen. Ich glaube, daß Gewohnheit und Erziehung hier mitzureden haben.

169. Was heißt es nun, daß ich auf dem Bild die Kugel '*schweben sehe*'?
   Liegt es schon darin, daß mir diese Beschreibung die nächstliegende, selbstverständliche ist? Nein; das könnte sie aus verschiedenen Gründen sein. Sie könnte z. B. einfach die herkömmliche sein.

163. "You can think now of *this*, now of *this*, as you look at it, can regard it now as *this*, now as *this*, and then you will see it now *this* way, now *this*." — *What* way? There is, after all, no further qualification.

* 164. But how is it possible to *see* an object according to an *interpretation*? —— The question presents it as a strange fact; as if something had been pressed into a mould it did not really fit into. But no squeezing, no pressing, took place here.

* 165. If it looks as if there were no room for such a form between other ones, you must find it in another dimension. If there's no room here, there will be in another dimension. |201|

(It is in this sense that there is no room for imaginary numbers in the continuum of real numbers. And this surely means: the application of the concept of imaginary numbers is less like that of real numbers than is revealed by the look of the *calculations*. It is necessary to descend to the application, and then the concept finds a different place — one which, so to speak, one never dreamed of.)

166. How would the following account do: "I can see something as whatever it can be a picture of"?

What this means is: the aspects in a change of aspects are *those* which, in certain circumstances, the figure could have *permanently* in a picture.

167. A triangle can really be *standing up* in one picture, hanging in another, and in a third represent something fallen over — in such a way that I, who am looking at it, say, not "It may also represent something fallen over", but "That glass has fallen over and is lying there in fragments". This is how we react to the picture.

168. Could I say what a picture must be like to produce this effect? No. There are, for example, styles of painting which do not convey anything to me in this immediate way, but do to other people. I think custom and upbringing have a hand in this.

169. What does it mean to say that I '*see the sphere floating in the air*' in a picture?

Is it enough that for me this description is the most suggestive, natural one? No; for it might be so for various reasons. It might, for instance, simply be the conventional description.

Was aber ist der Ausdruck dafür, daß ich das Bild nicht nur, z. B., so verstehe (weiß, was es darstellen *soll*), sondern so *sehe*? —— Ein solcher Ausdruck ist: "Die Kugel scheint zu schweben", "Man sieht sie schweben", oder auch, in besonderem Tonfall, "Sie schwebt!"

Das ist also der Ausdruck des Dafürhaltens. Aber nicht als solcher verwendet.

170. Wir fragen uns hier nicht, was die Ursachen sind und was in einem besonderen Fall diesen Eindruck hervorruft.

171. Und *ist* es ein besonderer Eindruck? — "Ich sehe doch etwas *anderes*, wenn ich die Kugel schweben, als wenn ich sie bloß daliegen sehe." — Das heißt eigentlich: Dieser Ausdruck ist gerechtfertigt! (Denn, wörtlich genommen, ist er ja nur eine Wiederholung.)

(Und doch ist mein Eindruck auch nicht der einer wirklichen schwebenden Kugel. Es gibt Abarten des 'räumlichen Sehens'. Die Räumlichkeit einer Photographie und die Räumlichkeit dessen, was wir durch's Stereoskop sehen.)

172. "Und ist es wirklich ein anderer Eindruck?" — Um es zu beantworten, möchte ich mich fragen, ob da wirklich etwas anderes in mir existiert. Aber wie kann ich mich davon überzeugen? —— Ich *beschreibe*, was ich sehe, anders.

173. Gewisse Zeichnungen sieht man immer als Figuren in der Ebene, andere manchmal, oder auch immer, räumlich.

Da möchte man nun sagen: Der Gesichtseindruck der räumlich gesehenen Zeichnungen ist räumlich; ist für's Würfelschema z. B. ein Würfel. (Denn die Beschreibung des Eindrucks ist die Beschreibung eines Würfels.)

174. Und es ist dann merkwürdig, daß unser Eindruck für manche Zeichnungen etwas Flaches, für manche etwas Räumliches ist. Man fragt sich: "Wo soll das enden?"

175. Wenn ich das Bild eines dahinjagenden Pferdes sehe, — *weiß* ich nur, daß diese Bewegungsart gemeint ist? Ist es Aberglaube, daß ich es im Bilde dahinjagen *sehe*? —— Und tut dies nun auch mein Gesichtseindruck?

176. Was teilt mir Einer mit, der sagt "Ich sehe es jetzt als . . ."? Welche Folgen hat diese Mitteilung? Was kann ich mit ihr anfangen?

But what is an expression for my not merely understanding the picture in this way, for instance (knowing what it is *supposed* to represent), but *seeing* it in this way? —— It is expressed by, say, "The sphere seems to float", "One sees it floating", or perhaps, in a special tone of voice, "It floats!"

This, then, is an expression for taking something to be so. But not being used as such.

170. Here we are not asking ourselves what are the causes and what produces this impression in a particular case.

171. And *is* it a special impression? — "Surely I see something *different* when I see the sphere floating from when I merely see it lying there." — This really amounts to: This expression is justified! (For, taken literally, it is no more than a repetition.) |202|

(And yet my impression is not that of a real floating sphere either. There are derivative forms of 'three-dimensional seeing'. The three-dimensional character of a photograph and the three-dimensional character of what we see through a stereoscope.)

172. "And is it really a different impression?" — In order to answer this, I'd like to ask myself whether there is really something different there in me. But how can I ascertain this? —— I *describe* what I see differently.

173. Certain drawings are always seen as flat figures, and others sometimes, or always, three-dimensionally.

Here one would now like to say: the visual impression of drawings seen three-dimensionally is three-dimensional; with the schematic cube, for instance, it is a cube. (For the description of the impression is the description of a cube.)

174. And then it is strange that with some drawings our impression should be something flat, and with others something three-dimensional. One wonders, "Where is this going to end?"

175. When I see the picture of a galloping horse — do I only *know* that this is the kind of movement meant? Is it superstition to think I *see* the horse galloping in the picture? —— And does my visual impression gallop too?

176. What does anyone tell me by saying "Now I see it as . . ."? What consequences has this information? What can I do with it?

177. Menschen assoziieren oft Farben mit Vokalen. Es könnte sein, daß für Manchen ein Vokal, wenn er öfters hintereinander ausgesprochen wird, seine Farbe wechselt. *a* ist für ihn z. B. 'jetzt blau —— jetzt rot'.

Es könnte die Äußerung "Ich sehe es jetzt als . . ." uns nicht mehr bedeuten, als die: "*a* ist für mich jetzt rot."

(Gekuppelt mit physiologischen Beobachtungen könnte auch dieser Wechsel uns wichtig werden.)

178. Da fällt mir ein, daß in Gesprächen über ästhetische Gegenstände die Worte gebraucht werden: "Du mußt es *so* sehen, so ist es gemeint"; "Wenn du es *so* siehst, siehst du, wo der Fehler liegt"; "Du mußt diese Takte als Einleitung hören"; "Du mußt nach dieser Tonart hinhören"; "Du mußt es *so* phrasieren" (und das kann sich auf's Hören wie auf's Spielen beziehen).

179. Die Figur

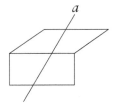

soll eine konvexe Stufe vorstellen und zur Demonstration von irgendwelchen räumlichen Vorgängen verwendet werden. Wir ziehen dazu etwa die Gerade *a* durch die Mittelpunkte der beiden Flächen. —— Wenn nun Einer die Figur nur auf Augenblicke räumlich sähe, und auch dann bald als konkave, bald als konvexe Stufe, so könnte es ihm dadurch schwer werden, unserer Demonstration zu folgen. Und wenn für ihn der flache Aspekt mit einem räumlichen wechselt, so ist es hier nicht anders, als zeigte ich ihm während der Demonstration gänzlich verschiedene Gegenstände.

180. Was heißt es, wenn ich, eine Zeichnung in der darstellenden Geometrie betrachtend, sage: "Ich weiß, daß diese Linie hier wieder zum Vorschein kommt, aber ich kann sie nicht so *sehen*"? Heißt es einfach, daß mir die Geläufigkeit des Operierens in der Zeichnung fehlt, daß ich mich nicht so gut in ihr 'auskenne'? — Nun, diese Geläufigkeit ist gewiß eines unserer Kriterien. Was uns vom räumlichen Sehen der Zeichnung überzeugt, ist eine gewisse Art des 'sich Auskennens'. Gewisse Gesten z. B., die die räumlichen Verhältnisse andeuten: feine Abschattungen des Verhaltens.

177. People often associate colours with vowels. It might be that for someone a vowel changed its colour when it was repeated over and over again. For him *a* is 'now blue —— now red', for instance.

An utterance of "Now I see it as . . ." might have no more significance for us than "*a* is now red for me".

(Linked with physiological observations, even this change might acquire importance for us.)

178. Here it occurs to me that in conversation on aesthetic matters we use the words "You have to see it like *this*, this is how it is meant"; "When you see it like *this*, you see where it goes wrong"; "You have to hear these bars as an introduction"; "You must listen out for this key"; "You must phrase it like *this*" (which can refer to hearing as well as to playing). |203|

179. This figure

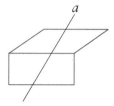

is supposed to represent a convex step and to be used in some kind of topological demonstration. For this purpose, for example, we draw the straight line *a* through the geometric centres of the two surfaces. —— Now, if someone saw the figure three-dimensionally only for a moment, and even then, now as a concave step, now as a convex one, this might make it difficult for him to follow our demonstration. And if for him the flat aspect alternates with a three-dimensional one, that is just as if I were to show him completely different objects in the course of the demonstration.

180. What does it amount to if I look at a drawing in descriptive geometry and say: "I know that this line appears again here, but I can't *see* it like that"? Does it simply amount to a lack of facility in operating with the drawing, that I don't 'know my way about' all that well? — Such facility is certainly one of our criteria. What convinces us that someone is seeing the drawing three-dimensionally is a certain kind of 'knowing one's way about': certain gestures, for instance, which indicate the three-dimensional relations — fine shades of behaviour.

Ich sehe, daß auf dem Bild der Pfeil das Tier durchdringt. Er hat es im Hals getroffen und ragt im Genick heraus. Das Bild sei eine Silhouette. — *Siehst* du den Pfeil — *weißt* du nur, daß diese beiden Stücke Teile eines Pfeils darstellen sollen?

(Vergleiche Köhlers Figur der einander durchdringen Sechsecke.)

181. "Das ist doch kein *Sehen*!" —— "Das ist doch ein Sehen!" — Beide müssen sich begrifflich rechtfertigen lassen.

182. Das ist doch ein Sehen! *Inwiefern* ist es ein Sehen?

183. "Die Erscheinung nimmt einen zuerst wunder, aber es wird gewiß eine physiologische Erklärung dafür gefunden werden." —
Unser Problem ist kein kausales, sondern ein begriffliches.

184. Würde mir das Bild des durchbohrten Tiers, oder der einander durchdringenden Sechsecke, für einen Augenblick nur gezeigt, und ich sollte es danach beschreiben, so wäre *das* die Beschreibung; sollte ich's zeichnen, so würde ich gewiß eine sehr fehlerhafte Kopie hervorbringen, aber sie würde eine Art Tier von einem Pfeil durchbohrt zeigen, oder zwei Sechsecke, die einander durchdringen. D. h.: Gewisse Fehler würde ich *nicht* machen.

185. Das erste, was mir an diesem Bild in die Augen springt, ist: es sind zwei Sechsecke.

Nun schaue ich sie an und frage mich: "Sehe ich sie wirklich *als* Sechsecke?" — und zwar die ganze Zeit, während sie vor meinen Augen sind? (Vorausgesetzt, daß sich ihr Aspekt dabei nicht geändert hat.) — Und ich möchte antworten: "Ich denke nicht die ganze Zeit an sie als Sechsecke."

186. Einer sagt mir: "Ich habe es sofort als zwei Sechsecke gesehen. Ja das war *alles, was* ich gesehen habe." Aber wie verstehe ich das? Ich denke, er hätte auf die Frage "Was siehst du?" gleich mit dieser Beschreibung geantwortet, auch hätte er sie nicht als eine von mehreren möglichen behandelt. Sie ist darin gleich der Antwort "Ein Gesicht", wenn ich ihm die Figur

gezeigt hätte.

I see that an animal in a picture is transfixed by an arrow. It has struck
it in the throat, and sticks out at the back of the neck. Let the picture
be a silhouette. — Do you *see* the arrow — or do you merely *know* that
these two bits are supposed to represent part of an arrow?

    (Compare Köhler's figure of interpenetrating hexagons.)

181. "But this surely isn't *seeing*!" —— "But this surely *is* seeing!" — It
must be possible to give both remarks a conceptual justification.

182. But this surely *is* seeing! *In what way* is it seeing?

183. "The phenomenon is at first surprising, but a physiological explanation of it will certainly be found." —
    Our problem is not a causal but a conceptual one.

184. If the picture of the transfixed animal or of the interpenetrating
hexagons were shown to me just for a moment and then I had to describe
it, *that* would be my description; if I had to draw it I'd |204| certainly
produce a very faulty copy, but it would show some sort of animal transfixed by an arrow, or two hexagons interpenetrating. That is to say:
there are certain mistakes that I'd *not* make.

185. The first thing to jump to my eye in this picture is: there are two
hexagons.
    Now I look at them and ask myself: "Do I really see them *as*
hexagons?" — and for the whole time they are before my eyes? (Assuming
that they have not changed their aspect in that time.) — And I'd like
to reply: "I'm not thinking of them as hexagons the whole time."

186. Someone tells me: "I saw it at once as two hexagons. Indeed that
was *all* I saw." But how do I understand this? I think he would have
given this description at once in answer to the question "What do you
see?", and wouldn't have treated it as one among several possibilities.
In this respect, his description is like the answer "A face" on being shown
the figure

187. Die beste Beschreibung, die ich von dem geben kann, was mir auf einen Augenblick gezeigt wurde, ist *das*: . . .
   "Der Eindruck war der von einem sich bäumenden Tier." Es kam also eine ganz bestimmte Beschreibung. — War das das *Sehen*, oder war es ein Gedanke?

188. Versuche nicht, in dir selbst das Erlebnis zu analysieren!

189. Es hätte ja auch sein können, daß ich das Bild zuerst als etwas anderes sah, und mir dann sagte "Ach, es sind zwei Sechsecke!" Der Aspekt hätte sich also geändert. Und beweist das nun, daß ich's tatsächlich als etwas Bestimmtes *sah*?

190. "Ist es ein *echtes* Seherlebnis?" Die Frage ist: Inwiefern ist es eins.

191. Es ist hier *schwierig*, zu sehen, daß es sich um Begriffsbestimmungen handelt.
   Ein *Begriff* drängt sich auf. (Das darfst du nicht vergessen.)

192. Wann würde ich's denn ein bloßes Wissen, kein Sehen, nennen? — Etwa, wenn Einer das Bild wie eine Werkzeichnung behandelte, es *läse*, wie eine Blaupause. (Feine Abschattungen des Benehmens. — Warum sind sie *wichtig*? Sie haben wichtige Folgen.)

193. "Es ist für mich ein Tier, vom Pfeil durchbohrt." Ich behandle es als das; dies ist meine *Einstellung* zur Figur. Das ist eine Bedeutung davon, es ein 'Sehen' zu nennen.

194. Kann ich aber auch im gleichen Sinne sagen: "Dies sind für mich zwei Sechsecke"? Nicht im gleichen Sinne, aber in einem ähnlichen.

195. Du mußt an die Rolle denken, welche Bilder vom Charakter der Gemälde (im Gegensatz zu Werkzeichnungen) in unserem Leben spielen. Und hier besteht durchaus nicht Einförmigkeit.
   Damit zu vergleichen: Man hängt sich manchmal Sprüche an die Wand. Aber nicht Lehrsätze der Mechanik. (Unser Verhältnis zu diesen beiden.)

196. Von dem, der die Zeichnung als dies Tier sieht, werde ich mir manches andere erwarten, als von dem, der nur weiß, was sie darstellen soll.

187. The best description I can give of what was shown me for a moment is *this*: . . .

"The impression was that of a rearing animal." So a perfectly specific description was given. — Was it *seeing*, or was it a thought?

188. Don't try to analyse the experience within yourself.

189. Of course, I might also have seen the picture first as something different, and then have said to myself "Oh, it's two hexagons!" So the aspect would have altered. And does this prove that I in fact *saw* it as something specific?

190. "Is it a *genuine* visual experience?" The question is: in what way is it one?

191. Here it is *difficult* to see that what is at issue is determination of concepts.
   What forces itself on one is a *concept*. (You must not forget that.)

192. When should I call it just knowing, not seeing? — Perhaps when someone treats the picture as a working drawing, *reads* it like a blueprint. (Fine shades of behaviour. — Why are they *important*? They have important consequences.) |205|

193. "To me it is an animal transfixed by an arrow." That is what I treat it as; this is my *attitude* to the figure. This is one meaning in calling it a case of 'seeing'.

194. But can I say in the same sense: "To me these are two hexagons"? Not in the same sense, but in a similar one.

195. You need to think of the role which pictures such as paintings (as opposed to working drawings) play in our lives. This role is by no means a uniform one.
   A comparison: proverbs are sometimes hung on the wall. But not theorems of mechanics. (Our attitude to these two things.)

196. From someone who sees the drawing as such-and-such an animal, what I expect will be rather different from what I expect from someone who merely knows what it is meant to represent.

197. Besser wäre vielleicht dieser Ausdruck gewesen: Wir *betrachten* die Photographie, das Bild an unserer Wand, als das Objekt selbst (Mensch, Landschaft, etc.), welches auf ihnen dargestellt ist.

198. Dies müßte nicht sein. Wir könnten uns leicht Menschen vorstellen, die zu solchen Bildern nicht dies Verhältnis hätten. Menschen z. B., die von Photographien abgestoßen würden, weil ihnen ein Gesicht ohne Farbe, ja vielleicht ein Gesicht in verkleinertem Maßstab, unmenschlich vorkäme.

199. Wenn ich nun sage "Wir betrachten ein Porträt als Menschen", — wann und wie lange tun wir dies? *Immer*, wenn wir's überhaupt sehen (und es nicht etwa als etwas anderes sehen)?

   Ich könnte das bejahen, und dadurch würde ich den Begriff des Betrachtens bestimmen. —— Die Frage ist, ob noch ein anderer, verwandter Begriff für uns wichtig wird, der eines so-Sehens (nämlich), das nur statthat, während ich mich mit dem Bild als dem Gegenstand (der dargestellt ist) beschäftige.

200. Ich könnte sagen: Ein Bild *lebt* nicht immer für mich, während ich es sehe.

   "Ihr Bild lächelt mich von der Wand an." Das muß es nicht immer tun, wenn gerade mein Blick darauf fällt.

201. Der H-E-Kopf. Man fragt sich: Wie ist es möglich, daß das Auge, dieser *Punkt*, in einer Richtung blickt? — "*Sieh, wie er blickt!*" (Und dabei 'blickt' man selbst.) Aber man sagt und tut das nicht in einem fort, während man das Bild betrachtet. Und was ist nun dieses "Sieh, wie er blickt!" — ist es der Ausdruck einer Empfindung?

202. (Ich strebe nicht mit allen diesen Beispielen irgend eine Vollständigkeit an. Nicht eine Klassifikation der psychologischen Begriffe. Sie sollen nur den Leser in den Stand setzen, sich in begrifflichen Unklarheiten zu helfen.)

203. "Ich sehe es jetzt als ein . . ." geht zusammen mit "Ich versuche, es als ein . . . zu sehen", oder "Ich kann es noch nicht als ein . . . sehen". Ich kann aber nicht versuchen, das konventionelle Bild eines Löwen *als* Löwen zu sehen, sowenig wie ein F als diesen Buchstaben. (Wohl aber z. B. als einen Galgen.)

204. Frage dich nun nicht "Wie geht es mit *mir*?" — Frage: "Was weiß ich vom Andern?"

197. Perhaps the following expression would have been better: we *view* the photograph, the picture on our wall, as the very object (the man, landscape, and so on) represented in it.

198. This need not have been so. We could easily imagine people who did not have this attitude to such pictures. Who, for example, would be repelled by photographs, because a face without colour, and even perhaps a face reduced in scale, struck them as inhuman.

199. I say: "We view a portrait as a human being" — when do we do so, and for how long? *Always*, if we see it at all (and don't, say, see it as something else)?

I might go along with this, and thereby determine the concept of viewing a picture. —— The question is whether yet another concept, related to this one, also becomes important to us: that, namely, of a seeing-as which occurs only while I am actually concerning myself with the picture as the object represented.

200. I could say: a picture is not always *alive* for me while I am seeing it.

"Her picture smiles down on me from the wall." It need not always do so, whenever my glance lights on it.

201. The duck-rabbit. One asks oneself: how can the eye, this *dot*, be looking in a direction? — "*See how it's looking*!" (And one 'looks' oneself as one says this.) But one does not say and do this the whole time one is looking at the picture. And now, what is this "See how it's looking!" — does it express a feeling? |206|

202. (In giving all these examples, I am not aiming at some kind of completeness. Not a classification of psychological concepts. They are only meant to enable the reader to cope with conceptual unclarities.)

203. "Now I see it as a . . ." goes with "I am trying to see it as a . . .", or "I still can't see it as a . . .". But I cannot try to see a conventional picture of a lion *as* a lion, any more than an F as that letter (though I may well try to see it as a gallows, for example).

204. Do not ask yourself: "How does it work with *me*?" — Ask: "What do I know about someone else?"

205. Wie spielt man denn das Spiel: "Es könnte auch *das* sein"? (*Das*, was die Figur auch sein könnte — und das ist das, als was sie gesehen werden kann — ist nicht einfach eine andere Figur. Wer sagt "Ich sehe

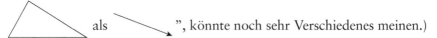 als ", könnte noch sehr Verschiedenes meinen.)

   Kinder spielen dieses Spiel. Sie sagen von einer Kiste z. B., sie ist jetzt ein Haus; und sie wird darauf ganz als ein Haus ausgedeutet. Eine Erfindung um sie gewoben.

206. Und *sieht* das Kind die Kiste nun als Haus?
   "Er vergißt ganz, daß es eine Kiste ist; es ist für ihn tatsächlich ein Haus." (Dafür gibt es bestimmte Anzeichen.) Wäre es dann nicht auch richtig zu sagen, er *sehe* sie als Haus?

207. Und wer nun so spielen könnte, und in einer bestimmten Situation mit besonderem Ausdruck ausriefe "Jetzt ist es ein Haus!" — der würde dem Aufleuchten des Aspekts Ausdruck geben.

208. Hörte ich Einen über das H-E-Bild reden, und *jetzt*, in gewisser Weise, über den besonderen Ausdruck dieses Hasengesichts, so würde ich sagen, er sehe das Bild jetzt als Hasen.

209. Der Ausdruck der Stimme und Gebärde aber ist der gleiche, als hätte sich das Objekt geändert und wäre nun endlich zu dem oder jenem *geworden*.
   Ich lasse mir ein Thema wiederholt und jedesmal in einem langsameren Tempo vorspielen. Endlich sage ich "*Jetzt* ist es richtig", oder "*Jetzt* erst ist es ein Marsch", "*Jetzt* erst ist es ein Tanz". — In *diesem* Ton drückt sich auch das Aufleuchten des Aspekts aus.

210. 'Feine Abschattungen des Benehmens.' —— Wenn sich mein Verstehen des Themas darin äußert, daß ich es mit dem richtigen Ausdruck pfeife, so ist das ein Beispiel dieser feinen Abschattungen.

211. Die Aspekte des Dreiecks: Es ist, wie wenn eine *Vorstellung* mit dem Gesichtseindruck in Berührung käme und für eine Zeit in Berührung bliebe.

212. Darin unterscheiden sich diese Aspekte aber vom konkaven und konvexen Aspekt der Stufe (z. B.). Auch von den Aspekten der Figur

* 205. How does one play the game: "It could also be *this*"? (*This* — which the figure could also be, which is what it can be seen as — is not simply another figure. Someone who said "I see ⟋‾△ as ⟍ " might still mean very different things.)

Here is a game played by children: they say of a chest, for example, that it is now a house; and thereupon it is interpreted as a house in every detail. A piece of fancy is woven around it.

206. And does the child now *see* the chest as a house?
"He quite forgets that it is a chest; for him it actually is a house." (There are certain signs of this.) Then would it not also be correct to say he *sees* it as a house?

207. And if someone knew how to play this game, and in a certain situation exclaimed with special expression "Now it's a house!" — he would be giving expression to the lighting up of an aspect.

208. If I heard someone talking about the duck–rabbit picture, and *now* he spoke in a certain way about the special expression of the rabbit's face, I'd say, now he's seeing the picture as a rabbit.

209. But the expression in one's voice and gestures is the same as if the object had altered and had ended by *becoming* this or that.
I have a theme played to me several times and each time in a slower tempo. Eventually I say "*Now* it's right", or "*Now* at last it's a march", "*Now* at last it's a dance". — In *this* tone of voice the lighting up of an aspect is also expressed. |207|

210. 'Fine shades of behaviour.' —— When my understanding of a theme is expressed by my whistling it with the correct expression, this is an example of such fine shades.

211. The aspects of the triangle: it is as if an *idea* came into contact, and for a time remained in contact, with the visual impression.

212. In this, however, these aspects differ from the concave and convex aspects of the step (for example). And also from the aspects of the figure

(ich werde sie "Doppelkreuz" nennen) als weißes Kreuz auf schwarzem Grund und als schwarzes Kreuz auf weißem Grund.

213. Du mußt bedenken, daß die Beschreibungen der miteinander abwechselnden Aspekte in jedem Fall von andrer Art sind.

214. (Die Versuchung, zu sagen, "Ich sehe es *so*", indem man bei "es" und "so" auf das Gleiche zeigt.) Eliminiere dir immer das private Objekt, indem du annimmst: es ändere sich fortwährend; du merkst es aber nicht, weil dich dein Gedächtnis fortwährend täuscht.

215. Jene beiden Aspekte des Doppelkreuzes (ich werde sie die Aspekte A nennen) ließen sich z. B. einfach dadurch mitteilen, daß der Betrachter abwechselnd auf ein freistehendes weißes und auf ein freistehendes schwarzes Kreuz zeigt.

Ja, man könnte sich denken, daß dies eine primitive Reaktion eines Kindes wäre, noch ehe es sprechen kann.

(Bei der Mitteilung der Aspekte A wird also auf einen Teil der Doppelkreuzfigur hingewiesen. — Den H- und E-Aspekt könnte man auf analoge Weise nicht beschreiben.)

216. Nur der 'sieht die Aspekte H und E', der die Gestalten jener beiden Tiere innehat. Eine analoge Bedingung gibt es für die Aspekte A nicht.

217. Den H-E-Kopf kann jemand einfach für das Bild eines Hasen halten, das Doppelkreuz für das Bild eines schwarzen Kreuzes, aber die bloße Dreiecksfigur nicht für das Bild eines umgefallenen Gegenstands. Diesen Aspekt des Dreiecks zu sehen, braucht es *Vorstellungskraft*.

218. Die Aspekte A sind nicht wesentlich räumliche Aspekte; ein schwarzes Kreuz auf weißem Grund nicht wesentlich eines, das eine weiße Fläche zum Hintergrund hat. Man könnte Einem den Begriff des schwarzen Kreuzes auf andersfärbigem Grunde beibringen, ohne ihm je andere als auf Papierbogen gemalte Kreuze zu zeigen. Der 'Hintergrund' ist hier einfach die Umgebung der Kreuzfigur.

(which I shall call a "double cross") as a white cross on a black ground and as a black cross on a white ground.

213. You must remember that the descriptions of the alternating aspects are of a different kind in each case.

214. (The temptation to say "I see it like *this*", pointing to the same thing for "it" and "this".) Always get rid of the idea of the private object in this way: assume that it constantly changes, but that you don't notice the change because your memory constantly deceives you.

215. Those two aspects of the double cross (I shall call them A aspects) might be reported simply by pointing alternately to a free-standing white and a free-standing black cross.

Indeed, one could imagine this as a primitive reaction in a child, even before he could talk.

(So in reporting A aspects, a part of the double cross is indicated. — The duck and rabbit aspects could not be described in an analogous way.)

216. Only someone conversant with the shapes of the two animals can 'see the duck–rabbit aspects'. There is no analogous condition for seeing A aspects.

217. Someone can take the duck–rabbit simply for the picture of a rabbit, the double cross simply for the picture of a black cross, but not the bare triangular figure for the picture of an object that has fallen over. To see this aspect of the triangle demands *imagination*. |208|

218. The A aspects are not essentially three-dimensional; a black cross on a white ground is not essentially a cross with a white surface in the background. One could teach someone the idea of the black cross on a ground of different colour without showing him anything other than crosses painted on sheets of paper. Here the 'background' is simply the surrounding of the cross.

Die Aspekte A hängen nicht in gleicher Weise mit einer möglichen Täuschung zusammen, wie die räumlichen Aspekte der Würfelzeichnung oder der Stufe.

219. Ich kann das Würfelschema als Schachtel sehen; — aber auch: einmal als Papier-, einmal, als Blechschachtel? — Was sollte ich dazu sagen, wenn jemand mich versicherte, *er* könnte es? — Ich kann hier eine Begriffsgrenze ziehen.

Denke aber an den Ausdruck '*empfunden*' bei der Betrachtung eines Bildes. ("Man fühlt die Weichheit dieses Stoffes.") (Das *Wissen* im Traum. "Und ich *wußte*, daß in dem Zimmer der . . . war.")

220. Eine *Art* der Aspekte könnte man "Aspekte der Organisation" nennen. Wechselt der Aspekt, so sind Teile des Bildes zusammengehörig, die früher nicht zusammengehörig waren.

221. Wie lehrt man ein Kind (etwa beim Rechnen) "Jetzt nimm *diese* Punkte zusammen!" oder "Jetzt gehören *die* zusammen"? Offenbar muß "zusammennehmen" und "zusammengehören" ursprünglich eine andere Bedeutung für ihn gehabt haben, als die, etwas so, oder so *sehen*. — Und das ist eine Bemerkung über Begriffe, nicht über Unterrichtsmethoden.

222. Ich kann im Dreieck jetzt *das* als Spitze, *das* als Grundlinie sehen — jetzt *das* als Spitze und *das* als Grundlinie. —— Es ist klar, daß dem Schüler, der nur eben erst mit dem Begriff Spitze, Grundlinie, etc. Bekanntschaft gemacht hat, die Worte "Ich sehe jetzt *das* als Spitze" noch nichts sagen können. — Aber das meine ich nicht als Erfahrungssatz.

Nur von dem würde man sagen, er sähe es jetzt *so*, jetzt *so*, der *imstande ist*, mit Geläufigkeit gewisse Anwendungen von der Figur zu machen.

Das Substrat dieses Erlebnisses ist das Beherrschen einer Technik.

223. Wie seltsam aber, daß dies die logische Bedingung dessen sein soll, daß Einer das und das *erlebt*! Du sagst doch nicht, nur der 'habe Zahnschmerzen', der das und das zu tun imstande sei. —— Woraus folgt, daß wir's hier nicht mit demselben Erlebnisbegriff zu tun haben können. Es ist ein anderer, wenn auch verwandter.

224. Nur von einem, der das und das *kann*, gelernt hat, beherrscht, hat es Sinn zu sagen, er habe *das* erlebt.

Und wenn das närrisch klingt, mußt du bedenken, daß der *Begriff* des Sehens hier modifiziert wird. (Eine ähnliche Überlegung ist oft nötig, um das Schwindelgefühl in der Mathematik zu vertreiben.)

The A aspects are not connected with the possibility of illusion in the same way as are the three-dimensional aspects of the drawing of a cube or step.

219. I can see the schematic cube as a box — but can I also see it now as a paper, now as a tin box? — What ought I to say, if someone assured me *he* could? — I can draw a conceptual boundary here.

Yet think of the expression "*felt*" in connection with looking at a picture. ("One feels the softness of that material.") (*Knowing* in dreams. "And I *knew* that . . . was in the room.")

* 220. One *kind* of aspect might be called 'organizational aspects'. When the aspect changes, parts of the picture belong together which before did not.

* 221. How does one teach a child (say in calculating) "Now take *these* dots together!" or "Now *these* belong together"? Clearly "taking together" and "belonging together" must originally have had another meaning for him than that of *seeing* in this way or that. — And this is a remark about concepts, not about teaching methods.

222. In the triangle I can see now *this* as apex, *that* as base — now *this* as apex, *that* as base. —— Clearly the words "Now I am seeing *this* as the apex" cannot so far have any significance for a learner who has only just met the concepts of apex, base, and so on. — But I do not mean this as an empirical proposition.

Only of someone *capable* of making certain applications of the figure with facility would one say that he saw it now *this* way, now *that* way.

The substratum of this experience is the mastery of a technique.

223. But how odd for this to be the logical condition of someone's having such-and-such an *experience*! After all, you don't say that one 'has toothache' only if one is capable of doing such-and-such. —— From this it follows that we cannot be dealing with the same concept of experience here. It is a different concept, even though related. |209|

224. Only of someone who *can do*, has learnt, is master of, such-and-such, does it makes sense to say that he has had *this* experience.

And if this sounds silly, you need to remember that the *concept* of seeing is modified here. (A similar consideration is often needed to dispel a feeling of dizziness in mathematics.)

Wir sprechen, machen Äußerungen, und erst *später* erhalten wir ein Bild von ihrem Leben.

225. Wie konnte ich denn sehen, daß diese Stellung zaghaft war, ehe ich wußte, daß sie eine Stellung und nicht die Anatomie dieses Wesens ist?

Aber heißt das nicht nur, daß ich *diesen* Begriff, der sich eben nicht *nur* auf Visuelles bezieht, dann zur Beschreibung des Gesehenen nicht verwenden könnte? — Könnte ich nicht dennoch einen rein-visuellen Begriff der zaghaften Stellung, des furchtsamen Gesichts haben?

226. Ein solcher wäre dann mit den Begriffen 'dur' und 'moll' zu vergleichen, die wohl einen Gefühlswert haben, aber auch einzig zur Beschreibung der wahrgenommenen Struktur gebraucht werden können.

227. Das Epitheton "traurig" auf das Strichgesicht angewendet, z. B., charakterisiert die Gruppierung von Strichen in einem Oval. Angewendet auf den Menschen hat es eine andere (obgleich verwandte) Bedeutung. (Das heißt aber *nicht*, daß der traurige Gesichtsausdruck dem Gefühl der Traurigkeit *ähnlich* sei!)

228. Bedenke auch dies: Rot und Grün kann ich nur sehen, aber nicht hören, — die Traurigkeit aber, soweit ich sie sehen kann, kann ich sie auch hören.

229. Denk nur an den Ausdruck "Ich hörte eine klagende Melodie"! Und nun die Frage: "*Hört* er das Klagen?"

230. Und wenn ich antworte: "Nein, er hört es nicht; er empfindet es nur" —— was ist damit getan? Man kann ja nicht einmal ein Sinnesorgan dieser 'Empfindung' angeben.

Mancher möchte nun antworten: "Freilich hör ich's!" —— Mancher: "Ich *höre* es eigentlich nicht."

Es lassen sich aber Begriffsunterschiede feststellen.

231. Wir reagieren anders auf den Gesichtsausdruck, als der, der ihn nicht als furchtsam (im *vollen* Sinne des Wortes) erkennt. — Nun will ich aber *nicht* sagen, wir spüren in den Muskeln und Gelenken diese Reaktion, und dies sei die 'Empfindung'. — Nein, wir haben hier einen modifizierten *Empfindungs*begriff.

232. Man könnte von Einem sagen, er sei für den *Ausdruck* in einem Gesicht blind. Aber fehlte deshalb seinem Gesichtssinn etwas?

We talk, we produce utterances, and only *later* get a picture of their life.

225. How could I see that this posture was hesitant before I knew that it was a posture, and not the anatomy of the creature?

But doesn't that mean only that I couldn't then use *this* concept, which doesn't refer *solely* to what is visual, to describe what is seen? — Couldn't I, for all that, have a purely visual concept of that hesitant posture, that timid face?

226. Such a concept would then be comparable to the musical concepts of 'major' and 'minor', which certainly have emotive value, but can also be used solely to describe a perceived structure.

227. The epithet "sad", as applied, for example, to the face of a stick-figure, characterizes the grouping of lines in an oval. Applied to a human being, it has a different (though related) meaning. (But this does *not* mean that a sad facial expression is *similar* to the feeling of sadness!)

228. Think of this too: I can only see, not hear, red and green — but to the extent to which I can see sadness, I can also hear it.

229. Just think of the expression "I heard a plaintive melody"! And now the question is: "Does he *hear* the plaint?"

230. And if I reply: "No, he doesn't hear it, he merely senses it" —— where does that get us? One cannot even specify a sense-organ for this 'sensing'.

Some would now like to reply: "Of course I hear it!" —— Others: 'I don't really *hear* it."

However, it is possible here to discern conceptual differences.

* 231. We react to a facial expression differently from someone who does not recognize it as timid (in the *full* sense of the word). — But I do *not* want to say here that we feel this reaction in our muscles and joints, and that this is the 'sensing'. — No, what we have here is a modified concept of *sensing*. |210|

232. One might say of someone that he was blind to the *expression* of a face. Would his eyesight on that account be defective?

Aber das ist natürlich nicht einfach eine Frage der Physiologie. Das Physiologische ist hier ein Symbol für das Logische.

233. Wer den Ernst einer Melodie empfindet, was nimmt der wahr? — Nichts, was sich durch Wiedergabe des Gehörten mitteilen ließe.

234. Von einem beliebigen Schriftzeichen — diesem etwa $\mathcal{H}$ — kann ich mir vorstellen, es sei ein streng korrekt geschriebener Buchstabe irgendeines fremden Alphabets. Oder aber, es sei ein fehlerhaft geschriebener; und zwar fehlerhaft auf die eine, oder andere Weise: z. B. schleuderhaft, oder typisch kindisch-ungeschickt, oder bürokratisch verschnörkelt. Es könnte in verschiedener Weise vom korrekt geschriebenen abweichen. — Und je nach der Erdichtung, mit der ich es umgebe, kann ich es in verschiedenen Aspekten sehen. Und hier besteht enge Verwandtschaft mit dem 'Erleben der Bedeutung eines Wortes'.

235. Es ist beinahe, als ob das 'Sehen des Zeichens in diesem Zusammenhang' ein Nachhall eines Gedankens wäre.
   "Ein im Sehen nachhallender Gedanke" — möchte man sagen.

236. Denk dir eine physiologische Erklärung für das Erlebnis. Es sei die: Beim Betrachten der Figur bestreicht der Blick sein Objekt wieder und wieder entlang einer bestimmten Bahn. Die Bahn entspricht einer besondern Form der Oszillation der Augäpfel beim Schauen. Es kann geschehen, daß eine solche Bewegungsart in eine andere überspringt und die beiden miteinander abwechseln (Aspekte A). Gewisse Bewegungsformen sind physiologisch unmöglich; daher kann ich z. B. das Würfelschema nicht als zwei einander durchdringende Prismen sehen. U. s. f. Dies sei die Erklärung. — "Ja, nun weiß ich, daß es eine Art *Sehen* ist." —— Du hast jetzt ein neues, ein physiologisches Kriterium des Sehens eingeführt. Und das kann das alte Problem verdecken, aber nicht lösen. — Der Zweck dieser Bemerkung war aber uns vor Augen zu führen, was geschieht, wenn uns eine physiologische Erklärung dargeboten wird. Der psychologische Begriff schwebt über dieser Erklärung unberührt. Und die Natur unsres Problems wird dadurch klarer.

237. Ich möchte sagen, daß, was hier aufleuchtet, nur so lange stehen bleibt, als eine bestimmte Beschäftigung mit dem betrachteten Objekt dauert. ("Sieh, wie er blickt.") —— 'Ich möchte sagen' — und *ist* es so? — Frage dich: "Wie lange fällt mir etwas auf?" — Wie lange ist es mir *neu*?

But this, of course, is not simply a question for physiology. Here the physiological is a symbol of the logical.

233. What does someone who senses the solemnity of a melody perceive? Nothing that could be conveyed by repetition of what was heard.

234. I can imagine some arbitrary cipher — this, for instance, $\mathcal{H}$ to be a strictly correct letter of some foreign alphabet. Or again, to be a faultily written one, and faulty in this way or that: for example, it might be slapdash, or typical childish awkwardness, or, like the flourishes in an official document. It could deviate from the correctly written letter in a variety of ways. — And according to the fiction with which I surround it, I can see it in various aspects. And here there is a close kinship with 'experiencing the meaning of a word'.

* 235. It is almost as if 'seeing the sign in this context' were an echo of a thought.
   "The echo of a thought in sight" — one would like to say.

* 236. Imagine a physiological explanation of the experience. Let it be this: When we look at the figure, our eyes scan it repeatedly, always following a particular path. The path corresponds to a particular pattern of oscillation of the eyeballs in looking. It can happen that one such pattern switches to another, and that the two alternate (A aspects). Certain patterns of movement are physiologically impossible; so, for example, I cannot see the schematic cube as two interpenetrating prisms. And so on. Let this be the explanation. — "Yes, now I realize that it is a kind of *seeing*." —— You have now introduced a new, a physiological, criterion for seeing. And this can conceal the old problem, but not solve it. — The purpose of this remark, however, was to bring out what happens when a physiological explanation is offered. The psychological concept hangs out of reach of this explanation. And this makes the nature of the problem clearer.

237. I'd like to say that what lights up here lasts only as long as I am occupied with the observed object in a particular way. ("See how it's looking!") —— 'I'd like to say' — and *is* it so? — Ask yourself, "How long am I struck by a thing?" — How long is it *new* to me?

238. Im Aspekt ist eine Physiognomie vorhanden, die nachher vergeht. Es ist beinahe, als wäre da ein Gesicht, welches ich zuerst *nachahme*, und dann hinnehme, ohne es nachzuahmen. — Und ist das nicht eigentlich genug der Erklärung? — Aber, ist es nicht zu viel?

239. "Ich bemerkte die Ähnlichkeit zwischen ihm und seinem Vater für ein paar Minuten, dann nicht mehr." — Das könnte man sagen, wenn sich sein Gesicht ändert und nur für kurze Zeit seinem Vater ähnlich sieht. Aber es kann auch heißen: Nach ein paar Minuten ist mir ihre Ähnlichkeit nicht mehr aufgefallen.

240. "Nachdem dir die Ähnlichkeit aufgefallen war, — wie lange warst du dir ihrer bewußt?" Wie könnte man diese Frage beantworten? —— "Ich habe bald nicht mehr an sie gedacht" oder "Sie ist mir von Zeit zu Zeit immer wieder aufgefallen" oder "Es ist mir einigemale durch den Kopf gegangen: Wie ähnlich sie doch sind!" oder "Ich habe gewiß eine Minute lang die Ähnlichkeit angestaunt". —— So etwa sehen die Antworten aus.

241. Ich möchte die Frage stellen: "Bin ich mir der Raumhaftigkeit, Tiefe, eines Gegenstandes (dieses Schranks z. B.), während ich ihn sehe, *immer bewußt?*" *Fühle* ich sie, sozusagen, die ganze Zeit? —— Aber stell die Frage in der dritten Person. — Wann würdest du sagen, er sei sich ihrer immer bewußt? wann das Gegenteil? — Man könnte ihn ja fragen, — aber wie hat er gelernt, auf diese Frage zu antworten? —— Er weiß, was es heißt "ununterbrochen einen Schmerz fühlen". Aber das wird ihn hier nur verwirren (wie es auch mich verwirrt).

Wenn er nun sagt, er sei sich der Tiefe fortwährend bewußt, — glaube ich's ihm? Und sagt er, er sei sich ihrer nur von Zeit zu Zeit bewußt (wenn er von ihr redet, etwa) — glaub ich ihm *das?* Es wird mir vorkommen, als ruhten diese Antworten auf falscher Grundlage. — Anders aber, wenn er sagt, der Gegenstand komme ihm manchmal flach, manchmal räumlich vor.

242. Es erzählt mir Einer: "Ich sah die Blume an, dachte aber an etwas anderes und war mir ihrer Farbe nicht bewußt." Versteh ich das? — Ich kann mir einen sinnvollen Zusammenhang dazu denken; es würde etwa weitergehen: "Dann plötzlich *sah* ich sie und erkannte, daß es die war, welche . . ."

Oder auch: "Hätte ich mich damals abgewandt, ich hätte nicht sagen können, welche Farbe sie hatte."

"Er blickte sie an, ohne sie zu sehen." — Das gibt's. Aber was ist das Kriterium dafür? — Es gibt da eben verschiedenerlei Fälle.

238. There is a physiognomy in the aspect, which then fades away. It is almost as if there were a face there which at first I *imitate*, and then accept without imitating it. — And isn't this really explanation enough? — But isn't it too much?

239. "I noticed the likeness between him and his father for a few minutes, and then no longer." — One might say this if his face were changing, and only looked like his father's for a short time. But it can also mean that, after a few minutes, I stopped being struck by the likeness.

240. "Once the likeness had struck you, how long were you conscious of it?" How might one answer this question? —— "I soon stopped thinking about it", or "It struck me again from time to time", or " 'I several times had the thought, how like they are!'", or "I marvelled at the likeness for at least a minute." —— This is more or less what the answers would look like.

241. I'd like to put the question: "Am I *conscious* of the three-dimensionality, the depth of an object (of this cupboard, for instance), the *whole* time I see it?" Do I, so to speak, *feel* it the whole time? |211| —— But put the question in the third person. — When would you say of someone that he was conscious of it the whole time? and when the opposite? — Of course, one could ask him — but how did he learn how to answer such a question? —— He knows what it means "to feel pain continuously". But that will only confuse him here (as it confuses me).

If he now says that he is continuously conscious of the depth — do I believe him? And if he says that he is conscious of it only from time to time (for example, when talking about it) — do I believe *that*? These answers will strike me as resting on a false foundation. — It will be different if he says that the object sometimes seems to him flat, sometimes three-dimensional.

242. Someone tells me: "I looked at the flower, but was thinking of something else and was not conscious of its colour." Do I understand this? — I can imagine a significant context, say his going on: "Then I suddenly *saw* it, and realized it was the colour which . . ."

Or again: "If I had turned away then, I could not have said what colour it was."

"He looked at it without seeing it." — There is such a thing. But what is the criterion for it? — Well, there is a variety of cases here.

243. "Ich habe jetzt mehr auf die Form, als auf die Farbe geschaut."
Laß dich durch solche Wendungen des Ausdrucks nicht verwirren. Vor allem,
denk nicht "Was mag da wohl im Aug, oder im Gehirn vor sich gehen?"

244. Die Ähnlichkeit fällt mir auf, und das Auffallen erlischt.
    Sie fiel mir nur für wenige Minuten auf, dann nicht mehr.
    Was geschah da? — Wessen kann ich mich entsinnen? Mein eigener
Gesichtsausdruck kommt mir in den Sinn, ich könnte ihn nachmachen.
Hätte Einer, der mich kennt, mein Gesicht gesehen, er hätte gesagt: "Es
ist dir jetzt etwas an seinem Gesicht aufgefallen." — Auch fällt mir ein,
was ich bei so einer Gelegenheit etwa hörbar, oder nur in mir selbst,
sage. Und das ist alles. — Und ist das das Auffallen? Nein. Das sind die
Erscheinungen des Auffallens; aber die *sind* 'was geschieht'.

245. Ist das Auffallen Schauen + Denken? Nein. Viele unsrer Begriffe
kreuzen sich hier.

246. ('Denken' und 'in der Vorstellung sprechen' — ich sage nicht "zu
sich selbst sprechen" — sind verschiedene Begriffe.)

247. Der Farbe des Objekts entspricht die Farbe im Gesichtseindruck
(dies Fließpapier scheint mir rosa, und es ist rosa) —— der Form des
Objekts die Form im Gesichtseindruck (es scheint mir rechteckig, und es
ist rechteckig) —— aber was ich im Aufleuchten des Aspekts wahrnehme,
ist nicht eine Eigenschaft des Objekts, es ist eine interne Relation zwischen ihm und andern Objekten.

248. Sehe ich wirklich jedesmal etwas anderes, oder deute ich nur, was
ich sehe, auf verschiedene Weise? Ich bin geneigt, das erste zu sagen.
Aber warum? —— Deuten ist ein Denken, ein Handeln; Sehen ein
Zustand.

249. Nun, die Fälle, in welchen wir *deuten*, sind leicht zu erkennen.
Deuten wir, so machen wir Hypothesen, die sich als falsch erweisen
mögen. —— "Ich sehe diese Figur als ein . . ." kann so wenig verifiziert
werden (oder nur in dem Sinne) wie "Ich sehe ein leuchtendes Rot". Es
besteht also eine Ähnlichkeit der Verwendung von "*sehen*" in beiden
Zusammenhängen.

250. Denk nur ja nicht, du wüßtest im vorhinein, was "*Zustand* des
Sehens" hier bedeutet! Laß dich die Bedeutung durch den Gebrauch *lehren*.

243. "Just now I looked at the shape rather than at the colour." Do not let such turns of phrase confuse you. Above all, don't wonder "What might be going on in the eyes or brain here?"

244. The likeness strikes me, and its striking me fades.
    The likeness only struck me for a few minutes, and then no longer did.
    What happened here? — What can I recall? My own facial expression comes to mind; I could reproduce it. If someone who knew me had seen my face, he would have said, "Something about his face struck you just now". — There further occurs to me what I say on such an occasion out loud or just to myself. And that is all. — And is this what being struck is? No. These are the manifestations of being struck; but they *are* 'what happens'.

245. Is being struck looking + thinking? No. Many of our concepts *cross* here.

246. ('Thinking' and 'talking in the imagination' — I do not say 'talking to oneself' — are different concepts.) |212|

247. The colour in the visual impression corresponds to the colour of the object (this blotting paper looks pink to me, and is pink) —— the shape in the visual impression to the shape of the object (it looks rectangular to me, and is rectangular) —— but what I perceive in the lighting up of an aspect is not a property of the object, but an internal relation between it and other objects.

248. Do I really see something different each time, or do I only interpret what I see in a different way? I'm inclined to say the former. But why? —— To interpret is to think, to do something; seeing is a state.

*   249. Well, it is easy to recognize those cases in which we are *interpreting*. When we interpret, we form hypotheses, which may prove false. —— "I see this figure as a . . ." can be verified as little as (or only in the same sense as) "I see a bright red". So there is a similarity in the use of "*see*" in the two contexts.

*   250. Just don't think you knew in advance what "*state* of seeing" means here! Let the use *teach* you the meaning.

251. Gewisses am Sehen kommt uns rätselhaft vor, weil uns das ganze Sehen nicht rätselhaft genug vorkommt.

252. Wer eine Photographie betrachtet, von Menschen, Häusern, Bäumen, dem geht Räumlichkeit an ihr nicht ab. Es wäre uns nicht leicht, sie als Aggregat von Farbflecken in der Ebene zu beschreiben, aber was wir im Stereoskop sehen, schaut noch in anderer Weise räumlich aus.

253. (Es ist nichts weniger als selbstverständlich, daß wir mit zwei Augen 'räumlich' sehen. Wenn die beiden Gesichtsbilder in eins verschmelzen, könnte man sich als Resultat ein verschwommenes erwarten.)

254. Der Begriff des Aspekts ist dem Begriff der Vorstellung verwandt. Oder: der Begriff 'ich sehe es jetzt als . . .' ist verwandt mit 'ich stelle mir jetzt *das* vor'.
   Gehört dazu, etwas als Variation eines bestimmten Themas zu hören, nicht Phantasie? Und doch nimmt man dadurch etwas wahr.

255. "Stell dir das so geändert vor, so hast du das andere." In der Vorstellung kann man einen Beweis führen.

256. Das Sehen des Aspekts und das Vorstellen unterstehen dem Willen. Es gibt den Befehl "Stell dir *das* vor!" und den: "Sieh die Figur jetzt *so*!"; aber nicht: "Sieh das Blatt jetzt grün!"

257. Es erhebt sich nun die Frage: Könnte es Menschen geben, denen die Fähigkeit, etwas *als etwas* zu sehen, abginge — und wie wäre das? Was für Folgen hätte es? —— Wäre dieser Defekt zu vergleichen mit Farbenblindheit, oder mit dem Fehlen des absoluten Gehörs? — Wir wollen ihn "Aspektblindheit" nennen — und uns nun überlegen, was damit gemeint sein könnte. (Eine begriffliche Untersuchung.)
   Der Aspektblinde soll die Aspekte A nicht wechseln sehen. Soll er aber auch nicht erkennen, daß das Doppelkreuz ein schwarzes und ein weißes Kreuz enthält? Soll er also die Aufgabe nicht bewältigen kön- nen: "Zeig mir unter diesen Figuren solche, die ein schwarzes Kreuz enthalten"? Nein, das soll er können, aber er soll nicht sagen: "Jetzt ist es ein schwarzes Kreuz auf weißem Grund!"
   Soll er für die Ähnlichkeit zweier Gesichter blind sein? — Aber also auch für die Gleichheit, oder angenäherte Gleichheit? Das will ich nicht festsetzen. (Er soll Befehle von der Art "Bring mir etwas, was so aus- schaut wie *das*!" ausführen können.)

251. We find certain things about seeing puzzling, because we do not find the whole business of seeing puzzling enough. |213|

252. Someone who looks at a photograph of people, houses and trees does not feel the lack of a third dimension in it. It would not be easy for us to describe a photograph as an aggregate of colour patches on a flat surface; but what we see in a stereoscope looks three-dimensional in a different way again.

253. (It is anything but a matter of course that we see 'three-dimensionally' with two eyes. If the two visual images were fused, one might expect a blurred image as a result.)

254. The concept of an aspect is related to the concept of imagination. In other words, the concept 'Now I see it as . . .' is related to 'Now I am imagining *that*'.
    Doesn't it take imagination to hear something as a variation on a particular theme? And yet one does perceive something in so hearing it.

255. "Imagine this changed like this, and you have this other thing." One can produce a proof in one's imagination.

256. Seeing an aspect and imagining are subject to the will. There is such an order as "Imagine *this*!", and also, "Now see the figure like *this*!"; but not "Now see this leaf green!".

257. The question now arises: Could there be human beings lacking the ability to see something *as something* — and what would that be like? What sort of consequences would it have? —— Would this defect be comparable to colour-blindness, or to not having absolute pitch? — We will call it "aspect-blindness" — and will now consider what might be meant by this. (A conceptual investigation.)
    The aspect-blind man is supposed not to see the A aspects change. But is he also supposed not to recognize that the double cross contains both a black and a white cross? So if told "Show me figures containing a black cross among these examples", will he be unable to manage it? No. He is supposed to be able to do that, but not to say: "Now it's a black cross on a white ground!"
    Is he supposed to be blind to the similarity between two faces? — And so also to their identity or approximate identity? I do not want to settle this. (He is supposed to be able to execute such orders as "Bring me something that looks like *this*!")

258. Soll er das Würfelschema nicht als Würfel sehen können? — Daraus würde nicht folgen, daß er es nicht als Darstellung (z. B. als Werkzeichnung) eines Würfels erkennen könnte. Es würde aber für ihn nicht von einem Aspekt in den andern überspringen. — Frage: Soll er es, wie wir, unter Umständen für einen Würfel *halten* können? — Wenn nicht, so könnte man das nicht wohl eine Blindheit nennen.

Der 'Aspektblinde' wird zu Bildern überhaupt ein anderes Verhältnis haben, als wir.

259. (Anomalien *dieser* Art können wir uns leicht vorstellen.)

260. Aspektblindheit wird *verwandt* sein mit dem Mangel des 'musikalischen Gehörs'.

261. Die Wichtigkeit dieses Begriffes liegt in dem Zusammenhang der Begriffe 'sehen des Aspekts' und 'erleben der Bedeutung eines Wortes'. Denn wir wollen fragen: "Was ginge dem ab, der die Bedeutung eines Wortes nicht *erlebt?*"

Was ginge z. B. dem ab, der die Aufforderung, das Wort 'sondern' auszusprechen und es als Zeitwort zu meinen, nicht verstünde, — oder Einem, der nicht fühlt, daß das Wort, wenn es zehnmal nach der Reihe ausgesprochen wird, seine Bedeutung für ihn verliert und ein bloßer Klang wird?

262. Vor Gericht z. B. könnte die Frage erörtert werden, wie Einer ein Wort gemeint habe. Und es kann dies aus gewissen Tatsachen geschlossen werden. — Es ist eine Frage der *Absicht*. Könnte es aber in ähnlicher Weise bedeutsam sein, wie er ein Wort — das Wort "Bank" z. B. — erlebt hat?

263. Ich hätte mit jemandem eine Geheimsprache vereinbart; "Turm" bedeutet Bank. Ich sage ihm "Geh jetzt zum Turm!" — er versteht mich und handelt danach, aber das Wort "Turm" kommt ihm in dieser Verwendung fremdartig vor, es hat noch nicht die Bedeutung 'angenommen'.

264. "Wenn ich ein Gedicht, eine Erzählung mit Empfindung lese, so geht doch etwas in mir vor, was nicht vorgeht, wenn ich die Zeilen nur der Information wegen überfliege." — Auf welche Vorgänge spiele ich an? — Die Sätze *klingen* anders. Ich achte genau auf den Tonfall. Manchmal hat ein Wort einen falschen Ton, tritt zu sehr, oder zu wenig hervor. Ich merke es und mein Gesicht drückt es aus. Ich könnte später über die Einzelheiten meines Vortrags reden, z. B. über die

258. Is he supposed to be unable to see the schematic cube as a cube? — It would not follow from this that he could not recognize it as a representation (a working drawing, for instance) of a cube. But for him it |214| would not switch from one aspect to the other. — Question: Is he supposed to be able to *take* it as a cube in certain circumstances, as we do? — If not, this could not very well be called a sort of blindness.

The 'aspect-blind' will have an altogether different attitude to pictures from ours.

259. (Anomalies of *this* kind are easy for us to imagine.)

260. Aspect-blindness will be *akin* to the lack of a 'musical ear'.

261. The importance of this concept lies in the connection between the concepts of seeing an aspect and of experiencing the meaning of a word. For we want to ask, "What would someone be missing if he did not *experience* the meaning of a word?"

What would someone be missing, who, for example, did not understand the request to pronounce the word "till" and to mean it as a verb — or someone who did not feel that a word lost its meaning for him and became a mere sound if it was repeated ten times over?

262. In a law court, for example, the question might be raised as to how someone meant a word. And this can be inferred from certain facts. — It is a question of *intention*. But could how he experienced a word — the word "bank", for instance — have been significant in a similar way?

263. Suppose I had agreed on a code with someone; "tower" means bank. I tell him "Now go to the tower!" — he understands me and acts accordingly, but he feels the word "tower" to be strange in this use; it has not yet 'absorbed' the meaning.

264. "When I read a poem or narrative with feeling, surely something goes on in me which does not go on when I merely skim the lines for information." — What processes am I alluding to? — The sentences have a different *ring*. I pay careful attention to intonation. Sometimes a word has the wrong intonation, stands out too much or too little. I notice this, and my face shows it. I might later talk about my reading in detail: for example, about the mistakes of intonation. Sometimes I visualize a

Unrichtigkeiten im Ton. Manchmal schwebt mir ein Bild, gleichsam eine Illustration vor. Ja, dies scheint mir zu helfen, im richtigen Ausdruck zu lesen. Und dergleichen könnte ich noch manches anführen. — Ich kann auch einem Wort einen Ton verleihen, der seine Bedeutung, beinahe als wäre das Wort ein Bild der Sache, aus den übrigen heraushebt. (Und dies kann natürlich durch den Bau des Satzes bedingt sein.)

265. Wenn ich beim ausdrucksvollen Lesen dies Wort ausspreche, ist es ganz mit seiner Bedeutung angefüllt. — "Wie kann das sein, wenn Bedeutung der Gebrauch des Wortes ist?" Nun, mein Ausdruck war bildlich gemeint. Aber nicht, als hätte ich das Bild gewählt, sondern es drängte sich mir auf. — Aber die bildliche Verwendung des Wortes kann ja mit der ursprünglichen nicht in Konflikt geraten.

266. Warum gerade *dies* Bild sich mir darbietet, ließe sich vielleicht erklären. (Denke nur an den Ausdruck und die Bedeutung des Ausdrucks "das treffende Wort".)

267. Wenn mir aber der Satz wie ein Wortgemälde vorkommen kann, ja das einzelne Wort im Satz wie ein Bild, dann ist es nicht mehr so verwunderlich, daß ein Wort, isoliert und ohne Zweck ausgesprochen, eine bestimmte Bedeutung in sich zu tragen scheinen kann.

268. Denke hier an eine besondere Art der Täuschung, die auf diese Dinge ein Licht wirft. — Ich gehe mit einem Bekannten in der Umgebung der Stadt spazieren. Im Gespräch zeigt es sich, daß ich mir die Stadt zu unsrer Rechten liegend vorstelle. Für diese Annahme habe ich nicht nur *keinen* mir bewußten Grund, sondern eine ganz einfache Überlegung konnte mich davon überzeugen, daß die Stadt etwas links vor uns liegt. Auf die Frage, *warum* ich mir denn die Stadt in *dieser* Richtung vorstellte, kann ich zuerst keine Antwort geben. Ich hatte *keinen Grund*, das zu glauben. Obgleich aber keinen Grund, scheine ich doch gewisse psychologische Ursachen zu sehen. Und zwar sind es gewisse Assoziationen und Erinnerungen. Z. B. diese: Wir gingen nämlich einen Kanal entlang, und ich war früher einmal, unter ähnlichen Umständen, einem gefolgt, und die Stadt lag damals rechts von uns. — Ich könnte die Ursachen meiner unbegründeten Überzeugung gleichsam psychoanalytisch zu finden trachten.

269. "Aber was ist das für ein seltsames Erlebnis?" — Es ist natürlich nicht seltsamer als jedes andere; es ist nur von andrer Art als diejenigen Erlebnisse, die wir als die fundamentalsten betrachten, die Sinneseindrücke etwa.

picture, an illustration, as it were. Indeed, this seems to help me to read with the correct expression. And I could mention more things of the same kind. — I can also give a word an intonation which makes its meaning stand out from the rest, almost as if the word were a portrait of the whole thing. (And this may, of course, depend on the structure of the sentence.) |215|

265. When I pronounce this word while reading expressively, it is completely filled with its meaning. — "How can this be, if meaning is the use of the word?" Well, what I said was intended figuratively. Not that I chose the figure: it forced itself on me. — But the figurative use of the word can't come into conflict with the original one.

266. Why precisely *this* picture suggests itself to me could perhaps be explained. (Just think of the expression, and the meaning of the expression "mot juste".)

267. But if a sentence can strike me as a painting in words, and even a single word in a sentence as a picture, then it is no more astonishing that a word uttered in isolation and without purpose can seem to carry a particular meaning within itself.

268. Think here of a special kind of illusion, which throws light on these matters. — I go for a walk in the environs of a city with a friend. As we talk, it emerges that I imagined the city to be on our right. Not only have I *no* reason that I am aware of for this assumption, but some quite simple consideration would be enough to make me realize that the city is a bit to the left ahead of us. I can at first give no answer to the question *why* I imagine the city in *this* direction. I have *no reason* to think so. But though I see no reason, still I seem to see certain psychological causes for it. In particular, certain associations and memories. For example, we were walking along a canal, and once before, in similar circumstances, I had followed a canal, and that time the city was on our right. — I might try, as it were psychoanalytically, to discover the causes of my unfounded conviction.

269. "But what a strange experience this is!" — Of course, it is not stranger than any other; it is simply of a different kind from those experiences which we regard as the most fundamental ones — sense impressions, for instance.

270. "Mir ist, als wüßte ich, daß die Stadt dort liegt." —— "Mir ist, als paßte der Name 'Schubert' zu Schuberts Werken und seinem Gesicht."

271. Du kannst dir das Wort "weiche" vorsprechen und es dabei einmal als Imperativ, einmal als Eigenschaftswort meinen. Und nun sag "Weiche!" — und dann "Weiche *nicht* vom Platz!" — Begleitet das *gleiche* Erlebnis beidemale das Wort — bist du sicher?

272. Wenn ein feines Aufhorchen mir zeigt, daß ich in jenem Spiel das Wort bald *so*, bald *so* erlebe, — zeigt es mir nicht auch, daß ich's im Fluß der Rede oft *gar* nicht erlebe? —— Denn, daß ich es dann auch bald *so*, bald *so* meine, intendiere, später wohl auch so erkläre, steht ja nicht in Frage.

273. Aber es bleibt dann die Frage, warum wir denn bei diesem *Spiel* des Worterlebens auch von 'Bedeutung' und 'Meinen' sprechen. —— Das ist eine Frage anderer Art. —— Es ist die charakteristische Erscheinung dieses Sprachspiels, daß wir, in *dieser* Situation, den Ausdruck gebrauchen: wir hätten das Wort in *der* Bedeutung ausgesprochen, und diesen Ausdruck aus jenem andern Sprachspiel herübernehmen.
    Nenn es einen Traum. Es ändert nichts.

274. Gegeben die beiden Begriffe 'fett' und 'mager', würdest du eher geneigt sein, zu sagen, Mittwoch sei fett und Dienstag mager, oder das Umgekehrte? (Ich neige entschieden zum ersteren.) Haben nun hier "fett" und "mager" eine andere, als ihre gewöhnliche Bedeutung? — Sie haben eine andere Verwendung. — Hätte ich also eigentlich andere Wörter gebrauchen sollen? Doch gewiß nicht. — Ich will *diese* Wörter (mit den mir geläufigen Bedeutungen) *hier* gebrauchen. — Nun sage ich nichts über die Ursachen der Erscheinung. Sie *könnten* Assoziationen aus meinen Kindheitstagen sein. Aber das ist Hypothese. Was immer die Erklärung, — jene Neigung besteht.

275. Gefragt, "Was meinst du hier eigentlich mit 'fett' und 'mager'?" — könnte ich die Bedeutungen nur auf die ganz gewöhnliche Weise erklären. Ich könnte sie *nicht* an den Beispielen von Dienstag und Mittwoch zeigen.

276. Man könnte hier von 'primärer' und 'sekundärer' Bedeutung eines Worts reden. Nur der, für den das Wort jene Bedeutung hat, verwendet es in dieser.

270. "I feel as if I knew the city was over there." —— "I feel as if the name 'Schubert' fitted Schubert's works and Schubert's face."

271. You can say the word "march" to yourself and mean it at one time as an imperative, at another as the name of a month. And now say "March!" — and then "March *no further*!" — Does the *same* experience accompany the word both times — are you sure?

272. If careful attention shows me that when I am playing this game I experience the word now *this* way, now *that* way — doesn't it also show |216| me that in the stream of speech I often don't experience the word *at all*? —— For the fact that I then also mean it, intend it, now like *this*, now like *that*, and maybe also explain it accordingly later, is, of course, not in question.

* 273. But the question then remains why, in connection with this *game* of experiencing a word, we also speak of 'the meaning' and of 'meaning it'. —— This is a different kind of question. —— It is a characteristic feature of this language-game that in *this* situation we use the expression "We pronounced the word with *this* meaning" and take this expression over from that other language-game.
   Call it a dream. It does not change anything.

274. Given the two concepts 'fat' and 'lean', would you be inclined to say that Wednesday was fat and Tuesday lean, or the other way round? (I am strongly inclined towards the former.) Now have "fat" and "lean" some different meaning here from their usual one? — They have a different use. — So ought I really to have used different words? Certainly not. — I want to use *these* words (with their familiar meanings) *here*. — I am saying nothing about the causes of this phenomenon now. They *might* be associations from my childhood. But that is a hypothesis. Whatever the explanation — the inclination is there.

275. Asked "What do you really mean here by 'fat' and 'lean'?", I could only explain the meanings in the usual way. I could *not* point them out by using Tuesday and Wednesday as examples.

276. Here one might speak of a 'primary' and 'secondary' meaning of a word. Only someone for whom the word has the former meaning uses it in the latter.

277. Nur dem, der rechnen gelernt hat — schriftlich oder mündlich — kann man, mittels dieses Begriffs des Rechnens begreiflich machen, was Kopfrechnen ist.

278. Die sekundäre Bedeutung ist nicht eine 'übertragene' Bedeutung. Wenn ich sage "Der Vokal *e* ist für mich gelb", so meine ich nicht: 'gelb' in übertragener Bedeutung — denn ich könnte, was ich sagen will, gar nicht anders als mittels des Begriffs 'gelb' ausdrücken.

279. Einer sagt mir: "Wart auf mich bei der Bank." Frage: Hast du, *als du das Wort aussprachst*, diese Bank gemeint? —— Diese Frage ist von der Art derjenigen: "Hast du, auf dem Weg zu ihm, beabsichtigt, ihm das und das zu sagen?" Sie bezieht sich auf eine bestimmte Zeit (auf die Zeit des Gehens, wie die erste Frage auf die Zeit des Redens) — aber nicht auf ein *Erlebnis* während dieser Zeit. Das Meinen ist sowenig ein Erleben, wie das Beabsichtigen.

Was unterscheidet sie aber vom Erlebnis? —— Sie haben keinen Erlebnisinhalt. Denn die Inhalte (Vorstellungen z. B.), die sie begleiten und illustrieren, sind nicht das Meinen oder Beabsichtigen.

280. Die Absicht, *in der* gehandelt wird, 'begleitet' nicht die Handlung, sowenig wie der Gedanke die Rede 'begleitet'. Gedanke und Absicht sind weder 'gegliedert' noch 'ungegliedert', weder einem einzelnen Ton zu vergleichen, der während des Handelns oder Redens erklingt, noch einer Melodie.

281. 'Reden' (ob laut, oder im Stillen) und 'Denken' sind nicht gleichartige Begriffe; wenn auch im engsten Zusammenhang.

282. Das Erlebnis beim Sprechen und die Absicht haben nicht das gleiche *Interesse*. (Das Erlebnis könnte vielleicht einen Psychologen über die '*unbewußte*' Absicht belehren.)

283. "Wir haben bei diesem Wort Beide an ihn gedacht." Nehmen wir an, jeder von uns hätte dabei die gleichen Worte im Stillen zu sich gesagt — und MEHR kann es doch nicht heißen. —— Aber wären diese Worte nicht auch nur ein *Keim*? Sie müssen doch zu einer Sprache gehören und zu einem Zusammenhang, um wirklich der Ausdruck des Gedankens an jenen Menschen zu sein.

284. Gott, wenn er in unsre Seelen geblickt hätte, hätte dort nicht sehen können, von wem wir sprachen.

277. Only to someone who has learnt to calculate — on paper or out loud — can one render intelligible, by means of this concept of calculating, what calculating in the head is.

278. The secondary meaning is not a 'metaphorical' meaning. If I say, "For me the vowel *e* is yellow", I do not mean: 'yellow' in a metaphorical meaning — for I could not express what I want to say in any other way than by means of the concept of yellow.

279. Someone tells me: "Wait for me by the bank." Question: Did you, *as you were saying the word*, mean this bank? —— This question is of the same kind as "Did you, on the way to him, intend to say such-and-such to him?" It refers to a definite time (the time of walking, as the former question refers to the time of speaking) — but not to an |217| *experience* during that time. Meaning something is as little an experience as intending.
  But what distinguishes them from an experience? —— They have no experiential content. For the contents (images, for instance) which accompany and illustrate them are not the meaning or intending.

280. The intention *with which* one acts does not 'accompany' the action any more than a thought 'accompanies' speech. Thought and intention are neither 'articulated' nor 'non-articulated'; to be compared neither to a single note which sounds during the acting or speaking, nor to a melody.

281. 'Talking' (whether out loud or silently) and 'thinking' are not concepts of a similar kind, even though they are in closest connection.

282. The *interest* of an experience one has while speaking and of the intention is not the same. (The experience might perhaps inform a psychologist about an '*unconscious*' intention.)

283. "At that word, we both thought of him." Let's assume that each of us said the same words to himself silently — and surely it can't mean MORE than that. —— But wouldn't these words too be only a *germ*? They must surely belong to a language and to a context, in order really to be the expression of the thought of that man.

284. If God had looked into our minds, he would not have been able to see there whom we were speaking of.

285. "Warum hast du mich bei diesem Wort angeschaut, hast du an
. . . gedacht?" —— Es gibt also eine Reaktion in diesem Zeitpunkt und
sie wird durch die Worte "Ich dachte an . . ." oder "Ich erinnerte mich
plötzlich an . . ." erklärt.

286. Du beziehst dich mit dieser Äußerung auf den Zeitpunkt des
Redens. Es macht einen Unterschied, ob du dich auf diesen, oder auf
jenen Zeitpunkt beziehst.
    Die bloße Worterklärung bezieht sich nicht auf ein Geschehnis im
Zeitpunkt des Aussprechens.

287. Das Sprachspiel "Ich meine (oder meinte) *das*" (nachträgliche
Worterklärung) ist ganz verschieden von dem: "Ich dachte dabei an . . ."
Dies ist verwandt mit: "Es erinnerte mich an . . ."

288. "Ich habe mich heute schon dreimal dran erinnert, daß ich ihm
schreiben muß." Welche Wichtigkeit hat, was dabei in mir vor sich ging?
—— Aber andererseits, welche Wichtigkeit, welches Interesse hat der
Bericht selbst? —— Er läßt gewisse Schlüsse zu.

289. "Bei diesen Worten fiel er mir ein." —— Was ist die primitive
Reaktion, mit der das Sprachspiel anfängt? — die dann in diese Worte
umgesetzt werden kann. Wie kommt es dazu, daß Menschen diese Worte
gebrauchen?
    Die primitive Reaktion konnte ein Blick, eine Gebärde sein, aber auch
ein Wort.

290. "Warum hast du mich angeschaut und den Kopf geschüttelt?" —
"Ich wollte dir zu verstehen geben, daß du . . ." Das soll nicht eine
Zeichenregel ausdrücken, sondern den Zweck meiner Handlung.

291. Das Meinen ist kein Vorgang, der dies Wort begleitet. Denn kein
Vorgang könnte die Konsequenzen des Meinens haben.
    (Ähnlich könnte man, glaube ich, sagen: Eine Rechnung ist kein
Experiment, denn kein Experiment könnte die besonderen Konsequenzen
einer Multiplikation haben.)

292. Es gibt wichtige Begleitvorgänge des Redens, die dem gedankenlosen Reden oft fehlen und es kennzeichnen. Aber *sie* sind nicht das
Denken.

285. "Why did you look at me at that word, were you thinking of . . . ?"
—— So there is a reaction at a certain moment, and it is explained by saying "I thought of . . ." or "I suddenly remembered . . ."

286. In saying this, you refer to the moment of speaking. It makes a difference whether you refer to this or to that moment.
    Mere explanation of a word does not refer to an occurrence at the moment of speaking.

287. The language-game "I mean (or meant) *this*" (subsequent explanation of a word) is quite different from this one: "I thought of . . . as I said it." The latter is akin to "It reminded me of . . ."

288. "I have already remembered three times today that I must write to him." Of what importance is what went on in me then? —— On the |218| other hand, what is the importance, the interest, of the report itself? —— It permits certain inferences.

289. "At these words he occurred to me." —— What is the primitive reaction with which the language-game begins — which can then be translated into these words? How do people get to use these words?
    The primitive reaction may have been a glance or a gesture, but it may also have been a word.

290. "Why did you look at me and shake your head?" — "I wanted to convey to you that you . . ." This is supposed to express not a symbolic convention but the purpose of my action.

291. Meaning something is not a process which accompanies a word. For no *process* could have the consequences of meaning something.
    (Similarly, I think, it could be said: a calculation is not an experiment, for no experiment could have the special consequences of a multiplication.)

292. There are important characteristic processes accompanying talking, which are often missing when one talks without thinking. But *they* are not the thinking.

293. "Jetzt weiß ich's!" Was ging da vor? —— Wußte ich's also *nicht*, als ich versicherte, jetzt wüßte ich's?

Du siehst es falsch an.

(Wozu dient das Signal?)

Und konnte man das 'Wissen' eine Begleitung des Ausrufs nennen?

294. Das vertraute Gesicht eines Wortes, die Empfindung, es habe seine Bedeutung in sich aufgenommen, sei ein Ebenbild seiner Bedeutung, — es könnte Menschen geben, denen das alles fremd ist. (Es würde ihnen die Anhänglichkeit an ihre Worte fehlen.) — Und wie äußern sich diese Gefühle bei uns? — Darin, wie wir Worte wählen und schätzen.

295. Wie finde ich das 'richtige' Wort? Wie wähle ich unter den Worten? Es ist wohl manchmal, als vergliche ich sie nach feinen Unterschieden des Geruchs: *Dies* ist zu sehr . . . , *dies* zu sehr . . . , — *das* ist das Richtige. —— Aber ich muß nicht immer beurteilen, erklären; ich könnte oft nur sagen: "Es stimmt einfach noch nicht." Ich bin unbefriedigt, suche weiter. Endlich kommt ein Wort: "*Das* ist es!" *Manchmal* kann ich sagen, warum. So schaut eben hier das Suchen aus, und so das Finden.

296. Aber 'kommt' nicht das Wort, das dir einfällt, in etwas besonderer Weise? Gib doch acht! —— Das genaue Achtgeben nützt mich nichts. Es könnte doch nur entdecken, was *jetzt* in *mir* vorgeht.

Und wie kann ich, gerade jetzt, überhaupt drauf hinhören? Ich müßte doch warten, bis mir wieder ein Wort einfällt. Aber das Seltsame ist ja, daß es scheint, als müßte ich nicht auf die Gelegenheit warten, sondern könnte mir's vorführen, auch wenn es sich nicht wirklich zuträgt. Und wie? — Ich *spiele* es. — Aber *was* kann ich auf diese Weise erfahren? Was mache ich denn nach? — Charakteristische Begleiterscheinungen. Hauptsächlich: Gebärden, Mienen, Tonfall.

297. Über einen feinen ästhetischen Unterschied läßt sich *Vieles* sagen — das ist wichtig. — Die erste Äußerung mag freilich sein: "*Dies* Wort paßt, *dies* nicht" — oder dergleichen. Aber nun können noch alle weitverzweigten Zusammenhänge erörtert werden, die jedes der Wörter schlägt. Es ist eben *nicht* mit jenem ersten Urteil abgetan, denn es ist das *Feld* eines Wortes, was entscheidet.

298. "Mir liegt das Wort auf der Zunge." Was geht dabei in meinem Bewußtsein vor? Darauf kommt's gar nicht an. Was immer vorging, war

293. "Now I know!" What went on here? —— So did I *not* know when I declared that now I knew?

You are looking at it in the wrong way.

(What is the signal for?)

And could the 'knowing' be called an accompaniment of the exclamation?

294. The familiar face of a word, the feeling that it has assimilated its meaning into itself, that it is a likeness of its meaning — there could be human beings to whom all this was alien. (They would not have an attachment to their words.) — And how are these feelings manifested among us? — By the way we choose and value words.

295. How do I find the 'right' word? How do I choose among words? It is indeed sometimes as if I were comparing them by fine differences of smell: *That* is too . . . , *that* is too . . . — *this* is the right one. —— But I don't always have to judge, explain; often I might only say, "It simply isn't right yet". I am dissatisfied, I go on looking. At last a word comes: "*That's* it!" *Sometimes* I can say why. This is simply what searching, that is what finding, is like here. |219|

296. But doesn't the word that occurs to you 'come' in a somewhat special way? Just pay attention! —— Careful attention is no use to me. All it could discover would be what is going on in *me, now.*

And how can I, precisely now, listen out for it at all? I would have to wait until another word occurs to me. But the curious thing is that it seems as though I did not have to wait for the occasion, but could display it to myself, even when it is not actually taking place. How? — I *act* it. — But *what* can I learn in this way? What do I imitate? — Characteristic accompaniments. Primarily: gestures, faces, tones of voice.

297. A *great deal* can be said about a subtle aesthetic difference — that is important. — The first remark may, of course, be: "*This* word fits, *that* doesn't" — or something of the kind. But then all the widespread ramifications effected by each of the words can still be discussed. That first judgement is *not* the end of the matter, for it is the *field* of a word that is decisive.

298. "The word is on the tip of my tongue." What is going on in my mind at this moment? That is not the point at all. Whatever went on

nicht mit jener Äußerung gemeint. Interessanter ist, was dabei in meinem Benehmen vorging. — "Mir liegt das Wort auf der Zunge" teilt dir mit: das Wort, das hierher gehört, sei mir entfallen, ich hoffe es bald zu finden. Im übrigen tut jener Wortausdruck nicht mehr, als ein gewisses wortloses Benehmen.

299. James will darüber eigentlich sagen: "Was für ein merkwürdiges Erlebnis! Das Wort ist noch nicht da und ist doch, in einem Sinne, schon da, — oder etwas ist da, was nur zu diesem Wort herauswachsen *kann.*" —— Aber das ist gar kein Erlebnis. Als Erlebnis *gedeutet* sieht es freilich seltsam aus. Nicht anders, als die Absicht, gedeutet als Begleitung des Handelns, oder aber –1 als Kardinalzahl.

300. Die Worte "Es liegt mir auf der Zunge" sind so wenig der Ausdruck eines Erlebnisses, wie die: "Jetzt weiß ich weiter!" — Wir gebrauchen sie in *gewissen Situationen*, und sie sind umgeben von einem Benehmen besonderer Art, auch von manchen charakteristischen Erlebnissen. Insbesondere folgt ihnen häufig das *Finden* des Worts. (Frage dich: "Wie wäre es, wenn Menschen *nie* das Wort fänden, das ihnen auf der Zunge liegt?")

301. Das stille, 'innerliche' Reden ist nicht ein halb verborgenes Phänomen, als nähme man es durch einen Schleier wahr. Es ist *gar nicht* verborgen, aber sein Begriff kann uns leicht verwirren, denn er läuft, eine weite Strecke, hart am Begriff eines 'äußern' Vorgangs entlang, ohne sich doch mit ihm zu decken.

(Die Frage, ob beim innerlichen Sprechen Kehlkopfmuskeln innerviert werden, und ähnliches, mag großes Interesse haben, aber nicht für unsere Untersuchung.)

302. Die enge Verwandtschaft des 'innerlichen Redens' mit dem 'Reden' drückt sich darin aus, daß sich hörbar mitteilen läßt, was innerlich geredet wurde, und daß das innerliche Reden eine äußere Handlung *begleiten* kann. (Ich kann innerlich singen, oder still lesen, oder kopfrechnen und dabei mit der Hand den Takt schlagen.)

303. "Aber das innerliche Reden ist doch eine gewisse Tätigkeit, die ich lernen muß!" Wohl; aber was ist hier 'tun' und was ist hier 'lernen'?

Laß dich die Bedeutung der Worte von ihren Verwendungen lehren! (Ähnlich kann man in der Mathematik oft sagen: Laß den *Beweis* dich lehren, *was* bewiesen wurde.)

was not what was meant by that expression. What is of more interest is what went on in my behaviour. — "The word is on the tip of my tongue" tells you: the word which belongs here has escaped me, but I hope to find it soon. — For the rest, the verbal expression does no more than some kind of wordless behaviour.

* 299. On this, James is really trying to say: "What a remarkable experience! The word is not there yet, and yet, in a certain sense, it is — or something is there, which *cannot* grow into anything but this word." —— But this is not an experience at all. *Interpreted* as an experience, it does indeed look odd. As does an intention, interpreted as an accompaniment of action; or again, like – 1, interpreted as a cardinal number.

300. The words "It's on the tip of my tongue" are no more the expression of an experience than "Now I know how to go on!" — We use them in *certain situations*, and they are surrounded by behaviour of a special kind, and also by some characteristic experiences. In particular, they are frequently followed by *finding* the word. (Ask yourself: "What would it be like if human beings *never* found the word that was on the tip of their tongue?") |220|

301. Silent, 'inner' speech is not a half hidden phenomenon, seen, as it were, through a veil. It is not hidden *at all*, but the concept may easily confuse us, for it runs over a long stretch cheek by jowl with the concept of an 'outer' process, and yet does not coincide with it.

(The question of whether laryngal muscles are innervated concurrently with internal speech, and similar things, may be of great interest, but not for our investigation.)

302. The close relationship between 'inner speech' and 'speech' comes out in that what was said inwardly can be communicated audibly, and that inner speech can *accompany* outer action. (I can sing inwardly, or read silently, or calculate in my head, and beat time with my hand as I do so.)

303. "But inner speech is surely a certain activity, which I have to learn!" Very well; but what is 'doing' and what is 'learning' here?

Let the use of words teach you their meaning. (Similarly, one can often say in mathematics: let the *proof* teach you *what* was being proved.)

304. "So rechne ich nicht *wirklich*, wenn ich im Kopf rechne?" — Du unterscheidest doch auch Kopfrechnen vom wahrnehmbaren Rechnen! Aber du kannst nur lernen, was 'Kopfrechnen' ist, indem du lernst, was 'Rechnen' ist; du kannst kopfrechnen nur lernen, indem du rechnen lernst.

305. Man kann sehr 'deutlich' in der Vorstellung reden, wenn man dabei den Tonfall der Sätze durch Summen (bei geschlossenen Lippen) wiedergibt. Auch Kehlkopfbewegungen helfen. Aber das Merkwürdige ist ja eben, daß man die Rede dann in der Vorstellung *hört*, und nicht bloß, sozusagen, ihr Skelett im Kehlkopf *fühlt*. (Denn das ließe sich ja auch denken, daß Menschen still mit Kehlkopfbewegungen rechneten, wie man mit den Fingern rechnen kann.)

306. Eine Hypothese, wie die, es ginge beim innerlichen Reden das und das in unserm Körper vor, ist für uns nur insofern von Interesse, als sie uns eine mögliche Verwendung der Äußerung "Ich sagte zu mir selbst . . ." zeigt; nämlich die, von der Äußerung auf den physiologischen Vorgang zu schließen.

307. Daß, was ein Andrer innerlich redet, mir verborgen ist, liegt im *Begriff* 'innerlich reden'. Nur ist "verborgen" hier das falsche Wort; denn ist es mir verborgen, so sollte es ihm selbst offenbar sein, *er* müßte es *wissen*. Aber er 'weiß' es nicht, nur den Zweifel, den es für mich gibt, gibt es für ihn nicht.

308. "Was Einer zu sich selbst im Innern spricht, ist mir verborgen" könnte freilich auch heißen, ich könne es zumeist nicht *erraten*, noch auch (wie es ja möglich wäre) aus den Bewegungen seines Kehlkopfs z. B. ablesen.

309. "Ich weiß, was ich will, wünsche, glaube, fühle, . . ." (u. s. f. durch alle psychologischen Verben) ist entweder Philosophen-Unsinn, oder aber *nicht* ein Urteil a priori.

310. "Ich weiß . . ." mag heißen "Ich zweifle nicht . . ." — aber es heißt nicht, die Worte "Ich zweifle . . ." seien *sinnlos*, der Zweifel logisch ausgeschlossen.

311. Man sagt "Ich weiß", wo man auch sagen kann "Ich glaube", oder "Ich vermute"; wo man sich überzeugen kann. (Wer mir aber vorhält, man sage manchmal "Ich muß doch wissen, ob ich Schmerzen habe!",

304. "So I don't *really* calculate, when I calculate in my head?" — After all, you yourself distinguish between calculating in the head and perceptible calculating! But you can only learn what 'calculating in the head' is by learning what 'calculating' is; you can only learn to calculate in your head by learning to calculate.

305. One can say things in one's imagination very 'distinctly', when one reproduces the intonation of one's sentences by humming (with closed lips). Movements of the larynx help too. But the curious thing is precisely that one then *hears* the talk in one's imagination and does not merely *feel* the skeleton of it, so to speak, in one's larynx. (For human beings could also well be imagined calculating silently with laryngal movements, as one can calculate on one's fingers.)

* 306. A hypothesis, such as that such-and-such goes on in our bodies when we talk silently to ourselves, is of interest to us only in that it points to a possible use of the expression "I said . . . to myself": namely, that of inferring the physiological process from the expression.

307. That what someone else says to himself is hidden from me is part of the *concept* of inner speech. Only "hidden" is the wrong word |221| here; for if it is hidden from me, it ought to be apparent to him, *he* would have to *know* it. But he does not 'know' it; only, the doubt which exists for me does not exist for him.

308. "What anyone silently says to himself is hidden from me" might, of course, also signify that I can for the most part not *guess* it; nor can I read it off from, for example, the movements of his larynx (which would be a possibility).

309. "I know what I want, wish, believe, feel, . . ." (and so on through all the psychological verbs) is either philosophers' nonsense or, at any rate, *not* a judgement a priori.

310. "I know . . ." may mean "I do not doubt . . ." — but does not mean that the words "I doubt . . ." are *senseless*, that doubt is logically excluded.

311. One says "I know" where one can also say "I believe" or "I suppose"; where one can satisfy oneself. (Someone who remonstrates with me that one sometimes does say "But I must know if I am in pain!",

"Nur du kannst wissen, was du fühlst" und ähnliches, der soll sich die Anlässe und den Zweck dieser Redensarten besehen. "Krieg ist Krieg!" ist ja auch nicht ein Beispiel des Identitätsgesetzes.)

312. Der Fall läßt sich denken, in dem ich mich davon überzeugen *könnte*, daß ich zwei Hände habe. Normalerweise aber kann ich's *nicht*. "Aber du brauchst sie dir ja nur vor die Augen zu halten." —— Wenn ich *jetzt* zweifle, ob ich zwei Hände habe, dann brauche ich auch meinen Augen nicht zu trauen. (Ebensogut könnte ich dann meinen Freund fragen.)

313. Damit hängt zusammen, daß z. B. der Satz "Die Erde hat Millionen von Jahren existiert" einen klareren Sinn hat, als der: "Die Erde hat in den letzten fünf Minuten existiert." Denn, wer das letztere behauptet, den würde ich fragen: "Auf welche Beobachtungen bezieht sich dieser Satz; und welche würden ihm entgegenstehen?" — während ich weiß, zu welchem Gedankenkreis und zu welchen Beobachtungen der erste Satz gehört.

314. "Ein neugeborenes Kind hat keine Zähne." — "Eine Gans hat keine Zähne." — "Eine Rose hat keine Zähne." — Das letztere — möchte man sagen — ist doch offenbar wahr! Sicherer sogar, als daß eine Gans keine hat. — Und doch ist es nicht so klar. Denn wo sollte eine Rose Zähne haben? Die Gans hat keine in ihren Kiefern. Und sie hat natürlich auch keine in den Flügeln, aber das meint niemand, der sagt, sie habe keine Zähne. — Ja wie, wenn man sagte: Die Kuh kaut ihr Futter und düngt dann damit die Rose, also hat die Rose Zähne im Maul eines Tiers. Das wäre darum nicht absurd, weil man von vornherein gar nicht weiß, wo bei der Rose nach Zähnen zu suchen wäre. ((Zusammenhang mit 'Schmerzen im Körper des Andern'.))

315. Ich kann wissen, was der Andere denkt, nicht was ich denke.

Es ist richtig zu sagen "Ich weiß, was du denkst", und falsch: "Ich weiß, was ich denke."

(Eine ganze Wolke von Philosophie kondensiert zu einem Tröpfchen Sprachlehre.)

316. "Das Denken des Menschen geht im Innern des Bewußtseins in einer Abgeschlossenheit vor sich, gegen die jede physische Abgeschlossenheit ein Offen-da-liegen ist."

Würden Menschen, die stets — etwa durch Beobachten des Kehlkopfs — die stillen Selbstgespräche des Andern lesen könnten, — würden die auch geneigt sein, das Bild von der gänzlichen Abgeschlossenheit zu gebrauchen?

"Only you can know what you feel", and similar things, should consider the occasion and purpose of these phrases. "War is war!" is not an example of the law of identity, either.)

312. It's possible to imagine a case in which I *could* satisfy myself that I had two hands. Normally, however, I *can't* do so. "But all you need do is to hold them up before your eyes!" —— If I am *now* in doubt as to whether I have two hands, I need not believe my eyes either. (I might just as well ask a friend.)

313. This is connected with the fact that, for example, the sentence "The Earth has existed for millions of years" makes clearer sense than "The Earth has existed for the last five minutes". For I'd ask anyone who asserted the latter: "What observations does this sentence refer to; and what observations would count against it?" — whereas I know to what context of ideas and what observations the former sentence belongs.

* 314. "A newborn child has no teeth." — "A goose has no teeth." — "A rose has no teeth." — This last at any rate — one would like to say — is obviously true! It is even surer than that a goose has none. — And yet it is far from clear. For where should a rose's teeth have been? The goose has none in its jaw. And neither, of course, has it any in its |222| wings; but no one means that when he says it has no teeth. — Why, suppose one were to say: the cow chews its food and then dungs the rose with it, so the rose has teeth in the mouth of an animal. This would not be absurd, because one has no notion in advance where to look for teeth in a rose. ((Connection with 'pain in someone else's body'.))

315. I can know what someone else is thinking, not what I am thinking.
　It is correct to say "I know what you are thinking", and wrong to say "I know what I am thinking".
　(A whole cloud of philosophy condenses into a drop of grammar.)

316. "Man's thinking goes on within the inner recesses of his mind in a seclusion in comparison with which any physical seclusion is a lying in full view."
　If there were people who always read the silent soliloquy of others — say by observing the larynx — would they too be inclined to use the picture of complete seclusion?

317. Spräche ich laut zu mir selbst, in einer Sprache, die die Anwesenden nicht verstehn, so wären meine Gedanken ihnen verborgen.

318. Nehmen wir an, es gebe einen Menschen, der immer richtig erriete, was ich im Gedanken zu mir rede. (Wie es ihm gelingt, ist gleichgültig.) Aber was ist das Kriterium dafür, daß er es *richtig* errät? Nun, ich bin wahrheitsliebend und gestehe, er habe es richtig erraten. — Aber könnte ich mich nicht irren, kann mich mein Gedächtnis nicht täuschen? Und könnte es das nicht immer, wenn ich — ohne zu lügen — ausspreche, was ich bei mir gedacht habe? — Aber so scheint es ja, es komme gar nicht drauf an, 'was in meinem Innern vorgegangen ist'. (Ich mache hier eine Hilfskonstruktion.)

319. Für die Wahrheit des *Geständnisses*, ich hätte das und das gedacht, sind die Kriterien nicht die der wahrheitsgemäßen *Beschreibung* eines Vorgangs. Und die Wichtigkeit des wahren Geständnisses liegt nicht darin, daß es irgend einen Vorgang mit Sicherheit richtig wiedergibt. Sie liegt vielmehr in den besondern Konsequenzen, die sich aus einem Geständnis ziehen lassen, dessen Wahrheit durch die besondern Kriterien der *Wahrhaftigkeit* verbürgt ist.

320. (Angenommen, daß die Träume uns wichtige Aufschlüsse über den Träumer geben können, so wäre das, was den Aufschluß gibt, die wahrhaftige Traumerzählung. Die Frage, ob den Träumer sein Gedächtnis täuscht, wenn er nach dem Erwachen den Traum berichtet, kann sich nicht erheben, es sei denn, wir führten ein gänzlich neues Kriterium für eine 'Übereinstimmung' des Berichts mit dem Traum ein, ein Kriterium, das hier eine Wahrheit von der Wahrhaftigkeit unterscheidet.)

321. Es gibt ein Spiel: 'Gedankenerraten'. Eine Variante davon wäre die: Ich mache dem A eine Mitteilung in einer Sprache, die B nicht versteht. B soll den Sinn der Mitteilung erraten. —— Eine andere Variante: Ich schreibe einen Satz nieder, den der Andere nicht sehen kann. Er muß den Wortlaut, oder den Sinn erraten. —— Noch eine: Ich stelle ein Jigsaw-Puzzle zusammen; der Andre kann mich nicht sehen, errät aber von Zeit zu Zeit meine Gedanken und spricht sie aus. Er sagt z. B.: "Wo ist nur dieses Stück!" — "*Jetzt* weiß ich, wie es paßt!" —— "Ich habe keine Ahnung, was hierher gehört" — "Der Himmel ist immer das schwerste" — u. s. f. — dabei aber brauche *ich* weder laut noch auch im Stillen zu mir selbst sprechen.

322. Alles das wäre Erraten von Gedanken; und wenn es tatsächlich nicht geschieht, so macht dies den Gedanken nicht verborgener, als den physischen Vorgang, den man nicht wahrnimmt.

317. If I were to talk to myself out loud in a language not understood by those present, my thoughts would be hidden from them.

318. Let's assume that there was a man who always guessed right what I was saying to myself in my thoughts. (It does not matter how he manages it.) But what is the criterion for his guessing *right*? Well, I'm a truthful person, and I confess that he has guessed right. — But might I not be mistaken, can my memory not deceive me? And might it not always do so when — without lying — I express what I have thought to myself? —— But now it does appear that 'what went on within me' is not the point at all. (Here I am drawing a construction line.)

319. The criteria for the truth of the *confession* that I thought such-and-such are not the criteria for a true *description* of a process. And the importance of the true confession does not reside in its being a correct and certain report of some process. It resides, rather, in the special consequences which can be drawn from a confession whose truth is guaranteed by the special criteria of *truthfulness*.

320. (Assuming that dreams can yield important information about the dreamer, what yielded the information would be truthful accounts of dreams. The question of whether the dreamer's memory deceives him when he reports the dream after waking cannot arise, unless we introduce a completely new criterion for the report's 'agreeing' |223| with the dream, a criterion which distinguishes a truth here from truthfulness.)

321. There is a game called 'thought guessing'. One variant of it would be this: I tell A something in a language that B does not understand. B is supposed to guess the meaning of what I say. —— Another variant: I write down a sentence which the other person can't see. He has to guess the words or the sense. —— Yet another: I am putting a jigsaw puzzle together; the other person can't see me, but from time to time guesses my thoughts and utters them. He says, for instance, "Now where is this bit?" — "*Now* I know how it fits!" —— "I have no idea what goes in here." — "The sky is always the hardest part", and so on — but *I* need not be talking to myself either out loud or silently at the time.

* 322. All this would be guessing thoughts; and even if I don't actually talk to myself, that does not make my thoughts any more hidden than an unperceived physical process.

323. "Das *Innere* ist uns verborgen." —— Die Zukunft ist uns verborgen.
— Aber denkt der Astronom so, wenn er eine Sonnenfinsternis berechnet?

324. Wen ich, mit offenbarer Ursache, sich in Schmerzen winden sehe,
von dem denke ich nicht: seine Gefühle seien mir doch verborgen.

325. Wir sagen auch von einem Menschen, er sei uns durchsichtig. Aber
es ist für diese Betrachtung wichtig, daß ein Mensch für einen andern
ein völliges Rätsel sein kann. Das erfährt man, wenn man in ein fremdes
Land mit gänzlich fremden Traditionen kommt; und zwar auch dann,
wenn man die Sprache des Landes beherrscht. Man *versteht* die
Menschen nicht. (Und nicht darum, weil man nicht weiß, was sie zu
sich selber sprechen.) Wir können uns nicht in sie finden.

326. "Ich kann nicht wissen, was in ihm vorgeht" ist vor allem ein *Bild*.
Es ist der überzeugende Ausdruck einer Überzeugung. Es gibt nicht die
Gründe der Überzeugung an. *Sie* liegen nicht auf der Hand.

327. Wenn ein Löwe sprechen könnte, wir könnten ihn nicht verstehn.

328. Man kann sich ein Erraten der Absicht denken, ähnlich dem
Gedankenerraten, aber auch ein Erraten dessen, was Einer nun tatsächlich
tun wird.
    Zu sagen "Nur er kann wissen, was er beabsichtigt" ist Unsinn; zu
sagen "Nur er kann wissen, was er tun wird" falsch. Denn die
Vorhersage, die im Ausdruck meiner Absicht liegt (z. B. "Sowie es fünf
Uhr schlägt, gehe ich nach Hause") muß nicht zutreffen, und der Andre
mag wissen, was wirklich geschehen wird.

329. Zweierlei aber ist wichtig: Daß der Andere in vielen Fällen meine
Handlungen nicht vorhersagen kann, während ich sie in meiner
Absicht vorhersehe. Und daß meine Vorhersage (im Ausdruck meiner
Absicht) nicht auf der gleichen Grundlage ruht, wie seine Vorhersage
meiner Handlung, und die Schlüsse, die aus diesen Vorhersagen zu ziehen,
ganz verschieden sind.

330. Ich kann der Empfindung des Andern so *sicher* sein, wie irgend eines
Faktums. Damit aber sind die Sätze "Er ist schwer bedrückt", "25 × 25 =
625" und "Ich bin 60 Jahre alt" nicht zu ähnlichen Instrumenten
geworden. Es liegt die Erklärung nahe: die Sicherheit sei von andrer *Art*.
— Sie scheint auf einen psychologischen Unterschied zu deuten. Aber
der Unterschied ist ein logischer.

323. "What is *internal* is hidden from us." —— The future is hidden from us. — But does the astronomer think like this when he calculates an eclipse of the sun?

324. If I see someone writhing in pain with evident cause, I do not think: all the same, his feelings are hidden from me.

325. We also say of a person that he is transparent to us. It is, however, important as regards our considerations that one human being can be a complete enigma to another. One learns this when one comes into a strange country with entirely strange traditions; and, what is more, even though one has mastered the country's language. One does not *understand* the people. (And not because of not knowing what they are saying to themselves.) We can't find our feet with them.

326. "I can't know what is going on in him" is, above all, a *picture*. It is the convincing expression of a conviction. It does not give the reasons for the conviction. *They* are not obvious.

327. If a lion could talk, we wouldn't be able to understand it.

328. It is possible to imagine a guessing of intentions similar to the guessing of thoughts, but also a guessing of what someone is actually *going to do*.

   To say "Only he can know what he intends" is nonsense; to say "Only he can know what he will do", wrong. For the prediction contained in my expression of intention (for example, "As soon as it strikes |224| five, I'm going home") need not come true, and someone else may know what will really happen.

329. Two points, however, are important: one, that in many cases someone else cannot predict my actions, whereas I foresee them in my intention; the other, that my prediction (in my expression of intention) does not rest on the same foundation as his prediction of my action, and that the conclusions to be drawn from these predictions are quite different.

330. I can be as *certain* of someone else's feelings as of any fact. But this does not make the sentences "He is very depressed", "25 × 25 = 625", and "I am 60 years old" into similar instruments. A natural explanation is that the certainty is of a different *kind*. — This seems to point to a psychological difference. But the difference is a logical one.

331. "Aber schließt du eben nicht nur vor dem Zweifel die Augen, wenn du *sicher* bist?" — Sie sind mir geschlossen.

332. Bin ich weniger sicher, daß dieser Mann Schmerzen hat, als daß 2 × 2 = 4 ist? — Aber ist darum das erste mathematische Sicherheit? —— 'Mathematische Sicherheit' ist kein psychologischer Begriff.
   Die Art der Sicherheit ist die Art des Sprachspiels.

333. "Seine Motive weiß nur er" — das ist ein Ausdruck dafür, daß wir *ihn* nach seinen Motiven fragen. — Ist er aufrichtig, so wird er sie uns sagen; aber ich brauche mehr als Aufrichtigkeit um seine Motive zu erraten. Hier ist die Verwandtschaft mit dem Fall des *Wissens*.

334. Laß es dir aber *auffallen*, daß es so etwas gibt, wie unser Sprachspiel: Das Motiv meiner Tat gestehen.

335. Die unsägliche Verschiedenheit aller der tagtäglichen Sprachspiele kommt uns nicht zum Bewußtsein, weil die Kleider unserer Sprache alles gleichmachen.
   Das Neue (Spontane, 'Spezifische') ist immer ein Sprachspiel.

336. Was ist der Unterschied zwischen Motiv und Ursache? — Wie *findet* man das Motiv, und wie die Ursache?

337. Es gibt die Frage: "Ist das eine zuverlässige Art, die Motive des Menschen zu beurteilen?" Aber um so fragen zu können, müssen wir schon wissen, was es bedeutet: "das Motiv beurteilen"; und das lernen wir nicht, indem wir erfahren, was '*Motiv*' ist und was '*beurteilen*' ist.

338. Man beurteilt die Länge eines Stabes und kann eine Methode suchen, und finden, um sie genauer, oder zuverlässiger zu beurteilen. Also — sagst du — ist, *was* hier beurteilt wird, unabhängig von der Methode des Beurteilens. Was Länge *ist*, kann man nicht mittels der Methode der Längenbestimmung erklären. — Wer so denkt, macht einen Fehler. Welchen? — Zu sagen "Die Höhe des Mont Blanc hängt davon ab, wie man ihn besteigt", wäre seltsam. Und 'die Länge immer genauer messen', das will man damit vergleichen, näher und näher an ein Objekt heranzukommen. Aber es ist in gewissen Fällen klar, in gewissen *nicht*, was es heiße "näher an die Länge des Objekts herankommen". Was "die Länge bestimmen" heißt, lernt man nicht dadurch, daß man lernt, was *Länge*, und was *bestimmen* ist; sondern die Bedeutung des Wortes "Länge" lernt man u. a. dadurch, daß man lernt, was Längenbestimmung ist.

331. "But if you are *certain*, aren't you are shutting your eyes in face of doubt?" — They've been shut.

332. Am I less certain that this man is in pain than that 2 × 2 = 4? — Is the first case therefore one of mathematical certainty? —— 'Mathematical certainty' is not a psychological concept.
   The kind of certainty is the kind of language-game.

333. "Only he knows his motives" — that is an expression of the fact that we ask *him* what his motives are. — If he is sincere, he will tell us them; but I need more than sincerity to guess his motives. This is where the kinship with *knowing* is.

334. Let yourself be *struck* by the existence of such a thing as our language-game of confessing the motive of my action.

335. We don't notice the enormous variety of all the everyday language-games, because the clothing of our language makes them all alike.
   What is new (spontaneous, 'specific') is always a language-game.

336. What is the difference between motive and cause? — How is the motive *discovered*, and how the cause?

337. There is such a question as "Is this a reliable way of judging people's motives?" But in order to be able to ask this, we must already know what "judging a motive" means; and we do not learn this by finding out what '*motive*' is and what '*judging*' is. |225|

338. One judges the length of a rod, and may look for and find some method of judging it more exactly or more reliably. So — you say — *what* is judged here is independent of the method of judging it. What length *is* cannot be explained by the method of determining length. — Anyone who thinks like this is making a mistake. What mistake? — To say "The height of Mont Blanc depends on how one climbs it" would be odd. And one wants to compare 'ever more accurate measurement of length' with getting closer and closer to an object. But in certain cases it is, and in certain cases it is *not*, clear what "getting closer and closer to the length of an object" means. What "determining the length" means is not learned by learning what *length* and *determining* are; rather, the meaning of the word "length" is learnt by learning, among other things, what it is to determine length.

(Darum hat das Wort "Methodologie" eine doppelte Bedeutung. "Methodologische Untersuchung" kann man eine physikalische Untersuchung nennen, aber auch eine begriffliche.)

339. Von der Sicherheit, vom Glauben möchte man manchmal sagen, sie seien Tönungen des Gedankens; und es ist wahr: sie haben einen Ausdruck im *Ton* der Rede. Denk aber nicht an sie als 'Gefühle' beim Sprechen, oder Denken!

Frag nicht: "Was geht da in uns vor, wenn wir sicher sind, . . . ?" — sondern: Wie äußert sich 'die Sicherheit, daß es so ist' in dem Handeln des Menschen?

340. "Du kannst zwar über den Seelenzustand des Andern völlige Sicherheit haben, aber sie ist immer nur eine subjektive, keine objektive." —— Diese beiden Wörter deuten auf einen Unterschied zwischen Sprachspielen.

341. Es kann ein Streit darüber entstehen, welches das richtige Resultat einer Rechnung ist (z. B. einer längeren Addition). Aber so ein Streit entsteht selten und ist von kurzer Dauer. Er ist, wie wir sagen, 'mit Sicherheit' zu entscheiden.

Es kommt zwischen den Mathematikern, im allgemeinen, nicht zum Streit über das Resultat einer Rechnung. (Das ist eine wichtige Tatsache.) — Wäre es anders, wäre z. B. der Eine überzeugt, eine Ziffer habe sich unvermerkt geändert, oder das Gedächtnis habe ihn, oder den Andern getäuscht, etc., etc., — so würde es unsern Begriff der 'mathematischen Sicherheit' nicht geben.

342. Es könnte dann noch immer heißen: "Wir können zwar nie *wissen*, was das Resultat einer Rechnung ist, aber sie hat dennoch immer ein ganz bestimmtes Resultat. (Gott weiß es.) Die Mathematik ist allerdings von der höchsten Sicherheit, — wenn wir auch nur ein rohes Abbild von ihr besitzen."

343. Aber will ich etwa sagen, die Sicherheit der Mathematik beruhe auf der Zuverlässigkeit von Tinte und Papier? *Nein.* (Das wäre ein Circulus vitiosus.) —— Ich habe nicht gesagt, *warum* es zwischen den Mathematikern nicht zum Streit kommt, sondern nur, *daß* es nicht zum Streit kommt.

344. Es ist wohl wahr, daß man mit gewissen Arten von Papier und Tinte nicht rechnen könnte, wenn sie nämlich gewissen seltsamen Änderungen unterworfen wären, — aber daß sie sich ändern, könnte ja doch nur wieder durch das Gedächtnis und den Vergleich mit andern Rechenmitteln sich ergeben. Und wie prüft man diese wieder?

(That's why the word "methodology" has a double meaning. A physical investigation may be called a methodological one, but also a conceptual investigation.)

* 339. One would sometimes like to say of certainty and conviction that they are tonalities of thought; and it is true that they receive expression in the *tone* of voice. But do not think of them as 'feelings' which we have in speaking or thinking.

Don't ask: "What goes on in us when we are certain that . . . ?" — but: How is 'the certainty that this is so' manifested in people's action?

340. "While you can have complete certainty about someone else's state of mind, still it is always merely subjective, not objective, certainty." —— These two words point to a difference between language-games.

341. A dispute may arise over the correct result of a calculation (say, of a rather long addition). But such disputes are rare and of short duration. They can be decided, as we say, 'with certainty'.

Mathematicians don't in general quarrel over the result of a calculation. (This is an important fact.) — Were it otherwise: if, for instance, one mathematician was convinced that a figure had altered unperceived, or that his or someone else's memory had been deceptive, and so on — then our concept of 'mathematical certainty' would not exist.

342. Even then it might still be said: "While we can never *know* what the result of a calculation is, for all that, it always has a quite |226| definite result. (God knows it.) Mathematics is indeed of the highest certainty — though we possess only a crude likeness of it."

343. But am I really trying to say that the certainty of mathematics is based on the reliability of ink and paper? *No.* (That would be a vicious circle.) —— I have not said *why* mathematicians do not quarrel, but only *that* they do not.

344. It is no doubt true that one could not calculate with certain sorts of paper and ink, if, that is, they were subject to certain strange alterations — but still, that they changed could in turn be ascertained only through memory and comparison with other means of calculation. And how, in turn, are these tested?

345. Das Hinzunehmende, Gegebene — könnte man sagen — seien *Lebensformen*.

346. Hat es Sinn, zu sagen, die Menschen stimmen in Bezug auf ihre Farburteile im allgemeinen überein? — Wie wäre es, wenn's anders wäre? — Dieser würde sagen, die Blume sei rot, die Jener als blau anspricht, etc., etc. — Aber mit welchem Recht könnte man dann die Wörter "rot" und "blau" dieser Menschen *unsere* 'Farbwörter' nennen? —
  Wie würden sie lernen, jene Wörter zu gebrauchen? Und ist das Sprachspiel, welches sie lernen, noch das, was wir den Gebrauch der 'Farbnamen' nennen? Es gibt hier offenbar Gradunterschiede.

347. Aber diese Überlegung muß auch für die Mathematik gelten. Gäbe es die volle Übereinstimmung nicht, so würden die Menschen auch nicht die Technik lernen, die wir lernen. Sie wäre von der unsern mehr, oder weniger verschieden, auch bis zur Unkenntlichkeit.

348. "Die mathematische Wahrheit ist doch unabhängig davon, ob Menschen sie erkennen, oder nicht!" — Gewiß: Die Sätze "Die Menschen glauben, daß 2 × 2 = 4 ist" und "2 × 2 = 4" haben nicht den gleichen Sinn. Dieser ist ein mathematischer Satz, jener, wenn er überhaupt einen Sinn hat, kann etwa heißen, daß die Menschen auf den mathematischen Satz *gekommen* sind. Die beiden haben gänzlich verschiedene *Verwendung*. —— Aber was würde nun *das* heißen: "Wenn auch alle Menschen glaubten, 2 × 2 sei 5, so wäre es doch 4." — Wie sähe denn das aus, wenn alle Menschen dies glaubten? — Nun, ich könnte mir etwa vorstellen, sie hätten einen andern Kalkül, oder eine Technik, die wir nicht "rechnen" nennen würden. Aber wäre das *falsch*? (Ist eine Königskrönung *falsch*? Sie könnte, von uns verschiedenen, Wesen höchst seltsam erscheinen.)

349. Mathematik ist freilich, in einem Sinne, eine Lehre, — aber doch auch ein *Tun*. Und 'falsche Züge' kann es nur als Ausnahme geben. Denn würde, was wir jetzt so nennen, die Regel, so wäre damit das Spiel aufgehoben, worin sie falsche Züge sind.

350. "Wir lernen Alle das gleiche Einmaleins." Das könnte wohl eine Bemerkung über den Arithmetik-Unterricht an unsern Schulen sein, — aber auch eine Feststellung über den Begriff des Einmaleins. ("In einem Pferderennen laufen die Pferde, im allgemeinen, so schnell sie nur können.")

345. What has to be accepted, the given, is — one might say — *forms of life*.

346. Does it make sense to say that people generally agree in their judgements of colour? — What would it be like if it were different? — One man would say that a flower was red, which another called blue; and so on. — But with what right could one then call these people's words "red" and "blue" *our* 'colour-words'? —

  How would they learn to use these words? And is the language-game which they learn still the one we call the use of 'colour names'? There are evidently differences of degree here.

347. But this consideration must apply to mathematics too. If there weren't complete agreement, then human beings wouldn't be learning the technique which we learn either. It would be more or less different from ours, perhaps even up to the point of unrecognizability.

348. "But mathematical truth is independent of whether human beings know it or not!" — Certainly, the propositions "Human beings believe that 2 × 2 = 4" and "2 × 2 = 4" do not have the same sense. The latter is a mathematical proposition; the other, if it makes sense at all, may perhaps mean: human beings have *arrived* at the mathematical proposition. The two propositions have entirely different *uses*. —— But what would *this* mean: "Even though everybody believed that 2 × 2 were 5, it would still be 4"? — For what would it be like for everybody to believe that? — Well, I could imagine, for instance, that people had a different calculus, or a technique which we wouldn't |227| call "calculating". But would it be *wrong*? (Is a coronation *wrong*? To beings different from ourselves it might look extremely odd.)

349. Of course, in one sense, mathematics is a body of knowledge, but still it is also an *activity*. And 'false moves' can exist only as the exception. For if what we now call by that name became the rule, the game in which they were false moves would have been abrogated.

350. "We all learn the same multiplication table." This might, no doubt, be a remark about the teaching of arithmetic in our schools — but also an observation about the concept of the multiplication table. ("In a horse-race, the horses generally run as fast as they can.")

351. Es gibt Farbenblindheit und Mittel, sie festzustellen. In den Farbaussagen der normal Befundenen herrscht, im allgemeinen, volle Übereinstimmung. Das charakterisiert den Begriff der Farbaussagen.

352. Diese Übereinstimmung gibt es im allgemeinen nicht in der Frage, ob eine Gefühlsäußerung echt, oder unecht ist.

353. Ich bin sicher, *sicher*, daß er sich nicht verstellt; aber ein Dritter ist's nicht. Kann ich ihn immer überzeugen? Und wenn nicht, macht er dann einen Denk- oder Beobachtungsfehler?

354. "Du verstehst ja nichts!" — so sagt man, wenn Einer anzweifelt, was wir klar als echt erkennen, — aber wir können nichts beweisen.

355. Gibt es über die Echtheit des Gefühlsausdrucks ein 'fachmännisches' Urteil? — Es gibt auch da Menschen mit 'besserem' und Menschen mit 'schlechterem' Urteil.

Aus dem Urteil des bessern Menschenkenners werden, im allgemeinen, richtigere Prognosen hervorgehen.

Kann man Menschenkenntnis lernen? Ja; Mancher kann sie lernen. Aber nicht durch einen Lehrkurs, sondern durch '*Erfahrung*'. — Kann ein Andrer dabei sein Lehrer sein? Gewiß. Er gibt ihm von Zeit zu Zeit den richtigen *Wink*. —— So schaut hier das 'Lernen' und das 'Lehren' aus. —— Was man erlernt, ist keine Technik; man lernt richtige Urteile. Es gibt auch Regeln, aber sie bilden kein System, und nur der Erfahrene kann sie richtig anwenden. Unähnlich den Rechenregeln.

356. Das Schwerste ist hier, die Unbestimmtheit richtig und unverfälscht zum Ausdruck zu bringen.

357. "Die Echtheit des Ausdrucks läßt sich nicht beweisen; man muß sie fühlen." — Wohl, —— aber was geschieht nun weiter mit diesem Erkennen der Echtheit? Wenn Einer sagt "Voilà ce que peut dire un cœur vraiment épris" — und wenn er auch einen Andern zu seiner Ansicht brächte, — welche weiteren Folgen hat es? Oder hat es keine, und *endet* das Spiel damit, daß dem Einen schmeckt, was dem Andern nicht schmeckt?

Es gibt wohl *Folgen*, aber sie sind diffuser Art. Erfahrung, also mannigfaltige Beobachtung, kann sie lehren; und man kann sie auch nicht allgemein formulieren, sondern nur in verstreuten Fällen ein richtiges, fruchtbares, Urteil fällen, eine fruchtbare Verbindung feststellen. Und

351. There is such a thing as colour-blindness, and there are ways of ascertaining it. There is, in general, complete agreement in the colour statements of those who have been diagnosed normal. This characterizes the concept of a colour statement.

352. There is in general no such agreement over the question of whether an expression of feeling is genuine or not.

353. I am sure, *sure*, that he is not pretending; but some third person is not. Can I always convince him? And if not, is there some mistake in his reasoning or observations?

354. "You don't understand a thing!" — this is what one says when someone doubts what we recognize as clearly genuine — but we cannot prove anything.

355. Is there such a thing as 'expert judgement' about the genuineness of expressions of feeling? — Here too, there are those with 'better' and those with 'worse' judgement.
   In general, predictions arising from judgements of those with better knowledge of people will be more correct.
   Can one learn this knowledge? Yes; some can learn it. Not, however, by taking a course of study in it, but through '*experience*'. — Can someone else be a man's teacher in this? Certainly. From time to time he gives him the right *tip*. —— This is what 'learning' and 'teaching' are like here. —— What one acquires here is not a technique; one learns correct judgements. There are also rules, but they do not form a system, and only experienced people can apply them rightly. Unlike calculating rules.

356. What is most difficult here is to express this indefiniteness correctly, and without distortion. |228|

357. "The genuineness of an expression cannot be proved; one has to feel it." — Very well —— but now, what happens further with this recognition of genuineness? If someone says "Voilà ce que peut dire un coeur vraiment épris" — and if he also brings someone else to the same view — what are the further consequences? Or are there none, and does the game *end* with its being to the taste of one but not of the other?
   There are certainly *consequences*, but of a diffuse kind. Experience — that is to say, varied observation — can inform us of them; and one can't formulate them in general terms; rather, only occasionally can one arrive at a correct and fruitful judgement, discover a fruitful connection.

die allgemeinsten Bemerkungen ergeben höchstens, was wie die Trümmer eines Systems aussieht.

358. Man kann wohl durch die Evidenz davon überzeugt werden, daß Einer sich in dem und dem Seelenzustand befinde, daß er z. B. sich nicht verstelle. Aber es gibt hier auch 'unwägbare' Evidenz.

359. Die Frage ist: Was *leistet* die unwägbare Evidenz?
Denk, es gäbe unwägbare Evidenz für die chemische Struktur (das Innere) eines Stoffes, so müßte sie sich doch nun durch gewisse *wägbare* Folgen als Evidenz erweisen.
(Unwägbare Evidenz könnte Einen davon überzeugen, dies Bild sei ein echter . . . Aber dies *kann* sich auch dokumentarisch als richtig erweisen.)

360. Zur unwägbaren Evidenz gehören die Feinheiten des Blicks, der Gebärde, des Tons.
Ich mag den echten Blick der Liebe erkennen, ihn vom verstellten unterscheiden (und natürlich kann es hier eine 'wägbare' Bekräftigung meines Urteils geben). Aber ich mag gänzlich unfähig sein, den Unterschied zu beschreiben. Und das nicht darum, weil die mir bekannten Sprachen dafür keine Wörter haben. Warum führe ich denn nicht einfach neue Wörter ein? —— Wäre ich ein höchst talentierter Maler, so wäre es denkbar, daß ich in Bildern den echten Blick und den geheuchelten darstellte.

361. Frag dich: Wie lernt der Mensch einen 'Blick' für etwas kriegen? Und wie läßt sich ein solcher Blick verwenden?

362. Verstellung ist natürlich nur ein besonderer Fall davon, daß Einer, z. B., eine Schmerzäußerung von sich gibt und nicht Schmerzen hat. Wenn dies überhaupt möglich ist, warum sollte denn dabei immer Verstellung statthaben, — dieses sehr spezielle Muster auf dem Band des Lebens?

363. Ein Kind muß viel lernen, ehe es sich verstellen kann. (Ein Hund kann nicht heucheln, aber er kann auch nicht aufrichtig sein.)

364. Ja es könnte ein Fall eintreten, in welchem wir sagen würden: "Dieser *glaubt*, sich zu verstellen."

And the most general remarks yield at best what look like fragments of a system.

358. One can indeed be convinced by the evidence that someone is in such-and-such a state of mind: that, for instance, he is not pretending. But there is also 'imponderable' evidence here.

359. The question is: what does imponderable evidence *accomplish*?

Suppose there were imponderable evidence for the chemical (internal) structure of a substance; still, it would have to prove itself to be evidence by certain consequences which *are* ponderable.

(Imponderable evidence might convince someone that a picture was a genuine . . . But this *may* be proved right by documentation as well.)

360. Imponderable evidence includes subtleties of glance, of gesture, of tone.

I may recognize a genuine loving look, distinguish it from a pretended one (and here there can, of course, be a 'ponderable' confirmation of my judgement). But I may be quite incapable of describing the difference. And this not because the languages I know have no words for it. Why don't I simply introduce new words? —— If I were a very talented painter, I might conceivably represent the genuine and the dissembled glance in pictures.

361. Ask yourself: How does a man learn to get an 'eye' for something? And how can this eye be used?

* 362. Pretending to be in pain, for example, is, of course, only a special case of someone producing expressions of pain without being in pain. If this is possible |229| at all, why should it always be pretending that is taking place — this very special pattern in the weave of our lives?

363. A child has much to learn before it can pretend. (A dog can't be a hypocrite, but neither can it be sincere.)

364. There might actually occur a case where we'd say: "This person *believes* he is pretending." |230|

365. Wenn die Begriffsbildung sich aus Naturtatsachen erklären läßt, sollte uns dann nicht, statt der Grammatik, dasjenige interessieren, was ihr in der Natur zu Grunde liegt? —— Uns interessiert wohl auch die Entsprechung von Begriffen mit sehr allgemeinen Naturtatsachen. (Solchen, die uns ihrer Allgemeinheit wegen meist nicht auffallen.) Aber unser Interesse fällt nun nicht auf diese möglichen Ursachen der Begriffsbildung zurück; wir betreiben nicht Naturwissenschaft; auch nicht Naturgeschichte, — da wir ja Naturgeschichtliches für unsere Zwecke auch erdichten können.

366. Ich sage nicht: Wären die und die Naturtatsachen anders, so hätten die Menschen andere Begriffe (im Sinne einer Hypothese). Sondern: Wer glaubt, gewisse Begriffe seien schlechtweg die richtigen, wer andere hätte, sähe eben etwas nicht ein, was wir einsehen, — der möge sich gewisse sehr allgemeine Naturtatsachen anders vorstellen, als wir sie gewohnt sind, und andere Begriffsbildungen als die gewohnten werden ihm verständlich werden.

367. Vergleiche einen Begriff mit einer Malweise: Ist denn auch nur unsere Malweise willkürlich? Können wir nach Belieben eine wählen? (Z. B. die der Ägypter.) Oder handelt sich's da nur um hübsch und häßlich?

365. If concept formation can be explained by facts of nature, shouldn't we be interested, not in grammar, but rather in what is its basis in nature? —— We are, indeed, also interested in the correspondence between concepts and very general facts of nature. (Such facts as mostly do not strike us because of their generality.) But our interest is not thereby thrown back on to these possible causes of concept formation; we are not doing natural science; nor yet natural history — since we can also invent fictitious natural history for our purposes.

366. I am not saying: if such-and-such facts of nature were different, people would have different concepts (in the sense of a hypothesis). Rather: if anyone believes that certain concepts are absolutely the correct ones, and that having different ones would mean not realizing something that we realize — then let him imagine certain very general facts of nature to be different from what we are used to, and the formation of concepts different from the usual ones will become intelligible to him.

367. Compare a concept with a style of painting. For is even our style of painting arbitrary? Can we choose one at pleasure? (The Egyptian, for instance.) Or is it just a matter of pretty and ugly? |231|

368. Wenn ich sage "Vor einer halben Stunde war er da" — nämlich aus der Erinnerung — so ist das nicht die Beschreibung eines gegenwärtigen Erlebnisses.

Erinnerungs*erlebnisse* sind Begleiterscheinungen des Erinnerns.

369. Erinnern hat keinen Erlebnisinhalt. —— Ist das nicht doch durch Introspektion zu erkennen? Zeigt *sie* nicht eben, daß nichts da ist, wenn ich nach einem Inhalt ausschaue? —— Das könnte sie doch nur von Fall zu Fall zeigen. Und sie kann mir doch nicht zeigen, was das Wort "erinnern" bedeutet, *wo* also nach einem Inhalt zu suchen wäre!

Die *Idee* von einem Inhalt des Erinnerns erhalte ich nur durch ein Vergleichen der psychologischen Begriffe. Es ist ähnlich dem Vergleichen zweier *Spiele*. (Fußball hat *Tore*, Völkerball nicht.)

370. Könnte man sich diese Situation denken: Einer erinnert sich zum erstenmal im Leben an etwas und sagt: "Ja, jetzt weiß ich, was 'Erinnern' ist, wie erinnern *tut*." — Wie weiß er, daß dies Gefühl 'Erinnern' ist? Vergleiche: "Ja, jetzt weiß ich, was 'bremseln' ist!" (er hat etwa zum erstenmal einen elektrischen Schlag gekriegt). —— Weiß er, daß es Erinnern ist, weil es durch Vergangenes hervorgerufen wurde? Und wie weiß er, was Vergangenes ist? Den Begriff des Vergangenen lernt ja der Mensch, indem er sich erinnert.

Und wie wird er in Zukunft wieder wissen, wie Erinnern tut?

(Dagegen könnte man vielleicht von einem Gefühl "Lang, lang ist's her" reden, denn es gibt einen Ton, eine Gebärde, die gewissen Erzählungen aus vergangenen Tagen angehören.)

368. When, on the basis of memory, I say: "He was here half an hour ago" — this is not the description of a present experience.

Memory *experiences* are accompaniments of remembering.

369. Remembering has no experiential content. —— Surely this can be seen by introspection! Doesn't *it* show precisely that there is nothing there, when I look out for a content? —— But it could only show this from case to case. And even so, it cannot show me what the word "remember" means, and hence *where* to look for a content!

I get the *idea* of a memory content only through comparing psycho-logical concepts. It is like comparing two *games*. (Soccer has *goals*, volleyball doesn't.)

370. Would this situation be conceivable: for the first time in his life someone remembers something and says: "Yes, now I know what 'remembering' is, what it *feels like* to remember". — How does he know that this feeling is 'remembering'? Compare: "Yes, now I know what 'tingling' is" (he has perhaps had an electric shock for the first time). —— Does he know that it is memory because it is caused by something past? And how does he know what the past is? After all, a person learns the concept of the past by remembering.

And how will he know again in the future what remembering feels like?

(On the other hand, one might, perhaps, speak of a feeling "Long, long ago", for there is a tone, a gesture, which go with certain tales of past times.) |232|

371. Die Verwirrung und Öde der Psychologie ist nicht damit zu erklären, daß sie eine "junge Wissenschaft" sei; ihr Zustand ist mit dem
der Physik z. B. in ihrer Frühzeit nicht zu vergleichen. (Eher noch mit
dem gewisser Zweige der Mathematik. Mengenlehre.) Es bestehen
nämlich, in der Psychologie, experimentelle Methoden *und Begriffsverwirrung*. (Wie im andern Fall Begriffsverwirrung und Beweismethoden.)
    Das Bestehen der experimentellen Methode läßt uns glauben, wir hät-
ten das Mittel, die Probleme, die uns beunruhigen, loszuwerden; obgleich Problem und Methode windschief aneinander vorbei laufen.

372. Es ist für die Mathematik eine Untersuchung möglich ganz analog unsrer Untersuchung der Psychologie. Sie ist ebensowenig eine
mathematische, wie die andere eine psychologische. In ihr wird *nicht*
gerechnet, sie ist also, z. B., nicht Logistik. Sie könnte den Namen einer
Untersuchung der 'Grundlagen der Mathematik' verdienen.

371. The confusion and barrenness of psychology is not to be explained by its being a "young science"; its state is not comparable with that of physics, for instance, in its beginnings. (Rather, with that of certain branches of mathematics. Set theory.) For in psychology, there are experimental methods *and conceptual confusion*. (As in the other case, conceptual confusion and methods of proof.)

The existence of the experimental method makes us think that we have the means of getting rid of the problems which trouble us; but problem and method pass one another by.

372. An investigation entirely analogous to our investigation of psychology is possible also for mathematics. It is just as little a *mathematical* investigation as ours is a psychological one. It will *not* contain calculations, so it is not, for example, formal logic. It might deserve the name of an investigation of the 'foundations of mathematics'.

Endnotes

Philosophical Investigations

§1(a) n. 1 We have translated from Wittgenstein's German, not from Augustine's Latin text.

§1(d) 'Von einer solchen war hier gar nicht die Rede': Anscombe's very free translation can be justified in the light of Wittgenstein's modifications of Rhees's translation (TS 226). He changed the original translation 'There was no question of any here; only . . .' to read: 'There was no question of such an entity "meaning" here, only . . .' thus making it clear *what* conception of meaning is under attack here. This is an authorial modification rather than a translation of the text, but its spirit is captured by Anscombe's rendering.

§11(b) 'hear them in speech, or see them written or in print': this translation is based on Wittgenstein's corrections to TS 226.

§16(c) Double-bracketed sentences are notes for the author to insert or consider inserting specific remarks from his notebooks or a new observation. Here, the double-bracketed note may be a reference to MS 124, 60 (cp. *Lectures on the Foundations of Mathematics* (Harvester Press, Sussex, 1976), Lecture XXI, p. 208); see also MS 107, 226f. (cf. *Philosophical Remarks* (Blackwell, Oxford, 1975), pp. 207f.), which is comparable to *Zettel* (Blackwell, Oxford, 1967), §691.

§19(a) 'Und unzähliges Andere' is unclear. Wittgenstein altered Rhees's translation (TS 226, §22 (p. 10)), from 'And countless others' to 'And countless other things'. We have followed his translation.

§20(a) The translation of the penultimate line of this paragraph is based on Wittgenstein's alterations to Rhees's translation.

§20(b) The rather free rendering of the concluding German sentence of this paragraph is based on Wittgenstein's modification to Rhees's translation.

§22(a) Frege used the word *Annahme* ('assumption') to signify the content of a possible assertion (see 'Function and Concept', repr. in his *Collected Papers on Mathematics, Logic, and Philosophy* (Blackwell, Oxford, 1984), p. 149; pp. 21f. in the original German pagination).

§22(d) Frege's assertion sign is the 'turnstile', |—, which is composed of the sign of assertion or judgement-stroke '|', and the content-stroke or horizontal '—', which is a function sign denoting a function from objects (including contents of possible judgements (assertions) or thoughts) to truth-values. See *The Basic Laws of Arithmetic*, vol. i (1893), §5 (cp. *Begriffschrift* (1879) (*Conceptual Notation and Related Articles* (Clarendon Press, Oxford, 1972)), §2).

Boxed remark between §22 and §23 has been relocated from the bottom of p. 11 in the first two editions. Immediately derived from TS 228, §432, it was inserted into TS 227(a) and (b) as handwritten slips in another hand, with the note 'Insertion at the end of §22'. In TS 227(b) this note was deleted, apparently in yet another hand. It is possible that this paragraph was intended as paragraph (e) of §22.

§25 Wittgenstein corrected Rhees's translation 'Commanding, asking, recounting' to 'Giving orders, asking questions, describing', and we have followed his correction, while translating *erzählen* by 'telling stories', rather than 'describing'.

Boxed remark between §28 and §29 has been relocated from the bottom of p. 14 in the first two editions. These two paragraphs are cut from TS 228, §522, and inserted between pp. 24 and 25 of the final typescript. In both copies of TS 227, the inserted slip has written on it the words 'Insertion at end of §28'.

Boxed remark between §35 and §36, paragraph (b): square brackets are used to indicate Wittgenstein's handwritten addendum on the slip of paper, cut from TS 228, §36, and inserted between pp. 30 and 31 of TS 227(a).

§38(a) 'the word "this" has been called the *real* name': a reference to Russell; see, e.g., *Theory of Knowledge — The 1913 Manuscript*, in *The*

Collected Papers of Bertrand Russell, vol. 7, ed. E. R. Eames in col-
laboration with K. Blackwell (Allen and Unwin, London, 1984), pp. 39f.,
and even more emphatically in 'The Philosophy of Logical Atomism',
repr. in *The Philosophy of Logical Atomism and Other Essays 1914–
1919*, ed. J. G. Slater, in *The Collected Papers of Bertrand Russell*, vol.
8 (Allen and Unwin, London, 1986), p. 170.

§39 Wittgenstein used the name 'Nothung', which is the name of
Siegfried's sword in Wagner's *Ring*, which was shattered. In TS 226, §46
(p. 27), Wittgenstein replaced the first occurrence of 'Nothung' by
'Escaliber' [*sic*], but not the subsequent occurrences — perhaps because
it then occurred to him that Excalibur was not shattered and reassem-
bled, and was therefore less apt to illustrate the point.

§46(b) 'Socrates says in the *Theaetetus*': see Plato, *Theaetetus* 201e–202b.
   The quotation from the *Theaetetus* is translated from Preisendanz's
German translation (Diederichs, Jena, 1925), which Wittgenstein used,
rather than from the original Greek. Note that Wittgenstein takes
Erklärung and *erklärungsweise* to mean description and descriptive language — as is evident in the first sentence of §49. F. M. Cornford's English
translation of the *Theaetetus* uses the phrase 'no account can be given
of them' where Preisendanz used 'gebe es keine Erklärung'; and where
Preisendanz had 'so seien auch seine Benennungen in dieser
Verflechtung zur erklärenden Rede geworden; denn deren Wesen sei die
Verflechtung von Namen', Cornford translated 'so the names are combined to make a description, a description being precisely a combination of names'.

§46(c) Russell's 'individuals': e.g. Russell, *Principia Mathematica*,
Introduction to 2nd edn (Cambridge University Press, Cambridge,
1927), II, 1, and his *Introduction to Mathematical Philosophy* (Allen
and Unwin, London, 1919), ch. 13.
   'and my "objects"': see *Tractatus Logico-Philosophicus* 2.01–2.032.

§47(b) Wittgenstein illustrated what he meant by 'an open curve composed of straight bits' in Rhees's translation (TS 226, §54 (p.32)),

namely: , by contrast with a continuous curve, namely .

§49(b) 'That was what Frege meant too, when he said that a word
has a meaning only in the context of a sentence': see Frege, *The*

Foundations of Arithmetic, tr. J. L. Austin, 2nd edn (Blackwell, Oxford, 1959), p. x, §§46, 60, 62, 106.

§51(b) Anscombe translated this as 'we must focus on the details of what goes on; must look at them *from close to*'. Our rendering is based on Wittgenstein's alteration to Rhees's translation (TS 226, §60 (p. 38)).

§54(b) 'aus der Praxis des Spiels': in TS 226, §62 (p. 40), Wittgenstein deleted Rhees's translation 'from the practice of the game' and replaced it with 'from the way the game is played'.

§65(a) 'Was allen diesen Vorgängen gemeinsam ist': Rhees translated *Vorgängen* as 'processes', which Wittgenstein corrected to 'procedures' (TS 226, §72 (p. 47)). Although it is natural to use the German *Vorgang* for any 'goings-on', it is unnatural to use either 'process' or 'procedure' for linguistic activities. So we have retained Anscombe's translation, but, for consistency's sake changed the word 'proceedings' in the opening sentence of §66(a) to 'activities'.

§66(a) 'singing and dancing games': this is Wittgenstein's preferred version in TS 226, §73 (p. 48).

Boxed remark between §70 and §71: in TS 227(b) this slip, cut from TS 228, §545, was inserted between pp. 59 and 60, together with the inscription 'On page 60'.

§71(b) 'Frege compares a concept to . . .': Wittgenstein is referring to *The Basic Laws of Arithmetic*, vol. ii (1903), §56. The German text runs as follows:

> Wenn man sich Begriffe ihrem Umfange nach durch Bezirke in der Ebene versinnlicht, so ist das freilich ein Gleichnis, das nur mit Vorsicht gebraucht werden darf, hier aber gute Dienste leisten kann. Einem unscharf begrenzten Begriffe würde ein Bezirk entsprechen, der nicht überall eine scharfe Grenzlinie hätte, sondern stellenweise ganz verschwimmend in die Umgebung überginge. Das wäre eigentlich gar kein Bezirk; und so wird ein unscharf definierter Begriff mit Unrecht Begriff genannt.

P. T. Geach, in Peter Geach and Max Black, eds, *Translations from the Writings of Gottlob Frege* (Blackwell, Oxford, 1960), p. 159, translated this as follows:

If we represent concepts in extension by areas on a plane, this is admittedly a picture that may be used only with caution, but here it can do us good service. To a concept without sharp boundary there would correspond an area that had not a sharp boundary-line all round, but in places just faded away into the background. This would not really be an area at all; and likewise a concept that is not sharply defined is wrongly termed a concept.

However, *Bezirk* means not 'area', but 'region', as in 'an administrative region marked on a map'.

§79(b) 'The German original runs:

'Unter "Moses" verstehe ich den Mann, der getan hat, was die Bibel von Moses berichtet, oder doch vieles davon. Aber wievieles? Habe ich mich entschieden, wieviel sich als falsch erweisen muß, damit ich meinen Satz als falsch aufgebe? Hat also der Name "Moses" für mich einen festen und eindeutig bestimmten Gebrauch in allen möglichen Fällen?'

Anscombe translated this as follows:

By "Moses" I understand the man who did what the Bible relates of Moses, or at any rate a good deal of it. But how much? Have I decided how much must be proved false for me to give up my proposition as false? Has the name "Moses" got a fixed and unequivocal use for me in all possible cases?

However Wittgenstein corrected Rhees's translation (TS 226, §86 (pp. 55–6)) thus:

by "Moses" I ~~understand~~ <<mean>> the man who did what the Bible records of Moses, or at any rate ~~a lot~~ <<much>> of it. But how much? Have I ~~come to any~~ deci[sion |ded] ~~as to~~ how much <<of it>> must ~~be shown~~ <<turn out>> to be false in order that I should ~~abandon~~ <<give up>> my ~~proposition~~ <<statement>> ~~as false~~? <<So>> ~~Has~~ <<is my use of>> the name "Moses" ~~for me~~ <<them>> ~~a~~ fixed and ~~clearly~~ <<unambiguously>> determined ~~use in~~ <<for>> all possible cases?

We have been guided by Wittgenstein's modifications to Rhees's translation.

§81 'F. P. Ramsey once emphasized in conversation with me that logic was a "normative science".' I. A. Richards remarked in *Scrutiny* I, 408 (1933) that 'a definition given by Charles Sanders Peirce . . . was a

favourite quotation of the late F. P. Ramsey: "Logic is the Ethics of thinking, in the sense in which Ethics is the bringing to bear of self-control
for the purposes of realizing our desires." '

§82 'was er unter "N" verstehe': Anscombe translated correctly 'What
he understood by "N"', but we have opted for 'What he meant by "N"'
in order to preserve continuity with Wittgenstein's preferred translation
of §79(b), line 3.

§85 'Also kann ich sagen, der Wegweiser lässt doch keinen // einen //
Zweifel offen': in TS 227(a) Wittgenstein deleted the *k* in *keinen* — which
makes much better sense. Hence we have changed the German text and
Anscombe's 'the signpost does after all leave no room for doubt' to 'the
signpost does after all leave room for doubt'.

§86(c) Anscombe translated the last sentence 'Und sind es die andern
Tabellen ohne ihr Schema?' as 'And are other tables incomplete without their schemata?'. But in TS 226, Wittgenstein added here the parenthesis 'are the other (abnormal) tables . . .', making it clear that he is
referring to the examples of abnormal schemata just discussed — hence
the addition of the definite article.

§88(b) 'colour edge': where two different coloured regions meet.

§89(a) 'Is logic in some way sublime' was Wittgenstein's preferred
translation (TS 226, §97 (p. 63)).

§89(b) 'Sie liege, so schien es, am Grunde aller Wissenschaften':
Wittgenstein preferred 'foundation' to 'basis'.
    'Denn die logische Betrachtung erforscht das Wesen aller Dinge':
Anscombe translated 'For logical investigation explores the nature of
all things.' Rhees translated *Wesen* as 'essence', which Wittgenstein
accepted. The matter is non-trivial. *Wesen* can do service both for 'essence'
and for 'nature'. Here, the conception of logical investigation under discussion is that which conceives of it as exploring the *essence* of all things.
See note on §92 below.

§89(c) Augustine: 'What, then, is time? I know well enough what it is,
provided that nobody asks me; but if I am asked what it is and try to
explain, I am baffled.' *Confessions* (Penguin Books, Harmondsworth,
1961), Bk. XI, §14 (tr. R. S. Pine-Coffin).

'ist etwas, worauf man sich *besinnen* muss': Anscombe had here 'is something that we need to *remind* ourselves of'. Wittgenstein changed a similar translation by Rhees (TS 226, §97 (p. 64)), substituting for 'remind' and 'recollect' the phrase 'call to mind'. We have followed this.

§90(a) Anscombe translated 'Erscheinungen *durchschauen*' as '*penetrate* phenomena'. We have opted for 'see right into' in order to conform to Wittgenstein's preferred translation of *durchschauen* in §92(a) (see end-note below).

'call to mind' (rather than 'remind ourselves') was Wittgenstein's pre-ferred translation of *besinnen* and *besinnt* (TS 226, §98 (pp. 64)).

§92(a) and (b) The fluidity of the German term *Wesen* is evident in this remark, making it singularly difficult to translate. For Wittgenstein is deliberately playing on the ambiguity of the German term. He himself changed Rhees's translation of *Wesen* as 'essence' to 'nature' in the first two occurrences, but left it in the third. In the fourth occurrence in para-graph (b) Wittgenstein first changed Rhees's 'The essence is hidden from us' to 'The nature is hidden to us'. He then wrote an alternative draft to this above it: namely, 'The essence is what's hidden'. We have not followed all his changes, which we suspect were precipitate and not fully thought through.

We have chosen to retain 'essence' in the first occurrence, since the conception being subjected to critical scrutiny is that according to which the essence of things is to be revealed by depth analysis. The sec-ond sentence of (a) concedes that we *are* trying to understand the *nature* of language. The concept of a language being, in Wittgenstein's view, a family-resemblance concept, language has no *essence*, i.e. defining char-acteristic marks (*Merkmale*); but it does not follow that it doesn't have a *nature* — just as propositions or numbers have a specifiable nature but no essence. In the third occurrence, 'essence' is the appropriate trans-lation, since what is again under discussion is the putative hidden essence that is to be dug out by analysis, and is not to be found by a surveyable ordering of familiar grammatical features of the uses of expressions. We have retained 'essence' for the fourth and final occurrence in paragraph (b), since the idea that the *Wesen* of language or of a proposition is hidden belongs to the conception that Wittgenstein is now criticizing, and is to be contrasted with the conception of the nature of language or proposition as being in full view, and to be rendered surveyable by an ordering of familiar features of usage.

§92(a) 'durch Ordnen *übersichtlich* wird': Anscombe had 'becomes sur-veyable by a rearrangement'. For *Ordnen* Wittgenstein had 'a process of ordering' (TS 226, §100 (p. 64)). We have followed this.

'was wir sehen, wenn wir die Sache durschauen': Anscombe had 'which we see when we look *into* the thing'. Wittgenstein corrected Rhees's trans-lation 'which we see when we look through the thing' to 'which we see when we see *into* the thing'.

§94 'die Sublimierung / sublimieren': Anscombe translated this as 'the subliming' and 'to sublime', but what Wittgenstein has employed here is a chemical trope: namely, 'the sublimation' and 'to sublimate'.

'der ganzen Darstellung': strictly speaking, this means 'of the whole (re)presentation', but Anscombe's translation: 'our whole account of logic' is a variant on Wittgenstein's changes to Rhees's translation (TS 226, §104 (p. 67)).

'ein reines Mittelwesen anzunehmen zwischen dem Satz*zeichen* und den Tatsachen': Wittgenstein changed Rhees's translation to read 'The tendency to assume a pure (immaterial) entity mediating between the propositional *sign* and the facts'.

§95 Unlike Anscombe, Rhees translated *Denken* as 'Thinking' (TS 226, §105 (p. 67)), which Wittgenstein retained. We have followed this translation.

§97 Rhees again translated *Das Denken* as 'Thinking' (TS 226, §107 (p. 68)), consistently with his translation of §95. Wittgenstein wrote 'Thought' above, but subsequently deleted this alteration, leaving Rhees's translation intact.

§98 'every sentence in our language "is in order as it is"': a reference to *Tractatus* 5.5563 — 'In fact, all the propositions of our everyday lan-guage, just as they stand, are in perfect logical order.'

§100 'vollkommenes': Anscombe, following Rhees (TS 226, §111 (p. 70)), translated this as 'perfect', but in the 3rd edition changed it to 'complete'. We have retained 'perfect' (which Wittgenstein did not delete in TS 226), since completeness is not at issue, and 'vollkommene Sprache' and 'voll-kommene Ordnung' were translated as 'perfect language' and 'perfect order' in §98 by both Rhees (with Wittgenstein's approval) and Anscombe.

'die Rolle, die das Ideal in unsrer Ausdrucksweise spielt': *Ausdrucks-weise*, strictly speaking, means 'mode of expression' or 'speech', but

Wittgenstein tentatively corrected this to 'language' in Rhees's translation (TS 226, §111 (p. 70)), and, like Anscombe, we have followed him.

Boxed remark between §104 and §105: its location is indicated by an asterisk after the first sentence of §104 and associated asterisk in a note in another's hand in TS 227(b). The reference is to M. Faraday, *The Chemical History of a Candle* (Hutchinson, London, 1907), p. 44.

Boxed remark between §108 and §109: printed in the first two editions as paragraphs (b)–(d) of §108, these three remarks (and the marginal note printed in square brackets) are from a handwritten note on a slip of paper, inserted between pp. 82 and 83 of TSS 227(a). Their proximate source is TS 228, §503. There is no clear indication as to where exactly to place it.

§109 'It was correct that our considerations must not be scientific ones': an allusion to *Tractatus* 4.111: 'Philosophy is not one of the natural sciences. (The word "philosophy" must mean something whose place is above or below the natural sciences, not beside them.)'
    'The feeling "that it is possible, contrary to our preconceived ideas, to think this or that" . . . could be of no interest to us': perhaps an allusion to Frank Ramsey's remark 'but it just *is* possible to think of such a thing' (MS 116, 51); see also MS 152, 93–5; *Philosophical Remarks* 304 (= MS 105, 23); *Zettel*, §272.

§122 'Übersicht', 'übersehbar', 'Übersichlichkeit', 'übersichtliche Darstellung': we have tried to preserve the reference to *view* and *survey* in translating *Übersicht* and its cognates, hence 'overview', 'surveyability', 'surveyable', and 'surveyable representation' as opposed to Anscombe's 'perspicuous representation'.

§124(d) 'A "leading problem of mathematical logic" ': Wittgenstein associated this phrase with Frank Ramsey (see MS 110, 189; *The Big Typescript* (Blackwell, Oxford, 2004), pp. 417f.; MS 115, 71).

§127 *Erinnerungen* can mean 'reminder', but in this context it signifies things remembered — not something that will *remind* one of the things one has learnt and knows full well, but those very things themselves. *The Big Typescript*, p. 419 (cp. MS 115, 164), just after a draft of an early version of *Investigations* §128 and before one of §129 has the remark 'Learning philosophy is *really* recollecting. We remember that we really

used words in this way.' Cf. MS 110, 131f., where he associates this with Socrates.

Boxed remark between §133 and §134: in previous editions, this was printed as paragraph (d) of §133. But it is in fact a slip cut from TS 228, §140, inserted on p. 91 of TS 227 with the editorial inscription 'p. 91 Footnote' in TS 227(a) and 'Note to p. 91' in TS 227(b).

§134 'Satz': this remark exemplifies all the problems that arise in translating the German *Satz* (see 'Editorial Preface', p. xiv). Although we have replaced most of Anscombe's uses of 'proposition' here by 'sentence', we have not done so in the cases of 'general propositional form', 'propositional schema', 'propositional variable' and 'our concept of a proposition', especially in view of the sequel in §§135–6.

Boxed remark between §138 and §139: this is the content of one of four slips inserted at this point in TS 227. A handwritten note in the margin makes it clear that the boxed remark is connected with §138. Originally, the printed remark was preceded by another version of PI §500 and followed by what are now the boxed remarks between §549 and §550. Presumably the lost copy of TS 227 contained instructions to the effect that only the present remark was to be printed at this point. The proximate source of this remark is TS 228, §82.

Boxed remarks between §139 and §140: these two remarks were written on a separate sheet of paper inserted between pp. 95 and 96 of the TS. The proximate source of (a) is TS 228, §363; that of (b) is TS 228, §335.

Boxed remark between §142 and §143: inserted on a slip of paper marked 'p. 99' between pp. 98 and 99 of TS 227(a), with a marginal handwritten note on the left of §142 reading 'Footnote: Slip attached'. The proximate source is TS 228, §357.

§144 'Indian mathematicians: "Look at this!" ': *Zettel*, §461, and MS 142, §146 (corrected numeration; §144 in Wittgenstein's numeration) clarify: 'I read somewhere that Indian mathematicians are (sometimes) content to use a geometrical figure accompanied by the words "Look at this!" as a proof of a theorem. This looking too effects an alteration in one's way of seeing (*Anschauungsweise*).' Cf. MS 161, 6; MS 110, 152.

Boxed remarks between §149 and §150: in TS 227(a) this pair of
remarks, typed on separate slips of paper, was inserted between pp. 103
and 104. In TS 227(b) the remarks are inserted between pp. 102 and
103. Their proximate sources are TS 228, §79 and §86.

Boxed remark between §165 and §166: in TS 227(a) this remark occurs
between pp. 115 and 116. The first paragraph is a handwritten addition above the typed paragraph (b). Paragraph (b) was cut from TS 228,
§395.

§169 The sequence of typographical symbols that were typed into TS
227 (and hence printed in earlier editions) were evidently a substitute
for a series of arbitrary squiggles, as in *Eine Philosophische Betrachtung* (Suhrkamp, Frankfurt, 1970), p. 182. We have accordingly reproduced those.

§226(a) 'working out the series $2x - 1$': Wittgenstein wrote '$x^2 + 1$',
which is a slip. Anscombe changed this to read '$2x + 1$', but the correct formula for this series is '$2x - 1$'.

§228 'A series presents us with *one* face . . . read the lips of a rule . . .':
Anscombe clearly disliked Wittgenstein's metaphor of the facial physiognomy of a rule of a series and accordingly suppressed it. This is unwar-
ranted, and we have restored it. This conceit links up with his
subsequent discussion of the physiognomy of word meaning (§568; see
also PPF §§38, 238, 294).

§§272–4 'Rotempfindung', 'Empfindung von Rot', 'die eigene Empfindung': Anscombe translated these words by the phrase 'sensation
of red' and 'the private sensation' (§274). However, there is no such
thing as a *sensation* of red (that is, no use of 'sensation' in 'sensation
of red' that is analogous to its use in 'sensation of pain'). The German
Empfindung is more pliable than the English 'sensation', although
even it is being stretched here. The sense of the passages is better conveyed by 'impression of red', which is suggested by Wittgenstein's use
of *Farbeindruck* ('colour impression') in §275 and §276, and both
Farbeindruck and *visueller Eindruck* ('visual impression') in §277.

§273 The quoted phrase 'uns Allen Gegenüberstehendes' is taken from
Frege's discussion of colour predicates in *The Basic Laws of Arithmetic*,
vol. i, preface, p. xviii.

§312 'Gesichtsempfindung' / 'Schmerzempfindung': as noted above, 'Empfindung' is more accommodating than 'sensation', but Gesichtsempfindung is stretching things to the limits, and perhaps beyond. We have opted for 'sensation of pain' / 'visual impression' for the sake of clarity, since there are no such things as visual sensations (save for sensations of glare).

§336 'A French politician . . .': MS 109, 177, suggests that the politician was Briand.

§339(a) 'the Devil took the shadow of Schlemihl from the ground': see Adelbert von Chamisso's tale Peter Schlemihls wundersame Geschichte. English-speaking readers will be more familiar with the similar conceit in James Barry's Peter Pan.

§339(b) 'numerals are actual, and numbers are non-actual, objects': a reference to Frege's Basic Laws of Arithmetic, vol. i, Introduction, p. xviii, where he argues that numerals are actual objects, whereas numbers are objective but not actual objects.

§342 William James's discussion of Ballard's reminiscences occurs in The Principles of Psychology (Holt, New York, 1890), vol. i, p. 266.

§351 'I can reply: "These words . . ." ': we have added the quotation marks here to match the previous quoted sentence.

§365 'Do Adelheid and the Bishop . . .': a reference to Goethe's Götz von Berlichingen, Act II, scene 1, in which the scene opens towards the end of a game of chess between Adelheid and the Bishop.

§370 'Frage nach dem Wesen der Vorstellung': Anscombe translated this, perfectly correctly, as 'the question as to the nature of the imagination' (for Wittgenstein is not claiming that 'the imagination' is defined by a set of necessary and sufficient conditions). But the price was to lose contact with the next remark (§371): 'Das Wesen is in der Grammatik ausgesprochen', which she translated as 'Essence is expressed by grammar'. To keep the continuity between §370 and §371, we have translated 'Frage nach dem Wesen der Vorstellung' in §370 as 'question of what imagination essentially is'.

§371 We have retained 'Essence' for Wesen, since one could hardly say 'Nature is expressed in grammar'. But it must be borne in mind that

Wesen does service for both 'essence' and 'nature' — thus leaving the question of whether the concept of the imagination is a family-resemblance concept wide open (see note to §92 above).

§373 '(Theology as grammar)': an allusion to a remark Wittgenstein attributed to Luther, who, he says, wrote somewhere that theology is the grammar of the word 'God'; see Alice Ambrose, ed., *Wittgenstein's Lectures, Cambridge, 1932–1935* (Blackwell, Oxford, 1979), p. 32, and 'Movements of Thought: Diaries 1930–1932, 1936–1937', repr. in translation in James C. Klagge and Alfred Nordmann, eds, *Ludwig Wittgenstein — Public and Private Occasions* (Rowman & Littlefield Publishers Inc., Lanham, Md., 2003), p. 211 (under 23 Feb. 1937).

§400 'und man könnte auch sagen, eine neue Empfindung: to repeat, *Empfindung* has a far broader extension than 'sensation'. Anscombe translated this as 'it might even be called a new sensation'. But this makes no sense. For what the proponent of 'the world as representation' has 'discovered' is a new way of conceiving, characterizing, his *experience of reality* (cf. §401). So we have opted for 'experience', rather than 'sensation' (cf. MS 120, 46v–47r, where 'neue Empfindung' and 'neue Erfahrung' appear to be used interchangeably in this context).

§402(a) "Ich sage zwar 'Ich habe jetzt die und die Vorstellung'": Anscombe translated this as "It's true I say 'Now I am having such-and-such an image'", and she translated 'die Vorstellungswelt ist *ganz* in der Beschreibung der Vorstellung dargestellt' as 'the description of the image is a *complete* account of the imagined world'. However, this remark is not concerned with an imagined world, but rather with the 'world as idea' or the 'world as experience' — the 'visual room' introduced in §398 and discussed in §§399–401. To make this clear, we have opted for 'visual image' (to avoid confusion with mental images that one may have when one imagines visibilia), and 'the 'visual world', which is the phrase Wittgenstein himself employed in his English lectures on this very theme. See 'Notes for Lectures on "Private Experience" and "Sense Data"', repr. in James C. Klagge and Alfred Nordmann, eds, *Ludwig Wittgenstein — Philosophical Occasions 1912–1951* (Hackett, Indianapolis, 1993), pp. 258–9, 272; cp. p. 275.

§436(a) ' "are evanescent, and, in their coming to be and passing away, tend to produce these others" ': We have not been able to identify this ostensible quotation. In MS 146, 27, this has no quotation marks.

§436(b) 'No words could be plainer or more commonly used. Yet their true meaning is concealed from us. We have still to find it out.' Augustine, *Confessions*, Bk XI, §22 (tr. R. S. Pine-Coffin).

§437 '("The hardness of the logical must".)': here Wittgenstein is quoting himself from TS 221, p. 228 (= TS 222, p. 97); *Remarks on the Foundations of Mathematics* (Blackwell, Oxford, 1978), Part I, §121, see also Part VI, §49).

§441(b) ' "For wishes themselves are a veil between us and the thing wished for" ': a quotation from Goethe's *Hermann und Dorothea*, Canto V, line 69, tr. D. Coogan in Goethe, *Hermann and Dorothea* (Frederik Ungar, New York, 1966).

§441(c) ' "Do I know what I long for before I get it?" ': Anscombe's mistranslation may be what Wittgenstein meant. The German is "Weiß ich, wonach ich lange, ehe ich es erhalte?", which means "Do I know what I reach for before I get [or grasp] it?". This single-sentence paragraph does not occur in MSS but only in the final TS. So it may have been dictated, and an error may have occurred in the typing. For what Wittgenstein may have dictated was 'wonach ich verlange' — 'what I long for'. We have therefore hesitantly stayed with Anscombe's version.

§454(a) ' "Everything is already there in . . ." ': this is not a quotation, but an exclamation that Wittgenstein thought peculiarly characteristic of the situation in which we find ourselves when we 'hit bedrock'. See MS 124, 140 and 184f.; MS 127, 143 and 145.

§458 Wittgenstein's punctuation here is confusing. We have changed the quotation marks and added italics in the translation.

§480 Wittgenstein has *Meinung* twice in the first sentence. Translating it by 'opinion', as Anscombe did, is perfectly correct, but renders the continuity of the remark with the preceding one less clear than in the German, so we have translated *Meinung* here by 'belief'.

§518(a) 'Socrates to Theaetetus': Plato, *Theaetetus* 189a. Schleiermacher's translation of the *Theaetetus*, which Wittgenstein apparently used here, has *vorstellt* ('imagines') here. The usual English translation is 'thinks', but *vorstellt* is Wittgenstein's term, and 'imagines' preserves continuity with §517.

§524(c) The note in double parentheses is apparently a reminder to insert a remark apropos this theme (which is an inversion of §464).

§534(c) The double parentheses suggest that Wittgenstein was undecided whether this remark should occur here or in §525.

§537 'Then perhaps I say, "I don't know what it would mean if this is a courageous face" ': the German runs 'Ich sage dann etwa: "Ich weiß nicht was das hieße, wenn dieses Gesicht ein mutiges Gesicht ist." Anscombe translated the cited remark as "I don't know what it would be for this to be a courageous face". But in MS 115, 23, Wittgenstein added parentheses to this sentence as follows '[Diesen Satz kann man nicht richtig stellen indem man statt "wenn" "daß" setzt, oder statt "ist" "wäre"]'. That is, Wittgenstein explains that this sentence is not tantamount to either 'I don't know what it would mean to say that this is a courageous face' or 'I don't know what it would mean if this were a courageous face'.

Boxed remarks beween §549 and §550: these two remarks do not occur in the two surviving typescripts of the *Investigations*. They occur in the first two editions at the foot of p. 147, which runs from §548 to §552. (a) derives from MS 110, 103 and 106 (BT 162); (b) from MS 110, 133 (also MS 114, 157).

§559 '((Meaning-bodies.))': this is apparently a note for Wittgenstein to insert a remark concerning the 'meaning-body' conception of significant combinatorial possibilities of words. The idea was that we are inclined to think that the use of a word *flows from its meaning*, that because it has the meaning it has, it can enter into just *these* significant combinatorial possibilities and not others. It is as if each word presented a single coloured surface, behind which was a colourless glass geometrical solid (cube, pyramid, etc.) that enabled the word to combine with certain words but not others, so that we could make a visible and significant picture only by means of words the meaning-bodies of which fit together. See *The Big Typescript*, p. 166; *Philosophical Grammar* (Blackwell, Oxford, 1974), p. 54; F. Waismann, *The Principles of Linguistic Philosophy* (Macmillan and St Martin's Press, London and New York, 1965), pp. 234–9; TS 302, 4f.; Gordon Baker, ed., *Voices of Wittgenstein* (Routledge, London, 2003), pp. 133–41. For examples of such a conception see Waismann *Principles of Linguistic Philosophy*, p. 234 n., where he cites Frege's *Basic Laws of Arithmetic*,

vol. ii, §§91, 158. This citation is derived from Wittgenstein's dictation to Waismann in *Voices of Wittgenstein*, p. 135, where *Basic Laws*, vol. ii, §207, is also cited. Other passages in Frege which Wittgenstein would not have known, but which bear out his remarks, are to be found in 'Logic in Mathematics', repr. in *Posthumous Writings* (Blackwell, Oxford, 1979), p. 225, and 'Foundations of Geometry I', repr. in *Collected Papers on Mathematics, Logic, and Philosophy*, p. 281.

§560 ' "The meaning of a word is what an explanation of its meaning explains" ': this is a self-quotation — see *The Big Typescript*, p. 34, where it occurs as the title of ch. 9, and where the first remark runs: ' "Meaning: what an explanation of meaning explains", that is: Let's not ask what meaning is, but instead let's examine what is called "an explanation of meaning".'

§568(b) '((Meaning — a physiognomy))': a note for Wittgenstein to insert here a remark about the physiognomy of word meaning. In MS 133, 39r, he noted: 'In the use of a word we see a physiognomy', and in MS 137, 4b, he cites (in quotation marks) 'The concept is not only a technique, but also a physiognomy'.

§571(b) 'and the psychologist observes the *utterances* [*Äusserungen*] (the behaviour) of the subject': Anscombe here translated *Äusserungen* as 'external reactions'. This is unsatisfactory. She translated a comparable passage in PPF, §28(b) (PI Part II, p. 179) 'What do psychologists record? — What do they observe? Isn't it the behaviour of human beings, in particular their utterances [*Äusserungen*]?' We have opted for 'utterances' here too, in order to ensure consistency between these two, related remarks.

§589 '(Luther: "Faith is under the left nipple.")': This, as suggested by Eike von Savigny (*Wittgensteins "Philosophische Untersuchungen — Ein Kommentar für Leser*, 2nd edn (Klostermann, Frankfurt am Main, 1996), vol. 2, p. 273), is probably a reference to Luther's sermon of 27 Dec. 1533: 'Es ligt nicht am euserlichen leben, sed unter dem lincken zitzen, das man wisse Christum esse Salvatorem' (*Dr Martin Luther's Werke, Kritische Gesamtausgabe* (H. Böhlaus Nachfolger, Weimar), vol. 37 (1910), p. 248), or his fourth sermon on Christmas Day 1544: 'Denn das du ein Christ seyest und Gott wolgefallest, solches ist nicht am eusserlichen leben gelegen, sonder unter dem lincken zuzen und im hertzen . . .' (ibid., vol. 52 (1915), pp. 63f.)

§606(b) '(("A quite particular expression"))': which of the many remarks on this theme Wittgenstein had in mind here is unclear. The theme is discussed in *The Blue and Brown Books* (Blackwell, Oxford, 1958), pp. 170–7 (see also MSS 120, 253; 130, 45; 150, 2f.).

§609(b) Wittgenstein discussed the idea of understanding as 'an atmosphere', and its apparently indescribable character *in extenso* in *The Blue and Brown Books*, pp. 144–85 (see especially pp. 155–7); see also MS 162(b), 56(r)ff. Which part of these extensive discussions he had in mind here is unknown. The quoted phrase 'An indescribable character' is probably an allusion to James, *The Principles of Psychology*, e.g. vol. i, pp. 251ff.

§610(b) '((I should like to say: "These . . ."))': It is unclear why this remark is enclosed in double parentheses. The reference to James is probably to *The Principles of Psychology*, vol. i, p. 251, where he remarks, 'our psychological vocabulary is wholly inadequate', to capture the indescribable difference between trying to recall A's name and trying to recall B's name.

§611(a) ' "Willing — wanting — too is merely an experience" ': the German reads ' "Das Wollen ist auch nur eine Erfahrung" ', which Anscombe translated as ' "Willing too is merely an experience" '. *Wollen*, however, serves both for 'willing' and for 'wanting', and to translate it and its cognates (in the sequel) *uniformly* by 'will' and 'willing' (as Anscombe did) can be misleading. By inserting '— wanting — ' we have tried to make it clear that Wittgenstein is speaking of wanting to do something (as in §613), as well as about philosophical conceptions of will and idea. The idiom of 'will' and 'idea' referred to in parentheses in the first sentence is Schopenhauer's, although Schopenhauer, unlike the British empiricists, insisted on the categorial distinctness of will and idea (representation).

§618(a) The reference to Augustine is to *Confessions*, Bk VIII, §8.

§621(b) It is unclear what this parenthetical note refers to. Note that neither James nor Russell argued that the *kinaesthetic sensations* are the willing, but, if anything, the *idea* of the normally associated kinaesthetic sensations — which allegedly causes the appropriate muscular contractions involved in a voluntary movement.

§639 'Meaning something, one wants to say, *develops*': the German runs: 'Die Meinung, möchte man sagen, *entwickelt sich*.' Strictly speaking,

Anscombe's translation, 'One would like to say that an opinion develops,' is correct. But it is clear from the MS source (MS 129, 166f.)
that what Wittgenstein had in mind was that *meaning* (something)
develops, evolves or unfolds. His Anglicized misuse of *Meinung* is quite
common (cf. §§186, 666; also MSS 128, 7; 116, 266).

§654 'as "proto-phenomena" ': a reference to Goethe's *Urphänomen*, or
'primal phenomenon' — conceived of as bedrock that does not call for
explanation (see Goethe, *Theory of Colours*, tr. C. L. Eastlake (MIT
Press, Cambridge, Mass., 1970), §§174–7.

Philosophy of Psychology — A Fragment
[*previously known as 'Part II'*]

§5 Following MS 144, we have run the third sentence on after the
second.

§9 In the light of MS 144, 5–6, we have amalgamated remark (c) and
(d) of p. 175 in the first two editions into a single remark.

§32, line 6 We have italicized 'as' to capture the emphasis given by 'eben'.

§34 The translation of the first sentence as 'There is a similarity here
to the way in which "physical object" and "sense impressions" stand
to each other' is warranted on the grounds that the colon after 'Es ist
hier wie mit dem Verhältnis' is meant to introduce two classes of expressions, not two classes of things. This interpretation is supported by
Remarks on the Philosophy of Psychology (Blackwell, Oxford, 1980),
vol. i, §289, which runs: 'It is here just as with talk of physical objects
and sense impressions. We have here *two* language-games, and their
mutual relations are complicated.'

§35 It is evident from the context that 'die *Intention*' here should be
translated as '*intentionality*' and not as Anscombe had it: '*intention*'.
In MS 108, 218f. and MS 145, 49f. Wittgenstein used the German word
'Intention' in this way.

§82 'for all that, does the service of a description': the German runs
'tut gleichwohl den Dienst einer Beschreibung'. Anscombe translated 'for
all that serves as a description'. But the occurrence of the noun *Dienst*

is not coincidental. A cry does not *serve* as a description, but it does the same *service* as one, since both the cry and the utterance of a description are criteria for ascribing pain to the person in question.

§108 We have added Wittgenstein's illustration here, which makes clear what he had in mind. See also *Last Writings on the Philosophy of Psychology* (Blackwell, Oxford, 1982), vol. i, §88.

§118 'derived from Jastrow': see J. Jastrow, *Fact and Fable in Psychology* (Houghton Mifflin, Boston, 1900). Wittgenstein refers to it as the 'duck–hare', but following Anscombe we have abided with the more usual name of 'duck–rabbit'.

'And I must distinguish between the "continuous seeing" of an aspect and an aspect's "lighting up".' Anscombe translated the latter phrase as 'the "dawning" of an aspect'. The German is *Aufleuchten*, which means 'lighting up' (as when a building is lit up by spotlights or a Christmas display of lights is turned on). Lighting up is an instantaneous event, whereas dawning is a gradual process; a thought cannot dawn on one in a flash. Moreover, 'dawning' is overly intellectual — as in 'it gradually dawned on me that things were thus-and-so'.

§136 As it stands, this remark is altogether misleading, since 'organization' is not compared with shape and colour in the visual impression; rather, 'organization' of the visual impression is compared with colour and shape. In MS 137, 127a, Wittgenstein wrote:

> Und das allein eliminiert für uns den Vergleich der 'Organisation des Gesichseindrucks' mit Farbe und Form. // Und das allein tut den Vergleich der 'Organisation' ~~des Gesichtseindrucks~~ mit ~~der~~ Farbe & Form im Gesichtsausdruck für mich ab. //

> And this suffices to eliminate for us the comparison of the 'organization of the visual impression' with colour and form. // And this suffices to dispose of the comparison of the 'organization' ~~of the visual impression~~ with form and colour in the visual expression for me.//

The attempted redraft is evidently poor (writing 'visual expression' instead of 'visual impression'), and has made matters more rather than less obscure. Although the confusion of 'impression' with 'expression' was eliminated in MS 144, and presumably in the missing TS 234, the remaining confusion of 'form and colour in the visual impression' persisted.

§151 'Compare a remark of Lewis Carroll's': MS 137, 135a, says that the remark is in *Alice Through the Looking Glass*. The reference is to ch. 1 in which writing in the Looking Glass world is reversed, and can be read only in a mirror, exemplified in the text by reproducing the hand-written first verse of 'Jabberwocky' in reverse. Of this Alice initially remarks 'It's all in a language I don't know.'

§153 we have amplified 'in a figure (1) for another figure (2)' to read 'in a certain figure (call it Figure 1) for another figure (call it Figure 2)' in order to avoid the impression that Wittgenstein is referring to two numbered figures somewhere in his text. We have adjusted §154 accordingly.

§§164 and 165 Anscombe translated 'eine Form' in both remarks by the same word, 'form'. But the two remarks come from separate contexts, §164 from MS 135, 176, and §165 from MS 135, 42. In the first of these remarks, 'eine Form' means *a mould*, but in the second it means *a logical form* (see *Remarks on the Philosophy of Psychology*, vol. 1, §1026).

§180(c) The reference to Köhler's figure of interpenetrating hexagons may be to his *Gestalt Psychology* (G. Bell and Sons Ltd, London, 1930), ch. 6.

§205 amalgates two remarks in the first two editions. The two paragraphs are a single remark in MS 137, 33a–b (cf. *Remarks on the Philosophy of Psychology*, vol. 2, §535), the latter being an elaboration on the former.

§§220–1 In the first two editions §221 was printed *before* §220. But Wittgenstein's instruction in MS 144 indicates that their order should be reversed — a change that makes better sense.

§231 'We react to the facial expression'. The printed German text here had *Gesichtseindruck* ('visual impression'), but it is a misprint, and should read *Gesichtsausdruck* ('facial expression'), as is evident from MS 138, 6b (under 21 Jan. 1949) — cf. *Last Writings on the Philosophy of Psychology*, vol. 1, §744: 'We *react* to a hesitant facial expression differently from someone who does not recognize it as hesitant (in the *full* sense of the word).' We have accordingly corrected both German and English.

'a modified concept of *sensing*': Anscombe had here 'a modified concept of *sensation*' (*Empfindungsbegriff*), but that is wrong. To recognize a facial expression as timid is not to have a *sensation* of any kind, but to *sense* something — to sense the timidity in the person's face.

§§235–6 were originally printed after §247 (as p. 212(b)–(c)) in the first two editions). Wittgenstein's instructions in MS 144 unequivocally indicate that they should occur after §234.

§§249–50 were run into one remark in the first two editions (p. 212(e)). We have separated them, as in MS 138, 10a–b, and MS 144, 74–5. This is the more cogent arrangement.

§273, third sentence   In place of Anscombe's addition of 'we say' (in the first two editions, p. 216(a)), we have added quotation marks to Wittgenstein's text.

§299 James: the reference is perhaps to *The Principles of Psychology*, vol. i, p. 253: 'And has the reader never asked himself what kind of mental fact is his *intention of saying a thing* before he has said it? It is an entirely definite intention, distinct from all other intentions, an absolutely distinct state of consciousness, therefore; and yet how much of it consists of definite sensorial images, either of words or of things? Hardly anything! Linger and the words and things come into the mind; the anticipatory intention, the divination is there no more. But as the words that replace it arrive, it welcomes them successively and calls them right if they agree with it, it rejects them and calls them wrong if they do not. It has therefore a nature of its own of the most positive sort, and yet what can we say about it without using words that belong to the later mental facts that replace it? The intention *to say so-and-so* is the only name it can receive.' See also vol. i, pp. 673f.: 'That nascent cerebral excitations can effect consciousness with a sort of sense of the immanence of that which stronger excitations would make us definitely feel, is obvious from what happens when we seek to remember a name. It tingles, it trembles on the verge, but does not come.'

§306 We have here changed the German text from 'beim innerlichen Rechnen' to 'beim innerlichen Reden', which corresponds to MS 144, 92 (cp. *Last Writings on the Philosophy of Psychology*, vol, 1, §865). This also accords better with the adjacent remarks, all of which concern saying things silently to oneself, and not specifically mental arithmetic.

§314, last line '((Connection with "pain in someone else's body".))'
In the 1930s, Wittgenstein toyed with the idea of the intelligibility of
feeling pain in another person's body (*Wittgenstein and the Vienna Circle*
(Blackwell, Oxford, 1967), p. 49; *Philosophical Remarks* (Blackwell
Oxford, 1975), p. 92; *The Blue and the Brown Books*, pp. 49ff.), on
the grounds that the criterion for pain location is where the sufferer
points, and it is conceivable that when asked where one has a pain,
one might (perhaps with eyes closed) point to someone else's body. It
is unclear what reminder this note is meant to be, in particular whether
Wittgenstein wished to reaffirm the intelligibility of pain in another's
body (see §302) or, arguably better, to put the supposition on the same
level as the statement that a rose has teeth in the mouth of an animal.

§322 The reference of 'es' in 'wenn es tatsächlich nicht geschieht' is unclear.
What is probably intended is the 'talking to myself' specified in the last
line of the previous remark. So we have added the elucidating phrase
'and even if I don't actually talk to myself'.

§339 'One would sometimes like to say of certainty and conviction
. . .': the German has 'Von der Sicherheit, vom Glauben möchte man
manchmal sagen . . .', which Anscombe translated 'We should sometimes like to call certainty and belief . . .'. But here *Glauben* means 'conviction', not 'belief'.

§362 'Verstellung ist natürlich nur ein besonderer Fall davon, . . .': In
the context from which this remark is drawn, namely MS 137, 52a–b,
it is evident that what is being asserted is not that pretending is a special case of someone's producing (say) . . . (as in Anscombe's translation), but rather that pretending to be in pain, for example, is a special
case of. . . .

Register

"PPF" steht für *Philosophie der Psychologie – Ein Fragment*, "Z" für "Zettel" (d.h. für eingerahmte Bemerkungen, die auf den genannten Paragraphen folgen), "V" für "Vorwort".

Aberglaube, 35 Z, 49, 110; PPF 175

Abgeschlossenheit, PPF 316

ableiten, 146, 162–4, 193, 479

Abmachung, 41

abrichten, Abrichtung, 5, 6, 86, 157–8, 189, 198, 206, 223, 441, 630; PPF 70

Abschattung, 254; PPF 180, 192, 210

Absicht, 210, 213–14, 247, 646
  eingebettet in Situation, 337
  Erinnerung an, 635–41, 645, 648, 653, 659–60
  kein Erlebnis, PPF 229
  und Gefühl, 588, 645
  und Handlung, 644, 659
  natürlicher Ausdruck, 647
  philosophische, 275
  und Tendenzerlebnisse, 591–2
  und Vorhersage, 629–31; PPF 98, 328–9

Adelheid (*Götz von Berlichingen*), 365

Ähnlichkeit, 9, 11, 66–7, 90, 130, 185, 430, 444; PPF 17, 111–13, 127, 134, 154, 239–40, 244, 249, 257

algebraischer Ausdruck, algebraische Formel, 146, 151, 152, 154, 179, 183, 189, 320

allgemein, PPF 73–4
  allgemeine Sachlage, 104
  allgemeine Sprache, 261

Alltag, alltäglich, tagtäglich, 93, 106, 116, 120, 129, 134, 197, 235, 244, 412, 436; PPF 161, 335

anähneln, 10

Analogie, 90, 140, 494, 613, 669

Analyse, analysieren, 39, 60–1, 63–4, 90–1, 383, 392–3, 413; PPF 188

Annahme, 22 Z; PPF 87–8, 98, 101, 106
  und Grund, PPF 268

Anweisung auf, 383, 449

Anwendung
  eines algebraischen Ausdrucks, 146–8
  eines Bildes, 140, 374, 422, 425
  einer Frage, 411
  eines Pfeils, 454
  einer Regel, eines Gesetzes, 147–8, 218

Dieses Register basiert auf dem von G. Hallett und C. Schwarck erstellten Register zu den *Philosophischen Untersuchungen* (1967).

Anwendung (*cont'd*)
des Verstehens, 146
eines Wortes, 84, 340
a priori, 97, 158, 251, 617; PPF 309
Arm, 612, 614, 616, 621–2, 624–5, 627;
PPF 59, 63
Aroma, 610
artfremd, 574
Artischocke, 164
Aspekt
Aufleuchten, Bemerken, 193–4;
PPF 113, 118, 140, 152–3, 207,
209, 239, 247
beschreiben, PPF 213, 215
des Doppelkreuzes, PPF 212, 215,
217, 257
des Dreiecks, PPF 162, 167, 211,
217, 222
des Gesichts, 536
des H-E-Kopfs, PPF 118, 120, 125,
128, 137, 152, 201, 208, 217
der Organisation, PPF 131, 134, 136,
220
eines Schriftzeichens, PPF 234
Sehen des Aspekts untersteht dem
Willen, PPF 256
stetiges Sehen des Aspekts, PPF 118
und Vorstellung, PPF 217, 234, 254,
256
des Würfelschemas, PPF 219, 236,
258
Aspektblindheit, PPF 257–8, 260
Aspektwechsel, PPF 129–30, 135,
166
assoziieren, Assoziation, 6, 53; PPF 50,
177, 268, 274
Ästhetik, ästhetisch, 77; PPF 178, 297
Atmosphäre, 165 Z, 173, 213, 594, 596,
607, 609; PPF 42, 50
auffallen, 129; PPF 237, 244–5, 334,
365
auffassen, Auffassung, 2, 4, 20, 28–9,
38, 48, 58, 109, 201, 363, 398, 401,
520, 539, 549, 557; PPF 8
Aufmerksamkeit, 33–4, 258, 268, 275,
411–12, 666–9, 674

Augenblick, 638, 642, 645; PPF 179,
184, 187
Augustinus, 1–4, 32, 89–90, 436, 618
Ausdruck, Miene, 21, 285, 536;
PPF 232
einer Absicht, natürlicher, 647
der Empfindung, 244, 288, 582
einer Erwartung, 452–3, 465, 574–7,
582
des Gedankens, 317–18, 335
und Meinen, 509; PPF 265
des Schmerzes, 288
bezogen auf Sprachspiel, 261; PPF 79
der Wahrnehmung, PPF 138
Ausdrucksform, Ausdrucksweise, 90–1,
93–4, 112, 194, 334, 339, 398,
402–3, 409, 426, 513, 617
ausführen, Ausführung eines Befehls,
53, 62, 74, 86, 431, 451, 461, 480,
519, 630; PPF 257
Ausländer, 20
Ausnahme, 142; PPF 349
Ausruf, 27, 244, 275, 295–6, 323, 586;
PPF 126, 138–9, 145, 293
Äußerung, 149, 152, 231, 571, 582,
585, 632; PPF 7
Automat, automatisch, 166, 169, 420;
PPF 19–21

Ball, Ballspiel, 83
Ballard, 342
Bank, PPF 262–3, 279
Bau, Bauen, Baustein, 2, 8, 10, 15,
20–1, 86, 364, 466, 491
Baum, 47, 418
Bedacht, 173–4
Bedeutung
und Anwendung, Verwendung, 41,
139, 197, 454, 556–7; PPF 303
Begriff der, 2, 5, 43, 120
und Deutung, 198, 652
erklären, 247, 533, 560; PPF 275
erleben, PPF 10, 234, 261–2
und Gebrauch, 30, 43, 138, 556, 561;
PPF 250
und Gefühl, 181–2, 542, 544–5

als Gegenstand, 1–2, 40, 45, 120
hören, 534
lernen, 77, 244, 590
in der Musik, 529
eines Namens, 39–43, 55, 79
ohne feste, 79–80, 163
als Physiognomie, Gesicht, 568;
    PPF 294
primäre und sekundäre, PPF 276
im Satz, 540
und Sprachspiel, PPF 273
verstehen, 138–9
vertauschte, PPF 16
vorführen, PPF 16
ins Wort aufgenommen, PPF 294
Bedeutungskörper, 559
Bedingtheit, 220; PPF 223
Bedürfnis, eigentliches, 108
Beethoven, Ludwig van, PPF 51
Befehl
    und Ausführung, Befolgung, Folgen,
        206, 345, 431, 433, 458–61
    als Bild, 519
    und Kluft, 431, 433, 503–6
    und Meldung, 19, 21
    verstehen, 6, 431, 451
    und Witz, 62
Befriedigung (befriedigt, unbefriedigt),
    88, 120, 438–40, 460
begleiten (Begleitvorgang,
    Begleiterscheinung), 152–3, 321,
    330, 673; PPF 43, 47, 76, 271,
    279–80, 291–3, 296, 299, 302, 368
Begriff
    analysieren, 383
    ausdehnen, 67
    begrenzt, verschwommen, 68–71,
        76–7, 98, 100–1
    drängt sich auf, PPF 191
    und Gebrauch, 532
    lehren, lernen, 208, 384
    und Malweise, PPF 367
    modifizieren, PPF 224, 231
    und Spiel, PPF 48, 369
    der Zahl, 67–8, 135
    und Zweck, 345

begrifflich (nicht kausal), PPF 67, 181,
    183, 202, 257, 338
Begriffsbestimmung, PPF 191
Begriffsbildung und Naturtatsachen,
    PPF 365–6
Begriffsgrenze, PPF 219
Begründung, 217
Behauptung, 21–4, 131, 402, 444, 447;
    PPF 87–8, 90, 97–8, 101–2, 106–7,
    110
Behaviourism, Behaviourist, 307–8
beherrschen
    Grundzahlenreihe, 185
    Spiel, 31
    Sprache, 33, 338, 508
    Technik, 150, 199, 692; PPF 222
Beispiel, 71, 75, 77, 133, 208–10, 593
Belehren, PPF 56, 58–9, 282
Belustigung, 42
Bemerken einer Ähnlichkeit, eines
    Aspekts, PPF 112–13, 125, 152–3
Benehmen, 244, 246, 267, 281, 288,
    304, 357, 393, 486, 571; PPF
    27–30, 32, 102, 105, 298, 300
    Ausdruck der Empfindung, 288
    und feine Abschattungen, PPF 192,
        210
benennen, Benennung, 1, 6–7, 15,
    26–8, 30–1, 38, 46, 49–50, 53, 244,
    275, 410
Benzol, 54
Beobachter, Beobachtung, 54, 417, 571,
    659; PPF 27–8, 67, 76, 86, 177,
    313, 316, 357
Berechtigung, 154–5, 378, 486, 557
bescheiden, 28 Z
Beschreibung
    als Abbildung einer Verteilung im
        Raum, PPF 70
    viele Arten der, 24, 291; PPF 160
    von Aspekten, PPF 213
    Benennen eine Vorbereitung zur,
        49
    eines Gefühls, PPF 63
    des Gesehenen, PPF 160, 225
    als Instrument, 291

Beschreibung (*cont'd*)
  als Methode der Philosophie,
    Grammatik, 109, 124, 486, 496
  und Name, 79
  eines seelischen Zustands, 24, 180,
    577, 588, 662; PPF 72, 79, 85, 90
  eines Vorgangs, 665; PPF 319
Besen, 60
besinnen, sich, 89–90, 475
Beulen, 119
Bewegung, 624–5; PPF 56, 59, 66
  grammatische, 401
Beweis, 310, 517, 578; PPF 255, 303,
  371
bewußt, 156, 159; vgl. unbewußt
Bewußtsein
  Aufmerksamkeit auf eigenes, 412
  bei Bewußtsein, 416–17
  Denken im Innern des Bewußtseins,
    PPF 316
  und Gehirnvorgang, 412
  haben, 390, 416, 418, 420
  eines Steins, 390, 418
  Vorgänge im Bewußtsein, PPF 298
  Wissen als Bewußtsein, 148
Bewußtseinszustand, 421
bezeichnen, 10, 13, 15, 39, 46, 55, 59,
  273–4
beziehen, sich, 10, 243–4, 273–4, 669;
  PPF 7, 286
Bild, 96, 139 Z, 194, 280, 291, 297,
  300–1, 368, 398, 515, 522, 526,
  548; PPF 23–6, 184–5, 195, 198,
  258, 360
  und Anwendung, 140, 374, 422, 425
  und Befehl, 519
  geistiges, inneres Bild, 6, 37, 73,
    139–40, 239, 301, 352, 367, 449,
    604–5, 663; PPF 133
  in der Philosophie, 59, 115, 191, 251,
    295, 352, 374, 422–7, 490, 573;
    PPF 55
  verstehen, 526
Bildente, 157
Bildgegenstand (-mensch, -tier), PPF 119
Bildhase, PPF 120–1, 128, 157

Blatt, Blattform, 73–4
blau, 33, 35 Z, 275
blind, Blindheit, 219, 281, 416,
    424; PPF 232, 257–8; vgl.
  Aspektblindheit, Farbenblindheit
Blume, 53
Boxer, 22 Z
brauchbar, unbrauchbar, 69, 88
Bremse, 6
bremseln, PPF 370
Brettspiel, 3, 31
Brille, 103
"bububu", 35 Z

Carroll, Lewis, 13; PPF 151
Charakteristiken des Benehmens,
  PPF 27
Charakteristisch, 35, 159–60, 175, 588,
  607; PPF 2, 273, 296, 300
cyrillisch, 159, 162

Darstellung, 50, 280, 435; PPF 147–8,
  158, 161, 258
"das", "dieses", 38–9, 45, 253, 398,
  410; PPF 111
Definition, definieren, 70, 75, 77, 182,
  354
  und Beschreibung, 49, 79, 665
  in Ethik, Ästhetik, 77
  hinweisende, 6, 28–30, 33, 38, 258
  von Namen, Farbnamen, 28–30, 33,
    38, 79, 239
  Schach durch Regeln definiert, 205
  wissenschaftliche, 79
  der Zwei, 28–9
Denken, denken
  etwas Einzigartiges, 95, 110
  und Glauben, 574–5
  Können Tiere, Maschinen, Sessel
    denken? 25, 359–61
  und Meinen, 22, 692–3
  Ordnung des Denkens, 336
  keine seelische Begleitung, 330–2, 427
  und Sprache, Sprechen, Welt, 32, 92,
    96–7, 110, 318, 327–32, 335–6,
    339, 342, 392; PPF 292

Vehikel des Denkens, 329
was nicht der Fall ist, 95
wie zu sich selbst reden, 32
Wozu denkt der Mensch? 466–70
Denkschema, 597
Denkweise, primitive, 597
Deutung, deuten, 28, 34, 85, 160, 198,
201, 210, 213, 506, 536, 539, 634,
637–8, 652–3, 656; PPF 116–17,
164, 248–9
Diät, einseitige, 593
Dienst, 304; PPF 23, 30, 82
Dimension, andere, PPF 35, 165
Dimensionierung, 267
Doppelkreuz, PPF 212, 215, 217, 257
Dreieck, PPF 162, 167, 211, 217, 222
Drittes, ausgeschlossenes, 352
Dunst, Dunstkreis, 5, 117, 607; PPF 35

Echtheit des Gefühlsausdrucks,
PPF 352, 354–5, 357
eindeutig, 79, 426; PPF 106
Eindruck, 259, 276–7, 280, 368, 600;
PPF 129–36, 170–5, 187
einfach, 4, 39, 45–8, 59, 97, 129–30
Einfluß, beeinflussen, 169–77, 484,
493
eins, 552
Einstellung, einstellen, eingestellt, 284,
310, 417, 441, 495, 575, 645–6,
672–3; PPF 22, 103, 193
Einteilung, Klassifikation, 17; PPF 202
Einzelheit, 51–2, 635–6
Element, 48–51, 53, 59
elliptisch, 19–20
empfinden als, 535
Empfindung, 290; PPF 47, 230
und Absicht, Aufmerksamkeit usw.,
582, 621, 624–6, 646–7, 669,
672
Benennen von, Deuten auf
Empfindungen, 244, 256, 258,
261–3, 268, 270, 298, 669
charakteristische, 151, 159–60
private, 246–8, 251, 270
des Steins, 284

Empfindungsäußerung, -ausdruck, 244,
256, 288
Empfindungsbegriff (modifizierter),
PPF 4, 231
empfindungslos durch Philosophieren,
348
empirisch, 109
Ende, 1, 326, 485; PPF 33
Entdeckung, entdecken, 119, 124–6,
133, 400, 511; PPF 296
Entscheidung, 186
Entschluß, 243, 588, 627, 631–2
entsprechen, 29, 39–40, 51, 53, 55, 60,
366
Erfahrung
gegenwärtige, 436
und Menschenkenntnis, PPF 355
und Rechtfertigung, 478, 480, 485,
495, 617
unabhängig von, 92
unmittelbare, PPF 117
und Wollen, 611
Erfahrungsbegriff, PPF 115
Erfahrungsmäßig, 79, 89, 97, 179,
193–5, 484
Erfahrungssatz, 85, 251, 295, 360;
PPF 222
Erfahrungstatsache, 194, 418, 466
erfassen, 89, 113, 116, 138–9, 153, 156,
191, 195, 197, 664
erfinden, Erfindung, 23, 27, 122, 126,
204, 257, 262, 401, 492, 525, 530,
549 Z; PPF 205
Erfolg, 320, 324
Erfüllung der Erwartung, 442, 444–5
erinnern, sich, 35, 56–7, 147, 165, 175,
177, 305–6, 379, 634–5, 645–6,
648, 651, 660–1
Erinnerungsbild, 56; PPF 58
Erinnerungserlebnis, PPF 368
Erinnerungsreaktion, 343
erklären, Erklärung, 3, 30, 49, 72–3,
142 Z, 145, 239, 288, 339, 429,
533, 560
und Abrichtung, 5
durch Beispiele, 69–71, 75, 208–10

erklären, Erklärung (*cont'd*)
des Denkens, 339, 598
mittels Gleichheit, 350–1
Grammatik erklärt nicht, 496
hat irgendwo ein Ende, 1, 87
kann mißverstanden werden, 28 Z,
34, 71, 87
muß fort, 109, 126, 654–5
private, 268
tiefere, 209
"unexakte", 88
Erleben einer Wortbedeutung, eines
Vorstellungsbilds, 509; PPF 10,
234, 261–2, 271–3, 279, 282
Erlebnis
begleitendes, charakteristisches,
34–5, 157, 165–6, 172–8, 322, 591,
645; PPF 279, 282, 299–300, 368
eigentliches, 649
gleiches, 350
Kriterium für ein Erlebnis, 509, 542;
PPF 146
merkwürdiges, seltsames, PPF 269,
299
Sprachliches als Erlebnis, 649
Erlebnisbegriff, PPF 223
Erlebnisinhalt, PPF 369
erraten, 33, 156, 161, 172, 210, 340,
636, 652; PPF 308, 318, 321–2,
328, 333
erwarten, 442, 444, 576–7, 582
Akt des Erwartens, 586
als etwas Unbefriedigtes, 438–9
Erwartung
zwei Arten, 577
ihr Ausdruck, 452–3, 465, 574, 582
und Empfindung, 582
ihre Erfüllung, 442, 444–5, 465
in Situation eingebettet, 581, 583,
586
als Zustand, 572
Erzählung, 524, 607, 652; PPF 264,
370
Ethik, 77
Evidenz, 638, 641; PPF 358–60
Evolution, PPF 55

Experiment, experimentelle, 23, 169,
265, 412, 490; PPF 32, 79, 291,
371

Faden, 67
Fähigkeit, 25, 151, 636; PPF 36, 257
Fahrplan, 265
falsch, fälschlich, 79, 112, 136–7,
241, 246, 288, 345, 429, 448, 515;
PPF 92, 161, 249, 348–9
Familie, Familienähnlichkeit, 67, 77,
164, 179, 236
Faraday, Michael, 104 Z
Farbe
Aufmerksamkeit auf Farbe richten,
33, 275, 277
benennen, 26
einfach oder zusammengesetzt, 47–8
die einem einfällt, 239
ihre Erklärung, 28 Z, 30, 72–3,
239
sich in eine Farbe vertiefen, 277
auf Farbe zeigen, 33, 35–6
unzerstörbar, 56–8
Farbeindruck, 275–7
Farbenblindheit, PPF 257, 351
Farbfleck, 76, 216, 526; PPF 252
Farbmuster, 1, 8, 16, 50, 56, 72–3
Farbname, Farbwort, 28, 30, 51;
PPF 346
Farburteil, PPF 346
Faser, 67
Fehler, 51, 54, 143, 189; PPF 178, 184,
338
feiern, 38
Feld eines Worts, PPF 297
Felsen, 217
"fett", PPF 274–5
Feuer, Flamme, 472–4, 480
Figur
(Bild, Gestalt), 74, 208, 420; PPF 35,
117–19, 121, 151, 153–4, 156, 166,
173, 179–80, 186, 193, 205, 212,
222, 236, 249, 256–7
(Spielfigur, Schachfigur), 108 Z, 136,
563

Fiktion, 22, 166, 307

Finger, 617; PPF 56–7, 61

Fleck, 216, 312, 443, 446; vgl.
Farbfleck, Schmerzfleck

Fliege, 284, 309

Folge, 207, 268, 620; PPF 176, 192,
257, 357, 359

folgen, einer Regel, einem Gesetz
folgen, 54, 125, 199, 201–2, 217,
219, 222, 232–3, 235, 237

folgern, Folgerung, 126, 322

Form
und Analyse, 60–1, 63
und Farbe, 21, 26, 33–6, 48
einer Figur, 31
eines Problems, 92, 123
des Satzes, 65, 114, 134, 136
der Sprache, 93, 111–12

Formel, 151–2, 154, 179, 183, 189–90,
320, 325, 521; PPF 34

formelle Einheit, 108

forschen, Forscher, Forschung, 89, 129,
206, 243, 308; PPF 55

fortsetzen, 145–6, 151, 154, 157, 179,
181, 183, 185, 208, 211–12, 305,
324–5, 634, 660; PPF 101, 103

Frage
anwenden, 411
und Behauptung, 22–3
und Erklärung, 87
grammatische, 47
philosophische, 47
psychologische, 377
verstehen, 516–17

Frege, Gottlob, 22, 22 Z, 49, 71

fremd, Fremder, 20, 32, 206, 596,
602; PPF 7, 158, 234, 263, 294,
325

führen lassen, 170, 172–3, 175, 177–8

Fundament, fundamental, 63, 87, 89,
125, 314; PPF 269

Funktion, 4, 11, 17, 21, 22, 27, 88,
92, 208, 260, 274, 280, 320, 556,
559

Funktionieren der Sprache, der
Wörter, 2, 5, 93, 304, 340

Furcht, sich fürchten, 142, 212, 472,
473, 476, 480, 537, 650; PPF 5,
72–5, 77, 83, 85

Fußball, PPF 369

Gans, PPF 314

Gebärde, 1, 44, 174, 185, 208, 288,
310, 330, 335, 433–4, 529, 550,
556, 673; PPF 6, 26, 209, 289, 296,
360, 370

Gebrauch, gebrauchen
und Bedeutung, 30, 41, 43, 120, 138,
197, 454, 532, 556–7, 561; PPF 15,
265
und Bedeutung lehren, 250, 330
Benennen als Vorbereitung zum
Gebrauch, 26
Definition erklärt Gebrauch, 30
und Gleichheit, 565–6
und Leben des Worts, 432
lehren, 9, 376; PPF 61
lernen, 9; PPF 346
und Praxis, 51
und Satz, 20
der Schachfigur, 31
ständiger, 198
und Wort, 1, 6, 9, 29, 30, 38, 79, 90,
138, 345, 378, 556

Gedächtnis, 53, 56, 159, 265, 271, 290,
333, 342, 604, 691; PPF 52, 214,
318, 320, 341, 344

Gedächtnisbild, 166

Gedächtnisphänomen, PPF 53

Gedanke
Ausdruck des Gedankens, 317–18,
335; PPF 139
blitzartiger, 318–20
nicht geheimnisvoll, 428
und Harmonie, 429
nachhallender, PPF 235
philosophischer, 299
seltsames Wesen, 428
und Zweck der Sprache, 304, 317,
501

Gedankenerraten, PPF 321–2, 328

Gedankenkreis, PPF 313

gedankenlos, 318, 330, 341; PPF 292
Gedicht, 13, 182, 282, 531, 533;
    PPF 264
Gefühl, fühlen
    und Absicht, 588
    gibt Bedeutung, Wahrheit, 544–5
    der Befriedigung, Unbefriedigung,
        439–40, 460
    der Bekanntheit, Unbekanntheit,
        Wohlvertrautheit, 596
    Beschreibung eines Gefühls, PPF 63
    der Bewegung, 624; PPF 59
    charakteristisches, 588
    als Deutung, 656
    erklären, PPF 61
    und Glauben, Sicherheit, PPF 339
    hypostasiert, 598
    der Raumhaftigkeit, Tiefe, PPF 241
    Schwindelgefühl, PPF 224
    der Überzeugung, 607
    nicht verborgen, PPF 324
    Wortgefühl, Wenn-Gefühl, 542;
        PPF 39, 41–4
Gefühlsausdruck, -äußerung, 142, 542;
    PPF 352, 355
Gefühlswert, PPF 226
Gegebenes, 23; PPF 345
Gegensatz, 20
Gegenstand, 38–9, 46–7, 293, 339, 373
    Physikalischer, 58, 253; PPF 34
Gegenteil nicht vorstellbar, 251
Geheimsprache, PPF 263
Gehirn, 149, 156, 158, 376; PPF 243
Gehirnvorgang, 412, 427
Geist, geistig, 25, 36, 51, 73, 76, 156,
    179, 184, 205, 306, 308, 333–4,
    337–8, 360, 363, 366, 452, 524,
    573–7, 592, 648, 673, 693; PPF 15,
    35, 54
    geistiges Auge, 56–7
    geistiger Mechanismus, 689
Geisteszustand, 608; PPF 90
Geläufigkeit, 159; PPF 180, 222
Geld, 120, 268, 294, 584
gemeinsam, Gemeinsamkeit, 65–7,
    71–3, 97, 172, 206, 273, 531

genau, Genauigkeit, 69–70, 88;
    PPF 338
Geometrie, PPF 180
Gepflogenheit, 198–9, 205, 337
Germanismen, 597
Geschichte, 23, 638, 644, 663
Gesetz, 147–8, 151, 352; PPF 27
    Bildungsgesetz, 143
    Identitätsgesetz, PPF 311
    Naturgesetz, 54, 325, 492
Gesicht, 171, 228, 409, 536–7, 583,
    606; PPF 17, 38, 50, 111–13,
    119, 124, 143, 150, 158, 186, 198,
    225, 232, 238–9, 244, 257, 270,
    294
Gesichtsausdruck, 24, 173, 285, 311,
    536, 665; PPF 227, 231, 244, 264
Gesichtsbild, 47; PPF 253
Gesichtseindruck, 354; PPF 131–2, 134,
    136, 173, 175, 211, 247
Gesichtssinn, 232
Gesichtszüge, 67, 537
Gestalt, 31, 73, 167, 312, 430; PPF 131,
    216
Geständnis, PPF 319
Geste, 45, 398, 610, 666; PPF 44, 180
gewinnen, 66
Gewißheit, 325
Gewohnheit, sich gewöhnen, 166, 200,
    508; PPF 168
gewöhnlich, 19–20, 60, 98, 105, 108,
    132, 156, 171, 318, 402, 412,
    417–21, 436, 494, 527; PPF 106,
    123, 274–5
    mit gewöhnlichen Dingen zugehen,
        94
Glaube, glauben, PPF 86–110
    Aussage, Satz glauben, 366, 578;
        PPF 348
    und Denken, 574–5; PPF 339
    und Empfindung, 260, 303, 310;
        PPF 19
    und Grund, 477–81
    und Introspektion, 587
    als Seelenzustand, 589; PPF 96–7
    unbefriedigt, 438–9

gleichförmig, Gleichförmigkeit, 11, 167, 208, 472

Gleichheit, 215–16, 223, 225–6, 254, 290, 330, 350, 376–8, 382, 565

Gleichheitszeichen, 558, 561; PPF 9

Gleichnis, 112; PPF 26

Gleichzeitigkeit, 176

Glück (im Spiel), 66

Goethe, Johann Wolfgang, PPF 51

Goldbach'scher Satz, 578

Gott, 234, 342, 346, 352, 426; PPF 284, 342

Gram, Grammuster, PPF 2

Grammatik
die sich aufdrängt, 304
ihre bildliche Darstellung, 295
und logische Möglichkeit, 520
und Naturtatsachen, PPF 365
Oberflächen-, Tiefengrammatik, 664
ohne Grammatik, 528
Platz des Wortes in der Grammatik, 29
Regeln der Grammatik, 496–7, 558
des Satzes, 353
Schwanken in der Grammatik, 354
Theologie als Grammatik, 373
fehlt Übersichtlichkeit, 122
Vorbild der Grammatik, 20
und Wesen, 371
eines Worts, Ausdrucks, 35 Z, 150, 165 Z, 182, 187, 199, 257, 293, 339, 350, 492, 657, 660, 693; PPF 106
Zweck der Grammatik, 497

grammatisch, grammatikalisch
Analyse, 392
Anmerkung, 232
Bemerkung, 574
Betrachtung, 90, 149 Z
Bewegung, 401
Fiktion, 307
Form, PPF 93
Frage, 47
Regel, 558
Satz, 251, 295, 458

Satzform, 21

Täuschung, 110

Unterschied, 149; PPF 62

Witz, 111

ein Zustand, 572–3

Grauen, PPF 6

Grenze, 68–9, 71, 76–7, 79, 88, 119, 143, 163, 499
Begriffsgrenze, PPF 219
Farbgrenze, 88

Grenzfall, 49, 385, 420

Grund, 89, 118, 169, 211–12, 324–6, 475–84, 607; PPF 125, 268, 326

Grundlage, V, 129; PPF 241, 329, 372

Grundzahlenreihe, 185

Grundzahlwort, 1, 9

haben, 283, 398

Hahn und Hühner, 493

Hand, 143, 268, 279; PPF 148, 302, 312

Handgriff, 12

Handlung, handeln
und Absicht, Gedanken, innerliches Reden, 36, 232, 490, 642; PPF 302
und Befehl, 23, 487, 505, 519
und Begründung, 217
und Regel, 198–201, 232
und Sicherheit, PPF 339
und Sprache, 207, 330, 486, 556
willkürliche, 613–14, 616, 627–9
ihr Zweck, PPF 290

Handlungsweise, 201, 206, 420, 489

Harmonie, 429

Härte des logischen Muß, 437

Hauptwort, 1

Heimat, 116

H-E-Kopf, PPF 118, 120, 125, 128, 137, 152, 201, 208, 217

herbeiführen, 611, 613–14

herkömmlich, PPF 169

heucheln, 250, 638; PPF 360, 363

hier, 410, 514

Hilfskonstruktion, PPF 318

Himmelsrichtung, 28

hineinpassen, 216; PPF 164
Hintergrund, V, 102, 422; PPF 218
hinweisend
  Definition, 6, 28–30, 33, 38
  Erklärung, 6, 27–8, 30, 32, 34, 38,
    362, 380
  Fürwort, 44, 411
  Lehren, 6, 8–9, 49, 51
Hinzunehmendes, PPF 161, 345
hoch, Höhe, 68, 279, 377, 670;
  PPF 338
Hof, PPF 35
hoffen, Hoffnung, 545, 572, 574, 577,
  583–5, 616; PPF 1, 78, 298
horchen, 233, 669, 671; PPF 104
hören, 165, 169, 534; PPF 228–30, 254,
  305
Hund, 250, 357, 650; PPF 1, 363
hypostasieren, 598
Hypothese, hypothetisch, 23, 82, 109,
  156, 325; PPF 249, 274, 306, 366

ich, Ich, 116, 398, 402–10, 514;
  PPF 86–107
ideal, Ideal, 81, 88, 98, 100–1, 103,
  105, 107, 194; PPF 133
Idealist, 402
Idee, 103, 187–8, 283, 304–5, 348, 420,
  556; PPF 369
identisch, Identität, 216, 253–4, 288,
  322, 404
Illusion, 311, 362
illustrieren, Illustration, 134, 139 Z,
  295, 663; PPF 116, 264, 279
imaginäre Zahl, PPF 165
impressionistisch, 368
inappellabel, 56
"individuals", 46
Indizien, 488
Induktion, induktiv, 135, 324–5
Inhalt, 217; PPF 10, 279, 369
  Erlebnisinhalt, PPF 279, 369
Inneres, innerlich, 24, 173–4, 256, 305,
  344, 348, 361, 376, 380, 398, 423,
  580, 659; PPF 35, 133–4, 301–3,
  306–8, 316, 318, 323

Institution, 199, 337, 380, 540, 584
Instrument, 50, 88, 291, 360, 421, 569;
  PPF 330
Intention, intendieren, 197, 205, 659;
  PPF 35, 272
Interesse, interessieren, 89, 108–9, 118,
  126, 166, 390, 412, 466, 570, 680;
  PPF 27, 36, 41, 52, 66, 114–15,
  282, 288, 301, 306, 365
interne Relation, PPF 247
Introspektion, 413, 551, 587, 677;
  PPF 369
Intuition, 186, 213–14, 659
irreführen, irreleiten, 73, 187, 213, 291,
  317, 356, 482, 640
irrelevant, 293, 636
Irrtum, sich irren, 51, 56, 110, 140,
  270, 288, 328; PPF 318
"ist", 20, 35 Z, 558; PPF 9

Jagd nach Chimären, 94
James, William, 342, 413, 610; PPF 299
Jastrow, Joseph, PPF 118
"Jetzt weiß ich's", 151
Jigsaw-Puzzle, PPF 321

Käfer, 293
Kalkül, 28 Z, 136, 559, 565; PPF 348
Kampf, 109
  Kampfspiel, 66
  Kampfstellung, 22 Z
Kartenspiel, 66
Käse, 142
Kategorie, kategorisch, PPF 111, 132
Katze, 647
Kaufmann, 1, 8
kausal, nichtkausal, 89, 195, 198, 220,
  613, 631; PPF 183
Kehlkopf, 376; PPF 305, 316
  Kehlkopfbewegungen, PPF 305,
    308
  Kehlkopfmuskeln, PPF 301
Kennzeichen, 545, 578
Kessel, Dampfkessel, 466, 469
Kette, V, 29, 85, 326
kinästhetisch, 621; PPF 56, 63

Kind, 5–7, 9, 27, 32, 66, 70 Z, 137,
    233, 244, 257, 282, 361, 420, 467,
    480, 539; PPF 119, 161, 205–6,
    215, 221, 314, 363
  Kinderzeichnungen, 148
  Kindheitstage, PPF 274
Kiste, 14; PPF 116–17, 205–6
Kitzel, 646
Klage, klagen, PPF 84–5, 229
Klang, 1, 31, 162, 171, 545; PPF 261
  Satzklang, 134
  Wortklang, 165
klar, Klarheit, 30, 47, 62, 81, 133, 142,
    314, 316, 318; PPF 314, 338, 354
klären, Klärung, 91, 160
Klarinette, 78
Klasse, 43, 66
Klassifikation, PPF 202
Klavier, Klavierstimmen, 666, 678,
    682
  Vorstellungsklavier, 6
Kleid, 195; PPF 335
Köhler, Wolfgang, PPF 180
kommen, Worte kommen, 165–6;
    PPF 296
Komplex, 48–9, 51, 53; PPF 37
komponieren, 233
konditional, 684
kongruent, PPF 127, 154
König, Schachkönig, 31, 35, 136, 563,
    567, 584
  Königskrönung, 584; PPF 348
konkret, 97; PPF 76
können, 30, 150–1, 182, 374, 497, 572;
    PPF 1, 224
Konsequenz, 486, 578, 626; PPF 291,
    319
konstruieren, Konstruktion, 75, 81, 98,
    149, 293, 366, 517
Kontrolle, kontrollieren, 265, 469
Kopfrechnen, 364, 366, 369, 385–6
Kopfschmerzen, 314
Kopfschütteln, 41–2, 556
Kopie, kopieren, 143; PPF 111, 131,
    135, 147, 151, 156, 184
Kopula, 20, 561

Körper, 36, 283, 286, 411
  Körper- und Bewußtseinszustände,
    421
Korrelat, 27, 96, 372; PPF 41
Krankheit, 255, 593
Kriterium
  für richtiges Erinnern, Erraten,
    Wiedererkennen, 56, 258, 625,
    633; PPF 318
  für Erlebnis, Gefühl, 509, 542;
    PPF 146
  für Fähigkeit, Können, 185, 238,
    385; PPF 36
  für Fehler, 51
  Geläufigkeit als Kriterium, PPF 180
  der Identität, 253, 288, 290, 322,
    377, 404
  für inneren Vorgang, 580
  für Lesen, 159–60, 164
  für Meinen, 190, 692
  für Passen, 182
  des Schmerzes, 315, 350–1
  für Sehen, PPF 242
  für Selbstgespräch, 344, 376
  für Selbstverständlichkeit, 238
  und Symptome, 354
  des Verstehens, 146, 182, 269
  für vorgestellte Farbe, 239, 377;
    PPF 60
  für Vorschweben, 141
  der Wahrhaftigkeit, PPF 319–20
  für Zustand der Seele, 149, 572–3
Kuh, 120, 449; PPF 314
Kummer, PPF 2–4, 6–8
Kunde, 356
Kurvenstück, 47

Labyrinth (der Sprache), 203
lächeln, 249, 351, 539, 583; PPF 5,
    149–50, 158, 200
Lampe, 62, 97
Landschaft, V, 398, 509; PPF 138, 160,
    197
Länge, 208–9, 251, 430; PPF 338
Längenmaß, 69
Laut, unartikulierter, 261

Leben
    gewöhnliches, menschliches,
        tierisches Leben, 105, 108 Z, 156,
        583; PPF 120, 195, 224
    von Zeichen, 339, 432, 592; PPF 224
Lebensform, 19, 23, 241; PPF 1, 345
Lebensluft, 103
Lebensteppich, Band des Lebens,
    PPF 2, 362
Lebewesen, lebender Mensch, 357, 420,
    430, 454
Leere, leer, 62, 107, 131, 293–4, 414,
    673; PPF 47
leerlaufen, 88, 132, 507
lehren, 6, 9, 53, 185, 190, 197, 208,
    362, 384, 556; PPF 61, 250, 355
Lehrer, 7, 145, 156–7, 362, 630;
    PPF 94, 355
Leichnam, 284
leisten, 60–1, 93, 183, 430, 546; PPF 359
lernen
    durch Abrichtung, 86
    Bedeutung, 77, 244, 361, 384–6, 590;
        PPF 338
    Gebrauch, 9, 26, 28 Z, 35, 179, 328,
        340, 376; PPF 303–4, 337–8,
        346–7, 350, 355, 361, 363, 370
    und können, 385
    Regeln, 31, 86, 162
    Spiel, 31
    Sprache, 9, 26, 32, 207, 338, 441, 495
Lernfähigkeit, 143–4
Lesemaschine, 156–7
lesen, 22, 86, 156–73, 375; PPF 264–5
letzte (Erklärung, Analyse, Instanz), 29,
    87, 91, 230
leugnen, 305–6, 308
Logik
    unserer Ausdrücke, Sprache, 38, 345
    ihre Exaktheit, Kristallreinheit, 105,
        107–8
    mathematische, symbolische, 124,
        134, 167
    als normative Wissenschaft, 81
    primitiveren, 554
    scheint aufgehoben, 108, 242

    Schluß der Logik, 486
    Sublimierung der Logik, 38, 89
    als Wesen des Denkens, 97
Logiker, 23, 81, 377
logisch
    ausschließen, 398; PPF 310
    Bedingtheit, 220
    Betrachtung, 89
    Konstruktion, 366
    möglich, 520–1, 566
    Unterschied, PPF 330
    Zirkel, 208
Logisch-philosophische Abhandlung,
    V, 23, 46, 97, 114
Logistik, PPF 372
Lokomotive, Eisenbahn, 12, 282
lösen, Lösung (Aufgabe), 91, 109, 125,
    133, 140, 351–2; PPF 131, 236
Löwe, PPF 203, 327
Lücke im Fundament, 87
Luft, in der Luft hängen, 87, 198, 380
Luftgebäude, 118
luftleerer Raum, 81
Luftwiderstand, 130
Lüge, lügen, 249, 355, 668; PPF 318
Luther, Martin, 589

"mager", PPF 274–5
Malweise, 401; PPF 168, 367
Mannigfaltigkeit
    des Gebrauchs, 10, 23, 38
    der Sprachspiele, 24; PPF 335
Manometer, 270
Märchen, 282
Marsbewohner, 139 Z
Maschine, Motor, 156–7, 193–4,
    270–1, 291, 359–60, 364, 491, 613,
    618; PPF 20
Maßstab, 11, 14, 131, 425, 430, 482;
    PPF 94, 198
Materialisation, PPF 158
materiell, 120, 398
Mathematik, mathematisch, V, 23,
    124–5, 189, 254, 334, 463, 517,
    544; PPF 224, 303, 322, 341–3,
    347–9, 371–2

Mathematiker, 144, 208, 240, 254;
  PPF 341, 343
mattsetzen, 316
Maus, 52
Mechanismus, 6, 156–7, 170, 270, 425,
  495, 559, 613, 689
Medium, 102, 177, 196, 308
mein, 246, 251, 253, 403–11
meinen
  eines Ausdrucks kein Erlebnis,
    kein begleitender Vorgang, 509;
    PPF 261–2, 271–3, 279, 291, 298
  Begriff des Meinens, 81, 125, 513
  und Erleben einer Wortbedeutung,
    509; PPF 10, 234, 261–2, 271–3,
    279, 282
  etwas meinen, 35 Z, 125, 276,
    455–7, 507, 511
  kein geistiges Handeln, kein
    Vorgang, keine Erfahrung, 19, 20,
    35, 60, 70 Z, 185–8, 334, 557,
    666–7, 674–80, 691–3; PPF 291
  ihn meinen, 661, 663, 686–7, 689,
    691; PPF 17
  Kriterium fürs Meinen, 190, 692
  "meinen" vs. "denken", 692–3
  etwas Privates, 358
  einen Satz meinen, 22, 81, 95, 358,
    507, 510, 592, 607
melden, Meldung, 19, 21; PPF 94–5,
  130, 138, 145
Melodie, 154, 184, 333; PPF 229, 233,
  280
Mengenlehre, 412, 426; PPF 371
Mensch, 281, 283, 360, 420
  und Bewußtsein, 281, 418, 420
  und Denken, 466–70
  primitive Menschen, 194
Menschenkenner, Menschenkenntnis,
  PPF 355
menschlich
  gemeinsame menschliche
    Handlungsweise, 206
  menschliches Benehmen, 281, 288,
    304, 393
Merkmal, 54, 134, 160, 166; PPF 58

messen, Messung, 23, 88, 242, 328, 330
Metapher, 356, 439
metaphysisch, 58, 116
Methode, 48, 133, 366, 548; PPF 221,
  338, 371
Methodologie, PPF 338
Miene, 21, 174; PPF 296
Mikroskop, 645–6
Milch, 498
mißverstehen, Mißverständnis, 10,
  28–9, 48, 71, 81, 87, 90–1, 93,
  100, 109, 120, 132, 201, 300, 314,
  345, 653
Mitleid, 287
mitteilen, Mitteilung, 280, 363, 522–3;
  PPF 5, 16, 20, 81
Mittelwesen, 94
Mittwoch und Dienstag, PPF 274–5
Modell, 141, 156; PPF 135
modellieren, 512
modifizieren, Modifikation, 14; PPF 1,
  224, 231
Möglichkeit, 20, 90, 97, 194, 253,
  520–1, 566
Moment, momentan, 184, 582, 638
Moore's Paradox, PPF 87, 98
Morgenzeitung, 265
Moses, 79, 87
Motiv, PPF 333–4, 336–7
Musik, musikalisch, 341, 523, 527, 529,
  531, 536; PPF 44, 260
müssen, 66, 81, 101, 131, 437
Muster, 1, 8 16, 50, 53, 56, 72–4, 293;
  PPF 2, 362
mutig, 536–7
Mythos, mythologisch, 221, 549 Z

nachahmen, 282, 285; PPF 150, 238
nachmachen, 208, 450; PPF 120, 149,
  244, 296
nähen, 195
Name, 1, 15, 27–8, 37–50, 55, 57–60,
  62, 64, 73, 79, 87, 116, 171, 244,
  256–7, 383, 410, 613, 680, 689–90;
  PPF 15, 50, 270
  eigentlicher, 38–9

Natur, 58, 114, 183, 185, 308, 441, 472, 549 Z; PPF 236, 365–6
Naturgeschichte, 25, 415; PPF 365
Naturgesetz, 54, 325, 492
Naturlaut, 310, 323
natürlich, 256, 595–6, 647
Naturnotwendigkeit, 372
Naturtatsache, 142 Z; PPF 365–6
Naturwissenschaft, 81, 89, 392; PPF 365
Negation, 547, 549–50
Nexus, 613
nichtkausales Herbeiführen, 613
Nichts, 304
Nimbus, 97
Nominalismus, 383
normal, 87, 141–3, 246, 288, 402, 509, 613; PPF 59, 312, 351
Notation, 18, 403, 562
Nothung, 39, 44
Notiz, 260, 319, 634
nützen, Nutzen, 15, 120, 185, 270, 312, 351, 397
nutzlos, 216

oben, 351
Oberflächengrammatik, 664
objektiv, PPF 340
Objektivität, 254
okkult, 38
Organisation, PPF 131, 134, 136, 220
Ornat, 426

Papagei, 344, 346
Paradigma, 50–1, 55, 57, 215, 300
Paradox, 95, 182, 201, 304, 412; vgl. Moore's Paradox
passen, 136–9, 182, 194, 216, 339, 409, 537, 572; PPF 50, 164, 270, 297, 321
Passiv, 47
Personenname, 27–8
Pfeil, 86, 454; PPF 162, 180, 184, 193
Pflanze, 70, 283, 312
Phänomen, 79, 108 Z, 176, 325, 363, 383, 436, 583; PPF 53, 86, 301
Phantasie, 342; PPF 254

Philosoph, 38, 116, 127, 255, 413, 514
Philosophen-Unsinn, PPF 309
Philosophie, 52, 81, 108–9, 119, 121, 124–6, 128, 133, 254, 309, 352, 393, 520, 599; PPF 315
philosophieren, 11, 15, 38, 131, 133, 194, 254, 261, 274, 295, 303, 348, 436, 592, 598
philosophisches Problem, 109, 123, 133, 308, 314
Photographie, 71, 486; PPF 59, 90, 171, 197–8, 252
Physik, physikalisch, 58, 108 Z, 194, 253, 401, 410, 493, 569, 571; PPF 34, 161, 338, 371
Physiognomie, 235, 568; PPF 238
Physiologie, physiologisch, 376, 632; PPF 177, 183, 232, 236, 306
Plan, 438, 653; PPF 12–13
pneumatisch, 109
Politiker, französischer, 336
Porträt, porträtieren, 522; PPF 143, 199
Prädikat, prädizieren, 104, 134, 136, 538
praktisch, 28 Z, 132, 268, 403, 411, 556
Praxis, 7, 21, 51, 54, 197, 202
primär, 656; PPF 276
primitiv, 2, 5, 7, 25, 146, 194, 339, 554, 597; PPF 82, 161, 215, 289
privat, 202, 243, 246, 248, 251, 256, 259, 262, 268–9, 272, 274–5, 280, 294, 311, 358, 380, 653; PPF 214
Projektionsmethode, 139, 141
Prozedur, 142
Prozeß, 308
psychisch, 321, 427, 454, 571
psychoanalytisch, PPF 268
Psychologe, 571; PPF 28, 114, 282
Psychologie, 377, 571, 577; PPF 28, 32, 371–2
psychologisch, 140, 213, 254, 274, 377, 589; PPF 32, 41, 202, 236, 268, 309, 330, 332, 369, 372
Puppe, 27, 282, 360; PPF 119

Quadrat, 47–9, 51, 53, 64, 74, 189
Qualität (und Quantität), 284

Ramsey, F. P., V, 81
Rätsel, rätselhaft, 23, 168; PPF 251,
   325
räumlich, 74, 108 Z, 539; PPF 148,
   158, 171, 173–4, 179–80, 218, 241,
   252–3
reagieren, 6, 157, 185, 189, 198, 206,
   495, 539; PPF 119, 128, 167, 231
Reaktion, 56–7, 143, 145, 284, 288,
   343, 630, 657, 659; PPF 215, 231,
   285, 289
Realist, 402
Rechnung vs. Experiment, PPF 291
rechtfertigen, Rechtfertigung, 182, 217,
   261, 265, 267, 289, 320, 323–5,
   382, 404, 460, 482, 485, 644;
   PPF 126, 161, 171, 181
Rechtschreibung, 121, 167
Regel, 142, 202, 207, 224–5, 231, 653
   abändern, 83–4
   Anwenden einer Regel, 218
   deuten, 85–6
   einer Regel folgen, 199, 202, 217,
     219, 222–3, 232, 235, 240
   der Grammatik, 497
   lernen, 31, 162
   präzise, 100–1
   und Rechtfertigung, 217
   und Schach, 197, 205
   des Spiels, 108 Z, 125, 205, 567;
     PPF 349
   der Sprache, 80–2, 497, 549 Z, 558
   des Sprachspiels, 53
   und Zweck, 567
   und Zweifel, 84–5, 87
regellos, 143, 163
regelmäßig, Regelmäßigkeit, 18, 73,
   163, 166, 169, 207, 208, 237, 630
Regelverzeichnis, 54, 197
Reihenornament, 208, 211
Reihenstück, 147, 228–9
rezeptiv, 172, 232, 672
Rohmaterial der Philosophie, 254

Rose, 514–15, 558; PPF 9, 314
Rotempfindung, 272
Russell, Bertrand, 46, 79
russisch, 20, 159

Satz, 19, 22–3, 49, 92–3, 98, 134–6,
   137, 225, 317, 421, 493, 513, 520,
   522, 527
   allgemeine Form des Satzes, 65, 114,
     134, 136
   Begriff des Satzes, 135
   denken, 22
   und Gebrauch, Verwendung, 21,
     134, 136, 195, 397
   und Grammatik, 353
   grammatischer Satz, 251, 295, 458
   mathematischer Satz, PPF 345
   meinen, 22, 81, 95, 358, 507, 510,
     592, 607
   philosophischer Satz, 85, 90
   verneinter, 447–8, 547–51, 554–7,
     549 Z
   verstehen, 80, 199, 513, 527, 531
Satzradikal, 22 Z
Satzschema, 134
Schach, 17, 31, 33, 47–9, 66, 108 Z,
   136, 149 Z, 197, 199, 200, 205,
   316, 337, 365, 563, 567; PPF 4, 36
Schatten, 194, 339, 448, 461
Schema, 47, 73, 86, 141, 163; PPF 135,
   173, 219, 236, 258
Schenken, 268
Schlag, mit einem Schlag, 139, 191,
   197, 318, 319
Schlemihl (Chamisso), 339
Schmerz, 281, 293, 295, 300, 302, 311,
   315, 384, 448–9
   des Anderen, 302–3, 350, 390; PPF
     314
   und Aufmerksamkeit, 666–7, 674
   benennen, 26, 244
   und Vorstellung, 300, 302, 311,
     391–3
   und Zweifel, 246, 288, 303
Schmerzäußerung, 245, 310; PPF 362
Schmerzbegriff, 282, 384

Schmerzbenehmen, 244, 281, 302, 304, 393

Schmerzempfindung, 154, 312; PPF 58

Schmerzflecken, 312

Schmerzgefühl, 351, 448

Schubert, Franz, PPF 270

Schweizer (Herr Schweizer), PPF 15

Seele, 1, 6, 37, 149, 188, 196, 283, 295, 357, 391, 422, 424, 454, 530, 573, 589, 648, 651, 652, 662, 676; PPF 11, 12, 22–5, 28–9, 76, 284

Seelenapparat, 149

Seelenleben, PPF 82

Seelenzustand, seelischer Zustand, 290, 577, 585, 652–3; PPF 29, 72, 79, 85, 102, 340, 358

"sehen", PPF 111

sehen, etwas als etwas sehen, PPF 121–2, 137, 166, 169, 171–6, 181–3, 185–7, 189–222, 254–61

Seherlebnis, PPF 117, 138–41, 146, 153, 156, 190

sekundär, 282; PPF 276, 278

Selbst, 413

Selbstbeobachtung, 586, 659

Sepia, 30, 50

siamesische Zwillinge, 253

sicher, Sicherheit, 320, 324–5, 474, 607; PPF 314, 330–2, 339–43, 353

Sinn
  und Analyse, 39, 60
  und Bild, Vorstellung, 352, 422, 426, 449
  gleicher Sinn, 20, 61, 183, 282, 556, 685; PPF 194, 348
  haben, 40, 47, 50, 138, 157, 227, 246, 253, 257, 366, 398, 453, 499
  eines Satzes, 20, 39–40, 44, 58, 79, 98–9, 117, 138, 197, 352, 395, 421, 502, 544; PPF 16, 37
  und Unsinn, 39, 282

Sinnesdatum, 366, 401, 486

Sinneseindruck, 354–5, 486; PPF 34, 60–1, 90, 269

sinnlos, 71, 157, 247, 358, 361, 500, 554; PPF 9, 80, 310

Sokrates, 46, 518

Solipsismus, 24, 402–3

"sondern", PPF 8, 261

Sonne, 88, 350–1, 607; PPF 323

Sorgfalt, 173

Spaten, 217

spezifisch, 322, 608; PPF 335

Spiegel, 285, 411

Spiel
  Ähnlichkeit zwischen Spielen (Familie), 61, 66–8; PPF 369
  Analogie der Sprache mit dem Spiel, 7, 81, 83, 108 Z, 125, 135, 182, 341, 562, 565
  erfinden, 204, 492
  und falsche Züge, 345; PPF 349
  lernen, 31, 54
  und Naturgeschichte, 25
  Sinn eines Spiels, 282
  und Sprachspiel, 42, 47, 49–51, 53, 57, 60, 64, 441; PPF 273
  Sprachspiel mit dem Wort "Spiel", 71
  wesentlich/unwesentlich für ein Spiel, 562, 564, 566–8

Spielfigur, Spielstein, 31, 35, 562, 565

Spielhandlung, 54

Spielregel, 108 Z, 567

Spinnennetz, 106

sprachähnlich, 7

Sprache
  allgemeine, 261
  beherrschen, 20, 33, 338, 508; PPF 1, 325
  als Berührungspunkt von Erwartung und Erfüllung, 445
  als Bild der Welt, 96–7
  und Denken, Meinen, 35 Z, 329–30, 341
  etwas Einzigartiges, 110
  erfinden, 491–2
  Grenze der Sprache, 499–500
  Grund der Sprache, 118
  als Instrument, 569
  Kleider der Sprache, PPF 335
  ein Labyrinth, 203

und Lebensform, 19, 23
lernen, 26, 32, 384
und Philosophie, 109, 116, 124
Praxis der Sprache, 7, 21, 51
private Sprache, 243, 245, 269, 275
und Regelmäßigkeit, 207
als System der Verständigung, 3
Übereinstimmung in der Sprache, 241
als Vehikel des Denkens, 329
und Verstehen, 54, 537
Werkzeug (Instrument) der Sprache,
    16, 50, 53, 569
Wesen der Sprache, 1, 92, 97
Zweck der Sprache, 304, 363, 491–2,
    496–7, 501
Sprachform, 25, 91, 111, 132
Sprachgebrauch, 58
Sprachlehre, PPF 315
Sprachlogik, 93
Sprachspiel, 2, 8, 21, 27, 48–51, 53, 60,
    64, 86, 143, 556, 630, 632; PPF 34,
    52, 94, 273, 287, 334, 346
Anfang, Ende, 290; PPF 289
Lügen als Sprachspiel, 249
das Neue ein Sprachspiel, PPF 335
normales Sprachspiel, 142, 288
als Primäres, 654–6
primitives Sprachspiel, 7, 146;
    PPF 161
Technik des Sprachspiels, 337
Traumerzählung als Sprachspiel,
    PPF 52
Verschiedenartigkeit der
    Sprachspiele, 23–4, 61, 195, 261,
    291; PPF 340
Verwandtschaft von Sprachspielen
    (Familie), 53, 64–5, 179, 630
Voraussetzung des Sprachspiels,
    PPF 31
Zug im Sprachspiel, 49
sprachwidrig, 40
sprechen, 25, 27, 32, 282, 318, 330,
    344, 347–8, 357; PPF 282
gedankenloses Sprechen, 341
in der Vorstellung, 344
Spruch, PPF 195

Sraffa, Piero, V
Stab, 251; PPF 338
stetiges Sehen, PPF 118
stöhnen, 257, 404, 406–7; PPF 30
Streit, 240, 588; PPF 341, 343
Strichgesicht, PPF 227
Strukturformel, 521
sublim, sublimieren, 38, 89, 94
Substrat, PPF 222
suchen, 77, 153, 165 Z, 334–5, 352,
    448, 462–3, 578, 654, 671, 685;
    PPF 62, 153, 295, 295, 314, 338,
    369
Superlativ, 192
Symbol, 193; PPF 232
symbolisch, 134, 219–21
Symbolismus, 18
Symptom, 354
System, 3, 143, 146, 152, 154–5, 189,
    325, 439; PPF 355, 357
Bezugssystem, 206
Dezimalsystem, 143
Maßsystem, 569
Nervensystem, 158
Regelsystem, 133
systematisch, 143

Tabelle, 1, 23, 53, 62, 73, 86, 162, 173,
    265
Tagebuch, 258, 270
Tat, 323, 459, 546
taub, 281, 416
taubstumm, 342, 348
Taufe, 38
Technik, 125, 150, 199, 205, 232, 262,
    337, 520, 557, 630, 692; PPF 222,
    347, 348, 355
Tendenz, 38, 94, 210, 591
Tendenzerlebnis, 591
Tennis, 66, 68
Theater, 23, 280, 365, 393; PPF 32
Theätetus (Platon), 46, 48, 518
Thema, 461, 523, 527, 531, 533;
    PPF 209, 210, 254
Theologie, 373
Theorie, 109

Therapie, 133
These, 128
tief, Tiefe, 89, 97, 111, 167, 209, 387,
    573, 583, 610; PPF 241
Tier, 25, 495, 647; PPF 1, 55
Ton, 21, 541, 582, 643; PPF 5, 98, 209,
    264, 339, 360, 370
  Tonfall, 21, 578, 607; PPF 74, 100,
    169, 264, 296, 305
  Unterton, 592
Tonart, 535, 536; PPF 178
Tönung, 339
Topf, 282, 297
tot, 284, 430, 432, 454, 455
Träger, 40–1, 43–4, 55, 283
Traum, träumen, 160, 358, 448;
    PPF 52–3, 219, 273, 320
Traumerzählung, PPF 52, 320
traurig, PPF 1, 227–8
Tricolore, 64
Typus, 23; PPF 40

Über-Ausdruck, -Begriff, -Bildnis,
    -Ordnung, 97, 192, 389
Übereinkunft, 355
übereinstimmen, Übereinstimmung,
    134, 139, 186, 201, 224, 234,
    241–2, 271, 352, 386, 416, 429,
    442, 465, 492, 538, 594, 607;
    PPF 320, 347, 351–2
überraschen, 326
übersehen, übersichtlich, 5, 92, 122,
    125, 352, 422
unbewußt, 149, 156, 171, 597; PPF 282
Unding, 108 Z; PPF 134
"und so weiter", 208
unendlich, 147, 186, 218, 229, 344,
    352, 426
unfehlbar, 215, 631
Unklarheit, begriffliche, PPF 206
Unsinn, unsinnig, 39, 40, 79, 119, 134,
    197, 246, 252, 282, 464, 448, 512,
    524, 540; PPF 19, 53, 309, 328
unwägbar, PPF 358–60
Urbild, 439
Urelement, 46, 48

Urmeter, 50
Urphänomen, 654
Ursache, 142, 177, 217, 324–5, 466,
    475–6, 593, 632; PPF 42, 114, 170,
    268, 274, 324, 336, 365

vag, Vagheit, 98, 100, 101
Variable, 134
Variation, 143, 420; PPF 2, 254
Vehikel, 329
verborgen, versteckt, 60, 91, 102, 126,
    129, 153, 164, 435; PPF 301,
    307–8, 317, 322, 323–4
verführen, 63, 93, 192, 294; vgl.
    verleiten, Versuchung
Vergleich, vergleichen, 20, 22–3, 50,
    71, 73, 77, 81, 104, 144, 308, 341,
    376, 400, 493, 522, 527, 604–5;
    PPF 127, 136, 195, 344, 369, 371
Vergleichsobjekt, 130–1
Verhalten, 157, 193, 344, 631; PPF 96,
    180
verifizieren, Verifikation, 272, 353;
    PPF 249
verleiten, 81, 171, 194, 322; vgl.
    verführen, Versuchung
Verneinung, 19, 251, 549, 549 Z, 551,
    554–7
verschwommen, 71, 77; PPF 160, 253
Verstand, 109, 119, 346
Verständigung, 2, 3, 22, 143, 242
verstehen
  Befehl, Frage verstehen, 431, 433,
    451, 505, 517
  Begriff des Verstehens, 150, 532
  Beschreibung, Bild, Zeichnung
    verstehen, 368, 526
  Erlebnis, innerer Vorgang des
    Verstehens, 153, 155, 322; PPF 36
  Gedicht, musikalisches Thema
    verstehen, 527, 531, 533; PPF 210
  Reihengesetz verstehen, 143, 147,
    152
  Satz, Sprache verstehen, 54, 81, 92,
    125, 199, 243, 355, 513, 525, 527,
    531, 652; PPF 317

Wort, Zeichen, Namen verstehen,
30, 87, 102, 139, 257, 261, 264,
269, 356
als Zustand, 146, 149 Z, 652
Verstellung, 249, 652; PPF 353,
358–60, 362–4
Versuchung (versucht sein), 20, 39,
143, 159, 182, 254, 277, 288, 334,
345, 374, 402, 520, 549 Z, 588;
PPF 101, 214; vgl. verführen,
verleiten
vertraut, Vertrautheit, 166–7, 596;
PPF 142, 294
verwandt, Verwandtschaft, 38, 47,
64–8, 76, 81, 88, 108, 150, 167,
224, 527, 538, 660; PPF 155, 199,
223, 223, 227, 234, 254, 260, 287,
302, 333
Vexierbild, PPF 131
visuelles Zimmer, 398–400
Vokal, PPF 177, 278
Volk, Volksstamm, 6, 200, 282, 385,
419
Völkerball, PPF 369
Volksschule, 351
Voraussetzung, 271, 631; PPF 31–3
Vorbild, 20, 131, 191–2, 302, 385;
PPF 135
Vorführung, 311; PPF 16, 296
vorgeben, 3, 156, 159, 365
vorhersagen, 193, 243, 629–32; PPF 98,
328–9
vorschweben, 20, 51, 59, 81, 139–41,
179, 210, 323, 329, 335, 352, 663;
PPF 17, 35, 264
Vorstellung
und Bild, 59, 141, 280, 300–1, 367,
389; PPF 17
und Denken, 338
von einer Gottheit, 346
motorische, PPF 18
des Schmerzes, 300–2, 311, 315,
391–3
Sprache der Vorstellung, 512
in der Vorstellung sprechen usw.,
168, 265–7, 344, 386; PPF 305

Vorstellungen vergleichen, 376–8,
382, 443
Wesen der Vorstellung, 370, 382
und Wirklichkeit, 386, 388–9, 393,
398, 443, 518; PPF 17
Vorstellungsbild, 166, 251, 265, 367;
PPF 11
Vorstellungserlebnis, PPF 10, 14
Vorstellungsklavier, 6
Vorstellungskraft, PPF 217
Vorstellungswelt, 402
Vorurteil, 108, 109, 131, 340

Waage, 142, 259
wahr, Wahrheit, 97, 136–7, 225, 282,
315, 437, 447, 544, 594; PPF
319–20, 348
Wahrhaftigkeit, PPF 319–20
Wahrheitsfunktion, 136
Wahrheitswert, 22
wahrnehmen, Wahrnehmung, 156, 417,
453; PPF 121, 128–30, 137–9, 247
wahrscheinlich, Wahrscheinlichkeit, 20,
158, 482, 484, 539
Wegweiser, 85, 87, 198
"weiche", PPF 271
Weil-Erlebnis, 176–7
weiterwissen, 151, 154–5, 179, 181,
323; PPF 300
Wellen der Sprache, 194
Welt, 96–7, 125, 205, 342; PPF 55
Weltanschauung, 122
Wenn-Gefühl, PPF 39, 41–4
Werkzeug, 11, 14–17, 23, 41–2, 53–4
Wesen
der Bezeichnung, 239
der Dinge, 89, 113, 116
in der Grammatik ausgesprochen,
371
Logik als Wesen des Denkens, 97,
105
der Negation, 547
der Sprache, 1, 46, 65, 92, 97, 113
verborgen, nicht verborgen, 92, 164,
371
wesensgleich, 399

Widerspruch, 58, 125, 201, 283; PPF 95

wiedererkennen, 35, 167, 270, 566, 602–4, 625; PPF 47

Wilde, 194

Wille, wollen, 19, 169, 174, 176, 338, 611–19, 621, 632, 635–8, 645, 659–60; PPF 93, 309

willkürlich, unwillkürlich, 168, 372, 497, 508, 520, 613–14, 616, 627–9; PPF 367

Wink, 355

wirklich, Wirklichkeit, 59, 131, 134, 188, 194, 352, 364–6, 386, 429, 438, 518

Wirkung, 28 Z, 145, 149, 160, 480, 498

Wirkungsweise, 193

wissen

    Äußerung des Wissens, 149

    und glauben, 481, 587, 138 Z; PPF 311

    Gott weiß, 426; PPF 342

    heißt beschreiben können, 378; PPF 57

    "Jetzt weiß ich's!", 147, 151, 179, 184, 409; PPF 236, 293, 321, 370

    und meinen, 187, 274, 398, 504, 679

    nur er/ich weiß, 156, 159, 246, 274, 293, 295, 303, 315, 378, 504; PPF 311

    und sagen, 78

    wer Schmerzen hat, 404, 409; PPF 311

    was ein Spiel ist, 75

    als Zustand der Seele, 149

Wissenschaft, wissenschaftlich, 79, 81, 89, 109; PPF 365, 371

Witz, 23, 62, 111, 142, 363, 564, 567

Wort

    und Atmosphäre, Charakter, Gefühl, 542–5; PPF 35, 37–50, 271–3

    und Bedeutung, Gegenstand, 1, 19, 30, 49, 120, 139, 544–5; PPF 274–8

    und Gebrauch, Verwendung, 1, 30, 34, 90, 116, 133, 139, 191, 196–7, 264, 345, 370, 378, 383, 556; PPF 7, 35

lehren, lernen, 1, 6, 9, 35, 49

    Seele eines Worts, 530

    Verstehen, 6, 29, 139, 264, 269; PPF 40

Wortart, 1, 17, 23

Wortbild, 167, 169–70, 291

Wörterbuch, 265

Worterklärung, 262, 268, 370

Wortgefühl, PPF 40

Wortgemälde, PPF 267

Wortsprache, 16

Wortstellung, 336–7

Wunsch, wünschen, 35, 437–41, 461, 546, 548, 614–16, 656

Würfelbild, Würfelschema, 74, 139–41; PPF 116, 135, 173, 218–19, 236, 258

Würfelspiel, 70 Z

Zahl, 10, 26, 28–9, 67–8, 135, 284, 339; PPF 133, 165

Zahlenarten, 67–8

Zahlenfolge, -reihe, 143, 145–6, 151, 185, 214, 226, 320

Zahlwort, 1, 8–10, 28

Zahnrad, 136

Zahnschmerzen, 257, 311–12, 665; PPF 223

Zeichen

    eigentliches, 105

    für eine Empfindung, 258, 260–1

    und Gebrauch, 51, 53, 82, 136, 198, 432–3

    für Wort und Satz, 49

Zeichnung, 23, 70, 141, 396, 425, 512 653; PPF 111–12, 132, 148, 150, 157, 173–4, 180, 192, 195–6, 218, 258

zeigen, 8–9, 33–7, 43, 71, 208, 275, 429, 454, 590, 669, 671

Zeit, 89–90, 108, 138, 196, 350, 607–8; PPF 58, 70, 285–6

zeitlos, 58

Zeitmessung, 88

zerstören, Zerstörung, 50, 55, 57, 59, 106, 118

Zeugnis, 386, 594

Zug (Charakterzug), 66, 168; PPF 27

Zug (Spielzug), 22, 33, 49, 345;
    PPF 349

Zukunft, 461, 480–1, 629; PPF 29, 323,
    370

zusammengesetzt, 39, 45–9, 59–60

Zustand
    der Mathematik, Psychologie, 125;
        PPF 371; vgl. Seelenzustand

Zuversicht, 325, 579

Zweck
    eines Begriffs, 69, 345, 385
    einer Beschreibung, 109, 609
    eines Bilds, 607

der Grammatik, 497

einer Handlung, PPF 290

und Philosophie, 127, 132

der Regel, 567

eines Satzes, 317, 416, 489, 501, 657

der Sprache, 304, 363, 492, 496, 501

des Wegweisers, 87

der Wörter, 5–6, 8, 565–6

Zweifel, zweifeln, 24, 84–5, 87, 142,
    157, 187, 197, 213, 246, 288,
    386, 408, 415, 578, 607, 652, 679;
    PPF 33, 64, 307, 310, 312, 331,
    354

zwingen, 140, 231, 299

Zwischenglied, 122

Index

Numbers refer to numbered remarks; 'brf *n*' is a boxed remark following remark *n*. 'PPF *n*' refers to *Philosophy of Psychology – A Fragment*, remark *n*. 'Pr' signifies a reference to Wittgenstein's Preface.

ability
- to ask a thing's name, 6, 31
asking a name presupposes –ies, 30
- to calculate in one's head, 385
criterion of an –, 182, 385; PPF 36
- is not a feeling, PPF 36
- to go on, 151, 154, 179, 183–4, 324–5, 660
grammar of 'able to' related to that of 'know', 150
- is grammatically a state, 572
knowing that one is able to, 388
- to learn, may come to an end, 143–4
- to play chess, brf 149; PPF 36
–ies required for the possibility of certain experiences, PPF 224
- to walk, 183
above/beneath, 351
accompaniment
- of a chess move, 33, 200
mental attitude doesn't accompany words like a gesture, 673
thought as – of speech, 330, 332
- of understanding, 152–3, 321
- of utterance, 20, 34, 35, 51, 56, 321

accord with a rule, *see* rule, accord with a
accuracy, 58, 158, 171, 254; PPF 112, 142, 338
act/action, 1, 7, 36, 612–25, 627
active/passive voice, 47
activity, 7, 23, 36, 156, 693; PPF 79, 349; *see also* mental act/activity
Adelheid, 365
aesthetics, 77; PPF 178, 297
affinities, 65–7, 76
agent, *doing* seems the real –, 620
agent/observer, 631
agreement, 61, 134, 208, 234, 241–2, 386, 429; PPF 346–7, 351–2
alphabet, 8, 137, 148, 160
analogy, 75, 83, 90, 140, 308, 494, 613, 669; *see also* likeness
analysis, 39, 60, 61, 63–4, 90–1, 92, 383, 392
and so on, 208, 229
animal
- belief, PPF 1
–s can't be hopeful, PPF 1
–s don't talk, 25
–s don't talk to themselves, 357

We are indebted to Fr G. Hallett's 1967 index to the *Investigations*.

animal (*cont'd*)
  evolution of higher –s and man,
    PPF 55
  picture of an – transfixed by an
    arrow, PPF 180, 184, 187, 193, 196
  see also cat, cock, cow, dog, lion
anticipating reality, 188
apple, 1
  wanting an –, 440
application
  – of an algebraic formula, 146–8
  – of an arrow as a pointer, 454
  – of brackets, 557
  – comes before the mind, 141
  – is the criterion of understanding,
    146
  – forced on one by a picture, 140
  – of imaginary numbers, PPF 165
  – of a picture, 140–1, 349, 374,
    422–5
  – of a rule, *see* rule, application of a
  – of a schema, 141
  – of a sentence-like formation, 520
  – of a word, *see* word, application
    of a
a priori, 97, 158, 251, 617; PPF 309
arbitrary, 372, 497, 508, 520; PPF 367
architectural requirement, 217
arm, movement of, 612, 614, 621–2,
    624–5, 627, 630
arrow, how it comes about that it
    points, 454
artichoke, 164
ashamed, 643–4
asking what something is called,
    see name, asking for the
aspect, PPF 111–261
  – blindness, PPF 257–60
  – change, PPF 124, 128, 129, 130,
    135, 152, 166, 179, 185, 189, 213,
    220, 257
  concept of an – related to concept
    of imagination, PPF 254
  continuous seeing of an –, PPF 118
  –s of a double cross, PPF 212–15,
    218, 236

aspect (*cont'd*)
  duck–rabbit –, PPF 152, 215, 216
  interpretation of an –, PPF 116–17
  knowing, rather than seeing, an –,
    PPF 192, 196
  lighting up of an –, PPF 118, 140,
    207, 209, 237, 247
  noticing an –, PPF 113
  organizational –s, PPF 220
  physiognomy of an –, PPF 238
  seeing an – demands imagination,
    PPF 217, 254, 256
  seeing an – and experiencing the
    meaning of a word, PPF 261
  seeing an – is subject to the will,
    PPF 256
  –s of a triangle, PPF 162, 211–12,
    217
assertion, 21, 22, 447
  of hesitancy, PPF 110
assertion-sign, 22
assertoric sentence, *see* sentence,
    assertoric
associative connection between word
    and thing, 6, 53, 256, 257
assumption, 187, 299; PPF 106–7
assumption (Fregean *Annahme*), 22,
    brf 22
astronomer, PPF 323
atmosphere, brf 165, 173, 213, 594,
    596, 607, 609; PPF 35, 42, 50
attention/attend, 275
  concentrating one's –, 33, 34, 258,
    263, 667
  – to one's consciousness, 412
  directing –, 6, 33, 268, 275, 277,
    411–12, 666, 669
  divided –, 666–7, 674, 678, 682
  –ing to a sensation, 258, 268, 668
attitude
  – to a drawing, PPF 192
  mental – does not accompany
    words, 673
  – to proverbs as opposed to
    theorems, PPF 195
  – of receptivity, 672

attitude (*cont'd*)
  – towards a soul, PPF 22
  struggle to maintain an –, 575
Augustine, 1–4, 32, 89, 90, 436, 618
Augustine's picture/conception of
      language, 1–4
automaton, 420; PPF 19–21

baby
  babble of a –, 282
  smile of a –, 249
balance, 259
Ballard, 342
bang, expecting a –, 442
baptism, 38
barometer, 354
bearer of a name, *see* name, bearer of a
because, 487
  experiencing the –, 176–7
  see also cause; motive; reason(s)
bedrock, 217
Beethoven, PPF 51
beetle, 293
behaviour
  change in the – of a reader, 157
  – characteristic of someone
      correcting a slip of the tongue, 54
  – as criterion for someone's talking
      to himself, 344
  – as criterion for understanding,
      misunderstanding and not
      understanding, 269
  description of –, PPF 32
  dog simulating pain –, 250
  don't say I am talking to myself on
      the basis of my –, 357
  – and doubt, 288
  – as expression of something mental,
      PPF 32
  fine shades of –, PPF 180, 192, 210
  – of a human being, 281, 283, 288
  pain –, 244, 246, 281, 300, 302, 304;
      PPF 324
  – of a point on a screen, PPF 27
  psychologists study –, 571
  psychology treats of –, PPF 28

behaviour (*cont'd*)
  report about – or state of mind,
      PPF 29–30
  shared human –, 206
behaviourism, 308
behaviourist, 307
being/non-being, 50; *see also*
      existence/exist
belief, PPF 86–110
  acting –, PPF 78
  cannot mistrust one's own –, PPF 91
  holding fast to a –, 575
  – and Moore's paradox, PPF 87, 98,
      105
  reasons for –, 475, 477–81, 578
  – in uniformity of nature, *see*
      uniformity of nature, belief in
  unsatisfied –, 439
to believe
  –ing that another isn't an
      automaton, PPF 19
  –ing that another is in pain, 303,
      310; PPF 19
  assertion of 'I believe' contrasted
      with supposition, PPF 88, 101
  assuming one –s, PPF 106–7
  –ing the chair will bear me, 575
  –ing Goldbach's conjecture, 578
  how one knows one –s, 587
  'I believe' throws light on my state,
      PPF 96–7
  introduction of 'I believe', PPF 95
  knowing what one –s, PPF 309
  –ing man has a soul, 422
  –ing one believes, 260
  –ing one is pretending, PPF 364
  seeming to –, PPF 99, 103
  –ing and state of mind, PPF 102
  –ing is not thinking, 574–5
  –ing that twice two is four, PPF 348
  use of 'I believe', PPF 86–90
  verb 'believe', PPF 93
  verb 'to believe falsely', PPF 92
belonging, *see* fitting/belonging
benzene, PPF 54
blindness, 424

blood-pressure, 270
blurred, 71, 76, 77, 253
body, 36, 283, 286, 359, 364, 391, 411
boiler, 466, 469
boundary, of a concept, *see* concept, boundary of
boundary line, 62, 69, 88, 163, 499
  purpose of a –, 499
  rigid/sharp –s, 68, 71, 76, 77, 99
box, 293, 425; PPF 116
boxer, brf 22
brain, 158, 412, 427
bridge, justifying choice of dimensions for, 267
bring about, 611, 613, 614
broomstick, 60
builder, and assistant, 2, 8, 21, 41, 42
building stones, 2, 7, 8, 10, 19–21, 86
  words for –, 2, 6, 7, 8, 9, 17, 21
bumps, 119
butter, rising in price, 693

calculate, 233–4, 236, 385–6; PPF 348
  –ing in the head/in the imagination, 364, 366, 369, 385–6; PPF 277, 304
calculation, correct result of a –, PPF 341–5
calculus, brf 28, 81, 136, 559, 565; PPF 348
call
  – someone, 27, 691
  – someone to mind, 691
carefulness, 173
Carroll, Lewis, 13; PPF 151
cat, 647
categorial difference, PPF 111
category, PPF 132
causal connection, 89, 195, 198, 613
  – irrelevant to logical investigation, 89
  – seen from inside/outside, 631
cause
  –s of concept formation, PPF 365
  – contrasted with object of emotion, 476
  – established by experiment, 169

cause (*cont'd*)
  experience of –, 169–70
  feeling the –, 169, 170, 175–7
  – of following a rule, 217
  –s are of interest to psychologists, PPF 114
  not interested in –s/our problems not causal, 217, 466; PPF 170, 183
  main – of philosophical diseases, 593
  –s of memory-feeling, PPF 370
  motive and –, PPF 336
  physical –s and cock call, 493
  – and prediction in expression of intention, 631–2
  psychological –s, PPF 228
  – and reason, 325, 475
  –s of unfounded conviction, PPF 268
certainty, 246, 320, 324–5, 474, 607, 679; PPF 330–2, 339–43, 353;
  see also uncertainty
chair, 1, 35, 47, 59, 80, 253, 361, 368, 486
chart
  colour, *see* colour-chart
  different ways of reading a –, 86
  – taking over the role of memory, 53
check, 136
checkmate, 316
cheese, weighing lump of, 142
chemical possibility, 521
chemical reaction, 56–7
chemistry, symbolism of, 18
chess
  ability to play –, brf 149; PPF 36
  –board, 47, 58
  – is a custom, 199
  – defined by its rules, 197, 205, 567
  intending to play –, 197, 205, 337
  – king, 31, 35, 136, 563, 567
  learning to play –, 31
  meaning of – pieces, 563
  – move, 33, 49, brf 108
  – pieces, 17, 33, 35, brf 108, 565
  real game of –, 365
  – rules, 197

chess (*cont'd*)
  skill in –, 66
  – translated into yells and stamping,
    200
chief, 419
child
  –'s ability to think, 32
  –ren's drawings, oddity of, PPF 148
  –ren give names to dolls, 27
  – learning language, 5, 6, 7, 9, 32
  – learning names of sensations, 244,
    257
  – playing with a ball, 66
  –ren playing with a chest as a
    house, PPF 205–7
  –ren playing at trains, 282
  – and pretending, 249; PPF 363
  –ren seen as automata, 420
chimeras, 94
choice, 219
church mode, 535
circle, 34
  not all lines are –s, PPF 108
circumstance
  – of asking what time it is, 607
  – that we call 'playing chess', 33
  – in which a concept loses its
    purpose, 385
  – under which a definition is given,
    29
  – dependence of criteria for reading,
    164
  – dependence of possibility of doubt,
    213
  – determine interpretation, 539
  – of drawing a line, 177
  – of the if-feeling, PPF 41
  – justifying claim of ability, 182–3
  – of an ostensive definition, 29, 35
  – of pointing, 35
  – in which a sample changes colour,
    56
  – in which a signpost is in order, 87
  – in which a supposition makes
    sense, 349
  – of the use of 'This is here', 117

circumstance (*cont'd*)
  –s warrant my saying I can go on,
    154–5, 179
  –s warrant saying that he meant,
    557
  – of a wish, 441
city, ancient – compared with
    language, 18
civic life, 125
clarity, 81, 133
classification, aim of, 17; PPF 202
clock, 266, 363, 607
clockwork, 318
clothing of our language, PPF 335
cock, 493
coffee, aroma of, 610
cogwheel, 136
colour
  attending to the –, 33, 72
  – blindness, PPF 351
  –chart, 1, 53, 73
  common –, 72
  consciousness of –, PPF 242
  defining – words, 28–30, 33, brf 28
  – edge, 88
  – 'exists', 58
  explaining the meaning of a – word,
    1, 16, 28, brf 28, 29, 30, 33, 35,
    brf 35, 50, 51, 73
  immersing oneself in a –, 277
  – impressions, 272–7; PPF 247
  indestructibility of –, 56–7
  judgements of –, PPF 346
  knowing from one's mental image
    what a – looks like, 388
  knowing what – to pick out, 239
  matter of course to call this – . . . ,
    238–9
  – names, 1, 26, 28, 29, 30, 33, 49,
    50, 51, 57, 58, 64; PPF 346
  – and private experience, 272–9
  sameness of –, 33, 56, 72, 208
  – samples, 1, 8, 16, 50, 53, 56, 57
  shades of –, 73
  simple or composite –, 47–8
  – statements, brf 35, 50; PPF 350

command, *see* orders/commands
common
  – colour in pictures, 72
  – feature, 71, 72, 73
  – order of possibilities in both world
    and thought, 97
  something – to, 65, 67
communicate, 363
communication, 2, 3, 242, 491; PPF 81
  point of –, 363
  possibility of –, 143
comparison
  of images, 376–7
  of impressions in recognition, 604–5
  mode of –, PPF 127
  of musical phrase with a sentence,
    527
  object of –, 50, 130
  possibility of –, 104
  – of words, to find the right one,
    PPF 295
complaint, PPF 84
complete/incomplete, 18
completeness, not aiming at, PPF 202
complex, 45, 48, 49, 53
compositeness, 47, 48, 59
composition
  – out of elements, 46, 47
  – of forces, 48
compositionalism, PPF 37
compulsion, logical/psychological, 140
concept
  analysing –s, 383
  blurred/sharp –s, 68, 71, 77
  boundary of –, 68, 69, 70, 71, 76;
    PPF 219
  – compared with a region, 71
  – compared with a style of painting,
    PPF 367
  – determination, PPF 191
  explaining the significance of a –,
    brf 142
  extending a –, 67
  –s are expressions of our interest,
    570
  – forces itself upon one, PPF 191

concept (*cont'd*)
  –formation, PPF 365–7
  –s are instruments, 569
  modified – of experience, PPF 222–6
  – of the past, PPF 370
  purely visual –, PPF 225
  purpose of a –, 385
  sameness of –, 76
  –s sometimes shade into one
    another, 544
  –s suitable for psychology, 577
  super-, 97
  –s touch and run side by side,
    PPF 108, 301
  usability of –, 69
conceptual (boundaries, confusions,
    differences, investigations,
    justifications, statements,
    unclarities), PPF 67, 181, 183,
    202, 219, 230, 257, 338, 371
confession, PPF 318–19
confidence, 325, 579; *see also* certainty
confronting, something – us all, 273
confusions, 16, 38, 132, 140, 339
conjuring trick, 308
connection, making a –/reporting a –,
    487, 682–5, 689
conscious act/activity, 156, 159
conscious of, 20, 156; PPF 240–2
consciousness, 358, 390, 412–21, 426
  awakening of –, PPF 55
  state of –, 148–9, 421
  – of a stone, 390, 418
conscious/unconscious, 149, 156, 281,
    418; PPF 282
conspicuousness, 600
constancy, 242; *see also* regularity
construction line, PPF 318
context, 156, 161, 403, 525, 539, 584,
    595, 638, 652, 665, 686; PPF 35,
    41, 47, 74, 75, 79, 235, 242, 283,
    313
  – of a sentence, 38, 49, 558; PPF 8,
    19, 38, 39, 249
continuing a series, *see* series,
    continuing a

contradiction, 58, 125

convention, 41, 355

conviction/convinced, 287, 333;
    PPF 100, 326, 339
  feeling of –, 607

copula, 20

corbel, sham, 217

coronation, 584; PPF 348

corpse, 284

correct/incorrect, 54, 145–6, 258

correctness, criterion of, 258

correspond, 20, 31, 36, 39, 40, 51, 53,
    55, 366, 521

court of appeal, final/highest, 56, 230

cow, 120, 449; PPF 314

criterion/criteria
  – for ability, 182
  – for being able to calculate in the
    head, 385
  – for being able to play chess,
    PPF 36
  – for being certain, PPF 339
  – for a body's changing weight, 182
  – for a body's fitting, 182
  – for colour of a mental image, 239
  – of correctness for remembering,
    258
  different kinds of – for method of
    projection before the mind, 141
  fluctuation of – with symptoms,
    354
  – for guessing thoughts right,
    PPF 318
  – for having had *that* experience,
    509
  – for how a formula is meant, 190
  – for identifying a sensation, 290
  – of identity for experiences of
    understanding, 322
  – of identity for mental images,
    376–8
  – of identity for pain, 253, 288
  – of identity of a person, 404
  – for the inner, 142
  – for inner states, PPF 36
  – for intention, 641

criterion/criteria (*cont'd*)
  – for knowing *qua* state of mind,
    149
  – for later saying, 542
  – for looking at something without
    seeing it, PPF 242
  – for having mastered rule of a
    series, 185
  – for meaning someone to continue
    a series, 692
  – for being in mental state, 572
  – for mistake, 51
  – for being of an opinion, 573
  outward –, 580
  physiological – for seeing, PPF 236
  – for reading, 159–60, 164
  – for recognizing the feeling of
    moving one's arm, 625
  – for remembering right, 56
  – for report's agreeing with a dream,
    PPF 320
  – for sameness of pain, 253
  – for saying the ABC to oneself, 376
  – for seeing a drawing three-
    dimensionally, PPF 180
  – for a sense-impression apprising
    one of shape and colour, PPF 60
  – for something's being a matter of
    course, 238
  – for talking to oneself, 344
  – for a thought's already having
    been completed, 633
  – for truth of a confession, PPF 319
  – for understanding/not
    understanding, 146, 182, 269
  – for visual experience, PPF 146

cry/crying, 24, 244, 296, 317, 543, 546;
    PPF 73, 82–5, 138, 145

crystal/crystalline, 97, 107–8

cube, drawing/picture of, 74, 140–1;
    PPF 218–19, 258

'cube', the word, 139

curse, 680–1

curve, continuous/open, 47

custom, 198, 199, 205, 337, 556;
    PPF 168

cylinder, 182, 439
Cyrillic, 159, 162

darkness of this time, Pr
deaf-mutes, 342, 348
debt, 294
decision, 31, 186, 588–9, 627, 631, 632
definition
   –s in aesthetics and ethics, 77
   agreement in –s, 242
   – of exactness, 69
   – inadequate to resolve paradoxes,
      182
   –s inessential, 70
   – of number two, 28
   ostensive –, 28–30, 33, 38, 258, 362
   – of plant, 70
   – of proper names, 28, 79
   – of 'S', 258
   scientific –s, 79
   – of 'two', 28–9
   unformulated –, 75
deity/God, 234, 346, 352, 426; PPF 284,
   342
demonstratives, *see* indexicals
dependence, causal vs. logical, 220
depth, 89, 111, 594
depth-grammar, 664
derive, brf 35, 162–4, 193, 479
description/describe
   – of alternating aspects, PPF 213
   – an aroma, 610
   a copy is an incomplete – of a visual
      experience, PPF 156
   a cry does the service of a –,
      PPF 82–3
   –s used to define proper names, 79
   exclamation is a – of a perception,
      PPF 139
   – of an impression, PPF 173
   language yields –s, 240
   multiplicity of kinds of –, 24, 290–2
   must be possible to give a – of
      destruction
   mythological – of the use of a rule,
      221

description/describe (*cont'd*)
   – of a new aspect, PPF 153
   – of an object in a picture, PPF 169
   –ing a private picture, 294
   – a representation of a distribution
      in a space, PPF 70
   –ing not on the same level as
      naming, 49
   – of a state of mind/mental state,
      180, 577, 585, 588; PPF 72–9,
      82–5, 90
   – of an unfamiliar object, PPF 142
   – of what is seen, PPF 158, 160, 184,
      186–7
   see also indescribability
destruction, 50, 55–8
determination
   by an act of meaning, 188, 190
   by algebraic formula, 189
   by a rule, 201, 218–21
   of what is not yet there, 437
device, 492; *see also* instrument of
   language; tools
diary, about recurrence of a sensation,
   258, 260, 270
dice, brf 70
dictionary, 265
discovery, 119, 124, 125, 133, 400
diseases, philosophical, 593; *see also*
   bumps; houses of cards; illness;
   therapy; treatment
disposition, 149; PPF 102
disputes, 53, 240, 402, 424; PPF 341
do/doing, 612, 620
dog, 250, 357, 650; PPF 1, 363
dogmatism, 131
doing the same, 34, 62, 226–7; *see also*
   rule and doing the same
doll, 27, 282, 360; PPF 119
double cross, PPF 212, 215–18, 257
doubt
   – which exists for me does not for
      him, PPF 307
   –ing has an end, PPF 33
   imaginability of –, 84
   possibility of –, 213

doubt (*cont'd*)
 senselessness of –, PPF 310
 shutting one's eyes in the face of –,
   PPF 331
 signpost leaves room for –, 85
 –ing what we recognize as genuine
   –, PPF 354
 –ing whether another is in pain,
   303
 –ing whether one has two hands,
   PPF 312
 –ing whether one meant, 679
 –ing whether one is in pain, 246,
   288
 –s about who Moses was, 87
draughts, 562
dreams, 160, 448; PPF 52–3, 219,
   320
duck–rabbit, PPF 118, 120, 125–8, 137,
   152, 201, 208, 215–17

Earth has existed for the last
   5 minutes, PPF 313
echo of a thought in sight, PPF 235
electric shock, 409
elliptical, 19, 20
emotion, manifestations of, 321;
   PPF 96
entertaining a proposition, 22
entertainment, 66
error, *see* mistake
essence, 1, 46, 65, 89, 92, 97, 113, 116,
   239, 370–4, 547; *see also* nature
essential/inessential, 62, 168, 173, 562,
   564, 568
ethics, 77
everyday, 81, 106, 116, 134, 197, 235,
   412; PPF 161, 335; *see also*
   normal; ordinary
evidence, 488, 638, 641
 imponderable –, PPF 358–60
evolution, PPF 55
exactness/inexactness, 28, 69, 70, 88,
   91
examples, as explanation, *see*
   explanation by examples

exclamation, 27, 231, 586; PPF 126,
   138–9, 293
excluded middle, 352
exhibit/exhibition, 201, 311–13;
   see also manifestation; utterance
exist/existence, 39, 41, 46, 50, 79
 necessary, 50
existence attributions, 46, 58
existing in and of itself, 46, 58
expectation, 576–7, 581–3
 an act of –, 586
 expression of an –, 452–3, 465, 574
 and its fulfilment/satisfaction, 442,
   444–5, 465
 – is grammatically a state, 572
 – and its object, 452–3
 – sometimes not a state of mind,
   577
 unsatisfied –, 438–9
experience
 –ing the because/cause, 170, 176–7
 characteristic/particular –, 34–5, 155,
   157, 165, 167, 171, 174
 – and expert judgement, PPF 355
 – of guidance, 172–3, 176
 inner private –, 243, 256–315
 intending, understanding, etc. are
   not –s, 34–5, 59, 165–6, 172–8,
   232, 322, 591, 645
 justification by –, 480, 485
 language-dependent –, 649;
   PPF 222–4
 meaning of an expression not an –,
   509
 –ing the meaning of a word,
   PPF 234, 261–7, 271–4
 – as a super concept, 97
 – of a tending, 591
 understanding, as an indefinable –,
   322
 visual –, *see* visual experience
 what – occasions saying "I'm
   conscious", 417–18
 willing, wanting, merely an –, 611
 word on the tip of one's tongue,
   not an –, PPF 299

experiment
  calculation not an –, PPF 291
  – establishes causal connections, 169
  psychological –, PPF 32
  result of an imagined –, 265
experimental method, PPF 371
expert judgement, PPF 355
explanation/explain
  accompaniments of –, 34
  – averts misunderstandings, 87
  – comes to an end, 1, 87, 654
  demand for –, 217
  effect of – depends on reaction, 145,
    288
  every – can be misunderstood,
    brf 28
  exact/inexact –, 88
  – by examples, 71, 75, 208–10
  grammar does not –, 496
  last/final –, 29, 87
  – of meaning, 1, 533, 560; PPF 286
  – of the meaning of a word, see
    word, explanation of a
  – of a musical theme, 527
  ostensive –, 28–36
  private –, see private explanation,
    and private ostensive definition
  –ing a proper name, 79, 82, 87
  rectification of –, 3
  – not training, 5
  – and understanding, see
    understanding and explanation
  –ing what a game is, see game,
    explaining what it is
  –ing what 'pain' means, see 'pain'
explorer, 206, 243
explosion, 576, 581–2
expression, facial, see face/facial
  expression
expression, form of, see form of
  expression

face/facial expression, 21, 285, 536–7,
  539, 583; PPF 17, 112–13, 119,
  150, 231–2
fact, 89, 95, brf 142, 471; PPF 365–6

Fahrenheit, 508
fairy tale, 282
faith, 589
familiarity/unfamiliarity, feelings of,
  129, 167, 596; PPF 35, 142;
    see also recognition/recognize
family
  – of cases, 164
  – of language-games, 179
family resemblance, 67–77, 108
Faraday, M., brf 104
fat/lean, PPF 274–5
fear
  – of being burned, 473, 480
  cry of –, PPF 74, 82–3, 85
  doubting someone else's –, 303
  expression of –, 142, 537
  object of –/cause of –, 476
  – utterance, PPF 5
  verbal expression of –, PPF 72–7
feeling
  ascribing –s to others, 283
  attending does not consist in –s, 34
  – a cause/an influence, 169–70, 234
  – of conviction/doubt, 607
  deep –, 583
  description of a –, PPF 63–6
  expression of expectation does not
    describe a –, 582
  –s of familiarity/unfamiliarity, 596
  genuineness of expressions of –s,
    PPF 355–62
  – gives the words 'meaning'/truth,
    544
  hidden –, PPF 324
  hypostatizing –s to explain thoughts,
    598
  if-feeling, PPF 39–44
  intention is not a –, 588, 645
  knowing what one feels, PPF 309,
    311
  – of a link between thoughts, 640
  making a chess move does not
    consist in –s, 33
  reading does not consist in –s,
    159–60

feeling (*cont'd*)
  report of emotion not learnt from
    –s, PPF 5–6
  – of satisfaction, 460
  tactile –s, 626
  see also genuineness of feelings;
    kinaesthetic sensations
fibres, overlapping, 67
fiction, 22, 307
fingers, crossing one's, 617
finite/infinite, *see* infinite/infinitely/
    infinity
fire, certainty that – will burn, 325,
    472–4, 477, 480
fit
  associated things seem to –,
    PPF 50–1
  everything –s into its shape, 216
  grammar of –, 182
  –ing is grammatically a state, 572
  meaning –s use, 139
  name –s a face, PPF 270
  pin –s socket, 194
  solid cylinder –s hollow one, 182
  'true' –s a proposition, 137
fitting/belonging, 136–9
flower, 53
fly
  in fly-bottle, 309
  a wriggling –, 284
follow/following a rule, 185–242
  – is analogous to obeying an order,
    206
  – blindly, 219
  – definite rules, 83
  how am I able to –, 217
  – not intimation, 222–3, 230
  one person, once in a lifetime –s a
    rule, 199
  physiognomy of –, 235
  – is a practice, 202
  – 'privately', 202
  – of a series, 143–7, 185–92, 213–38
  when we – things don't turn out,
    125
  what we call '–', 201

foreign country, 32
foreigner, 20
foreknowledge, 629–32; PPF 329;
    see also prediction
forgetting which colour this is the
    name of, 57
formation rule, 143
form of expression, 90, 94, 334, 356,
    398, 402, 409, 426, 513
form of life, 19, 23, 241; PPF 1, 345
forms of our language, 111, 112
formula, 146, 151, 152, 154, 179, 183,
    185–90, 226, 320; PPF 34
foundations, 87, 89
four consecutive sevens, 352, 516
Frege, G., 22, brf 22, 49, 71
French adjective, 538
French politician, 336
friction, 107
full-stop, 22
function, 5, 11, 17, 22, 27, 208, 260,
    304, 556, 559; *see also* language,
    function of; sentence, function
    of a; word, function(s) of

gambling, brf 70
game
  ball –, 83
  – a blurred concept, 71
  board –, 3, 31, 66
  card –, 66
  comparing –s, PPF 369
  concept of a –, 66–71, 75, 135
  definition of –, 3
  – determined by its rules, 567
  essential/inessential part of a –,
    562–8
  explaining what a – is, 69, 71, 75
  false moves in a –, 345
  – a family resemblance concept, 66,
    68, 69
  inventing a – that is never played,
    204
  knowing what a – is, 74
  learning to play a –, 31, 54
  perfect –, 100

game (*cont'd*)
  piece in a –, 17, 31, 33, 35
  playing a –, 3, 200, 282
  rules of a –, 3, 31, 54, 84, brf 108,
    125, 205, 567–8; PPF 349
  something common to all –s, 66
  still playing a –, 200
  use of words compared with –s, 7,
    81, 83, 182
gaps, 84, 87
gaze, 412
general propositional form, *see*
  proposition, general form of
genuineness of feelings, 606;
  PPF 352–61
Germanisms, 597
gesture, 1, 174, 208, 288, 310, 330, 335,
  433–4, 528, 529, 550, 590, 610,
  673; PPF 6, 26; *see also* pointing
ghost, 360
gift, right hand to left hand, 268
given, the, PPF 345
glasses, pair of, 103
  frame of –, 114
globe, 351
God, *see* deity
Goethe, PPF 51
going on in the same way, 185,
  215–16, 223–8
going to, 631–2, 635–9, 641, 645, 660;
  PPF 7, 328
Goldbach's conjecture, 578
'good', 77
goose, PPF 314
grammar
  aim of –, 497
  arbitrariness of –, 497, 520
  basis of –, PPF 365
  comparison with a paradigm in –,
    20
  – deficient in surveyability, 122
  – describes rather than explains, 496
  drop of –, PPF 315
  – expresses essence, 371–3
  oscillation/fluctuation between
    natural science and –, 79, 392

grammar (*cont'd*)
  pictorial representation of –, 295
  place/post in –, 29, 257
  purpose of –, 497
  surface/depth –, 664
  theology as –, 373
  – tries to force itself on us, 304
  – and verification, 353
  what – permits, 520
grammatical
  – difference, 149
  – fiction, 307
  – illusion, 110
  – inquiry, 90
  – joke, 111
  – movement, 401
  – proposition, *see* proposition,
    grammatical
  – question, 47
  – remark, 232, 574
grasping the meaning of a word,
    see understanding, at a stroke
grief, PPF 2–4, 67, 68
groan, 404, 406–7; PPF 30
grounds/well-grounded, 320
guess, 32, 33, 210, 266, 340, 607, 652;
  PPF 308, 318, 321–2, 328
guidance, 143–4, 170, 172–3, 175,
  177–8, 234, 237
gun, 442

hail/hailstones, PPF 9
hand, 268; PPF 312
handles, 12
hardness, state of, 572
hardness of the logical 'must', *see*
  logical 'must', hardness of
harmony, between thought and reality,
  429
hatred, 642
'having' experience/pain, *see* ownership
  of experience
headache, studying, to clarify problem
  of sensation, 314
hearing/sensing a plaintive/solemn
  melody, PPF 229–30, 233

hearing something as a variation on a
theme, PPF 254
heptagon, construction of, 517
hexagon, two interpenetrating –s
(Köhler), PPF 180, 184–6, 189,
194
hidden, 60, 91, 92, 102, 126, 129, 153,
164, 435, 559; PPF 301, 307, 317,
322–6
highway, 426
hocus-pocus, 454
hope, 545, 574, 583–6; PPF 1, 78
horror, PPF 5–6
house, last, 29
houses of cards, 118
human being, 6, 26, 241, 243, 257,
281–8, 360, 361, 415, 416, 418,
466–8, 495, 656; PPF 19–23, 25
human being, behaviour of, see
behaviour, of a human being
human being, living, 281, 420, 430
hunch, 469, 607
hypothesis, 82, 109, 156, 325; PPF 249,
306

I, 398, 404–10
idea, 73
ideal, 81, 88, 98, 100–1, 103, 105
idealists, 402–3
identity
criterion of –, 253–4, 288, 322, 404
law of –, 215–16; PPF 311
numerical/qualitative –, 253–4
–/self-identity, 215–16
see also same
if-feeling, PPF 39–44
illness, 255
illusion, 80, 96, 97, 110; PPF 268
image-mongery, 390
images, see mental image
imaginability, as guarantor of sense,
251, 395–7, 449, 451, 517
imagination
concept of – related to concept of
an aspect, PPF 254
experiments in the –, 265, 267

imagination (cont'd)
intentionality of the –, 518
keyboard of the –, 6
language of – excludes nonsense,
512
looking at a clock in one's –, 266
looking up a table in the –, 265
nature of –, 370
– needed to hear something as,
PPF 254
object of –, 443
pain in the –, see pain, in the
imagination
powers of –, 251
proof producible in the –, PPF 255
rehearsing a tune in the –, 184
seeing aspects of a triangle
demands –, PPF 217
talking in the –, see talking to
oneself in the imagination
'imagination', ask how – is used, 370
imagine
– Beethoven writing . . . , PPF 51
can't – anything senseless, 512
can't – the opposite, 251
–ing a colour, 382, 386
content of experience of –ing,
PPF 10
describing what one –s, 367–8
experience of –ing, PPF 14
grammar of –ing, brf 35
–ing pain, 300–2, 311, 391–4
a painted picture of how one –s
something, 280
–ing red, 443, 451
–ing something is not necessary for
understanding a sentence, 396, 449
–ing is subject to the will, PPF 256
when I – something goes on, 363
when I – something I have got
something . . . , 398
imponderable, PPF 358–60
impression
auditory –s, 671
– of a balance, 259
– of colour, 272–8

impression (*cont'd*)
  comparing –s and recognition, 604
  deep –, 167
  – of inconspicuousness/ordinariness,
    600
  – of a picture-duck, PPF 157
  private – of a picture, 280
  – of a room, 368
  – of a rule, 259
  tangled –, PPF 160
  – of timidity, 536
  – of unfamiliarity, 596
  see also sense impression; visual
    impression
impressionistic picture, 368
inarticulate sound, 261
incorporeal process, 339
indefinable word, 182
independent, 57, 92, 157, 265, 620;
    PPF 102, 338, 348
indescribability
  of aroma of coffee, 610
  of simples, 46, 49
indexicals ('this', 'that'), 8, 9, 16, 38,
    44, 45, 117, 410, 514
Indian mathematicians, 144
individuals, Russellian, 46
induction, 324–5, 472–85
inference, 486, 599; PPF 96
infinite/infinitely/infinity, 147, 218, 229,
    344, 427
  – expansion of π, 352
infinitesimal calculus, 18
influence, 169–70, 175, 177, 491
  feeling/experiencing an –, 169–70,
    171, 176
information/informs, brf 35, 280, 481;
    PPF 20
inner
  – activity of listening, 671
  – clock, 607
  – experience, 174, 243, 256, 645
  – (internal) is hidden
  – life, 24
  – object, PPF 134
  – ostensive definition, 380

inner (*cont'd*)
  – picture, PPF 133, 158
  – process, 305, 580; PPF 36
  – speech, PPF 301–3, 307, 301;
    see also talking to oneself
  – states, PPF 36
  – voice, 213, 232–3
inquiry, turning the – round, 108
insignificant, boundaries of the –, 79
inspiration, 232
institution, 199, 337, 380, 540, 584
instrument of language, 50, 57, 291,
    360, 421, 569; *see also* device; tool
intangible, 175, 358, 421, 607–8
intend
  act of –ing, 197
  –ing construction of a sentence in
    advance, 337
  –ing to deceive, 638
  –ing not an experience, PPF 279
  guessing what I –, 210
  only you/he can know what
    you/he –, 247; PPF 328
  –ing to play chess, 197, 205
  rules contained in act of –ing, 197
  –ing to say something, 591–2
  –ing to write to a person, 681
  see also mean (meinen)
intention
  – not an accompaniment of intended
    act, PPF 280, 299
  accompaniments of an –, 646
  actions foreseen in –, 629–31;
    PPF 329
  apparent independence of custom/
    technique, 205
  ashamed of my –, 644
  certainty of/evidence for –, 641
  – embedded in a situation, 337
  evidence for –, 641
  – and experience of tending, 591
  – and expression of uncertainty,
    247
  – and feeling, 588
  guessing –s, 210; PPF 328
  – and inner experience, 645

intention *(cont'd)*
 – and knowing what one was going
   to do, 633–60
 – and mental process, 205
 natural expression of –, 647
 nature of –, 174
 – and prediction, 631–2; PPF 98,
   328–9
 remembering an –, 635, 648, 653, 660
 reporting a past –, 656
 – and as it were saying to oneself,
   658
 – and self-revelation, 659
 unconscious –, PPF 282
intentionality, 428–65; PPF 35
intermediate links, 122, 161
internal relation, PPF 247
interpretation/misinterpretation, 28, 32,
   34, 85, 111, 160, 170, 194, 198,
   201, 210, 213, 215, 506, 536, 539,
   634, 637–8, 656; PPF 116–17, 164,
   248, 299
intimation, 171, 222, 230, 232, 237
introspection, 413, 551, 587, 677;
   PPF 369
intuition, 186, 213–14, 659
'is', 558, 561
'is', sign of identity, PPF 9
is/is called, 27–31, 33–5, brf 35, 38

James, William, 342, 413, 610; PPF 299
Jastrow, J., PPF 118
jigsaw puzzle, PPF 321
joy
 characteristic expression of –, 142
 pattern of –, PPF 1–2
judgement, 242; PPF 297, 309, 346,
   355, 356, 357, 360
justification, 155, 169, 182, 217, 261,
   265, 267, 289, 320, 324, 325,
   378, 485, 486, 527; PPF 161, 171;
   see also reason(s); warrant

kinaesthetic sensations, 621, 624;
   PPF 56–62, 66
knife and fork, PPF 122

knob, 270
know
 –ing the ABC, 148–9
 –ing the application of the rule of a
   series, 147–8, 187
 –ing the future, 461
 –ing is grammatically a state, 572
 –ing how one's finger is moving,
   PPF 57
 –ing how to go on, 151, 179, 180–1,
   183–4, 211–14, 323, 324; PPF 300
 –ing I must, PPF 311
 –ing a language, 20
 –ing and not being able to say, 75,
   78
 not – what one wishes for, 441
 –ing one is in pain, 246
 –ing one's way about, 203
 only he can – what he intends,
   PPF 328
 only he –s, 156
 only you can – if you had that
   intention, 247
 –ing rather than seeing, an aspect,
   PPF 192
 –ing something that happens, 20
 –ing a state of consciousness,
   process or ability, 148–9
 –ing a tune, 184
 –ing what one believes, PPF 309
 –ing what one feels, PPF 309
 what one has to – before one can
   ask for a name, 30
 –ing what one is going to do, 629,
   631–2
 –ing what one was going to say,
   633–7
 –ing what one wants, PPF 309
 –ing what one wishes for, 441;
   PPF 309
 –ing what pain is from one's own
   case, 293, 295
 –ing what someone looks like, 450
 –ing what a word means, 75, 78
 –ing whether another has
   experience, 272

'know'
  '–' means expression of uncertainty
    is senseless, 247
  grammar of – related to 'can', 'is
    able to', 'understands', 150
  "I can't know what is going on in
    him" is a picture, PPF 326
  "I know . . ." does not mean that
    "I doubt" is senseless, PPF 310
  "I know . . ." said where one
    can also say "I believe" or
    "I suppose", PPF 311
  '–', use as exclamation ("Now I
    know"), 151
  '–', used as normal, 246
knowledge, 363
  exclamation of –, PPF 293; see also
    understanding, exclamation of
  expression of –, 75
  – of other people, PPF 355
  temporal character of –, 148
Köhler, W., PPF 180

lamp, 62
language
  agreement in –, 241
  – and analogy with games, 83;
    see also language-game
  animals don't use –, 25
  Augustine's description of –, 1–3, 32
  clothing of our –, PPF 335
  completeness/incompleteness of –, 18
  – consisting only of orders, reports,
    questions, 2, 18, 19
  – contains the possibility of different
    forms of sentences, 20
  – as correlate of the world, 96
  a dream of –, 358
  essence of/nature of –, 1, 65, 92, 97
  everyday –, 81, 120, 134; see also
    language, ordinary
  excluding a form of words from –,
    500
  expectation and fulfilment meet in –,
    445
  – is a family of structures, 108

language (cont'd)
  forms of –, 5, 25, 65, 111, 112, 132
  – is founded on convention, 355
  function of –, 2, 92, 304
  how can one wish to interpose –
    between pain and its expression,
    245
  ideal/perfect –, 81, 98
  – idling, 132
  – of imagination, 512
  imagining a –, 19
  innate knowledge of –, 495
  – is an instrument, 569
  instruments of –, 16, 50
  interpreting an unknown –, 206–7
  – is interwoven with activities, 7
  invention of –, 492
  – a labyrinth of paths, 203
  – lack of formal unity, 108
  learning a foreign –, 32
  learning/teaching of –, 1, 5, 6, 7, 9,
    26, 32, 77, 495
  – is like ancient city, 18
  limits of –, 119, 499, 540
  logic of our –, 38
  new types of –, 23
  only in – can I mean something by
    something, brf 35
  – is in order as it is, 98
  an order in our knowledge of –,
    132
  ordinary –, 98, 105, brf 108, 132,
    243, 402, 436, 494
  primitive –, 2, 5, 7, 25
  – private, see private language
  problems solved through an insight
    into the workings of –, 109
  purpose of –, 363, 491, 496–8, 501
  reform of –, 132
  regimentation of –, 130
  – and regularity, 207
  samples are part of –, 16
  seas of –, 194
  – of sense-impressions, 355
  sign, see sign-language
  something common to all –, 65

language (*cont'd*)
  spatio-temporal phenomenon of –, brf 108
  – suggests a body, 36
  tools of –, 16, 23
  – of a tribe, 6
  understanding a –, 199
  uniqueness of –, 110
  use of –, 1, 7, 25, 58, 81, 124, 132
  – as vehicle of thought, 329
  what words in this – signify, 10, 13, 15
  working of –, 5, 109
'language'
  grammar of, 492
  has a humble use, 97
language-game
  abrogation of the normal –, 288
  beginning of a –, 290; PPF 289
  – of confessing one's motive, PPF 334
  essence of a –, 65
  everyday – has to be accepted, PPF 161
  explanation of concept of a –, 7
  – with the expression of sensation, 288
  – with 'he is in pain', 300
  image of pain enters the –, 300
  instruments of a –, 50, 53, 55, 57
  kind of certainty is kind of –, PPF 332
  –s losing their point, 142
  lying is a –, 249
  move in a –, 22, 49
  multiplicity of –s, 24; PPF 335
  names in a –, 41, 42, 44, 49, 55, 57
  new kinds of –s, 23
  –s as objects of comparison, 130
  – with 'pain' begins with utterance, 290
  – with 'physical object' and 'sense impression', PPF 34
  playing our – always rests on tacit presupposition, PPF 31

language-game (*cont'd*)
  –s not preliminary studies for future regimentation, 130
  primitive – needs no justification, PPF 161
  – as proto-phenomenon, 654–6
  – of reporting dreams, PPF 52
  – for *Theaetetus*, 48
  varieties of –, 23, 24; PPF 335
  – of writing down a series, 143–7
law of excluded middle, 352, 356
leaf, 73–4
learn
  ability to –, 143
  – expert judgement, PPF 355
  – a game, 31, 54
  "I have –ed English", 381
  – language, *see* language, learning/teaching of
  – mental arithmetic, 385
  – to talk, 5
length, 29, 47, 69; PPF 338
lever, 6, 12
light, point of, PPF 27
likeness, *see* noticing a likeness
lion, if a – could talk, PPF 327
listening, 669, 671
living beings, 281, 284, 357, 420, 430
locked in a room, 99
locomotive, cabin of, 12
logic
  crystalline purity of –, 107–8
  – the essence of thought, 97
  – of our expressions, 345
  – of our language, 93
  – a normative science, 81
  philosophy of –, brf 108
  proposition and word – deals with, 105
  rigour of –, 108
  – seems abolished, 108, 242
  – is something sublime, 89
  sublimating – of our language, 38, 94
  – for a vacuum, 81
  no vagueness in –, 101

logical
  – circle, 208
  – construction, 366
  – 'must', hardness of, 437
  – possibility, 512, 520–1, 566
logicians, 23, 81, 377
look
  – and see, 66, 340
  see how it's –ing, PPF 201
  –ing plus seeing, PPF 245
  – for someone, 462–3
  way of –ing at things, 144
  –ing without seeing, PPF 242
loom, 414
Luther, M. 589
lying, 249, 668

machine
  could a – think, 359–60
  the human body a –, 359
  – as symbol, 193–4
major/minor, concepts of, in music,
  PPF 226
man, old, brf 139
manifestation (*Äusserung*), 149, 152,
  453, 582, 585; PPF 1, 96, 244;
  see also exhibition; utterance
manometer, 270
map, 653
Martian, brf 139
mastery
  – of a game, 31
  – of a language, 33, 338
  – of a technique, 150, 199, 692;
    PPF 224
  – of use of language, PPF 1
mathematical
  certainty, PPF 330, 332, 341–3
  – conjecture, 578
  – discovery 124–5
  – facts, 254
  – investigation, PPF 372
  – problems, 334
  – proof, 517, 578; PPF 255, 303,
    371
  – proposition, PPF 348

mathematical (*cont'd*)
  sense of a – proposition, 544
  – truth, PPF 348
mathematicians, 208, 240, 254;
  PPF 341, 343
mathematics
  agreement in –, PPF 347
  – is a body of knowledge, PPF 348
  changes in –, 23
  feeling of dizziness in –, PPF 224
  foundations of –, PPF 372
  – and philosophy, 124–5, 254
matter of course, 238, 260, 524;
  PPF 93, 253
meaning (*Bedeutung*)
  Augustine's picture of –, 1–2, 5
  – not an aura, 117
  – body, 559
  – and compositionality, PPF 9,
    15–16, 37
  – conceived as object corresponding
    to a word, 1, 2, 5, 39–40, 42, 120,
    316
  cry is full of –, 543
  – not determined by interpretations
    alone, 198
  displaying the –, PPF 15–16
  experiencing the – of a word,
    PPF 234, 261–7, 271–4
  explanation of –, 560
  family of –, 77
  – and feeling, 544–5
  fixed/fluctuating –, 79
  – is not hidden, 60, 164, 435
  – and interpretation, *see*
    interpretation/misinterpretation
  keeping hold of understanding a –,
    PPF 11
  let the use teach you the –, PPF 250,
    303
  metaphorical –, PPF 278
  myth of –, brf 549
  – of a name and destruction of
    bearer, 55
  – a physiognomy, 568; PPF 294
  primary/secondary –, PPF 275–8

meaning (*Bedeutung*) (*cont'd*)
– of a proper name, 79
sameness/difference of –, 19, 140,
   154, 183, 551, 552–3, 555–6, 558,
   561; *see also* sense, sameness of
– of a sentence, *see* sentence,
   meaning of
– and significance/being full of
   meaning, 543–5
– of 'this', 45
– and use, 1, 9, 10, 20, 30, 35, 40,
   41, 43, 120, 138, 139, 197, 247,
   532, brf 549, 556–7, 561; PPF 7, 9,
   14, 265, 303
of a word, *see* word, meaning of
words without –, 13
word has a – only in the context of
   a sentence, 49
mean (*meinen*)
–ing and aiming, 689, 691
–ing an analysed sentence, 60
–ing as a condition of sense, 507,
   509, 511, 513
depth grammar of –ing, 664
–ing and directing one's attention,
   666–7, 674
–ing, doubt and certainty, 679
–ing emphatic negation, 557
grammar of –ing, brf 35, 693
–ing *him*, 661, 663, 680–1, 686–91
how can one –, 19–20, 665
how an order is –t, 186–8
how someone –t a word, 504, 557;
   PPF 262
"I didn't – that sort of game",
   brf 70
"I – my words to quieten him", 648
–ing and intending, PPF 279
knowing what one –s, 147, 274, 504
making sense because one –s it, 357
mental act of –ing, 454, 592, 665,
   693
–ing the pain or the piano tuning,
   666–9, 674, 678, 682
–ing by pointing, 670–1
remember having –t, 661

mean (*meinen*) (*cont'd*)
–ing a senseless sequence of words,
   358, 508, 512, 540–1
seriously –ing something, 590, 677
–ing someone, 663, 680, 686
–ing something, concept of, 125,
   513
–ing something determining steps in
   advance, 190
–ing something develops, 639
–ing something like going towards
   someone, 455–7
–ing something not an activity, 675
–ing something not an affection of
   the mind, 676
–ing something not an experience,
   PPF 279
–ing something privacy of, 358
–ing something not a process, 34–5,
   675; PPF 291
–ing something by a sentence, 19,
   20, brf 35, 95, 102, 125, 358,
   507–14, 540
–ing something not thinking of it,
   PPF 287
–ing something by a word, 33,
   brf 35, 276, 665
–ing such-and-such contrasted with
   thinking of such-and-such, 686–7,
   692, 693; PPF 287
–ing – thinking – a sentence, 22, 81,
   540, 692–3
trying to –, 510
–ing and wanting to say, 334
'meaning' and 'vouloir dire', 657
measure/measurement, 50, 69, 242,
   328, 330, 553, 569; PPF 94, 338
melody, plaintive, PPF 229–30
membrane, 276
memory
   a –, 265, 343
   chart taking over role of –, 53
   commit to – the connection between
      sign and sensation, 258
   content of –, PPF 369
   correct –, 265

memory (cont'd)
    criterion for remembering right, 56
    – of a dream, PPF 52–3
    – experiences, PPF 368
    –image, 56, 166, 239; PPF 58
    linguistic –ies, 649
    – conceived as agent of comparison, 604
    – reaction, 343; PPF 289
    – report, importance of, PPF 288
    strange – phenomenon, 342
    what does my – show me, 648, 651
    see also remember
mental accompaniments, see accompaniment
mental act/activity
    of inner speech, PPF 303
    – of listening, 671
    meaning something as a –, 592, 665, 693
    naming as a –, 38
    negating as a –, 547
    pointing as a –, 36
    reading as a special –, 156
mental image
    asking what –s are, 370
    – of a colour, what it looks like, 386, 388
    comparing –s, 376–82
    – of a cow, 449
    description of a –, 367
    either a – floats before his mind or it does not, 352
    – evoked by words, 6, 139–41, 239
    experiencing a –, PPF 10
    intentionality of –, PPF 17
    keeping hold of a –, PPF 11
    picture of a –, 280
    –s are private, 251
    – as representation of signs, 366
    – as super-likeness, 389
    table of –s in the imagination, 265
    using words to evoke –s, 6
    what makes my – of him a – of him, PPF 17
    see also impression; visual image

mental process, 20, 152–4, 167, 303, 305–8, 332, 361, 363, 366, 452
mental state
    description of a –, 24, 180
    intangibility of –, 608
    isolating one minute of a –, 584–5
    philosophical problem of –s, 308
    understanding is not a –, 146, brf 149
    see also state of mind
message, 356
metaphor, 356, 439; PPF 278
metaphysical, 58, 116
method
    experimental –, PPF 371
    – in philosophy, 133
    – of projection, see projection, method of
    – of proof, PPF 371
methodology, PPF 338
microscope, 645–6
mimic, 450
mind
    apparatus of the –, 149
    call to –, see recollect/recollections/ call to mind
    –'s eye, 56, 57
    having an idea in –, 73
    having a picture/sample/ before the –, 6, 37, 56, 73
    meaning staying before the –, PPF 11
    – an odd kind of being, 196
    one doesn't say "his – is in pain", 391
    if one sees the behaviour of a living being, one sees its –, 357
    does psychology treat of behaviour, not of the –, PPF 28
    – seems to be able to give a word meaning, PPF 54
    state of –, 149; PPF 29; see also mental state
    what has a – to do with a stone, 283
mistake, 51, 54, 140, 143, 270, 288
misunderstanding, 10, 29, 48, 71, 87, 90, 91, 93, 111, 120, 143, 201, 314

model, 141
money, 120, 265
monologue, 243
Mont Blanc, 78; PPF 338
mood, manifestations of, PPF 96
Moore's paradox, PPF 87, 95, 98, 105
morning paper, 265
Morse-code, 167
Moses, 79, 87
motion, relative/absolute, brf 138
motive, PPF 333–7
motor imagery, PPF 18
mourn, PPF 81
mouse, 52
multiplication table, PPF 350
music, playing with/without thought, 341
musical
 – ear, PPF 260
 – phrase and the feeling it gives, PPF 45–9
 – theme, 531; PPF 209–10
 – theme tells me itself, 523
 understanding a – theme, 527

name
 asking for the –, 6, 27, brf 28, 30–1
 bearer of a –, 40, 43, 44, 45, 55
 diversity of category of –s, 28, 38
 explanation of use of/meaning of –s, 38, 43, 410
 –s and faces, 171
 inventing a –, 27
 meaning of a –, 1, 6, 10, 39–43, 55–8, 79
 model of object and –, 293
 –s of objects, 1, 6, 7, 15, 26, 27, 39
 personal – ostensively defined, 28, 40
 proper –, 28, 39, 40, 41, 55, 87; PPF 15, 50–1
 proper –, definition of, 79
 real –, 38, 39
 – relation, 37–8, 244, 259
 –s of sensation, 243–4, 256, 270–1, 275

name (cont'd)
 –s of simples/indestructibles, 39, 46, 48, 49, 50, 55, 57–9
 –tag, 15, 26
 use of a –, 1, 6, 7, 8, 9, 11, 26, 27, 28, 30, 31, 383
 words conceived as –s, 1–2, 383
naming, 7, 15, 26, 27, 38, 46, 49, 257
naming the non-existent, 41, 42, 50
naming vs. describing, brf 35, 46, 49, 50
natural history, 25, 415; PPF 365
natural law, 54
nature, 92
nature, general facts of, brf 142; PPF 365–6
nature of, 58, 89, 92, 101, 105, 114, brf 142, 174, 183, 308, 399, brf 549; see also essence
necessity, objective, 372
negation, 447–8, 547–57
 – and intentionality, 446–8
nervous system, 158
nominalism, 383
nonsense/senseless, 39, 40, 79, 119, 247, 252, 282, 464, 498–500, 511–13, 524; PPF 19, 22, 309
normal/abnormal
 – cases, 141–2
 – learner, 143
normative science, 81
Nothing, a –, 304
Nothung, 39, 44
noticing
 an aspect, PPF 113
 causes of –, PPF 114
 – a likeness, PPF 112–13, 239–40, 244, 257
noughts and crosses, 66
number
 concept of a –, 68, 135
 – a family resemblance concept, 67–8
 –s imaginary and real, PPF 165
 naming –s, 26
 and numerals, 143, 339; PPF 133

number (*cont'd*)
- one, 553–4
- 1 interpreted as a cardinal –, PPF 299
ostensive definition of –, 28–9
pointing to a –, 33, 35
- two, 28–9
–word, 1, 8, 9, 10, 28
nuts, 28

obey an order, 206, 345
object-name model, 293
objects of comparison, 130–1
objects in *Tractatus*, 46
objective certainty, PPF 340
observation, 417, 659; PPF 67–9, 76, 86, 313
opining, grammatically a state, 572–3
opinion, 241; PPF 22
order, in our knowledge of our use of language, 132
order, perfect, 98, 105
ordering (arranging), 92
orders/commands, 2, 8, 18, 19, 20, 21, 23, 25, 60, 61, 62, 199, 206, 207, 208, 212, 345, 431, 433, 449, 451, 458–61, 498, 505–6, 519
ordinariness, 600
ordinary, *see* language, ordinary
ornament, 270
ornamental pattern, 208, 211
orthography, 121
ostensive definition, 6, 28, 29, 30, 33, 38, 362
ostensive definition, private –, *see* private ostensive definition
ostensive explanation, 6, 27, brf 28, 30, 32, 34, 38, 380
ostensive teaching, 6, 9, 49
ownership of experience, 253, 294, 398–403

pace, definition of a –, 69
pain
absence of –, 448
another person can't have my –, 253

pain (*cont'd*)
bearer of –, 253, 283, 286, 302
- behaviour, 244, 246, 257, 281, 288, 296, 302, 304; PPF 30, 324
concept of –, 384
criteria of –, 350–1
- and cry of complaint, PPF 84
- and doubt, 246, 288, 303, 408
duration of –, brf 149
exhibiting –, 311, 313
expression of –, 142, 244–5, 288, 317; *see also* pain behaviour
feeling – in another's body, PPF 314
grammar of – must be prepared, 257
having –, 253, 261
having the same –, 253, 350
identity of –, 253, 288, 350
- in the imagination/imagining, 300–2, 315, 391–4
inanimate –, 282–4
knowing whether I am in –, 246, 251, 288, 303, 408; PPF 311
knowing who is in –, 404
- location, 253, 626; PPF 58–9, 66
- of a machine, 359
meaning the –, 665–8
- and mental process, 154
momentary –, PPF 3
my –, 246, 251, 253, 289, 310, 403–9; PPF 84
naming, 256–7, 262–3
- of others, 302–3, 350, 391; PPF 324, 332
- patches, 312
picture of –, 300
secondary concept of –, 282
- simulation/pretence, 249–50; PPF 362–4
- of a stone, 283–4, 288, 390
- of a stove, 351–2
symptoms of –, 271
'pain', 244, 271, 288, 300, 315
painting, 295, 401, 518, 520; PPF 35, 38, 51, 168, 195, 267, 367
style of, PPF 367

paradigm, in grammar/language-game,
    20, 50, 51, 55, 57; *see also* sample
paradox, 95, 182, 201, 304, 412, 421
Paris, 50
parrot, 344, 346
parts of speech, 1
passive voice, 47
past, concept of the, 656; PPF 370
paths, familiar, leading off, 525, 534
patience (game of), 66, 248
pattern in the weave of our lives,
    PPF 2, 362
perceive/perception, 92, 104, 170, 229,
    417, 453; PPF 121, 128–30, 137–9,
    226, 233, 247, 254, 322, 341;
    see also observation
person, 404–6
    criteria of identity of a –, 404
    – may be transparent to us, PPF 325
phenomena, possibilities of, 90
philosopher
    –'s metaphysical use of words, 116
    –'s nonsense, PPF 309
    work of the –, 127
philosophical
    – diseases, 593
    – investigation, importance of, 118
    – paradoxes, 182
    – problems, 109, 110–11, 123, 125,
        133, 308, 314
    – proposition/statement, 85, 90
    – superlative, 192
    – treatment, 254–5
    – understanding, 122
philosophy
    aim in –, 309
    become insensitive by doing –, 348
    cloud of – condensed into drop of
        grammar, PPF 315
    – contrasted with science, 109
    dead-end in –, 436
    depth of –, 111
    no discoveries in –, 109, 125
    – and dogmatism, 131
    no explanations in –, 126
    give – peace, 133

philosophy (*cont'd*)
    no hypotheses in –, 109
    no inferences in –, 599
    – leaves everything as it is, 124
    – and mathematics, *see* mathematics
        and philosophy
    method of –, 133, brf 133
    – must not interfere with use of
        language, 124
    nothing hidden in –, 126
    – is prior to all inventions, 125
    – is purely descriptive, 109, 124
    raw material of –, 254
    – and recollections, 126
    results of –, 119
    no second-order –, 121
    – only states what everyone
        concedes, 599
    – struggles against bewitchment, 109
    – and surveyability, 122, 125
    no theory in –, 109
    theses in –, 128
    when doing –, 11, 15, 52, 81, 131,
        194, 254, 261, 274, 295, 303, 393,
        520, 592, 598
photograph, 71, 486; PPF 59, 90, 171,
    197, 198, 252
physical object, 58, 253
    explaining the concept of – in terms
        of 'what is really seen', PPF 161
'physical object' and 'sense-
    impression', PPF 34
physics, 410, 571; PPF 371
physiology, 376, 632; PPF 177, 183,
    236, 306
π, 208, 352, 516
pianola, 157
piano-tuning, 666, 678, 682
pictorial likeness, PPF 17
picture
    affinity of –s, 76
    application of a –, 349, 374, 422–7
    choosing words compared with
        choosing –s, brf 139
    – compared with mental image, 389
    – and description, 291

picture (cont'd)
  duck–rabbit –, PPF 118, 120, 125–9,
    137, 152, 157
  – forcing a use on one, 140
  – of a galloping horse, PPF 175
  genre –s, 522
  –s give pleasure, 524
  "I can't know what is going on in
    him" is a –, PPF 326
  – illustration to a story, 663
  impressionistic –, 368
  indistinct –, 71
  inner –, PPF 133
  – of an inner/mental process, 305–8
  – of a mental image, 280
  – in the mind, 6, 37, 139, 141
  multicoloured –s, 72
  – object, PPF 119
  – and its object, 518
  – of pain, 300
  puzzle –, PPF 131
  role of –s in our lives, PPF 195
  – and sentence-radical, brf 22
  sharp/blurred –, 71, 76–7
  – of the soul, PPF 23–5
  understanding a –, 526
  upside-down –, PPF 150
  – and use of a word, 139, brf
    139–40
  – viewed as the object it represents,
    PPF 197
  – and visual impression, PPF 166–75
  – and what it tells me, 523
pigment, 57
pity, 287, 403
place in language/grammar, 29, 31
plaint, PPF 229
plan, 438; PPF 12–13
plant, definition of, 70
poem, 531, 533
point, movement of, PPF 27
pointing
  arrow's –, 454
  – with one's attention, 275, 411
  – to the bearer of a name, 43–5
  characteristic experience of –, 35

pointing (cont'd)
  – to a chess piece, 31, 35
  – at a/the colour, brf 28, 33, 35–6,
    73, 429
  – doesn't explain what 'imagination'
    means, 370
  –gesture, 8, 44–5, 71, 185, 398
  – and indexicals, 9, 38, 117
  listening/looking compared with –,
    669, 671–2
  – at a mental image, 382
  – at a/the number, 9, 28, 29, 33
  – at objects, 6, 7, 8, 9, 33, 34, 35,
    117, 669, 670
  – to a paradigm, 51
  – is part of the language-game, 669
  – to a place, 8, 9, 71, 208
  – at a sensation, 258, 275, 298, 411,
    669
  – at a/the shape, 33, 34, 35, 36
  – to what is in common, 72
  when I say "I am in pain", I don't
    point to a person, 404
  – while telephoning, 670
  see also ostensive definition;
    ostensive explanation
point of, 62, 142, 564–7
politician, French, 336
portrait, PPF 199–200
possibility/possible
  a priori order of –ies, 97
  – of having the same pain, 253
  logical –, see logical possibility
  – of movement, 194
  – of phenomena, 90
  – state of affairs, 520
posture, PPF 225
pot, 282, 297
pot, boiling, 297
practice
  following a rule is a –, 202
  in –, 54, 132, 323, 556, 607
  linguistic –, 21
  – of playing, 197
  – of the use of language, 7, 51
practice/practising, 54

prediction, 193, 243, 629–32; PPF 98,
    328–9, 355
prefix "I think", "I believe", 24
prejudice, 340
preparation, 26, 31, 49
presupposition, PPF 31–4
pretence/pretending, 156, 159, 249–50;
    PPF 353, 358, 362–4
primary element, 46, 48–51, 53, 59
primitive
    – explanation, 339
    – expression of sensation, 244
    – forms of language, 2, 5, 7, 25
    – language-game, 1–21, 146; PPF 161
    – logic, 554
    – mode of thought, 597
    – people, 194
    – reaction, PPF 289
private
    – definition, 262, 268, 380
    – exhibition of pain, 311
    – experience, 272, 274
    – explanation, 262, 268
    – impression, 272–8, 280
    – language, 243–315
    – map, 653
    – mental image, 251, 280
    – object, 374; PPF 214
    – ostensive definition, 258, 262–3,
        380
    – picture, 294
    – sensations/mental images/
        impressions, 243–8, 251, 256, 272,
        275–7, 280, 294
    – transition, 380
'private'/'privately', 202, 256
probable, 158, 482, 484
process
    incorporeal –, 339
    inner –, 305; see also mental process
    inner – stands in need of outward
        criteria, 580
    intending is not a –, 34, 205
    interpreting is not a mental –, 34
    knowing is not a mental –, 148,
        363

process (cont'd)
    looking like a statement of a
        mental –, 303
    meaning something is not a
        mental –, PPF 291
    mental – corresponding to
        multiplication on paper, 366
    –es in the mental sphere, 571
    momentary –, 638
    naming is not an occult –, 38
    odd –, 196
    outer –, PPF 301
    philosophical problem of mental –es,
        308
    reading is not a particular –, 165,
        167
    remembering is not a mental –,
        305–6
    thinking is not a –, 330–2, 427
    understanding is not a mental –,
        152, 154; PPF 36
projection
    lines of, 141
    method of, 139, 141, 366
promise, 226
proof, PPF 303, 354
proper name, see name, proper
prophecy, 21, 461
proposition
    concept of a –, 135
    – equivalent to language, thought,
        world, 96
    essence of a –, 92
    – fits 'true' and 'false', 137
    general form of –, 65, 95, 114,
        134–6
    grammatical –, 251, 295, 360, 458
    lack of formal unity of –, 108
    negation of a –, 447
    negation of an a priori –, 251
    – as a picture, 96, 520, 522
    – is a remarkable thing, 93–4
    – and truth, 136, 225
    – and what makes it true, 437
propositional schema/variable, 134
proto-phenomenon, 654

proverbs, hung on the wall, PPF 195
psychological
  causes, PPF 268
  concepts, PPF 202
  experiment, PPF 32
psychologists, 571; PPF 28, 114, 282
psychology
  concepts suitable for –, 577
  confusion and barrenness of –,
    PPF 371
  subject matter of –, 571
purpose, 2, 5, 6, 8, 62, 87, 88, 109,
    127, 132, 208, 220, 257, 263, 304,
    317, 345, 385; PPF 80, 290, 311

quality, transition from quantity to –,
    284
question, 19, 21–5

rails, 218
rain, 22, brf 35, 354, 356, 540; PPF 89,
    105, 107, 109
rainbow, 47
Ramsey, F. P., Pr, 81
react/reaction, 6, 143, 145, 198, 206,
    284, 343, 495, 659; PPF 167, 289
reading, 22, 156–71
  – expressively, PPF 264–7
  – silently, how taught, 375
reading-machine, 156–7
realists, 402
reason(s), 169, 211–12, 217, 325, 326,
    477–85; PPF 268, 326
  – and causes, 475–85, 487–90, 493
receptivity, 232
recognition/recognize, 35, 270, 285,
    378–81, 388, 448, 596, 602–5, 625;
    PPF 141–5, 149–50, 152
recollect/recollections/call to mind, 89,
    90, 127, 335, 342; PPF 159
red/'red', 1, 20, brf 28, 51, 53, 57, 58,
    239, 272–3, 377, 380–1, 386, 429,
    443, 446
referring/reference, 10, 27, 243–4,
    273–4, 669, 685; PPF 7, 286
region, 71, 88

regularity, 189, 207–8, 223, 237, 242
relation, see internal relation; name
    relation
religion, PPF 23
remember, 35, 56, 271, 305–6, 601,
    634–7, 645, 648, 660–1; PPF 369,
    370; see also memory
report, 19, 21, 23, 144, 199, 207, 270,
    386, 421, 525, 585–6, 656–7, 683;
    PPF 5–6, 94, 138
represent
  how a sentence –s, 435
  what a drawing –s, 683, 691
representation
  means of –, 50
  medium of –, 397
  – and mental image, 280, 366;
    PPF 18
  – and method of projection, 366
  mode of –, 50, 104, 403
  – of what is seen, PPF 146–7
ring-a-ring-a-roses, 7
rod, every – has a length, 251
role, of pictures, see pictures, role of
role, of a word, see word, role of a
rose
  – is red in the dark, 514–15
  – has no teeth, PPF 314
rule
  accord with a –, 198, 201, 217, 224
  application of a –, 147–8, 201, 218,
    292, 380
  – for application of a rule, 84, 86
  changing –s, 83–4
  – and choice, 219
  compulsion by a –, 231
  in conflict with a –, 201
  – for construction of a proposition,
    102
  – contained in the act of intending,
    197
  correct –, brf 549
  definite –, 81, 83
  – and doing the same, 189, 223,
    225–7
  entanglement in –s, 125

rule (*cont'd*)
essential/inessential –s, 562, 564,
567–8
– and exception, 142
following, *see* following a rule
– in the form of a chart, 53, 86
– in the form of a table, 162
formulating the –s, 31
– of a game, *see* game, rules of a
grasping a –, 201
guidance by a –, 234, 237, 292;
see also guidance
impression of a –, 259
interpreting –s, 85–6, 198
– for interpreting a map, 653
knowing the –, 31
learning a –, 31, 54, 162
making the –s up as we go along, 83
mythological description of the use
of a –, 221
nod of a –, 223
point of a –, 567
– and practice, 202
– present in the mind, 102, 197, 205
– by which he proceeds, 82
– produces its consequences, 238
read the lips of the –, 228
– and regularity, 208, 223, 237
roles of a –, 53
– as tool of a game, 54
– traces the lines to be followed,
219
vagueness of –s, 69–70, 75, 79–80,
83, 88, 98, 100
'rule'
– related to 'accord', 224
– related to 'same', 225; *see also*
regularity; rule, and doing the
same
Russell, B., 46, 79
Russian, 20, 159

sadness, PPF 227–8
same, 20, 61, 62, 140, 208, 215, 223–6,
253–4, 350, 377–8, 551, 552, 556;
PPF 194; *see also* identity

sample
– is a means of representation, 50, 53
at the mercy of a –, 56
– in the mind, 56, 57, 73
– as part of language, 16, 50, 55, 56
– of shape, 74
shape of –, 73
use of a –, 1, 8, 74
satisfaction/non-satisfaction, 429–65
satisfaction, feeling of, 440–1, 460
satisfy oneself that things are so,
PPF 311–12
savages, like – when we do
philosophy, 194
saw off the branch, 55
saying things to oneself, 346–8
as it were –, 658; *see also* talking to
oneself
scaffolding, 240
schema, 73, 86, 134, 141, 163
Schlemihl, 339
Schubert, F., PPF 270
scientific definitions, *see* definitions,
scientific
Scot, Mr, PPF 15
scruples, 120
secondary meaning, *see* meaning,
primary/secondary
seduce, *see* temptation
'see', two uses of, PPF 111
seeing
concept of –, PPF 160, 224
– contrasted with merely knowing,
– an aspect, PPF 192, 196
– and interpreting, PPF 116–17,
163–4, 248–9
– a likeness, PPF 111
– an object in a picture, PPF 169, 175
a physiological criterion for –,
PPF 236
– and seeing as, PPF, 121–2, 137,
166, 167, 169, 171–6, 181–3,
185–7, 189–222, 254–61
– is a state, PPF 248, 250
– and thinking, PPF 140, 144, 163,
180, 187

seeing (*cont'd*)
  – three-dimensionally, PPF 148, 171, 173–4, 179–80, 241, 252, 253
  way of –, 74
  – what is in common, 72
  whole business of – is puzzling, PPF 251
self, 413
self-observation, 586, 659; *see also* introspection
sensation, 243–315
  absurd to say that a body has –, 286
  criterion of identity for a –, 253, 290
  diary about recurrent –s, 258
  directing one's attention on a –, 263, 268, 283, 298
  doubting whether one has a –, 246, 288
  having –s, 246, 281, 283–4
  I don't identify my – by means of criteria, 290
  kinaesthetic, *see* kinaesthetic sensations
  language-game begins with expression of –, 290
  my –, 246, 253, 256, 258, 263, 270, 283, 288–90, 293, 295, 302–3, 310–13, 411
  names of –s, 243–4, 256
  naming –s, 257
  natural expression of –, 256, 288, 293
  private –s, 243, 246, 248, 257
  recognizing a –, 270
  reference to –s, 243–4
  – S, 258, 260–1, 270
  sign for –, 261
  stone having –s, 283–4, 288
  words for –s tied up with natural expressions of, 256
sense
  analysing the –, 39
  – and application, 319
  circumstance dependence of –, 117
  determinate/indeterminate –, 99
  determining the –, 352
  disintegration of –, PPF 9, 16

sense (*cont'd*)
  lacking –, 499, 500
  making –/no –, 40, 44, 47, 117, 157, 357–8, 395, 498–500, 511, 513
  – of a mathematical proposition, 544
  sameness of –, 20, 61, 183
  seeming to fix the –, 426
  – isn't senseless, 500
  – of a sentence, 39, 44, 60, 98–9, 138, 358, 395, 421, 500, 502, 513, 685; PPF 37
  – and use, 20, 421–2; PPF 55, 89
sense data, 366, 401
sense impression, 354–5, 486; PPF 34, 60–1, 69, 90, 129, 269; *see also* visual impression
senseless, senselessness, *see* nonsense/senseless
sensing the emotion in a melody, PPF 228–30, 233
sentence
  assertoric –, 22, 24
  – as combination of names, 1
  degenerate –, 19
  elliptical –, 19, 20
  every – is in order as it is, 98
  – as expression of thought, 317, 501
  function of a –, 21, 27
  grammatical form of a –, 21
  how a – represents, 435
  – as instrument, 421
  kinds of –s, 23
  – that logic deals with, 105
  – makes sense, 513
  meaning a –, 81
  meaning of a –, 19, 20, 544
  sense of a –, *see* sense, of a sentence
  understanding a –, *see* understanding, a sentence
  use of a –, 20, 27, 117, 278, 449
  vague –, 98
  word has a meaning only in the context of a –, 49
sentence-radical, brf 22
sentential context, *see* context, of a sentence, 38

series
  beginning of a –, 218
  continuing a – correctly, 143,
    145–6, 151–2, 185–90, 214, 226,
    324
  face of a –, 228
  pattern in the segment of a –, 229
set theory, 412, 426; PPF 371
'sew a dress', 195
shadow, 194, 339, 448
shame, 643–4
shape, 26, 33–6, 48, 73
sharpness, of concepts, 71, 76–7
shopkeeper, 1, 8
Siamese twins, 253
sight, objects of, PPF 111
sign
  arbitrary –s, 508
  – for a broken tool, 41–2
  – of emphasis, 4
  every – by itself seems dead, 432
  – given by a rule, 82, 86
  idea of a –, 105
  kinds of use of –s, 23
  life of a –, 432
  – may sometimes be a word,
    sometimes a sentence, 49
  propositional –, 94, 102
  real –, 105
  use of –s explained by paradigms,
    51, 53
  – is what is given in giving an order,
    503–4
  what –s signify, 10
signal, of being able to go on, 180
signify, 10, 13, 15, 39, 51, 55, 56, 196,
    239, 256, 264
signify sensations/impressions, 243–5,
    256, 273–4
sign-language, 348
signpost, 85, 87, 198
similarities, in the large/in the small,
    66
simile, 112
simple constituent parts, 47
simples, 39, 46–8

singing
  – from sheet music, 22
  – a tune from memory, 333
situation, 49, 57, 166, 172, 218, 393,
    417, 448, 552, 539, 581, 587, 591,
    592, 633, 637, 645, 662; PPF 207,
    273, 300, 370
sketches of a landscape, Pr
skill, 66
sky, 275
slip of the tongue, 54
smile, 249, 539, 583; PPF 149, 150
Socrates, 46, 518
solipsism, 24, 402–3
solution, 140
Something/a Something, 261, 293, 296,
    304, 358
sorrow, pattern of, PPF 2
soul, 422, 573, 589; PPF 22–5
  of words, see words, soul of
sound, direction of, PPF 57
sound-sample, 16
spade, my – is turned, 217
speaking with tongues, 528
speak of someone, 344, 687–9; PPF 17,
    283–4
speech, in the imagination, see talking
    to oneself in the imagination
speech and thought, see thought, and
    speech
sphere, 251; PPF 169, 171
spider's web, repair with our fingers,
    106
spirit, 36
spiritual activity, 36
spontaneous generation, 52
Sraffa, P., Pr
standard metre, 50
state, 36, 91, 146, 148, 149, brf 149,
    157, 183, 388, 413, 421, 448, 572,
    573, 589; PPF 248, 250, 371
state of mind, 149, 290, 577, 585,
    588, 607–8, 652, 653, 661, 662;
    PPF 29, 72, 73, 79, 85, 90, 96–7,
    102, 340, 358; see also mental
    state

stereoscope, PPF 171, 252
stipulation, 88
stone
    – having consciousness, 390, 418
    – having sensations, 284
    turning to –, 283, 288
stove, has the same experience as I,
    350–1
strive, 623; PPF 123
style of painting, PPF 367
subjective certainty, PPF 340
sublimate, 38, 94
sublime, 89
sun, five o'clock on the –, 350–1
super-expression, 192
superlative, philosophical, *see*
    philosophical superlative
super-likeness, 389
super-order, 97
superstition, brf 35, 49, 110
supposition, 349; PPF 87; *see also*
    assumption; presupposition
surface grammar, 664
surprise, PPF 152, 183
surprise, absence of, 628
surroundings, 250, 412, 540, 583, 584,
    603; *see also* circumstance;
    context; situation
surveyable representation, 122
surveyable/surveyability, 92, 122, 125
symbolic logic, 134
symptom, 321, 354

table of correlation, 1, 62, 86, 162–3;
    see also chart
table in the imagination, 265
table that wobbles, 79
tailor, 195
taking something as something,
    PPF 123
talk
    – about things, 27
    animals don't –, 25, 357
    child learns to –, 5
    –ing to oneself aloud, 243, 260;
        PPF 246

talk (*cont'd*)
    –ing to oneself in the imagination,
        32, 168, 243, 344, 346–8, 357, 361,
        376; PPF 246, 301–3, 305–8
    pot –s to itself, 282
    thinks quicker than one –s, 318
    –ing without thought, 330; PPF 292
tall, 279
tapestry of life, PPF 2
teacher, 6, 7, 49, 143–5, 156–7, 362
teaching, 5, 9, 53–4, brf 70, 143, 185,
    190, 197, 208–11, 361–2; PPF 221,
    355
teaching, ostensive, *see* ostensive
    teaching
technique, 125, 150, 199, 205, 232, 262,
    337, 520, 557, 692; PPF 348, 355
telling stories, 23, 25
temptation, 254, 277, 288, 294, 299,
    345, 374, 520
tending, experience of, 591
tennis, 66, 68
testimony, 386, 594
'that', *see* indexicals
Theaetetus, 46, 48, 518
theology, as grammar, 373
therapy, brf 133
theses, 128
think
    –ing aloud, 331
    analysing concept of –ing, not
        phenomenon, 383
    animals do not –, 25
    –ing apparently unique, 95, 110
    believing is not –ing, 574
    chair is –ing to itself, 361
    as if the child could – but not
        speak, 32
    concept of –ing unlike concept of
        talking, PPF 281
    –ing different from talking in the
        imagination, PPF 246
    explanation of –ing requires a
        feeling, 598
    –ing not an incorporeal process,
        339

think (*cont'd*)
 is one infallible in saying one is
  –ing, 328
 to interpret is to –, PPF 248
 interrupting –ing, 328
 knowing what someone else is –ing,
  PPF 315
 location of –ing, 361
 machine –ing, 359–60
 pneumatic conception of –ing, 109
 privacy of –ing, PPF 316–22
 processes accompanying talking are
  not –ing, PPF 292
 purpose of –ing, 466–70
 –ing a sentence, 19, 22, 511
 –ing of someone, 686–90; PPF 283–9
 –ing surrounded by a nimbus, 97
 –ing not talking in the imagination,
  PPF 246
 –ing and thought-schema, 597
 what –ing is, 327–32
 –ing what is not the case, 95
 –ing of what one sees, PPF 139–40
 why does man –, 466–70
 word order of –ing, 336
 –ing in words, 329
 see also thought, and speech
'think'
 grammar of, 339
 meaning of –, 316, 328, 332, 339
 the word – is an instrument, 360
'this', *see* indexicals
thought
 – not an accompaniment of speech,
  PPF 280
 conveying –s, 304, 317, 501
 – as correlate of the world, 96
 the echo of a – in sight, PPF 235
 essence of –, 92, 97
 expression of –, 317–18, 335, 501,
  531; PPF 139–40
 feelings seem to explain our –s,
  598
 finding the right expression for one's
  –s, 335
 guessing –s, PPF 318, 321–2

thought (*cont'd*)
 harmony between – and reality, 429
 –s in the head/mind/soul, PPF 24
 hidden –s, PPF 317, 322
 lightning-like –, 318–20
 links between –s, 640
 – neither articulated nor non-
  articulated, PPF 280
 –s occupying us, 577
 – process, 427
 – seems an accompaniment of
  speech, 330, 332
 speaking/writing with –, 318
 – and speech, 327, 330, 335–6, 338,
  341–2, 540
 speed of –, 318–19
 strangeness of/uniqueness of –, 95,
  97, 110, 428, 430
 tonalities of –, PPF 339
 wordless –s, 342
'thought', 332
'till', ambiguity of, PPF 8, 261
time, 88, 89, 90, 196, 266, 363, 607;
  PPF 7
timelessness, 58
timetable, 265
tingling, PPF 370
tip (hint), PPF 355
tone of voice, 21, 578, 582; PPF 74, 98,
  264, 339
tool-box, 11
tools, 11, 14, 15, 16, 17, 23, 41–2, 53,
  54
toothache, 257, 665
Tractatus Logico-Philosophicus, Pr, 23,
  46, 97, 114
training, 5, 6, 9, 27, 86, 189, 198, 206,
  223, 630
trains, children playing at, 282
translation, 243, 265, 342, 459, 597;
  PPF 7
treatment, 254
tree, 47, 418
triangle, aspects of, PPF 162, 167, 211,
  222
tricolor, 64

trisecting an angle with compass and
    rule, 334, 463
'true', interwoven with 'proposition',
    136, 225
true/false, 136–7, 241
truism, 95
truth, 136
    – functions, calculus of, 136
    – and truthfulness, 544; PPF 319–20
    – value, 22
try, 618–19, 622; PPF 123; *see also*
    strive
turn to stone, *see* stone, turning to
type/token, 48

uncertainty, 24, 97, 247; PPF 66, 95
unconscious, *see* conscious/unconscious
understanding
    – apparently reaches deeper than
        examples, 209–10
    – as atmosphere, 609
    – compared with mental processes,
        154
    – compared with mental states,
        brf 149
    concept of –, 513, 532
    concomitants of –, 152–3, 321
    criterion of –, 146, 182, 269
    deeper –, 209–10
    duration of –, brf 149
    effecting an –, 6
    exclamation of –, 151, 179, 183, 323;
        PPF 293
    – and explanation, 28–34, 71–3,
        87, 141, 145, 185, 208–10, 257,
        516
    – a further analysed sentence, 60
    grammar of –, 150, 182
    – a grammatical proposition, 251
    grounds for saying one –s, 147
    idea of – smells fishy, 348
    – as indefinable experience, 322
    – not an inner process, 152–4, 321,
        396; PPF 36
    interruption of –, brf 149
    knowing one understands, 138

understanding (*cont'd*)
    – a language, is to have mastered a
        technique, 199
    manifestations of –, 152
    – the meaning of a word, 138, 197
    medium of –, 102
    – as a mental process, 153–4
    – mere signs, 503–4
    – a musical theme, 527, 533
    "Now I understand", 151
    – in one's heart, PPF 26
    only I can understand, 256
    – an order, 6, 431, 433, 451, 505–6
    ostensive definition will help me
        understand, 30
    – people in a strange country;
        PPF 325
    – a picture, 526
    – a poem, 531, 533
    – as a process, 431; PPF 36
    – a question, 516–17
    – the rule of a series, 146
    – a sentence, 60, 81, 138, 199, 332,
        396, 513, 514, 525, 527, 531
    – as source of correct use, 146
    – as a state, 146
    – at a stroke, 138–9, brf 138, 151–2,
        154–5, 320–1; PPF 13
    sudden –, *see* understanding, at a
        stroke
    – the system of natural numbers,
        143, 146
    thinking one understands, brf 138,
        517
    – a thought in a flash, 319–20
    utter a sentence with –, 332
    in what signs do we understand,
        433
    – a word, 6, 10, 29–30, 33, 87, 102,
        117, 122, 138–9, brf 149, 196–7,
        257, 264, 269, 288; PPF 40
    – the word 'pain', 256–7, 264, 269,
        293–5, 315
'understand'
    – closely related to 'know', 150
    meaning of –, 532–3

uniform, 208
uniformity of nature, belief in, 472–82
unlimited, 209
unsatisfied, *see* satisfaction/non-
satisfaction
unverifiable, *see* verifiable/unverifiable
usage, 198, 199
use
– of the assertion sign, 22
– and depth/surface grammar, 664
describing the –, 82, 124, 156, 242,
496
– is extended in time, 138
figurative –, PPF 265
grasping the –, 138–9, 179, 191, 195,
197, 274
– of language, *see* language, use of
– and meaning, 30, 40–3, 117, 120,
138, 139, 190, 197, 532, 552, 556,
561; PPF 250, 265, 303
– of money, 120
– of a person's name, 27, 79
primitive kinds of –, 5
sameness of –, 20, 35, 565
– of a sentence, 20–1, 23, 117, 397,
435
– of a sign its living breath, 432
– and understanding, 29, 146 288
can the whole – come before my
mind, 139
use of a word
compare – with games and calculi,
81
everyday/ordinary –s, 116; PPF 15,
106
– not everywhere regulated by rules,
68
failure to understand the –, 196
kinds of –, 10, 23, 38
know the use when you know what
the word stands for, 264
–s laid out in advance, 142
look at the – to know how word
functions, 340
misunderstandings about –, 90, 196
naming is preparatory for the –, 26

use of a word (*cont'd*)
ostensive definition explains the –,
30
overview of –, 122
philosophical –, 116
teaching the –, 6–10, 16
utterance (Äusserung), 310, 440, 571,
631, 632, 656–7; PPF 7, 17, 28,
76, 87, 96, 98, 102, 122, 177, 224;
see also manifestation

vacuum, logic for a, 81
vague, 98, 100, 101; *see also* blurred;
boundary line, rigid/sharp
vase, 33
vehicle, 329
verifiable/unverifiable, 272, 353;
PPF 249
visual experience, PPF 117, 138–41,
146, 153, 156, 188–90; *see also*
visual impression
visual image, 47, 402; PPF 253;
see also mental image; visual
impression
visual impression, 272–7, 312, 354;
PPF 131–6, 151, 170–5, 187, 211,
247
visual room, 398–402
visual world, 402
vocal expression, 606
voluntariness, 611–31
vowels, and colours, PPF 177, 278

walk, 183
want, knowing what one –s, PPF 309
wanting, 611–29
war, PPF 311
warrant, 154–5, 378, 481, 557
water, falling/jumping into, 187
weaving, 414
weight/weighing, 142, 182, 572
Weltanschauung, 122
wheel, idle, 271
will, the, 174, 176, 617–19; PPF 256
willing, 611–29
willing subject, 618

winning and losing, 66
wish
  – and its fulfilment, 437–41, 461
  knowing what one –es, PPF 309
  –ing not a means to bring about
    movement, 614
  –ing that something
    should/shouldn't happen, 548
  –ing and voluntary action, 616
word
  – absorbs/assimilated its meaning,
    508–9; PPF 263, 294
  application of a –, 80, 84, 100,
    140–1, 264, 340, 349, 383
  apt –, brf 139
  one calculates, operates, with –s,
    449
  choosing between –s, brf 139
  choosing the right –, PPF 294–5
  –s are also deeds, 546
  description of use of a –, 10
  dissatisfaction with what are called
    '–s', 105
  every – signifies something, 13
  everyday use of –s, 116
  –s and exclamations, 27
  explanation of a –, 28, brf 28, 29,
    30, 31, brf 35, 288, 560
  face of a –, PPF 38
  function(s) of –s, 1, 5, 11, 17, 274,
    280, 340, 556, 559
  grasping the meaning/use of a – at a
    stroke, 138–9, 191, 195, 197
  hearing a – as having this meaning,
    534
  – as instrument, 360
  kinds of –, 1, 17, 23, 45
  knowing the meaning of a –, 139;
    PPF 14
  – in the language-game in which it
    is at home, 116
  learning the meaning of a –, 1, 7, 9,
    brf 28, 35, 77
  meaning of a –, 1, 2, 5, 13, 30, 40,
    41, 43, 49, 55, 57, 80, 140, 257,
    560; PPF 8–16, 37

word (cont'd)
  meaning of a – determined by use,
    139
  meaning of a – fitting another, 138
  meaning of a – not an
    accompaniment, 120
  meaning of a – not an aura, 117
  meaning of a – not a Something we
    have in mind, brf 139
  metaphysical use of –s, 116
  one – sentence, 19–20
  operating with –s, 1, 449
  ostensive teaching of –s, see
    ostensive teaching
  physiognomy of –s, PPF 38, 294
  place of a – in grammar/language,
    post at which stationed, 29
  playing with a –, 67
  preparation for the use of a –, 26
  purpose of a –, 4, 6
  role of a –, 16, brf 28, 30, 156,
    182
  soul of –s, 530
  sound or shape of a –, 31
  teaching of a –, 6, 7, 9
  – on the tip of one's tongue,
    PPF 298–300
  uniform appearance of –s, 11
  unregulated use of a –, 68
  use of –s, 6, 7, 8, 9, 10, 11, 20, 21,
    29, 30, 38, 41, 43–5, 49, 58, 82,
    90, 116, 133, 142, 196, 556, 561,
    565–6, 664
  use of a – before the mind, 139,
    PPF 35
  use of a – extended in time, 138
  use of a – stands in need of
    justification, 261
  use of a – without a justification,
    289
  what is a – really, brf 108
  what –s signify, 10
  –s without meaning, 13, 39, 41
word/sentence distinction, 19, 27, 49
word–thing association, 6
world, 96–7, 342, 402; PPF 55